BEGINNING

Windows® 8 Application Development

István Novák
György Balássy
Zoltán Arvai
Dávid Fülöp

WILEY

John Wiley & Sons, Inc.

Beginning Windows® 8 Application Development

Published by
John Wiley & Sons, Inc.
10475 Crosspoint Boulevard
Indianapolis, IN 46256
www.wiley.com

Published simultaneously in Canada

ISBN: 978-1-118-01268-0
ISBN: 978-1-118-22183-9 (ebk)
ISBN: 978-1-118-23562-1 (ebk)
ISBN: 978-1-118-26050-0 (ebk)

Manufactured in the United States of America

10 9 8 7 6 5 4 3 2 1

For general information on our other products and services please contact our Customer Care Department within the United States at (877) 762-2974, outside the United States at (317) 572-3993 or fax (317) 572-4002.

Wiley publishes in a variety of print and electronic formats and by print-on-demand. Some material included with standard print versions of this book may not be included in e-books or in print-on-demand. If this book refers to media such as a CD or DVD that is not included in the version you purchased, you may download this material at http://booksupport.wiley.com. For more information about Wiley products, visit www.wiley.com.

Library of Congress Control Number: 2012943021

CREDITS

Acquisitions Editor
Mary James

Project Editor
Kevin Shafer

Technical Editor
Alex Golesh

Production Editor
Kathleen Wisor

Copy Editor
Kim Cofer

Editorial Manager
Mary Beth Wakefield

Freelancer Editorial Manager
Rosemarie Graham

Associate Director of Marketing
David Mayhew

Marketing Manager
Ashley Zurcher

Business Manager
Amy Knies

Production Manager
Tim Tate

Vice President and Executive Group Publisher
Richard Swadley

Vice President and Executive Publisher
Neil Edde

Associate Publisher
Jim Minatel

Project Coordinator, Cover
Katie Crocker

Compositor
Jeff Lytle, Happenstance Type-O-Rama

Proofreaders
Jennifer Bennet, Word One
Sarah Kaikini, Word One
Louise Watson, Word One

Indexer
Johnna VanHoose Dinse

Cover Designer
Ryan Sneed

Cover Image
© Donall O Cleirigh/iStockPhoto

ABOUT THE AUTHORS

ISTVÁN NOVÁK is an associate and the chief technology consultant of SoftwArt, a small Hungarian IT consulting company. He works as a software architect and community evangelist. In the last 20 years, he participated in more than 50 enterprise software development projects. In 2002, he co-authored the first Hungarian book about .NET development. In 2007, he was awarded with the Microsoft Most Valuable Professional (MVP) title, and in 2011 he became a Microsoft Regional Director. As the main author, he contributed in writing the *Visual Studio 2010 and .NET 4 Six-In-One* book (Indianapolis: Wiley, 2010), and he is the author of *Beginning Visual Studio LightSwitch Development* (Indianapolis: Wiley, 2011). He holds master's degree from the Technical University of Budapest, Hungary, and also has a doctoral degree in software technology. He lives in Dunakeszi, Hungary, with his wife and two teenage daughters. He is a passionate scuba diver. You may have a good chance of meeting him underwater at the Red Sea in any season of the year.

GYÖRGY BALÁSSY teaches web development as a lecturer at the Budapest University of Technology and Economics. He is a founding member of the local MSDN Competence Center (MSDNCC), having an important role in evangelizing the .NET platform as a speaker, book author, and consultant. Balássy provided leadership in the foundation of the Hungarian .NET community as a key evangelist on Microsoft events, technical forums, and as the head of the Portal Technology Group in the MSDNCC. He is a regular speaker on academic and industrial events, presenting in-depth technical sessions on .NET, ASP.NET, Office development, and ethical hacking, with which he won the Best Speaker and the Most Valuable Professional awards in SharePoint, ASP.NET, and IIS multiple times. He was also selected to be a member of the ASPInsiders group. Since 2005, Balássy has been the Microsoft Regional Director in Hungary. You can visit his blog at `http://gyorgybalassy.wordpress.com` or reach him at `balassy@aut.bme.hu`.

ZOLTÁN ARVAI is a software engineer specializing in client application development and front-end architectures. He's very passionate about user experience and next-generation user interfaces. He's been a freelancer the last seven years, working on several .NET projects, mainly in the enterprise software development world. Arvai was honored with the Microsoft Most Valuable Professional (MVP) award in 2009, and has been recognized three times as a Silverlight MVP. He is a frequent speaker at local Microsoft events. Arvai has co-authored Hungarian books about Silverlight 4.0 and Windows Phone 7.5. He lives in Budapest, Hungary, where he enjoys playing jazz on his old piano, and is a big fan of meeting different cultures all over the world.

DÁVID FÜLÖP is a Hungarian software developer who spent the past decade building .NET and, later, Silverlight applications. Apart from writing code and writing books about writing code, he's been a freelance software development trainer teaching developers of various companies, and giving lectures to college students at the University of Óbuda. Also, he's a recurring presenter at local Microsoft-related developer events. In his free time, he does karate, plays online, and furiously tries to learn the Klingon language.

ABOUT THE TECHNICAL EDITOR

ALEX GOLESH is a Chief Technology Officer (CTO) at Sela (located in Seattle). He is an international expert who specializes in Windows 8, Windows Phone, XNA, Silverlight, and Windows Presentation Foundation (WPF). Golesh is currently consulting for various enterprises worldwide, architecting and developing Windows 8, Windows Phone, Rich Internet Applications (RIA), and Smart Client solutions. He has been developing training samples and courses for various product groups at Microsoft (in Redmond, WA). He conducts lectures and workshops, and leads projects worldwide in the fields of Windows 8, Windows Phone, RIA, and Smart Client. He has conducted Windows Phone 7, WPF, and Silverlight trainings in Israel, India, Sweden, and Poland as a part of the Microsoft Early Adoption Program. He has received recognition as a Microsoft Most Valuable Professional (MVP) for four years in a row.

ACKNOWLEDGMENTS

WRITING THIS BOOK WAS A GREAT ADVENTURE! Just a few weeks after I had completed my previous book, Paul Reese called and asked me to participate in a book about Windows 8. I did not hesitate, and immediately said "yes." I'm happy that Paul took a chance on me again, and hope he'll be content with the result.

This book wouldn't have been completed on time without Kevin Shafer and Mary E. James. Kevin not only did amazing editorial work, but also undertook the burdens of adjusting the book again and again as Microsoft changed the terminology of Windows 8. Mary always kept the book on the right track, and encouraged us when we had to revise previously completed chapters because of breaking changes in a new release of Windows 8.

I'd also like to thank Kim Cofer for thoroughly reading the manuscript, removing ambiguities, and translating complex paragraphs to simple and tangle-free sentences. Alex Golesh not only reviewed the book from technical point of view, but also suggested great ideas to make the exercises in this book easier to follow and understand. I'm very grateful for his help.

I would not have been able to create this book without such a great authoring team. So, I'd like to thank György, Zoltán, and Dávid for adding their hearts and souls to this adventure. It was great to work with you!

Finally, I owe many kisses to my wife and daughters for letting me spend so many hours in my study, working on this book. I'll keep my promise, and we'll spend the remaining weekends of this summer together.

—ISTVÁN NOVÁK

WRITING THIS BOOK WAS REALLY DIFFICULT, but definitely one of the most exciting tasks I've ever completed. Windows 8 is so exciting, and there is so much to tell and write about the possibilities and brilliant technological solutions that it seemed almost impossible to fit all this information into a single book.

I would have never succeeded without the help of István Novák, Kevin Shafer, and Mary E. James. Thank you for leading me on the right path with my chapters to make this book as awesome as it has turned out to be.

I'd also like to thank György and Dávid for contributing to this book, and putting all the hard work into this project. It was really great and fun to work with you guys!

I'd also like to thank Kim Cofer and Alex Golesh, who thoroughly read my chapters and made sure that the silly mistakes I made would never see the sunlight. Thank you for all your suggestions and your hard work.

I'm very grateful for the chance to work on this project. It was a real adventure. Thank you all for your help.

Last, but not least, Adrienn, thank you for supporting me all the way, and accepting that I couldn't be with you on those long nights. I promise I'll make it up to you.

—Zoltán Arvai

FIRST OF ALL, I'D LIKE TO THANK ZOLTÁN AND ISTVÁN for inviting me on board to participate in writing my first non-Hungarian book. You do know how much fun it was! Thank you for guiding me, and keeping me from making all my sample apps Trek- or South Park-related. I'd also like to thank György, who made the book complete with his invaluable chapters.

I'd like to thank to the editorial crew at Wiley: Kevin Shafer for the incredibly insightful advice on making every page better, and Mary E. James for helping me with the book writing process. Kim Cofer deserves all my appreciation for making my English-like sentences really English. The book's readability improved a lot thanks to Kim. Last, but not least, I'd like to thank Alex Golesh, our Technical Editor, who was always there to make the book thorough by providing another vital point of view on every matter.

Finally, I'd like to thank my parents, Gyuri and Zsuzsa, and my girlfriend, Dóri, for their support while I was living like a hermit for days, living my life aloof with my laptops when a deadline was near. I hope you can forgive the short bursts of complete lack of interest in socializing, sleeping or eating, just like our cats, Seven and Cica could.

—David Fülöp

CONTENTS

INTRODUCTION

DURING ITS 27 YEARS OF LIFE, Windows has undergone several big changes. Without a doubt, both users and developers perceive a big leap from Windows 7 to Windows 8! When Microsoft began development of the newest Windows version, it totally re-imagined the operating system. Instead of patching the previous versions and just adding new or mandatory features, Microsoft started developing Windows 8 from the ground up by defining the user experience as one of the top priorities.

The new operating system was previewed at the beginning of summer in 2011. At the Build developer's conference held in Anaheim, California, in September 2011, Microsoft publicly released the Developer Preview version of Windows 8. Moreover, conference attendees were given an Intel-based quad-core Samsung tablet with Windows 8 Developer Preview installed. This event provided big momentum and built anticipation for the release of Microsoft's newest operating system. Windows 8 was no longer just a concept. It was actually touchable — figuratively and physically.

Windows 8 introduces a new kind of application, referred to as *Windows 8 style apps*. These apps provide a novel approach for the users by means of a new user interface (UI)—such as the authentically digital user experience of the design, the fluent and responsive application screens, and the experience of browsing and installing apps from the Windows Store. These new apps not only provide a unique and pleasurable user experience, but developers can also take advantage of novel tools, APIs, and programming techniques!

WHO THIS BOOK IS FOR

This book was created with the variety of programmers and software developers in mind. Although the tools and the programming languages for creating Windows 8 applications have matured and are used by millions of programmers all around the world, the majority of concepts and APIs are fairly new.

If you have experience with C++ programming or (in the realm of .NET) with C#/Visual Basic, or you have experience creating web pages with HTML and JavaScript, you'll be able to use your existing skills and learn the new concepts and APIs. The chapters of this book are built on each other. If you read them from the beginning to the end, you'll get to know the fundamentals of designing and creating Windows 8 style apps — even if you're a novice programmer, or if you've just turned to Windows development.

The first part of the book prepares you for Windows 8 style app development. It provides an overview of the most important concepts and tools, and explains the architectural basics of the new development platform. If you're a seasoned Windows programmer, you can skip Chapter 1 and Chapter 4.

The second part of the book starts by explaining the essential principles that are the key traits of modern app development, and these are used in the subsequent chapters.

The four programming languages that can be used for creating Windows 8 style apps are C++, C#, Visual Basic, and JavaScript. The size and scope of this book would have doubled if all four languages had been treated in detail, so C# is used in most of the samples and exercises. If you have web development experience, or you're interested in programming apps with web technologies, Chapter 6 focuses on HTML5, CSS3, and JavaScript. If you're using C++ today, Chapter 13 treats that great programming language in the context of Windows 8 apps.

WHAT THIS BOOK COVERS

Windows 8 promises that you can run every Windows 7 application on the new version of the operating system. Moreover, you can use existing technologies and tools to develop applications on Windows 8. This book focuses on the Windows 8 style app development that is brand new and not available in any previous versions of the operating system. It treats the existing technologies only in the context of Windows 8 style app development.

After reading this book, you will be familiar with the following general areas:

➤ The architectural basics of the new application development platform

➤ The fundamental new principles and traits of Windows 8 application development — using both .NET languages and HTML/JavaScript

➤ The basics of Windows 8 style app development using the HTML5/CSS3/JavaScript web technologies

➤ The XAML markup used to create a Windows 8 style app UI with the built-in UI controls

➤ The creation of a more complex UI with multiple pages and new commanding surfaces introduced in Windows 8

➤ The fundamental APIs of Windows Runtime, which is used to create full-fledged applications that leverage touch and tablet features

➤ The scenarios in which the C++ programming language is the right choice

➤ The distribution and sale of your apps in the Windows Store

You learn about these topics through hands-on exercises that walk you through the use of Microsoft Visual Studio 2012 Express for Windows 8 in tandem with Microsoft Expression Blend to create Windows 8 style apps.

HOW THIS BOOK IS STRUCTURED

This book is divided into three sections that will help you understand the concepts behind Windows 8 application development as well as become familiar with the fundamental tools and techniques.

➤ The first part provides a quick overview that presents the fundamental changes brought into application development by Windows 8 — including the user experience scenarios, UI concepts, application architecture, and tools.

➤ In the second part, the numerous hands-on exercises enable you to learn the main concepts, fundamental techniques, and best practices of Windows 8 style application development.

➤ The third part introduces a few advanced topics that help you to step toward becoming a professional Windows 8 app developer.

Most chapters first establish a context and treat the essential concepts, illustrated with figures and code snippets. You learn how to use these concepts through hands-on exercises, in which you build Windows 8 apps from scratch and improve the ones you built earlier. Each exercise concludes with a "How It Works" section that explains how (including all important details) the exercise achieves its objective.

Part I: Introduction to Windows 8 Application Development

Windows 8 totally changes the landscape of application development with the new style of app. In this part, you become acquainted with the fundamental concepts, technologies, and tools that make it possible to leverage these great features.

➤ **Chapter 1: "A Brief History of Windows Application Development"**—Windows 8 represents the biggest leap in the entire lifetime of the operating system family. Here you learn how the operating system evolved during the past 27 years, and then you traverse the development technologies and tools as they developed in tandem with Windows.

➤ **Chapter 2: "Using Windows 8"**—Windows 8 changes a lot in terms of the UI. It was built with a more touch-centric approach in mind. Although the user may learn these things intuitively, for a developer, it is imperative to know all the nooks and crannies of using the Windows 8 UI. After reading this chapter, you will get the sense of building really engaging and intuitive apps that users use not just to complete a task but enjoy using.

➤ **Chapter 3: "Windows 8 Architecture from a Developer's Point of View"**—Windows 8 provides a new development model via a new kind of application — Windows 8 style apps — while still allowing for the development of traditional desktop applications. Here you learn the architecture of components that help you to develop these kinds of apps, including the cornerstone, Windows Runtime.

➤ **Chapter 4: "Getting to Know Your Development Environment"**—Microsoft provides great tools to leverage the magnificent Windows 8 technologies. In this chapter, you learn about the two fundamental tools you are going to utilize while developing your apps: Visual Studio 2012 and Expression Blend.

Part II: Creating Windows 8 Applications

In this part, you learn the indispensable concepts and patterns you need to know about developing Windows 8 applications. You start with modern principles and move toward creating application UIs. Having this knowledge, you shift to techniques and components that enable you to develop full-fledged Windows 8 style apps.

> ➤ **Chapter 5: "Principles of Modern Windows Application Development"**—Before you start to program, you must understand the basic principles of modern Windows application development. Here you learn about the key concepts of the Windows 8 design language, and then you explore and try out the brand new asynchronous programming patterns in C# and JavaScript.

> ➤ **Chapter 6: "Creating Windows 8 Style Applications with HTML5, CSS, and JavaScript"**— Windows 8 enables web developers to build on their past experiences because they can utilize their existing HTML, CSS, and JavaScript knowledge. This chapter provides a brief overview of these technologies in regard to Windows 8 style app development.

> ➤ **Chapter 7: "Using XAML to Create Windows 8 Style User Interfaces"**—In this chapter, you learn about the basics of developing Windows 8 style application UIs using eXtensible Application Markup Language (XAML). XAML provides a way to develop the UI with a rich set of tools, including layout management, styles, templates, and data binding, as you will discover here.

> ➤ **Chapter 8: "Working with XAML Controls"**—Windows 8 provides a number of predefined UI controls, including buttons, text boxes, lists, grids — any many more — that can be used in XAML. In this chapter, you learn not only how to use these controls, but how to transform and customize them, and how to utilize Expression Blend.

> ➤ **Chapter 9: "Building Windows 8 Style Applications"**—Windows 8 style applications use a set of patterns to provide a uniform user experience. Here you learn about patterns that determine how your application can implement the same user interaction experience as the new apps that are shipped as a part of Windows 8. You also learn important details about integrating your apps with the operating system's Start screen.

> ➤ **Chapter 10: "Creating Multi-Page Applications"**—In this chapter, you learn how to create applications with multiple pages. You start by studying the navigation concepts used in Windows 8 style apps, and you get acquainted with the UI controls that support paging. Visual Studio provides two project templates — the Grid Application template and the Split Application template — that are great for starting your multi-page apps. Here you discover the details surrounding these templates.

> ➤ **Chapter 11: "Building Connected Applications"**—Modern applications often leverage services available on the Internet, such as weather information, financial services, social networks, and many others. In this chapter, you learn how to utilize Windows 8 features that enable you to develop connected applications using these Internet services as building blocks.

➤ **Chapter 12: "Leveraging Tablet Features"**—Windows 8 is very focused on tablets with touchscreen devices and various sensors. Here you discover the APIs that enable you to integrate touch experience and sensor information into your apps to provide a great tablet-aware user experience.

Part III: Advancing to Professional Windows 8 Development

The topics treated in this part widen your knowledge of Windows 8 style app development. Here you learn concepts and techniques that enable you to start creating professional apps and even monetize them through the Windows Store.

➤ **Chapter 13: "Creating Windows 8 Style Applications with C++"**—The C++ programming language has experienced a renaissance because of its performance characteristics. Now you can develop Windows 8 style apps with C++. In this chapter, you learn how the newest version of C++ supports Windows 8 apps, and in which scenarios C++ is the best choice.

➤ **Chapter 14: "Advanced Programming Concepts"**—In this chapter, you learn several concepts that enable you to develop more advanced Windows 8 style apps, such as hybrid projects that mix several programming languages, background tasks, and querying input devices and touch capabilities.

➤ **Chapter 15: "Testing and Debugging Windows 8 Style Applications"**—Creating high-quality apps is important if you want to achieve success with them. Here you learn how to write additional code to test your application logic to ensure that your code behaves exactly the way it should. You will also learn indispensable debugging techniques to find the root causes of malfunctions in your code.

➤ **Chapter 16: "Introducing the Windows Store"**—As a developer, you can submit your application to the Windows Store to enable users to buy and install it seamlessly. In this chapter, you learn about the prerequisites and the flow of the submission process, as well as other tools that help you in this workflow.

WHAT YOU NEED TO USE THIS BOOK

Windows 8 supports two separate hardware platforms. One of them is the Intel platform (just as all previous Windows versions have supported it), including the 32-bit x86 and 64-bit x64 versions. The other one is based on the ARM processor architecture (typically used on mobile phones and touchscreen tablet devices), and this platform (Windows on ARM) is new in the Windows family of operating systems.

To create Windows 8 style applications, you need the development tools, and those run only on the Intel platform. So, you must install either the x86 or the x64 version of Windows 8 on your computer used for development. As of the writing of this book, Windows on ARM is not available.

You can use Microsoft Visual Studio 2012 and Microsoft Expression Blend to create Windows 8 style apps. If you have an appropriate Microsoft Developer Network (MSDN) subscription, you may have licenses for using these tools. Otherwise, you can download Microsoft Visual Studio 2012 Express for Windows 8 — including Expression Blend — for free. This book uses the Express version. Owing to the development tools, the Windows 8 style apps you create will run on both the Intel and ARM platforms.

CONVENTIONS

To help you get the most from the text and keep track of what's happening, we've used a number of conventions throughout the book.

TRY IT OUT

The "Try It Out" is an exercise you should work through, following the text in the book.

1. It usually consists of a set of steps.

2. Each step has a number.

3. Follow the steps through with your copy of the database.

How It Works

After each "Try It Out" exercise, the code you've typed is explained in detail.

As for styles in the text:

➤ We *highlight* new terms and important words when we introduce them.

➤ We show keyboard strokes like this: Ctrl+A.

➤ We show filenames, URLs, and code within the text like so: `persistence.properties`.

➤ We present code in two different ways:

```
We use a monofont type with no highlighting for most code examples.
We use bold to emphasize code that is particularly important in the present
    context or to show changes from a previous code snippet.
```

SOURCE CODE

As you work through the examples in this book, you may choose either to type in all the code manually, or to use the source code files that accompany the book. All the source code used in this book is available for download at `http://www.wrox.com`. When at the site, simply locate the book's title (use the Search box or one of the title lists) and click the Download Code link on the book's detail page to obtain all the source code for the book.

> **NOTE** *Because many books have similar titles, you may find it easiest to search by ISBN; this book's ISBN is 978-1-118-01268-0.*

Once you download the code, just decompress it with your favorite compression tool. Alternatively, you can go to the main Wrox code download page at `http://www.wrox.com/dynamic/books/download.aspx` to see the code available for this book and all other Wrox books.

ERRATA

We make every effort to ensure that there are no errors in the text or in the code. However, no one is perfect, and mistakes do occur. If you find an error in one of our books (like a spelling mistake or faulty piece of code), we would be very grateful for your feedback. By sending in errata, you may save another reader hours of frustration, and at the same time, you will be helping us provide even higher quality information.

To find the errata page for this book, go to `http://www.wrox.com` and locate the title using the Search box or one of the title lists. Then, on the book details page, click the Book Errata link. On this page, you can view all errata that has been submitted for this book and posted by Wrox editors. A complete book list, including links to each book's errata, is also available at `www.wrox.com/misc-pages/booklist.shtml`.

If you don't spot "your" error on the Book Errata page, go to `www.wrox.com/contact/techsupport.shtml` and complete the form there to send us the error you have found. We'll check the information and, if appropriate, post a message to the book's errata page and fix the problem in subsequent editions of the book.

P2P.WROX.COM

For author and peer discussion, join the P2P forums at `p2p.wrox.com`. The forums are a web-based system for you to post messages relating to Wrox books and related technologies, and to interact with other readers and technology users. The forums offer a subscription feature to e-mail you topics of interest of your choosing when new posts are made to the forums. Wrox authors, editors, other industry experts, and your fellow readers are present on these forums.

At `http://p2p.wrox.com`, you will find a number of different forums that will help you, not only as you read this book, but also as you develop your own applications. To join the forums, just follow these steps:

1. Go to `p2p.wrox.com` and click the Register link.
2. Read the terms of use and click Agree.
3. Complete the required information to join, as well as any optional information you wish to provide, and click Submit.

4. You will receive an e-mail with information describing how to verify your account and complete the joining process.

> **NOTE** You can read messages in the forums without joining P2P, but in order to post your own messages, you must join.

Once you join, you can post new messages and respond to messages other users post. You can read messages at any time on the web. If you would like to have new messages from a particular forum e-mailed to you, click the Subscribe to this Forum icon by the forum name in the forum listing.

For more information about how to use the Wrox P2P, be sure to read the P2P FAQs for answers to questions about how the forum software works, as well as many common questions specific to P2P and Wrox books. To read the FAQs, click the FAQ link on any P2P page.

PART I

Introduction to Windows 8 Application Development

1

A Brief History of Windows Application Development

WHAT YOU WILL LEARN IN THIS CHAPTER:

➤ Understanding how the Windows operating system began, and how it evolved over the past 27 years

➤ Grasping the different historical tools and technologies that have characterized Windows development

➤ Perceiving the paradigm shift of Windows 8 and using it for application development

➤ Getting to know Windows 8 style applications

Windows 8 represents the biggest leap in the entire lifetime of this operating system. It is not simply a new version that updates old capabilities and adds a number of requested and trendy features. But, as Microsoft emphasizes, the operating system has been "re-imagined." Without knowing where Windows 8 comes from, it is difficult to understand the paradigm shift it brings.

In this chapter, you first learn how the operating system has evolved over the last 27 years, and then you learn about the development technologies and tools as they evolved in tandem with Windows.

THE LIFE OF WINDOWS

When the very first version of Microsoft Windows was released on November 20, 1985, it was designed to be geared toward graphical user interfaces (GUIs). Microsoft created Windows as an extra component for its MS-DOS operating system, and Windows totally changed the landscape for personal computers. The first version of Windows used very simple graphics, and it was more of a front end to MS-DOS than a real operating system.

From Windows 3.1 to 32-bit

Almost seven years passed after the first version was introduced before Windows 3.1 was released in March 1992. This 16-bit operating system allowed *multitasking* — in an environment where users were not used to seeing it. The new version of Windows contained virtual device drivers that could be shared between DOS applications. Because of its *protected mode*, Windows 3.1 was capable of addressing several megabytes of memory — the default address mode used by the 8086 family of central processing units (CPUs) allowed only 640 KB at that time — without the need for any virtual memory manager software. Computer users living in that era might remember the startup splash screen of this operating system, as shown in Figure 1-1.

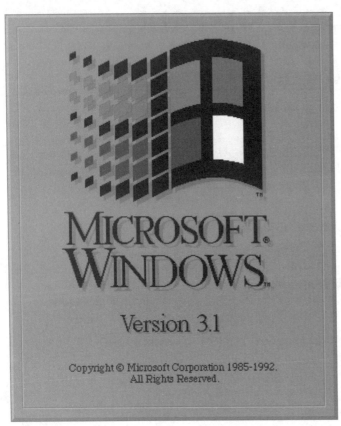

FIGURE 1-1: The splash screen of Windows 3.1

> **NOTE** Multitasking *is a capability of operating systems that allow the running of multiple tasks (also known as* processes*) during the same period of time. These tasks share the computer's resources, such as the CPU and memory. The operating system switches among the tasks while executing them. Each task runs for a small amount of time, and because of fast switching, they seem to run simultaneously.*
>
> Protected mode *is an operational mode of x86-compatible CPUs that enables special features such as virtual memory handling and multitasking.*

Released in August 1995, Windows 95 was a 32-bit operating system that supported *preemptive multitasking* — in other words, the operating system was capable of interrupting a task without any active contribution by the task. Windows 95 no longer was an add-on for MS-DOS, but now represented a full-fledged operating system (a fact that was debated for a long time). A few other Windows versions followed (specifically, Windows 98 and Windows Me), before Windows XP was released in October 2001.

Windows XP and Windows Vista

With its famous logo shown in Figure 1-2, Windows XP became the most popular version of Windows. Weird as it may seem, this success (in terms of its huge installed base) was only partly because of the new user experience (XP stands for "eXPerience") it offered when it was released. Similarly, innovations such as the GDI+ graphical subsystem, the fast user switching, ClearType font rendering, 64-bit support, and much more, also only partially contributed to the success of this version of Windows. Actually, the primary boost to XP's success was the unpopularity of Windows Vista — its successor.

FIGURE 1-2: The Windows XP logo

Released in November 2006, Windows Vista appeared with a brand-new design, and it offered a very improved security — in contrast to XP, which required three service packs to remove its security issues and pains. Although this could have been enough to achieve a greater popularity than its predecessor, Vista required improved hardware as a price for its new features. Most enterprises that had spent a significant part of their IT budget stabilizing XP — after Windows XP Service Pack 3 (SP3)—simply did not deem it reasonable to migrate to Vista. Vista soon became the shortest-living operating system in the Windows family.

Windows 7 Blots Out Vista Fiasco

As Steven Sinofsky (the president of Microsoft's Windows division) confessed several times, Microsoft had learned its lesson even before it started to design Windows 7, which was released in July 2009, two years and eight months after Vista. Windows 7 contains significant performance improvements over Windows XP and Vista, including boot time, shutdown time, better task scheduling on multi-core CPUs (that is, CPUs with more than one processor), search, and much more. The user experience improved a lot, and Windows 7 introduced new features such as jump lists, Aero Peek, Aero Snap, and many other small things that made it easier to navigate among application windows, as well as organize them on the screen.

Windows 7 definitely provided a successful way to blot out the Vista fiasco. For the Windows team, it would have been easy to follow the direction designated by Windows 7, but the team instead undertook a most compelling challenge.

The Paradigm Shift of Windows 8

Although Windows was born in an era where personal computers became part of everyday life, it still remained an operating system created with enterprises and information workers in mind. Most functions offered by the operating system actually wanted — or sometimes forced — the users to work in the way wired into the system. Users could not perform any actions before getting acquainted with concepts such as files, directories, security groups, permissions, shares, the registry, and so on. This approach mirrored how the designers assumed that users should interact with the system.

> **NOTE** Because of the applications that swarmed out to available system resources, the Windows operating system needed periodic maintenance by way of cleanups, disk defragmentation, virus checks, service pack installations, and so on. Although each new version made some great improvement toward lightening or automating this burden, the onus never faded away completely.

Microsoft Takes the First Steps Toward Consumers

Apple's consumer-centric products such as iPhone and iPad showed the world that there was another approach making it possible to interact with computer software in an intuitive way — without having any idea what a file, a directory, the system registry, or an application installation procedure was. Microsoft seemed to not understand this approach for a long time, but the sales figures of the market forced the company to shift its focus to consumer-centric devices and operating systems.

The first serious change in Microsoft's behavior could be seen in the middle of February 2010 at the Mobile World Congress (in Barcelona, Spain), where the company first introduced Windows Phone 7 to the public. Windows Phone 7 was totally about the consumer experience. The visual design, its simplicity, and its gentle, well-hit animations highlighted the user interface (UI), and so the usage of this device became very intuitive. The market appraised this change, and now — almost a year after the Windows Phone 7.5 "Mango" release — Microsoft is the third competitor in the mobile operating system (OS) market, and is getting closer and closer to Apple's iOS and Google's Android.

> **NOTE** The Windows operating system family did have editions for embedded devices (Windows Embedded) and mobile phones (Windows CE and Windows Mobile), which were available before Windows Phone 7.

Windows 8 Appears on the Scene

The consumer-centric approach of Windows Phone 7 became a part of the operating system experience with the release of Windows 8. When you start the operating system (the boot time has significantly decreased in comparison to Windows 7), the new Windows 8 Start screen does not remind you of the former desktop with the taskbar at the bottom. Instead, you are faced with a set of tiles, each representing an application, as shown in Figure 1-3.

FIGURE 1-3: The Windows 8 Start screen

This new Start screen is a clear message to consumers. Windows is not only an operating system for information workers and seasoned computer users, but it is also a consumer device designed with multi-touch sensitivity, tablets, and slates in mind. The surface of the Start screen is very intuitive, and most people can immediately start playing with it without any guidance. Users having experience with touch-screen smartphones and tablets find it natural to use the Start screen, launch applications, scroll, zoom, and apply the gestures they have already learned with other devices.

Those people who use Windows to run business applications (such as Word, Excel, or PowerPoint), or any other enterprise-specific system's UI, may find this change to the Windows UI discipline unusual. Well, Windows was designed with total compatibility for existing applications, so it has a desktop mode as well. When launching an application that was created for any of the previous Windows versions (or one that simply does not use the Windows 8 style UI), the application will run in the well-known desktop environment. For example, when a user starts Excel, it opens in desktop mode, as shown in Figure 1-4.

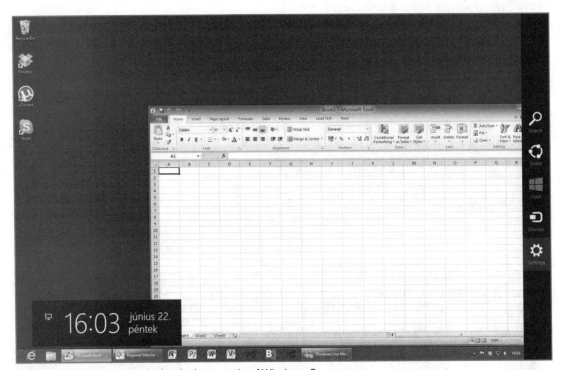

FIGURE 1-4: Excel running in the desktop mode of Windows 8

This is the second face of Windows 8 — familiar to everyone who used Windows before. If you did not see the Start menu and the status indicator displaying the current date and time, you might think you were using Windows 7.

The new Windows 8 Start screen is not just a simple addition to Windows 7. Behind this simple screen, there is a brand-new world of consumer-centric applications, called *Windows 8 style applications*. Instead of using a desktop full of icons and rectangular windows of applications, users see only one application at a time, which possesses the full screen. No window caption, close button, sizable border, or any other element (called "chrome" in the user experience terminology) detracts the user's sight from the application. The Weather application shown in Figure 1-5 is a great example of this new style.

FIGURE 1-5: The Weather application in Windows 8

In this book, you learn all about this new UI paradigm, and most importantly, you will acquire a command of developing such a new style of applications. Before diving deeply into the development aspects of Windows 8 style applications, you should understand a bit about the history of Windows development.

HISTORY OF APIS AND TOOLS

The Windows story would be pretty lame without applications running on the platform, and developers creating these programs. Microsoft has always been a company building a strong developer community around its products, including its flagship, Windows.

> **NOTE** *The importance of this community is often voiced by Microsoft leaders. When you surf the Internet searching for "Steve Ballmer," you can't miss the videos where he passionately starts shouting "developers, developers, developers, ..." and repeats this word a dozen times.*

In 2012, the Windows platform turned 27 years old. During its long life, not only the operating system, but also its *application programming interfaces (APIs)* and the related development tools improved vastly. From this point of view, Windows 8 represents the biggest leap that has ever happened in Windows's history. To understand why this can be said, it is worth a look back in time, right to the very first moments of Windows application development.

The Power of C

Although, in today's world, programming Windows applications is very common, it was not at the very beginning of the life of Windows. At that time, programmers who grew up with MS-DOS applications perceived the Windows approach as being weird — as if it had been turned inside out. Though a clean-cut MS-DOS application controlled everything, and it called operating system functions when they were needed, Windows followed a crazy path! The operating system controlled the application, and called it whenever it wanted to goad the program into doing something, such as refreshing the UI or executing a menu command.

And this was not the only outrage against poor developers. Using the C programming language — that was "the" language of the time — writing the simplest "Hello, world" application in MS-DOS was a piece of cake, as shown here:

```
#include <stdio.h>

main()
{
    printf("Hello, world");
}
```

Well, to achieve the same result, Windows required some more work. It demanded writing "scaffolding" code around the single `printf` function, and you could call it anything but intuitive, as shown in Listing 1-1.

LISTING 1-1: The "Hello, world" program à la Windows 3.1 (extract)

```
#include <windows.h>

/* Export the entry point to be called by Windows */
long FAR PASCAL _export WndProc(HWND, UINT, UINT, LONG)

/* The entry point of the application */
int PASCAL WinMain(HANDLE hInstance, HANDLE hPrevInstance,
    LPSTR lpszCmdParam, int nCmdShow)
{
    static char szApplication[] = "HelloW";
    HWND hwnd;
    MSG msg;
    WNDCLASS wndClass;

    /* Create a Window class */
    if (!hPrevInstance)
    {
        wndClass.Style = CS_HREDRAW | CS_VREDRAW;
```

```
            wndClass.lpfnWndProc = WndProc;
            /* A few code lines omitted for the sake of brevity */
            wndClass.hbrBackground = GetStockObject(WHITE_BRUSH);
            wndClass.lpszMenuName = NULL;
            wndClass.lpszClassName = szApplication;
            RegisterClass(&wndClass);
        }

    /* Create a window instance for the class */
    hwnd = CreateWindow(szApplication,
        "My Hello World Program",
        WS_OVERLAPPEDWINDOW,
        /* A few parameters omitted for the sake of brevity */
        hInstance,
        NULL);
    /* Initiate displaying the window */
    ShowWindow(hwnd, nCmdShow);
    UpdateWindow(hwnd);

    /* Manage the message loop */
    while (GetMessage(&msg, NULL, 0, 0))
    {
        TranslateMessage(&msg);
        DispatchMessage(&msg)
    }
}

/* Processing messages */
long FAR PASCAL _export WndProc(HWND hwnd, UINT message,
    UINT wParam, LONG lParam)
{
    HDC hdc;
    PAINTSTRUCT ps;
    RECT rect;

    switch (message)
    {
        case WM_PAINT:
            hdc = BeginPaint(hwnd, &ps);
            GetClientRect(hwnd, &rect);
            DrawText(hdc, "Hello, world", -1, &rect,
                DT_SINGLELINE | DT_CENTER | DT_VCENTER);
            EndPaint(hwnd, &pd);
            return 0;

        case WM_DESTROY:
            PostQuitMessage(0);
            return 0
    }
    return DefWindowProc(hwnd, message, wParam, lParam);
}
```

This program contains many lines of code, because it was written over an API that offered only low-level operating system functions. Although this source code is long, it uncovers important internal details of Windows. All of them are still in the heart of Windows 8, of course, in an improved form:

➤ At the very beginning, the program creates a window class by setting up the fields of the wnd-Class structure and using the RegisterClass method. The *window class* is a concept that identifies a procedure (called *window procedure*) that processes messages sent to the window.

➤ The program creates a window (with the CreateWindow method) using the registered window class, and then displays it with the ShowWindow method. The UpdateWindow method sends a message to the window in order to repaint its UI.

➤ The soul of the application is the *message loop*, as shown here:

```
while (GetMessage(&msg, NULL, 0, 0))
{
    TranslateMessage(&msg);
    DispatchMessage(&msg)
}
```

This loop obtains messages from a queue, translates key presses to equivalent messages (for example, as if a mouse were used), and then dispatches them to the appropriate window procedure.

➤ If the message loop is the soul, the window procedure is the heart. In Listing 1-1, WndProc is called by the message loop. Its message parameter contains the code of the message (the event to handle), and a switch statement wraps the pieces of code snippets processing individual messages.

➤ The WM_PAINT message tells the window that it should repaint itself. With the BeginPaint method, it obtains a device-context resource to use for drawing in the client area of the window. This device context is then used to write the "Hello, World" message in the middle of the window. ReleasePaint releases this device context — which happens to be a very limited resource in the system.

You can imagine how time-consuming and painful Windows development was at that time — because programmers were forced to use low-level operating system constructs through the Windows API.

C++ Takes Over C

In 1983, only a few years after Brian Kernighan and Dennis Ritchie published the first edition of C (1978), Bjarne Stroustrup created a new language that added object-oriented aspects to C. This language was C++, and it soon became popular in the Windows platform, too.

C++ allows encapsulating data and functionality in classes, as well as supporting object inheritance and polymorphism. With these features, the flat API of Windows could be presented as a smaller set of entities that grouped data structures and API operations into a logical context. For example, all the operations related to create, display, and manage windows on the UI could be put into a class named Window.

The C++ approach helped developers have a better overview of the API, and lowered the entry barrier to Windows programming. For example, the essential parts of the "Hello, World" program described in Listing 1-1 could be organized around objects, as shown in Listing 1-2.

LISTING 1-2: The blueprint of the "Hello, World" program in C++ (extract)

```cpp
// --- Class representing the main program
class Main
{
  public:
    static HINSTANCE hInstance;
    static HINSTANCE hPrevInstance;
    static int nCmdShow;
    static int MessageLoop( void );
};

// --- Class representing a window
class Window
{
  protected:
    HWND hWnd;
  public:
    HWND GetHandle( void ) { return hWnd; }
    BOOL Show( int nCmdShow ) { return ShowWindow( hWnd, nCmdShow ); }
    void Update( void ) { UpdateWindow( hWnd ); }
    virtual LRESULT WndProc( UINT iMessage, WPARAM wParam, LPARAM lParam ) = 0;
};

// --- The class representing this program's main window
class MainWindow : public Window
{
    // --- Implementation omitted for brevity
};

// --- Extract from the implementation of the Main class
int Main::MessageLoop( void )
{
    MSG msg;

    while( GetMessage( (LPMSG) &msg, NULL, 0, 0 ) )
    {
        TranslateMessage( &msg );
        DispatchMessage( &msg );
    }
    return msg.wParam;
}

LRESULT MainWindow::WndProc( UINT iMessage, WPARAM wParam, LPARAM lParam )
{
    switch (iMessage)
    {
        case WM_CREATE:
```

continues

LISTING 1-2 *(continued)*

```
            break;
        case WM_PAINT:
            Paint();
            break;
        case WM_DESTROY:
            PostQuitMessage( 0 );
            break;
        default:
            return DefWindowProc( hWnd, iMessage, wParam, lParam );
    }
    return 0;
}
```

With the object-oriented approach offered by C++, object behaviors could be packaged into reusable code libraries. Programmers could create their programs based on these libraries so that they needed to define only the behaviors that differed from the built-in ones. For example, they had to override the `Paint()` method in Listing 1-2 to repaint the UI of their window objects.

Windows programming changed a lot with C++ and object libraries. Microsoft created two libraries, Microsoft Foundation Classes (MFC) and Active Template Library (ATL), which are still maintained and available in their flagship development environment, Visual Studio.

> **NOTE** *You will soon learn more about the Visual Studio development environment.*

Visual Basic

Applications written in the C or C++ programming languages expose a lot of details about how Windows works. In a few instances, it is important to know these things, but in most cases, it could be frustrating and detract developers from focusing on the real application functionality.

Released in May 1991, Visual Basic dramatically changed this programming style. Instead of exposing internal Windows details, Visual Basic concealed them from programmers, and offered high-level constructs such as forms, controls, modules, classes, and code-behind files. Instead of writing dozens of lines to achieve very simple functionality, the Visual Basic language enabled developers to focus on the real business of their applications. The "Hello, World" program could be written in one line:

```
MsgBox("Hello, World!")
```

No window class setup, no window registration, no message loop programming! The high-level concepts of the language made it totally unnecessary to deal with scaffolding details. All of this was implemented by the Visual Basic run time.

Using a graphical Integrated Development Environment (IDE), this way of application development is still the most preferred and most productive approach. Programmers graphically design the dialog box windows (or *forms*, in Visual Basic terminology) of the application by dragging UI elements (controls) from the toolbox of the IDE, and dropping them to the form's surface. Each control has several event handlers that respond to the events arriving from the environment — such as when the user clicks a button or changes the selection in a combo box. Programming is actually writing the code that handles these events.

In 1993, Microsoft developed a binary standard, the component object model (COM), which allowed the creation of reusable objects that can be consumed by other applications. A number of technologies are built upon COM, such as Object Linking and Embedding (OLE), which made it possible to automate applications. The versions of Visual Basic released after 1993 were created with COM and OLE in mind. This approach was so successful that a dialect of the language, Visual Basic for Applications (VBA), became the programming language of Microsoft Office macros.

Delphi

Visual Basic was not the only programming environment that had gone off the beaten track of C and C++. Originally developed by Borland, Delphi used the Object Pascal programming language. Whereas Visual Basic was an object-based language (it supported classes with encapsulated data and functions, but did not allow object inheritance), Object Pascal was a real object-oriented language. The IDE of Delphi (its first version was released in 1995) was very similar to the Visual Basic IDE. Delphi was designed to be a Rapid Application Development (RAD) tool that supported developing database applications, including simple ones and even enterprise systems.

The product evolved very fast, with five versions released in the first five years of its life. Delphi was the first tool capable of compiling 32-bit applications for Windows. Similar to Visual Basic controls, it provided more than 100 visual components (organized into Delphi's Visual Component Library) that developers could immediately put into practice. In addition, developers could easily create their own visual components, and add them to the existing library.

The Emergence of .NET

In 2002, the .NET Framework provided fresh momentum to Windows development. .NET programs are compiled into an intermediate language called Microsoft Intermediate Language (MSIL). This intermediate code is transformed to executable CPU-specific operations during run time by a just-in-time (JIT) compiler. This new approach brought several important paradigms into Windows development, including the following:

➤ Prior to the release of .NET, each language (and development environment) used its own runtime library. Learning a new language used to mean learning a new runtime library as well. With .NET, all languages use the same run time. In 2002, only two programming languages were supported by Microsoft (C# and Visual Basic.NET). Today, more than 100 .NET languages are in use. Microsoft itself added F# to this list, and the company also supports IronPython and IronRuby (which are driven by their own communities).

➤ Using a garbage-collection mechanism, the runtime environment manages memory allocation and object destruction automatically. This behavior helps increase productivity, and allows developers to create less error-prone code.

Garbage collection also reduces the chance of writing programs with memory leaks.

➤ Instead of low-level API methods, programmers can work with objects that cover the complexity of the APIs behind the scenes. Instead of dealing with nitty-gritty, internal Windows details, developers can use high-level abstraction, thus boosting productivity.

➤ .NET provides a great level of cooperation between COM and .NET objects. The .NET code can not only access COM objects, but it also provides objects that can be consumed by the COM world.

.NET is called *managed environment*, and its languages are called *managed languages* — as a distinction from *native languages* such as C, Object Pascal (Delphi), and C++, which compile CPU-specific code.

> **NOTE** *The .NET Framework was not the first managed runtime environment. This distinction belonged to Java, which was released by Sun Microsystems in 1995. .NET was Microsoft's answer to the Java phenomenon, and a number of its features were inspired by Sun's Java implementation.*

Released in tandem with the .NET Framework, Visual Studio played an important role in the success of .NET. Visual Studio shipped with about two dozen project templates to boost the start of Windows application development. Today, the Ultimate edition of Visual Studio contains more than a hundred project templates.

> **NOTE** *You learn more about Visual Studio in Chapter 4.*

Visual Studio templates are very powerful. For example, you can create the application shown in Figure 1-6 with a few clicks by using the Windows Forms Application template.

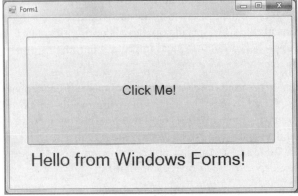

FIGURE 1-6: A simple Windows Forms application created with Visual Studio

With the tools of Visual Studio, you can easily establish the visual properties of the window shown in Figure 1-6. Listing 1-3 shows the only code that you should add manually in this example.

LISTING 1-3: The code behind the form in Figure 1-6

```csharp
using System;
using System.Windows.Forms;

namespace HelloWorldWinForms
{
    public partial class Form1 : Form
    {
        public Form1()
        {
            InitializeComponent();
        }

        private void button1_Click(object sender, EventArgs e)
        {
            label1.Text = "Hello from Windows Forms!";
        }
    }
}
```

Although .NET was harnessed with rich object libraries and great tools, it still used the API that was based on the design of the first Windows versions.

New UI Technologies

For a long time, the Windows UI was managed by the Graphics Device Interface (GDI) API that evolved to GDI+ with the release of Windows XP. GDI and GDI+ are raster-based APIs, and all standard Windows UI controls used them for rendering themselves. The only way a developer could change the default visual appearance of any standard control was to override the Windows event that rendered the UI of the controls.

When the Windows Presentation Foundation (WPF) graphical subsystem was introduced in the .NET Framework 3.0 (and later as a built-in component of Windows Vista), the GDI paradigm was totally changed. Instead of creating the UI in an imperative way (that is, using instructions written in a programming language), WPF employs eXtensible Application Markup Language (XAML), a derivative of eXtensible Markup Language (XML), to describe UI elements. WPF also leverages the great hardware-accelerated capabilities of graphics processing units (GPUs) built into the computers.

Silverlight (Microsoft's rich Internet application framework) uses XAML to define the user interface, too. Listing 1-4 shows a very simple XAML sample implementing the "Hello, World" application in Silverlight.

LISTING 1-4: The "Hello, World" applications' MainPage.xaml file

```xml
<UserControl x:Class="HelloFromSL.MainPage"
    xmlns="http://schemas.microsoft.com/winfx/2006/xaml/presentation"
    xmlns:x="http://schemas.microsoft.com/winfx/2006/xaml"
    xmlns:d="http://schemas.microsoft.com/expression/blend/2008"
```

continues

LISTING 4-1 *(continued)*

```
    xmlns:mc="http://schemas.openxmlformats.org/markup-compatibility/2006"
    mc:Ignorable="d"
    d:DesignHeight="300" d:DesignWidth="400">

    <Grid x:Name="LayoutRoot" Background="White">
        <TextBlock FontSize="48">Hello from Silverlight</TextBlock>
    </Grid>
</UserControl>
```

This code produces the page shown in Figure 1-7. The text in this figure is displayed as a result of the boldface code line in Listing 1-4.

FIGURE 1-7: The output of Listing 1-4

WPF and Silverlight are great technologies. Using them is like replacing a 1930s Lamborghini engine (the GDI/GDI+ type one) with a state-of-the-art one produced in 2012 (WPF/Silverlight). These technologies not only define the UI, but also can declare its dynamic behavior using no (or a minimal amount of) code. These technologies connect the UI with the logic (model) layer of an application. Following are some important features of these technologies:

➤ These technologies are designed and tailored so that you can create rich, powerful desktop or Internet applications to produce a superior user experience. In addition to providing simple UI elements (such as text boxes, buttons, lists, combo boxes, images, and so on), they also provide the freedom to create content with *animation* and *media elements*, such as video and audio. In contrast to the traditional (some may even say boring) UI approach with rectangular UI elements, WPF and Silverlight enable you to change the entire face of an application.

➤ They provide a very flexible *layout system* that makes it easy to create layouts you can automatically adapt to a number of factors (such as available screen size, number of items displayed, size of the displayed elements, and magnification).

➤ *Styles* and *templates* are features that contribute to a smooth cooperation between developers and designers. Developers implement the logic of the application, so they never set the visual properties of the UI directly. Instead, they signal programmatically that the state of the UI is changed. Designers create the visuals of the UI, taking into account the possible states of the UI.

➤ Silverlight and WPF declaratively (in other words, no code required) apply *data binding* — that is, a technology used to connect elements of the UI to data, or other UI elements. Data binding works in cooperation with styles, templates, layouts, and even animations. This mechanism is especially useful in line-of-business (LOB) applications. With the help of data-binding information coming from the database and processed by the application's logic, elements can be declaratively bound to the UI elements.

> **NOTE** *A layout system is used to arrange the elements on the UI. With a flexible layout system (such as the one behind WPF, Silverlight, and Windows 8), you can define relationships among UI elements, and those are automatically placed on the UI at run time. For example, you can define a layout system so that it should arrange UI controls in two columns, and distribute them evenly.*
>
> *Styles and templates in WPF and Silverlight are used similarly as styles and templates in document publishing systems. A style collects common attributes of UI elements; a template is a skeleton with placeholders for the content of a UI element.*

The primary virtue of WPF and Silverlight is probably the fact they can help in the clear separation of UI-related tasks belonging to developers from tasks carried out by designers. With today's consumer-centric applications, this is an obvious advantage over approaches where the tasks of developers and designers are mingled.

> **NOTE** *XAML plays a very important role in the Windows 8 style applications, as you learn in Chapter 3.*

CATCH-22 OF WINDOWS APPLICATION DEVELOPMENT

During the evolution of Windows application development, technologies and related techniques branched out. One branch consisted of the native development, which started with the C programming language in the very early days of Windows. The other branch consisted of the managed development, which uses the .NET Framework, along with its managed technologies and languages.

Because of CPU-specific code compilation and the low-level access to Windows API and system resources, native applications can provide great performance that cannot be beaten by managed technologies. However, when writing business applications, using native code is less productive and more cumbersome than employing managed code with the .NET Framework. Because business applications generally work with databases, the performance overhead of managed languages cannot be perceived at all — the application spends most of its time communicating with underlying services and databases.

When Windows application developers are looking for the right technology and tool for a certain application, they may find themselves in the same predicament as Yossarian, the bombardier in Joseph Heller's novel, *Catch-22* (New York: Alfred A. Knopf, 1995).

In many situations, especially when writing desktop applications, there is no optimal choice between native and managed development. Although WPF and Silverlight would be great technologies for spectacular applications, they are not available from native code. WPF and Silverlight are not embedded into the operating system deeply enough. For example, launching a WPF application takes time while the WPF subsystem loads into the memory. In many cases where computing capacity is required, .NET produces much poorer results than native code.

Visual Studio is a great example of this schizophrenic situation. It uses a mixed codebase. Most of the components are implemented in C++, and certain parts in C# (using WPF). The splash screen should be immediately popped up on the screen after the user launches the application. It is implemented in C++ with GDI+, so WPF would not have been fast enough. The code editor of Visual Studio is implemented in WPF, because it has a rich and easy-to-use toolset for hosting such a complex component with a great UI.

In LOB application development, productivity is the most important factor. The performance advantage of native code development does not add much value to an application, because, in most cases, the database tier is the performance bottleneck. Using managed code, the programming phase of a business application is generally much faster and less error-prone.

So, when writing a desktop application, native code provides the optimal performance, but, in this case, you cannot use the rich toolset of WPF and Silverlight. When you move to managed code, you may gain productivity, but lose final application performance. In your final despair, you can go on with some "mule" solution — just as Visual Studio does, but, in this case, you undertake a lot of overhead. It's not an easy decision, is it?

This situation totally changes with Windows 8. Web developers with HTML5/cascading style sheets 3 (CSS3)/JavaScript experience, seasoned C++ programmers, and developers growing up on .NET, can all feel that their knowledge is enough and appropriate for starting Windows 8 style application development. There is no privileged camp of geeks like C programmers happened to be at the very beginning of the Windows era. Everyone can use the same technologies and the same tools — all without compromise. How is this possible? Chapter 3 explains how.

SUMMARY

The Windows platform has evolved amazingly in the past 27 years. It has transformed from a simple MS-DOS extension to a complex and full-fledged operating system used in the majority of personal computers all around the world. Windows was designed with information workers and seasoned computer users in mind. Although, in every version, it moved closer and closer to less-advanced users, it never could become the operating system of such a simple consumer device as Apple's iPhone or iPad.

Windows 8 changes this. In addition to the traditional desktop mode familiar to all its users, the operating system has a new face with Windows 8 style applications that provide an intuitive user experience — the application possesses the full screen and the full attention of the user.

Not only has the operating system changed, but the development tools and APIs have changed and been significantly improved. Unlike in the past when only C and C++ programmers were privileged to create Windows applications, today C++, Visual Basic, C#, and Delphi programmers can also develop applications with their favorite IDEs. Depending on the chosen language and tool, programmers must use different APIs and technologies. Whereas native programming languages (such as C, C++, and Delphi) offer CPU-specific code and better performance, managed code is more productive for developing LOB applications, and they can easily access the modern UI technologies such as WPF and Silverlight.

Windows 8 style applications provide the same API that is available both in native code and managed code — without compromises. Moreover, this API is available for HTML5/CSS3/JavaScript developers, too.

Windows 8 changes not only the UI of the operating system, but also the way in which you can interact with it. In addition to supporting the traditional input devices such as the keyboard and the mouse, it provides first-class support for interacting with the operating system and Windows 8 style applications — with support for multi-touch gestures, a stylus, and through sensors such as the gyroscope and accelerometer.

In Chapter 2, you learn about all these new things when using Windows.

EXERCISES

1. What was Microsoft's first operating system in the Windows family that was designed and developed totally with consumers in mind?

2. Do Windows 8 style applications have window captions and borders?

3. List the programming languages that are frequently used for Windows application development.

4. What stack of languages can web developers use to create Windows 8 style applications with Windows 8?

> **NOTE** *You can find answers to the exercises in Appendix A.*

▶ **WHAT YOU LEARNED IN THIS CHAPTER**

TOPIC	KEY CONCEPTS
Windows operating system	Windows is the family of operating systems that started with Windows 1.0, released on November 20, 1985, as an extra component of the MS-DOS operating system. The family has also included members for embedded devices (Windows Embedded) and mobile phones (Windows CE, Windows Mobile, and Windows Phone). The current versions are Windows 8 and Windows Phone 7.5.
Windows APIs	The applications working on Windows can access the underlying services of the operating system through the Windows application programming interfaces (APIs).
The C and C++ programming languages	As two programming languages that can be used for developing Windows applications, C and C++ exploit all the features of the operating system, including hardware-specific and very low-level ones. These languages have been used for application development since the early days of Windows. C++ extends C with object-oriented features, and has become a very mature programming language over the past 25 years.
The Visual Basic programming language	Released in 1991, Visual Basic is a revolutionary programming language that significantly reduces the programming efforts required by providing high-level UI concepts such as forms, controls, and events. The language also provides a seamless integration with component object model (COM)/Object Linking and Embedding (OLE) components.
.NET Framework	The Microsoft .NET Framework is a runtime environment that sits between the operating system and the applications. Its primary role is to provide access to all services of the underlying operating system in a managed way that enables developers to be productive. C# and Visual Basic .NET are the two most frequently used languages to create applications for the .NET Framework.
WPF and Silverlight	Windows Presentation Foundation (WPF) and Silverlight are modern and sophisticated UI platforms running on the .NET Framework. They enable you to create applications with a rich UI, including flexible layout, multimedia elements, and animation. They use advanced techniques such as styles, templates, and data binding to provide a very efficient way to tie the UI layer of applications with the underlying logic.

Windows 8 **style applications**	Windows 8 style applications are a new form of applications introduced in Windows 8. These are totally different from the traditional desktop applications because of their visual appearance and ways of managing user interactions. Windows 8 style applications possess the full screen (that is, they do not have an application chrome), and no longer require users to display and manage multiple windows within the application.

2

Using Windows 8

WHAT YOU WILL LEARN IN THIS CHAPTER:

- ➤ Using Windows 8 with the mouse and keyboard
- ➤ Using Windows 8 with multi-touch devices
- ➤ Leveraging the features of the Start screen, Live Tiles, and the charm bar
- ➤ Switching to the desktop and using traditional Windows applications

Windows 8 changes a lot in terms of the user interface (UI). It was built with a more touch-centric approach in mind. The desktop has a few slightly changed features, but most of the traditional, mouse-based workflows remain untouched. On the new Windows 8 style interface, virtually everything is new. Live Tiles aren't just shortcuts; Windows 8 style applications aren't handled like traditional Windows apps. Even the Start screen contains features the old Start menu didn't.

Although the user may learn these things intuitively, for a developer, it is imperative to know all the nooks and crannies of using the Windows 8 UI. Only with extensive knowledge of these capabilities can you build really engaging and intuitive apps that users use not just to complete a task, but enjoy doing so.

TWO WORLDS, ONE OPERATING SYSTEM

Windows 8 has two distinct UIs: the ordinary desktop UI (which probably you are used to) and the completely different and new Windows 8 UI. Why is the Windows 8 UI so important?

In the past few decades, users have experienced the triumph of the mouse over nearly every other controlling device on PCs. For an ordinary Windows user, using a mouse is considered to be the easiest way to use a desktop computer's graphical user interface (GUI). In addition to the mouse, power users rely on the keyboard, too. Keyboard shortcuts such as Ctrl+Alt+Del and special keys, like the Windows key, speed up their work.

Microsoft built its Windows operating systems on the assumption that you will use a mouse and a keyboard to control the operating system and the programs. This premise led Microsoft to create a GUI, which coordinates user interactions performed with these devices. It is always assumed that you have a pixel-precise pointer, and you can click on a small icon without any trouble.

Smaller devices such as Personal Digital Assistants (PDAs) and smartphones used to have hardware buttons or styluses to operate their interfaces. Because of their size, these devices are less effective when creating content than when consuming it. That being said, mimicking the desktop GUI on these devices might not have been the best choice. However, at the time when smartphones and PDAs started to become common, it was the best choice. The operating systems of these smart devices tried to re-create a simplified GUI of their bigger, desktop counterparts to preserve the user experience and ease the learning curve as much as possible.

In 2001, Microsoft created a third category of devices: the tablet PC. Tablet PCs were basically small laptops with reversible touchscreens. They were fully capable computers, but they were more mobile. With the touchscreen, you were able to manipulate the objects on the screen in a more natural way, without using a mouse or keyboard.

Because of its inherent shortcomings, the form factor of the tablet PC had little impact on the market back then. They were small devices — but still heavy. They were good devices for content creation and consumption — but they lacked a long battery life, and so on. Along with the hardware-related issues, a more pressing problem hindered tablet PCs from prevailing: the absence of a GUI like those built for (multi-) touchscreens. Windows XP merely enabled users to use their fingers instead of the mouse pointer.

In the past decade, another type of GUI has risen. Ordinary cell phones have become bigger and smarter. At one point, they became much like PDAs — digital companions, organizers, and content-consuming devices. However, if you look at a contemporary big-screen smartphone, you almost never find a stylus. And, more importantly, the GUI is totally different from what you'd find on a Windows desktop PC or on an older PDA.

This new kind of GUI was built from the ground up to let you manipulate objects on the screen naturally without using some additional hardware device like a stylus or keys. You can simply touch objects on the screen with your fingers, without any pointer or using a hardware device. The majority of these devices have a multi-touchscreen, so they can recognize manipulations done with multiple fingers — commonly referred to as *multi-touch gestures*. These features enable a more natural way to interact with your handheld device.

Though it is possible to use smartphones for content consumption like browsing the web or reading documents, the small, 3- to 4-inch screen often becomes a hurdle. Laptop computers are considered to be the other extreme. They are too big, too heavy, too noisy, and not mobile enough to do such simple tasks. They were built to let you do everything a computer can do. As content creation devices, they provide unparalleled possibilities, but this comes at a price.

To fill the gap between smartphones and laptops, a third kind of device reappeared — with a twist. They are still called tablets (sometimes *slates*), but most of the time they lack the hardware keyboard. They have 7- to 10-inch multi-touchscreens and only a handful of hardware buttons. Some of them have styluses, but primarily they leverage touch gestures as a user interaction method. And, because of this, they have inherited smartphone operating systems with a touch-centric GUI. Using these tablets often feels really natural, even for someone who hasn't used a computer yet.

The new kind of tablet can be considered a descendant of the smartphone. Unlike the older devices, they share almost nothing with desktop PCs, but they are decent content-consuming devices. Their GUI is completely different. They require different interaction methods to be powerful, and, just as importantly, they don't run the same applications.

Operating systems built on one of these UIs are predestined to be best for only one of two worlds. They are either good for a content-consuming device or for a content-creating device, but not for both.

Today's hardware has evolved to the point where the original tablet concept could become real, without all the illnesses it had ten years ago. Software, however, just isn't ready yet, because no operating system fits both of the two distinct usage methods.

With Windows 8, Microsoft created the first operating system that tries to be best of both worlds by providing a mix of the two UI paradigms. The well-known desktop applications are best suited for content-creating scenarios (such as writing books or programs), whereas Windows 8 style apps are best at consuming content (such as reading the aforementioned books).

The two-faced makeup of Windows 8 makes it the first operating system to be flexible enough to let you choose the method you want to use for any device that runs the operating system. Whether you are using a new-generation tablet with an external keyboard dock, an ultrabook with a built-in keyboard and a touchscreen, or a powerful laptop or desktop PC, you can always use the same, familiar operating system. Additionally, your Start screen, your settings, and your Windows 8 apps follow you through all the devices you use.

The seemingly complex nature of the Windows GUI and the improvements in the core of the operating system let you, the developer, build apps that run on every device that has a 7- to 70-inch screen (and, of course, adheres to certain hardware requirements). The apps are equally engaging when used with a multi-touchscreen, or controlled with a mouse and a keyboard. This no-compromise operating system offers a new level of comfort for the users, and, just as importantly, an unprecedented market opportunity for developers.

INPUT METHODS

If your device or PC has USB ports, you can use the mouse and the keyboard to interact with it. But with Windows 8, it is important to be aware of the other methods you can use to control a device.

Multi-Touch Input

Whereas the previous versions of Windows were primarily for desktop and laptop computers, Windows 8 opens up possibilities for a whole new range of devices — ARM-based tablets, tablets built on x64 architecture, the new ultrabooks, and so on. A common feature of these is the multi-touch-capable, capacitive touchscreen. While building Windows 8 style apps, it is best to create the UI with that in mind.

Microsoft helps you with two things in building touch-centric apps:

➤ The out-of-the-box controls that arrive with Visual Studio 2012 for Windows 8 style apps are suited for mouse and touchscreen use as well. You learn about these controls in later chapters of this book.

➤ Microsoft ensures a consistent usage of specific single- and multi-touch gestures throughout the operating system, and a clear and concise way to describe them. These are user interactions done with one or two fingers.

Following are all the gestures defined for Windows 8. It is a good practice to keep them in mind, because all Windows users will know them, and you can build your apps to adhere to this quasi-standard.

➤ **Tap** — This is the main interaction with an object on the screen, such as starting an app by touching its Live Tile on the Start screen. You can think of this as the touch counterpart of a mouse click.

➤ **Tap and Hold** — This is a secondary interaction with an object, such as bringing up the context menu by touching the object for a second without releasing it. This is much like the right-click with the mouse.

➤ **Slide** — Programs without any kind of list are very rare. Scrolling a list usually means clicking (or tapping) a scrollbar to move the view. Though this is still possible to do, it is much more natural for touchscreen users to move the view by touching the list with one finger, and flicking it. The list will *pan*, or scroll in that direction.

➤ **Swipe** — Use this gesture to select an object on the screen. A swipe is similar to a slide. You touch an object with one finger, and pull it down slightly without releasing it. When you stop and release, you complete a swipe gesture. If you don't stop moving your finger downward, when you release the screen, it'll likely to be interpreted as a slide gesture.

➤ **Pinch** — This multi-touch gesture involves two fingers touching the screen at the same time, and moving them toward each other or apart. Usually, this gesture is linked to zooming effects, either magnifying or shrinking an image or any other object.

➤ **Rotate** — This gesture is performed by using two fingers to touch the screen, and turning around a center point (which can be one of the fingers). This gesture can be used for turning or rotating an object.

➤ **Swipe from the Edge** — As you see later in this chapter, edges and corners of the screen have important functions in Windows 8. Thus, a swipe gesture on one of the edges on the screen might be used to activate something useful. For example, if you swipe from the right edge of the touchscreen, you will always open the charm bar (which, as you learn later in this chapter, contains the Start button and several other useful features). If you swipe from the bottom of the screen, that usually activates the context bar for application commands (which you also learn more about later in this chapter).

Figure 2-1 shows all these gesture interactions.

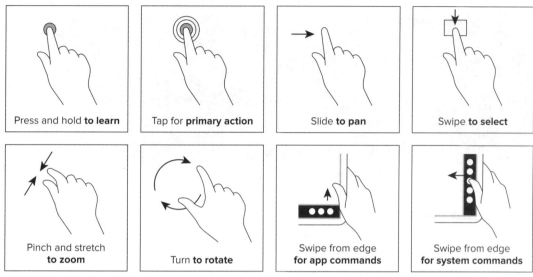

FIGURE 2-1: Windows 8 touch gestures

NOTE *You can find more detailed information about gestures at* http://msdn
.microsoft.com/en-us/library/windows/apps/hh761498.aspx.

The Software Keyboard

A lot of Windows 8 devices will be too small to have a hardware keyboard. Keyboard input on these devices is done by using an on-screen, software keyboard. When a user taps in a text box (or some other control that awaits keyboard input), the software keyboard automatically pops up on the bottom of the screen. On smaller screens, this means that the keyboard takes up most of the space. Thus, when designing an app that receives alphanumeric user input, you must ensure that the control is sized well enough to fit the smallest screen resolution when the software keyboard is open.

Windows 8 ships with multiple software keyboard layouts, which help you to be able to type on the keyboard as comfortably as possible. On certain layouts, the size of the buttons can be modified, too. However, the layout of the software keyboard and the size of the buttons don't affect the space the whole keyboard requires.

Figure 2-2 shows the new "two thumbs" keyboard layout, which helps you to type comfortably only with your thumbs while holding a Windows 8 tablet with both of your hands. The vertical ellipsis in the upper-left corner lets you choose the size of the buttons (with the biggest setting being shown in the figure).

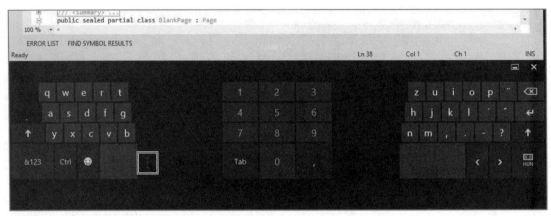

FIGURE 2-2: The software keyboard with a special layout

Other Input Devices

Most of the time, your apps will be used in conjunction with either a mouse or touchscreen. But that doesn't mean that other input devices aren't supported by Windows 8.

Some devices — mostly handheld ones — are equipped with a *stylus*. A stylus is a touchscreen aid that provides much greater precision than using bare fingers. But, because a stylus is not common, you should build the UI for normal touch input.

A more important kind of input device is the sensor. The vast majority of new Windows 8 tablets are going to have built-in equipment to detect the device's location and attitude (the way you hold the device), among other things. If the device or computer has a sensor, its data can be used in your Windows 8 style app.

Following are some examples of sensors:

➤ A global positioning service (GPS) tells you the geographical location of the device.

➤ An accelerometer informs you about the change of the device's velocity.

➤ A gyroscope tells you the rotation speed of the device.

➤ A magnetometer or compass tells you the angle of the north direction.

➤ An ambient light sensor informs you about the lighting conditions of the device's surroundings.

You can incorporate the sensory input into your app easily by using the APIs provided by Microsoft, and this gives you the opportunity to create more engaging or easy-to-use applications.

LOGGING IN

Logging in to the operating system is not really an important thing from a Windows 8 app developer's standpoint — apart from the fact that you can't write apps if you don't log in. But it is worth noting that Windows 8 was built to be used with Microsoft Accounts (which is basically a new name for Live ID), as opposed to plain, local user accounts on every computer.

> **NOTE** *Windows Live is Microsoft's collection of online services. You can access them via* `http://live.com`. *Windows Live includes mail, calendar, online storage, and instant messaging functionality. You can access all of these for free by creating a Microsoft Account at* `http://live.com`.

This means that if you log in with your Live ID e-mail address and password, Windows 8 enables you to reach everything stored in Live Services as easily and seamlessly integrated as possible. For example, if you open `http://live.com` in Internet Explorer, you'll be logged in immediately with the login and password you use to log in to Windows. Or, if you want to select a picture in an app, you'll see not only images on the computer you're using, but all the images you store on your SkyDrive — just as though they were stored locally. (Of course, this is true only if the computer can access the Internet to get these pictures from SkyDrive.)

> **NOTE** *SkyDrive is Microsoft's free online storage technology. If you have a Microsoft Account (formerly known as Windows Live ID), you get 5 GB of free storage space that you can use to make your photos and documents available online at* `http://www.skydrive.com`. *You can make these files privately or publicly accessible, or you can share them with others.*

When you build an app, you can leverage this Live integration, and allow your app to use the user information and data just as seamlessly as if it were built by Microsoft into Windows 8. The first time the user starts the app and it tries to log in to Windows Live, the user is presented with a screen that asks for permissions for the app. After the user reads the details and clicks or taps OK, the app will be able to do all the things the user has approved — reading e-mails, accessing personal data, downloading or uploading files to SkyDrive, and so on. The user can revoke these permissions at any time.

In addition to Microsoft Accounts, using ordinary local accounts is still a possibility.

Two new login types are also worth mentioning. Because strong passwords might take a long time (and some effort) to type, this can be especially cumbersome on a touchscreen device without a hardware keyboard. Windows 8 lets you create an image and/or a personal identification number (PIN) login, in addition to the traditional strong password login.

Picture password lets you choose a picture, draw three figures on it (points, lines, and circles), and the next time you have to log in, lets you log in without having to type a possibly long password. You just have to repeat drawing the three figures in the same sequence and at the same places — which is very easy using a touchscreen.

The *PIN password* option simply lets you choose a four digit personal identification number, which is easier to type in than a long password.

THE START SCREEN

After logging on to your Windows 8 device, the first screen you encounter is the new Start screen. Windows 8 takes a giant and bold leap — the Start menu you knew for decades is no more. However, as you will see, every function the old Start menu had lives on in the Start screen, so you will get used to it very fast.

Evolution of the Start Menu

Basically, the Start screen represents an evolution of the Start menu. As a result of this evolution, instead of icons or plaintext, you get the fascinating Live Tiles. If you are familiar with Microsoft's latest mobile phone operating system (Windows Phone 7), you already have the gist of these. If you are new to the Windows 8 design, they might seem like simply bigger icons. But they can do much more — they can contain rich and changing content!

The *Calendar Live Tile* synchronizes with your online calendars (Windows Live, Hotmail, Exchange, and so on), and presents you with information about your next appointment. When you look at your *Messaging Live Tile*, you can see how many instant messages are waiting to be answered. On the *Weather Live Tile*, you can see basic weather information, and the *People Tile* tells you about status updates for your friends on various social networks. Figure 2-3 shows the Start screen in action.

FIGURE 2-3: The Windows 8 Start screen

These Live Tiles represent applications and programs, just like the Start menu did before. But they also provide basic information regarding the purpose of the application. So, you don't even have to start these applications — you just take a glance on your Start screen, and all the important information is available right there.

Of course, it is very likely that you will want to have more Live Tiles than can fit on one screen. The number of tiles placed vertically on your Start screen is adapted to the resolution of your screen, so on a bigger monitor, you will automatically get more rows of tiles. However, your tiles can overflow horizontally. By leveraging this feature, you can place an arbitrary number of Live Tiles on your Start screen. You learn more about placing Live Tiles on the Start screen later in this chapter.

A *list control* is a basic programming and UI concept that you should be aware of. A list control is a part of an application that represents an arbitrary number of UI elements, usually in a unified manner. Under All Programs in the Windows 7's Start menu, you can see a basic example of a list control — all your programs represented as icons and simple strings.

The item panel in Windows Explorer is a more complex list control. It can represent the contents of a folder in many ways (small or large icons, details, or a simple list), and it has grouping and sorting capabilities.

List controls may be different from each other, but they share a few common features that every Windows user has become familiar with over the years.

Because the Start screen is a kind of list control, it shares these usability features. If you happen to use a mouse and a keyboard, scrolling the Start screen works just as you would think. There is a scrollbar at the bottom of the Start screen, which you can use to move the view to the left or the right. Just like any list control you may have previously encountered, you can use the wheel on your mouse to scroll the Start screen. Additionally, try to put your mouse pointer on the right edge, and move it to the right. As you can see on Figure 2-4, the view moves to the right.

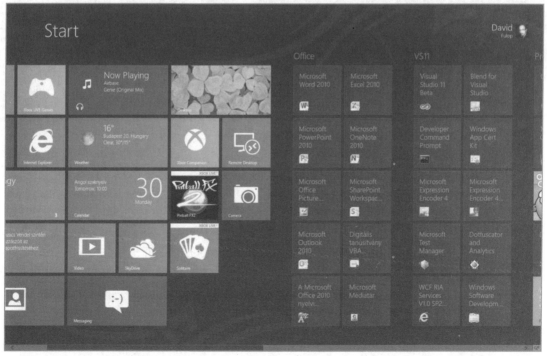

FIGURE 2-4: Sliding the Start screen

If you have a touchscreen device, you can leverage the natural user interactions. Just touch the Start screen anywhere (except the very edges of the screen), and slide your finger horizontally. The view follows your gesture.

Although scrolling or sliding the screen can be quite convenient, there is a way to look at all the Live Tiles from a zoomed-out view. The zoomed-out view shrinks your Live Tiles on the Start screen, and lets you see all of them at once. This way you can quickly jump to a point (a particular Live Tile) in lieu of having to scroll through all of them. Figure 2-5 shows the Start screen in zoomed-out view.

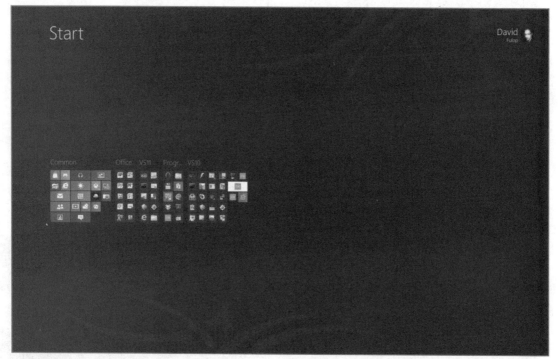

FIGURE 2-5: The Start screen in zoomed-out view

You dive into using and managing Live Tiles, as well as using the zoomed-out view, a bit later in this chapter. However, let's first see how you can look for apps on the Windows 8 Start screen.

Browsing and Searching for Installed Apps

In a way, your apps define the capabilities of your entire system. Therefore, adding new features and facilities means adding and installing new apps. You could quickly find yourself in a situation where you have more apps than you want to appear on the Start screen as Live Tiles.

> **NOTE** By the way, there is no point in having all the apps pinned to your Start screen — you surely won't use every single app equally frequently.

Certainly, you will prioritize, and hide (unpin) some apps. Where (or more specifically, how) can you find these apps?

In previous versions of Windows, the Start menu's All Programs section was the central place to list all the installed software, browse the installed software, and search for a particular application. As stated earlier, every function of the old Start menu lives on in the Start screen — but you won't find a Live Tile named, "All Programs."

On the Apps screen, you see groups identified by letters. These contain apps whose names start with the letters in the group's name. Some of them have a very less-than-expressive name (such as "Windows System"). These groups are like folders in the old Start menu. They contain programs that were installed along with each other, and they are accordingly tied together by some relationship.

The new Apps screen (and its features) helps you to be able to browse in your numerous apps — a fast and fluid experience compared to the old Start menu with one long list.

This is an efficient way to get to the app you have been looking for. Ever since the release of Windows Vista, the old Start menu had a rather splendid trait — searching programs. Upon opening the Start menu, you were presented with a text box, and you just had to start typing. The Start menu filtered its contents. When you knew that you were looking for something specific like the Control Panel, you just clicked Start, typed **co**, and clicked the Control Panel icon without having to go through a long list.

In Windows 8, you can leverage this familiar workflow, as you see in the next exercise. Also, you learn how to browse applications that have already been installed on your computer or device, and how to pin apps on the Start screen.

TRY IT OUT **Browsing, Searching for Apps, and Pinning Apps on the Start Screen**

To browse or search for apps in the Start screen, follow these steps:

1. With the mouse, right-click any empty area (that is, anywhere but a Live Tile) of the Start screen. The bottom menu appears with one command, "All apps," as shown in Figure 2-6. When using a touchscreen device, use the "swipe from the edge" gesture on the bottom of the screen to achieve the same effect.

FIGURE 2-6: The "All apps" command in the bottom menu of the Start screen

2. Click or tap the "All apps" icon. The Live Tiles disappear, and you are now presented with the list of all the software installed on your system, as shown in Figure 2-7. You can scroll this list, just like you would scroll the Start screen itself, and you can click any icon or name to start the appropriate program. (You don't have to do that right now, but if you did so, you could use your keyboard's or device's Start button to get back to the Start screen. You learn more about this later.)

3. To search for an app by its name or affiliation to other apps, use the mouse wheel while pressing the Ctrl button on your keyboard, or make a pinch gesture on the screen to shrink the icons. The icons on the Apps screen merge into groups, as shown in Figure 2-8. Click a group to focus on the apps of that group.

Apps
9GAG - Learn to read Korean in 15...
Adobe Reader X
BackgroundTransfer
Calendar
Camera
Cut The Rope
Desktop
FileAccessSample
FilePickerSample
Finance
HttpClient
Internet Explorer
Mail
Maps
Messaging
Microsoft SQL Server 2000 Sampl...
Microsoft Web Platform Installer
Music
Opera
People
Photos
Pinball FX2
Recycle Bin
Remote Desktop
SkyDrive
Solitaire
Store
Video
Weather
Windows Defender
Windows Reader
Xbox Companion
Xbox LIVE Games
DivX Plus
Check for Updates
Codec Settings
DivX Plus Player
DivX Support
Post DivX® video to your website
Register
Why Buy DivX Pro
Dropbox
Dropbox
Dropbox Website
Media Player Classic - Ho...
Changelog
Media Player Classic - Home Cinema a...
Media Player Classic - Home Cinema x64
Microsoft Expression
Blend for Visual Studio
Microsoft Expression Encode...
Microsoft Expression Encode...
Microsoft Expression Encode...
Microsoft Office
A Microsoft Office 2010 nyelvi...
Digitális tanúsítvány VBA-projektekhez
Microsoft Access 2010
Microsoft Excel 2010
Microsoft InfoPath Designer 2010
Microsoft InfoPath Filler 2010
Microsoft Médiatár
Microsoft Office 2010 Upload Center
Microsoft Office Picture Manager
Microsoft OneNote 2010
Microsoft Outlook 2010
Microsoft PowerPoint 2010
Microsoft Publisher 2010
Microsoft SharePoint...
Microsoft Word 2010
Microsoft Silverlight
Microsoft Silverlight
Microsoft Silverlight 3 SDK
Welcome
Microsoft Silverlight 4 SDK
Welcome
Microsoft Silverlight 5 SDK
Welcome
Microsoft SQL Server 2008
Import and Export Data (64-bit)
SQL Server Error and Usage...
SQL Server Installation Center...
Microsoft SQL Server 2008...
Data Profile Viewer
Execute Package Utility
Import and Export Data (32-bit)
Reporting Services Configuration...
SQL Server Configuration...
SQL Server Installation Center...
SQL Server Management Studio

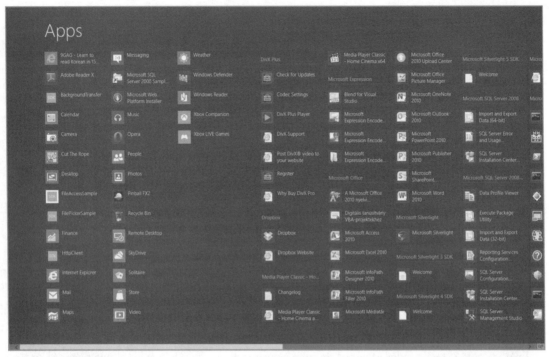

FIGURE 2-7: The Apps screen

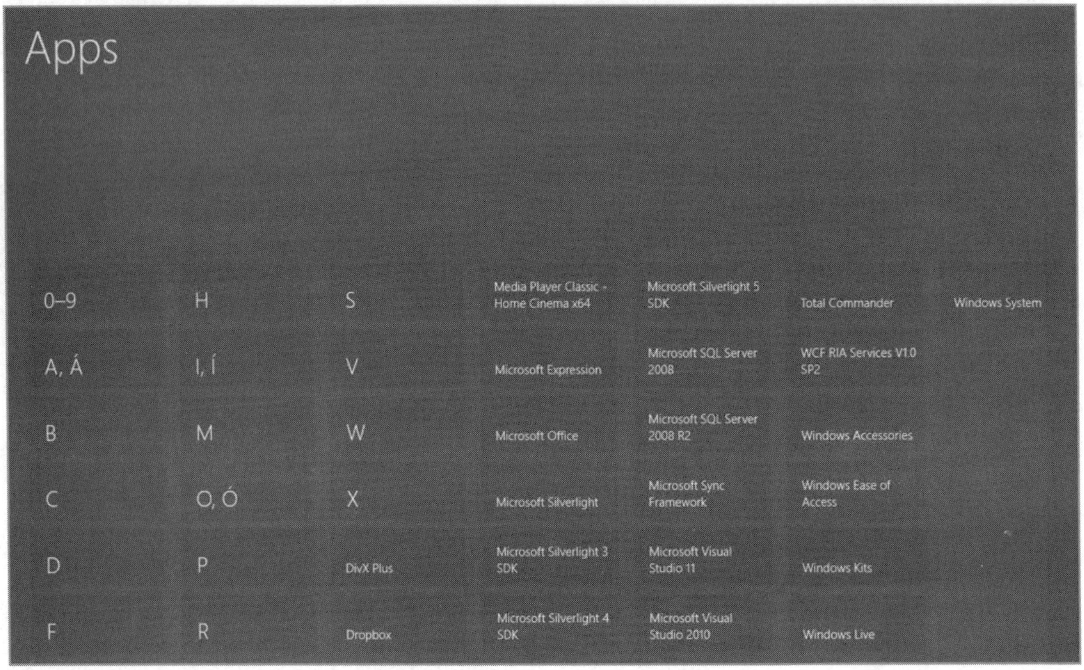

Apps
0–9
A, Á
B
C
D
F
H
I, Í
M
O, Ó
P
R
S
V
W
X
DivX Plus
Dropbox
Media Player Classic - Home Cinema x64
Microsoft Expression
Microsoft Office
Microsoft Silverlight
Microsoft Silverlight 3 SDK
Microsoft Silverlight 4 SDK
Microsoft Silverlight 5 SDK
Microsoft SQL Server 2008
Microsoft SQL Server 2008 R2
Microsoft Sync Framework
Microsoft Visual Studio 11
Microsoft Visual Studio 2010
Total Commander
WCF RIA Services V1.0 SP2
Windows Accessories
Windows Ease of Access
Windows Kits
Windows Live
Windows System

FIGURE 2-8: Application groups in the Apps screen

4. Press the Start button on your keyboard or your touchscreen device to return to the Start screen.

   If your keyboard doesn't have a Start button, move your mouse cursor to the lower-right corner of your screen to open the charm bar. If you use a touchscreen device that has no hardware Start button, use the "swipe from the edge gesture" on the right side of the screen to do the same.

   Five icons appear, overlapping the content of the screen. Click (or tap) the blue window-shaped icon in the middle to return to the Start screen. (You learn more about the charm bar later in this chapter.)

5. To search for an app, start typing on your keyboard when the Start screen is open.

   For example, press C. The same Apps screen appears that you already met in this "Try It Out" exercise — with two differences. First, it's now filtered down to showing only the apps whose name starts with the letter "c". Second, on the right side of the screen, a sidebar appears. This contains the text box you've been typing into, and some other things as well.

   Achieving the same with a touchscreen device that lacks a hardware keyboard is a bit trickier. To open the Search bar that you can use to look for apps, use the "swipe from the edge" gesture on the right edge of the screen. This brings out the charm bar, as shown in Figure 2-9. Then tap the upper-most icon of the charm bar, called Search. The familiar Apps screen shows up, with a sidebar on the right. This sidebar contains a text box. Tap in the text box to bring up the virtual keyboard, and tap the "c" key.

6. Press or tap the "o" key. The apps are filtered again, so now you can see only apps whose name contains "co," as shown in Figure 2-10.

7. To pin the Control Panel app on the Start screen, right-click or swipe down the app's icon to choose it. This brings up the context bar on the bottom of the screen, as shown in Figure 2-11. The context bar contains four icons. Click or tap the first one that reads "Pin to Start." The context bar disappears, and if you return to the Start screen, you'll find the Control Panel on the very right end of the screen. (You may have to scroll to find it.) The next time you select the Control Panel this way, the first button on the context bar will read "Unpin from Start." By clicking or tapping that icon, you can reverse this, and erase the Live Tile from your Start screen.

FIGURE 2-9: The charm bar with the Search command

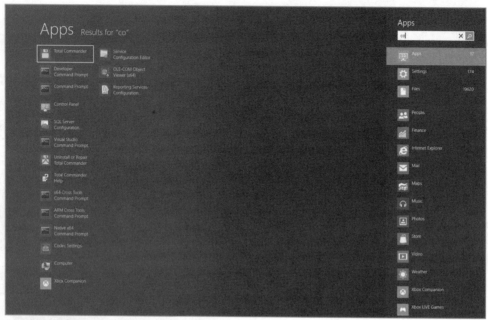

FIGURE 2-10: Applications with "co" in their names

FIGURE 2-11: A selected app icon with the opened context bar

NOTE *You aren't restricted to looking for only the first word of the name of an app. The filtering algorithm looks for the entered substring in every word of the name of an application. For example, if you type* **c**, *the icon of "Windows Media Center" will appear on the list, because one of the words in its name starts with "c."*

Both the charm bar and the Search function are central features of Windows 8, which you learn about later in this chapter. But now let's see what you can do with the central parts of the Start screen — Live Tiles.

Using Live Tiles

As you learned earlier, a Live Tile could be considered a shortcut because it represents an application. But Live Tiles aren't merely grown-up icons. They channel out some of the data consumed by the application to let you be more efficient. You don't have to open an e-mailing application to see whether you have new e-mails waiting. You just have to take a peek at the app's Live Tile.

Actually, some applications could have more than one Live Tile. For example, you can tell certain weather apps to pin a Live Tile on the Start screen that shows the weather of one city, and pin another Live Tile to show information on another. This feature is optional, though. The only applications that provide this feature are the ones that were prepared (programmed) to do so.

To start an application, just click its Live Tile (or tap it, if you use a touchscreen device). On most of the Live Tiles, this action causes the app to simply start. But it's good to know (not just as a developer) that special Live Tiles (secondary tiles) can contain some initialization information for the app. This feature (called *deeplinking*) allows the user to not just start the application, but specify what part of the app he or she wants to use. For example, if the user pins a Live Tile about the weather of Budapest using the aforementioned weather application, and later starts the weather app through this Live Tile, the app will open and show the forecast on Budapest.

Now, let's take a look at the basic operations with and on Live Tiles.

The Context Bar of a Live Tile

When you use Windows (or any graphical desktop operating system, for that matter), you are introduced to the notions of context and pop-up menus. These provide extra operations on a graphically represented object — whether that is an icon on the desktop, or the desktop itself. Context menus appear in Windows 8 in a more controlled manner — at least in terms of place and design. When you right-click the Start screen to bring up the context bar, you see Windows 8's context menu.

Every Live Tile has its own context menu, and, of course, the items residing in those menus may vary a bit. When you bring up the context bar of Windows 8 style apps, you will probably find the following buttons:

➤ **Pin/Unpin from Start** — Clicking (or tapping) this button makes the selected Live Tile appear on the Start screen, or disappear from it — as you have already seen in the previous "Try It Out" exercise.

➤ **Uninstall** — Clicking or tapping this button erases the app behind the selected Live Tile from your device. You can reverse the effect by installing the app again from the Windows 8 Marketplace.

➤ **Larger/Smaller** — Some apps provide two kinds of the same Live Tile — a small, square-shaped one, and a twice-as-big, rectangular one, which provides more information. When a Live Tile is selected, and the app linked to it can have these two sizes of tiles, you will see a button either called Larger or Smaller on the context menu. These let you choose whether you want to use a small or a double-sized Live Tile with this app, but they appear only if the application supports large tiles.

➤ **Turn live tile off/on** — This button lets you turn off the notifications on a Live Tile, or turn them on again. When turned off, a Tile shows only a default icon representation of the app. These buttons appear only if the application behind the Tile supports notifications.

Windows 8 style apps are just half of the story. Windows 8 can run traditional Win32/.NET apps, too. When one of these apps is pinned on the Start screen, its corresponding Live Tile isn't really live; it will not be updated. Traditional software applications currently lack the means to do this. Also, the context bar of these programs will be a bit different.

When bringing up the context bar of traditional apps, in addition to the buttons of context bars for Windows 8 style apps, you will mostly find the following buttons:

➤ **Pin to taskbar** — You can use this button to permanently pin this program on the desktop's taskbar.

➤ **Open new window** — Use this button to open a new instance of the application on the desktop.

➤ **Run as Administrator** — Use this button to run the application on the desktop with Administrator privileges. Note that you don't need to be an Administrator to see this button, but upon using it, you will be prompted to type in an administrator's password.

➤ **Open file location** — Use this button to open the folder that contains the executable file for the application in Windows Explorer — and, of course, on the desktop.

As you can see, all of these buttons are related to the Windows desktop. Another difference from Windows 8 style apps is that you won't find Larger/Smaller and "Turn live tile on/off" buttons on the context bar for obvious reasons. In the next exercise you learn how to use the context bar of a Live Tile.

TRY IT OUT   Using the Context Bar of a Live Tile

To change the size of Live Tiles or turn them on/off with the context bar, follow these steps:

1. To bring up the context bar, right-click or swipe a Live Tile. For example, right-click or swipe the Music Live Tile. The Live Tile you've clicked receives a small frame and a mark on the top-right corner. Also, the context bar appears, as shown in Figure 2-12.

2. Click or tap the Smaller button on the context bar to make the Music Live Tile smaller. Note that the context bar automatically disappears after the operation, as shown in Figure 2-13.

FIGURE 2-12: The context bar of the Music Live Tile

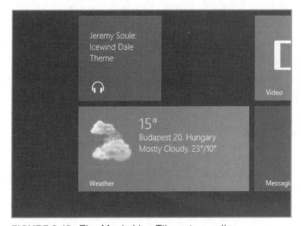

FIGURE 2-13: The Music Live Tile gets smaller

3. Right-click or swipe the Music Live Tile again. Click or tap the Larger button. The Live Tile becomes double-sized again.

4. To turn off updates of a Live Tile, first right-click or swipe the Music Live Tile. Then click or tap the "Turn live tile off" button on the context bar. The Live Tile will cease to update its contents; only a musical note will appear on it.

5. To turn updates back on, right-click or swipe the Music Live Tile. Click or tap on the "Turn live tile on" button. When you play music with the app, updates will appear again on the Tile.

How It Works

Live Tiles could be considered as small apps themselves — except that they have to be connected to a "real" application. When you build a Windows 8 style application, you are able to send status updates to the application's Live Tile through a third component, called a *background task*. The operating system calls the background agent from time to time, and lets it send two kinds of updates to the Live Tile — one for the smaller Live Tile and one for the larger version. By clicking or tapping the "Turn live tile off" button on the context bar, you can prevent the Live Tile from receiving these updates.

> **NOTE** *While the previously described scenario is the most common way for Live Tiles to work, there are special situations. You will learn more about Live Tiles in Chapter 9.*

You can select more than one Live Tile with the right-click action or the swipe gesture. When multiple Live Tiles are selected, only the "Unpin from Start" or the "Clear selection" button appears. The latter lets you deselect all the selected Live Tiles. To clear the selection of a single Live Tile, right-click the Live Tile again, or swipe it again.

Relocating Live Tiles

Live Tiles reside on the Start screen in a clean, ordered fashion. A column of tiles is comprised of two small (square) Live Tiles, and when tiles reach and occupy the final row (determined by the screen resolution), the next tile is placed in a new column.

To provide and maintain a consistent and familiar experience when using any Windows 8 device, the operating system will not allow anyone to change this layout mechanism. Customization, however, is well within reach. Apart from the actions previously described, users are able to assemble Live Tiles into groups, or simply transpose them to change the ordering.

Let's try changing the ordering.

TRY IT OUT Reordering Live Tiles

To reorder Live Tiles, follow these steps:

1. Move to the Start screen. Click and hold the left mouse button on a Live Tile. Budge the mouse slightly in any direction. All the other tiles freeze and go astern relative to the one you're holding, but the Live Tile you are holding onto has the same size it had. Also notice that it became semi-transparent.

    To do this on a touchscreen device, swipe the Live Tile downward, and don't release it until it completely unsnaps from its place.

2. Move the Live Tile freely in any direction. The other Live Tiles will move away to make room for the Live Tile you try to relocate, as shown in Figure 2-14.

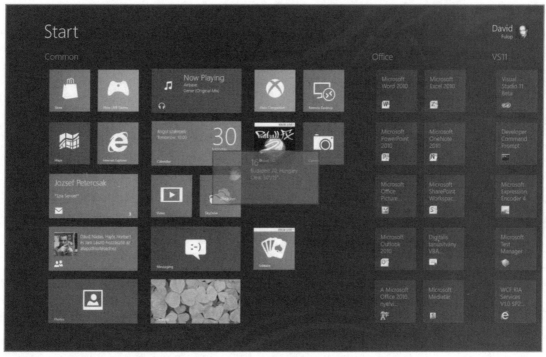

FIGURE 2-14: Relocating a Live Tile

3. Release the left mouse button or your finger when you have found the place where you want the Live Tile. The new order and layout will be preserved.

How It Works

When you unsnap a Live Tile from its place, Windows 8 understands that you want to place that Live Tile somewhere else on the Start screen. To help you do that, all the other Live Tiles freeze and shrink. When you move the Live Tile to a new place, the other Live Tiles automatically move away to show you how they are going to be arranged if you place the dragged Live Tile there.

Live Tile Groups

As you might have already noticed, Live Tiles on the Start screen are divided into groups. This grouping is very subtle. The only thing that gives it away is the bigger horizontal space between two columns of Live Tiles. Also, groups can have their own names, which are shown above the Live Tiles.

Creating a Live Tile Group

Creating Live Tile groups is fairly easy, but, oddly, you won't find a command button for this task on the context bar. When you drag a Live Tile to a new location, and the Live Tile hovers between two groups, a thick, light gray horizontal line appears. If you release the dragged Live Tile, it becomes the first item in a new Live Tile group.

Using Live Tile Groups

When you create a new Live Tile group, it has no name. If you want to give a name to the group, or you want to place it somewhere else among the other groups, you can enter the zoomed-out view of the Start screen. In this view, you see all the Live Tiles and groups at once. You cannot select individual Live Tiles in this overview, but you can select the groups (one at a time). Selecting a group opens up the context bar on the bottom of the screen with one command that reads "Name group." Selecting this command lets you add a name to the group, or modify it if it already exists.

Rearranging groups works somewhat similarly to relocating Live Tiles. In the zoomed-out view, you can select a Live Tile group, and drag it to where you want to place it. As you drag the group, the other groups move away to make space for the dragged one.

TRY IT OUT   **Managing Live Tile Groups**

To create a new Live Tile group, give it a name, and then place it somewhere else among the other groups, follow these steps:

1. Open the Start screen. Grab a Live Tile by clicking it and moving it away while still holding the left mouse button down. If you use a touchscreen device, swipe the Live Tile, and don't release it. When the Tile snaps out of its place, you can move it. Drag the Live Tile horizontally until it's directly above a bigger gap between the Live Tiles. (This is the separator between groups.) A thick gray line appears between the groups, as you can see in Figure 2-15. Release the Live Tile.

FIGURE 2-15: Creating a Live Tile group

2. Enter the zoomed-out view. You can achieve this by pressing the Ctrl key and using the mouse wheel, or by making a pinch gesture on the Start screen. If your mouse doesn't have a wheel, click the bottom-right corner of the screen. Figure 2-16 shows a Start screen in zoomed-out view.

3. Right-click or swipe the new group you just created in Step 1. This opens the context bar on the bottom of the screen. It has one command button: "Name group." Click or tap it, and in the pop-up window that appears above the context bar, give a name to the yet unnamed group. Figure 2-17 shows this step. When you have typed the name, click or tap on the Name button below the text box.

FIGURE 2-16: Zoomed-out view

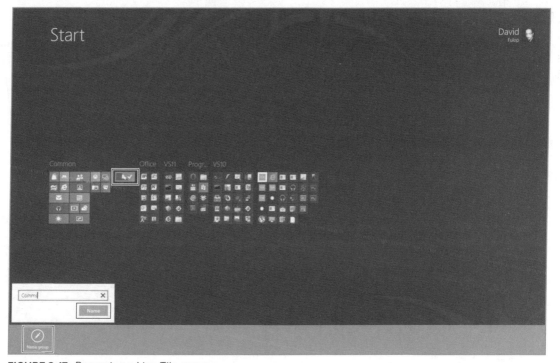

FIGURE 2-17: Renaming a Live Tile group

4. While still in the zoomed-out view, click and hold (or swipe) the group you created in Step 1. Move the mouse or your finger while holding on to the group. After moving a few pixels, the group snaps out of its place. Drag the group sideways until an adjacent group changes its place to make room for the group you are dragging, as shown in Figure 2-18. Release the mouse button or your finger to place the group there.

FIGURE 2-18: Arranging Live Tile groups

5. Click or tap anywhere on the screen to exit the zoomed-out view.

How It Works

Live Tile groups help you categorize the Live Tiles on your Start screen. You create a new group by placing a Live Tile between two groups, or on the edge of the Start screen. When you create a group, it is unnamed, but by selecting it in zoomed-out view you can name the group. Also in this overview view, you can change the arrangement of the groups.

Using Windows 8 Style Apps

Windows 8 and Windows 8 style apps are designed to be controlled easily with a mouse or with the touchscreen, too. There are a few (multi-) touch gestures with which you can accomplish specific tasks with — such as closing an app or switching between apps. Therefore, some differences exist between using Windows 8 style apps and using the good old Windows desktop and programs running on it, and you must be aware of these differences.

Closing a Windows 8 Style App

First of all, you can't really close a Windows 8 style app (unless, of course, you kill by using code, or by using the Task Manager). You can tell the operating system that you'd like the running application to be closed, but it won't release the app for a while.

This is mostly unimportant from a "how to use Windows 8" perspective, but as a result of this and several other design decisions, Windows 8 style apps don't have a close button. In fact, they don't have a frame, a header, or anything that could be considered *chrome*. (Microsoft usually refers to things in the design that have no function as chrome.)

Furthermore, Windows 8 style apps have no window; they are always full screen — except when used in split screen, but let's not get into that just yet. Therefore, closing a Windows 8 style app could be difficult at first, because most of these apps won't have a close button.

To close a Windows 8 style app, you can use a simple gesture that can be done with one finger or with the mouse. If you grab the "header" of the application (that is, the top few pixels of the screen), and drag it down to the bottom edge of the screen, the app closes, and you are thrown back to the Start screen.

It's really easy to use this gesture, and you should build your apps according to its implications. Don't place buttons or any other command controls too near to the top edge of the app. If it is not necessary, don't incorporate a "close" button in your app, because the users will be accustomed to using the gesture described previously.

Switching between Windows 8 Style Apps

What happens if you want to switch to another Windows 8 style app when using one? When you run a Windows 8 style app, it consumes all the pixels on your screen. There is no taskbar in Windows 8, so you can't just click the app's icon.

If your computer has a keyboard, you can use the old Alt+Tab or Windows key+Tab shortcuts to switch between apps. To do this with the mouse entirely, or to do this on a touchscreen device, you have to learn about another mouse movement or another gesture.

If you want to switch between Windows 8 style apps using a mouse, move the mouse to the top-left corner of the screen. The thumbnail picture of the app previously used will appear. If you click it, the current app goes to the background, and switches places with the last used one. If you don't click it, but move the mouse pointer down along the left edge of the screen, a black stripe appears, and on this stripe, every Windows 8 style app that runs in the background appears. You can click any of them to bring that one app to the screen.

If you use a touchscreen device, the method of switching apps is somewhat different. If you want to switch between apps, use the "swipe from the edge" gesture on the left side of the screen. The thumbnail picture of the previous app will appear. If you keep dragging this picture with your finger, and release it somewhere on the screen, it becomes active and full-screen again. With this gesture, you can go through all the running Windows 8 style apps.

To choose the exact app you want to switch to, use the "swipe from the edge" gesture on the left, and when the previous app's thumbnail appears, swipe it back to the edge. This opens the same black sidebar that you can see when using the mouse to access the running apps. When the apps sidebar is open, you can release the screen, and the sidebar will stay open. Then, just tap the app you want to reactivate.

> **NOTE** *It is worth noting that the thumbnail of the Start screen always resides on the bottom of the apps sidebar. If you click or tap this thumbnail, you get back to the Start screen. The app you've been using won't close. It just gets sent to the background.*

Using Multiple Windows 8 Style Apps at the Same Time

It is very likely that you will want to run two apps at the same time without having to switch back and forth between them. To support this very common scenario, Windows 8 style apps have three visual states.

Apart from the full-screen state that is the default, apps can be "filled" or "snapped." When you want to use two apps at the same time, one of them can be *snapped*, meaning it consumes only a small portion on one side of the screen. Meanwhile, another Windows 8 app can be *filled*, which means it takes up the rest of the space. By clicking or tapping and holding the narrow line between a snapped and filled app, and dragging the separator horizontally, you can make the apps switch their state (one from snapped to filled, and the other vice versa). Or, if you drag the line all the way to the edge of the screen and then release it, the app that was behind the line will be closed.

In the following "Try It Out" exercise, you will see these features in action by using their corresponding mouse- or touch-gestures.

TRY IT OUT   **Using Windows 8 Style Apps**

To become familiar with basic tasks with Windows 8 apps, follow these steps:

1. On the Start screen, click or tap an app's Live Tile to start the app. For example, start the Music app.

2. When the app is running, move the cursor to the top-left corner of the screen, and move it slightly downward. The sidebar appears with the currently running Windows 8 apps. To bring out this sidebar using a touchscreen, use the "swipe from the edge" gesture on the left edge, and immediately swipe back to the edge. Figure 2-19 shows an open sidebar.

3. Click or tap on the Start screen's thumbnail on the bottom of the sidebar to get back to the Start screen.

4. On the Start screen, click or tap on another app's Live Tile. For example, start the Weather app.

5. When it's running, repeat the process described in Step 2 to open the sidebar of the running apps.

6. Click or tap on the topmost thumbnail in the sidebar. This brings you back to the previously used app (the Music app). (Actually, you can do this by simply moving the mouse to the top-left corner, and clicking the thumbnail without opening the sidebar.)

7. Grab the header of the app. If you use a mouse, move the cursor toward the top edge of the screen until it becomes a small hand. Then click and hold the left mouse button, and move the cursor toward the bottom of the screen. Doing the same by using a touchscreen is very similar. Swipe the top edge of the screen to grab the app. The app shrinks to about half or third of its original size.

8. Drag the app toward either the left or right side of the screen, and release the left mouse button or your finger when it's near enough to the edge. This makes the app enter the snapped

FIGURE 2-19: The sidebar shows the running Windows 8 apps

state. While dragging the app, a pale vertical line appears that shows that if you release the dragged app, it'll be snapped to the nearer side of the screen. The bigger half of the screen will remain gray or empty. This area can show a filled app.

9. To fill the remaining empty space of the screen with the previous app, move the cursor to the top-left corner of the screen, and click the thumbnail of the last used app. If you use a touchscreen device, just use the "swipe from the edge" gesture on the left side of the screen. Figure 2-20 shows this stage.

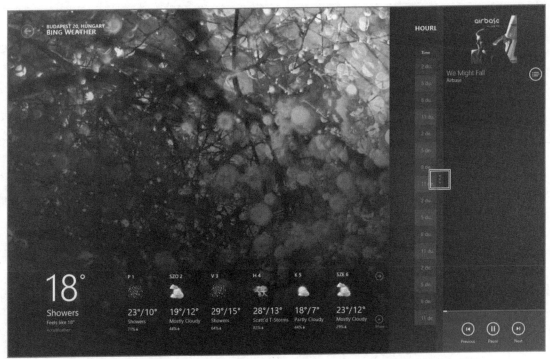

FIGURE 2-20: Filled-state Windows 8 app on the left, Snapped-state Windows 8 app on the right

10. To modify the division of the screen between the two apps, click and hold (or tap and hold if you are using a touchscreen) on the narrow dark gray line that separates the snapped and filled app. (It is highlighted in Figure 2-20.) Move the mouse or your finger toward the farther end of the screen until the filled app moves away. Release the mouse or the touchscreen to swap the ratios of screen size between the two apps.

11. Grab the separator line again, and move it to the nearest side of the screen. When you release it, the snapped app disappears, and the previously filled app becomes full screen.

12. To close the running app, first grab the header of it, just as you did in Step 7. Then move the app down to the very bottom of the screen. It'll become transparent if you move it close enough to the edge.

13. Release the mouse button to close the app. If you use a touchscreen device, don't release your finger before swiping it down to the bottom edge.

How It Works

Windows 8 style apps need a way for users to perform common tasks easily either by touch or by mouse. If you want to switch to another app, you can do it by moving the cursor to the top-left corner and clicking one of the thumbnails, or by swiping in the other running apps from the left edge. If you want to use two apps at the same time, you can split the screen into a smaller and a larger portion. Each can be filled by an app that can handle the snapped or filled layout style. To close a Windows 8 app, just grab its header, pull it down to the bottom edge of the screen, and then release it.

THE WINDOWS CHARM BAR

A few common tasks of the operating system need a central place to be easily accessible at any time. These tasks include things like getting back to the Start screen (akin to pressing the Windows button in previous Windows versions to open the Start menu), searching, switching between apps, and managing devices or settings. Moreover, because Windows 8 style apps fill the entire screen, these functions must be invisible, but still readily accessible.

As you have learned, app switching is tied to the left side of the screen. Gestures performed on the top edge are related to closing an app, or changing its size between the three layout states. The bottom edge of the screen is used to bring up a command or context bar. That leaves only the right edge to contain all the important operating system functions that are yet to be placed.

Introducing the Charm Bar

No matter whether you are on the Start screen, working in a Windows 8 style app, or on the desktop, if you move the mouse to one of the right corners of the screen (or use the "swipe from the edge" gesture on the right side of it), five buttons will appear on the right side. This is the *charm bar*.

The charm bar is sort of a central hub you use to work with your apps and with the operating system in general. It always contains the same five buttons — Start, Search, Share, Devices, and Settings — and it's always there, one swipe or mouse move away. Applications cannot override this behavior.

Figure 2-21 shows the Start screen with an open charm bar.

Also, when you open the charm bar, a little information box appears on the lower-left side of the screen that tells you the current date and time, the strength of the network signal, and the remaining battery strength.

The Start Button

With its central position and different color from all the other buttons, the Start button really stands out as something special. Given the important

FIGURE 2-21: The open charm bar

function of the Start button in previous Windows versions throughout history, this is quite under-standable. Note that, in Windows 8, there is no permanent Start button on the screen, and if you have a touchscreen device that lacks a hardware keyboard, without this button you have no means to return to the Start screen.

When you click or tap the Start button while using some app, it opens the Start screen. When you click or tap it again (while the Start screen is open), you are returned to the last app you used. This may seem like a somewhat different behavior from the previous Windows versions, but it is exactly the same. The difference actually lies in the new Start screen. It takes up the whole screen, not just a small portion of it like the Start menu did. But the app you were running when you clicked or tapped Start keeps running in the background; it is not suspended.

> **NOTE** *It is worth noting that on a computer equipped with a mouse, you can always use the Start screen's thumbnail (as you did already in the last "Try It Out" exercise). Move the cursor to the bottom-left corner of the screen while using a Windows 8 app, and click the thumbnail that appears.*

The Search Button

Finding files or apps on the PC or the device quickly is really important. Windows Vista made it quicker by placing a search box in the Start menu itself. In the earlier "The Start Screen" section and in its corresponding "Try It Out" exercise, you learned how to use this feature to find apps. But Windows 8 can do more!

When you bring out the charm bar, and click or tap the Search button, you'll get to the app search page you saw earlier. By default, Windows will look for apps that contain the text you type in their names. But, below the text box you type into, you can see three buttons: Apps, Settings, and Files. As you type, numbers appear on these buttons. These numbers tell you how many apps, Windows settings, or files have the text you typed in their names, and how many files contain the text you're looking for.

The Search screen shows only apps as you type, but when you click or tap the Settings or Files button, apps disappear, and you are presented with the filtered list of Windows settings or files. When looking for files, even categories show up on the top of the Search screen to help you speed up your search. Figure 2-22 shows the Search screen in Files mode.

When you build a Windows 8 app, you can set it up as a search provider. This means that the app is working with data that can be searched from outside the app — from the Windows Search screen. Provided that you indicated to Windows that your app can search in its data, Windows will enable you to search the app's data without having to start the app first.

Under the three main buttons are the apps that indicate to Windows that they have a search function inside them. When you click (or tap) one of these icons, the corresponding app is started, and you are immediately presented with the search results inside that app.

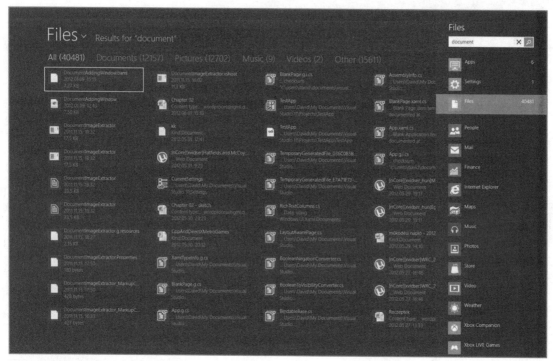

FIGURE 2-22: Searching files

The Share Button

Sharing information — links, documents, and so on — has become an everyday task over the past decade. Usually, this requires starting an app that "has" the information (like a browser that can open a specific web page), then starting another app that can be used to communicate with others (like an e-mail-client), then setting up the sharing method (creating a new e-mail), and copying the information from one app to another.

With Windows 8, this commonplace task becomes part of the system, which, in turn, simplifies it to save you time and effort. The Share button on the charm bar can be used in an app that can share data with other apps, to bring up a sidebar that enumerates the apps that accept this data. Clicking or tapping on one of the apps brings up that app, and immediately sets up everything it can, to be able to share the information with someone as quickly as possible (like creating an e-mail, and setting the sender and the message body).

In the following exercise, you can see how easy this is.

TRY IT OUT Sharing via the Charm Bar Apps

Follow these steps to share some data between apps using the Windows charm bar:

1. Start Internet Explorer (IE) by clicking or tapping its Live Tile on the Start screen.

2. Navigate to www.microsoft.com by clicking or tapping into the text box on the bottom of the app, and then typing the URL. When you have finished typing, press Enter, or tap on the arrow next to the text box.

3. When the page is opened, open the charm bar by moving the mouse cursor to the top or bottom-right corner of the screen, or by doing a swipe gesture on the right edge of the screen. Click or tap on the Share button on the charm bar to make Windows list all the apps that can accept and share the URL that is opened in IE. Until you install other apps, only the Mail app will show up in the list. Figure 2-23 shows the sidebar that lists the accepting apps.

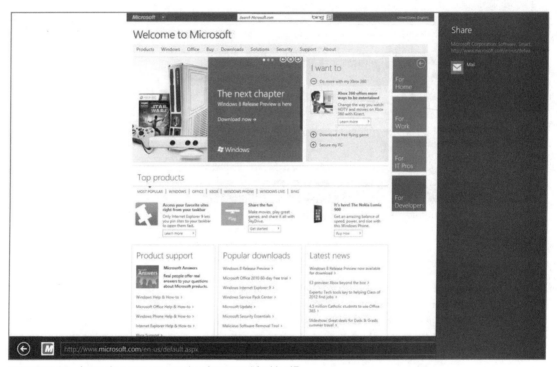

FIGURE 2-23: Apps that can accept the data provided by IE

4. Click or tap the Mail app's icon. The Mail app opens on the right side of the screen, and it immediately shows an e-mail that is almost ready to be sent. Figure 2-24 shows what you should see on your device.

5. Type an e-mail address into the text box of the Mail app (you can click or tap on the suggested addresses to speed up the process), and click or tap the Send button on the top-right corner of the app. (It is highlighted in Figure 2-24.) The Mail app indicates that the e-mail is being sent, and then it vanishes.

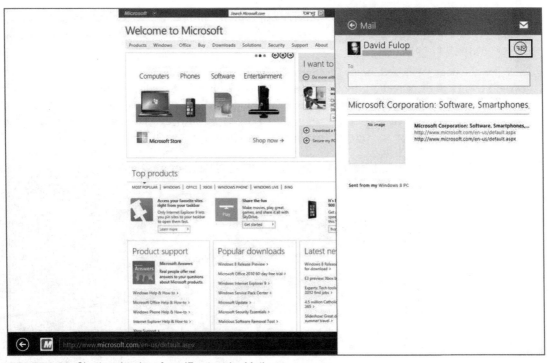

FIGURE 2-24: Sharing the data from IE using the Mail app

How It Works

Windows 8 apps can indicate to Windows that they can share some kind of data or information with other apps. An app can send this data to another one that can accept it. When using a Windows 8 app, bring out the charm bar and select the Share button to start sharing. Then select the app that you'd like to receive the information. The app that is the target of the sharing will receive the data through Windows, and can process (do whatever it wants with) it.

The Devices Button

PCs and tablets aren't standalone, monolithic hardware. They almost always can connect to some kind of peripherals — external monitors, input devices, docks, and so on. Desktop PCs have a constant set of these most of the time, because they aren't moved a lot. Laptops and tablets, on the other hand, are mobile devices, and they might be used in different environments all the time. Different environments could lead to different peripherals. If you use your laptop while travelling, you use it all by itself, but when you arrive back at your office, you'll probably connect a mouse and a second screen to it.

The Devices button lets you access these connected external hardware devices in one central place. You don't have to go to the Control Panel or My Computer to see the devices. Just open the charm bar, and click or tap on the Devices button to see a list of them.

The Settings Button

The last button on the charm bar is "everything else" that is useful in the everyday use of your device. When you click or tap on the Settings button, the Settings bar opens. This contains slightly different things when opened from Windows 8 (that is, when opened from the Start screen, or while using a Windows 8 app), than when opened from the desktop. (You learn more about the desktop shortly.) Figure 2-25 shows the Settings Bar opened in Windows 8 mode.

On the lower end of the Settings bar you will find six icons. From left to right (and from top to bottom), these include the following:

➤ **Network** — This indicates whether your PC or device has an active local area network (LAN) or Internet connection, and the signal strength (when using Wi-Fi). Clicking or tapping it opens the Networks sidebar that you can use to connect to networks.

➤ **Volume** — This shows the volume setting of the speakers or headphones attached to the computer. Clicking or tapping it opens the volume slider, which you can use to adjust this setting.

➤ **Brightness** — This shows the brightness setting of the screen, if available. Clicking or tapping this icon opens the brightness slider, which you can use to adjust this setting.

➤ **Notifications** — Some applications (and Windows 8 itself) can create pop-up (or *toast*) notifications. These are little boxes that appear on the screen with some information, and they disappear after a few seconds. By clicking or tapping this

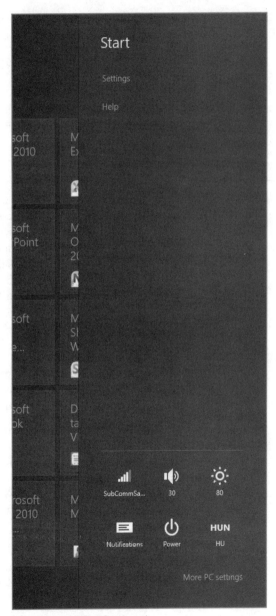

FIGURE 2-25: The Settings bar

button, you can enable or disable these notifications to stop all the apps that might be disturbing you.

➤ **Power options** — Click or tap on this button to shut down, restart, hibernate your PC, or send it to sleep mode. Available power options may vary, depending on various other settings or policies.

➤ **Keyboard locale** — This icon indicates the current locale and layout of the software and hardware keyboards. Click or tap on this button to switch to another keyboard layout.

Under these six buttons is a link that reads "More PC settings." If you click or tap on it, the PC Settings app opens. Here you can manage the most important settings of your computer.

The Settings bar can function as a settings page for your app. You can add custom content to it, and by using these, the user can manage the active app's settings.

THE WINDOWS DESKTOP

As you learned in Chapter 1, Windows has a very long history — one that dates back to the early 1990s. Microsoft has always kept backward compatibility as a primary goal when releasing new incarnations of its operating systems. Windows 8 changes a lot of things with its Windows 8 UI, Windows 8 style apps, and turning the Start menu into a full-screen Start screen. After logging in, you were always presented with the Windows desktop — the place where all the programs run in separate windows. Now, in Windows 8, you are immediately sent to the Start screen. What happened to the desktop, and what about the non-Windows 8 apps you used to use?

Introducing the Desktop App

On the Start screen, you'll find a somewhat unique app, called the Desktop app. When you click or tap it, you get to the good old Windows desktop that hasn't changed too much since Windows 7. Note that if you unpin it for some reason, you can always pin it back from the Apps search page. See the earlier section, "The Start Screen," for more information.

It is imperative to understand that the Desktop app itself can be treated like any other Windows 8 app! You can close it by pulling it down. You can make it snapped or filled, and it'll show up as any ordinary app on the apps sidebar on the left side of the screen when you open the sidebar. What makes it special is that it runs all the legacy desktop apps created for previous Windows versions, and all the non-Windows 8 apps created for Windows 8. Figure 2-26 shows the Desktop app in filled-state while another Windows 8 app is taking the snapped position.

Apart from starting the Desktop app itself from the Start screen, there is another way to switch to the Windows desktop. When you start a non-Windows 8 app in Windows 8, that app immediately starts the Desktop app. This is quite reasonable, because without this behavior, starting non-Windows 8 apps would result in a lot of running (but inaccessible) desktop apps.

If the Desktop app is closed, all the desktop programs it was running are kept running in memory. Nothing will happen to them; they are just inaccessible until you re-open the Desktop app.

FIGURE 2-26: The Desktop app and another Windows 8 app sharing the screen

Switching between Desktop Programs

If you have a keyboard, you can switch between all the programs (Windows 8 and non-Windows 8 apps as well) by pressing and holding the Alt key, pressing the Tab key repeatedly, and releasing the Alt key when you reach the app or desktop program you want to use.

On a touchscreen device that lacks these keys, you can just bring the Desktop app to the foreground, and tap an application's icon on the taskbar. Of course, mouse users can do the same by clicking the icon, just like in older Windows versions.

Desktop apps won't show up on the apps sidebar on the left side of the screen, only the Desktop app itself that runs them.

Where Is the Start Button?

In Windows 8, Microsoft decided to break the tradition of putting a Start button on the bottom-left corner of the screen. But this doesn't mean you have to learn a new workflow to open the Start screen.

Between the left edge of the screen and the leftmost icon on the taskbar, there is always a small empty space. When you move the mouse cursor to this bottom-left corner of the screen, the thumbnail of the Start screen appears. Click it to open the Start screen. It's really not that different from what you've done in previous Windows versions.

Of course, pressing the Windows key on a keyboard results in the same effect.

For touchscreen users, the previously described options are available to open the Start screen from anywhere, including the Desktop app. You can open the charm bar by swiping the right edge of the screen, and then just tap on the Start button. Or, you can swipe the left edge to open the app bar, and then tap the Start screen thumbnail in the bottom of the sidebar.

SUMMARY

With Windows 8, you can harness the power of a new breed of applications and infrastructural services. Windows 8 applications provide a way to build tablet-friendly applications while preserving all the advantages of traditional desktop software. With the aid of Windows 8, you can build apps that will run on a wider spectrum of devices — desktops, laptops, and tablets. By leveraging multi-touch gestures and mouse gestures, the functionality of corners and edges, share, and search contracts, you can build more intuitive applications — but this comes at a price. As a developer, you must know how to use the UI effectively, either with mouse or with a touchscreen.

The purpose of the Start screen is not just to serve as a full-screen Start menu. Users are more likely to pin an app on the Start screen if its Live Tile continually provides them with useful information.

The charm bar is a central place where users look for features like searching and sharing things. If an app provides searching and/or sharing functions, it is a good practice to provide these by hooking up the app to the Search and Share hubs on the charm bar.

In Chapter 3, you learn a few internal details about the architecture of Windows 8 to understand what components help you build Windows 8 style applications.

EXERCISES

1. How can you switch to the previous Windows 8 style application by touch?

2. Where can you look for an application that doesn't have a Live Tile on the Start screen?

3. How can you make a Live Tile stop refreshing its content?

4. How can you close a Windows 8 style app?

5. How can you share data in one app with another app?

6. How can you switch to the Windows Desktop app to run a desktop app?

> **NOTE** *You can find answers to the exercises in Appendix A.*

► **WHAT YOU LEARNED IN THIS CHAPTER**

TOPIC	KEY CONCEPTS
Multi-touch gestures	The tap, press-and-hold, slide, swipe, pinch, swipe from the edge, and rotate gestures let the user interact with an app more intuitively and naturally when using a touchscreen device.
Login modes	Although the traditional password login is still available, you can use a four-digit personal identification number (PIN) password and a more touch-friendly picture login, too.
Start screen	This is the descendant of the old Start menu. This is the central screen to work with your PC or tablet.
Live Tile	A Live Tile is a shortcut to an app, but it can show information that is continuously updated from the background, even when the corresponding app is not running. Live Tiles reside on the Start screen, and can be grouped.
Apps sidebar	You can open the Apps sidebar on the left side of the screen, and it shows all the currently running Windows 8 apps.
Full screen, snapped, filled	Windows 8 apps can have these three layout states. The screen of the device can accommodate one full-screen app, or a snapped and a filled one. The snapped app resides on either side of the screen, and can provide full functionality, despite the smaller size. The filled app takes all the remaining screen space left by the snapped app.
Charm bar	The charm bar is a central place in Windows 8 that you use to do common tasks. Here you can find the Search and the Share buttons, which serve as hubs for apps providing searching or sharing features, respectively. The Start button is also placed in the charm bar.
Share	This button on the charm bar provides you with the option to send data from one app to another.
The Windows desktop	This is the place where all the non-Windows 8 apps reside and run. It still has a central and crucial function on desktop and laptop PCs, and is accessible by starting a non-Windows 8 app, or by starting the Desktop app itself from the Start screen.

3

Windows 8 Architecture from a Developer's Point of View

WHAT YOU WILL LEARN IN THIS CHAPTER:

➤ Understanding the separate technology stacks for Windows 8 style applications and desktop applications

➤ Grasping the role of Windows Runtime in developing Windows 8 style applications

➤ Getting to know which programming languages can be used to access Windows Runtime application programming interfaces (APIs)

➤ Understanding the new features of .NET Framework 4.5

➤ Choosing the appropriate programming language and technology stack to create your own Windows 8 applications

When you develop applications, you generally use a set of technologies that work together. The Windows development platform provides a plethora of tools, techniques, and technologies. In the last decade, the number of these components increased tremendously. Windows 8 provides a new development model via a new kind of application — Windows 8 style apps — that support several programming languages (C++, C#, Visual Basic, JavaScript), and still keeps the number of related technology components low. Windows 8 still allows developing traditional desktop applications.

In this chapter, you learn about the architecture of components that help you to develop Windows 8 apps. You start with getting to know the difference between desktop and Windows 8 app development technology stacks. As you will learn, the key component of Windows 8 app development is the Windows Runtime, so you will learn about its structure and benefits. Choosing the appropriate technology for a particular application is not easy. This chapter concludes with a section that helps you to make this decision easier.

WINDOWS 8 DEVELOPMENT ARCHITECTURE

As you have learned, Windows 8 enables you to develop a new kind of application — Windows 8 style applications — while traditional desktop applications still run on Windows. Moreover, you can still use your favorite tools and technologies to develop Windows 8 style applications.

The architects of Windows 8 made an important decision when they created a new stack of architecture layers for Windows 8 style applications. Therefore, in Windows 8, you have two fundamental stacks of technologies (one for Windows 8 style applications, and one for desktop applications) that can be used side-by-side, as shown in Figure 3-1.

> **NOTE** *An* architecture layer *is a set of components having the same role (for example, communicating with the operating system). A stack of architectural layers mirrors how the services of those layers are built on each other.*

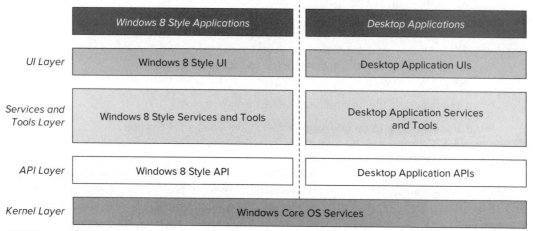

FIGURE 3-1: Windows 8 has separate stacks of architectural components for Windows 8 style applications and desktop applications

Although these Windows 8 style applications and desktop applications use the same operating system kernel, you have some important things to consider when it comes to application development. Table 3-1 provides a comparison of the two kinds of applications.

TABLE 3-1: Desktop Applications and Windows 8 Style Applications

DESKTOP APPLICATIONS	WINDOWS 8 STYLE APPLICATIONS
Desktop applications can be programmed either on top of the Win32 application programming interface (API) that dates back to 1995 (and many of its parts even to 1991), or with the .NET Framework that uses managed base classes. As you learned in Chapter 1, "A Brief History of Windows Application Development," you have a wide variety of language, tool, and technology choices for desktop applications. Although the richness of options is a great thing, from an application development point of view, it can be a disadvantage. Depending on the aim of your application — or your intention — you may pick up a mix of languages or technologies to program the expected functionality.	Windows 8 style applications represent a new approach. They are about providing a first-class user experience with multi-touch and sensors, and they are very sensitive in terms of user interface (UI) responsiveness. Imagine an application where you can drag an object on the screen with your finger, rather than experiencing a choppy response as you move the object across the screen with your mouse. To ensure the perfect experience, the API used for Windows 8 style applications should support UI responsiveness natively. Of course, Windows 8 style apps still support perfect mouse and keyboard integration.
Most desktop applications display windows and dialog boxes on the screen, and wait for user input, response, or confirmation. Sometimes these applications show more than one modeless dialog box (that is, dialogs that let you you switch back to the main applications without closing the dialog) over the main window. While working, the user must shift from one window to another, often focusing on distinct tasks simultaneously, sometimes unconsciously.	Windows 8 style application development is about providing an intuitive UI where the application owns the full screen. This approach does not encourage using dialog boxes popped up on the screen, but rather suggests using application pages, just as web applications running in the browser do. Windows 8 style applications can be deployed through Windows Store, and must conform with UI and user experience guidelines published by Microsoft in order to pass the certification process.
Desktop applications generally require a standard setup procedure that incorporates a few screens that guide the user through the installation steps. The whole process may take a minute (or even more) while all files and resources are copied to the computer, and necessary registrations take place. Removing an application also follows a standard procedure, and it requires the user to start with the Control Panel.	Windows 8 style applications are for consumers who are not necessarily familiar with concepts like files, the registry, and setup procedures. These users expect to be able to add an application to their portfolio with a simple touch or click, and all the other steps are automatically done by the system. These users want to be able to remove programs with the same ease — not caring how Windows implements this procedure behind the scenes.

As you can see, as a result of a consumer-centric approach to this information technology, expectations for Windows 8 style applications are very different compared to traditional desktop applications. The Windows architect team decided to create a separate subsystem for Windows 8 style applications, and also a distinct API to build them.

Before diving into the details of this new API, let's first take a look at the architectural components of traditional desktop applications.

Desktop Application Layers

To build traditional desktop applications, the developer has available a wide variety of application types with related component stacks. It is funny (but not surprising) how the word "traditional" now has a totally different meaning than it used to have a few years ago (say, perhaps five years ago). Although, with the emergence of Windows 8, you can call all the application stacks shown in Figure 3-2 "traditional," the managed application stack was quite new in 2002, and the Silverlight stack is the youngest, available since 2008.

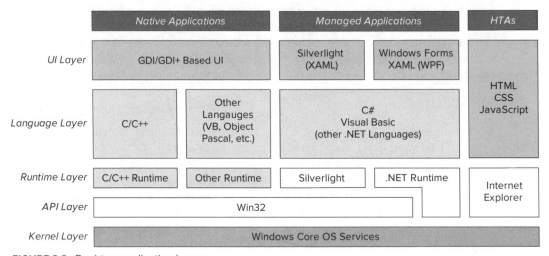

FIGURE 3-2: Desktop application layers

> **NOTE** Do not feel intimidated if you do not know all the technologies depicted in Figure 3-2. The aim of this figure is to show you the variety of technology components related to desktop application development. If you are interested any of them in particular, search the MSDN (http://msdn.microsoft.com) using their names.

Notice in Figure 3-2 the relationship between the Language Layer and the UI Layer. As you can see, the chosen programming language fundamentally determines the stack of technologies you can use to create your desktop application.

For native applications, choosing C or C++ (or other native languages such as Visual Basic, Object Pascal, and so on) that are compiled directly to CPU-specific code means that you must use graphics device interface (GDI) or GDI+ technologies for the UI.

With managed applications, you could still use GDI and GDI+. (In .NET, they are used under the alias of Windows Forms.) A more modern and powerful choice is Windows Presentation Foundation (WPF)—which is based on eXtensible Application Markup Language (XAML)—or its younger (but not less powerful) sibling, the Silverlight XAML.

> **NOTE** *While* native applications *are compiled directly to CPU-specific code,* managed applications *are translated to an intermediate language (IL). When you run a managed application, the IL is transformed to CPU-specific code by a just-in-time (JIT) compiler.*

Though it is not common to create desktop applications with HTML and related technologies, you can create them using HTML Applications (HTAs).

Your language preference also determines the available runtime libraries and environments you can use while programming (the Runtime Layer shown in Figure 3-2). These libraries contain operations that are natively used by the language to access operating system services, such as displaying values, managing files, or communicating through the network. With native applications, each language used to have in its own language run time, such as Microsoft Foundation Classes (MFC) and Active Template Library (ATL) for C/C++, VB Runtime for Visual Basic (the good old Basic language before the emergence of .NET), or Visual Component Library (VCL) for Delphi (Object Pascal).

.NET eliminated this by introducing its own Base Class Library that is available in all .NET languages, including C# and Visual Basic (as well as other popular .NET languages such as F#, IronPython, IronRuby, and others). Nonetheless, this uniform picture got a bit blurred with the release of Silverlight, which has yet another .NET run time available both in browser applications (such as Internet Explorer, Firefox, Safari, and in a few others) and in desktop applications. The Silverlight Base Class Library is only a subset of runtime types available in .NET.

The runtime libraries of native applications are built on top of the Win32 API (shown in the API Layer in Figure 3-2), which is a flat API with tens of thousands (actually unrelated) entry points that invoke Windows Core OS Services (the Kernel Layer in Figure 3-2). In contrast, .NET has its own runtime environment — called Common Language Runtime (CLR)—that provides a better abstraction of the Win32 API in forms of objects that package related data structures and operations into reusable types.

Imagine that you're an architect who wants to create the development component stack for Windows 8 style applications. Would you merge it with the existing desktop application technologies? Perhaps, but nonetheless, the architect team at Microsoft decided to create a new, independent set of APIs to get rid of the technology fragmentation.

Windows 8 Style Application Layers

With the consumer-centric approach of the Windows 8 operating system, Microsoft now faces new challenges. Creating an intuitive, multi-touch-enabled, always-responsive UI is only one of the challenges. A bigger challenge is establishing a platform that supports developers the right way, allowing them to use the technology and tools they know, and most importantly of all, to be productive.

The Challenge

Microsoft has a very strong development community working with Windows. A vast number of developers have experienced the "consumerization" of IT through web application development. However, only a very small number of developers are familiar with Windows-based consumer devices, namely Windows Phone developers. For a long time, Windows Phone was the only real consumer device from Microsoft.

Many web developers and hobbyists around the world — more than the whole Microsoft community camp — have experience with consumer application development for the Android (Google) or iOS (Apple) platforms. Windows 8 is intended to be an operating system that attracts not only professional Windows developers, but also those who are not closely related to the Microsoft community.

Microsoft seems to have begun gearing up very late in the competition for winning over consumers. Creating new devices and their operating systems is one important step to meeting the competition, but without having a great development platform and strategy, it would not be possible to provide quality applications that were good enough to strengthen Windows, and provide quality alternatives to consumers.

Microsoft has always provided great development tools that have been continuously evolving over time, tools that have offered great productivity. Instead of betting on only one programming language for its platform (such as what Apple and Google do), Microsoft accommodates a plethora of programming languages, and lets its developers choose the one they intend to work with. Providing the best platform for creating consumer applications is definitely a key factor to attaining a better market position.

Microsoft has answered this challenge with the development platform for Windows 8 style applications.

Architecture Layers Overview

By creating an independent stack of layered components for Windows 8 style applications, Microsoft has introduced a new concept that casts off the issues of traditional desktop application development, and reimages the idea of Windows API and language run times. This new concept embraced the support for multiple languages over a single programming API, as shown in Figure 3-3.

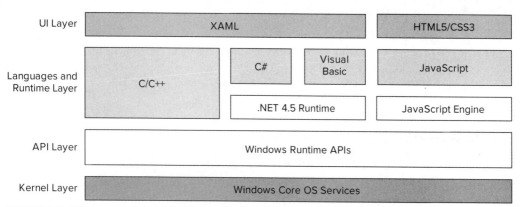

FIGURE 3-3: Windows 8 style application technology layers

You can derive a few important things from Figure 3-3.

All Windows 8 style applications have one ultimate API layer — Windows Runtime — to talk to Windows Core OS Services, and there is no other API a program would need to access them. Independently of the programming language used, every service is available without any limitation, so that you can access from C++, C#, Visual Basic, and JavaScript, too.

HTML and CSS are used by millions of developers all around the world to create websites and web pages. These developers use JavaScript to add (sometimes complex) UI logic to their web pages. In the Windows 8 style application model, Microsoft augmented the potential for JavaScript to access the full set of APIs offered through Windows Runtime.

The newest standard of HTML (HTML5), combined with Cascading Style Sheets 3 (CSS3) and JavaScript, is more powerful than its predecessors. HTML5 sites can natively play multimedia and display vector graphics — leveraging the hardware acceleration of the graphics processing unit (GPU) in the computer. Over the past couple of years, thousands of new websites have been built with HTML5 to provide the user experience of a new era. All this power can be immediately used by developers familiar with HTML and JavaScript technologies to create Windows 8 style applications.

In Windows 8, the core of the XAML-based WPF and Silverlight technologies has become a part of the operating system — rewritten in native code. The UI of C++, C#, and Visual Basic applications can be defined in XAML. The same XAML produces the exact same UI in every language — without constraints or barriers. Because of the uniform UI technology and the same APIs providing access to the operating system services, application models are the same for C++, C#, and Visual Basic.

If you compare the desktop application architecture layers in Figure 3-2 with Windows 8 style application layers in Figure 3-3, you can immediately see that the latter is simpler by means of runtime, API, and UI technology choices. Independent of whether you are a web developer, a C++ fan, or a .NET programmer, the entry barrier for creating Windows 8 style applications is actually lowered when compared to creating traditional desktop applications.

Your preference of programming language determines only the UI technology you must utilize in your programs. JavaScript is tied to HTML, whereas other languages (C++, C#, and Visual Basic) are bound to XAML. Generally, developers use more than one programming language and markup language, and they are used to being multilingual, so to speak. Learning a new language should be a motivating rather than a restraining force, however, dealing with separate runtime libraries and components is pretty cumbersome.

Windows 8 style application development strides over this issue. Regardless of your programming language of choice, you must learn only a single set of APIs — provided by Windows Runtime.

UNDERSTANDING WINDOWS RUNTIME

Without a doubt, Windows Runtime is the key component in the Windows 8 style application architecture. It represents a big leap in the evolution of the programming model, similar to what the .NET Framework did in 2002. The Microsoft team responsible for this great architectural piece describes Windows Runtime as "the solid, efficient foundation for building great Windows 8 style apps."

In Chapter 1, you learned that the Win32 API contains a flat set of operations and data structures. The language run times utilized before .NET provide libraries that conceal most of the API operations, and expose a simpler set of objects and functions to make common programming tasks easier. The .NET Framework adds a runtime environment to these objects with extra features like garbage collection, exception handling, communication support between applications, and much more.

Although language runtime libraries and the .NET Framework have been continuously evolving for a long time, they still do not expose all data structures and operations proffered by the Win32 API. The main reason for this plight is that the runtime components utilizing Win32 are created separately from the services of the operating system.

This situation totally changed with Windows 8. Windows Runtime is an organic part of the operating system. It is not an additional component to be installed separately, such as the Windows Software Development Kit (Windows SDK). Every time a new Windows 8 build is created, the APIs and Windows Runtime are built together with the other parts of the operating system. Let's take a closer look at the power of this great new component.

Windows Runtime Architecture Overview

Just as Windows 8 was designed with the user experience in mind, Windows Runtime was designed with a focus on the developer experience. Modern development environments such as Visual Studio (which you learn more about in Chapter 4, "Getting to Know Your Development Environment") provide great tooling to make developers more productive.

Windows Runtime Design Principles

A good example of a productive tool is IntelliSense, which watches the context as you are typing the code, and automatically offers a list of possible continuations. As shown the example in Figure 3-4, IntelliSense provides a list of expressions that may follow the `this` member in the context of the `MainPage` method. IntelliSense not only displays the list of appropriate members, but it also displays a short explanation of the selected member (`AllowDrop`) in a tooltip. The team responsible for the design of Windows Runtime continuously kept in mind that the new API should be very easy to use with powerful tools like IntelliSense.

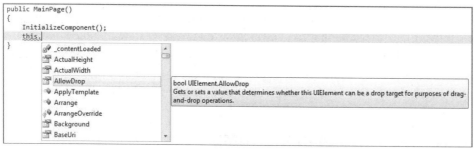

FIGURE 3-4: IntelliSense makes developers more productive

The smooth user experience of Windows 8 can be delivered only by applications that keep the UI responsive. In the past, the biggest issues with Windows were bound to the lazy and rugged behavior of the operating system and its applications. For example, the user started to drag an object on the screen by moving the mouse fluently, but the object moved in a "bitty" fashion.

The asynchronous programming model provides a great remedy for this kind of issue. The model does not block the UI while performing long or resource-intensive computations in the background. The APIs of Windows Runtime were established with asynchrony in the mind. The design team made a tough decision: *All operations that may take more than 50 milliseconds are implemented as asynchronous operations.* The new versions of the C# and Visual Basic programming languages shipped with Visual Studio 2012 and support this programming model, as you will learn in Chapter 5.

> **NOTE** *Do not be intimidated by concepts you are unfamiliar with, such as "asynchronous programming" or "UI blocking." Chapter 5, "Principles of the Modern Windows Application Development," provides a detailed overview of these concepts. For now, understand that asynchrony provides a way to push long operations into the background, while letting the UI remain responsive.*

The Windows team has always invested a lot in providing backward application compatibility with every new Windows release. Windows Runtime is designed and established so that applications keep running in new Windows versions. If an API changes an operation in a new version of the operating system, the older operation versions still remain available in parallel with the new one, so they can be used side-by-side. Each application uses the version of the operation with which it was created.

The Building Blocks of Windows Runtime

Reflective of Microsoft's design principles, Windows Runtime is not simply a set of APIs. It is a real runtime environment that binds the operating system services with the Windows 8 style applications built on them, independently of the programming language used to implement a particular application. This runtime environment is composed from several building blocks, as shown in Figure 3-5.

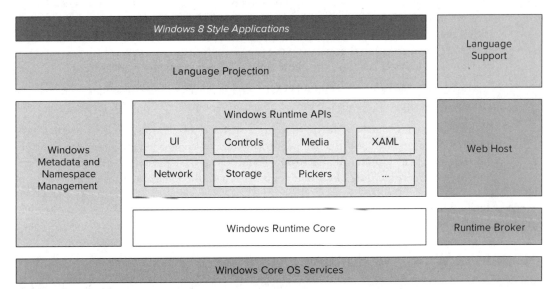

FIGURE 3-5: The building blocks of Windows Runtime

Windows OS are exposed to Windows 8 style applications through the Windows Runtime core block, which (as its name suggests) is the essence of the runtime environment. This core block wraps the low-level services into types and interfaces. On top of the core are many APIs, each of which is responsible for a certain kind of common operating system task. Although in Figure 3-5 only a few of them are shown, more than two dozen APIs are available.

You do not have to remember each type, interface, or even the API in which a certain type or functionality can be found, because Windows Runtime has its own metadata describing information about them. Moreover, the elemental types are grouped into hierarchical namespaces — such as objects in the .NET Framework, or in the Java Runtime — so it is quite easy to find them.

> **NOTE** *You learn more about Windows Runtime shortly.*

Programming languages have different characteristics, and they use disparate conventions. At the top of the APIs and the metadata block, there is a thin layer, Language Projection, which is responsible for exposing the APIs in a language-specific way. Windows 8 style applications access Windows Runtime APIs through this layer.

> **NOTE** *You learn more about this layer later in this chapter.*

A few other components shown in Figure 3-5 complete the environment where Windows 8 style applications can fully exploit the capabilities of the operating system through Windows Runtime:

➤ Your application might access specific system resources (such as the webcam, the microphone, or the Internet) where the user's permission is required. These resources can be accessed only through the Runtime Broker component that asks the user whether he or she allows the access to the resource — the first time an operation tries to use it. For example, if you create an application that picks up the user's photo from the webcam, Runtime Broker does not let the system capture the photo unless the user explicitly enables it.

➤ As you already learned, you can use HTML5 and JavaScript to create Windows 8 style applications. These apps — because of their web nature — run in a web host.

➤ Each language has some specific runtime support (for example, runtime libraries that support the language, such as the `printf` C++ function, or `append` JavaScript method, or the `String.Split` operation available from C# and Visual Basic). These can be found in the Language Support building block that cooperates with the Language Projection layer.

Some of the building blocks shown in Figure 3-5 play an important role in everyday programming activities. In the next few sections, you learn more details about them.

Metadata in Windows Runtime

Providing a way to use metadata in Windows Runtime is a very important feature in Windows 8 style application development. It is an indispensable resource to make the architecture more robust, the APIs more discoverable, and, in the long run, developers more productive. Well, the different development technologies behind Windows are a bit scattered by means of metadata format they utilize:

➤ The Win32 API is a large collection of data structures and operations that can be accessed through Dynamic Link Libraries (DLLs) sitting in the System32 folder under your Windows installation directory. These libraries include kernel32.dll, user32.dll, netapi32.dll, avicap32.dll, and many more. DLLs have many operation entry points. However, having only plain .dll files, you cannot tell what operations they contain, and how to invoke them, because they are not self-descriptive.

➤ The component object model (COM) that Microsoft introduced in 1993 was a binary standard that allowed developers to write the interfaces of objects in Interface Definition Language (IDL). An .idl file can be compiled into a Type Library (.tbl file) that represents metadata related to COM objects.

➤ The .NET Framework promoted type metadata into a first-class citizen. In .NET, *types* are the objects that provide you with utilizable operations, and *type metadata* describes the available operations. Assembly files (the binary files resulting from the compilation of the source code written in any of the .NET languages) are self-descriptive. They contain the metadata about types and operations encapsulated into the assembly.

The way .NET handles metadata is magnificent! However, metadata can be bound only to managed types. Many Win32 operations simply do not have a .NET type wrapping them. Using these types from managed code requires creating a definition that substitutes the missing metadata. Such definitions are laborious to describe, and you need documentation about the operation you intend to use. One such an example is the definition of the capCreateCaptureWindow operation that can be found in the avicap32.dll:

```
[DllImport("avicap32.dll", EntryPoint="capCreateCaptureWindow")]
static extern int capCreateCaptureWindow(
    string lpszWindowName, int dwStyle,
    int X, int Y, int nWidth, int nHeight,
    int hwndParent, int nID);
```

If you create a wrong definition (for example, you use double X instead of int X), your source code will compile, but will raise a runtime error, causing you to spend a lot of effort to find and troubleshoot this issue.

Metadata Format

The designers of Windows Runtime were inspired by the .NET Framework when architecting the metadata subsystem. They decided to use the metadata format utilized by .NET assemblies, which has already proven its adequacy over the past ten years. The designers chose the format used by .NET Framework 4.5 (the newest version of .NET, released in tandem with Windows 8).

Metadata files provide information about each of the APIs available in Windows Runtime. They are installed with Windows 8, and so they can be found on each computer with Windows 8 independently, even if that machine is used for development or just for another business. These files are machine-readable, and you can examine their content, as you learn in the following exercise.

TRY IT OUT   Peeking into Windows Runtime Metadata

Windows Runtime metadata files are located under the Windows installation folder. They have a.winmd extension, and you can examine their content with the ILDASM utility.

To examine the metadata files, follow these steps:

1. In the Start screen, click the Desktop tile, and then, from the taskbar, select Windows Explorer.

2. Navigate to the System32\WinMetadata folder under your Windows installation directory. If your operating system is installed to the default location, you can find this folder under C:\Windows. If you provided a different location during the setup of Windows, choose that folder.

3. This folder lists more than a hundred files, each with a name starting with Windows, and having the .winmd extension, as shown in Figure 3-6. These files represent the metadata information of Windows Runtime APIs.

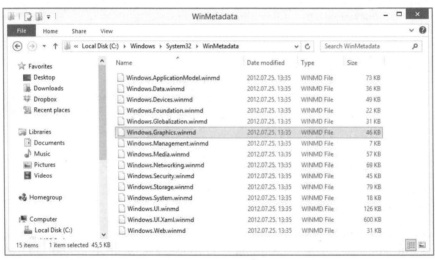

FIGURE 3-6: Windows Runtime metadata files in the System32\WinMetadata folder

4. Scroll down to the Windows.Graphics file. Right-click it and select the Open With command from the context menu. A pop-up appears on the screen, and there you can associate an application with the .winmd file type. Scroll down to the bottom of the pop-up, and select, "Look for an app on this PC," as shown in Figure 3-7.

5. The Open With dialog box pops up on the screen. In the File Name text box, type the C:\Program Files (x86)\Microsoft SDKs\Windows\v8.0A\bin\NETFX 4.0 Tools path (or navigate to this path using the Open With dialog box). Click Open. The dialog box is populated with the files in this folder. Scroll down to `ildasm` and click Open again.

6. The `ILDASM` utility opens and displays the metadata tree of the `Windows.Graphics.winmd` file. Expand the `Windows.Graphics.Display` node, and then the `Windows.Graphics.Display` `.ResolutionScale` node. You can discover all types defined in this metadata file, and also the enumeration values of the `ResolutionScale` type, as shown in Figure 3-8.

FIGURE 3-6: Associating .winmd files with an application

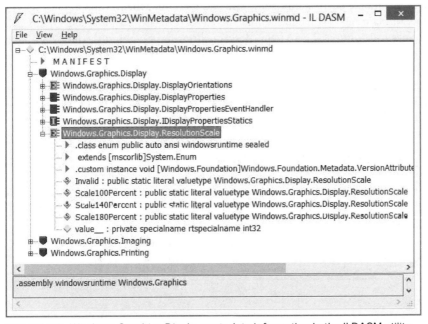

FIGURE 3-8: Windows.Graphics.Display metadata information in the ILDASM utility

7. In the ILDASM application window, double-click the MANIFEST node. A new window opens to display the manifest information of the metadata file, as shown in Figure 3-9.

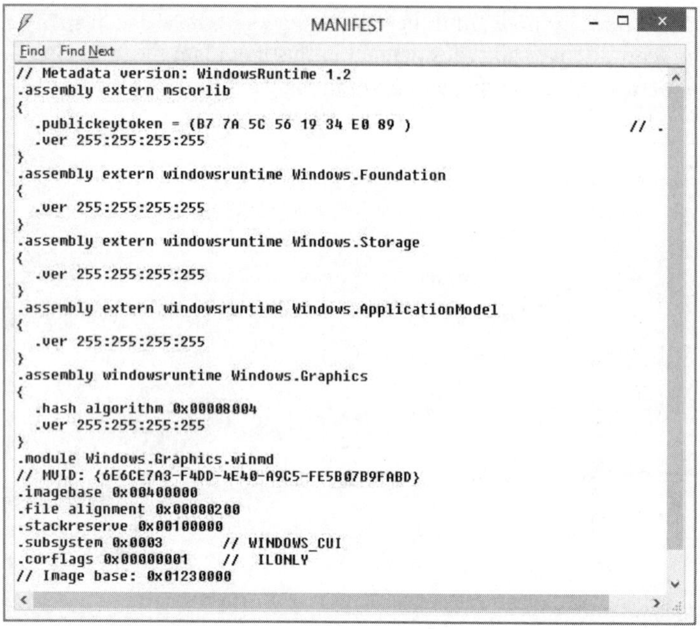

```
// Metadata version: WindowsRuntime 1.2
.assembly extern mscorlib
{
  .publickeytoken = (B7 7A 5C 56 19 34 E0 89 )              // .
  .ver 255:255:255:255
}
.assembly extern windowsruntime Windows.Foundation
{
  .ver 255:255:255:255
}
.assembly extern windowsruntime Windows.Storage
{
  .ver 255:255:255:255
}
.assembly extern windowsruntime Windows.ApplicationModel
{
  .ver 255:255:255:255
}
.assembly windowsruntime Windows.Graphics
{
  .hash algorithm 0x00008004
  .ver 255:255:255:255
}
.module Windows.Graphics.winmd
// MVID: {6E6CE7A3-F4DD-4E40-A9C5-FE5B07B9FABD}
.imagebase 0x00400000
.file alignment 0x00000200
.stackreserve 0x00100000
.subsystem 0x0003      // WINDOWS_CUI
.corflags 0x00000001   // ILONLY
// Image base: 0x01230000
```

FIGURE 3-9: The manifest information of the Windows.Graphics metadata file

The manifest of a metadata file carries important information about the file and about the types described in the file. In Figure 3-9, you can see that there is a `.module Windows.Graphics.winmd` entry with several lines following it. These items describe information about the metadata file. You see three entries starting with `.assembly extern`, and these are references to other metadata information related to types used within the `Windows.Graphics` metadata file. The first reference, `mscorlib`, is the main system component of the .NET 4.5 Common Language Runtime (CLR). The other two, `Windows.Foundation` and `Windows.Storage`, respectively, are other `.windm` files — as can be inferred from the `windowsruntime` modifier tag they have.

8. Open other metadata files from the `System32\WinMetadata` folder, and examine their structure. When you have finished, close all open ILDASM instances.

How It Works

The `System32\WinMetadata` folder contains essential `.windm` files. In Step 5, you associated the `.winmd` file extension with the ILDASM utility. In Step 6, you peeked into the metadata of the `Windows.Graphics.Display.ResolutionScale` type. In Step 7, you examined how the `.winmd` manifest describes dependencies on external metadata files.

Namespaces

As you experienced in the previous exercise, Windows Runtime types have hierarchical names. For example, the enumeration with the resolution scale values has the full name of Windows.Graphics .Display.ResolutionScale. The last tag of this name is the type's simple name, and prefix tags form the namespace hierarchy. The top-level namespace is Windows. It has an embedded namespace, Graphics, and Graphics embeds Display.

> **NOTE** *.NET, Java, and C++ programmers are familiar with the concept of namespaces. Windows Runtime uses the namespace with exactly the same semantics as applied in .NET.*

Namespaces are important concepts when managing the vast amount of types you utilize while creating your applications. If you had only type names poured into a big pool, it would be very difficult to find them and guess what type is the appropriate one for a certain task.

Another issue would be naming types. You cannot guarantee that no one else uses the same type. name that you use. For example, when you name your type Circle, there is a great likelihood that someone else will use the same name. If you buy a package of custom UI components, there already may be a Circle type. How will your application know which Circle type to use at a certain location of the source code, and whether you intend to use your own Circle or the purchased one?

Namespaces are great constructs that help you to group objects into categories. Using well-designed namespace hierarchies makes you more productive, because you can find appropriate types for a certain task easily. For example, when you are about to display images on the screen, first you will look them in the Windows.Graphics.Imaging namespace, because its name suggest that such types exist there.

Namespaces also help you avoid conflicting type names. If you put your own types into their own namespaces (for example, you put Circle into the MyCompany.Shapes namespace), they won't clash with types from other programmers or companies.

Types can have pretty long full names. Fortunately, all programming languages that manage the concept of namespaces offer some kind of constructs to avoid full names, and allow writing only the simple names. Let's take a look at a few examples.

C# offers the using clause to help resolve type names:

```
using Windows.UI.Xaml;

namespace MyAppNamespace
{
  class MyClass: UserControl
  {
    public MyClass()
    {
      // ...
      selectedItem = this.FindName(itemName) as ListBoxItem;
      // ...
    }
  }
}
```

Visual Basic offers the same construct with the `Imports` keyword:

```vb
Imports Windows.UI.Xaml

Namespace MyAppNamespace

  Class MyClass
    Inherits UserControl

    Public Sub New()
      ' ...
      selectedItem = TryCast(Me.FindName(itemName), ListBoxItem)
      ' ...
    End Sub
  End Class
End Namespace
```

It is not surprising that C++ offers the same concept with the `using namespace` clause, too:

```cpp
using namespace Windows::UI::Xaml;

namespace MyAppNamespace
{
  class MyClass: UserControl
  {
    public MyClass()
    {
      // ...
      selectedItem = dynamic_cast<ListBoxItem^>(this->FindName(itemName);
      // ...
    }
  }
}
```

The `using`, `Imports`, and `using namespace` constructs in C#, Visual Basic, and C++, respectively, instruct the compiler that type names should be looked up in the specified namespaces. This mechanism allows writing only `ListBoxItem` type names in your programs, because the compiler will check the `Windows.UI.Xaml` namespace as well. Otherwise, you would have to write the full `Windows.UI.Xaml.ListBoxItem` name.

> **NOTE** Of course, objects in Windows Runtime namespaces can be accessed from JavaScript programs, too. In JavaScript, you can use a different mechanism, as you learn in Chapter 6, "Creating Windows 8 Style Applications with HTML5, CSS, JavaScript, and jQuery."

Language Projections

Programming languages have their own characteristics. Fans of a particular programming language like to work with the language because of its attributes, such as readability, high-performance constructs, functionality, low syntax noise, and so on. When creating Windows 8 style applications, you can use several languages — with different syntax and semantic approaches. However, it was a challenge for Windows Runtime designers to allow using all services from these very different languages.

The Language Projections layer is responsible for transforming Windows Runtime APIs to the shape of the language. Because of this transformation, programmers can use the APIs as if those were the part of the language's native runtime libraries.

The best way to understand what the Language Projection layer does is to take a look at a simple example. The `Windows.Storage.Pickers` namespace contains a type named `FileOpenPicker` that enables you to select a file from a folder. Using the C# programming language, you can use the following code to configure this dialog box for picking up picture files:

```
using Windows.Storage.Pickers;
// ...
FileOpenPicker openPicker = new FileOpenPicker();
openPicker.ViewMode = PickerViewMode.Thumbnail;
openPicker.SuggestedStartLocation = PickerLocationId.PicturesLibrary;
openPicker.FileTypeFilter.Add(".jpg");
openPicker.FileTypeFilter.Add(".jpeg");
openPicker.FileTypeFilter.Add(".png");
```

The same task can be rewritten using JavaScript, as shown in this code snippet:

```
var openPicker = new Windows.Storage.Pickers.FileOpenPicker();
openPicker.viewMode = Windows.Storage.Pickers.PickerViewMode.thumbnail;
openPicker.suggestedStartLocation =
    Windows.Storage.Pickers.PickerLocationId.picturesLibrary;
openPicker.fileTypeFilter.replaceAll([".png", ".jpg", ".jpeg"]);
```

The identifiers highlighted in bold represent Windows Runtime API types. All of them start with an uppercase letter and use Pascal case, both in C# and JavaScript. The identifiers with italic typeface are members of Windows Runtime types. As you can see, they use Pascal case in C# and Camel case in JavaScript. This is done by the Language Projection layer! Whereas the C# language projection renders member names with Pascal case, the JavaScript language projection uses Camel case — according to JavaScript conventions.

> **NOTE** *Using* Pascal case *and* Camel case *means writing identifiers in which words are joined without spaces, with each element's initial letter capitalized within the compound, respectively. Whereas Pascal case uses uppercase for the first letter (such as "P" in "PicturesLibrary"), Camel case has a lowercase letter (such as "v" in "viewMode").*

The task of the Language Projection layer does not stop at syntax sugar. In Windows Runtime API, the `FileFilterType` property of the `FileOpenPicker` type is a vector (or array) of string elements (`FileExtensionVector`). The C# language projection renders this property as a `List<string>` (list of strings), and so the file extensions can be added with the `Add` method of the `List<string>` type, as shown here:

```
openPicker.FileTypeFilter.Add(".jpg");
openPicker.FileTypeFilter.Add(".jpeg");
openPicker.FileTypeFilter.Add(".png");
```

The JavaScript language projection renders the `fileFilterType` property to an array of strings, and so the `replaceAll` function can be used to set up the content of the array, as shown here:

```
openPicker.fileTypeFilter.replaceAll([".png", ".jpg", ".jpeg"]);
```

Visual Studio also leverages the features of the Language Projection layer. As shown in Figure 3-10 and Figure 3-11, respectively, IntelliSense in C# and in JavaScript proffers the appropriate continuations, depending on the language.

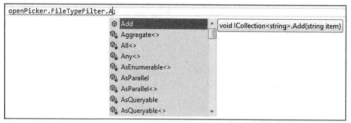

FIGURE 3-10   IntelliSense proffers members of the List<string> type in C#

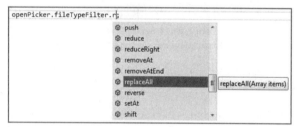

FIGURE 3-11   IntelliSense proffers array operations in JavaScript

With language projection, you do not need to utilize different tools to access and seize the operating system services depending on the programming language. You perceive all Windows Runtime services as if those were the part of the chosen programming language's runtime environment.

Benefits of Windows Runtime

As you have learned, Windows Runtime is a new modern API over Windows Core OS Services, and it is more natural to use from many programming languages, including C++, C#, Visual Basic (.NET), and HTML/JavaScript. This modernization allowed Windows Runtime architects to rethink how a contemporary operating system should support application development:

➤   Windows Runtime provides an easy access to hardware such as a Global Positioning System (GPS) unit, sensors, camera, or other modern hardware devices — with a few lines of code. Although, in the past, you had to write a several dozen lines of code to create the first "Hello, world" program in C with Windows 3.1, Windows Runtime enables you to take a picture with the built-in camera in about five lines of code.

➤   Applications run in a security *sandbox*. This means that only those operations are executed that are deemed safe within the current security context. For example, if an application wants to turn on the microphone, this operation is thought unsafe unless the user explicitly confirms that he or she allows using the microphone.

➤ The old Win32 API was a separate layer over the core operating system services. Windows Runtime is an integral part of the operating system tuned for developer experience. Windows Runtime is not only easier to use than Win32, but it is more stable and has improved memory management to allow less memory consumption and faster memory management.

➤ Modern hardware devices and the always-responsive UI cannot work without an asynchronous programming model. Windows Runtime supports asynchrony natively.

What's not in Windows Runtime

By now, you have learned that Windows Runtime is the key component to developing Windows 8 style applications. All services of the operating system exposed through Windows Runtime can be consumed from C++, C#, Visual Basic, and JavaScript. Before you put an equation sign between Windows 8 style applications and Windows Runtime, you should know that Windows 8 style applications can leverage other operating system components that are not available in Windows Runtime.

Applications written in the C or C++ programming languages are compiled directly to CPU-specific machine instructions that can be directly executed on the CPU. These applications can directly access the native operating system components responsible for rendering the UI, controlling input devices, managing sensors, communicating with the GPU, and much more. Most of these components may add extra value to Windows 8 style applications. For example, game programmers can leverage the high-performance graphics capabilities of DirectX APIs, such as Direct2D, Direct3D, DirectWrite, XAudio2, and XInput.

> **NOTE** *Microsoft DirectX is a collection of multimedia and game APIs. These APIs eliminate several additional layers between applications and the hardware hosting the specific function to provide the high performance required by multimedia and game applications. Direct2D is the two-dimensional graphics API, and Direct3D is designed for three-dimensional graphics game development. DirectWrite is a text-layout and glyph-rendering API that was shipped with Windows Vista first, and is still available in Windows 8.*
>
> *When Microsoft set out to develop its gaming console, the X was used as the basis of the name "Xbox" to indicate that the console was based on DirectX technology.*

These APIs provide a very thin layer between your application and the hardware they access, and use low-level data structures to move information to and from the app and the hardware. Although services available through Windows Runtime are safe with regard to UI responsibility and system stability, these APIs are tuned for performance — requiring more control within your application.

Using C++, you can create Windows 8 style applications that leverage DirectX API features. For example, you can create great calligraphic texts with DirectWrite, as shown in Figure 3-12.

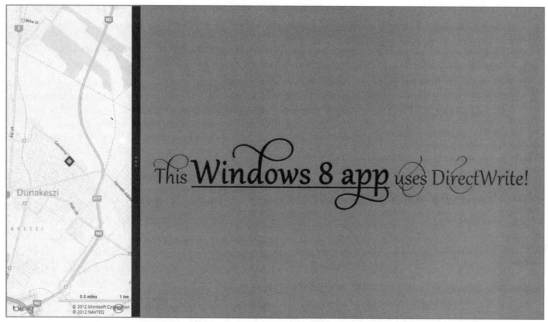

FIGURE 3-12: Windows 8 style application using the DirectWrite API

Although these components are not available through Windows Runtime, and you can access them directly only from C++, mechanisms in C# and Visual Basic utilize these APIs in managed code. As of this writing, you can find a few open source projects on CodePlex (`http://www.codeplex.com`) that target using DirectX on Windows 8 from C#. Although these are in a very initial state, in a few months they may improve a lot.

.NET FRAMEWORK 4.5

Two programming languages that support Windows 8 style applications — C# and Visual Basic — run over the .NET Framework. Windows 8 has been released with a new version of .NET Framework — version 4.5. The development architecture picture would not be complete without understanding what's new in this version, and how .NET Framework cooperates with Windows Runtime.

The Installation Model of .NET Framework 4.5

Since 2002 (when .NET 1.0 was released), there have been several ways for a new .NET Framework release to cooperate with previous releases, as shown in Figure 3-13. Although the first three versions (1.0, 1.1, and 2.0) were shipped with different CLR versions that could run side-by-side on the same computer, subsequent versions followed a different path.

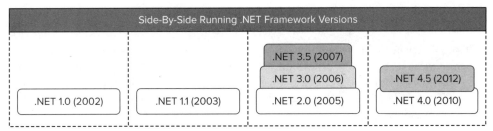

FIGURE 3-13   The relation of .NET versions

When .NET Framework 3.0 was released in 2006, it did not install its own CLR. It was simply an addition to version 2.0 and used its runtime core. The same thing happened with .NET 3.5 in 2007. It was an addition to .NET 3.0, and still used the CLR released with .NET 2.0.

In 2010, .NET 4.0 was released, again with its own CLR, encapsulating the enhanced forms of Base Class Libraries coming from .NET 3.5. Theoretically, in 2010, you could install four CLR versions side-by-side on your computer: CLR 1.0, CLR 1.1, CLR 2.0, and CLR 4.0. The newest .NET Framework, version 4.5, added more salt to the installation models used before. Instead of adding a new CLR side-by-side or new Base Class Libraries on top of the CLR 4.0 runtime, .NET 4.5 is an in-place update (that is, an update that not only adds new files, but overwrites existing ones) that changes both the CLR 4.0 runtime (it upgrades it to CLR 4.5) and also extends the prior Base Class Libraries.

> **NOTE** *An in-place operating system update or .NET CLR update is always a big risk from a compatibility point of view. With the .NET Framework 4.5 release, Microsoft undertook this risk, and spent much effort to cope with potential incompatibility issues. Microsoft set up a compatibility lab, reviewed all bug fixes and new features, and ran old tests unchanged.*

Window Runtime Integration

The .NET CLR has always had integration features with other legacy technologies, such as COM and P/Invoke (Platform Invoke to access the Win32 API). With .NET Framework 4.5, the CLR natively integrates with Windows Runtime. C# and Visual Basic programmers now can use Windows Runtime types with the same ease, as if those were .NET types.

Windows Runtime types are native types. They actually use a new and modern version of COM that does not require object registration, and so their operations cannot be called directly from managed code. However, the .NET CLR and the language compilers arrange everything behind the scenes, and you do not need to deal with the details of calling the native Windows Runtime object from your managed code.

If you take a look back at Figure 3-2 and Figure 3-3, you can see that both the desktop application and Windows 8 style application development stacks contain a .NET Runtime box. You may think this means that two different .NET Frameworks exist, one for the desktop applications and one for Windows 8 style applications. Fortunately, there is only one.

The Base Class Library available to Windows 8 style applications (Windows Runtime applications) is restricted to services that are considered "safe" for a Windows 8 application to use. When you try to build your existing .NET source code, some parts would not compile, because those might be using some .NET Base Class Library functions that are not found in Windows Runtime, or are not thought "safe" in Windows 8 apps.

> **NOTE** Generally, all operations are taken into account as "safe" that do not jeopardize UI responsiveness.

Asynchrony Support

As you have learned, asynchronous programming is a key technique to provide UI responsiveness, and Windows Runtime was designed with asynchrony in mind. The results of the Windows Runtime design process inspired the .NET Framework team, and they added asynchrony support to many components of the framework. The .NET Base Class Libraries contain hundreds of changes and improvements, including the following most significant ones:

➤ The key interfaces of the Base Class Library (for example, file I/O operations) support asynchrony.

➤ Data access procedures in ADO.NET (the foundational data access technology in .NET), and network communication components in Windows Communication Foundation (WCF), also handle asynchronous constructs as first-class operations.

➤ ASP.NET supports asynchronous pipelines when processing requests and creating responses. ASP.NET MVC 4 provides asynchronous controllers.

➤ The Task Parallel Library — introduced in .NET Framework 4.0 — was designed with asynchronous programming in mind. In .NET Framework 4.5, its thread-management was improved with new types managing synchronization and various timeout scenarios.

Although the asynchronous programming patterns provide better UI responsiveness and improved throughput, it is quite difficult to apply them, and they are pretty error-prone. With .NET Framework 4.5, the C# and Visual Basic compilers provide two new keywords (`async` and `await` in C#, `Async` and `Await` in Visual Basic) that take over all complexity related to these patterns.

> **NOTE** You learn more about these keywords in Chapter 6.

Other New Features

Although the main novelty of .NET Framework 4.5 is Windows Runtime integration and enhanced support of asynchronous programming, many other tiny improvements make developers more productive. There are many new features in .NET Framework 4.5, but explaining them is far beyond the scope of this book. If you would like to obtain more information about them, the best starting point is the .NET Framework Development Center on MSDN at `http://msdn.microsoft.com/netframework`.

PICKING THE APPROPRIATE TECHNOLOGY FOR YOUR PROJECT

This chapter has shown you a wide variety of technologies and programming languages that you can use to create Windows 8 applications. Sometimes the most difficult decision is choosing the appropriate language and technology stack for your project. This section contains a few hints to help you make the optimal decision.

In addition to the programming language and development technology, there is another important consideration scarcely mentioned before. Windows 8 totally changes not only the way users work with applications, but also the way they discover, install, and remove programs. This new installation model may inspire you to create Windows 8 style applications instead of desktop apps, so this might be a good time to take a brief overview of it.

The Windows Store

In previous Windows operating systems, you had to create installation kits and deploy your applications by running those kits on the target computers. Your users had to understand a few technical details of the installation process, such as selecting the target folder, installing prerequisites, adding shortcuts to the desktop, and so on. Often, the installation process was a source of fear — will this installation override something on your computer to prevent other applications from running properly? Further, unnecessary applications had to be removed and often cleanup utilities were needed to remove the garbage heap left by those apps.

The consumer-centric approach cannot work without a significantly easier way of obtaining and releasing applications. Windows 8 style applications can be installed only from the Windows Store, which is an online service. As a developer, you can upload your application to the Windows Store, where it goes through an approval process before users can discover and install it. As a user, you can find an application in the Windows Store and, after buying it (or choosing to try it free, or even using it free when the application allows it), let the operating system install the app for you. If you do not need the application any more, Windows 8 will instantly uninstall it and take care of the cleanup process — releasing all resources held by the app.

> **NOTE** Using the Windows Store is very easy for consumers who want to buy and run Windows 8 style applications. However, developers need to know more details about uploading their programs and leveraging Windows Store features in order to monetize them. Chapter 16, "Introducing the Windows Store," is dedicated entirely to this topic.

Windows 8 or Desktop Applications?

The first thing you should decide is whether you want to create Windows 8 style applications or desktop applications. Table 3-2 helps with your decision by distinguishing a few points of consideration.

TABLE 3-2: Helping Points to Choose between Windows 8 Style and Desktop Applications

USE WINDOWS 8 STYLE APPLICATIONS WHEN...	USE DESKTOP APPLICATIONS WHEN...
You have no, or very little, experience in Windows programming.	You have more experience in Windows programming — moreover, you're a seasoned Windows programmer.
You're focusing on applications with a superior user experience.	You're focusing on applications where you intend to utilize the UI technologies (Windows Forms, WPF, or Silverlight) you already know.
You have a relatively small UI codebase to reuse.	You have a large amount of code related to the UI, and you want to reuse the knowledge carried by that codebase.
Your application works on a single Windows computer. Your application's primary focus is providing a UI for services and remote components accessed through the Internet (or company intranet).	Your application is distributed into several components, including UI, business services, and databases. UI application components use legacy, vendor-specific, or proprietary communication technologies to access other services.
Your application intends to leverage the user experience and device features offered by mobile devices, such as a tablet.	Your application is primarily used on desktop computers and/or integrates with existing applications.
You want to leverage the easy application deployment model offered by the Windows Store.	You need a more complex deployment model than provided by the Windows Store.
You can use (that is, you are allowed to use) C++, C#, Visual Basic, or JavaScript programming languages to create your application.	Besides the set of C++, C#, Visual Basic, and JavaScript, you need to use other programming languages heavily to create your application.

If you participate in a complex project, you obviously cannot use the Windows 8 style technology stack for the entire project — often you need to do server-side development. However, it is worth examining the UI components of your system that you can put through and that might be implemented as Windows 8 style applications.

> **NOTE** *This book is dedicated to Windows 8 style application development, and does not intend to cover traditional desktop development technologies such as WPF and Silverlight. If you are also interested in these technologies, Wrox offers you a wide selection of great books. Visit the Wrox website (*www.wrox.com*) for more information.*

Choosing a Programming Language

As you learned earlier in this chapter, you can use several languages for Windows 8 style application development — C++, C#, Visual Basic, and JavaScript. If you prefer any of them, do not hesitate to start using that language.

If you have no or very little experience with Windows programming, or are uncertain which language would have the shortest learning curve, here are several clues to help with your decision:

➤ If you have experience with web page design and website creation, you certainly know HTML, and probably have experience with CSS and JavaScript. Start creating your first Windows 8 style programs with JavaScript.

➤ If you have used macros in Microsoft Word and Excel, Visual Basic is probably the language you should start with.

➤ If your experience is about programming algorithms rather than UI, then C++ and C# are your best choices. C# is probably easier to learn; C++ provides more control over low-level programming constructs.

One of the best things about Windows 8 style application programming is that you are not obligated to stick to only one language! You can even use more than one programming language within an application. For example, if you have web programming experience with JavaScript, you may create your UI with HTML and JavaScript, but still consume more complex application logic written in C# and high-performance algorithms programmed in C++.

Even if you start application development with one of these languages, it is worth learning other ones — because each of them has its own strength. When you have short deadlines or want to be more open toward other platforms, knowing several languages and getting used to mixing them reasonably is invaluable.

SUMMARY

Windows 8 provides a new application development model called the Windows 8 style application model. However, you can still leverage the technology stack of desktop application development used with previous Windows versions.

Windows 8 style applications have their own technology stack. Four programming languages — C++, C#, Visual Basic, and JavaScript — can be used to create Windows 8 apps. Independently of the language used, all operating system services required by these apps can be accessed through a new component called Windows Runtime — and, from this perspective, languages are co-equal.

Windows Runtime is a modern programming surface over the core Windows services. Although it is implemented in native code, it provides namespaces, object metadata, and asynchronous operations. Each programming language has a Language Projection layer that mimics Windows Runtime. This layer was created with the particular language in mind.

C# and Visual Basic use the .NET Framework 4.5, which integrates with Windows Runtime natively, so types in Windows Runtime can be used as easily as any .NET Base Class Library types.

In Chapter 4, you learn the fundamental tools that you can use to create Windows 8 style applications. You are going to create a few simple apps to whet your appetite.

EXERCISES

1. List the programming languages that can be used to create Windows 8 style applications in Windows 8.

2. Which UI technologies are supported in Windows 8 style applications?

3. What is the component that allows accessing Windows core services from all Windows 8 programming languages?

4. Why is Windows Runtime superior over the traditional Win32 APIs?

5. What is the application deployment model offered by the Windows Store?

> **NOTE** *You can find answers to the exercises in Appendix A.*

▶ **WHAT YOU LEARNED IN THIS CHAPTER**

TOPIC	KEY CONCEPTS
Windows 8 programming languages	Windows 8 style applications can be created with the following languages: C/C++, C#, Visual Basic, JavaScript.
XAML	In Windows 8, eXtensible Application Markup Language (XAML) is used to declare and implement the user interface (UI) of apps programmed in C++, C#, and Visual Basic.
HTML	In Windows 8, the newest HyperText Markup Language (HTML) version, HTML5, is used in tandem with Cascading Style Sheets 3 (CSS3) to create application UI with the JavaScript programming language.
Windows Runtime	Windows Runtime is the application programming interface (API) that Windows 8 style applications can use to access the underlying operating system services.
Windows Runtime objects	In contrast to Win32 (which uses flat operations), Windows Runtime provides meaningful objects with related operations and data structures. These objects are self-descriptive. They provide metadata information about themselves. Using this metadata, applications can easily consume the exposed operations.
Namespaces	Windows Runtime objects are organized into hierarchical namespaces. Objects in separate namespaces can use the same simple name.
Language Projection layer	Windows Runtime objects and operations can be accessed from each Windows 8 programming language as if Windows Runtime were tied to that particular language. This behavior is provided by the Language Projection layer.
Asynchronous programming model	Windows Runtime offers an asynchronous programming model to provide UI responsiveness. Operations that may block the UI are implemented in an asynchronous manner — they push the processing to a background thread while keeping the UI responsive.
.NET Framework 4.5	.NET Framework 4.5 is the newest version of the .NET Framework released in tandem with Windows 8. It provides native integration with Windows 8, and adds asynchrony to many Base Class Libraries.
Windows Store	Windows 8 style applications can be installed only from the Windows Store, which is an online service. Developers can upload their applications to the Store, where they go through an approval process before users can buy and install them.

Getting to Know Your Development Environment

➤ Discovering the indispensable tools you can utilize to develop your Windows 8 style applications

➤ Learning about the Visual Studio and Expression Blend IDEs

➤ Creating your first Windows 8 style application with Visual Studio

➤ Discovering a few useful features of the Visual Studio IDE

➤ Enhancing the user experience with Expression Blend

WROX.COM CODE DOWNLOADS FOR THIS CHAPTER

You can find the wrox.com code downloads for this chapter on the Download Code tab at www.wrox.com/remtitle.cgi?isbn=012680. The code is in the Chapter04.zip download and individually named, as described in the corresponding exercises.

Windows 8 development is a great thing, because of Windows Runtime, the powerful programming languages, and the rendering technologies. Microsoft provides great tools to leverage these magnificent technologies, too. In this chapter, you learn about the two fundamental tools you will utilize while developing your apps: Visual Studio 2012 and Expression Blend.

First, you create a simple Windows 8 app with Visual Studio. The exercises in this chapter help you get acquainted with using the Visual Studio integrated development environment (IDE), and help you understand the basic steps of Windows 8 app development. The user experience is a key success factor for your Windows 8 apps. To understand how a great design tool supports enhancing your user interfaces (UIs) in a few steps, you modify your sample application with Expression Blend.

After reading this chapter, you'll be ready to dive into the details of Windows 8 app development and use these great productivity tools.

INTRODUCING THE TOOLSET

In Chapter 3, you learned that Windows 8 has a complete technology stack for building Windows 8 style applications. It supports four programming languages — C++, C#, Visual Basic, and JavaScript. Developers working with JavaScript can use HTML5 and CSS3 to create the user interface of their applications, and fans of the other programming languages can leverage eXtensible Application Markup Language (XAML) when establishing the UI.

These technologies are great, but without the right toolset, developers cannot use them efficiently. The flagship development tools of Microsoft run on Windows 8, and you can leverage them to design and implement your Windows 8 style applications:

➤ Microsoft Visual Studio 2012 is the ultimate development environment that supports all Windows 8 languages and the full technology stack for Windows 8 style application development.

➤ Microsoft Expression Blend is a great tool that helps UI designers establish a professional application UI in a fairly productive way.

Visual Studio 2012

Visual Studio is an integrated development environment from Microsoft. Its roots date back 21 years. The newest version is the 11th major version and is called Visual Studio 2012. This is the ultimate tool that you can use to develop applications for all Microsoft platforms, including Windows 8 and its predecessors, .NET Framework, Windows Phone, Silverlight, and Windows Azure. During the past 21 years, Visual Studio went through many changes while it attained its current form.

A Brief History of Visual Studio

Application development on the first couple of Windows operating system versions was a privilege for developers working with the C programming language. With those Windows versions, creating an application meant writing source code in a text editor, performing manual steps to compile the application, and linking the resulting binaries into an executable file.

Visual Basic dramatically changed this landscape in May 1991 when version 1.0 was released. This product made development really visual (in contrast to the C language tools used before) with the introduction of concepts such as forms, controls, modules, classes, and code-behind files.

Because of the success of Visual Basic, Microsoft built a plethora of tools and languages with the visual composition feature. Visual C++ with the Microsoft Foundation Classes (MFC) library (released in February 1993) proved that the C++ language could be used as a productive tool for creating great UIs in a simple way, too. In 1995 (a year that was full of news about the Java programming language), Microsoft created the Visual J++ language, with its own Java virtual machine (JVM).

The architect team at Microsoft recognized that the visual aspect of an application can be totally separated from the programming language used to create it. They created a product — Visual Studio 97 — that bundled Visual Basic 5.0, Visual C++ 5.0, Visual FoxPro 5.0, Visual J++, and Visual InterDev. The next version of the IDE, named Visual Studio 6.0, was released in June 1998.

As an answer for the success of the Java platform, Microsoft released the .NET Framework in February 2002. .NET Framework 1.0 was released in tandem with Visual Studio.NET. This Visual Studio version integrated several programming languages and tools into the same IDE. Developers could use four languages out-of-the-box: Visual Basic.NET, Visual C#, Visual C++, and Visual J#. Except for J#, these languages are still available in Visual Studio 2012.

Visual Studio Editions

Microsoft has always endeavored to build a large developer community around its tools, and has created specialized editions targeting certain audiences — including hobbyists and students, as well as professional and enterprise developers. The same product — Visual Studio — can be used by single developers coding for fun, or by professional developers working on large enterprise projects. The trend to have a free Express version of Visual Studio in addition to the editions offered to enterprise developers started in 2005. Since then, each new Visual Studio release has its related Express version.

Although, in the beginning, Express versions were released on a programming language basis (Visual C# Express, Visual Basic Express, Visual Web Developer Express), Microsoft later changed this trend to release them according to application type (Visual Studio Express for Windows Phone, Visual Studio Express for Windows 8). Also, new tools (such as unit testing) started to become part of the Express versions.

The newest Visual Studio 2012 supports the following editions:

> **Visual Studio 2012 Express for Windows 8** — This is a free version that you can download from Microsoft Developer Network (MSDN). With this tool, you can develop full-fledged Windows 8 style applications. Unit tests and Team Foundation Server (Microsoft's source control and team management tool) integration are also available.

> **Visual Studio 2012 Professional/Premium/Ultimate** — These editions are not free; you must pay for the features and services they provide. The Professional edition is designed for freelance developers who work in small teams. The Premium edition targets enterprise projects, and the Ultimate edition provides tools for architects and project managers to be used in large projects with several dozen team members.

In this book, you use the Visual Studio 2012 Express for Windows 8 edition because it contains every tool you need for Windows 8 style application development — and it's free.

Installing Visual Studio 2012 Express for Windows 8

Before you can create Windows 8 style applications with Visual Studio 2012 Express for Windows 8, you must install it on your computer. In the following exercise, you download and install the product.

TRY IT OUT Installing Visual Studio 2012 Express for Windows 8

To install Visual Studio 2012 Express for Windows 8, follow these steps:

1. Visit the Windows 8 style apps Dev Center site on MSDN (`http://msdn.microsoft.com/en-us/windows/apps/default`). Select the "Download the tools and SDK" link to get to the "Downloads for developers" page.

2. Click the "Download now" button, and when your browser asks whether you want to run or save the application, choose Run. In a few seconds, the Visual Studio 2012 Express for Windows 8 installer launches.

3. Check "I agree to the License terms and conditions", and click the INSTALL text at the bottom of the screen, as shown in Figure 4-1.

4. Depending on your Windows 8 settings, the User Access Control dialog box may pop up asking you if you want to allow the installer program to make changes on your computer. If it pops up, click Yes; otherwise, the installation will be cancelled.

5. The installation process starts. It downloads the packages to set up on your computer, installs them, and configures them. You can follow this process with two progress bars, as shown in Figure 4-2.

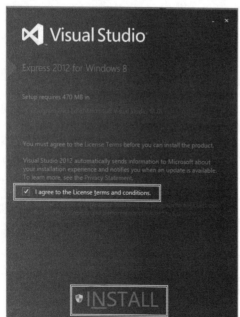

FIGURE 4-1: The Start screen of the Visual Studio 2012 Express for Windows 8 installer

FIGURE 4-2: You can follow the progress of the installation.

The Acquiring bar shows the progress of package download, while the Applying bar displays the progress of installation and configuration.

6. In about 15 minutes, all Visual Studio 2012 Express components will be installed on your computer. At the bottom of the installation screen, click the LAUNCH link to start the IDE. The splash screen appears for a few seconds while the IDE is configured, and then the main window is displayed with the Start Page, as shown in Figure 4-3.

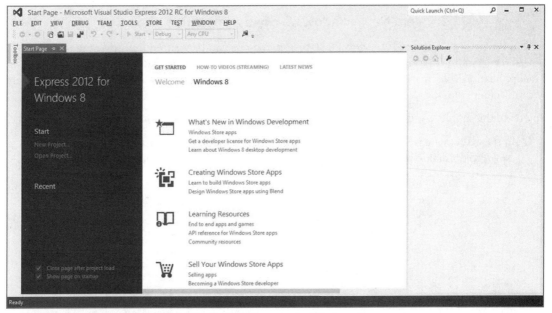

FIGURE 4-3: The Start Page of Visual Studio 2012 Express for Windows 8

Now, Visual Studio is ready. It's very easy to create Windows 8 style applications in this IDE with a few clicks, as you learn later in this chapter.

> **NOTE** *Right after the first launch, Visual Studio asks you to acquire a developer license. This license is required to submit apps to the Windows Store, as you will learn in Chapter 16. When the Developer License dialog appears, select Cancel.*

A SHORT TOUR OF THE VISUAL STUDIO IDE

The Visual Studio IDE has gone through a modernization and a cleanup since the previous release (Visual Studio 2010). The product team worked very hard to make the IDE faster (providing shorter startup and project load times), more frugal in terms of memory consumption, and easier to use. In this section, you learn about the IDE by creating a simple application.

Creating a New Project

In the Visual Studio IDE, your current work is represented by a *solution*. A solution groups smaller units of application artifacts, called *projects*. A project is the smallest unit that can be built independently. In the following exercise, you learn how to create a project.

TRY IT OUT | **Create a New Windows 8 Style Application**

As you learned in Chapter 3, Windows 8 style applications can be written in four languages (C++, C#, Visual Basic, and JavaScript). In this exercise, you use the C# language and the XAML UI technology. The application you create does not do anything exciting. It simply shows four rectangles on the screen with different colors, and displays text as you tap or click the rectangles.

To create the simple Windows 8 style app, follow these steps:

1. In the main menu, select the File ⇨ New Project command to select the type of project to create. The New Project dialog box appears and displays a number of project templates, as shown in Figure 4-4.

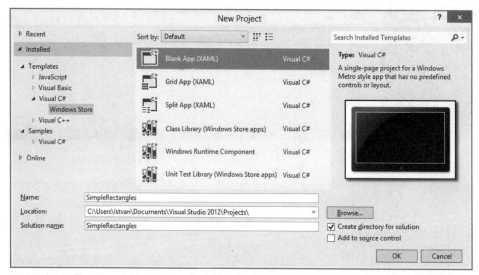

FIGURE 4-4: The New Project dialog box with the Visual C# Blank Application template

2. The left pane of the dialog box displays a hierarchy of categories. Under the Installed node, extend Templates and then Visual C#. Click the "Windows Store" node to display the available project templates for this category. Select the Blank Application template, name it `SimpleRectangles`, and then click OK.

The root node represents the solution that has one project — the node directly beneath the root. The project has child nodes, such as the `Properties`, `References`, `Assets`, and `Common` folders, the `App.xaml` file, and others. The IDE also opens the `App.xaml.cs` file for editing.

FIGURE 4-5: The Solution Explorer with the project

How It Works

When you selected the Blank Application template in Step 2 and specified its name, Visual Studio created a copy of the template files and replaced a few placeholders in the template with the application's name (`SimpleRectangles`). Immediately after the template was copied, the IDE opened it and showed its structure in the Solution Explorer window.

If you were to run the app, it would display only a blank page. In the next exercise, you design the app's page.

TRY IT OUT Designing a Page

To design the application's page, follow these steps:

1. In Solution Explorer, double-click the `MainPage.xaml` node. The IDE opens the file in design view, as shown in Figure 4-6. This view is divided into a design pane (top) that shows a preview of the page, and a XAML pane (bottom) that contains the XAML code describing the definition of the page.

> **NOTE** *When you open a page (or any XAML) file in Visual Studio, loading the design preview may take a few seconds. During this time, a box with "Loading designer..." text is displayed in the preview pane.*

2. At the bottom-left corner of the design pane, use the combo box to change the zoom factor so that you can see the whole design preview. Depending on the size of the display you have, 66.67%, 50%, or 33.33% may be the right scale.

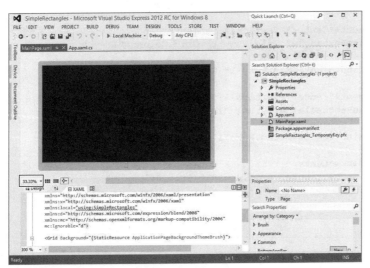

FIGURE 4-6: Designing the MainPage.xaml file

3. In the XAML pane, scroll down to the empty line between the <Grid …> and </Grid> elements, and start typing **<Grid .RowD**. As you type, the IntelliSense technology built into Visual Studio automatically displays a completion list, as shown in Figure 4-7. In this list, the RowDefinitions entry is highlighted as the suggested completion for "RowD." Press Tab, and the suggested completion is applied. Press ">" to close the XAML tag, and the editor automatically creates the closing </Grid.RowDefinitions> tag for you, as shown in Figure 4-8.

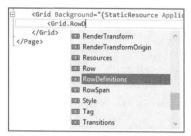

FIGURE 4-7: The completion list displayed by IntelliSense

```
<Grid Background="{StaticResource ApplicationPageBackgroundThemeBrush}">
    <Grid.RowDefinitions></Grid.RowDefinitions>
</Grid>
```

FIGURE 4-8: The completed expression

4. Copy the following boldfaced code into the XAML pane:

```
<Grid Background="{StaticResourceApplicationPageBackgroundThemeBrush}">
    <Grid.RowDefinitions>
        <RowDefinition />
        <RowDefinition />
    </Grid.RowDefinitions>
    <Grid.ColumnDefinitions>
        <ColumnDefinition />
        <ColumnDefinition />
    </Grid.ColumnDefinitions>
    <TextBlock Text="Behind Red" Grid.Row="0" Grid.Column="0"
        FontSize="48"
        HorizontalAlignment="Center" VerticalAlignment="Center" />
    <Rectangle Name="RedRectangle" Grid.Row="0" Grid.Column="0"
        Fill="Red" />
    <TextBlock Text="Behind Green" Grid.Row="0" Grid.Column="1"
        FontSize="48"
        HorizontalAlignment="Center" VerticalAlignment="Center" />
    <Rectangle Name="GreenRectangle" Grid.Row="0" Grid.Column="1"
        Fill="Green" />
    <TextBlock Text="Behind Blue" Grid.Row="1" Grid.Column="0"
        FontSize="48"
        HorizontalAlignment="Center" VerticalAlignment="Center" />
    <Rectangle Name="BlueRectangle" Grid.Row="1" Grid.Column="0"
        Fill="Blue" />
    <TextBlock Text="Behind Yellow" Grid.Row="1" Grid.Column="1"
        FontSize="48"
        HorizontalAlignment="Center" VerticalAlignment="Center" />
    <Rectangle Name="YellowRectangle" Grid.Row="1" Grid.Column="1"
        Fill="Yellow" />
</Grid>
```

5. The design preview is refreshed according to the XAML UI definition you have just typed in, as shown in Figure 4-9.

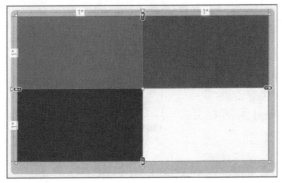

FIGURE 4-9: The preview of the page

How It Works

When you work with C++, C#, or Visual Basic programming languages, XAML is the technology used to define the UI of a Windows 8 style app. When you created the project in the previous exercise, the IDE created the `MainPage.xaml` file for you as the default application page.

In Step 3 and Step 4 you added a grid declaration that divided the screen into two rows and two columns, and each cell of the grid contained a `TextBlock` and a `Rectangle` element. In each cell, the rectangle was put in front of the text, because `TextBox` declarations preceded `Rectangle` declarations.

As you change the content of the XAML pane, the preview is continuously refreshed, as shown in Figure 4-9.

Although you designed the layout of the page, you have not added any behavior to the application yet. In the following exercise, you add a few code lines that allow the user to click or tap a rectangle to reveal the text behind it.

TRY IT OUT Adding and Editing Event-Handler Code

Windows 8 style applications follow the well-known event pattern. When the user interacts with the application, an event is raised by the operating system. In the code, you can write an event-handler method that responds to the specific event.

To add event-handler code to the page you designed in the previous exercise, follow these steps:

1. If you closed the `MainPage.xaml` file in the previous exercise, open it by double-clicking it in Solution Explorer.

2. In the XAML pane, select the `<Rectangle>` element with the `Name="RedRectangle"` attribute. On the right side of the main window, under Solution Explorer, you can see the Properties window, as shown in Figure 4-10. If you can't see it, press Alt+Enter to display it.

3. To the right of the Name field, you see two icons. Click the second one (as highlighted in Figure 4-10) to display the events of the selected rectangle. Scroll down to the Tapped event, type **RectangleTapped**, and press Enter.

4. The IDE opens the `MainPage.xaml.cs` file and creates a new event-handler method named `RectangleTapped`.

FIGURE 4-10: The Properties window

> **NOTE** *The* `MainPage.xaml.cs` *file is called a* code-behind file, *because it contains code that is associated with the UI defined by the* `MainPage.xaml` *file. If you expand the* `MainPage.xaml` *node in Solution Explorer, you'll see that it nests the* `MainPage.xaml.cs` *file.*

5. Append the following code line after the last line at the top of the `MainPage.xaml.cs` file that starts with using:

C#
```
using Windows.UI.Xaml.Shapes;
```

6. Type the following boldfaced code into the body of the `RectangleTapped` method:

C#
```
private void RectangleTapped(object sender,
        TappedRoutedEventArgs e)
{
    RedRectangle.Fill.Opacity = 1.0;
    GreenRectangle.Fill.Opacity = 1.0;
    BlueRectangle.Fill.Opacity = 1.0;
    YellowRectangle.Fill.Opacity = 1.0;
    var rectangle = sender as Rectangle;
    if (rectangle != null)
    {
        rectangle.Fill.Opacity = 0.25;
    }
}
```

7. Click the Mainpage.xaml tab under the IDE's toolbar to get back to the page's design view, and have a look at the `<Rectangle>` element with which you associated the event-handler method:

```
<Rectangle Name="RedRectangle" Grid.Row="0" Grid.Column="0"
    Fill="Red"
    Tapped="RectangleTapped" />
```

The IDE automatically associated the `RectangleTapped` method with the `Tapped` event of the `<Rectangle>` element. Copy the following boldfaced code by selecting it and then pressing Ctrl+C, and then paste it to the other three `<Rectangle>` elements by pressing Ctrl+V:

```
<TextBlock Text="Behind Red" Grid.Row="0" Grid.Column="0"
    FontSize="48"
```

```
            HorizontalAlignment="Center" VerticalAlignment="Center" />
        <Rectangle Name="RedRectangle" Grid.Row="0" Grid.Column="0"
            Fill="Red"
            Tapped="RectangleTapped" />
        <TextBlock Text="Behind Green" Grid.Row="0" Grid.Column="1"
            FontSize="48"
            HorizontalAlignment="Center" VerticalAlignment="Center" />
        <Rectangle Name="GreenRectangle" Grid.Row="0" Grid.Column="1"
            Fill="Green"
            Tapped="RectangleTapped" />
        <TextBlock Text="Behind Blue" Grid.Row="1" Grid.Column="0"
            FontSize="48"
            HorizontalAlignment="Center" VerticalAlignment="Center" />
        <Rectangle Name="BlueRectangle" Grid.Row="1" Grid.Column="0"
            Fill="Blue"
            Tapped="RectangleTapped" />
        <TextBlock Text="Behind Yellow" Grid.Row="1" Grid.Column="1"
            FontSize="48"
            HorizontalAlignment="Center" VerticalAlignment="Center" />
        <Rectangle Name="YellowRectangle" Grid.Row="1" Grid.Column="1"
            Fill="Yellow"
            Tapped="RectangleTapped" />
```

Now, the SimpleRectangles application is ready to run.

How It Works

You can use the Properties window to set up attributes of the selected element, or associate the element's events with event-handler methods. In Step 3, you created a new event-handler method and associated it with the Tapped event of the Rectangle element named RedRectangle. This event is raised when you tap the element or click it with the mouse.

The code you added in Step 6 makes all rectangles opaque, and sets the selected rectangle to be almost transparent. So, the text hidden by it can be seen because of the transparency.

In Step 7, you edited the XAML definition to associate the Tapped event of the other three rectangles (green, blue, and yellow) with the RectangleTapped method.

You have created the first Windows 8 style application. It is now time to run it. In the following exercise, you learn how to start your application from Visual Studio, and then how to debug it.

TRY IT OUT   Running and Debugging the Project

To start the application, follow these steps:

1. Press Crtl+F5, or use the Debug ⇨ Start Without Debugging menu command. Visual Studio builds and deploys your project, and then immediately starts it. The application displays the four rectangles.

2. Tap any of the rectangles (if you have a tablet), or click any of them with the mouse pointer. The rectangle gets darker, and displays the text behind it. For example, when you tap or click the green rectangle, it displays the "Behind Green" text, as shown in Figure 4-11.

Behind Green

FIGURE 4-11: The SimpleRectangles application in action

3. Press Alt+F4 to close the application. As soon as it is closed, the Start screen is displayed. Use your fingers or the mouse to slide the screen until you reach the rightmost tiles. You can discover the tile of the `SimpleRectangles` application, as shown in Figure 4-12.

4. Click the Windows button or tap the Desktop tile in the Start screen to get back to Visual Studio IDE.

5. Open the `MainPage.xaml.cs` file, scroll down to the `RectangleTapped` method, and click the editor margin to the left from the beginning of the `if (rectangle != null)` line. This click adds a breakpoint to the line, as shown in Figure 4-13.

FIGURE 4-12: The SimpleRectangles tile in the Start screen

```
    var rectangle = sender as Rectangle;
    if (rectangle != null)
    {
        rectangle.Fill.Opacity = 0.25;
    }
```

FIGURE 4-13: Creating a breakpoint within the RectangleTapped method

6. Press F5 or use the Debug ⇨ Start Debugging command to launch the application in debug mode. The application starts the same way as before.

```
        var rectangle = sender as Rectangle;
        if (rectangle != null)
        {
            rectangle.Fill.Opacity = 0.25;
        }
```

FIGURE 4-14: The execution stops at the breakpoint.

7. Tap or click the screen. The RectangleTapped event is raised, and the program execution stops at the selected breakpoint, as shown in Figure 4-14.

8. Press F10 twice, and the program execution moves to the rectangle.Fill.Opacity = 0,25; line. Press F5, and the program runs again — until you click the screen again.

9. Stop the application by pressing Shift+F5 when you're within the Visual Studio IDE, or by pressing Alt+F4 if you're within the SimpleRectangles application.

> **NOTE** *Be careful not to use the Alt+F4 key combination while you're in Visual Studio, because it will close the IDE. The Shift+F5 key combination is a shortcut for the Debug ⇨ Stop Debugging command. You can use Shift+F5 to finish debugging when you're in the IDE.*

How It Works

As this exercise demonstrated, you can start your application either with or without debugging, using the F5 or Ctrl+F5 key, respectively. In both cases, Visual Studio compiles the application, immediately deploys it, and creates a corresponding tile in the Start screen, as was shown in Figure 4-12.

You can add breakpoints to your code. When the application is launched, any time the execution reaches a breakpoint, the application stops, and the IDE shows the file with the breakpoint, highlighting your current position.

> **NOTE** *You can find the complete code to download for this exercise on this book's companion website at* www.wrox.com *in the folder* SimpleRectangles-VS *within the* Chapter04.zip *download.*

Using Samples and Extensions

Peeping into sample applications can help you accelerate your learning curve. The designers of Visual Studio kept this thought in mind, and integrated the IDE with the Samples Gallery website (http://code.msdn.microsoft.com). This community website is a hub for Windows programming code samples, and you can find thousands of great source code projects. In this website, you can search for samples by specifying tags, programming languages, Visual Studio versions, and other criteria. When you find an interesting sample, you can download it and open it with Visual Studio. Moreover, you can upload your own sample applications.

Creating a New Project from a Sample

Although the website is very intuitive to use, you first must download a sample and then open it in the IDE. Instead of using a browser to find and download an interesting sample, you can open it directly from the IDE, as you learn in the next exercise.

TRY IT OUT   **Create a New Project from a Sample Application**

To create a project from a sample application, follow these steps:

1. With the File ⇨ Close Solution menu command, close the SimpleRectangles project and all its related files in the IDE.

2. Use the File ⇨ New Project menu command, or press the Ctrl+Shift+N key combination to create a new sample project. The New Project dialog box pops up.

3. Click the Online node (the bottommost) in the dialog box. The IDE connects to a few Visual Studio–related websites — including the Samples Gallery site — and retrieves information that is displayed within the dialog box. Under the Online node, two main folders are displayed: Templates and Samples.

4. Click the small triangle to the left of the Templates folder to collapse it.

5. Under the Samples folder, expand the JavaScript node, then expand Desktop, and click HTML5. The dialog box displays the available sample programs written in JavaScript and tagged with HTML5, as shown in Figure 4-15.

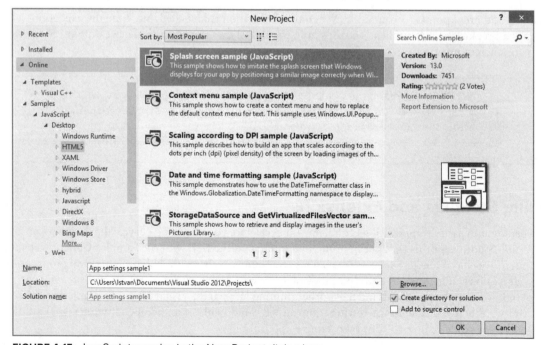

FIGURE 4-15: JavaScript samples in the New Project dialog box

6. Select the Splash Screen Sample (JavaScript) item and click OK. Visual Studio downloads the sample code, and installs it on your computer. Before the installation, you must agree with the license terms displayed in the "Download and Install" dialog box, as shown in Figure 4-16. Click Install.

7. Visual Studio creates a new project using the installed sample, and opens the `description .html` document that explains the details about this sample.

8. Run the project by pressing Ctrl+F5. The application starts, and you can immediately use it. Close the application by pressing the Alt+F4 key combination.

9. Press the Windows key to switch back to Visual Studio. In the IDE, you can use the Solution Explorer to browse project files and discover how `SplashScreenSample` works.

FIGURE 4-16: The Download and Install dialog box

How It Works

In Step 3, when you clicked the Online node, the IDE queried a few websites for template and sample categories. In Step 5, when you traversed through the sample hierarchy, the IDE queried the Samples Gallery site for JavaScript projects in the Desktop/HTML5 category and displayed them. When you selected the `SplashScreenSample` item, it installed the sample files and created a new solution based on this project.

While you browse the samples, the right pane of the New Project dialog box displays a bit more information about the sample. If you want to know more about the selected sample, you can click the More Information link that opens the page of the sample on the Samples Gallery site.

It is worth looking at the sample projects when you want to learn new Windows 8 features. The Windows SDK team uploaded more than 100 Windows 8 examples to the Samples Gallery site.

Installing and Using Extensions

Visual Studio 2012 has a great feature called Extensions Manager (referred as Extensions and Updates in Visual Studio 2012) to help with discovering, downloading, and managing Visual Studio Extensions from Visual Studio Gallery (`http://visualstudiogallery.com`). By using this feature, you can find templates, visual controls, and tools uploaded to the gallery. In the next exercise, you learn how to use the Extension Manager for downloading and installing tools.

TRY IT OUT Using the Visual Studio Extension Manager

In this exercise, you install the free NuGet extension. To install it, follow these steps:

1. Use the Tools ⇨ Extensions and Updates command in the menu to launch the Extensions and Updates dialog box. This dialog box is a hub to managing (that is, downloading, installing, disabling, and removing) all extensions that you want to utilize within the IDE. By default, the dialog box lists all your installed extensions, as shown in Figure 4-17.

FIGURE 4-17: The Extensions and Updates dialog box displaying all installed extensions

2. Click the Online tab. The IDE queries the Visual Studio Gallery and the Samples Gallery to collect information about available extensions. Click the Visual Studio Gallery node to display available extensions.

3. Select the NuGet Package Manager item in the list, and click the Download button. The selected extension is downloaded and the VSIX Installer program is started. Click Install.

> **NOTE** Depending on your security settings in Windows 8, the User Account Control dialog box may ask you to confirm that you allow the VSIX Installer program to make changes on your computer.

4. In a few seconds, VSIX Installer configures the NuGet Package Manager extension. Click Close to exit VSIX Installer.

5. Click the Installed tab. Now you can see the NuGet Package Manager in the list, as shown in Figure 4-18. Most extensions require a Visual Studio restart, as the message displays at the bottom of the dialog box. Click Restart.

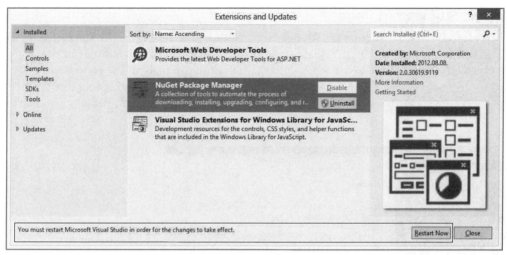

FIGURE 4-18: The Extension Manager dialog box now displays the NuGet Package Manager.

6. When Visual Studio is restarted, go to the Tools menu. You can discover the Library Package Manager item there, which has been placed there by the NuGet Package Manager, as shown in Figure 4-19.

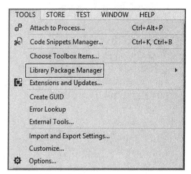

How It Works

Visual Studio has an extensibility model that allows installing add-ins, templates, tools, controls, samples, and other artifacts that integrate into the IDE. All of them can be handled with the Extension Manager dialog box that helps you to discover, install, and manage them. Most extensions need to carry out configuration steps that can be done only at Visual Studio startup time, so to use them, you must restart Visual Studio.

FIGURE 4-19: The NuGet Package Manager added a new menu item.

A Few Useful Things to Learn about the IDE

The Visual Studio IDE is a real workbench that provides a vast number of useful tools and functions to create your software in a productive way. This book would at least double in size if it intended to tell you all the important details about the IDE.

The majority of improvements in Visual Studio 2012 were about simplifying the UI and making it cleaner. In this section, you learn a few things that will make working with the IDE easier.

The Visual Studio Start Page

When you start Visual Studio, the IDE displays a well-organized screen, the Start Page, as shown in Figure 4-20. If you have used Visual Studio before, this page may be familiar to you. This page is a hub to starting your everyday work with the IDE. You can load any of your recent projects, start a new one, or open an existing project file. If you are new to Visual Studio, the Start Page provides you with the most useful links to start application development, including Windows 8 style applications.

FIGURE 4-20: The Visual Studio Start Page

This page provides you with two options that help you manage the visibility of the Start Page, as highlighted in Figure 4-20. Setting the first option closes the Start Page when you load a project into the IDE. The second option enables you to control whether the Start Page should be displayed when Visual Studio starts. Sometimes you may like to use the Start Page when it is momentarily not visible. Use the View ➪ Start Page command to display it.

Window Management

While you are working with Visual Studio, you generally use several documents (such as code files and designer surfaces) and a bunch of tools (such as the Solution Explorer, the Toolbox, the Properties windows, and so on). Respectively, you work with *document windows* and *tool windows*. It is not always easy to place them in the right place so that you can use the best layout needed to be productive.

The IDE provides you with simple (but still powerful) window management features that support multiple monitors. You can change the layout of the workbench with drag-and-drop window operations, as shown in Figure 4-21. You have several ways to arrange windows in the IDE:

➤　You can tab-dock document or tool windows to the editing frame. For example, `MainPage` `.xaml.cs` and `App.xaml.cs` in Figure 4-21 are arranged this way.

➤ You can dock tool windows to the edge of a frame in the IDE, or tab-dock them to the editing frame. In Figure 4-21, you can see the "Find in Files" dialog box is docked to the right edge of the editing frame. As you drag "Find in Files" by its caption, a guiding diamond appears in the middle of the editing frame. As you move the window and the mouse overlays on the rightmost guiding icon, a "ghost frame" shows the new dock position of the dialog box. You can accept this position by releasing the left mouse button, or move the window to another position.

➤ You can float windows over or outside the IDE.

➤ You can display windows on multiple monitors by simply dragging a window to another monitor.

➤ You can minimize (auto-hide) tool windows along the edge of the IDE. In Figure 4-21, the Toolbox window at the left edge of the screen is auto-hidden. Move the mouse and click Toolbox to show this tool window.

➤ At any time, you can reset window placement to the original layout with the Windows ➪ Reset Window Layout command.

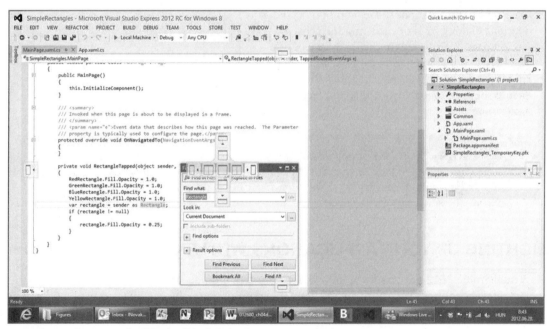

FIGURE 4-21: Dragging the "Find in Files" dialog box to a new dock position

Using Quick Launch

Visual Studio has thousands of available commands. You can find most of them easily in the menus or toolbars. However, it is not always straightforward. For example, when you have a project open in the IDE and you want to create a new project, you probably look for the New Project command in the Project menu and not in the File menu (where this command is actually located).

Visual Studio 2012 introduced a new search tool named Quick Launch. It is located at the top-right corner of the IDE, where search boxes in most programs and web pages are located. You can use the Ctrl+Q key combination to immediately move the focus to Quick Launch.

It is pretty easy to use this tool. Simply type a part of the command you are looking for and the IDE searches for the commands, options, and files you may be asking for. For example, when you type **project** in the Quick Launch box, you'll see the list of available commands, options, and files, as shown in Figure 4-22.

You can use the up and down arrow keys with the Enter key, or the mouse to invoke the appropriate command. For example, when you click the Project and Solutions ⇨ General option, the Options dialog box is opened, and the chosen option page is displayed. In the list, you can use the Ctrl+Q key combination to show all results and move around the result categories (such as menus, options, open documents, and recently used commands).

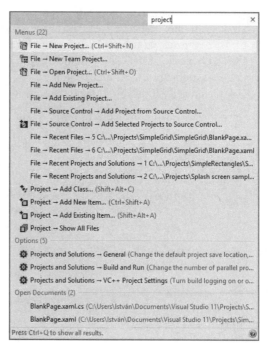

FIGURE 4-22: Quick Launch search results for "project"

> **NOTE** The IDE has many useful functions that make your efforts easier and more productive. In the subsequent chapters of this book, you learn about these features in more detail.

LIGHTING UP YOUR APPLICATIONS WITH EXPRESSION BLEND

Visual Studio 2012 Express for Windows 8 is your free ultimate tool to create Windows 8 apps. It provides the toolset to establish application UI and program the logic managing user interactions. When you installed Visual Studio, another great tool, Expression Blend for Visual Studio 2012, was also installed on your computer.

Blend is a member of Microsoft's Expression product family. This tool is intended for UI designers to produce modern, attractive, and unique application pages using the XAML or HTML technologies. Although it's a designer's product, it's not just about graphical design, but also can be used for designing and creating an application, as you learn in this section.

Starting Expression Blend with a Visual Studio Solution

The `SimpleRectangles` application you created earlier in this chapter could have been constructed with Expression Blend, too. Whereas Visual Studio puts the emphasis on creating the application in a way that programmers are used to making it, Blend focuses on the design of the UI. These two tools mirror the sharing of tasks between a developer and a designer. The great thing is that a Windows 8 style application project created in Visual Studio can be opened in Expression Blend, and vice versa.

To learn more about using Expression Blend, in the next exercises, you add an animation to the `SimpleRectangles` project.

TRY IT OUT   Starting Expression Blend with a Visual Studio Solution

To start enhancing the `SimpleRectangles` application with Visual Studio Blend, follow these steps:

1. Go to the Start screen (if you're in Desktop mode, press the Windows button) and click the Blend for Visual Studio tile.

> **NOTE** *If you cannot find the Blend for Visual Studio tile, start typing* **Blend**.
> *Windows automatically goes into the search screen and displays all applications having "Blend" in the name. Right-click Blend for Visual Studio and, in the application bar, select "Pin to Start." From this point on, you'll find the application tile pinned to the Start screen.*

It is worth repeating the search process and using the "Pin to Taskbar" command in the application bar. After this simple action, Blend for Visual Studio will be accessible from the taskbar in Desktop mode with one click.

2. Expression Blend starts in a few seconds. Select the File ⇨ Open Project/Solution command (or press Ctrl+Shift+O), and the Open Project dialog box opens.

3. Navigate to the folder where you saved the `SimpleRectangles` project when you created it. Select the `SimpleRectanges.sln` file, and click Open. The Blend IDE opens the solution and displays its structure in the Projects window.

4. Double-click the `MainPage.xaml` file and the IDE displays it in the middle of the main window, as shown in Figure 4-23.

> **NOTE** *The screenshot you see in Figure 4-23 uses a light color scheme to provide better contrast in printing. You will see darker colors, because Blend uses the dark theme by default. You can use the Workspace tab of the Options dialog box (File ⇨ Options) to change the theme from dark to light, or vice versa.*

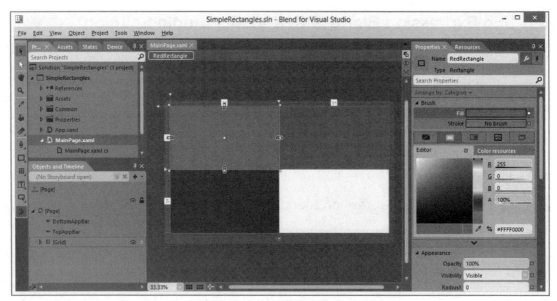

FIGURE 4-23: The SimpleRectangles solution opened in Blend for Visual Studio

5. In the Projects window, expand the `MainPage.xaml` node and double-click the `MainPage.xaml.cs` node right beneath. The file opens and shows the C# code, just as though you were within the Visual Studio IDE.

6. Click the X icon in the `MainPage.xaml.cs` tab to close the code editor.

How It Works

Blend for Visual Studio can open the solution files created with Visual Studio, and understands the structure of solutions with Windows 8 app projects. You can use the Blend IDE to create and modify a UI, and you can read and edit the related code, too.

Although this exercise did not demonstrate it, you can even create a new Windows 8 application project in Blend with the File ⇨ New Project command.

Blend has a set of tool windows that help you to design the UI. Figure 4-23 shows the most important ones:

➤ The Projects tool window displays the structure of files and folders in the solution, similar to what Solution Explorer does in Visual Studio.

➤ The Toolbox at the left edge of the screen contains the set of tools you can utilize to edit the page open in the design surface.

➤ The "Objects and Timeline" tool window shows the hierarchy of visual elements constituting the UI. In Figure 4-23, you can see that the page (`MainPage.xaml`) is composed from three elements: `BottomAppBar`, `TopAppBar`, and `[Grid]`. `[Grid]` is expandable, so it nests other elements, as the little triangle indicates.

➤ The middle of the screen is the designer surface. This is where you can drag and drop UI elements, as well as move, size, and manage them.

➤ Each object that builds up the UI has attributes that can be edited in the Properties window — to the right of the design surface.

The Blend IDE does not look very complicated (in contrast to other designer-centric applications, like Adobe's Photoshop), yet it is very powerful, as you learn in the next exercises.

Adding an Animated Object to the UI

The `SimpleRectangles` application changes the opacity of a rectangle when the user taps or clicks it. Let's now extend it with a fly-in animation effect. When the rectangle is tapped or clicked, text will fly in the screen.

TRY IT OUT Create a Text Block with Expression Blend

To create a text block that will fly in when any of the rectangles is tapped or clicked, follow these steps:

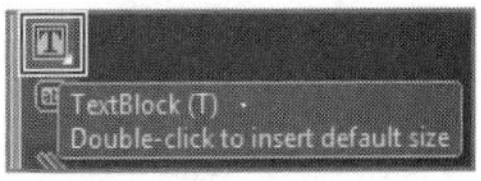

1. In the Toolbox, click the TextBlock tool, as shown in Figure 4-24. The TextBlock tool is now selected.

2. In the designer surface, draw a rectangle above the red and green rectangles (and outside of the tablet border) in the middle of the screen, as shown in Figure 4-25. To draw the rectangle, click the design surface where you want to put its top-left corner, and, without releasing the left mouse button, move the pointer into the position of the bottom-right corner. While you move the mouse, Blend displays the dimensions of the rectangle, as highlighted in Figure 4-25. Make the rectangle about 700 pixels wide and 100 pixels high.

FIGURE 4-24: The TextBlock tool

3. Click the Properties window, and type **FlyInRectangle** into the Name box, as shown in Figure 4-26. This will be the name of the control you can use when writing code.

FIGURE 4-25: Drawing the TextBlock rectangle

FIGURE 4-26: Setting the name of the TextBlock in the Properties window

4. In the Toolbox, click the black mouse pointer tool, which selects the TextBlock you have just drawn. In the Properties window scroll down to the Text section, and set the size of the text to 24 points (24 pt), as shown in Figure 4-27.

5. In the Text section, click the second (paragraph mark) tab, and set the horizontal alignment to Center, as shown in Figure 4-28.

6. In the designer surface, double-click the TextBlock's rectangle to select its text, and type **You've tapped the screen** to change the default "TextBlock" text. The design surface is updated, as shown in Figure 4-29.

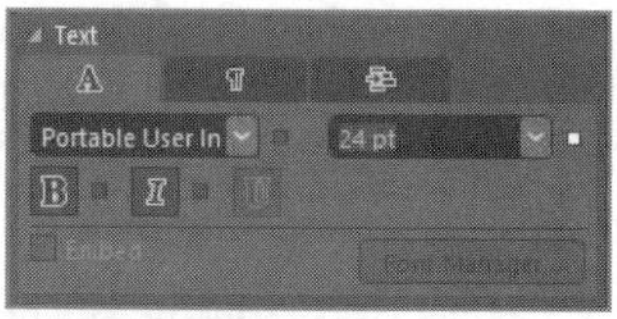

FIGURE 4-27: Setting the text size to 24 points

How It Works

You can use the Toolbox to pick a UI element and place it on the design surface. In this exercise, you used the TextBlock tool to put a box of text on the `MainPage.xaml` page. You used the Properties window to set the name, the size, and the horizontal alignment of the text. In addition, you changed the default text.

FIGURE 4-28: Setting the horizontal text alignment to Center

The new TextBlock UI element was added to the hierarchy of the page's UI elements, and was displayed in the "Objects and Timeline" tool window, as shown in Figure 4-30.

FIGURE 4-30: The FlyInRectangle added to the UI element hierarchy

FIGURE 4-29: The updated design surface

Now you are ready to compose an animation for the `FlyInRectangle` UI element. Creating an animation with Blend is fairly easy. With the help of a storyboard, you can do it in a few steps, as you learn in the next exercise.

TRY IT OUT Creating an Animation with Blend

To create an animation that moves the `FlyInRectangle` element, follow these steps:

1. In the "Objects and Timeline" tool window, click the New button (the plus sign, as shown in Figure 4-31) to create a new storyboard. The Create StoryBoard Resource dialog box opens. Type **FlyInStoryboard** in the Name (Key) text box, and click OK.

2. The storyboard object is created, and recording mode is started, as the "FlyInStoryboard timeline recording is set on" label indicates at the top of the design surface. The timeline pane is displayed in the "Objects and Timeline" tool window, as shown in Figure 4-32.

FIGURE 4-31: The New button in the "Objects and Timeline" dialog box

FIGURE 4-32: The timeline pane

This pane contains a horizontal scale representing the seconds in the timeline. A small yellow arrow and a vertical yellow line beneath the 0 value indicate that the design surface displays the initial state of the storyboard.

3. Click the 2 scale value on the timeline. The yellow arrow and line now indicate that the design surface represents the state of the storyboard at 2 seconds.

4. Click the "You've tapped the screen" text and move it into the middle of the screen. Because the storyboard is in recording mode, with this simple move, you instructed the designer that you want to create a storyboard that animates the text so that it moves into the selected location 2 seconds after the storyboard starts.

5. In the timeline pane, there is a little play button. Click it. The storyboard starts and animates the text, moving from its initial location to the new position you designated in the previous step.

6. In the "Objects and Timeline" tool window, expand the `FlyInRectangle` node. This node nests a new `RenderTransform` node that represents the change of the text's position (the little animation you added in Step 4), as shown in Figure 4-33.

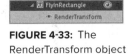

FIGURE 4-33: The RenderTransform object nested by FlyInRectangle

7. Click the `RenderTransform` node to change its attributes in the Properties window. The animation you set up is a bit unnatural, because the text moves with a constant speed. It would be more natural if it started slowly, and after acceleration, it slowed again before stopping. You can make this change easily in the Easing section of the Properties window, as shown in Figure 4-34. You can see a diagram there displaying how the animated property (in this case, the position of the text block, marked by the vertical axis) changes over time (marked by the horizontal axis).

8. In the bottom-left and top-right diagram corners you find two grips. To change the diagram, click and move them one by one into a new position, as shown in Figure 4-35.

9. In the "Objects and Timeline" tool window, click the `FlyInStoryboard` name (directly beneath the tool window's tab) to display the related attributes in the Properties window.

10. In the Properties window, check the AutoReverse box. Click the Play button in the timeline to see that now the text block flies in and then automatically flies out.

11. Save all changes with the File ⇨ Save All command.

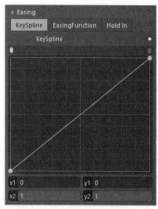 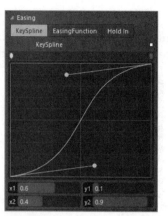

FIGURE 4-34: The original easing of the RenderTransform object

FIGURE 4-35: The modified easing of the RenderTransform object

How It Works

The key object of creating animations is the storyboard you added to the page in Step 1. The storyboard uses a timeline to define the states of objects on the design surface. In Step 3 and Step 4, you defined two states — two separate positions — of the text block "You've tapped the screen." The storyboard recorded how the properties of the text block had changed. When you played the storyboard in Step 5, the property values of the text block were calculated for every frame between 0 and 2 seconds (about 30 frames for each second), and that is what you perceived as a fluent animation.

In Step 7 and Step 8 you changed the way the property values were calculated. The diagram in Figure 4-35 showed how the properties change over time. You could see that at the beginning and at the end of the animation the properties changed slowly over time (the diagram was flat), whereas in the middle of the animation, properties changed faster (the diagram was steeper).

In many cases, you'll discover that it's great to use the AutoReverse flag you set in Step 10. You do not need to create a new storyboard to mirror the animation. Setting this flag automatically does it for you.

Starting the Animation

You have done almost everything. The final step is to trigger the storyboard when you tap or click the screen. It's easy; you can do it in Blend, as you learn in the next exercise.

> **TRY IT OUT** Starting the Animation

To start the animation you created in the previous exercise, follow these steps:

1. In the Projects tool window, double-click the `MainPage.xaml.cs` file to open it. Locate the `RectangleTapped` event-handler method at the bottom of the file.

2. Add the following two lines to the end of the method:

```C#
FlyInStoryBoard.SkipToFill();
FlyInStoryboard.Begin();
```

3. In the menu, select the Project ⇨ Run Project command. The Blend IDE builds the projects (just as if you were using Visual Studio), deploys it, and starts the `SimpleRectangles` application.

4. When the application starts, try tapping or clicking the rectangles. You can check that the animation starts every time you tap or click a rectangle. If you tap or click two rectangles in quick succession (within 2 seconds), you can check that the animation always starts from the beginning.

How It Works

The code lines you added in Step 2 simply stop and then start the animation from the beginning. As you experienced in Step 3, Expression Blend also can build and deploy your Windows 8 style apps.

> **NOTE** You can find the complete code to download for this exercise on this book's companion website at `www.wrox.com` in the folder `SimpleRectangles-Blend` within the `Chapter04.zip` download.

Using Visual Studio and Blend Together

In the previous exercises, you learned about only a few features of Blend. Expression Blend provides you with rich functionality, many advanced features (including amazing UI editing capabilities), support for data binding, sample data, styling, and templates. Although many design features of Blend are also integrated into Visual Studio 2012, Blend is still the tool for designers.

In real Windows 8 style application projects, Blend and Visual Studio are used in tandem. Typically, developers work in Visual Studio to create the basic UI and write the logic behind the application. Designers use Blend to enhance the UI with rich animation effects, media, and nice layouts.

In the following chapters of the book you see many examples of how these two great tools constitute an ultimate toolset to create Windows 8 applications.

SUMMARY

Windows 8 provides great technologies to host Windows 8 style applications. However, without the right toolset, developers cannot use them efficiently. Microsoft delivers those tools that make application development easy:

➤ Microsoft Visual Studio 2012 is the ultimate development environment that supports all Windows 8 languages and the full technology stack for Windows 8 style application development. It has a free version, Visual Studio 2012 Express for Windows 8, which you can download from MSDN.

➤ Microsoft Expression Blend is a tool that targets UI designers to establish a professional application UI in a fairly productive way. A free version of Blend is also available.

You can create, develop, build, and run Windows 8 style applications both in Visual Studio and in Blend. Visual Studio provides a great coding experience, and Blend is the tool you need to edit a great-looking and modern UI.

In Chapter 5, you learn more about the principles of Windows 8 style application development, and get acquainted with the fundamentals of asynchronous programming.

EXERCISES

1. Which free development tool supports all Windows 8 languages?

2. How can you look for sample Windows 8 applications?

3. Which tool window lists the structure of your Visual Studio projects?

4. If you want to start your application in Visual Studio, which commands can you use?

5. Which Visual Studio feature can you use to quickly find commands or options?

6. What is the key object in creating animations with Expression Blend?

> **NOTE** You can find answers to the exercises in Appendix A.

▶ **WHAT YOU LEARNED IN THIS CHAPTER**

TOPIC	KEY CONCEPTS
Visual Studio 2012 Express for Windows 8	This tool is a free member of the Visual Studio 2012 family. You can download it from the MSDN website. This tool contains all features you need to create, debug, and deploy Windows 8 style applications.
Creating a new application project	Use the File ⇨ New Project command (Ctrl+Shift+N) to display the New Project dialog box. Under the Installed Templates tab, select the programming language you intend to work with, and then select the target template. Type the name of your application and optionally change the project's location. Click OK to create the project.
Creating a new project from a sample	Use the File ⇨ New Project command (Ctrl+Shift+N) to display the New Project dialog box. Select the Online tab, and then expand the Samples tab. The dialog box lets you browse the online samples. You can also use the search box at the top-right corner of the dialog box to filter samples. When you find the sample you are looking for, type the name of your application and optionally change the project's location. Click OK to create the project from the specified sample.
Installing Visual Studio extensions	Use the Tools ⇨ Extension Manager command to open the Extension Manager dialog box. In this dialog box, select the Online Extensions tab to browse the Visual Studio Gallery for controls, templates, and tools, or the Sample Gallery for project samples. If you find an extension, you can immediately start using it by clicking the Download button. When you install an extension, you may need to restart Visual Studio. In this case, Extension Manager will notify you.
Finding a command with Quick Launch	In Visual Studio 2012, the Quick Launch tool lets you easily find commands without traversing through the menu structure. Click the Quick Launch search box in the top-right corner of the IDE's main window, or press Ctrl+Q. As you type an expression, the IDE lists matching commands, options, and open document names. You can click an item in the result list, and Visual Studio starts the appropriate command, or navigates you to the selected document.
Opening Visual Studio Projects in Expression Blend	Expression Blend can open Windows 8 style application projects created with Visual Studio. After starting Blend, use the File ⇨ Open Project command (Ctrl+Shift+O), and select the appropriate solution file. Blend opens the solution and shows its structure in the Projects tool window.

PART II
Creating Windows 8 Applications

5

Principles of Modern Windows Application Development

WHAT YOU WILL LEARN IN THIS CHAPTER:

➤ Grasping the concepts of the Windows 8 design language

➤ Understanding the difference between synchronous and asynchronous programming

➤ Using the new asynchronous patterns in C# 5.0

➤ Creating asynchronous logic in JavaScript

WROX.COM CODE DOWNLOADS FOR THIS CHAPTER

You can find the wrox.com code downloads for this chapter on the Download Code tab at `www.wrox.com/remtitle.cgi?isbn=012680`. The code is in the `Chapter05.zip` download and individually named, as described in the corresponding exercises.

In this part of the book, you learn about creating Windows 8 applications. Windows 8 supports numerous programming languages, including JavaScript, C#, and C++, and you will see all of them in the following chapters.

Before you start to program, however, you first must understand the basic principles of modern Windows application development. In this chapter, you learn about the key concepts of the Windows 8 design language, and then you explore and try out the asynchronous programming patterns in C# and JavaScript.

WINDOWS 8 STYLE APPLICATIONS

Before you learn about the principles and characteristics of the new Windows 8 style applications, you must first turn back the clock to understand what brought the Windows 8 design language to life. So, let's look into the history and talk about retro-style applications.

A long time ago, when people started to use computers, they needed aids to understand how the various computer software worked. To simplify the user's life, software developers started using metaphors and built their software on concepts that were well-known from real life. Probably the most widely used metaphor is the "desktop." With modern operating systems that follow this metaphor, users see documents and applications on their computer as very similar to what they might see on their desk in the real physical world.

Although the desktop metaphor is more than 40 years old (according to Wikipedia) it was first introduced by Alan Kay at Xerox PARC in 1970), you can find the same concepts in today's devices. New devices have much more powerful hardware that has helped to portray objects on the desktop more realistically.

For example, if you look at the home screen of even the smallest cell phone today, you can see icons that are beautifully painted. Numerous colors, shadows, and three-dimensional (3-D) effects make them look like the original objects in the physical world. If you start an e-book reader application, you will probably first see a bookshelf that looks absolutely real with a wooden texture and well-aligned books. Then, when you open an e-book, it opens like a real book, and animations make you feel like you are reading a physical book when you turn the pages.

This is the *iconographic design style* that uses metaphors from the physical world, and portrays objects with hyper-realistic graphics in the digital world.

However, the world has changed since these concepts were born. A new generation of users has grown up that doesn't need aids to understand and use computers. Instead of the gorgeous graphics, people now prefer simplicity and productivity. Users don't care anymore if an application is drawn beautifully or super-beautifully, but they are delighted with applications that can help them to quickly solve their problems. In today's fast-paced world, consuming information quickly is the key to success. This is called the *infographic design style*, and the user interfaces (UIs) of Windows 8 style applications follow these principles.

What Is the Windows 8 Design Language?

Microsoft created a new design language for Windows 8 that follows the infographic design principle. Although every application has its own appearance, they have common patterns and common themes that help users to understand and use them in a similar way. By following the same design concepts in your application that the operating system is using, you can help your users to be more productive with your software.

Although the origins of this design language can be found in earlier versions of the Windows Media Center and the Zune media player applications, it was with Windows Phone 7 that Microsoft fully committed to this new direction and made this language prominent. Since then, the dashboard of Xbox 360 has been adapted to this design, and Windows 8 relies heavily on it as well. In the future, you will probably see more and more applications adopting these concepts.

> **NOTE** *For Windows 8, you can create two kinds of applications: classic desktop applications and new Windows 8 style applications. You are not forced to use Windows 8. However, the Windows 8 concepts may be much more usable on devices with touch support. Thus, if you are targeting tablets or other devices where users can control the application with touch gestures, consider using Windows 8.*

General Design Principles for Windows 8 Applications

The first thing you probably notice about Windows 8 is that it is definitely different from what you are used to. Windows 8 breaks with the old conventions, and you must be open-minded if you want to accept it.

FIGURE 5-1: A Windows 8 style icon with simplified graphic

The first thing you have to take into account is that software and devices are part of a digital world. If you see a photo of a book on your phone or computer, it reminds you of reading, because your brain connects the digital photo to the physical book. But your brain doesn't need a perfect photo or a realistic image to have that connection, because you know that it is just a digital copy of an analog object on your device. With that, you can simplify the image — as you can see in Figure 5-1 — while keeping its original purpose.

Your software doesn't need to copy the analog world into the digital world. It doesn't have to look like something else — it actually is a digital application. Authenticity and simplicity can help users to understand programs faster, which is very important in the infographic design style.

The second thing you have to realize is why you create your applications. It is primarily for producing and consuming information. In this case, you must put the information into the center, and get rid of everything that doesn't help the production and the consumption of it (remember, simplicity). The focus should be on the content, and not the frame that holds it. If your users are working with the content, then all the windows, borders, lines, and background images — the so-called *chrome* — are not so important to them. You can use them if they help your original goal, but not simply to make your application look fancy.

NOTE *Remember, most people use mobile devices these days, and all the extra chrome you use in your application consumes power and can degrade the precious battery life.*

Just take a look at any of the built-in Windows 8 style applications. These are not running within a window, but instead are running in full screen to give space for the content. Windows 8 style applications even hide the classic Windows taskbar to free up some screen real estate (remember, mobile devices have small screens), and help the users to concentrate on the current application.

Today, users are flooded with data from various sources, so they really appreciate when the information is tailored to their needs. On a tablet device, the application may know who you are, where you are, in which position you hold the device, who is around you, and what information are you interested in right now. The application can customize itself to deliver content that is personal, relevant, and connected. If the device supports touch gestures, you can interact directly with the content, which is another level of user experience that rises above using the classic mouse and keyboard combo.

In the Windows 8 design language, content is king, and if you want to use it wisely, you need good typography. Typefaces, font sizes, colors, and whitespace are the keys to displaying the information in a easily readable format. Microsoft provides recommendations about the best practices, and even provides controls and typefaces you can use for free without extra licensing.

Animations are also important in the Windows 8 design language, because motion can further help the user to understand the software. The consistent use of animations makes your application more intuitive, even if the user doesn't consciously care about them. You can use fast and fluid animations to signal to the user that your application is responsive, and bring the interface to life.

But wait a minute! What happens with the unique appearance of your application if you use the same layout, fonts, animation, and style as any other application? Windows 8 provides a set of design principles that Microsoft believes can make applications better by answering the usability challenges. This set is not a rigorous list of expectations your application should meet in order to run on Windows 8. You can definitely brand your application while you are following the Windows 8 design principles. Just look at the built-in applications or the applications that are available from the Windows Store, and you will see that they are different and reflect the brand of the author. Be inspired by the design language, but balance between Windows 8 and your own style.

Application Structure and Navigation Models

Windows 8 style applications are next-generation software in the sense that they are targeting not only desktop PCs and laptops, but also the latest handheld tablet devices. Tablet devices support touch gestures, and they often come without any other input device (including mouse and keyboard). The Windows 8 operating system is fully prepared for running on tablets (for example, it has a virtual keyboard that enables you to enter text on a touchscreen), and you should also design your application for gesture-based control. In fact, Microsoft recommends designing your Windows 8 style application for touch-first experience, meaning that you should design and optimize for gestures as the primary input method.

> **NOTE** *Although touch gestures are the primary input method for Windows 8 style applications, you can use them fully with mouse and keyboard as well.*

Unfortunately, gestures present two problems:

➤ Users can't work with their fingers as precisely as they can with a mouse. This means you must enlarge the touch targets on your UI.

➤ Touch gestures are not easy to explore. This type of input works beautifully only if the gestures are used consistently across the system, because, in this way, users must learn them once, and can use the same gestures everywhere, even in your applications.

Fortunately, Microsoft developed a navigation system for Windows 8 style applications that solves these problems.

> **NOTE** *You can read more about touch gestures in Chapter 14, "Advanced Programming Concepts."*

The basic unit of navigation in a Windows 8 style application is the *page*. As you may guess, the name comes from the web, because these application pages work very much like web pages. The user works with one page at a time, and navigation means going from one page to another. No windows or pop-ups appear that could break this consistency and complicate the UI.

You can organize your pages into a flat system or into a hierarchical system.

In the flat system, all pages reside at the same hierarchical level. This pattern is best for applications that contain only a small number of pages and the user must be able to switch between the tabs. Games, browsers, or document-creation applications often fall into this category. In these applications, the user can switch between the pages using the navigation bar (or *nav bar*) on the top of the screen, as shown in Figure 5-2.

You can represent your pages in any way on the navigation bar, but a typical technique is the use of thumbnails.

The hierarchical system is more familiar to people because it follows the same pattern in which website pages are organized. The hierarchical pattern is best for applications that have a large number of pages that can be grouped into multiple sections.

The root of the hierarchy is a *hub page*, which is the entry point of the application. On the hub page, users can get a glimpse of what is available in the sections of the application, so this first page should engage the users and draw them into the section pages. You can see an example of the hub page in Figure 5-3 from the Bing Finance application. This welcome page is an at-a-glance summary of the most important and relevant data in the application.

FIGURE 5-2: The Windows 8 style Internet Explorer with the tab navigation bar

FIGURE 5-3: The hub page of the Bing Finance application

From the hub page, users can navigate to the second level of the application, the *section pages*. Section pages often contain lists that can be grouped, sorted, and filtered. In Figure 5-4, you can see the section page of the Bing Finance application that lists the stocks available in the application.

From the list on the section page, users can select a single item and navigate to the third level of the hierarchy, the *detail page*. Detail pages may contain all information about the selected item, and the layout may vary depending on the type of the content. In Figure 5-5, you can see the detail page of a single stock in the Bing Finance application.

Users can go deeper in the hierarchy by activating (touching) an item on the screen, or can go back by using the Back button at the top of the page. Naturally, if your application is simpler, you can omit the hub page or the section page to make a more shallow hierarchy.

In Chapter 2, "Using Windows 8," you learned about the charm bar and the app bar. The charm bar can slide in from the right, and the app bar can slide up from the bottom of the screen to display more options to the user. Both bars are extensible, and you can add your application-specific options to them.

The app bar should contain contextual commands, and can even pop-up menus when they have too many commands. The charm bar includes the Settings charm, which provides a single access point to all settings that are relevant in the user's current context. This means you should add your application's settings to the settings charm as well. In Figure 5-6, you can see how the built-in Weather application extends the Settings charm to include its options.

FIGURE 5-4: The Watchlist section page of the Bing Finance application

FIGURE 5-5: The detail page of a stock in the Bing Finance application

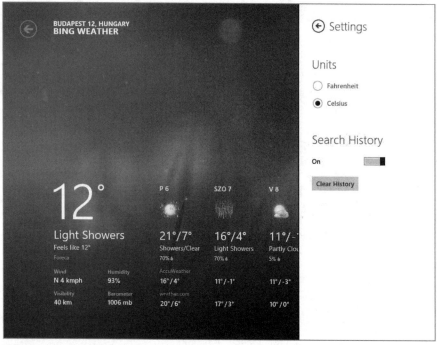

FIGURE 5-6: The Settings charm of the Weather application

At first, you may think that the navigation concept with the app bar, charm bar, nav bar, hierarchy, and Back button is really complex. Perhaps that's true. However, if all these concepts are used consistently across the operating system and the applications, there's no doubt that the users will sooner or later master them, and, at the end of the day, hopefully they will even enjoy them.

Now let's take a look at how to create a basic Windows 8 style application.

TRY IT OUT Creating a Basic Windows 8 Application

To create your first Windows 8 style application, follow these steps:

1. Start Visual Studio 2012 by clicking its icon on the Start screen.

2. Select File ⇨ New Project (or press Ctrl+Shift+N) to display the New Project dialog box.

3. Select the Installed ⇨ Templates ⇨ Visual C# ⇨ Windows Store category from the left tree, and then select the Grid Application project type in the middle pane, as shown in Figure 5-7.

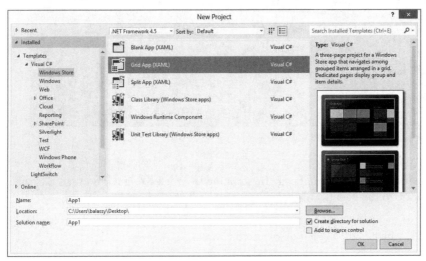

FIGURE 5-7: The New Project dialog box

4. Click OK. Visual Studio creates an empty project skeleton and opens the main `App.xaml.cs` file in the code editor.

5. Start the application by clicking the Debug ⇨ Start Without Debugging menu item. Visual Studio compiles and starts the application, and you will have a Windows 8 style application running, as shown in Figure 5-8.

6. View the groups in the application by scrolling from left to right.

7. Click one of the group titles to open the group detail page.

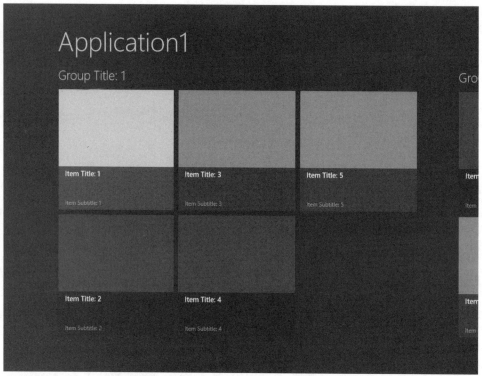

FIGURE 5-8: The default Grid Application type

8. Review the content on the group detail page by scrolling from left to right, and then click one of the items to navigate to the item details page.

9. View the content of the item detail page, and then navigate back to the home screen by clicking the Back button twice, which is the big left arrow on the top of the screen.

How It Works

According to the project template you selected, Visual Studio generated an empty skeleton that contains everything you need to start creating your Windows 8 style application in C#. You can open the Solution Explorer window by clicking the View ➪ Solution Explorer menu item (or simply pressing Ctrl+Alt+L), where you can see all the files within your project, as shown in Figure 5-9.

The application contains three pages: the homepage, the group detail page, and the item detail page. In the Solution Explorer window (and also in your project folder), you can find the GroupedItemsPage. xaml, the GroupDetailPage.xaml, and the ItemDetailPage.xaml files that represent these pages.

The generated files also contain code to implement the navigation between the pages. You can locate these code lines by double-clicking the GroupedItemsPage.xaml.cs file. (You may need to open the hierarchy by clicking the arrow triangle on the left of the GroupedItemsPage.xaml file.) Scroll down to the lines that start with this.Frame.Navigate.

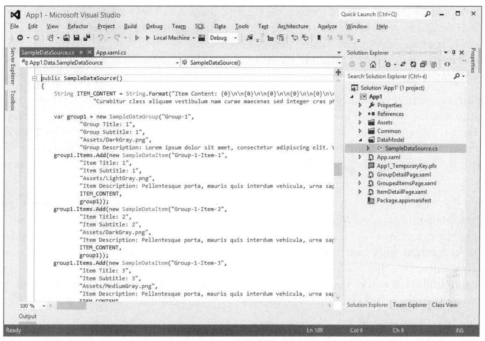

FIGURE 5-9: The content of the project folder in the Solution Explorer window

The data displayed in the application (the groups and the items) are hard-coded into the template, because the application doesn't connect to any data source. You can view the hard-coded data by double-clicking the `SampleDataSource.cs` file within the `DataModel` folder in the Solution Explorer window, then scrolling down to the `SampleDataSource` class as shown in Figure 5-9.

ASYNCHRONOUS DEVELOPMENT PLATFORM

Every year, client applications rely more and more heavily on data they download from the network. Because the amount of transferred data is increasing significantly, the latency of the network more often results in frozen applications that cause serious headaches not only for end users, but also for developers.

As the number of the connecting clients grows on the server side, the server should be able to scale and manage the increased workload. However, clients usually request data that the server must fetch from external services or databases before the requests can be processed. Even while the server is just waiting for the external data, its resources are allocated for the current request, which limits the scalability of the server.

A well-known programming practice, to solve both the UI responsiveness and the server scalability issues, is to design your software to do multiple things simultaneously. For example, while one part of your application is downloading data over the network (which can take a while), another part of your application can be responsible for reacting to mouse and keyboard events (which are generated by the user). If your application can handle these UI events, the user will feel that the application is working and responsive, and he or she will be satisfied, even if the network is slow. Otherwise, your program will appear to be frozen, which definitely ruins the user's experience.

You have already seen several applications that follow this design. For example, you can browse your favorite website while you are copying files on your hard disk and listening to your favorite music in the background. To achieve this, the operating system is continuously switching over the running applications and giving them a very short time to execute. After this short time-slice has elapsed, the operating system switches to the next application, and lets it execute for the next time slice.

However, if you look under the covers, the operating system is switching not between applications, but between smaller units called *threads*. A thread is the smallest unit of processing that can be scheduled by the operating system. Every single application can create multiple threads and perform different tasks on them, and the operating system will take care of executing these threads simultaneously. This concept is called *multithreading*, and you enjoy its benefits when you browse multiple websites on multiple tabs within your web browser, or when you compose a new e-mail in your mailing program while the previous one is being sent in the background.

As you may guess, multithreaded applications are usually more user friendly than classic applications that do all their tasks on a single thread. However, creating multithreaded applications is not easy, and nowadays developers try to avoid these challenges in their code. As you see later in this chapter, the concurrent execution increases the complexity of your application, and makes your code less readable and less maintainable.

Introduction to Asynchronous Programming

You should write code in the same way that you think. When you are thinking logically, your brain creates a continuous series of thoughts that are tightly linked together. Thankfully, programming languages have a long history of supporting developers who express this way of thinking in programming logic — as a sequence of discrete steps that are executed one after the other. This is called *synchronous programming*, and because this is the simplest way of coding, most developers prefer to write synchronous code.

All programs consist of *tasks*, which are shorter or longer units of jobs that should be completed. As you can see in the synchronous programming model shown in Figure 5-10, when you arrange your tasks in a synchronous model, the next task can start only when the previous one is fully completed.

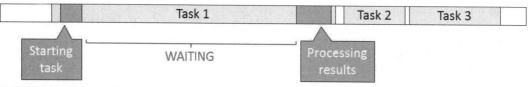

FIGURE 5-10: The synchronous programming model

Because the tasks are always completed in a definite order, the output of an earlier task is always available for the later one. In other words, the later tasks depend on the previous tasks.

Problems arise when a task takes too long to complete, because it performs a long-running computation-intensive operation, reads a large file from a slow disk, or connects to a server that has a slow response time. Because, by default, the operating system allocates a single thread to every process, that single thread will be busy waiting for the result of the long-running operation, and will not be able to respond to any (UI) events. In this case, the thread is *blocked*.

Although the program is actually running (that is, it is very busy doing nothing but waiting), the end user will feel that the program is frozen, which is a very poor user experience. In today's world of smart mobile devices and touch-driven applications, your users are very sensitive to a rich user experience, and your application must be always responsive, independently of everything — the speed of the network, the disk, or the CPU. To achieve this ideal user experience, you must do your best to avoid blocked threads.

A natural solution to this problem is to move from the single-threaded synchronous model to the threaded model, which you can see in Figure 5-11.

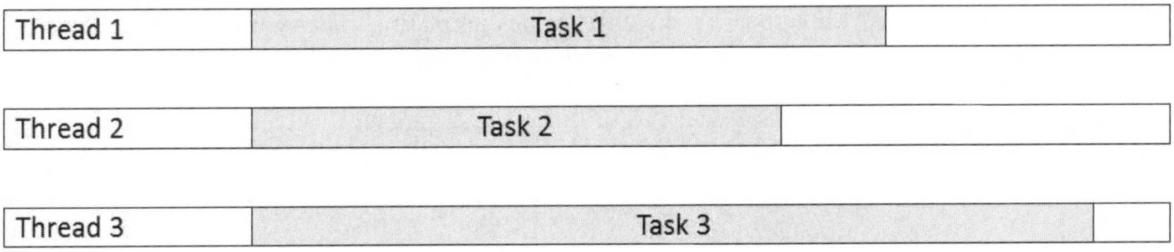

Thread 1	Task 1	
Thread 2	Task 2	
Thread 3	Task 3	

FIGURE 5-11: The threaded synchronous model

In this model, each task is executed on a separate thread, and the underlying operating system takes care of executing them simultaneously. With this model, you can move the long-running task to a background thread and respond to the UI event in a UI thread to keep the application responsive. Because the operating system does the heavy lifting of managing the threads by allocating CPU time slices to them and switching between them, it seems to be a convenient solution, even if you have more threads than CPUs.

Still, it is not.

When you write a multithreaded application, you face some nasty problems. For example, if you have a data structure that is used by multiple threads, how can you ensure that the concurrent access is done safely? In other words, are you sure you can write thread-safe code? Do you know how to marshal data between threads, which means if you have a value on one thread, how can you pass it to another thread? Will the user be able to cancel the long-running process? Propagating an exception is another problem. If you have an error on a background thread, how can you forward it to the UI thread? How can the background thread signal progress to the user?

Although the problems represented by these questions can be properly solved, the solutions require a skilled programmer, and often result in the use of complex logic.

With a slightly simplified model, you can achieve very similar results and get rid of many of those questions. This requires the use of the *asynchronous programming model* shown in Figure 5-12.

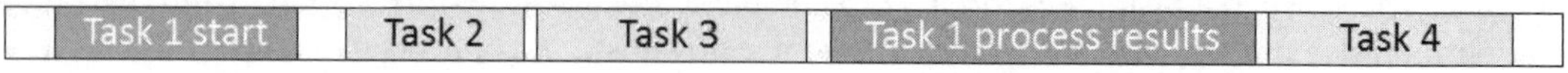

| Task 1 start | Task 2 | Task 3 | Task 1 process results | Task 4 | |

FIGURE 5-12: The asynchronous programming model

In the asynchronous programming model, multiple tasks are executed on the same thread. However, the long tasks are divided into smaller units to make sure they don't block the thread for a long time. This is a great difference compared to the synchronous model, in which the tasks are executed sequentially as single, complete units. In the synchronous model, the next task can start only after the previous one is completed. But in the asynchronous model, the next task can start as soon as the previous one yields execution to it. The second task does not have to wait until the first task fully completes.

For example, if the task is to download a file from a website, you can send the request (which is a quick operation), and then you can release the thread to respond to UI events. As shown in Figure 5-13, when the network card signals that the response has arrived from the server, you can then process the results. Although the tasks will not be completing faster with this model, your application will produce a much more pleasant user experience.

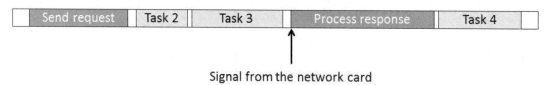

Signal from the network card

FIGURE 5-13: Downloading without blocking

Because your tasks are interleaved on a single thread, you have no more problems with thread safety, data marshaling, exception propagation, progress reporting, cancellation, and so on.

Unfortunately, the asynchronous model is still not perfect. The penalty is that after rewriting your synchronous code to the asynchronous model, you will hardly recognize it. It's your duty to divide your tasks into smaller, non-blocking units, and make sure they release the thread when they no longer need it. This usually means writing code that starts a task, does something else, and then finally processes the results in a callback function. It takes a long time to implement, and the resulting code is difficult to read and difficult to maintain, because you completely lose the continuous flow of control.

The dilemma is obvious. Do you please the user with a responsive system, or do you please the developer with simple code that is joy to write? When you use .NET, you can do both.

Evolution of Asynchronous Programming on the .NET Platform

Since the first release of the .NET Framework, the platform has had built-in support for asynchronous programming. Throughout the numerous versions of the framework over the past ten years, multiple approaches have evolved, and now you have several design patterns you can use to create asynchronous logic in .NET.

With the first .NET Framework, you could use the *Asynchronous Programming Model (APM)*. In the APM, asynchronous operations were implemented with two methods (`BeginOperationName` and `EndOperationName`) that started and completed the asynchronous operation (`OperationName`), respectively. You can see it in action in the following code snippet, which downloads a file asynchronously. (This code may be found in the `NetFx\ NetFxAsyncHistory\APMForm.cs` downloadable code file.)

```
private void StartDownload( string url )
{
  HttpWebRequest req = (HttpWebRequest) WebRequest.Create( url );
  IAsyncResult result = req.BeginGetResponse( this.OnResponse, req );
}

private void OnResponse( IAsyncResult result )
{
  HttpWebRequest req = (HttpWebRequest) result.AsyncState;
  HttpWebResponse resp = (HttpWebResponse) req.EndGetResponse( result );
  Stream str = resp.GetResponseStream();
  // TODO: process the response stream here
}
```

The `BeginGetResponse` method was used to kick off the asynchronous download and to register a callback method to be called by the framework when the asynchronous operation was completed. The `BeginGetResponse` method returned an `IAsyncResult` instance that you could use to query the current state of the asynchronous operation. When the download was completed, the framework called the specified `AsyncCallback` callback, where you could call the `EndGetResponse` method to get the results and complete the download.

This was all you had in .NET 1.0, and, as you can see, it works, but requires a whole bunch of code. Besides, the APM does not support exception handling, cancellation, and progress-monitoring explicitly. These were all up to you to implement.

The second major version of the .NET Framework focused on the events and the delegates, and introduced the *Event-based Asynchronous Pattern (EAP)*. The advantage of the EAP was that it was implemented with only a single method name (`OperationNameAsync`) for the asynchronous operation (`OperationName`). But before calling this method, you had to register the callback method that was called when the operation was completed.

The following code snippet shows how you could use the `WebClient` class that implemented EAP to download a string. (This code may be found in the `NetFx\NetFxAsyncHistory\EAPForm.cs` downloadable code file.)

```
private void StartDownload( string url )
{
  WebClient wc = new WebClient();
  wc.DownloadStringCompleted += this.OnCompleted;
  wc.DownloadStringAsync( new Uri( url ) );
}

private void OnCompleted( object sender,
  DownloadStringCompletedEventArgs e )
{
  string result = e.Result;
  // TODO: Process the string result here.
}
```

This is much less code and seems much cleaner, right? However, if you were to imagine a whole application built around these few lines of code, you would realize that it is very difficult to understand which code block runs when, even if they run on a single thread asynchronously. You can't easily follow the path of execution, because your code reflects a totally mixed control flow. What's more, if you rewrite this code with lambda expressions (that is, a new, compact language syntax introduced in C# 3.0), you get code in which you write down first what will be executed later. (This code may be found in the NetFx\NetFxAsyncHistory\EAPForm.cs downloadable code file.)

```
WebClient wc = new WebClient();
wc.DownloadStringCompleted += ( s, args ) =>
{
  string result = args.Result;
  // TODO: Process the string result here.
};
wc.DownloadStringAsync( new Uri( url ) );
```

In this example you have only a single callback, but other classes (for example, the BackgroundWorker class) may require multiple callbacks, and when you review your code, the control flow will look completely inside out. And this is only a single operation. Things just get worse if you want to complete multiple tasks asynchronously. In addition, the exception-handling issue is not solved either, because how could you propagate an exception to the caller when that call is already returned?

To solve all these difficulties, the .NET Framework 4.0 introduced a completely new approach, named the *Task-based Asynchronous Pattern* (*TAP*). Before TAP, when developers wanted to solve a problem asynchronously, they had to figure out the path of execution, and as you saw previously, it resulted in callbacks and mixed flows of control. The primary goal of TAP is to make developers work with asynchronous code just as they do with synchronous code, and help them clearly see the flow of control.

To achieve this, a new set of classes called the *Task Parallel Library* (*TPL*) was added to .NET 4.0. The most important thing in the library is the Task class that gives developers the option to break with the "path of execution" way of thinking and focus on the "unit of work." An instance of the Task class refers to a value that will be delivered at some point in the future. You don't have to care about how and on which thread this value is computed. All you have to know is that it takes some time to deliver the result, and you can use the Task object to prevent the blocking of the current execution flow until the result arrives.

With the Task object, you can query the status of the asynchronous execution, wait for its completion, and get the result value. There is even a generic version of this class, Task<TResult>, that you can use to access the result of the asynchronous operation in a strongly typed way.

The following code snippet shows how you can use the Task class to download a web page. (This code may be found in the NetFx\NetFxAsyncHistory\TAPForm.cs downloadable code file.)

```
Task.Factory.StartNew( () =>
{
  WebClient wc = new WebClient();
  string result = wc.DownloadString( url );
  // TODO: Process the string result here.
} );
```

With tasks, you can write asynchronous logic very similar to your earlier synchronous code. It's no surprise that Microsoft favors this approach, and .NET 4.5 contains new methods that return `Task` instances directly. For example, the `WebClient` class has a new method called `DownloadStringTaskAsync` (the `TaskAsync` postfix is the naming convention for methods that return `Task` objects) that further simplifies your job, as shown here. (This code may be found in the `NetFx\ NetFxAsyncHistory\TAPForm.cs` downloadable code file.)

```
WebClient wc = new WebClient();
var task = wc.DownloadStringTaskAsync( url );
// TODO: Process the task.Result string here.
```

So far, you have seen several ways to execute code asynchronously, and all of them were provided by the .NET Framework Base Class Library. The benefit of this architecture is that these classes are available for all .NET languages. But because this makes the solution generic, you cannot fully utilize the productivity and cannot enjoy the comfort of your favorite programming language. On the other hand, a language-specific solution could be more convenient for the developers working with that language. However, it would be available only for them.

Microsoft has experience in this area, because it used a similar approach with Language Integrated Query (LINQ) in .NET 3.0. LINQ relies heavily on a set of extension methods that do the heavy lifting on `IEnumerable` instances, but the language syntax in C# makes the usage of them much cleaner, and results in more readable code. Because this solution has proven advantages, Microsoft did the same again, and as you see later in this chapter, direct language support was added for tasks in C# 5.0. With the new language syntax, you will never write another callback.

> **NOTE** *The code snippets in this chapter show how you can initiate and complete an asynchronous operation, but don't deal with the details of processing the result. That alone can be complex in desktop applications. There is one important rule you should keep in mind when you create a graphical user interface (GUI) application with asynchronous logic: code running on a background thread must not touch the UI directly! For example, this means that you cannot display a value in a window directly from an asynchronous callback. Check the companion code for this chapter available for download from* www.wrox.com *to see an example of how to solve this issue with the* Invoke *method in Windows Forms applications.*

Asynchronous Programming with C# 5.0

In C# 5.0, Microsoft further simplified asynchronous programming by adding two new keywords to the language. The new keywords were inspired by the `await`/`async` pattern in F#, and they unquestionably make your code much cleaner. However, you will definitely need some time to fully understand how they work. But after you become familiar with the new syntax, asynchronous programming turns into a joy!

The two new keywords are the `async` modifier and the `await` operator. When you use them, always keep in mind that their primary goal is to cut down the syntactical burden you face with when you use the `Task` class, just like LINQ does with the `select` keyword and the extension methods on `IEnumerables`. With the new keywords, you can transfer to the compiler the mechanical job of turning a synchronous method to asynchronous logic.

Let's take a look at them in more detail with the help of a short example. The following code snippet shows a synchronous method that contains a `WebClient.DownloadString` call, which may take a long time to execute. (This code may be found in the `CS5\CS5Async\Form1.cs` downloadable code file.)

```
private void DownloadSync( string url )
{
  WebClient wc = new WebClient();
  string result = wc.DownloadString( url );
  this.txtStatus.Text = result;
}
```

You can convert this code to an asynchronous method by using the new keywords:

```
private async void DownloadAsync( string url )
{
  WebClient wc = new WebClient();
  string result = await wc.DownloadStringTaskAsync( url );
  this.txtStatus.Text = result;
}
```

The boldface code indicates the changed parts of the code. First you use the `async` modifier on a method or a lambda expression to indicate to the compiler that the code block is asynchronous. The method that is marked with the `async` modifier is referred to as an *async method*.

Second, within the `async` method, you probably have multiple lines of code, but at some point, the execution reaches an operation or function call that takes a long time to execute. This is the point where you *really* want asynchrony to avoid blocking the current thread.

> **NOTE** *Traditionally, you would subscribe to a completion event with a callback handler here, and return the control to the caller. The* `await` *operator does this. If you apply the* `await` *operator to the long-running function call within an asynchronous method, it instructs the compiler to subscribe the rest of this method as the continuation handler of that task, and then returns to the caller immediately. When the task completes, the task invokes the continuation, which runs in the synchronization context of the caller.*

Note that the asynchronous methods are for *managing* asynchrony, and not for *creating* asynchrony. Asynchronous methods don't start new threads; instead, they use the well-known callbacks under the hood, but they spare you from the mechanics of creating them. In fact, the compiler does the heavy lifting by generating the code that fully manages the control flow. To make it work, the awaited operation must return a `void`, a `Task`, or a `Task<T>` instance. This looks like a serious restriction at first, but you will realize in practice that it fully serves your needs and helps standardize your code.

In the next "Try It Out" exercise, you create a classic Windows Forms application that downloads content from the network, while keeping the UI responsive using the new `async` and `await` keywords in C#.

GETTING C# 5.0

To work with the new C# language elements, you need a version of the C# compiler that understands them. If you have Visual Studio 2012 and .NET Framework 4.5, you are ready to go, because they come with C# 5.0. However, you can try the new syntax even if you have only Visual Studio 2010 by installing the Visual Studio Async Community Technology Preview (CTP) available at `http://msdn.microsoft.com/en-us/vstudio/gg316360`. The Async CTP is essentially a minor patch to Visual Studio that upgrades the C# compiler and code editor to understand the `async` and `await` keywords. As of this writing, Version 3 is available, which is compatible with Visual Studio Express, Silverlight 5, Windows Phone SDK 7.1, and the Roslyn CTP.

> **NOTE** *You can find the complete code to download for this exercise on this book's companion website at* `www.wrox.com` *in the folder* `CS5TryItOut` *within the* `Chapter05.zip` *download.*

TRY IT OUT Writing Synchronous Code

To create a desktop application that becomes unresponsive during long operations, follow these steps:

1. Start Visual Studio and create a new Windows Forms Application project.

2. Open `Form1` in the designer and drop a `TextBox` and a `Button` onto it from the Common Controls section of the Toolbox. You will use the button to start a long-running operation, and the text box to display messages about the current status of the operation.

3. Open the Properties window, and, for the Name property of the `TextBox`, enter **txtStatus**, and for the Name property of the `Button`, enter **btnStart**. In the Text property for the `Button`, enter **Start**. Change the Multiline property of the text box to **true** and arrange the controls as shown in Figure 5-14.

FIGURE 5-14: The layout of the controls in the designer

4. Double-click the Start button to switch to code view and generate an event-handler stub for it.

5. To make your later code more readable, create the following short method, which adds the specified message to the text box in a new line, to the `Form1` class:

```
private void Write( string message )
{
   this.txtStatus.Text += message + "\r\n";
}
```

6. Enter the following code to use the new `Write` method to display some status messages when the application is started and when the event handler is running. This code also changes the mouse cursor to indicate that the application is busy.

```
public Form1()
{
  InitializeComponent();
  Write( "Ready." );
}

private void btnStart_Click( object sender, EventArgs e )
{
  this.Cursor = Cursors.WaitCursor;
  Write( "Click event handler started." );
  // TODO: The real work comes here...
  Write( "Click event handler ended." );
  this.Cursor = Cursors.Default;
}
```

7. Compile and start the application to test that the messages are displayed when you click the Start button, as shown in Figure 5-15.

8. Enter the following code to create the `DoWork` method after the `btnStart_Click` method that runs the long-running operation. This method downloads a page from the Internet and returns its length.

FIGURE 5-15: Displaying the default messages

```
private int DoWork()
{
  string result = new WebClient().DownloadString(
    "http://gyorgybalassy.wordpress.com" );
  return result.Length;
}
```

To make this code compile, you must add the following `using` directive to the top of the file:

```
using System.Net;
```

9. Replace the `TODO` comment you entered in Step 6 in the `btnStart_Click` event handler with the following lines of code, which starts the download and displays the results:

```
int length = DoWork();
Write( "Download completed. Downloaded bytes: " + length.ToString() );
```

At this point, your code should look like this:

```
using System;
using System.Net;
using System.Windows.Forms;

namespace WindowsFormsApplication1
```

```csharp
{
  public partial class Form1 : Form
  {
    public Form1()
    {
      InitializeComponent();
      Write( "Ready." );
    }

    private void btnStart_Click( object sender, EventArgs e )
    {
      this.Cursor = Cursors.WaitCursor;
      Write( "Click event handler started." );
      int length = DoWork();
      Write( "Download completed. Downloaded bytes: " + length.ToString() );
      Write( "Click event handler ended." );
      this.Cursor = Cursors.Default;
    }

    private int DoWork()
    {
      string result = new WebClient().DownloadString(
        "http://gyorgybalassy.wordpress.com" );
      return result.Length;
    }

    private void Write( string message )
    {
      this.txtStatus.Text += message + "\r\n";
    }
  }
}
```

10. Compile and start the application. Click the Start button, and notice that you must wait about 3 seconds before the messages shown in Figure 5-16 are displayed.

How It Works

This code shows you a classic synchronous implementation of downloading content from a network.

FIGURE 5-16: Synchronous execution

The Button on the user interface you created in Step 2 is used to start the download, and the multiline TextBox is used to provide some feedback for you to know what is currently happening.

The Write method you created in Step 5 is a helper method that simplifies adding new lines of messages to the status text box. The "\r\n" string in the Write method takes care of writing the messages in new lines.

When the application starts, the "Ready" message is displayed, and the program is waiting for user actions. When the user clicks the Start button, the btnStart_Click event handler you created in Step 6 is executed, which changes the mouse cursor and displays the "Click event handler started" status message. After that, the DoWork method you created in Step 8 is called, which is the essence of the application because it is performing the download operation by using the `DownloadString` method of the `WebClient` class. Note that this is a synchronous method, which blocks the execution until the desired content is fully downloaded from the Internet. While this method is blocking the thread, the application cannot process other UI events, and the window becomes unresponsive.

To keep the example simple, only the length of the downloaded content is returned from the `DoWork` method and then displayed by the remaining part of the click event handler.

The code you now have as a result of this "Try It Out" exercise is completely synchronous, and the `DownloadString` call blocks the thread until the content is fully downloaded. Because the call is on the UI thread, the application is totally unresponsive. Notice that you can't even move or close the window during the download.

The next exercise walks you through how to solve this problem.

> **NOTE** You can find the complete code to download for this exercise on this book's companion website at www.wrox.com in the folder CS5TryItOut within the Chapter05.zip download.

TRY IT OUT   Using Asynchronous Callbacks

To solve the thread-blocking problem with asynchronous callbacks, follow these steps:

1. Using the final code from the previous "Try It Out" exercise, you will now use the asynchronous version of the `DownloadString` method. Replace the previous `DoWork` method from Step 8 of the previous exercise with the following two methods:

```
private void DoWork()
{
  Write( "DoWork started." );

  WebClient wc = new WebClient();
  wc.DownloadStringCompleted += OnDownloadCompleted;
  wc.DownloadStringAsync( new Uri( "http://gyorgybalassy.wordpress.com" ) );

  Write( "DoWork ended." );
}

private void OnDownloadCompleted( object sender,
  DownloadStringCompletedEventArgs e )
{
  Write( "Download completed. Downloaded bytes: " + e.Result.Length.ToString() );
}
```

In this case, you first subscribe to the `DownloadStringCompleted` event of the `WebClient` instance with the `OnDownloadCompleted` event handler, and then start the download asynchronously.

2. Because, in this case, the callback is responsible for displaying the result length on the UI, simplify the method call in the btnStart_Click event handler to this:

```
DoWork();
```

At this point your code should look like this:

```
using System;
using System.Net;
using System.Windows.Forms;

namespace WindowsFormsApplication1
{
  public partial class Form1 : Form
  {
    public Form1()
    {
      InitializeComponent();
      Write( "Ready." );
    }

    private void btnStart_Click( object sender, EventArgs e )
    {
      this.Cursor = Cursors.WaitCursor;
      Write( "Click event handler started." );
      DoWork();
      Write( "Click event handler ended." );
      this.Cursor = Cursors.Default;
    }

    private void DoWork()
    {
      Write( "DoWork started." );

      WebClient wc = new WebClient();
      wc.DownloadStringCompleted += OnDownloadCompleted;
      wc.DownloadStringAsync( new Uri(
        "http://gyorgybalassy.wordpress.com" ) );

      Write( "DoWork ended." );
    }

    private void OnDownloadCompleted( object sender,
      DownloadStringCompletedEventArgs e )
    {
      Write( "Download completed. Downloaded bytes: " +
        e.Result.Length.ToString() );
    }

    private void Write( string message )
    {
      this.txtStatus.Text += message + "\r\n";
    }
  }
}
```

3. Compile and test your application. Notice that now you can barely see the mouse wait cursor, and the "started" and "ended" messages are displayed almost instantly. The application remains responsive in spite of the fact that the "Download completed" result message is displayed a few seconds later, as you can see in Figure 5-17.

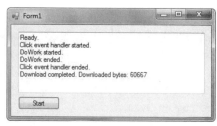

FIGURE 5-17: Asynchronous execution

How It Works

The `DownloadStringAsync` method you entered in Step 1 initiates the download on a background thread, then immediately returns. Because it doesn't block the UI thread, the rest of the `DoWork` method and the button event handler can execute. Because the button event handler returns very quickly, the message loop of the application can continue, and the application can respond to further UI messages.

The `OnDownloadCompleted` method you entered in Step 1 is a callback method that is called when the `WebClient` object has fully downloaded the content from the given URL. But, before the download is started asynchronously, you must specify which method serves as the callback, and you do that by subscribing to the `DownloadStringCompleted` event in the following line:

```
wc.DownloadStringCompleted += OnDownloadCompleted;
```

When the `OnDownloadCompleted` callback method is called, it gets the result of the download in the `Result` property of the `e` parameter, whose length is then displayed on the UI using the `Write` method.

The problem with this approach is that your code doesn't reflect the flow of control. Your click action triggers an event handler that calls a method, then both the method and the handler return. However, the job is not yet completed, because, at some point in the future, the callback will finish it by displaying the results to the user.

Before reading any further, take a moment to think about how you would change your code if you had to download content from another URL if the first download fails, or the result is too small. Yes, you would probably need another callback.

> **NOTE** You can find the complete code to download for this exercise on this book's companion website at `www.wrox.com` in the folder `CS5TryItOut` within the `Chapter05.zip` download.

TRY IT OUT | **Working with the New Asynchronous Keywords in C#**

To use new `async` and `await` keywords in C#, follow these steps:

1. Locate the `DoWork` method you entered in the previous "Try It Out" exercise, and replace it with the following code that uses the new `async` and `await` keywords:

```
private async void DoWork()
{
```

```
    Write( "DoWork started." );

    WebClient wc = new WebClient();
    string result = await wc.DownloadStringTaskAsync(
      new Uri( "http://gyorgybalassy.wordpress.com" ) );
    Write( "Download completed. Downloaded bytes: " + result.Length.ToString() );

    Write( "DoWork ended." );
}
```

> **NOTE** Note that if you use the Visual Studio Async CTP with Visual Studio 2010, you must add a reference to the `AsyncCTPLibrary.dll` file or your code won't compile. To add a reference, right-click the References branch in the Solution Explorer window, and then click Add Reference to open the Add Reference dialog box. Click the Browse button and select the `AsyncCTPLibrary.dll` from the folder where you earlier installed the Visual Studio Async Community Technology Preview.

2. Build and test your application. You should see the result shown in Figure 5-18.

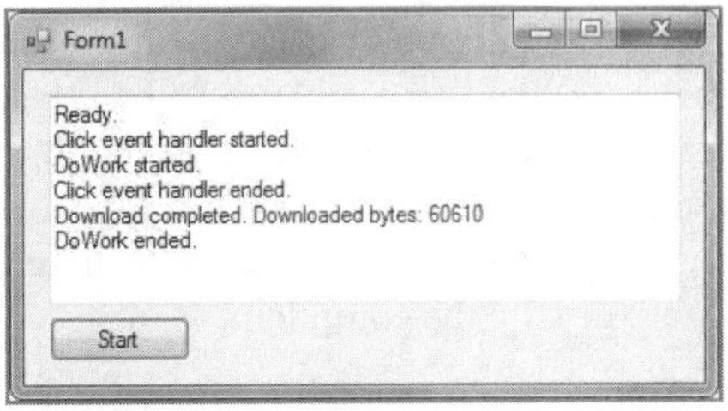

3. To further simplify your code, you can even turn the `btnStart_Click` event handler you created in the previous "Try It Out" exercise to an asynchronous method by using the `async` and `await` keywords directly in it.

FIGURE 5-18: The control flow with an asynchronous method

```
private async void btnStart_Click( object
sender, EventArgs e )
{
  this.Cursor = Cursors.WaitCursor;
  Write( "Click event handler started." );

  WebClient wc = new WebClient();
  string result = await wc.DownloadStringTaskAsync(
    new Uri( "http://gyorgybalassy.wordpress.com" ) );
  Write( "Download completed. Downloaded bytes: " + result.Length.ToString() );

  Write( "Click event handler ended." );
  this.Cursor = Cursors.Default;
}
```

4. With the new syntax, it is very easy to examine the results and add a fallback download to your code. You do this the same as you would do with synchronous code, right after the previous download, as shown here:

```
private async void btnStart_Click( object sender, EventArgs e )
{
  this.Cursor = Cursors.WaitCursor;
  Write( "Click event handler started." );

  WebClient wc = new WebClient();
```

```
string result = await wc.DownloadStringTaskAsync(
  new Uri( "http://gyorgybalassy.wordpress.com" ) );
if( result.Length < 100000 )
{
  Write( "The result is too small, download started from second URL." );
  result = await wc.DownloadStringTaskAsync(
    new Uri( "https://www.facebook.com/balassy" ) );
}
Write( "Download completed. Downloaded bytes: " + result.Length.ToString() );

Write( "Click event handler ended." );
this.Cursor = Cursors.Default;
}
```

How It Works

After modifying the application in Step 1, and then building and testing the application in Step 2, you can see from the output shown in Figure 5-18 that the control flow is totally different at this time. The DoWork method is started, but when the execution reaches the awaited method, the control is returned to the caller, and the event handler completes. When the awaited method is ready to return its result, the execution is continued with the remaining part of the asynchronous method. The code looks entirely synchronous, because the magic with the callbacks is done fully by the compiler.

In Step 3, you learned how you can get rid of the DoWork method while keeping the same behavior, as shown in Figure 5-19.

FIGURE 5-19: The control flow with an asynchronous event handler

Now that you are familiar with the new keywords available in C# 5.0, let's take a look at how to implement cancellation in C# 5.0.

> **NOTE** *You can find the complete code to download for this exercise on this book's companion website at* www.wrox.com *in the folder* CS5TryItOut *within the* Chapter05.zip *download.*

TRY IT OUT **Implementing Cancellation in C# 5.0**

To cancel a long-running asynchronous operation using C# 5.0, follow these steps:

1. To support cancellation on the UI, drop a Button control onto Form1 from the Toolbox. For its Name property, enter **btnCancel**, and for its Text property, enter **Cancel**. Double-click the Cancel button in the designer to generate an empty btnCancel_Click event-handler method.

2. The preferred pattern to implement cancellation relies on a lightweight object called a *cancellation token*. Enter the following code to add a CancellationTokenSource object to the Form1 class that you will use later to signal the cancellation to the long-running operation:

```
private CancellationTokenSource cts;
```

3. Now you can implement the event handler of the Cancel button you generated in Step 1 to signal the cancellation by entering the following code:

```
private void btnCancel_Click( object sender, EventArgs e )
{
  Write( "Cancellation started." );
  this.cts.Cancel();
  Write( "Cancellation ended." );
}
```

4. In the previous "Try It Out" exercise, you already used the DownloadStringTaskAsync method in the btnStart_Click event handler. This method supports cancellation if you supply a cancellation token in its second parameter:

```
cts = new CancellationTokenSource();
WebClient wc = new WebClient();
string result = await wc.DownloadStringTaskAsync(
  new Uri( "http://gyorgybalassy.wordpress.com" ), cts.Token );
```

At this point your code should look like this:

```
using System;
using System.Net;
using System.Windows.Forms;

namespace WindowsFormsApplication1
{
  public partial class Form1 : Form
  {
    private CancellationTokenSource cts;

    public Form1()
    {
      InitializeComponent();
      Write( "Ready." );
    }

    private async void btnStart_Click( object sender, EventArgs e )
    {
      this.Cursor = Cursors.WaitCursor;
      Write( "Click event handler started." );

      cts = new CancellationTokenSource();
      WebClient wc = new WebClient();
      string result = await wc.DownloadStringTaskAsync(
        new Uri( "http://gyorgybalassy.wordpress.com" ), cts.Token );
      if( result.Length < 100000 )
      {
        Write( "The result is too small, download started from second URL." );
        result = await wc.DownloadStringTaskAsync(
          new Uri( "https://www.facebook.com/balassy" ) );
      }
      Write( "Download completed. Downloaded bytes: " + result.Length.ToString() );

      Write( "Click event handler ended." );
```

```
          this.Cursor = Cursors.Default;
        }

      private void btnCancel_Click( object sender, EventArgs e )
      {
        Write( "Cancellation started." );
        this.cts.Cancel();
        Write( "Cancellation ended." );
      }

       private void Write( string message )
       {
          this.txtStatus.Text += message + "\r\n";
       }
    }
}
```

5. Compile and test your application by starting and immediately cancelling the download. Notice that the exception shown in Figure 5-20 is thrown.

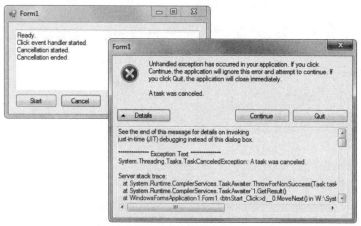

FIGURE 5-20: A TaskCanceledException is thrown

6. To make your code failsafe, you should wrap the awaited method within the btnStart_Click event handler in a try-catch block:

```
try
{
  string result = await wc.DownloadStringTaskAsync(
    new Uri( "http://gyorgybalassy.wordpress.com" ), cts.Token );
  Write( "Download completed. Downloaded bytes: " + result.Length.ToString() );
}
catch( TaskCanceledException )
{
  Write( "Download cancelled." );
}
```

7. Run this code and note that the download is gracefully cancelled this time, as shown in Figure 5-21.

8. You can even use the cancellation mechanism to implement a timeout. For this, you must call the `CancelAfter` method of the `CancellationTokenSource` before the asynchronous operation is kicked off with the `DownloadStringTaskAsync` method call within the `try` block you created in Step 6:

FIGURE 5-21: Download with cancel

```
cts = new CancellationTokenSource();

WebClient wc = new WebClient();
try
{
  cts.CancelAfter( 100 );
  string result = await wc.DownloadStringTaskAsync(
    new Uri( "http://gyorgybalassy.wordpress.com" ), cts.Token );
  Write( "Download completed. Downloaded bytes: " + result.Length.ToString() );
}
catch( TaskCanceledException ex )
{
  Write( "Download cancelled." );
}
```

How It Works

The `CancellationTokenSource` you created in Step 2 is the standard way of implementing cancellation in .NET. When the event handler of the Cancel button you created in Step 3 calls the `Cancel` method of the `CancellationTokenSource`, it sets an internal flag that indicates to that asynchronous task that a cancellation is requested. To associate the current cancellation token instance with the current asynchronous method, you pass it as a method parameter to the `DownloadStringTaskAsync` method in Step 4.

Internally, the `DownloadStringTaskAsync` method periodically checks the token, and if a cancellation was requested, it then aborts the download. For some reason, the creators of the .NET Framework decided that cancellation is an exceptional operation. Therefore, it always raises a `TaskCanceledException`, which you can handle gracefully with the `try-catch` block you added in Step 6. Without this wrapping, the exception would crash the application.

In Step 8, you saw another usage of the `CancellationTokenSource` object for implementing timeouts. Internally, this code initializes a `System.Threading.Timer` object with the specified timeout. When the timer fires, it calls the `Cancel` method of the `CancellationTokenSource` object. Because this is actually a cancellation, the same `TaskCanceledException` is thrown, and it's up to you to detect that a timeout or a user-initiated cancellation has happened.

At this point, you have learned how to create user-friendly applications with asynchronous logic. In the next section, you apply this knowledge to Windows 8 and Windows Runtime.

Asynchronous Development on Windows Runtime

In Windows 8, Windows Runtime gave Microsoft the opportunity to completely redesign the application programming interfaces (APIs) of Windows. Now history repeats itself, because the same thing happened when Microsoft started working on the .NET Framework more than ten years ago. At that time, one of the original goals was to create an advanced, object-oriented API on top of the low-level `Win32` functions that you can access easily from any .NET language. This goal was reached. However, the challenges have recently changed.

As you learned earlier in this chapter, asynchronous programming became more and more important during the evolution of rich, interactive UIs. The .NET Framework continuously adapts to this new challenge by providing newer and newer methods to support the asynchronous approach. Although the architects of the .NET Framework at Microsoft do their best to offer more and more simple syntax for creating asynchronous logic, .NET developers remain the same. Microsoft realized that if a developer is given a choice of a synchronous versus an asynchronous API, most developers choose the synchronous one because of its simplicity. Even if there is a clean syntax for asynchronous methods, the synchronous logic is easier to understand.

Microsoft kept this in mind when it designed Windows Runtime, and followed a simple rule: If an API is expected to run more than 50 milliseconds, the API is asynchronous. This means that there is no way to call it synchronously. You must go the asynchronous path, whether you like it or not. The idea behind this serious decision is to ensure that Windows 8 style applications always respond to user input, and never provide a poor user experience.

> **NOTE** *You will find asynchronous-only APIs in various parts of Windows Runtime, especially when you are doing a filesystem or a network operation. According to Microsoft, about 15 percent of the full Windows Runtime is an asynchronous-only API. If you have already done some Silverlight or Windows Phone development, you will hardly notice them, because those platforms follow similar rules for network access.*

In the next exercise, you learn how to use the new asynchronous file-open dialog box called the File Open Picker.

> **NOTE** *You can find the complete code to download for this exercise on this book's companion website at* www.wrox.com *in the folder* WinRTTryItOut *within the* Chapter05.zip *download.*

TRY IT OUT   Using the File Open Picker

Before starting this exercise, ensure that you have JPG image files in your My Pictures folder. You can copy some from the C:\Windows\Web\Wallpaper folder to the My Pictures folder so that your application will be able select them.

To try the new File Open Picker, follow these steps:

1. Start Visual Studio 2012 by clicking its icon on the Start screen.

2. Select File ⇨ New Project (or press Ctrl+Shift+N) to display the New Project dialog box.

3. Select the Installed ⇨ Templates ⇨ Visual C# ⇨ Windows Store category from the left tree, and then select the Blank Application project type in the middle pane, as shown in Figure 5-22.

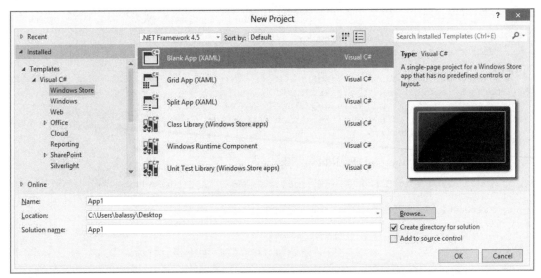

FIGURE 5-22: The New Project dialog box

4. Click OK. Visual Studio creates an empty project skeleton and opens the main `App.xaml.cs` file in the code editor.

5. Open the Solution Explorer window by clicking the View ⇨ Solution Explorer menu item (or by pressing Ctrl+Alt+L).

6. Double-click the `MainPage.xaml` file to open it in the designer. Note the notification in the middle of the design pane, which indicates that the designer is still loading. Be patient while the designer completely loads and the image of the UI of your application is displayed.

7. Open the Toolbox window by clicking the View ⇨ Toolbox menu item (or by pressing Ctrl+Alt+X).

8. Open the Common XAML Controls section in the Toolbox, and then drag and drop a `Button` control onto the design surface.

9. Double-click the button on the designer surface to generate the event-handler method that is called when the user clicks the button. Visual Studio switches to code view in the `MainPage.xaml.cs` file, and you can see the newly generated `Button_Click_1` event handler.

10. Scroll to the top of the file and add the following `using` statements:

```
using Windows.Storage;
using Windows.Storage.Pickers;
using Windows.UI.Popups;
```

11. Scroll down to the `Button_Click_1` method and add the `async` modifier to its signature. Then add the following lines of code to the body of the method:

```
FileOpenPicker picker = new FileOpenPicker
{
  ViewMode = PickerViewMode.Thumbnail,
  SuggestedStartLocation = PickerLocationId.PicturesLibrary,
};
picker.FileTypeFilter.Add(".jpg");
StorageFile file = await picker.PickSingleFileAsync();
MessageDialog dlg = new MessageDialog(
  "Selected: " + file.Path, "Selection completed");
await dlg.ShowAsync();
```

At this point, your method should look like this:

```
private async void Button_Click_1(object sender, RoutedEventArgs e)
{
  FileOpenPicker picker = new FileOpenPicker
  {
    ViewMode = PickerViewMode.Thumbnail,
    SuggestedStartLocation = PickerLocationId.PicturesLibrary,
  };
  picker.FileTypeFilter.Add(".jpg");
  StorageFile file = await picker.PickSingleFileAsync();
  MessageDialog dlg = new MessageDialog(
    "Selected: " + file.Path, "Selection completed");
  await dlg.ShowAsync();
}
```

12. Start the application by clicking the Debug ➪ Start Without Debugging menu item. Visual Studio compiles and starts the application.

13. Click your only button in the application to open the file picker. Select any image file, and then click the Open button. The file picker closes, and the full path of the selected file is displayed in a pop-up dialog box.

How It Works

In this exercise, you created a Windows 8 style application that allows the user to select an image file from his or her `My Pictures` folder.

In Steps 8 and 9, you added a button control onto the main page of your application, and generated the method that is called by Windows when the user clicks the button.

You can use the `Windows.Storage.Pickers.FileOpenPicker` class to display the standard Windows 8 style file selection UI to your user. Because its namespace is not included in the source file by default, you added it in Step 10. In this step, you also added two other namespaces that are used in your code.

In Step 11, you added the code that first shows the file picker, and then displays the full path of the selected file in a pop-up dialog box. In the first two statements, you configured the file picker to start in the My Pictures folder of the user, show only JPEG files, and display these files as thumbnails.

The PickSingleFileAsync method displays the file picker. Note that its name ends with Async, which means that it is an asynchronous method. Therefore, you must add the await keyword before the call, and the async keyword to the signature of the hosting function.

The result of the operation is a Windows.Storage.StorageFile object that describes the selected file. Its Path property contains the full path of the selected file, and that is what you display in the pop-up dialog box.

You use the Windows.UI.Popups.MessageDialog class to display a new Windows 8 style pop-up dialog box to the user. Note that the ShowAsync method that you use to accomplish this is also asynchronous, which is why you must use the await keyword before it.

The return value of the PickSingleFileAsync method is of type PickSingleFileOperation that implements the IAsyncOperation<StorageFile> interface. This interface is one the most important interfaces in Windows Runtime because it is the standard for asynchronous APIs, and you will use it very frequently.

Earlier in this chapter, you learned about the Task and Task<T> types in the .NET Framework that refer to a value that will be delivered at some point in the future. Windows Runtime and .NET are very close to each other, but Windows Runtime is not equal to the .NET Framework, and its features must be available for other languages that cannot access the .NET Framework (such as JavaScript) as well.

To abstract the differences, Windows Runtime provides its own future type in the form of the IAsyncOperation interface. All asynchronous APIs in Windows Runtime return an IAsyncOperation or IAsyncOperation<T> object, and you can use its Completed property to set a callback method that is called when the asynchronous operation is completed, and its GetResults method to return the result in the form of an object of type T.

If you recall in an earlier "Try It Out" exercise, there was no IAsyncOperation<StorageFile> in the code. Instead, the PickSingleFileAsync method directly returned a StorageFile object. That's part of the magic the await keyword does. It not only takes care of the asynchronous execution, but also unwraps the result and returns the raw result object without the packaging.

Because the IAsyncOperation is provided not by the .NET Framework but rather Windows Runtime, you can utilize its power even if you write a Windows 8 style application in JavaScript.

Asynchronous Programming with JavaScript Promises

Earlier in this chapter, you learned how Microsoft made the asynchronous coding patterns first-class citizens in its developer technologies — in the .NET Framework, in C#, and in Windows Runtime. However, Windows Runtime is open for developers who have a web development background, and directly supports JavaScript as well. In this section, you learn how you can apply asynchronous patterns in JavaScript, using a new concept called *promises*.

JavaScript is a single-threaded language, which means that any long-running or waiting operation that blocks this single thread can make your application look frozen. It's been a known behavior for a long time in the web world, and it's no surprise that most of these long-running operations (typically network calls) are implemented using callbacks. However, as you saw earlier in this chapter, callbacks often result in complicated code that is difficult to maintain.

Windows Runtime implements the *Common JS Promises/A* proposal to overcome these problems. A *promise* is a JavaScript object that returns a value at some time in the future, just like tasks in C#. All asynchronous Windows Runtime APIs that are exposed to Windows 8 style applications are wrapped in promise objects, so you can work with them in a natural way in JavaScript.

The most frequently used method on a promise object is the `then` function, which takes three parameters:

```
then( fulfilledHandler, errorHandler, progressHandler )
```

➤ In the `fulfilledHandler` parameter, you can specify a callback method that is called when the promise completes successfully, or, in other words, is fulfilled.

➤ In the `errorHandler` parameter, you can optionally specify a callback method that is called when the promise completes with an error.

➤ In the `progressHandler` parameter, you can optionally specify a callback that is called when the promise object provides progress information. Note that not all promise objects can signal progress.

> **NOTE** *You can read the original Promises/A proposal at* `http://wiki.commonjs.org/wiki/Promises/A`*.*

Now that you understand the basic concepts of promises, you can use them in practice. In the next exercise, you create a Windows 8 style application in JavaScript that uses promises to asynchronously search for content on Twitter.

> **NOTE** *You can find the complete code to download for this exercise on this book's companion website at* `www.wrox.com` *in the folder* `JSTryItOut` *within the* `Chapter05.zip` *download.*

TRY IT OUT **Creating a Simple Twitter Client with JavaScript Promises**

To create a Windows 8 style application in JavaScript, follow these steps:

1. Start Visual Studio 2012 by clicking its icon on the Start screen.

2. Select File ➪ New Project (or press Ctrl+Shift+N) to display the New Project dialog box.

3. Select the Installed ➪ Templates ➪ JavaScript ➪ Windows Store category from the left tree, and then select the Blank App project type in the middle pane, as shown in Figure 5-23.

FIGURE 5-23: The New Project dialog box

4. Click OK. Visual Studio creates an empty project skeleton and opens the main `default.js` file in the code editor.

5. Start the application by clicking the Debug ➪ Start Without Debugging menu item. Visual Studio compiles and starts the application, and you will have your first JavaScript Windows 8 style application running. You can see that, as its name implies, the application is really blank. It displays only the "Content goes here" text on its surface.

6. Exit the application by pressing ALT+F4, or using the close gesture if you are using a device that supports touch gestures.

7. Return to Visual Studio, and open the Solution Explorer window by selecting the View ➪ Solution Explorer menu item (or by pressing Ctrl+Alt+L).

8. In the Solution Explorer window, you can see the three main files for the application:

➤ The `default.html` file contains the markup that describes the user interface of your application.

➤ The `default.css` file in the `css` folder defines the look and feel of your application.

➤ The `default.js` file in the `js` folder contains your application logic.

9. Double-click the `default.html` file to open it in the code editor. Find the `<body>` and `</body>` tags in the code, and replace that content with the following:

```
<p>Enter a keyword to search for on Twitter:</p>
<div>
  <input type="text" id="txtKeyword" value="Budapest" />
  <button id="btnSearch">Search</button>
</div>
<div id="divStatus">Ready.</div>
<div id="divResult"></div>
```

10. Double-click the `default.css` file within the `css` folder in the Solution Explorer to open it in the code editor. Find the `body{ }` section at the top of the file, and replace it with the following content:

```
body { padding: 30px; }
#txtKeyword { width: 500px; }
#divStatus { padding: 10px; }
#divResult { padding: 10px; margin-top: 10px; line-height: 2em; }
```

11. Double-click the `default.js` file within the `js` folder in the Solution Explorer to open it in the code editor. Find the `if` block within the `app.onactivated` event-handler function with the "Initialize your application here" comment. Add the following code into it:

```
var btnSearch = document.getElementById("btnSearch");
btnSearch.addEventListener("click", onSearchButtonClicked);
```

12. Append the following function code block to the end of the `default.js` file:

```
function onSearchButtonClicked(e) {
    var txtKeyword = document.getElementById("txtKeyword");
    var divStatus = document.getElementById("divStatus");
    var divResult = document.getElementById("divResult");

    var url = "http://search.twitter.com/search.json?q=" + txtKeyword.value;

    WinJS.xhr({ url: url })
      .then(
        function complete(result) {
          divStatus.style.backgroundColor = "lightGreen";
          divStatus.innerHTML = "Downloading " + result.response.length +
                                " bytes completed. <br />";

          var hits = JSON.parse(result.responseText).results;

          for (var i = 0; i < hits.length; i++) {
            divResult.innerHTML += hits[i].text + "<br/>";
          }
        },

        function error(e) {
          divStatus.style.backgroundColor = "red";
          divStatus.innerHTML = "Houston, we have a problem!";
        },

        function progress(result) {
          divStatus.style.backgroundColor = "blue";
          divStatus.innerHTML = "Downloaded " + result.response.length +
              " bytes. <br />";
        }
      );
}
```

13. Start the application by clicking the Debug ➪ Start Debugging menu item (or by pressing F5).

14. Enter any keyword (or accept the default keyword) and click the Search button. The results should resemble those shown in Figure 5-24.

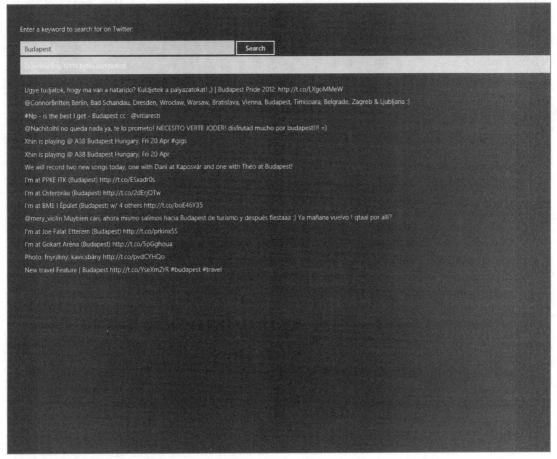

FIGURE 5-24: The Twitter search application in action

How It Works

According to the project template you selected, Visual Studio generated an empty skeleton that contains everything you need to start creating your Windows 8 style application in JavaScript. You reviewed the generated template code in Step 7 and Step 8.

In Step 9, you created the markup that describes the structure of your application page. It contains two input controls, a text field named txtKeyword, and a button named btnSearch. The markup also contains two div elements (divStatus and divResult) that act as placeholders for the output. Note that the id attribute contains the names of the elements that you can use to refer to them in your application code and in style sheets.

In Step 10, you used cascading style sheets (CSS) to define the look and feel of your UI elements.

In the next steps, you added the logic to your application. In Step 11, you subscribed to the click event of the search button with the `onSearchButtonClicked` event handler. This function is called when the user clicks the Search button. You added this event-handler function in Step 12.

The `onSearchButtonClicked` event handler you added in Step 12 sends an asynchronous search request to Twitter, and displays the results. In the first three lines of the function, you created shortcut variables for the UI elements. In the fourth line, you built the URL for Twitter search from the keyword the user entered into the text input field.

The `WinJS.xhr` method is one of the most important functions when creating a Windows 8 style application in JavaScript, because it enables you to communicate asynchronously over the network using promises. The `WinJS.xhr` function returns a promise object, and you can call its `then` method to specify the `complete`, the `error`, and the `progress` callbacks. These callbacks are specified as three function type parameters for the `then` function. Note that you don't have to name these functions; names are used here only for making the code more readable.

The first callback (`complete`) is called when the asynchronous download successfully completes. In the first two lines, you set a friendly light green background color and a status message for the user. Then you parsed the text data that was returned by Twitter to a `hits` object, which is an array that contains the result hits. Then, with the `for` loop, you iterated through the results, and added them one by one to the results pane.

The second callback (`error`) is called when the asynchronous download completes with an error. If you want to test it, enter a single apostrophe (`'`) into the search input field and click the Search button. This error handler displays a constant error message on a red background.

The third callback (`progress`) is called when the `WinJS.xhr` function reports progress. This function displays the number of downloaded bytes in the status pane with a blue background. On most networks, the download is really fast, so you must really open your eyes to catch it. If you blink, you'll miss it.

If you have tested the application without attaching the debugger (by using the Debug ⇨ Start Without Debugging menu item, or by pressing Ctrl+F5), you have probably realized that sometimes the Search button doesn't work. The root cause is that the event subscription code is not perfect, but now that you have learned how promises work, you can fix it in the next exercise.

> **NOTE** *You can find the complete code to download for this exercise on this book's companion website at* `www.wrox.com` *in the folder* `JSPromisesTryItOut` *within the* `Chapter05.zip` *download.*

TRY IT OUT Using Promises at Application Initialization

To optimize the application initialization code, follow these steps:

1. Open the `default.js` file in the code editor and delete the following code that you added in the previous "Try It Out" exercise:

```
var btnSearch = document.getElementById("btnSearch");
btnSearch.addEventListener("click", onSearchButtonClicked);
```

2. Find the code line that starts with `args.setPromise` in the `app.onactivated` function and change it to the following:

```
args.setPromise(WinJS.UI.processAll().then(function () {
  var btnSearch = document.getElementById("btnSearch");
  btnSearch.addEventListener("click", onSearchButtonClicked);
}));
```

3. Start the application without attaching the debugger using the Debug ⇨ Start Without Debugging menu item (or by pressing Ctrl+F5), and test the application.

How It Works

The `WinJS.UI.processAll` function initializes the UI elements you have defined in the HTML markup, and returns a promise that is fulfilled when the initialization is successfully completed. Using the `then` function, you can ensure that you attach your code that subscribes to the click event of the Search button only after the markup is initialized.

In the previous exercises, you called the `then` method as a procedure, without using its return value. However, its return value is really valuable, because the `then` function returns a promise, too, which, of course, also has a `then` function that returns another promise, and so on. This allows you to chain multiple `then` functions and even multiple asynchronous operations in a very natural way.

In the previous "Try It Out" exercises, you first created a Windows 8 style application that searches on Twitter. In the next exercise, you extend the previous application and save the search results into a file. Note that now you will have multiple asynchronous operations that should execute in the following order:

1. Download the search results from Twitter.

2. Create a target output file.

3. Write the results to the output file.

Thankfully, Windows Runtime provides asynchronous methods that return promises to achieve this goal.

> **NOTE** You can find the complete code to download for this exercise on this book's companion website at www.wrox.com in the folder `JSChainingPromisesTryItOut` within the `Chapter05.zip` download.

TRY IT OUT   Chaining Promises

To learn how you can chain promises, follow these steps:

1. In Visual Studio, open the project you created in the previous exercise, and open the `default.js` file.

2. Find the `onSearchButtonClicked` function and add the following line to its top:

```
var content;
```

3. Find the `complete` function of the `then` method and add the following line to its end:

```
content = result.responseText;
```

4. Remove the semicolon (`;`) from the end of the `then` method and replace it with the following lines of code:

```
.then(
  function () {
    var folder = Windows.Storage.ApplicationData.current.temporaryFolder;
    return folder.createFileAsync("temp.txt",
      Windows.Storage.CreationCollisionOption.replaceExisting);
  }
)
.then(
  function (storageFile) {
    divStatus.innerHTML += "Saving the results to " + storageFile.path + "<br />";
    return Windows.Storage.FileIO.writeTextAsync(storageFile, content);
  }
)
.then(
  function () {
    divStatus.innerHTML += "Done.";
  }
);
```

At this point, your `onSearchButtonClicked` function should look like this:

```
function onSearchButtonClicked(e) {
  var content;
  var txtKeyword = document.getElementById("txtKeyword");
  var divStatus = document.getElementById("divStatus");
  var divResult = document.getElementById("divResult");

  var url = "http://search.twitter.com/search.json?q=" + txtKeyword.value;

  WinJS.xhr({ url: url })
    .then(
      function complete(result) {
        divStatus.style.backgroundColor = "lightGreen";
        divStatus.innerHTML = "Downloading " + result.response.length +
                        " bytes completed. <br />";

        var hits = JSON.parse(result.responseText).results;
```

```
            for (var i = 0; i < hits.length; i++) {
              divResult.innerHTML += hits[i].text + "<br/>";
            }

            content = result.responseText;
          },

          function error(e) {
            divStatus.style.backgroundColor = "red";
            divStatus.innerHTML = "Houston, we have a problem!";
          },

          function progress(result) {
            divStatus.style.backgroundColor = "blue";
            divStatus.innerHTML = "Downloaded " + result.response.length +
                " bytes. <br />";
          }
      )
      .then(
        function () {
          var folder = Windows.Storage.ApplicationData.current.temporaryFolder;
          return folder.createFileAsync("temp.txt",
            Windows.Storage.CreationCollisionOption.replaceExisting);
        }
      )
      .then(
        function (storageFile) {
          divStatus.innerHTML += "Saving the results to " + storageFile.path +
              "<br />";
          return Windows.Storage.FileIO.writeTextAsync(storageFile, content);
        }
      )
      .then(
        function () {
          divStatus.innerHTML += "Done.";
        }
      );
    }
```

5. Start the application by pressing Ctrl+F5 and search for any keyword on Twitter. Note that now the results are not only shown, but also saved to a file whose path is displayed in the green status pane. You can see an example output in Figure 5-25.

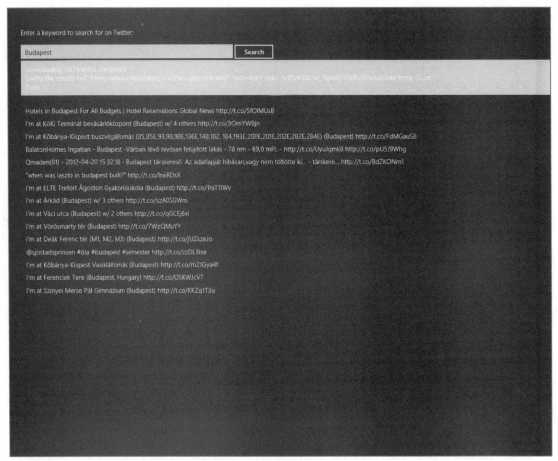

FIGURE 5-25: Saving the results in the Twitter search application

6. Use Windows Explorer to browse to the folder that is displayed in the green status pane and verify the content of the `temp.txt` file.

How It Works

In Step 2, you created a local variable named `content`, and in Step 3 you saved the raw result that was returned from Twitter into this variable. This is the content that is later written into the output file.

In Step 4, you added three new `then` blocks to the end of the asynchronous process chain. Note that although the `then` function can accept up to three parameters, in this simple example, you defined only the first one, which is called when the promise successfully completes. You can omit the error and the progress handler if you don't want to use them.

In the first new `then` block, you used the `createFileAsync` function of Windows Runtime to create a file named `temp.txt` in the temporary files folder of the application. As you might guess from its name, the `createFileAsync` function is an asynchronous function, and like all asynchronous functions, it returns a promise object.

The next `then` block uses this promise object, which will be fulfilled when the file is successfully created. Having the file in place, you used the `writeTextAsync` function to save the content into it. `writeTextAsync` is also an asynchronous function that returns a promise object.

The last `then` block handles the completed event of this promise object and displays a simple message when the whole process successfully completes.

SUMMARY

Windows 8 brings a new generation of applications that are optimized to answer the challenges of today's execution environments. Modern applications are more often executed on touch-driven devices, and used by people who are expecting the best user experience.

The Windows 8 design language is a key pillar to delivering a great user experience on mobile devices, as well as in the desktop world. The new infographic design concept breaks with the traditional iconographic design style, and focuses on the content instead of the chrome around it. By following the Windows 8 design principles you can create user-friendly applications that fit perfectly into Windows 8.

To have the best user experience, you need applications that are fast and fluid. In a time of large data structures and high-latency network communications, you cannot reach this goal with the classic single-threaded programming model. You must use asynchronous programming techniques, and Windows Runtime forces you to do so, by providing only asynchronous APIs for numerous features.

Thankfully, the top two programming languages in Windows 8 (C# and JavaScript) have direct support for asynchronous programming. In C# 5.0, you have two new keywords (`async` and `await`) you can use to create asynchronous methods without using callbacks and breaking the linear flow of control in your source code. In JavaScript, you can use promises to write asynchronous logic that is complex, but easy to read and maintain.

EXERCISES

1. What is the Windows 8 design language?

2. What types of applications are best for flat and for hierarchical navigation patterns?

3. What is the difference between the threaded and the asynchronous execution model?

4. How does C# 5.0 support asynchronous programming?

5. What are JavaScript promises?

> **NOTE** *You can find answers to the exercises in Appendix A.*

▶ **WHAT YOU LEARNED IN THIS CHAPTER**

TOPIC	KEY CONCEPTS
Iconographic design style	The iconographic design style is a design concept that uses metaphors from the physical world, and portrays objects with hyper-realistic graphics in the digital world.
Infographic design style	The infographic design style is a design concept that focuses on the information and the content, instead the frame that contains it.
Flat navigation	Flat navigation is a navigation pattern in which all pages reside at the same hierarchical level.
Hierarchical navigation	Hierarchical navigation is a navigation pattern in which the pages of the application are grouped into multiple sections and levels.
Thread	The thread is the smallest unit of execution that can be scheduled by the operating system.
Asynchronous programming model	In the asynchronous programming model, multiple tasks are executed on the same thread, but long tasks are divided into smaller units to ensure that they don't block the thread for a long time.
Task object	A `Task` is a .NET object that refers to a value that will be delivered at some point in the future.
`async` and `await`	`async` and `await` are two new keywords in C# 5.0 that you can use to create asynchronous methods.
`IAsyncOperation<T>`	The `IAsyncOperation<T>` interface is the future type used in Windows Runtime.
JavaScript promise	A promise is a JavaScript object that follows the Common JS Promises/A proposal, and returns a value at some time in the future.

Creating Windows 8 Style Applications with HTML5, CSS, and JavaScript

WHAT YOU WILL LEARN IN THIS CHAPTER:

➤ Understanding the basics of HyperText Markup Language, cascading style sheets, and JavaScript

➤ Accessing Windows Runtime from HTML5 applications

➤ Creating Windows 8 style applications with JavaScript

WROX.COM CODE DOWNLOADS FOR THIS CHAPTER

You can find the wrox.com code downloads for this chapter on the Download Code tab at www.wrox.com/remtitle.cgi?isbn=012680. The code is in the Chapter06.zip download and individually named, as described in the corresponding exercises.

Earlier in this book, you learned that Windows 8 brings new opportunities to web developers. Traditionally, web developers could use their technologies to create websites that consist of programming logic running on a web server, and a user interface (UI) that can be accessed only via a web browser. Windows 8 changes this landscape by allowing web developers to reuse their existing knowledge to create applications that run on the desktop. Technologies that previously lived only on web servers and inside web browsers are now first-class citizens for creating classic rich client applications.

This chapter provides a brief overview of these technologies. First, you learn about how to create a classic web page and how to design it, and then you learn how to use the same technologies for creating full desktop applications on Windows 8.

> **NOTE** *This chapter contains a short introduction to HTML5, CSS and JavaScript. If you already have experience with these technologies, you can skip the introduction and jump to the, "HTML5 Applications on Windows Runtime," section in this chapter.*

HTML5 AND CSS ON THE WEB

When Tim Berners-Lee invented the World Wide Web, he needed a language to describe content that is richly decorated with images, arbitrarily formatted, and consisted of pages that were connected together. Because there was no such language in 1989, he created the *HyperText Markup Language (HTML)*, which has become the standard for building web pages.

In the past 20 years, HTML has been slowly (but constantly) changing to follow the new requirements of the emerging Internet. Today, most websites are built using HTML4, but since the World Wide Web Consortium (W3C) published the Working Draft of HTML5 in January 2008, more and more browser vendors have started supporting the new features, which opens the road for web creators to utilize the advantages of HTML5.

HTML was originally designed to describe the static content of web pages, and today this is the primary purpose of this language. However, when discussing HTML5, it often encompasses a broader scope. The term HTML5 is commonly used as an umbrella term, which covers more than 100 specifications that are used by next-generation websites. These technologies are developing standards for supporting the new requirements to play multimedia, store data, work with files, access the user's geographic coordinates, make websites functional offline in the browser, and so on.

In this chapter, you first learn about the enhancements of the HTML language itself in version`5. Later in this chapter, you get a sneak peek into the related standards, because many of them are also available for Windows 8 applications.

Getting to Know HTML5 Technologies

In the strictest sense, HTML5 is the next version of the HTML standard that inherits most of its features from HTML4, makes a few of them obsolete, and extends them with new ones. Because the language itself is made up of HTML elements and their attributes, this essentially means that HTML5 adds new elements and attributes to the language.

You can group the new elements and attributes into the following categories:

- ➤ Semantic and structural elements
- ➤ Media elements
- ➤ Form elements and input types
- ➤ Drawing

New Semantic and Structural Elements

Previously, web developers mainly used the `div` container element to wrap simple elements into a bigger section, so they could refer to them as a whole and format them. For example, `div` elements are used to create headers, menus, and footers, too. Today, the markup code of most web pages is built up of numerous meaningless `div` elements embedded into each other, which are difficult to maintain.

HTML5 introduces new structural elements such as `header`, `nav`, `footer`, `figure`, `summary`, `aside`, and so on. These new elements not only help you to understand your markup more easily, but because they provide semantics to the code, they help search engines and screen readers understand the purpose of a particular content section.

New Media Elements

Previously, if a web developer wanted to embed an audio or video file into a web page, he or she was forced to rely on third-party browser plug-ins, because there was no direct support for multimedia in the browser. However, these plug-ins raise numerous questions related to their deployment, stability, and security on the desktop. Additionally, browser plug-ins are not available on most mobile devices, which makes the multimedia content unavailable on these devices.

To solve all these problems, HTML5 introduces new media elements, like `audio`, `video`, `track`, and so on. With these new elements, browsers are able to play multimedia content natively, without requiring the user to install any third-party plug-ins.

New Form Elements and Input Types

Forms are integral parts of the HTML standard because they are used to post data to the server. Although previous HTML versions had strong support for forms, they left tons of repetitive work for the web developers. For example, if you want to let your users enter a number, a date, an e-mail address, or a URL into a form, all you could give him or her was a generic text box, and then it was your task to validate the entered input and check if it was a valid number, date, or e-mail address.

To make your life easier, HTML5 introduces new input types, like color, date, time, e-mail, and so on. All you have to do is set your input to these types, and the browser will render the proper input field (for example, a date picker for dates) and will do the appropriate input validation, too.

Drawing

HTML5 introduces the new `canvas` element, which you can use to draw graphics on-the-fly via scripting. Because the graphics are no longer hard-coded into your web pages, they can adapt themselves to the devices, or the current state of your page, and they can even be interactive. Some browsers even support hardware-accelerated rendering for `canvas`, which makes the web a perfect environment for graphics-intensive applications and games.

As you can see, HTML5 extends the previous version in several areas. The common theme among these areas is that these new features help you to create modern websites with very clean markup, with much less coding, and without browser plug-ins.

First Steps with HTML

Before you create your first web page with HTML5, you must learn the basic syntax of HTML elements. If you understand the syntax, it is much easier to understand how your page works.

An HTML page consists of *HTML elements*. An HTML element usually contains content decorated with some markup. The following is a sample element that renders the text with strong typography:

```
<strong>This will be printed in bold in most browsers.</strong>
```

The first part of the element is the *opening tag* that is followed by the content, and finally the element is finished by the *closing tag*. Very important is the fact that the set of tags are fixed by the HTML standard, so you cannot invent new tags, because the web browsers will not understand them.

The `strong` tag in the previous example instructs the browser to render the content of the element with strong highlight (that means boldfaced letters in most browsers). The tags are separated from the content using angle brackets (<>), and the closing tag is differentiated from the opening tag with a forward slash character (/) after its opening angle bracket.

Some elements do not have content, and you mark them with *self-closing tags*. Self-closing tags are single tags with a forward slash (/) before the closing angle bracket. For example, the following `br` tag instructs the browser to render a line break:

```
<br />
```

Some elements require additional parameters to work properly. For example, the `img` element renders an image, but you must define which image file should be displayed. You can use *HTML attributes* on those elements that expect this kind of additional configuration. Attributes are name-value pairs that you define within the opening tag. The following example shows how you can use the `src` attribute of the `img` tag to display the image file `budapest.png`:

```
<img src="budapest.png" />
```

A single element can have multiple attributes separated by whitespace. For example, the `img` tag can have an `alt` attribute, too, that may contain alternate text that is displayed when the image cannot be rendered for some reason:

```
<img src="budapest.png" alt="A nice photo of Budapest, capital of Hungary." />
```

The next thing you must keep in mind regarding HTML elements is that you cannot overlap them. That means you can embed one element fully into another, but you cannot embed it partly. The following example correctly uses the `em` element to emphasize and the `strong` element to force the content even more. Most browsers render the `em` element with italic-faced and the `strong` element with boldfaced letters. In this example, the word `important` will be bold and italic.

```
<strong>The is <em>important!</em></strong>
```

Note that the full `em` element is within the `strong` element. However, if you re-order the closing tags, you will get incorrect markup, because the outer `strong` element is closed before the inner `em` element, as shown here:

```
<strong>This is <em>important!</strong></em>
```

This is called *overlapping*. You must avoid it (even if many web browsers render it correctly without any errors).

> **NOTE** *If you want to be sure that your markup is correct, use the W3C Markup Validation Service available at* `http://validator.w3.org`*.*

This is the basic syntax of the HTML language, and you use it in the next "Try It Out" exercise to create a web page. After the exercise, you learn how you can add some fancy design to it.

> **NOTE** *You can find the complete code to download for this exercise on this book's companion website at* `www.wrox.com` *in the folder* `HTML\TryItOut` *within the* `Chapter06.zip` *download.*

TRY IT OUT   Creating a Web Page with HTML5

To create an HTML web page, follow these steps:

1. Start Visual Studio 2012 by clicking its icon on the Start screen.

2. Select File ➪ New ➪ Web Site (or press Alt+Shift+N) to display the New Web Site dialog box.

3. Select the Installed ➪ Templates ➪ Visual C# category from the left tree, and then select the ASP.NET Empty Web Site project type in the middle pane.

4. Click OK, and Visual Studio creates an empty project skeleton.

5. Open the Solution Explorer window by selecting the View ➪ Solution Explorer menu item (or by pressing Ctrl+Alt+L). In the Solution Explorer window, right-click the WebSite1 item and select Add ➪ Add New Item. In the Add New Item dialog box, select the HTML Page template and enter **default.html** in the Name text box. Click Add.

6. Visual Studio creates a new HTML file with some default content and opens it in the editor. Find the `<title>` and `</title>` tags and replace them with the following code:

```
<title>My first webpage</title>
```

7. Find the `<body>` and `</body>` tags and add the following code between them:

```
<h1>Hello World!</h1>

This is a link that opens the
<a href="http://wrox.com" target="_blank">Wrox homepage</a>
on a new browser window.

<h2>Text elements</h2>

<p>
  This is a paragraph with a line break and
  <br />
  some <strong>important</strong> information.
```

```html
</p>

<h2>Lists</h2>

<section>
  <h3>Numbered list</h3>
  This is a numbered list of programming languages:
  <ol>
    <li>JavaScript</li>
    <li>C++</li>
    <li>C#</li>
  </ol>
</section>

<section>
  <h3>Bulleted list</h3>
  This is a bulleted list of colors:
  <ul>
    <li>red</li>
    <li>white</li>
    <li>green</li>
  </ul>
</section>

<h2>Form elements</h2>

<form>
  <label for="txtName">Name:</label>
  <input type="text" id="txtName" /> <br />

  <label for="txtEmail">E-mail:</label>
  <input type="email" id="txtEmail" /> <br />

  <label>Gender:</label>
  <label for="radFemale">Female</label>
  <input id="radFemale" name="gender" type="radio" />
  <label for="radMale">Male</label>
  <input id="radMale" name="gender" type="radio" />
  <br />

  <label for="selContinent">Continent:</label>
  <select id="selContinent">
    <option>Asia</option>
    <option>Africa</option>
    <option>North America</option>
    <option>South America</option>
    <option>Antarctica</option>
    <option selected="selected">Europe</option>
    <option>Australia</option>
  </select>
  <br />

  <label for="chkAccept">I accept the terms:</label>
  <input id="chkAccept" type="checkbox" />
```

```
    <br />

    <button>Save</button>
</form>
```

8. Start the application by clicking the Debug ⇨ Start Without Debugging menu item (or by pressing Ctrl+F5). Visual Studio starts the developer web server and opens the page in your default web browser. The results should resemble those shown in Figure 6-1.

FIGURE 6-1: Basic web page without any formatting

How It Works

In this exercise, you created a simple web page that demonstrates the most commonly used HTML elements.

In Step 5, you created a basic HTML page skeleton that contains the elements that appear in most web pages.

The `<!DOCTYPE html>` declaration in the first line tells the browser that it should follow the HTML5 standard when processing this page.

After the `DOCTYPE` comes the root `html` element, which encloses a `head` and a `body` element. The `body` contains the content of the page, and the `head` contains additional information about the page for the browser. In Step 6, you set the title of the page, which is displayed on the browser tab that renders the page.

In Step 7, you added the markup that defines the page content. The first line contains an h1 element that renders the top-level heading on the page. The markup also contains h2 and h3 elements, which are responsible for displaying the second-level and third-level headings, respectively.

After the top heading, there is a sentence that contains an a (anchor) tag that transforms its content into a clickable hyperlink. Note that the sentence is broken into three lines in the source code, separated by line breaks and multiple whitespaces, but it is rendered in a single line by the browser. This is because the formatting of the markup doesn't influence the rendered page. If you want the browser to do something, you must explicitly tell it to do so by using a tag. That's why so many <br /> tags exist in the markup that create line breaks.

After the second-level Text elements heading, there is a <p> tag that defines a paragraph, which provides good practice for wrapping longer content.

The ul and ol elements define an unordered (bulleted) and an ordered (numbered) list, respectively, which contain the list items defined by the li elements. The two lists with the corresponding introduction sentences and headings are wrapped into section elements. The section element is a new HTML5 tag that you can use to divide your page into smaller sections, with or without changing the visual representation of its content.

The form element defines a form that contains input elements. The form itself is not necessarily used for gathering data from the user, but it is a good practice to use it that way. Within the form element, input elements render the text boxes, radio buttons, and the check box based on the value of their type attribute. The select element transforms its option sub-elements into a combo box in the browser.

Note the label tags that contain the text for the input elements. The connections between the labels and the input elements are created using the for and the id attributes. The for attribute of the label refers to the id input element to which the label belongs. If you click the label text in the browser, the focus is set to the corresponding input element.

At the bottom of the form, there is a button that doesn't do much at this point. Later, you write some client-side code to react to user clicks.

In the previous exercise, you created a web page by defining its content using HTML markup. Because you didn't define how the browser should render it, the content is displayed with the default (a bit modest) style. In the next section, you learn how you can customize the visual look and feel of your web pages.

Styling Pages with CSS

Originally, HTML was an independent standard in the sense that you could use it to define the structure of the content, as well as the visual representation of the content. You could use HTML elements like big, center, and color, and attributes like align, height, and width to define how you wanted to render your page in the browser.

You can still use these elements and attributes in today's websites, but they were removed from HTML5, because they have two important drawbacks:

➤ Using these elements and attributes makes your code more complex and difficult to read. Other HTML elements define the structure and semantics of the content, but these presentation elements define the visual representation of the content. Mixing the "what" with the "how" results in unnecessary complexity.

➤ When you use these presentational HTML elements, you tightly couple the content with the design. The content and the definition of how to display it in the browser resides in the same HTML file, and it is very difficult to give a new look to your page independently from the content.

Both of these disadvantages point to a direction of separating the structural and semantic parts of the content from the visual representation of the content. This separation has the following advantages:

➤ Separating the design from the content helps you to create much more maintainable code. One file contains the HTML content, and another file contains the presentation semantics.

➤ You can easily change the content and the visual presentation independently from each other. If you are a web developer or content manager, you must alter only the HTML file. But if you are a web designer, you must change only the design file.

➤ It's much easier to create consistent design, because you can easily attach the design to all your web pages within your website.

For many years, there was a standard to help with this separation, called *cascading style sheets (CSS)*. Thanks to its obvious advantages, CSS was a widely used technology among web creators for many years, and it is the technology you can now use to define the look and feel of your Windows 8 style application.

First Steps with CSS

Before styling your previously created web page with CSS, you must learn how CSS works.

You can describe the look and feel of some content by using *CSS declarations*. CSS declarations are property name-value pairs that define position, size, color, border, font, and so on. In the following example, you can see the `text-align`, `color`, and `margin` properties:

```
text-align: center;
color: red;
margin. 5px 10px;
```

Syntactically, the property name and the value are separated by a colon (`:`), and multiple declarations are separated by a semicolon (`;`).

You can attach the CSS settings directly to the HTML element you want to format by using its `style` attribute. In the following example, you can see a custom-formatted HTML paragraph:

```
<p style="font-style: italic; border: 1px solid blue; margin-left: 30px;
          width: 300px; padding: 10px; text-align: center;">
  Everything is difficult for one, nothing is impossible for many.
     (István Széchenyi)
</p>
```

This paragraph is rendered by the browser in a blue-bordered box with italic and centered text. The box has a slight internal margin (padding), and it is indented by setting a larger left margin, as you can see it in Figure 6-2.

This technique is called *inline style*, and although it works as expected and concentrates all formatting into the single `style` attribute, it does not detach the formatting from the content, because if you want another similarly formatted paragraph, you must repeat all style settings.

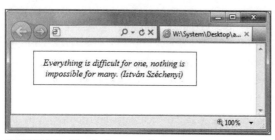

FIGURE 6-2: Simple formatted content

A better approach is to use a *style block*. The style block is an HTML `style` element within the page, which can contain multiple formatting rules, as you can see in the following code snippet:

```
<style type="text/css">
  /* Style rules come here… */
</style>
```

With style blocks, you can concentrate all style definitions you use into a single location within the page. You can easily reuse them within the same page. However, if you want to use the same style on multiple pages, you must repeat the style block on those pages.

To solve this, you can move all style settings into an external file, called the *external style sheet*. The external style sheet is a plain-text file (usually named with a `.css` extension) that you attach to multiple pages using the HTML `link` tag within the `head` section of the page, as shown here:

```
<link href="style.css" rel="stylesheet" type="text/css" />
```

External style sheets are the most commonly used approach, because with them, you can easily reuse your existing formatting definitions on multiple pages in your website, and you can still manage your design in a single central location. If you follow the best practices, you must modify only the CSS file when you redesign your website.

Another benefit of this approach is that the browser must download the CSS file only once, and can store it in the download cache. When the next page refers to the same CSS file, the browser doesn't have to download it, sparing network bandwidth and rendering the page much faster.

However, if you detach the style definition from the content with style blocks or external style sheets, you must specify which part of the page you want to format with it. This is where *CSS selectors* come into the picture. With CSS selectors you can attach a style definition to the following:

➤ All instances of an HTML tag (such as to all `h1` headings)

➤ Multiple HTML elements

➤ A single HTML element

If you want to format all occurrences of an HTML tag, you can select them by the name of the tag. For example, if you want to format all `h2` second-level headings to have underlined text, you can use the following *CSS rule* that consists of a selector and a declaration:

```
h2 { text-decoration: underline; }
```

In this case, the CSS selector is `h2`, and it attaches the CSS declarations in the following `{}` block to all `h2` elements in the page. A single CSS rule can contain multiple CSS selectors, and can contain multiple CSS declarations, too.

If you want to format multiple elements in the page, you can use *CSS class selectors*. Within a style sheet, you can define a new CSS class by giving it a name and typing a period (`.`) before it, as you can see in the following example:

```
<style type="text/css">
  .famous
  {
    font-style: italic;
    font-size: 120%;
  }
</style>
```

Then you can attach your new class to any HTML element using the `class` HTML attribute, as shown here:

```
<p class="famous">Albert Wass</p>
```

Note that the CSS class itself does not define the name of the tag you can format with it. That means you can attach the same CSS class to various HTML elements, as shown here:

```
<span class="famous">László Bíró</span>
```

> **NOTE** *A good practice is to name your classes based on their purpose and not on how they look, because if you redesign your site, they will probably look different, but will serve the same purpose. For example, a class named* highlight *is good, because it clearly tells what it is used for, regardless of how exactly it highlights the content. But a class named* bigredtext *may look strange after you change the look and feel of your site, and you decide to highlight content with blue borders and yellow background, instead of red color and larger letters.*

Now you know how you can style all or some elements in a page. However, if you want to format only a single HTML element, classes are overkill. Thankfully, there is a third type of CSS selector you can use to select a single HTML element — by its HTML `id` attribute. The `id` attribute, as the name suggests, must contain an arbitrary value that uniquely identifies a single element within the page. You can refer to this value by the *CSS id-selector* that starts with a # sign, as you can see in the following example:

```
<style type="text/css">
  #first
  {
    font-weight: bold;
    color: red;
  }
</style>

<p>
  Lake <span id="first">Balaton</span> is the largest lake in Central Europe.
</p>
```

> **NOTE** *What if you want to format a few words, and you won't have an HTML element that contains only those words? In this case, you can use the inline* span *element to wrap your content, as you can see in the following example:*
>
> ```
> <p>
>     Did you know that <span class="important">Harry Houdini</span>
>         was born in Budapest?
> </p>
> ```
>
> *If you want to format a larger part of your page, you can wrap that into an HTML* div *element. Both the* span *and* div *elements can have* style, class, *and* id *attributes that you can use to format the wrapped content.*

Now that you have learned about the three basic types of selectors, you are ready to combine them. For example, you can select only those list items (li elements) that have the important class attached (which is useful if the important selector is also attached to other elements):

```
<style type="text/css">
  .important
  {
    color: red;
  }

  li.important
  {
    font-variant: small-caps;
  }
</style>

<p class="important">
  This paragraph will be rendered with red letters.
</p>

<ul>
  <li>orange</li>
  <li class="important">apple</li>
  <li>grape</li>
</ul>
```

In the preceding example, the paragraph and the second list item will be rendered as red, thanks to the `important` CSS class. Additionally, the second list item will be rendered in small capitals, because of the `li.important` mixed selector.

HTML elements inherit most of their style settings from their parent element, which is very useful because you don't have to define every style setting on every element. If you format a parent element, its style will be propagated to its child element. Because the `body` is the outermost element that wraps all content elements, it is a good practice to define page-level settings on the `body` element, as you can see in the following example:

```
body
{
  font-family: Verdana, Arial, Sans-Serif;
  font-size: 75%;
}
```

This selector sets the font family and font size for all elements on the page, because these CSS attributes are inherited. However, not all CSS properties behave this way, and CSS has a very good reason for that. For example, the `border` property is not inherited, because in most cases, when you add a border to an element, you don't want to add a similar border to all of its child elements.

Now you know that a value of a CSS property can come from various sources:

- ➤ From the default style of the browser
- ➤ From an external style sheet
- ➤ From an in-page style block
- ➤ From an inline `style` attribute
- ➤ From a parent element

Another aspect of CSS that relies on the element hierarchy is hierarchical selectors. With *descendant selectors*, you can select elements that are a descendant of another. In the following code snippet, you can see two CSS rules. The first applies to all links (HTML anchors), but the second applies only to those links that are used within a list item.

```
a { text-decoration: none; }
li a { text-decoration: none; }
```

Of course, you can also use class and ID selectors with hierarchical selectors, too. The following CSS rule applies to all links that have the `error` class within a list item that has the `errors` value in its `id` attribute:

```
li#errors a.error { font-weight: bold; }
```

This section briefly introduced the syntax of CSS. However, it could only present the most frequently used parts of it, which you will probably also use in your Windows 8 application. If you want to learn about pseudo-classes, pseudo-elements, child, adjacent sibling, and attribute selectors, visit the "Understanding CSS Selectors" article in the MSDN Library at `http://msdn.microsoft.com/en-us/library/aa342531.aspx`.

> **NOTE** *If you want to be sure that your style sheet is correct, use the W3C CSS Validation Service available at* `http://jigsaw.w3.org/css-validator/`.

Now you have everything you need to style a full web page. In the next exercise, you format your previously created HTML5 web page with CSS.

> **NOTE** *You can find the complete code to download for this exercise on this book's companion website at* `www.wrox.com` *in the folder* `CSS\TryItOut` *within the* `Chapter06.zip` *download.*

TRY IT OUT Using CSS Features to Add Design and Layout to a Web Page

To learn how you can format the web page you created in the previous exercise with CSS, follow these steps:

1. Start Visual Studio 2012 by clicking its icon on the Start screen.

2. Select File ➪ Open ➪ Web Site (or press Alt+Shift+O) to display the Open Web Site dialog box. Select the folder where you created the website in the previous exercise, and click Open.

3. Open the Solution Explorer window by selecting the View ➪ Solution Explorer menu item (or by pressing Ctrl+Alt+L). In the Solution Explorer window, right-click the `WebSite1` item and select Add ➪ Add New Item. In the Add New Item dialog box, select the Style Sheet template, and enter **default.css** in the Name text box. Click Add.

4. Visual Studio creates a new CSS file with some default content and opens it in the editor. Replace the template-generated content with the following code, and then press Ctrl+S to save your changes:

```
body {
    font-family: "Segoe UI";
    font-size: 11pt;
    font-weight: 300;
    line-height: 1.36;
    margin: 20px;
}

h1, h2, h3 {
    color: #8c2633;
    clear: both;
    font-weight: 200;
}
h1 { font-size: 42pt; margin-top: 0; margin-bottom: 10px; }
h2 { font-size: 20pt; margin-bottom: 5px; }
h3 { font-size: 11pt; margin: 0; }

a { text-decoration: none; }
```

```
a:hover { text-decoration: underline; }

.left-column  { width: 60%; float: left; margin-right: 10%; }
.right-column { width: 30%; float: left; }

form { line-height: 2; }

label {
  display: inline-block;
  width: 120px;
}
label[for^=rad] { width: auto; }

input[type=radio] { margin-right: 20px; }
input[type=checkbox] { padding: 0; }

button {
  background-color: rgba(182, 182, 182, 0.7);
  line-height: 1;
  border-width: 0;
  padding: 6px 8px 6px 8px;
  min-width: 80px;
  margin-left: 124px;
}
```

5. In the Solution Explorer window, double-click the `default.html` file to open it in the editor. Add the following code before the closing `</head>` tag:

```
<link rel="stylesheet" type="text/css" href="default.css" />
```

6. Scroll down and add the `class="left-column"` attribute to the first `section` element, and the `class="right-column"` attribute to the second `section` element. At this point, your `section` elements should look like this:

```
<section class="left-column">
  <h3>Numbered list</h3>
  This is a numbered list of programming languages:
  <ol>
    <li>JavaScript</li>
    <li>C++</li>
    <li>C#</li>
  </ol>
</section>

<section class="right-column">
  <h3>Bulleted list</h3>
  This is a bulleted list of colors:
  <ul>
    <li>red</li>
    <li>white</li>
    <li>green</li>
  </ul>
</section>
```

7. Start the application by clicking the Debug ⇨ Start Without Debugging menu item (or by pressing Ctrl+F5). Visual Studio starts the developer web server and opens the page in your default web browser. The results should resemble those shown in Figure 6-3.

FIGURE 6-3: The formatted web page

How It Works

In this exercise, you formatted the previously created web page with CSS. In Step 4, you created the CSS code in a separate CSS file, and in Step 5 you connected it to the HTML page.

The first CSS rule you added in Step 4 formats the body element. Because the body element contains all content, this rule efficiently defines the font style and the line spacing for all elements on the page.

The second CSS rule defines the text color and the font weight for all h1, h2, and h3 headings on the page. This rule applies to all headings, and it is followed by three separate rules that define the different font sizes and margins for the three heading levels.

After the heading rules are two rules that format the links on the page. The a selector applies to all links and removes the underlines. The a:hover selector applies only to those links that are currently selected by the mouse and displays the underline.

The .left-column and the .right-column selectors place the two section elements next to each other. By default, the section is a block element, which means that it is as wide as the page. By reducing the width and using the float property, you can place it in a single line.

The next form selector applies to the form element, and increases the 1.36 line spacing inherited from the body to 2. This gives a little vertical space between the input elements within the form.

The following CSS rules format the form content. To align all input elements vertically, you must make the labels the same width. However, label is an inline element, which means you can't set its width and height properties, because they work only with block elements. You can combine the inline and the block behavior by setting the display property to inline-block. As you can see, the label selector formats all label elements to 120 pixels wide. However, this would cause problems for the labels of the radio buttons, so the next line fixes it:

```
label[for^=rad] { width: auto; }
```

This is a really tricky selector applying to all input elements that have a for attribute that starts with rad. Within the square brackets ([]), you can define filters for HTML attributes and their values. The next two CSS rules use the same technique to format the radio buttons and the check box on the page.

Finally, the button is formatted on the bottom of the page. Note how you removed its border by setting the border width to zero, and aligned it to the other input controls by setting its left margin.

In the previous exercise, you customized the look and feel of an HTML page. However, the page is still static, which means it doesn't react to user actions. If you want to create an interactive page, you have to learn how you can write code that runs in the browser.

Running Client-Side Code

The HTML and the CSS standards provide you with an elegant and convenient way to create a web page, and define the look and feel of it. However, these standards focus on the static content, and they don't give you any option to create interactive pages. To create web pages that can react to user actions and change dynamically, you need some code that can execute on the client side, within the browser.

Currently, only one language is supported by all major browsers without installing any plug-ins, and allows you to create client-side logic: JavaScript. JavaScript is an interpreted, object-oriented, dynamic scripting language, which means it has types, operators, core objects, and methods. Its syntax comes from the Java language, which itself inherits from the C language, so if you know the C language or C#, many coding structures will be familiar to you.

First Steps with JavaScript

Just like many other languages, the basic building blocks of the JavaScript language are the types. It has five basic types: number, string, boolean, object, and function.

When you declare a variable, you don't have to specify its type. It is automatically inferred by the browser from the value you store in the variable:

```
var a = 9;              // Number
var b = "Hello World!"; // String
var c = true;           // Boolean
```

JavaScript is a *dynamic language*, which means that the types are associated with values, not with variables. As a result, you can change the type of a variable by storing a different type of value in it, which naturally can change how the various operators work on the variable:

```
var d = 9;          // d is of type Number
var e = d + 27;     // e is 36
d = 'September';    // d is of type String now
var f = d + 2;      // f is 'September27'
```

This dynamic nature provides the power of the language. For example, you can create an object and dynamically add properties to it later when you need them, as shown here:

```
var city = { Name: 'Budapest', Population: 2551247 };
city.Founded = 1873;
// Here you can access the values as city.Name, city.Population and city.Founded.
```

Note that you don't have to specify the class you want to instantiate. Instead, you just define the values you want to store in the object. JavaScript is an object-oriented language with objects, but without classes.

Functions are also first-class citizens in JavaScript. They can take zero or more parameters, and can optionally return a value using the `return` statement, as shown here:

```
function add( a, b )
{
  return a+b;
}
```

Function parameters are also weakly typed, which means that it's up to you how you use them. For example, you can call the previous `add` function with number or string parameters, as shown here:

```
add(5, 21);            // returns 26
add('Hello', 'World'); // returns 'HelloWorld'
```

You can even omit any number of parameters from the end of the parameter list, as shown in the following:

```
add(1998);   // This returns "NaN" which means "Not-a-Number",
             // that indicates that the return value is not a legal number.
```

If you don't give a value to a function parameter, or don't assign a value to a variable, it becomes `undefined`:

```
add('May');  // Returns 'Mayundefined'
```

You can check whether a variable has a value by testing it against `undefined`:

```
function add( a, b )
{
  if( b !== undefined )
    return a+b;
  else
    return a;
}
add('May');          // Returns 'May'
add('May', 'a');   // Returns 'Maya'
```

A very unique feature of JavaScript is that functions behave just like any other variables; therefore, you can use them in objects as well. For example, you can create an object that has properties and functions, as shown here:

```
function getPerson( title, firstName, lastName )
{
  return {
    Title: title,
    FirstName: firstName,
    LastName: lastName,
    getDisplayName: function()
    {
      return title + ' ' + firstName + ' ' + lastName;
    }
  };
}
var p = getPerson( 'Dr.', 'James', 'Plaster');  // The parts of the
                                                // name are accessible
                                                // via the p.Title,
                                                // p.FirstName and
                                                // p.LastName properties here.

var name = p.getDisplayName();                  // name is 'Dr. James Plaster'
```

You can also pass functions as parameters, just like any other variables:

```
function getEnglishName( firstName, lastName )
{
  return firstName + ' ' + lastName;
}

function getHungarianName( firstName, lastName )
{
  return lastName + ' ' + firstName;
}

function getPerson( firstName, lastName, nameFunc )
{
  return {
    FirstName: firstName,
    LastName: lastName,
```

```
    getDisplayName: function()
    {
      return nameFunc( firstName, lastName );
    }
  };
}

var en = getPerson( 'ErnÐ', 'Rubik', getEnglishName ).getDisplayName();
var hu = getPerson( 'ErnÐ', 'Rubik', getHungarianName ).getDisplayName();
// en is 'ErnÐ Rubik' and hu is 'Rubik ErnÐ' here
```

You can even use functions as parameters without giving them a name and inline them in the function call, as shown here:

```
var p = getPerson( 'Flórián', 'Albert', function(fn, ln) {
  return fn + ' ' + ln;
} );
var en = p.getDisplayName();     // en is 'Flórián Albert'
```

> **NOTE** *This is just a short introduction into the JavaScript language, focusing on the features that you use later in this chapter when you create Windows 8 style applications in JavaScript. You can read more about JavaScript in the W3Schools JavaScript Tutorial at* http://www.w3schools.com/js.

In the next exercise, you use JavaScript to react to a user action on the web page you created in the previous exercise.

> **NOTE** *You can find the complete code to download for this exercise on this book's companion website at* www.wrox.com *in the folder* JavaScript\TryItOut *within the* Chapter06.zip *download.*

TRY IT OUT   Adding Client-Side Code to a Web Page

To learn how you can use JavaScript to add interactivity to the web page you created in the previous exercise, follow these steps:

1. Start Visual Studio 2012 by clicking its icon on the Start screen.

2. Select File ➪ Open ➪ Web Site (or press Alt+Shift+O) to display the Open Web Site dialog box. Select the folder where you created the website in the previous exercise and click Open.

3. Open the Solution Explorer window by selecting the View ➪ Solution Explorer menu item (or by pressing Ctrl+Alt+L). In the Solution Explorer window, right-click the WebSite1 item and select Add ➪ Add New Item. In the Add New Item dialog box, select the JavaScript File template and enter **default.js** in the Name text box. Click Add.

4. Visual Studio creates a new JavaScript file and opens it in the editor. Add the following code to the default.js file, and then press Ctrl+S to save your changes:

```
function load() {
  var btn = document.getElementsByTagName('button')[0];
  btn.disabled = true;

  btn.addEventListener('click', function (event) {
    var lbl = document.getElementById('lblMessage');
    var txt = document.getElementById('txtName');
    var name = txt.value;

    txt.addEventListener('keypress', function () {
      lbl.innerText = '';
    });

    lbl.innerText = name.length === 0 ?
      'Please enter your name!' :
      'Thank you, ' + name + '!';

    event.preventDefault();
  });

  var chk = document.getElementById('chkAccept');
  chk.addEventListener('click', function (event) {
    btn.disabled = !this.checked;
  });
}
```

5. In the Solution Explorer window, double-click the default.html file to open it in the editor. Add the following code before the closing </head> tag:

```
<script type="text/javascript" src="default.js"></script>
```

At this point, your head element should look like this:

```
<head>
  <title>My first webpage</title>
  <link rel="stylesheet" type="text/css" href="default.css" />
  <script type="text/javascript" src="default.js"></script>
</head>
```

6. Scroll down and add the following attribute to the opening <body> tag:

```
onload="load();"
```

At this point, your <body> tag should look like this:

```
<body onload="load();">
```

7. Scroll down and add the following element between the closing </button> and </form> tags:

```
<span id="lblMessage" />
```

8. In the Solution Explorer window, double-click the `default.css` file to open it in the editor. Add the following code to the end of the file:

```
#lblMessage { color: red; }
```

9. Start the application by clicking the Debug ⇨ Start Without Debugging menu item (or by pressing Ctrl+F5). Visual Studio starts the developer web server and opens the page in your default web browser.

Note that you cannot click the Save button, because it is disabled when the page loads. Check the "I accept the terms" check box and the Save button becomes enabled.

Click the Save button and a "Please enter your name!" error message appears. Enter your name in the Name text box, and note that the error message disappears as soon as you start typing into the text box. Click the Save button again and a "Thank you" message appears next to the button, as shown in Figure 6-4.

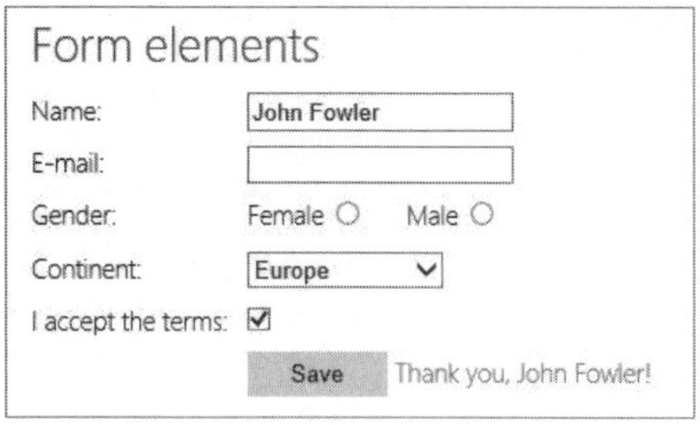

FIGURE 6-4: The interactive form

How It Works

In this exercise, you added JavaScript logic to your web page that runs on the client within the browser.

In Step 4, you created the JavaScript code in a separate JavaScript file, and then you connected it to the HTML page by adding a `script` tag into the `head` in Step 5.

In Step 6, you attached an event handler to the `load` event of the `body` element, which executes the `load` function in the `default.js` file after the `body` element is completely loaded into the browser. The order of the actions is important, because the JavaScript code refers to the page elements. So, first the page must be completely loaded.

In Step 7, you added a new placeholder element to the page that is used by the JavaScript code to display the messages, and then in Step 8 you formatted this element with CSS.

The `load` function you added in Step 4 accesses the HTML elements on the page, and modifies them according to the user actions. The most commonly used technique to reference an HTML element from JavaScript is to use the `document.getElementById` function, which uses the value of the `id` attribute of the element. The `document.getElementsByTagName` function has a similar purpose, but it returns the list of elements with the specified tag name.

When the page loads, the `load` function is immediately executed. It first gets a reference to the Save button by its name, then disables the button. Next, you used the `addEventListener` function to attach an event handler to the click event of the Save button.

The *event handler* is a code block that is executed when the user clicks the button. This code first gets a reference to the label that displays the messages and the Name text box. The following code gets the entered text from the Name text box and stores it in the `name` variable:

```
var name = txt.value;
```

Then, you subscribed a simple handler to the `keypress` event of the Name text box, which is called every time when the user presses a key while typing into the text box. The handler is just a single line that clears the message by setting it to an empty text.

The next three code lines (which is a single expression) display the appropriate message based on the length of the entered name:

```
lbl.innerText = name.length === 0 ?
    'Please enter your name!' :
    'Thank you, ' + name + '!';
```

This is how you can read it. When the name is empty, the message is "Please enter your name!"; otherwise, the name is "Thank you [name comes here]!". Actually, this is the short form of the following code:

```
if(name.length === 0)
{
    lbl.innerText = 'Please enter your name!';
}
else
{
    lbl.innerText = 'Thank you, ' + name + '!';
}
```

The last `event.preventDefault();` code line within the `click` event handler is required to suppress the default action that the browser would perform when the button is clicked. In this case, the browser would post the form to the server, which you want to avoid.

After the button click event handler, the last three code lines attach an event handler of the `click` event of the check box. Within the event handler, the `this` object refers to the HTML element to which the handler is attached, which is the check box in this case, so you can use its `checked` property to query whether the user checked or unchecked it. According to this value, the button is enabled or disabled with a single line of code, which is the short form of the following:

```
if(this.checked === true)
{
    btn.disabled = false;
}
else
{
    btn.disabled = true;
}
```

In this exercise, you learned the basic JavaScript techniques to manipulate objects on the page. In the subsequent parts of this chapter, you learn how you can use this knowledge to create a Windows 8 style application.

> **NOTE** If you would like to learn more about HTML5, CSS and JavaScript, you can find quick tutorials about these technologies at http://www.w3schools.com.

HTML5 APPLICATIONS ON WINDOWS RUNTIME

Earlier in this chapter, you learned the basic technologies that web developers use to create applications that run in the web browser. Traditionally, it was only the web browser that understood HTML, CSS, and JavaScript, and was capable of executing complex application logic built with these technologies. If a developer wanted to utilize web technologies in a desktop application, he or she had to embed the web browser into the application, because desktops were not able to execute web code directly.

However, with Windows 8, Microsoft extended this web platform for client applications, and now you can create a Windows 8 style application that runs fully on the client using HTML, CSS, and JavaScript. The Windows 8 platform contains everything built in that is required to execute web code natively.

In Figure 6-5, you can see how Windows 8 style applications written in JavaScript compare with the traditional desktop applications. On the right, you can see that for desktop applications, the web browser is responsible for hosting and running the JavaScript application code. On the other hand, for Windows 8 style applications, Microsoft provides a JavaScript Engine (codename "Chakra") that hosts and executes the HTML, CSS, and JavaScript code of the application.

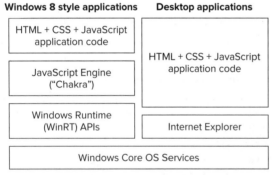

FIGURE 6-5: The difference between Windows 8 style and desktop applications

You can also note another component for Windows 8 style applications called the Windows Library for JavaScript, which you learn about in the next section.

The Windows Library for JavaScript (WinJS)

If you are a web developer, you can love or hate JavaScript. You can love JavaScript because it is a very powerful and flexible programming language. It is fully focused on the web, and you can write quite complex logic with very few lines of code, thanks to its weakly typed nature. However, writing good code or debugging faulty code is another story. JavaScript coding and debugging tools are not as advanced as the C# and Visual Basic tools, because of the characteristics of the language.

JavaScript developers usually solve this problem by using client-side libraries that provide ready-made solutions for the typical programming tasks. With libraries, you can speed up your application development, and give standard solutions for similar problems. Several libraries are available for download, but none of them is optimized for Windows 8. To make a developer's life easier, Microsoft created a new library called the *Windows Library for JavaScript (WinJS)* that contains tons of useful namespaces, classes, and functions that you can rely on when you create your Windows 8 style application in JavaScript.

WinJS provides the following components:

➤ Helper functions to organize your code into namespaces and classes

➤ A `WinJS.Promise` object that encapsulates the functionality of JavaScript promises and is used by all asynchronous functions in WinJS

➤ An application model that manages the life cycle of your application

➤ A navigation framework that you can use to create multi-page user interfaces

➤ Template-based data binding to seamlessly flow data from the storage variables to the UI elements

➤ User interface (UI) controls that wrap and enhance the typical HTML controls

➤ Default CSS styles and animations to build UIs consistent with other Windows 8 style applications and the Windows 8 OS itself

➤ Helper functions that solve typical coding tasks

As you can see from this list, WinJS is a huge and very useful library that provides natural integration of Windows Runtime features into the JavaScript programming language.

CREATING WINDOWS 8 STYLE APPLICATIONS WITH JAVASCRIPT

In the next sections, you learn about the various aspects of creating Windows 8 style applications with JavaScript. First, you learn about the new filesystem application programming interface (API), then about the data binding services of Windows Runtime for JavaScript. After understanding data management, you learn about querying device properties and adding direct touch manipulation to your application. In the final sections of this chapter, you create images and Windows 8 style animations dynamically.

> **NOTE** *Because of the limitations of this book, this chapter cannot show you every detail of creating Windows 8 style applications in JavaScript. Note that JavaScript is a first-class citizen on the Windows 8 platform, and you can access all Windows Runtime features from JavaScript, just like from C# or Visual Basic.*

Accessing the Filesystem

Windows Runtime provides a brand new API for applications that require access to the filesystem to read and write files. Because file operations can be lengthy, methods of the new API are asynchronous, thus forcing developers to avoid blocking the UI thread and creating responsive applications. In JavaScript, you can conveniently manage the asynchronous methods via promises, and chain them using the `then` method.

The `FileIO` class in the `Windows.Storage` namespace provides the following methods for reading and writing files:

➤ appendLinesAsync

➤ appendTextAsync

➤ readBufferAsync

➤ readLinesAsync

➤ readTextAsync

➤ writeBufferAsync

➤ writeBytesAsync

➤ writeLinesAsync

➤ writeTextAsync

These methods can work on an `IStorageFile` instance that provides information about the file and its content, and ways to manipulate them. You typically get an `IStorageFile` object by showing the user the file open or the file save pickers. *File pickers* are very similar to the old file open and file save dialog boxes, but they are completely redesigned for Windows 8 style applications. You can find the `FileOpenPicker` and the `FileSavePicker` classes in the `Windows.Storage.Pickers` namespace.

In the next exercise, you create a simple Notepad-like application, which you can use to open, edit, and save text files.

> **NOTE** *You can find the complete code to download for this exercise on this book's companion website at* www.wrox.com *in the folder* FileSystem\TryItOut *within the* Chapter06.zip *download.*

TRY IT OUT   Accessing the Filesystem from an HTML5 Application

Before starting this exercise, ensure that you have TXT text files (that is, plaintext files) on your desktop. You can use Notepad to create some plaintext files with simple content. In this exercise, you create an application that displays the content of these files.

To learn how you can access the filesystem from an HTML5 application, follow these steps:

1. Start Visual Studio 2012 by clicking its icon on the Start screen.

2. Select File ➪ New Project (or press Ctrl+Shift+N) to display the New Project dialog box.

3. Select the Installed ⇨ Templates ⇨ JavaScript ⇨ Windows Store category from the left tree, and then select the Blank App project type in the middle pane.

4. Click OK. Visual Studio creates an empty project skeleton and opens the main `default.js` file in the code editor.

5. Open the Solution Explorer window by selecting the View ⇨ Solution Explorer menu item (or by pressing Ctrl+Alt+L).

6. In the Solution Explorer window, double-click the `default.html` file to open it in the code editor.

7. Find the content between the `<body>` and the `</body>` tags, and replace it with the following code:

```html
<p>
  <button id="btnOpen">Open...</button>
  <button id="btnSave">Save as...</button>
  Selected file:
  <span id="lblPath">(No file selected, click Open to select a file)</span>
</p>
<textarea id="txtContent" style="width: 100%; height: 100%;"></textarea>
```

8. Click the Save icon on the toolbar (or press Ctrl+S) to save your changes. Close the editor tab of the `default.html` file to return to editing the `default.js` file.

9. Find the `Initialize your application here` comment line within the `app.onactivated` event handler, and add the following code right after it:

```javascript
var btnOpen = document.getElementById('btnOpen');
btnOpen.addEventListener('click', onOpenButtonClicked);

var btnSave = document.getElementById('btnSave');
btnSave.addEventListener('click', onSaveButtonClicked);
```

10. Append the following code to the end of the `default.js` file:

```javascript
function onOpenButtonClicked() {
  var picker = new Windows.Storage.Pickers.FileOpenPicker();
  picker.suggestedStartLocation = Windows.Storage.Pickers.PickerLocationId.desktop;
  picker.fileTypeFilter.replaceAll(['.txt', '.ini', '.log']);

  picker.pickSingleFileAsync().then(function (file) {
    if (file !== null) {
      var lblPath = document.getElementById('lblPath');
      lblPath.innerText = file.path;

      Windows.Storage.FileIO.readTextAsync(file).then(function (content) {
        var txtContent = document.getElementById('txtContent');
        txtContent.value = content;
      });
    }
  });
}

function onSaveButtonClicked() {
  var txtContent = document.getElementById('txtContent');
```

```
var content = txtContent.value;

var picker = new Windows.Storage.Pickers.FileSavePicker();
picker.suggestedStartLocation = Windows.Storage.Pickers.PickerLocationId.desktop;
picker.fileTypeChoices.insert('Plain text', ['.txt']);
picker.pickSaveFileAsync().then(function (file) {
  if (file !== null) {
    Windows.Storage.FileIO.writeTextAsync(file, content).then(function () {
      var dlg = new Windows.UI.Popups.MessageDialog(
        'Your content is successfully saved to ' + file.path, 'Save completed');
      dlg.showAsync();
    });
  }
});
}
```

11. Start the application by clicking the Debug ⇨ Start Debugging menu item (or by pressing F5). The results should resemble those shown in Figure 6-6.

12. Click Open to start the File Open Picker. Select a file, and then click Open in the lower-right corner in the picker dialog box. Your application loads the content into the editable area, as shown in Figure 6-7.

13. Change the text in the editable area, and then click Save as to save your changes into a new file. Enter a name for the file in the bottom of the File Save Picker, and then click Save in the lower-right corner of the picker dialog box.

14. Click Close to dismiss the pop-up message dialog box that notifies you about the result of the save operation, as shown in Figure 6-8.

FIGURE 6-6: The main screen of the text editor application

FIGURE 6-7: The main screen of the text editor application after a file is opened

FIGURE 6-8: The notification dialog box after successful save

How It Works

According to the project template you selected, Visual Studio generated an empty skeleton that contains everything you need to start creating your Windows 8 style application in JavaScript. This project contains two main files:

➤ The `default.html` file contains the HTML markup that defines the UI elements of your application.

➤ The `default.js` file contains the JavaScript logic that defines the behavior of your application.

In Step 7, you created the UI of your application in the `default.html` file. The UI consists of two buttons (Open and Save), a `span` element that displays the path of the selected file, and a `textarea` that provides the text-editing features. Note that all the `buttons`, the `span`, and the `textarea` elements have `id` attributes, which are required in order to reference them later from JavaScript code.

In Step 9, you extended the initialization code of the application. As you learned earlier in this chapter, the `WinJS.UI.processAll` function is responsible for initializing the markup of your Windows 8 style application. Because it returns a promise, you can use the `then` function to run your custom initialization code right after the markup initialization is successfully completed.

Here you initialized the two buttons by attaching an event handler to them. First, you used the `document.getElementById` function to get a reference to the button using the value of its `id` attribute, and then you called the `addEventListener` function to subscribe with a custom function to the `click` event of the button. This ensures that your function is called when the user clicks the button. The same logic is repeated once for the Open button and once for the Save button, with different handler functions.

In Step 10, you added the event handler functions for the Open and the Save buttons.

The `onOpenButtonClicked` function is called when the user clicks the Open button. In this function, you first created an instance of the `FileOpenPicker` class, and configured the folder in which it will open and the type of files it will show. After configuring the picker, you used the `pickSingleFileAsync` function to open the picker dialog box. Note that this is an asynchronous function that returns a promise, so you could use the `then` function to handle its return value. The `pickSingleFileAsync` function returns a `StorageFile` instance, which your code receives directly in the `file` parameter of the `then` function. If the user closes the picker dialog box without opening a file, the `file` parameter contains `null` value.

After the user selects a file, you display the path of the file on the UI. For this, you used the HTML `span` element as a placeholder for the path, and replaced its default using its `innerText` property.

To read the content of the selected file, you used the `readTextAsync` function of the `FileIO` class. Note that this is also an asynchronous function, which returns the string content of the file that is displayed in the `textarea` element on the UI.

The `textarea` element provides built-in features to edit its content, so your logic contains no special code for handling any events during editing.

When the user clicks the Save As button, the `onSaveButtonClicked` function is called. First, you used the `value` property of the `textarea` to retrieve the edited text and stored it in the `content` variable. Then, you instantiated the `FileSavePicker` class, which behaves very similarly to the `FileOpenPicker` class. After you configured its default folder and file type, you used the `pickSaveFileAsync` function to open the picker dialog box. This asynchronous function returns a `StorageFile` instance that can be `null` if the user canceled the save dialog box. Next, you used the `writeTextAsync` function of the `FileIO` class to write the string content to the target file. After the save function was returned asynchronously, you created a new `MessageDialog` instance, and called is `showAsync` method to display the notification dialog box about the successful save.

Managing Data

Data management is a key component of every application. The data is read from a database, from a file, or from a network service, and then it is displayed on the UI. The user searches the data and modifies it, and later the changes are propagated back to the original data source. The data is flowing first from the data source to the UI, and then from the UI to the data source.

Because data management is a typical programming task, modern programming environments have several features to make it easier. Typically, they have data source components that you can use to connect to the database, file, or network service, and UI controls that can display the data and provide input features to the users. The connection between the data source and the UI components is set up via data binding.

Data binding ensures that there is seamless data flow to and from the UI elements. One-way data binding pumps the data from the storage variable to the UI, and ensures that the UI is updated automatically when the underlying data is changed. Two-way data binding extends the functionality of the one-way binding by pumping the data back to the underlying data source after the data is modified on the UI.

Based on the size and structure of the data, two types of binding exist:

➤ *Simple binding* connects a single value to a single property of a single UI element. For example, you can display a name, stored in a string variable, in a text box.

➤ *List binding* connects multiple values to a UI element that can manage lists. For example, you can take a list of country names stored in a string array and display it in a table or a combo box.

In Windows 8, the WinJS supports only one-way binding, which means you can easily pump data from a variable to the UI. To handle data modifications, you must wire up event handlers for change events of the UI elements, and manually write the modified data back to the data source.

You can define your binding in a declarative or programmatic way. With *declarative binding*, you extend the HTML markup with expressions that describe which properties of the data object should be bound to an attribute of the current element. For example, the following `img` element renders an image whose URL is stored in the `avatarUrl` property of the data object:

```
<img data-win-bind="src: avatarUrl" />
```

The WinJS also supports *programmatic binding*. This means that you can use objects and functions in the WinJS.Binding namespace to set up and manipulate data bindings from your JavaScript code. For example, the following code displays an image whose URL is stored in the data.avatarUrl property:

```
var data = WinJS.Binding.as({ avatarUrl: 'myphoto.png' });
data.bind('avatarUrl', function (newValue, oldValue) {
    var target = document.getElementById('picture');
    target.src = newValue;
});
```

In the next exercises, you create an image browser application, and learn how you can declaratively bind data in an HTML5 Windows 8 style application.

TRY IT OUT   **Using Simple Data Binding in an HTML5 Application**

Before starting this exercise, ensure that you have image files in your Pictures Library folder. If you need images, you can find some in the C:\Windows\Web folder. In this exercise, you create an HTML5 Windows 8 style application that displays these image files.

To learn how you can use data binding in an HTML5 application, follow these steps:

1. Start Visual Studio 2012 by clicking its icon on the Start screen.

2. Select File ⇨ New Project (or press Ctrl+Shift+N) to display the New Project dialog box.

3. Select the Installed ⇨ Templates ⇨ JavaScript ⇨ Windows Store category from the left tree, and then select the Blank App project type in the middle pane.

4. Click OK. Visual Studio creates an empty project skeleton and opens the main default.js file in the code editor.

5. Open the Solution Explorer window by selecting the View ⇨ Solution Explorer menu item (or by pressing Ctrl+Alt+L).

6. In the Solution Explorer window, double-click the default.html file to open it in the code editor.

7. Find the template-generated content between the <body> and the </body> tags and replace it with the following code:

```
<h1>
  Your
  <span data-win-bind="innerText: name"></span>
  Library
</h1>
```

8. Click the Save icon on the toolbar (or press Ctrl+S) to save your changes.

9. In the Solution Explorer window, double-click the default.css file within the css folder to open it in the code editor.

10. Add the following code to the end of the file:

```
h1 {
  margin: 20px;
```

```
    }

h1 span {
    font-weight: bold;
}
```

11. Click the Save icon on the toolbar (or press Ctrl+S) to save your changes.

12. In the Solution Explorer window, double-click the `default.js` file within the `js` folder to open it in the code editor.

13. Find the `WinJS.UI.processAll()` function call within the `app.onactivated` event handler and replace it with the following code:

```
args.setPromise(WinJS.UI.processAll().then(function () {
    var lib = Windows.Storage.KnownFolders.picturesLibrary;
    var data = WinJS.Binding.as({ name: lib.name });
    var element = document.getElementById('span');
    WinJS.Binding.processAll(element, data);
}));
```

14. Click the Save icon on the toolbar (or press Ctrl+S) to save your changes.

15. Open the Solution Explorer window by selecting the View ⇨ Solution Explorer menu item (or by pressing Ctrl+Alt+L). In the Solution Explorer window, double-click the `package.appxmanifest` file to open it in the manifest editor.

> **NOTE** The manifest file is an XML file that contains all information that is used during the deployment process. You can read more about the manifest file in Chapter 9.

16. In the manifest editor, go to the Capabilities tab and check the Pictures Library Access option in the Capabilities list.

17. Start the application by clicking the Debug ⇨ Start Debugging menu item, or by pressing F5. The results should resemble those shown in Figure 6-9.

FIGURE 6-9: The main screen of the image browser application

How It Works

According to the project template you selected, Visual Studio generated an empty skeleton that contains everything you need to start creating your Windows 8 style application in JavaScript.

In Step 7, you created the UI of your application in the `default.html` file. The simple UI contains only an `h1` heading element with the words "Your" and "Library," and a `span` element that acts as a placeholder between them. This placeholder will render the name of the library. Note the `data-win-bind` attribute of the `span` element, which defines that the `name` property of the data source object, is bound to the `innerText` property of the `span` element.

In Step 10, you used CSS to slightly modify the look and feel of your application by adding a margin around the heading, and by highlighting the name of the library with boldfaced text.

In Step 13, you extended the initialization code of the application. Because the `WinJS.UI.processAll` function returns a promise, you can use the `then` function to run your custom initialization code right after the markup initialization is successfully completed.

First, you created a reference to the `Pictures Library` folder. It is a well-known folder, and Windows Runtime provides a property to access it conveniently.

Next, you used the `as` function of the `WinJS.Binding` class to store the name of the `Pictures Library` in the local `data` variable in an observable way.

Next, you created a reference to the HTML `span` element that is the root element in the markup hierarchy to where the data should be bound.

Finally, you used the `WinJS.Binding.processAll` function to connect the UI element with the data source, and update all bindings and transfer the values from the data source objects to the UI controls. This causes the name of the `Pictures Library` displayed in the heading.

This application accesses the `Pictures Library`, which is a security-sensitive operation and, by default, not allowed to any application. To solve this, your application must explicitly request permission to access the `Pictures Library`. This is a feature of your application, and you must indicate it to Windows 8 by using the manifest file of your application. This is why you had to check the Pictures Library Access option among the application Capabilities in Step 15. If you run your application in Debug mode without checking this option, you receive the exception shown in Figure 6-10.

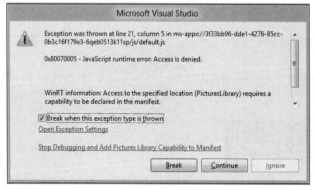

FIGURE 6-10: The Access Denied exception thrown only in Debug mode

In the previous exercise you learned how you can bind a single data value to an attribute of a single HTML element. This is called *simple binding*. In the next exercise you learn how you can bind multiple values to a single UI control using *list binding*.

TRY IT OUT   **Using List Binding in an HTML5 Application**

To learn how you can use list binding in an HTML5 application, follow these steps:

1. Open the application you created in the previous exercise.

2. Open the `default.html` file in the code editor and insert the following code right after the closing `</h1>` tag:

```
<div id="tmpl" data-win-control="WinJS.Binding.Template">
  <div>
    <img src="#" data-win-bind="alt: name; src: url; title: path" />
    <br>
    <span class="name" data-win-bind="innerText: name"></span>
    <br />
    <span class="date" data-win-bind="innerText: date"></span>
  </div>
</div>

<div id="lv"
  data-win-control="WinJS.UI.ListView"
  data-win-options="{itemDataSource : files.dataSource, itemTemplate:
      select('#tmpl')}">
</div>
```

3. Click the Save icon on the toolbar (or press Ctrl+S) to save your changes.

4. In the Solution Explorer window, double-click the `default.css` file within the `css` folder to open it in the code editor.

5. Add the following code to the end of the file:

```
#lv.win-listview
{
  height: 500px;
  width: 500px;
}

#lv .win-container {
  margin: 20px;
  padding:  10px;
}

#lv .win-item {
  width:  205px;
  height: 165px;
}

#lv .win-item img {
  width: 192px;
  height: 120px;
}

.name {
  font-weight: bold;
```

```
    }

    .date {
      font-size: small;
    }
```

6. Click the Save icon on the toolbar (or press Ctrl+S) to save your changes.

7. In the Solution Explorer window, double-click the `default.js` file in the `js` folder to open it in the code editor.

8. Create a global variable by adding the following code to the top of the file:

```
var files = new WinJS.Binding.List;
```

9. Find the `WinJS.Binding.processAll(element, data);` line and add the following code after it:

```
lib.getItemsAsync().then(function (items) {
  items.forEach(function (item) {
    if (item.isOfType(Windows.Storage.StorageItemTypes.file)) {
      files.push({
        url: URL.createObjectURL(item),
        name: item.name,
        path: item.path,
        date: item.dateCreated
      });
    }
  });
});
```

10. Start the application by clicking the Debug ⇨ Start Debugging menu item (or by pressing F5). The results should resemble those shown in Figure 6-11.

Note that if you hover the mouse over an image, a tooltip pops up containing the full path of the image. Additionally, if you have more than four images, you can scroll the list horizontally.

How It Works

In this exercise, you extended your existing code with a `ListView` control that displays the images in your `Pictures Library` using declarative data binding.

In Step 2, you added two `div` elements to the page. The second `div` element is marked with the `data-win-control` attribute, and it is transformed into a `WinJS.UI.ListView` control when the `WinJS.UI.processAll` function

FIGURE 6-11: The image browser application with images

is executed. This `div` element has a `data-win-options` attribute that contains the settings for the `ListView` control:

➤ The `itemDataSource` property defines the object that contains the data to display by the `ListView` control. In this case, it is the `dataSource` property of the `files` object created in a later step.

➤ The `itemTemplate` property points to another HTML element in the page that is used to render a single item in the `ListView`. In this case, it is the `div` element that precedes the `ListView`. Because the template is referenced by the `ListView`, the template must be declared before the `ListView` within the page.

The template `div` is also marked by the `data-win-control` attribute, and it is transformed into a `WinJS.Binding.Template` instance. Within the template, the `data-win-bind` attributes connect the properties of the data source to the properties of the HTML elements.

In Step 5, you added some CSS classes that control the rendering of the `ListView`. The `ListView` uses nine built-in CSS classes, and you can use these classes to customize the rendering of the whole control and the containing items. Here you used the `win-listview`, the `win-container`, and the `win-item` classes to change the default look and feel of the `ListView`.

In Step 8, you created a global variable that is used as the data source for the `ListView`. `ListView` supports any data type that implements the `IListDataSource` interface. The WinJS provides several types of `IListDataSource` objects, and the `WinJS.Binding.List` is one of them.

In Step 9, you populated the data source with the data of the files in your `Pictures Library` folder. With the `getItemsAsync` and the `forEach` functions, you asynchronously enumerated through all items in the library, and added a custom-shaped object about every file to the data source. The data source contains a single object about every file with a `url`, a `name`, a `path`, and a `date` property. You can see in Step 2 that you referenced these properties in the item template of the `ListView`.

You have seen in the previous exercise that data binding provides a convenient way to display data from a variable on the UI. In the next exercise, you see that data binding builds a live connection between the data source and the UI control, and can update the UI automatically when the underlying data changes. To demonstrate this, you extend your image library browser application and provide remove functionality for the image list.

> **NOTE** *You can find the complete code to download for this exercise on this book's companion website at* www.wrox.com *in the folder* Binding\TryItOut *within the* Chapter06.zip *download.*

TRY IT OUT   Updating the Data Source

To learn how you can update the underlying data source using list binding in an HTML5 application, follow these steps:

1. Open the application you created in the previous exercise.

2. In the Solution Explorer window, double-click the `default.js` file in the `js` folder to open it in the code editor.

3. Find the following code block:

```
args.setPromise(WinJS.UI.processAll().then(function () {
  var lib = Windows.Storage.KnownFolders.picturesLibrary;
  var data = WinJS.Binding.as({ name: lib.name });
  var element = document.getElementById('span');
  WinJS.Binding.processAll(element, data);

  lib.getItemsAsync().then(function (items) {
    items.forEach(function (item) {
      if (item.isOfType(Windows.Storage.StorageItemTypes.file)) {
        files.push({
          url: URL.createObjectURL(item),
          name: item.name,
          path: item.path,
          date: item.dateCreated
        });
      }
    });
  });

  // Place code in this exercise here.
}));
```

4. Add the following lines of code into the line that is marked with the "Place code in this exercise here" comment in the previous code snippet:

```
var lv = document.getElementById('lv');
lv.addEventListener('iteminvoked', function (eventObj) {
  eventObj.detail.itemPromise.then(function (listViewItem) {
    var binding = files.dataSource.createListBinding();
    binding.fromIndex(listViewItem.index).then(function (dataItem) {
      files.dataSource.remove(key);
      binding.release();
    });
  });
});
```

At this point, your code should look like this:

```
args.setPromise(WinJS.UI.processAll().then(function () {
  var lib = Windows.Storage.KnownFolders.picturesLibrary;
  var data = WinJS.Binding.as({ name: lib.name });
  var element = document.getElementById('span');
  WinJS.Binding.processAll(element, data);

  lib.getItemsAsync().then(function (items) {
    items.forEach(function (item) {
      if (item.isOfType(Windows.Storage.StorageItemTypes.file)) {
        files.push({
          url: URL.createObjectURL(item),
          name: item.name,
          path: item.path,
          date: item.dateCreated
        });
```

```
      }
    });
  });

  var lv = document.getElementById('lv');
  lv.addEventListener('iteminvoked', function (eventObj) {
    eventObj.detail.itemPromise.then(function (listViewItem) {
      var binding = files.dataSource.createListBinding();
      binding.fromIndex(listViewItem.index).then(function (dataItem) {
        var key = dataItem.key;
        files.dataSource.remove(key);
        binding.release();
      });
    });
  });
}));
```

5. Start the application by clicking the Debug ⇨ Start Debugging menu item (or by pressing F5). Click any of the images. If you did everything right, the clicked image should disappear from the list, and the list should re-order itself. Don't worry; the image files are not deleted from your disk.

How It Works

In this exercise, you extended your existing `ListView` control with a custom event handler that removes an item from the data source of the `ListView`.

The first two lines of the code you added in Step 4 attached a new event handler to the `iteminvoked` event of the `ListView` control. The `iteminvoked` event is raised when the user clicks or taps (on a touch-based device) on one of the items in the list.

In this event handler, you first accessed the clicked item of the `ListView` using the `detail` property of the event handler's `eventObj` parameter. Using the `itemPromise` property of this object, you can handle the clicked item as a promise, and chain a `then` function to it. When the promise is fulfilled, the inline function of the `then` function is called, and the clicked item is passed to it in the `listViewItem` parameter. The `listViewItem` object represents the visible object that is rendered by the `ListView`. Note that this is not the original data item, just a projected version of it that is displayed on the UI.

This is where data binding comes into the picture. Data binding can help you to get back the underlying data item from the list view item. The list view item has an `index` property, and you used the `fromIndex` function, which returns the original data item that is the source of the list view item.

The next step is to request the data source to remove this data item. To manipulate any data item in the data source, you must reference it via its unique identifier, called the *key*. When you add items to the data source, you can create a unique key to every item, or if you don't do that, the data source creates one automatically. You can get the key of the data item via its `key` property. In this code, you used this key to call the `remove` function of the data source to remove the specified item.

In the last line of this code block, you called the `release` function of the binding object, which signals the binding that you are finished with all modifications, and it should notify all subscribed UI controls about the changes. This causes the `ListView` to remove the specified item from the UI, and automatically re-order itself.

In the previous three exercises, you learned how you can use data binding to render and manipulate data on the UI. Data binding is a very powerful tool because it helps you eliminate several lines of code, so you will use it every day when you create data-driven applications.

Respecting the User's Device

Previously, client applications could run only on classic desktop computers and laptops. But Windows 8 brings a new type of device to the picture: the tablet. The tablet differs significantly from the desktops and laptops, because it provides new types of interactions. You can take a tablet with you, hold it in your hand in landscape or portrait mode, and control the applications using touch gestures. Tablets usually have a set of built-in sensors that your applications can access to detect the position of the device, the location of the user, the light level in the environment, and so on.

> **NOTE** *You can read more about sensors in Chapter 12.*

Windows 8 can run on a broad range of devices, and your application must gracefully handle the various characteristics of these devices. Even if your application doesn't rely on the built-in sensors, it must respect at least the different screens of the various devices. Your application must adapt itself to the four characteristics of the screen:

➤ **Size** — This is the physical size of the display of the device.

➤ **Resolution** — This is the number of pixels in the display. The minimum resolution to have all Windows 8 features enabled is at least 1366 × 768 pixels.

➤ **Orientation** — This indicates how the user is holding the device in his or her hand (that is, in landscape or portrait mode).

➤ **Mode** — On Windows 8, the user can run Windows 8 style applications in full-screen mode or in snapped mode. In full-screen mode, the application consumes the whole screen, whereas in snapped mode, the application is docked in a 320 pixels-wide column to the edge of the screen.

Windows Runtime provides APIs to query the device parameters and react to screen changes. To provide the best user experience, your Windows 8 style application must use these APIs to optimize itself to the current display conditions. When the user rotates the device or changes the application from full-screen mode to snapped mode, you can reposition or resize your UI elements.

In the next exercise, you create a picture browser application that adapts itself to the various screen sizes.

> **NOTE** *You can find the complete code to download for this exercise on this book's companion website at* www.wrox.com *in the folder* ViewState\TryItOut *within the* Chapter06.zip *download.*

Creating Flexible Layout

Before starting this exercise, ensure that you have at least ten image files in your `Pictures Library` folder. If you need images, you can find some in the `C:\Windows\Web` folder.

To learn how you can create an application that reacts to screen size changes, follow these steps:

1. Start Visual Studio 2012 by clicking its icon on the Start screen.

2. Select File ➪ New Project (or press Ctrl+Shift+N) to display the New Project dialog box.

3. Select the Installed ➪ Templates ➪ JavaScript ➪ Windows Store category from the left tree, and then select the Blank App project type in the middle pane.

4. Click OK. Visual Studio creates an empty project skeleton and opens the main `default.js` file in the code editor.

5. Open the Solution Explorer window by selecting the View ➪ Solution Explorer menu item (or by pressing Ctrl+Alt+L).

6. In the Solution Explorer window, double-click the `default.html` file to open it in the code editor.

7. Find the template-generated `<p>Content goes here</p>` content between the `<body>` and the `</body>` tags and replace it with the following code:

```html
<div id="tmpl" data-win-control="WinJS.Binding.Template">
  <section>
    <img src="#" data-win-bind="src: url" />
    <div>
      <span class="name" data-win-bind="innerText: name"></span>
      <br />
      <span class="date" data-win-bind="innerText: date"></span>
    </div>
  </section>
</div>

<div id="host">
  <div id="lv" data-win-control="WinJS.UI.ListView"
              data-win-options="{ itemDataSource: data.items.dataSource,
                                  itemTemplate: select('#tmpl'),
                                  layout: {type: WinJS.UI.GridLayout} }" />
</div>
```

8. Add the following code right before the closing `</head>` tag:

```html
<script src="/js/data.js"></script>
```

9. Click the Save icon on the toolbar (or press Ctrl+S) to save your changes.

10. In the Solution Explorer window, double-click the `default.css` file within the `css` folder to open it in the code editor.

11. Add the following code to the end of the file:

```css
#host {
  height: 100%;
  width: 100%;
```

```css
}

#lv {
  height: 100%;
  width: 100%;
}

  #lv .win-item {
    width: 410px;
    height: 350px;
    padding: 10px;
  }

    #lv .win-item img {
      width: 400px;
      height: 300px;
    }

.name {
  font-weight: bold;
}

.date {
  font-size: small;
}
```

12. Click the Save icon on the toolbar (or press Ctrl+S) to save your changes.

13. In the Solution Explorer, right-click the js folder and select Add ⇨ New item. In the Add New Item dialog box, select JavaScript File and enter **data.js** into the Name text box. Click OK.

14. Add the following code into the data.js file:

```javascript
(function () {
  "use strict";

  var images = new WinJS.Binding.List;
  var lib = Windows.Storage.KnownFolders.picturesLibrary;

  lib.getItemsAsync().then(function (items) {
    items.forEach(function (item) {
      if (item.isOfType(Windows.Storage.StorageItemTypes.file)) {
        images.push({
          url: URL.createObjectURL(item),
          name: item.name,
          date: item.dateCreated
        });
      }
    });
  });

  WinJS.Namespace.define("data", {
```

```
    items: images
  });
})();
```

15. Click the Save icon on the toolbar (or press Ctrl+S) to save your changes.

16. Open the Solution Explorer window by selecting the View ➪ Solution Explorer menu item (or by pressing Ctrl+Alt+L). In the Solution Explorer window, double-click the `package.appxmanifest` file to open it in the manifest editor.

17. In the manifest editor, go to the Capabilities tab and check the Pictures Library Access option in the Capabilities list.

FIGURE 6-12: Starting the application in the Simulator

18. Start the application by selecting the Simulator on the toolbar, as shown in Figure 6-12.

You can see the running application in Figure 6-13.

FIGURE 6 13: The image browser application in the Simulator

Note that you can scroll the application horizontally to see all images.

19. Use the rotate icon on the right (shown in Figure 6-14) to rotate the Simulator from landscape mode to portrait mode.

FIGURE 6-14: The rotate icons of the Simulator

You can see the application in portrait mode in Figure 6-15. Note that although the images are automatically rotated, the layout is less than optimal, because the application doesn't use the full device screen.

Rotate the application back to landscape mode using the buttons on the right of the Simulator.

20. Drag the top edge of the application and move it to the left of the screen (within the Simulator) to switch it to snapped mode, as shown in Figure 6-16.

FIGURE 6-15: The application in portrait mode

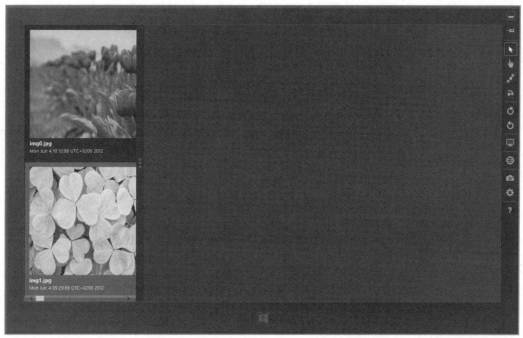

FIGURE 6-16: The application in snapped mode

If the application doesn't switch to snapped mode, it is probably because the Simulator runs with too low of a resolution. Windows 8 requires at least 1366 × 768 resolution to support snapped mode. You can use the Change Resolution button on the right of the Simulator to simulate this screen size, as shown in Figure 6-17.

Note that although the size of the application automatically adapted to the snapped mode, the images are too large and scrolling the list horizontally is not convenient.

FIGURE 6-17: The Change Resolution feature in the Simulator

In the next steps you optimize the application to automatically adapt to the portrait and snapped modes.

21. Open the `default.css` file from the Solution Explorer. Add the following code to the end of the file:

```
@media screen and (-ms-view-state: snapped) {
  #lv .win-item {
    width: 100%;
    height: 210px;
    padding: 5px;
  }

    #lv .win-item img {
      width: 280px;
```

```
        height: 210px;
      }

      #lv .win-item div {
        display: none;
      }
    }

@media screen and (-ms-view-state: fullscreen-portrait) {
  #lv .win-item {
    width: 100%;
    height: 310px;
  }

      #lv .win-item div {
        display: inline-block;
        margin-left: 10px;
        height: 300px;
        vertical-align: bottom;
        font-size: 20pt;
      }

    .date {
      font-size: 14pt;
    }
  }
```

22. Open the `default.js` file from the Solution Explorer. Find the code line that starts with `var activation` and add the following code after it:

```
var appView = Windows.UI.ViewManagement.ApplicationView;
var appViewState = Windows.UI.ViewManagement.ApplicationViewState;
```

23. Find the code line `args.setPromise(WinJS.UI.processAll());` and replace it with the following code:

```
args.setPromise(WinJS.UI.processAll().then(function () {
  window.addEventListener('resize', onResize);
}));
```

24. Find the code line `app.start();` and add the following two functions after it:

```
function onResize(eventArgs) {
  refresh(appView.value);
}

function refresh(newViewState) {
  var newLayout;

  switch (newViewState) {
    case appViewState.snapped:
      newLayout = new WinJS.UI.ListLayout();
      break;
```

```
      case appViewState.filled:
        newLayout = new WinJS.UI.GridLayout();
        break;
      case appViewState.fullScreenLandscape:
        newLayout = new WinJS.UI.GridLayout();
        break;
      case appViewState.fullScreenPortrait:
        newLayout = new WinJS.UI.ListLayout();
        break;
    }

    var lv = document.getElementById('lv').winControl;
    WinJS.UI.setOptions(lv, {
      layout: newLayout
    });
}
```

25. Run and test the application in landscape, portrait, and snapped modes in the Simulator. Note that the application now fully adapts its layout to the available screen size, and changes the scroll direction according to the view mode, as shown in Figures 6-18 and 6-19.

FIGURE 6-18: The optimized layout in portrait mode

FIGURE 6-19: The optimized layout in snapped mode

How It Works

In this exercise, you created an image browser application that is very similar to the one you created in previous exercises. However, this version respects the user's device.

In Step 7, you created the UI of the application. This application uses a `WinJS.UI.ListView` control to display the images from your `Pictures Library` folder. Note the configuration parameters of the `ListView` control set in the `data-win-options` attribute:

➤ The `itemDataSource` property configures the data object that will be bound to the `ListView` control. You created the `data.items.dataSource` object in Step 14 in the `data.js file` you connected to this page in Step 8.

➤ The `itemTemplate` property points to the `div` element above the `ListView` that is used to define the layout and the content of every single item in the list.

➤ The `layout` property is very important here, because it defines the layout of the whole list. The default that you set here is the `WinJS.UI.GridLayout` object that provides horizontal scrolling, and renders the items in multiple rows and columns. This is the default rendering that is used in landscape mode.

In Step 11, you used CSS to define the look and feel of your application. Note that you referred to the `ListView` control by its `id` attribute (`#lv`), and formatted the list items with the built-in `.win-item` CSS class of the `ListView` control.

In Steps 13 and 14, you created the data source object of the `ListView`. The code is very similar to the code you have seen earlier in this chapter, but this time the code is completely isolated from other parts of the application. The self-executing function (note the `()` at the bottom) provides code encapsulation, and the `define` function in the last code line ensures that only the necessary data is published from this scope.

In Steps 18–20, you tested the default behavior of the application. Windows 8 automatically re-renders your application when the view state of the application changes. However, it doesn't know how to use the screen effectively. That is completely up to your application.

In Step 21, you added two sets of CSS rules that are wrapped into `@media` blocks. These `@media` blocks are *media queries* that rely on the `-ms-view-state` property to apply the CSS rules only when the application is in snapped and portrait modes. The CSS rules defined in these media queries are added to the rules that are defined previously without any media query block. For snapped mode, the `div` element (which renders the texts) is hidden, and the images are scaled to 280×210 pixels to fit into the 320-pixel width of the snapped mode. For portrait mode, the texts are rendered not below, but on the right of the image with larger font.

Media queries are very powerful when you change the look and feel of your application, but you cannot use them to change its behavior. In this example, you had to add some code to change the scrolling direction of the `ListView` according to the view state.

In Step 24, you added a `refresh` function that changes the layout of the `ListView` from `GridLayout` to `ListLayout`, because `GridLayout` provides horizontal scrolling, and `ListLayout` provides vertical scrolling that is much better for snapped and portrait modes.

In Step 23, you ensured that the list layout is refreshed when the user changes the screen size of the application. For this, you subscribed the `onResize` event handler to the `resize` event.

As you saw in the previous exercise, creating flexible UIs is very easy with HTML5 and CSS3 in Windows 8. Media queries provide a convenient way to change the look and feel of your application using only CSS, and Windows 8 provides events and APIs to fine-tune your application in JavaScript code.

Scrolling and Zooming

Touch gestures are the primary way of interacting with Windows 8 style applications on modern, touch-based devices. Direct manipulation is a natural way of controlling applications, but only if the gestures are used consistently in the operating system and all applications. Microsoft did profound research to develop the Windows 8 touch-interaction scheme, and integrated the best implementation of touch handling deep into the operating system. To ensure that gestures are handled consistently and optimally in every application, the controls in the WinJS have built-in support for touch interactions.

Because a lot of content cannot fit on small screens, the two basic interactions are scrolling and zooming. You can scroll content using a slide and zoom with a pinch gesture. Users quickly become familiar with the scroll and zoom gestures, because they can navigate within the Windows 8 Start screen and other Windows 8 style interfaces with them as well.

In the next exercise, you create an image browser application in that you can zoom, pan, and scroll using touch gestures.

> **NOTE** *You can find the complete code to download for this exercise on this book's companion website at* `www.wrox.com` *in the folder* `Zoom\TryItOut` *within the* `Chapter06.zip` *download.*

TRY IT OUT   **Implementing Zooming and Panning**

To learn how you can create an application in which you can zoom and pan using touch gestures, follow these steps:

1.   Start Visual Studio 2012 by clicking its icon on the Start screen.

2.   Select File ⇨ New Project (or press Ctrl+Shift+N) to display the New Project dialog box.

3.   Select the Installed ⇨ Templates ⇨ JavaScript ⇨ Windows Store category from the left tree, and then select the Blank App project type in the middle pane.

4.   Click OK. Visual Studio creates an empty project skeleton and opens the main `default.js` file in the code editor.

5.   Open the `C:\Windows\Web\Wallpaper\Nature` folder in Windows Explorer and copy the `img1.jpg`, `img2.jpg`, `img3.jpg`, and `img4.jpg` files to the clipboard.

6.   Switch back to Visual Studio and open the Solution Explorer window by selecting the View ⇨ Solution Explorer menu item (or by pressing Ctrl+Alt+L). Right-click the `images` folder and click Paste.

7.   In the Solution Explorer window, double-click the `default.html` file to open it in the code editor.

8.   Find the template-generated `<p>Content goes here</p>` content between the `<body>` and the `</body>` tags and replace it with the following code:

```
<div class="step">
  <img src="images/img1.jpg" />
</div>
```

9.   Double-click the `default.css` file within the `css` folder in the Solution Explorer window to open it in the editor. Add the following code to the end of the file:

```
.step {
  overflow: auto;
  -ms-content-zooming: zoom;
  -ms-content-zoom-limit-min: 10%;
  -ms-content-zoom-limit-max: 500%;
  width: 100%;
  height: 100%;
}

  .step img {
    width: 100%;
    height: 100%;
  }
```

10. Start the application by selecting the Simulator on the toolbar, as shown in Figure 6-20.

If you have a device that supports touch gestures, you can also run the application without the Simulator. But if your computer supports only mouse and keyboard, the Simulator can help you to test your application and simulate various touch gestures.

11. On the right of the Simulator, you can see buttons that you can use to simulate touch gestures. If you hover your mouse over them, a tooltip pops up, as shown in Figure 6-21.

FIGURE 6-20: Starting the application in the Simulator

FIGURE 6-21: The touch buttons of the Simulator

12. Click the Touch emulation pinch/zoom button of the Simulator and hover your mouse over the image displayed by your application. Hold down the left mouse button and rotate the mouse wheel forward (away from you) to zoom in or backward (toward you) to zoom out.

13. Click the Basic touch mode button of the Simulator (the second button from the top), and hover your mouse over your application. Move the mouse while holding down the left button to pan the enlarged image.

How It Works

In this exercise, you created a simple image viewer application that lets you zoom and pan using touch gestures.

In Step 8, you created the simple UI of the application. Note that the image is displayed with a classic img tag that is wrapped into a div element. The div element has a CSS class named step that you defined in Step 9.

You implemented the zooming and panning feature using only CSS in Step 9 for the step class. Only the -ms-content-zooming: zoom and the overflow: auto CSS declarations are required to enable zooming. With the -ms-content-zoom-limit-min and the -ms-content-zoom-limit-max properties, you defined the minimum and the maximum zoom level. The former one is required if you want to enable zooming out, because the default minimum zoom level is 100 percent.

As you saw in the previous exercise, implementing zooming and panning is very easy using nothing more than CSS. In the next exercise, you extend the previous application with scrolling.

> **NOTE** You can find the complete code to download for this exercise on this book's companion website at www.wrox.com in the folder ZoomAndScroll\ TryItOut within the Chapter06.zip download.

TRY IT OUT   Implementing Scrolling

To learn how you can create an application in which you can scroll using touch gestures, follow these steps:

1. Start Visual Studio and open the application you created in the previous exercise.

2. Open the Solution Explorer window by selecting the View ➪ Solution Explorer menu item (or by pressing Ctrl+Alt+L).

3. In the Solution Explorer window, double-click the `default.html` file to open it in the code editor.

4. Find the `<body>` element and replace its content (what you added in the previous exercise) with the following:

```
<div id="scroller">
  <div class="step">
    <img src="images/img1.jpg" />
  </div>
  <div class="step">
    <img src="images/img2.jpg" />
  </div>
  <div class="step">
    <img src="images/img3.jpg" />
  </div>
  <div class="step">
    <img src="images/img4.jpg" />
  </div>
</div>
```

5. Double-click the `default.css` file within the `css` folder in the Solution Explorer window to open it in the editor. Add the following code to the end of the file:

```
#scroller {
  overflow: auto;
  display: -ms-flexbox;
  width: 100%;
  height: 100%;
}
```

6. Start the application by selecting the Simulator on the toolbar. Click the Basic touch mode emulation icon on the right of the Simulator to enable touch gestures. Hover your mouse over the image, then hold down the left mouse button and move the image to left. Note that the image scrolls and the next image appears on the right.

7. Switch back to Visual Studio and add the following two code lines to the `#scroller` CSS rule:

```
-ms-scroll-snap-type: mandatory;
-ms-scroll-snap-points-x: snapInterval( 0%, 100% );
```

At this point your code should look like this:

```
#scroller {
  overflow: auto;
  display: -ms-box;
  width: 100%;
```

```
    height: 100%;
    -ms-scroll-snap-type: mandatory;
    -ms-scroll-snap-points-x: snapInterval( 0%, 100% );
}
```

8. Start the application in the Simulator and scroll the images using touch gestures. Note that now you always see a full image, because the scrolling is snapped to image boundaries.

You can test that the zooming and panning feature you created in the previous exercise also works.

How It Works

In this exercise, you extended the previous image viewer application with scrolling features, so your users now can use natural touch gestures to switch between the images.

In Step 4, you changed the UI of the application to display not only a single image, but four images. The images are independently wrapped into `div` separate elements with the `step` CSS class attached, which provides the zooming features as you learned in the previous exercise. All four images are wrapped into an outer `div` named the `scroller` that provides the scrolling functionality.

In Step 5, you configured the `scroller div` in CSS. To implement scrolling, you added the `overflow: auto` and the `display: -ms-box` CSS rules. With these two rules, the `div` automatically becomes scrollable using touch gestures.

In Step 7, you configured the snapping behavior of the scrolling. By setting the `-ms-scroll-snap-type` property to `mandatory`, you defined that the scrolling is always adjusted so that it will land on a snap-point. The snap-point that is selected is the one that is closest to where the scroll position would normally stop.

In the `-ms-scroll-snap-points-x` property, you defined where snap-points will be located along the x-axis. The `0%` means the left edge and the `100%` means the right edge of the image. The `snapInterval` defines that the specified distance should be repeated along the x-axis.

Canvas Graphics in Windows 8 Style Applications

Many applications require a drawing surface, where users can paint custom shapes, render text, and manipulate images on the fly. This challenge has been solved for a long time on the desktop, but in the browser, programmatic drawing was a painful issue before HTML5.

HTML5 introduces the `<canvas>` element, which provides a rectangular area where you can draw anything you want using the canvas drawing API. With the `canvas` element, you can do the following:

➤ Draw shapes

➤ Fill them with colors

➤ Create gradients and patterns

➤ Render texts and images

➤ Manipulate pixels

In short, you can use `canvas` to dynamically create raster images in JavaScript.

It's important to note that the `canvas` element behaves like a real canvas: it remembers only the last painted image. `canvas` doesn't support layers, objects, or event handlers, so you cannot manipulate the previously created graphics. If you want to modify the image, you must redraw the canvas.

The disadvantage of this low-level API is that you cannot easily add interactivity to your drawings. On the other hand, this direct image drawing is really fast in modern web browsers. The latest browsers also support hardware-accelerated rendering that further speeds up the canvas operations, and makes the `canvas` element a perfect host even for graphics-intensive applications and games.

In Windows 8, you can use the canvas API in your Windows 8 style applications. In the next exercise, you learn the basics of the canvas API by drawing a smiling face in JavaScript.

> **NOTE** *You can find the complete code to download for this exercise on this book's companion website at* `www.wrox.com` *in the folder* `Canvas\TryItOut` *within the* `Chapter06.zip` *download.*

TRY IT OUT   Drawing on the Windows 8 Canvas

To learn how you can draw on the canvas in a Windows 8 style application, follow these steps:

1. Start Visual Studio 2012 by clicking its icon on the Start screen.

2. Select File ⇨ New Project (or press Ctrl+Shift+N) to display the New Project dialog box.

3. Select the Installed ⇨ Templates ⇨ JavaScript ⇨ Windows Store category from the left tree, and then select the Blank App project type in the middle pane.

4. Click OK. Visual Studio creates an empty project skeleton and opens the main `default.js` file in the code editor.

5. Open the Solution Explorer window by selecting the View ⇨ Solution Explorer menu item (or by pressing Ctrl+Alt+L). Double-click the `default.html` file to open it in the code editor.

6. Find the template-generated `<p>Content goes here</p>` content between the `<body>` and the `</body>` tags and replace it with the following code:

```
<canvas id="canvas" width="400" height="400"></canvas>
```

7. In the Solution Explorer window, double-click the `default.css` file within the `css` folder to open it in the editor.

8. Add the following code to the end of the `default.css` file:

```
canvas {
   background-color: White;
   border: 3px solid orange;
   margin: 15px;
}
```

9. In the Solution Explorer window, double-click the `default.js` file within the `js` folder to open it in the editor.

10. Find the line that contains `args.setPromise(WinJS.UI.processAll());` and add the following code lines after it:

```
var canvas = document.getElementById('canvas');
var ctx = canvas.getContext('2d');

var line = '#000';
var head = '#ffff00';
var eye = '#fff';
var pupil = 'green';
var mouth = '#FF0000';
var nose = 'BLACK';

ctx.save();

ctx.shadowColor = "#999";
ctx.shadowBlur = 20;
ctx.shadowOffsetX = 5;
ctx.shadowOffsetY = 5;

ctx.fillStyle = head;
ctx.beginPath();
ctx.arc(200, 200, 100, 0, Math.PI * 2, false);
ctx.fill();

ctx.restore();

ctx.strokeStyle = line;
ctx.lineWidth = "2";
ctx.stroke();

ctx.strokeStyle = mouth;
ctx.beginPath();
ctx.moveTo(135, 225);
ctx.quadraticCurveTo(200, 285, 265, 225);
ctx.stroke();

ctx.moveTo(135, 225);
ctx.quadraticCurveTo(200, 310, 265, 225);
ctx.stroke();

ctx.strokeStyle = line;
ctx.fillStyle = eye;
ctx.lineWidth = '1';

ctx.beginPath();
ctx.arc(160, 160, 15, 0, Math.PI * 2, false);
ctx.stroke();
ctx.fill();

ctx.beginPath();
ctx.arc(240, 160, 15, 0, Math.PI * 2, false);
ctx.stroke();
ctx.fill();

ctx.fillStyle = pupil;
ctx.beginPath();
```

```
ctx.arc(162, 162, 6, 0, Math.PI * 2, false);
ctx.fill();

ctx.beginPath();
ctx.arc(238, 162, 6, 0, Math.PI * 2, false);
ctx.fill();

ctx.save();

ctx.fillStyle = nose;
ctx.translate(200, 190);
ctx.rotate(45 * Math.PI / 180);

ctx.beginPath();
ctx.fillRect(0, 0, 16, 16);
ctx.fill();

ctx.restore();

ctx.font = '48px Calibri';
var text = 'Smile!';
var textSize = ctx.measureText(text);
var textx = 200 - textSize.width / 2;
ctx.strokeText(text, textx, 360);
ctx.fillText(text, textx, 360);
```

11. Start the application by clicking the Debug ➪ Start Debugging menu item (or by pressing F5). The results should resemble those shown in Figure 6-22.

How It Works

In this exercise, you created a simple Windows 8 style application that draws a smiling face on the canvas.

In Step 6, you added the `canvas` element to your HTML markup that hosts the drawing. Note that you explicitly specified the width and the height of the `canvas` element in the markup, which is very unusual, because, as you learned earlier, CSS is a much better place for these types of layout settings.

However, `canvas` is not an ordinary element! The `width` and the `height` attributes control the size of the coordinate space. If these attributes are missing, the coordinate space of the canvas defaults to 300 pixels width and 150 pixels height. Then, when you specify the width and the height for the canvas in CSS, the 300 × 150 pixels coordinate space is stretched to the specified size, which usually results a distorted drawing. To ensure that the drawing is not stretched, you should define the width and the height in the HTML. In this case, the canvas is 400 pixels wide and 400 pixels high.

In Step 8, you added the CSS settings for the `canvas` element. As you can see, you can control the borders, the background color, and the layout of the canvas, just like any other HTML element.

FIGURE 6-22: The drawing on the canvas

In Step 10, you added the code that renders the drawing. With the first two lines of code, you created the context object that exposes the API you can use to draw on the canvas.

Next, in the six code lines that begin with `var`, you defined the colors that you used later for styling fills and strokes. Note that you can define the colors in several ways, using their names, their RGB codes, uppercase, lowercase, and so on.

Next, with the first `ctx.save()` function, you saved the current drawing context. It is required, because the next lines that start with `ctx.shadow` change the shadow settings. Because these settings are global, all drawing elements inherit them later. The first object that is drawn is the yellow circle using the `arc` and the `fill` functions. Because shadow is only required for this object, the original context is restored with the `ctx.restore` function right after the circle is drawn.

The next three lines of code draw a 2-pixel black line around the previously drawn circle:

```
ctx.strokeStyle = line;
ctx.lineWidth = "2";
ctx.stroke();
```

In the next step, you drew the mouth with two lines. The first `quadraticCurveTo` function drew the upper lip, and the second drew the lower lip.

After the mouth, you drew the eyes with four circles. First, the style of the eyes is set to white fill color and thin black stroke with the following lines:

```
ctx.strokeStyle = line;
ctx.fillStyle = eye;
ctx.lineWidth = '1';
```

Next, you drew the left eye and the right eye, and then the left pupil and the right pupil.

After the eyes, you drew the nose. The nose is a bit tricky, because it is a rotated rectangle. With the `translate` function, you moved the canvas origin from the upper-left corner to the center of the location of the nose, and then rotated the coordinate space by 45 degrees with the `rotate` function. At this point, the coordinate space is positioned as shown in Figure 6-23.

Because you wanted to apply this transformation only to the nose rectangle, the context is saved before drawing the nose, and then restored.

With the last six lines of code, you displayed the "Smile!" text under the face. `measureText` is a very useful function, because you can use it to calculate the required width for any text using the font size and font face currently set in the context. In this example, you used it to correctly position the text in the horizontal center of the drawing. Finally, with the `strokeText` and the `fillText` functions, you rendered the outlined text.

FIGURE 6-23: The translated and rotated coordinate space

Using the Windows 8 Animation Library

Animations play an important role on the Windows 8 platform, because they bring Windows 8 style applications to life. Good animations are not just beautiful, but they also enhance the user experience by giving users the confidence of knowing what has happened, or what will happen. Animations are an integral part of the Windows 8 design language.

However, creating good animations is difficult. Although animations can add beauty and unique personality to your application, they must be consistent throughout the whole platform to be purposeful and not distracting. Additionally, in the world of battery-powered devices, animations must be optimized and fully respect the user's device.

To answer these challenges, Microsoft provides the Windows 8 Animation Library, which helps you to easily add optimized and consistent animations to your Windows 8 style application. The Windows 8 Animation Library covers the following scenarios:

➤   Application navigation

➤   Animating content

➤   Revealing or hiding UI elements

➤   Animating collection changes

➤   Animating selections

Just like many other functions within the WinJS, animations are also using promises. To provide a fast and fluid user experience, animations are played on a separate thread and not blocking the UI. The functions are all asynchronous, and return promise objects that you can use to chain animations. Internally, the animations are built on standards-based CSS3 animations and transitions, and optimally utilize the hardware capabilities of the device.

In the next exercise, you create a Windows 8 style application and enhance the user experience by adding the most common animations.

> **NOTE** *You can find the complete code to download for this exercise on this book's companion website at* `www.wrox.com` *in the folder* `Animation\TryItOut` *within the* `Chapter06.zip` *download.*

TRY IT OUT   Using the Windows 8 Animation Library

To learn how you can use the Windows 8 Animation Library in a Windows 8 style application, follow these steps:

1. Start Visual Studio 2012 by clicking its icon on the Start screen.

2. Select File ➪ New Project (or press Ctrl+Shift+N) to display the New Project dialog box.

3. Select the Installed ⇨ Templates ⇨ JavaScript ⇨ Windows Store category from the left tree, and then select the Blank App project type in the middle pane.

4. Click OK. Visual Studio creates an empty project skeleton and opens the main `default.js` file in the code editor.

5. Open the Solution Explorer window by selecting the View ⇨ Solution Explorer menu item (or by pressing Ctrl+Alt+L). Double-click the `default.html` file to open it in the code editor.

6. Find the template-generated `<p>Content goes here</p>` content between the `<body>` and the `</body>` tags and replace it with the following code:

```html
<h1>Animations</h1>

<h2>Content</h2>

<p id="content1">
  Lorem ipsum dolor sit amet, consectetuer adipiscing elit, sed diam nonummy nibh
  euismod tincidunt ut laoreet dolore magna aliquam erat volutpat. Ut wisi enim ad
  minim veniam, quis nostrud exerci tation ullamcorper suscipit lobortis nisl ut
  aliquip ex ea commodo szeretlek. Tucsok autem vel eum iriure dolor in hendrerit
  in vulputate velit esse molestie consequat, vel illum dolore eu feugiat nulla
  facilisis at vero eros et accumsan et iusto odio dignissim qui blandit praesent
  luptatum zzril delenit augue duis dolore te feugait nulla facilisi.
</p>

<p id="content2">
  At vero eos et accusamus et iusto odio dignissimos ducimus qui blanditiis
  praesentium voluptatum deleniti atque corrupti quos dolores et quas molestias
  excepturi sint occaecati cupiditate non provident, similique sunt in culpa qui
  officia deserunt mollitia animi, id est laborum et dolorum fuga. Et harum quidem
  rerum facilis est et expedita distinctio. Nam libero tempore, cum soluta nobis est
  eligendi optio cumque nihil impedit quo minus id quod maxime placeat facere
  possimus, omnis voluptas assumenda est, omnis dolor repellendus. Temporibus autem
  quibusdam et aut officiis debitis aut rerum necessitatibus saepe eveniet ut et
  voluptates repudiandae sint et molestiae non recusandae. Itaque earum rerum hic
  tenetur a sapiente delectus, ut aut reiciendis voluptatibus maiores alias
  consequatur aut perferendis doloribus asperiores repellat.
</p>

<button id="btnShow">Show content</button>
<button id="btnNext">Next content</button>
<button id="btnHide">Hide content</button>

<h2>Panels</h2>

<p>
  <button id="btnShowPanel">Show panel</button>
  <button id="btnHidePanel">Hide panel</button>
</p>

<div id="panel">
  <p>Hello from a side panel!</p>
</div>
```

You can write any content between the <p> tags. For example, you can copy and paste the well-known Lorem ipsum placeholder text (as shown here) from `http://lipsum.com`.

7. In the Solution Explorer window, double-click the `default.css` file within the `css` folder to open it in the editor.

8. Replace the template-generated content with the following code:

```css
body        { margin: 15px; }
p           { line-height: 1.8em; }
h2          { margin-top: 20px; }
#content1 { opacity: 0; }
#content2 { display: none; }
#btnNext   { display: none; }
#btnHide   { display: none; }

#panel
{
  position: fixed;
  right: 0px;
  top: 0px;
  width: 450px;
  height: 100%;
  background-color: #323232;
  opacity: 0;
  z-index: 1;
}

#panel p
{
  position: absolute;
  top: 45%;
  text-align: center;
  width: 100%;
}
```

9. In the Solution Explorer window, double-click the `default.js` file within the `js` folder to open it in the editor.

10. Find the line that contains the `Initialize your application here` comment and add the following code lines after it:

```javascript
var headings = document.querySelectorAll('h1, h2');
WinJS.UI.Animation.enterPage(headings, { top: '100px', left: '500px' });

btnShow.addEventListener('click', onBtnShowClicked);
btnNext.addEventListener('click', onBtnNextClicked);
btnHide.addEventListener('click', onBtnHideClicked);

btnShowPanel.addEventListener('click', onBtnShowPanelClicked);
btnHidePanel.addEventListener('click', onBtnHidePanelClicked);
```

11. Scroll down and insert the following code after the `app.start();` line:

```
function onBtnShowClicked() {
  WinJS.UI.Animation.enterContent(content1);
  btnShow.style.display = 'none';
  btnNext.style.display = 'inline';
}

function onBtnNextClicked() {
  WinJS.UI.Animation.exitContent(content1).then(function() {
    content1.style.display = 'none';
    content2.style.display = 'block';
    btnNext.style.display = 'none';
    btnHide.style.display = 'inline';
    return WinJS.UI.Animation.enterContent(content2);
  });
}

function onBtnHideClicked() {
  WinJS.UI.Animation.exitContent(content2);
  content1.style.display = 'block';
  content2.style.display = 'none';
  btnShow.style.display = 'inline';
  btnNext.style.display = 'none';
  btnHide.style.display = 'none';
}

function onBtnShowPanelClicked() {
  panel.style.opacity = '1';
  WinJS.UI.Animation.showPanel(panel);
}

function onBtnHidePanelClicked() {
  WinJS.UI.Animation.hidePanel(panel).then(function () {
    panel.style.opacity = '0';
  });
}
```

11. Start the application by clicking the Debug ➪ Start Debugging menu item (or by pressing F5). Note that the titles are flying to their final positions from the lower-right corner when the application starts.

12. Click the "Show content" button. Note that the paragraph text doesn't appear immediately, but fades in and floats to its final position.

13. Click the "Next content" button. Note that the paragraph text changes to a longer text, and the controls on the page move down to provide enough screen real estate for the new content.

14. Click the "Show panel" button. Note that a narrow panel slowly flies in from the right without changing the other content on the page. You can see it in Figure 6-24.

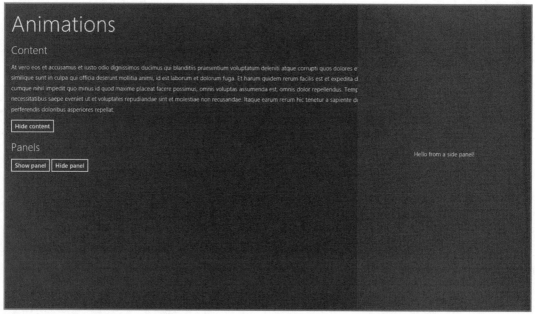

FIGURE 6-24: The animations sample

Click the "Hide panel" button to fly-out the panel.

15. Click the "Hide content" button to hide the paragraph text and return the application to its start state.

How It Works

In this exercise, you created a simple Windows 8 style application that demonstrates some basic animations using the Windows 8 Animation Library.

In Step 6, you created the basic markup of the application. Note the following in the HTML:

➤ An `h1` and two `h2` tags that render the title and the headings of the application.

➤ Two `p` tags that contain the content that is animated when you click the "Show content," "Next content," and "Hide content" buttons. The first paragraph is displayed when the application starts, and it switches over to the second paragraph when you click the "Next content" button.

➤ The buttons are rendered using `button` elements.

➤ The right panel is created using a `div` element.

➤ Most elements have an `id` attribute to make them uniquely accessible from JavaScript and CSS code.

In Step 8, you set the visual appearance of the elements on the page using CSS.

You used the `display:none` CSS declaration to completely hide elements, and the `opacity:0` declaration to make elements invisible. The difference between the two is that invisible elements continue to consume screen space, whereas hidden elements are completely removed from the UI, thus giving up their space to other elements.

Note how the `panel div` is transformed to a full-height box and moved to the right side of the page using the `position`, `right`, `top`, `width`, and `height` properties. The `z-index` property ensures that the panel is rendered on another layer above the other UI elements.

In Step 10, you added some code that runs when the application starts.

The first line of code creates a JavaScript list with all headings (`h1` and `h2` elements) on the page. The second line animates these elements using the `enterPage` animation of the Windows 8 Animation Library. Note the second parameter of the `enterPage` function that sets the offset from where the headings fly into their final positions. In this case, the headings appear at 500 pixels right and 100 pixels down from their final positions when the page loads, then the `enterPage` animation moves them to the position defined in HTML and CSS. This offset setting is used here only for demonstration purposes. Microsoft recommends setting the `offset` parameter to `null` to create Windows 8 style animations.

The next five code lines in the application initialization code attach event-handler functions to the `click` event of the buttons on the page. Note that you can directly access the HTML objects on the page without calling `document.getElementById` by using their `id` defined in the HTML markup.

In Step 11, you implemented the event-handler functions that are executed when the user clicks the buttons on the UI.

You used the `style.display` property to show or hide the UI elements. Setting this property to `'none'` hides the element. Setting this property to `'inline'` or `'block'` displays the inline or block elements accordingly. The `style.opacity` property behaves similarly. When you set it to `0`, the element becomes invisible. When you set it to `1`, the element becomes visible.

When you click the "Show content" button, the `onBtnShowClicked` function is called that starts the `enterContent` animation for the paragraph text, hides the "Show content" button, and displays the "Next content" button. Because the `enterContent` function starts the animation asynchronously, the buttons are changing while the text is still animating. The effects are simultaneous.

When you click the "Next content" button, the `onBtnNextClicked` function is called. This event handler starts the `exitContent` animation asynchronously, and uses the `then` function to execute additional code only after the animation is completed. After the first paragraph text is slowly faded out, the "Next content" button is hidden and the "Hide content" button is shown. Finally, the `enterContent` animation is started that fades in the second paragraph.

The `onBtnHideClicked` function is called when you click the "Hide content" button, and it uses the `exitContent` animation and the `style.display` property to restore the elements to their original state.

The `onBtnShowPanelClicked` and the `onBtnHidePanelClicked` functions are called when you click the "Show panel" and the "Hide panel" buttons accordingly. When you click the "Show panel" button, the `showPanel` animation starts and flies the panel in from the right of the screen. When you click the "Hide panel" button, the `hidePanel` animation flies the panel out from the screen. Here you can see another example of effect chaining using the `then` function. The panel is made invisible using the `style.opacity` property only after the `hidePanel` moved it out from the screen.

SUMMARY

In the browser, HTML, CSS, and JavaScript have already been proven to be suitable for creating real-world applications. In the past few years, the techniques and the practices have evolved, and web developers also have become ready to implement complex solutions using mature patterns with pure HTML and JavaScript. With Windows 8, Microsoft opens the Windows developer platform to web developers by enabling them to reuse their existing knowledge and develop Windows 8 style applications. The same technologies that power all websites are now first-class citizens on the client as well.

The features and services of Windows Runtime are fully available to JavaScript applications. A specific component, the Windows Library for JavaScript (WinJS), ensures that JavaScript developers can access these features and services in a well-known and natural way, regardless of the characteristics and limitations of the language.

Additionally, this library provides helpers to common coding tasks to make the lives of developers easier. With the WinJS controls, you can quickly create Windows 8 style applications that can easily manage data using declarative or programmatic data binding. The Windows 8 Animation Library helps you to add beauty, energy, motion, and personality to your applications via device-optimized animations.

EXERCISES

1. In what four groups can you sort the new HTML5 elements?

2. What is the Windows Library for JavaScript (WinJS)?

3. What is data binding?

4. What are CSS media queries?

5. Why should you use the Windows 8 Animation Library instead of implementing your own animations in JavaScript?

> **NOTE** You can find answers to the exercises in Appendix A.

▶ **WHAT YOU LEARNED IN THIS CHAPTER**

TOPIC	KEY CONCEPTS
HTML5	HTML5 is the next generation of the HyperText Markup Language standard that enables you to create rich Internet applications in the browser.
Windows Library for JavaScript (WinJS)	The Windows Library for JavaScript (WinJS) is a JavaScript code library that publishes system-level features and helpers for common coding patterns to simplify creating Windows 8 style applications in JavaScript.
`document.getElementById` and `document.getElementsbyTagName`	With the `document.getElementById` and the `document.getElementsByTagName` functions, you can get references to DOM elements in JavaScript code.
`addEventListener`	With the `addEventListener` function, you can attach a function to a DOM element to react to user actions.
Simple binding	Simple binding is a type of data binding that connects a single data value to a single UI element.
List binding	List binding is a type of data binding that connects an array of values to a complex UI element that can handle multiple values in a list or table.
`WinJS.UI.ListView`	`ListView` is a WinJS control that provides the standard listing behaviors in Windows 8 style applications.
`@media`	The `@media` keyword introduces a CSS media query that you can use to tailor your CSS selectors to devices with specific capabilities.
Snapped mode	Snapped is one of the display modes of Windows 8 style applications. In snapped mode, the application is docked to the edge of the screen in a 320-pixel-wide frame.
`canvas`	`canvas` is an HTML5 element that enables you to create raster graphics with JavaScript.

Using XAML to Create Windows 8 Style User Interfaces

WHAT YOU WILL LEARN IN THIS CHAPTER:

➤ Understanding what XAML is and how it can be used to describe the user interface

➤ Understanding the layout management mechanism

➤ Understanding what resources are and how to share them in the application

➤ Getting to know basic controls you can use in Windows 8 style applications

➤ Getting acquainted with the powerful data-binding engine in Windows 8 style applications

WROX.COM CODE DOWNLOADS FOR THIS CHAPTER

You can find the wrox.com code downloads for this chapter on the Download Code tab at www.wrox.com/remtitle.cgi?isbn=012680. The code is in the Chapter7.zip download and individually named, as described in the corresponding exercises.

In this chapter, you learn about the basics of developing Windows 8 style applications using eXtensible Application Markup Language (XAML). This chapter begins with a look at how the layout management works, and how to create reusable components with resources, followed by an introduction to basic controls and the animation and media framework supported by Windows 8 style applications. By the end of this chapter, you'll have learned how to restyle the user interface (UI) with styles and templates, and will become familiar with data-handling scenarios.

DESCRIBING THE USER INTERFACE USING XAML

A couple of years ago, functionality was all that mattered. People were content with completing a task simply by using a favorite tool. Even if the tool was not that easy to use, the developers of the tool could still remain competitive in the market.

When developing new-generation applications, you must embrace new requirements and standards that set the bar higher in terms of user experience, innovation, creativity, and responsiveness. Expectations are much higher today. A competitive product must have an outstanding user experience in terms of usability, visual design, content, and data representation. The holy grail of software design today is to build a product that people love.

These new requirements have changed the need for tools and technologies quite a bit. Not so long ago, Windows Forms was the most popular UI technology in the Microsoft Developer Stack. Developers loved it because it was very easy to use, and it was a productive technology to use to build Windows client applications. Functional requirements were met relatively easily.

But today's new requirements have quickly rendered Windows Forms obsolete. Although Windows Forms was an effective technology, it had a major weakness — a very rigid control model. To change the visual look of a control like a button or a list-based control takes quite a lot of work. Designing innovative user experiences with it is almost impossible, and, at the very least, it is very difficult to achieve.

> **NOTE** *When designing user interfaces, first you must define the layout of your screen using panels. Next, you must place controls on the panels such as buttons, other controls displaying lists, or whatever makes sense to you. You should build a layout that handles different resolutions and aspect ratios of display devices. After the basics are complete, you can use nice animations and some visual customization to improve the look of your application.*

Windows Forms was not the only technology that suffered from these symptoms. Many other Microsoft and non-Microsoft technologies shared the same fate.

Microsoft realized this soon enough. In the .NET Framework 3.0, Microsoft released a new technology called Windows Presentation Foundation (WPF). WPF was designed to enable developers to build any UI they could think of with the freedom to build innovative experiences. The technology itself introduced a few new and very important concepts:

➤ **A brand-new control model** — WPF divides controls into two main categories — controls that have one child, and controls that have many children. (You learn more about what controls are and how to use them later in this chapter.) That's pretty much it. This is all that WPF includes as a contstraint. For example, you can have a `Button` control and place another `Button` inside it. You can then add a `ListBox` inside the inner `Button`. This doesn't make too much sense, of course, but it does show the flexibility of the new control model introduced in WPF.

➤ **Declarative UI** — WPF includes a new way to describe the UI. You no longer need to write code and logic to build the UI. You can do this entirely declaratively with an XML-based language called eXtensible Application Markup Language (XAML). If you've ever done any web development using HyperText Markup Language (HTML), this concept should be very familiar to you.

➤ **Vector graphics** — WPF introduces a UI that incorporates vector graphics. Vector graphics use math to render the contents, rather than pixels. The components are composed of curves and lines, and notof dots. This means that, with different resolutions and with different dots-per-inch (DPI) values, the UI remains visually pleasing. Scaling up and scaling down can be performed easily without the loss of quality. In XAML-based UIs, you should always see crisp and perfect fonts and drawings.

➤ **Styles and templates** — The new controls are built from primitives and basic shapes. These little visuals compose the visual tree of the controls. Using templates and styles, you can change or entirely replace the visual tree of any control while still keeping all the functionality that the control represents.

The new concepts were quite successful, so Microsoft decided to build a web technology that supports XAML-based development. The codename of the project was WPF Everywhere (WPF/E), and it was later introduced to the public as Silverlight.

XAML became strategically very important to Microsoft. Today, XAML is found throughout Microsoft products. You can use XAML to build WPF, Silverlight, or Windows Phone applications. As a matter of fact, XAML is used in Windows Workflow Foundation (WF) 4.0 to define long-running workflows and display them visually.

When you are developing Windows 8 style applications, you can choose from two different technologies. You can build the UI using HTML5 and JavaScript, or you can choose XAML.

XAML by itself is just an XML document, and nothing else. A very powerful parser processes the elements in this document. This means that no matter what you add to this document, an instance will be created from it.

The syntax is fairly straightforward. Most of the time, the syntax comes from the XML specification, but some nice additions make XAML more powerful.

In the following code sample, a new `Button` control is created and its `Content` property is set to `"Hello XAML"`. You can set properties on objects using the *attribute syntax*. By using this approach, the attributes on the XAML element map to properties on the object itself.

```
<Button Content="Hello XAML"/>
```

The following code creates a rectangle with a gradient brush. You could easily specify a simple color like "White" or "Black" by using attribute syntax. However, you might want to fill your rectangle with a much more sophisticated color. A gradient brush would be a perfect choice. It contains a list of *gradient stops* that define the colors that appear in the gradient brush. You must switch to a different syntax called the *property syntax* to describe the assignment of this complex value. In the following example, the rectangle's `Fill` property is set to a `LinearGradientBrush`:

```
<Rectangle Width="100" Height="100">
    <Rectangle.Fill>
        <LinearGradientBrush EndPoint="0.5,1" StartPoint="0.5,0">
            <GradientStop Color="Black"/>
```

```
            <GradientStop Color="#FF1875AA" Offset="1"/>
          </LinearGradientBrush>
      </Rectangle.Fill>
  </Rectangle>
```

The following code demonstrates the use of *markup extensions*. Later in this chapter, you learn about bindings, resources, and referencing other objects. These features are available through markup extensions. Markup extensions require a special syntax with curly braces, as shown here:

```
<TextBlock Text="{Binding FirstName}" Foreground="{StaticResource whiteBrush}"/>
```

At this point, you shouldn't worry about what all this code means. All you have to be familiar with is the syntax in XAML.

USING NAMESPACES

If you have created applications in object-oriented languages, you know that different components and controls can co-exist with the same name, but with different namespaces. *Namespaces* are logical containers for your code. They are meant to help you avoid element name conflicts. This is not just XAML-specific. The standard XML specification defines XML namespaces and syntax. Microsoft provides a nice additional capability to map directly to Common Language Runtime (CLR) namespaces.

When you add a XAML element to the document, by default, the XAML parser tries to resolve that type in the default namespace. If the type is located in a different namespace, you must explicitly reference that namespace using the `xmlns:prefix` attribute. The prefix serves as a shortcut for the full namespace. So, whenever you want to reference an object from a specific namespace, you must reference it like `prefix:MyControl`, where `prefix` is the custom shortcut name for that specific namespace.

The default namespace is an `xmlns` declaration without a specified prefix. In Windows 8 style applications, the default namespace in XAML is `http://schemas.microsoft.com/winfx/2006/xaml/presentation`, which maps directly to the `Windows.UI.Xaml.Controls` namespace. This is where all the basic controls are located.

In the next exercise, you learn how to create your first Windows 8 style application using XAML.

> **NOTE** *You can find the complete code to download for this exercise on this book's companion website at* www.wrox.com *in the* GreetMeApplication *within the* Chapter07.zip *download.*

TRY IT OUT   **Building the GreetMe Application with XAML**

In this exercise, you create a simple Windows 8 style application using XAML. You place a `Button` control on the UI and handle its `Click` event. When the event is raised, you'll greet the user.

1. Open Visual Studio 2012 and create a new Windows 8 style application project. For the Name of the project, enter **GreetMeApplication**.

2. After the project loads, ensure that `MainPage.xaml` is the file you are currently editing.

3. To add a `Button` control to the UI, locate the `Grid` panel with the name `LayoutRoot` and add the following code inside the `Grid` element:

```
<StackPanel HorizontalAlignment="Center" VerticalAlignment="Center"
        Orientation="Horizontal">
    <TextBlock Text="Your name: "/>
    <TextBox x:Name="txtName" Text="" Width="200" Margin="8,0,8,0"/>
    <Button Content="Greet Me" />
</StackPanel>
```

4. To subscribe to the `Click` event of the `Button` control, change the `Button` declaration to the following code:

```
<Button Content="Greet Me" Click="Button_Click"/>
```

5. To write the event handler for the `Click` event, right-click the XAML code editor and select View Code. A new file named `MainPage.xaml.cs` opens up. Add the following code inside the `MainPage` class:

```
private void Button_Click(object sender, RoutedEventArgs e)
{
    var dialog = new Windows.UI.Popups.MessageDialog("Hello "+txtName.Text);
    dialog.ShowAsync();
}
```

6. Run the application by pressing F5. Type your name into the `TextBox` and click the GreetMe button. Figure 7-1 shows the result.

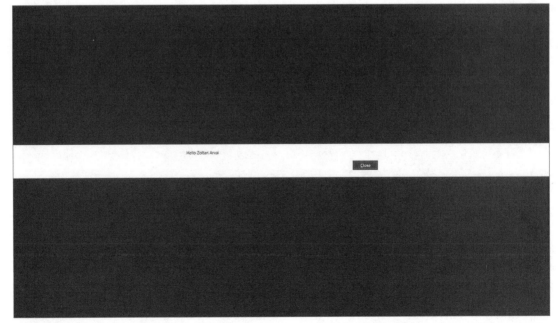

FIGURE 7-1: Running the GreetMe application

How It Works

This is a very simple application, but there is a lot to learn here. When you created the project in Step 1, Visual Studio prepared the project structure for you. Figure 7-2 shows the created structure in the Solution Explorer window.

In the `Assets` folder, you'll see some graphics for your application, such as logos and splash screen pictures. You also have two XAML files. One of them is `App.xaml`, which represents the application object. This object is the first one to be created when your application runs. In `App.xaml`, you can see from the `x:Class` attribute that the `Application` object is `GreetMeApplication.App`. In Solution Explorer, you can see that under `App.xaml` is a code-behind file called `App.xaml.cs`. A *code-behind* file contains code that is joined with markup-defined objects, in this case the `App` object. If you open it, you'll see the following code:

FIGURE 7-2: The project structure in the Solution Explorer window

```
sealed partial class App : Application
{

    public App()
    {
        this.InitializeComponent();
        this.Suspending += OnSuspending;
    }

    protected override void OnLaunched(LaunchActivatedEventArgs args)
    {
        // Do not repeat app initialization when already running, just ensure that
        // the window is active
        if (args.PreviousExecutionState == ApplicationExecutionState.Running)
        {
            Window.Current.Activate();
            return;
        }

        if (args.PreviousExecutionState == ApplicationExecutionState.Terminated)
        {
            //TODO: Load state from previously suspended application
        }

        // Create a Frame to act navigation context and navigate to the first page
        var rootFrame = new Frame();
        if (!rootFrame.Navigate(typeof(MainPage)))
        {
            throw new Exception("Failed to create initial page");
        }

        // Place the frame in the current Window and ensure that it is active
        Window.Current.Content = rootFrame;
        Window.Current.Activate();
```

```
    }

    private void OnSuspending(object sender, SuspendingEventArgs e)
    {
        var deferral = e.SuspendingOperation.GetDeferral();
        //TODO: Save application state and stop any background activity
        deferral.Complete();
    }
}
```

This is where the application object is created. Inside the OnLaunched method, a Frame control is created. The Frame control is responsible for navigating between different pages, just like a web browser, but in this case, these pages are XAML-based views. Using the Frame (named *rootFrame*), control navigation is initiated to the MainPage. This is why MainPage is displayed immediately after the application runs. The Frame control is not yet part of the visible Window, so the Frame is set as the current content of the window.

You can see some additional code regarding execution states and suspending events. You don't have to worry about that right now. This code is related to the application lifecycle. You'll learn more about this in the Chapter 9.

The Grid panel stretches inside MainPage. Panels are used to create the layout. You'll learn more about this in this chapter. For now, think about panels like containers for controls such as the Button control. The x:Name attribute of the Grid specifies the name of the variable you can use to reference the panel from code-behind, or from XAML code. In this case, the name of the variable is LayoutRoot. Later, you see that this name is quite common. The first item on a page is usually a panel with the name LayoutRoot.

In Step 3, a StackPanel is placed inside LayoutRoot and is positioned in the center of the screen using the HorizontalAlignment and the VerticalAlignment properties. The TextBlock control is used to display simple text, and the TextBox control is used to accept user input. Note that the TextBox control is named txtName. The third element in the StackPanel is a Button control. To display the "Greet Me" string inside the Button control, its Content is set to "GreetMe".

In Step 4, you set the Click event to point to a method named Button_Click. The Click event is used to react to a user action. When the user clicks on a button, the Click event is raised. You can subscribe to these events using event handlers. In this case, the Button_Click event handler will be notified when the Click event is raised. The XAML parser looks for this method inside the MainPage class. In the code-behind file called MainPage.xaml.cs, the MainPage class must implement this method.

In Step 5, the body of the event handler, you use a DialogMessage to greet the user. The DialogMessage displays the "Hello" string appended by the text typed into the TextBox named txtName.

UNDERSTANDING THE LAYOUT MANAGEMENT SYSTEM

When you are creating the UI of an application, one of the most difficult problems you face is adapting to the different display resolutions, aspect ratios, and DPI settings. If you consider the future of Windows 8 regarding the possible display screens and hardware (such as tablets, desktop PCs, notebooks, televisions, and so on), this seems like it may be a really tough challange. So, you must be very careful when building the UI and ensure that it scales and adapts well to the different scenarios. XAML-based Windows 8o style applications have a very flexible layout management system that significantly helps you meet these requirements.

At the heart of the layout management system lies the `Panel` class. XAML-based Windows 8 style applications have a number of `Panel` classes that offer a great deal of flexibility and strategy when it comes to laying out the visual elements on the UI.

A New Concept: Dependency Properties

Before learning about the details of layout management, you should be aware of a new concept. In XAML-based Windows 8 style applications, a new kind of property has been introduced called a *dependency property*. The most substantial base class in the framework is `DependencyObject`. Every control, panel, and shape inherits from this class. Only `DependencyObject`s can have dependecy properties.

Most of the time, you don't have to worry at all about these properties being dependency properties, but you should know that only dependency properties support data binding, animation, and styling. All controls are derived from the `DependencyObject` class, and most (but not all) of their properties are dependency properties, which means that you'll get all the advantages when working with control properties.

Taking Dependecy Properties One Step Further with Attached Properties

Designing a UI control model is not an easy task, especially if you want to keep things as simple and as flexible as possible. Panels are the heart of a layout management system. A *panel* is a simple container for controls. It's the panel's responsibility to arrange these children elements according to a certain logic. In many technologies, controls have properties for specific panels. If you set these properties and add the controls to a panel, the panel would know how to arrange the controls. But this means that the composer of the control must know what kind of panels exist in the framework, and what kind of properties should be supported.

This would introduce a very rigid model. What if you wanted to create a new kind of panel that would support a circular arrangement and that would place the elements into predefined slots? There is no way for the author of a control to know in advance that someday there will be this really cool panel you create, and it would need a `SlotIndex` property on the control.

If you can't add a property to a control during development, then you should attach it later. This is what the *attached properties* are all about. You can set a dependency property on an object that belongs to a different type. Attached properties are basically dependecy properties.

You can think of this as saving a special value for an instance into a memory area, and then later, if you need that value, you can check that area to see if someone has already saved the value for the given instance. The beauty of attached properties is that you don't have to deal with any of these problems and steps. In XAML, they almost look as though they were properties of the control.

The following code demonstrates the declaration of an attached property called `SlotIndex` in the `CircularPanel` class:

```
// Attached property representing an index
public static readonly DependencyProperty SlotIndexProperty =
    DependencyProperty.RegisterAttached("SlotIndex", "Int32",
    "MyPanels.CircularPanel",...)
```

The following code shows how you would use it:

```
<Button Content="Press Me" local:CircularPanel.SlotIndex="1"/>
```

The `Button` control doesn't know anything about `CircularPanel` or `SlotIndex`. This information is only valuable for your `CircularPanel` class. You defined the `SlotIndex` property in the `CircularPanel` class, but still you set it on the `Button` control.

> **NOTE** `CircularPanel` *is an imaginary panel, and is not part of Windows 8 style applications.*

Properties Affecting the Size and Layout of a Control

When it comes to layout, it's not always about panels. The control itself has a couple of properties that have a huge impact on its size and the layout.

➤ **Width** and **Height** properties — You get the results you expect by setting explicit values for `Width` and `Height` properties. The control takes up the necessary space to grow to the proper size. If you do not provide an explicit value, these properties default to `Auto`, which means that the real size of the control is determined by other factors.

➤ **Margin** property — The `Margin` property is a collection of four numbers specifing the `Left`, `Top`, `Right`, and `Bottom` margins (in that order). You can use a negative number for a `Margin` value to indicate that `Margin` has a direct effect on the final size and position of the control.

➤ **Padding** property — The `Padding` property is a collection of four numbers specifying the `Left`, `Top`, `Right`, and `Bottom` paddings (in that order). Paddings are defined on controls with content. The padding value determines the distance between the container control and the edges of the contained control.

➤ **HorizontalAlignment** property — This property determines whether the control is aligned to `Left`, `Center`, `Right`, or `Stretched` in the horizontal space.

➤ **VerticalAlignment** property — This property determines whether the control is aligned to `Top`, `Center`, `Bottom`, or `Stretched` in the vertical space.

All panels respect the `Width`, `Height`, and `Margin` properties. However, aligment properties are not always taken into account. This behavior depends on the type of the panel, and its own layout algorithm.

The Canvas Panel

The Canvas panel is the most basic panel with the most simple layout strategy. When you add a control to the panel, it is displayed in the top-left corner. If you want to specify how far it should be located from the top-left corner, you can use the Canvas.Left and the Canvas.Top attached properties. In the following code and in Figure 7-3, you can see that a button is placed onto a Canvas panel at location 120,100:

```
<Canvas>
    <Button Canvas.Left="120" Canvas.Top="100"/>
</Canvas>
```

The Canvas panel has a third attached property called Canvas.ZIndex. If two controls overlap each other, the last control added to the panel's Children collection is on top. If you want to change the order, you should set the ZIndex on the children to reflect the appropriate ordering of the elements.

This is pretty much all you need to know about the Canvas panel to get started. The simple layout strategy means that the layout algorithm will be very fast, which could be important with regard to performance optimalizations.

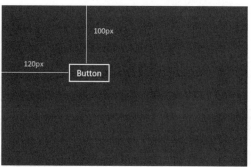

FIGURE 7-3: Button control placed inside a Canvas

There is one more thing you should note in Figure 7-3. The size of the Button control takes up only the necessary space to be capable of rendering its inner content. This is because the Width and Height properties are not set on the Button control, so it defaults to Auto. In this case, Auto means that the Canvas panel decides the final width and height of the properties, and according to the Canvas, the Button only needs the space to render its content appropriately. If you set the Width and Height properties to a specific value, the control fills the space it needs.

The StackPanel Panel

The StackPanel is a fairly straightforward panel as well. It places its children one after the other horizontally or vertically, depending on its Orientation property. The StackPanel doesn't have any attached properties. If the Orientation is set to Vertical, the StackPanel's layout algorithm takes the HorizontalAlignment property into account, but not the VerticalAlignment. If the Orientation is set to Horizontal, StackPanel's layout algorithm takes the VerticalAlignment property into account, but not the HorizontalAlignment property.

The following code has two StackPanels with a horizontal and a vertical orientation. Figure 7-4 shows the specified layout:

```
<StackPanel Orientation="Horizontal">
    <Button Content="Left" HorizontalAlignment="Left"/>
    <Button Content="Center" HorizontalAlignment="Center"/>
    <Button Content="Right" HorizontalAlignment="Right"/>
```

```
        <Button Content="Strech" HorizontalAlignment="Stretch"/>
    </StackPanel>

    <StackPanel Orientation="Vertical">
        <Button Content="Top" VerticalAlignment="Top"/>
        <Button Content="Center" VerticalAlignment="Center"/>
        <Button Content="Bottom" VerticalAlignment="Bottom"/>
        <Button Content="Strech" VerticalAlignment="Stretch"/>
    </StackPanel>
```

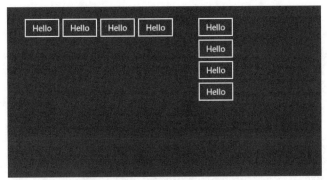

FIGURE 7-4: StackPanels with horizontal and vertical orientations

The Grid Panel

The `Grid` panel is a little bit more complex with a more sophisticated layout strategy. As its name suggests, this panel supports grid-like layouts with rows and columns. The children of the panel are always placed inside a cell. If no rows or columns are defined, the `Grid` panel has a single cell that fills the entire area of the `Grid` panel.

Defining Rows and Columns

You can defines rows and columns by adding `RowDefinitions` and `ColumnDefinitions` to the `Grid` panel. By default, the rows and columns divide the available space equally. You can change this behavior by setting the `Height` and `Width` properties on the `RowDefinition` and `ColumnDefinition` items. The `Height` and `Width` properties support the following three different values:

➤ **`Auto`** — `Auto` means that the row or column should be sized to fit the content.

➤ **Fixed value** — By providing explicit values, you can ensure that the `Height` and `Width` values are not affected by any other values, and that the rows or columns are taking up the required space.

➤ **Star sizing** — The *star value* means that the remaining space should be occupied. The *remaining* word is the key here. After rows and columns with `Auto` and fixed sizes get their space, the remaining space can be occupied by the star-sized rows and columns. If more rows are star-sized, these rows divide the remaining space equally. A star can have a number associated with it that represents its proportion.

Let's take a look at a simple example:

```
<Grid>
    <Grid.RowDefinitions>
        <RowDefinition Height="Auto"/>
        <RowDefinition Height="100"/>
        <RowDefinition Height="1*"/>
        <RowDefinition Height="1*"/>
        <RowDefinition Height="2*"/>
    </Grid.RowDefinitions>
</Grid>
```

The previous code snippet contains only the layout code, so it is not visible without content. In the this configuration, the first row of the `Grid` is sized to the content of the first row. The second row is `100px`. The remaining space is divided between row numbers 3, 4, and 5. And their proportions from the remaining space are 25 percent, 25 percent, and 50 percent, respectively. Figure 7-5 shows the layout with the `Grid` panel.

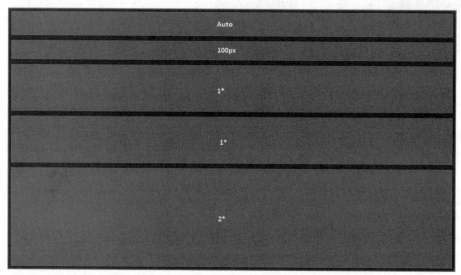

FIGURE 7-5: Complex layout with the Grid panel

Placing a Control Inside a Grid

To specify the row or column index for the control, you should use the `Grid.Rows` and `Grid.Columns` attached properties. The following code places the `Button` control into the second row and the third column. (Indexing is starting from 0.)

```
<Button Grid.Row="1" Grid.Column="2"/>
```

In terms of layout, placing a control inside a cell of a `Grid` means that the control can take up all the space the cell offers. You can adjust the place and size of the control inside the cell using the alignment and margin properties of the control.

Controls may span over multiple rows or columns. You can achieve this with the `Grid.RowSpan` and the `Grid.ColumnSpan` properties.

The VariableSizedWrapGrid Panel

Using the `VariableSizedWrapGrid` panel, you can create layouts very similar to the one seen on the home screen of Windows 8. The layout strategy of this panel is quite simple.

The panel arranges its children controls from left to right, or top to bottom, according to the `Orientation` property while there is available free space. When there is no more available space for another element, the panel starts to use a new row or column.

You can also specify the maximum number of rows or columns using the `MaximumNumberOfRowsOrColumns` property. If the `Orientation` is set to `Horizontal`, the `MaximumNumberOfRowsOrColumns` property constrains the number of rows. If the `Orientation` is set to `Vertical`, the `MaximumNumberOfRowsOrColumns` property constrains the number of columns.

The layout is more or less uniform using this panel. If you want more control over the space given to each control inside the panel, you can set the `ItemHeight` and `ItemWidth` properties. By assigning values to these properties, you can ensure that every item in the panel has the same fixed cell size.

Sometimes you'll want to allocate more space for an item. Using the `VariableSizedWrapGrid.ColumnSpan` and the `VariableSizedWrapGrid.RowSpan` attached properties, you can specify that an item spans over multiple rows or columns.

Let's take a look at a simple example:

```
<VariableSizedWrapGrid ItemHeight="150" ItemWidth="150" MaximumRowsOrColumns="3" >
    <Rectangle Margin="8" Fill="LightGreen" VariableSizedWrapGrid.ColumnSpan="2"
        VariableSizedWrapGrid.RowSpan="2"/>
    <Rectangle Margin="8" Fill="Red"/>
    <Rectangle Margin="8" Fill="Red"/>
    <Rectangle Margin="8" Fill="Red"/>
    <Rectangle Margin="8" Fill="Red"/>
    <Rectangle Margin="8" Fill="Red"/>
    <Rectangle Margin="8" Fill="Red"/>
    <Rectangle Margin="8" Fill="Red"/>
    <Rectangle Margin="8" Fill="Red"/>
    <Rectangle Margin="8" Fill="Red"/>
    <Rectangle Margin="8" Fill="Red"/>
    <Rectangle Margin="8" Fill="Red"/>
    <Rectangle Margin="8" Fill="Red"/>
    <Rectangle Margin="8" Fill="Red"/>
    <Rectangle Margin="8" Fill="Red"/>
    <Rectangle Margin="8" Fill="Red"/>
    <Rectangle Margin="8" Fill="Red"/>
</VariableSizedWrapGrid>
```

In this example, the `VariableSizedWrapGrid` panel has 18 rectangles to arrange. The values set for the `ItemWidth` and `ItemHeight` properties mean that each rectangle has a width and height of 150 pixels. The only exception is the first rectangle, which has the `VariableSizedWrapGrid` `.ColumnSpan` and the `VariableSizedWrapGrid.RowSpan` attached properties set to `2`. These settings ensure that the rectangle spans over two rows and two columns, thus having a size of 300 by 300. You can see the result in Figure 7-6.

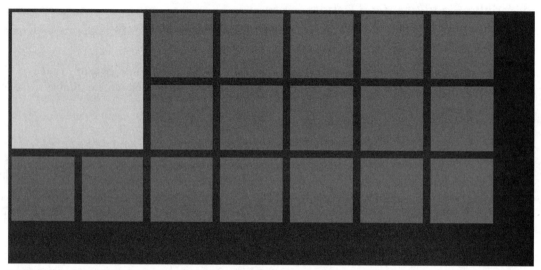

FIGURE 7-6: Complex layout with the VariableSizedWrapGrid panel

> **NOTE** *You can use other layout containers such as the* `CarouselPanel` *or the* `WrapGrid` *panel, but these panels are limited to be used only in an* `ItemsPanelTemplate`. *In Chapter 8, you learn more about customizing the layout of* `ItemsControls` *using the* `ItemsPanelTemplate`.

In the next excercise, you learn how to to build flexible layouts with XAML in Windows 8 style applications.

TRY IT OUT Building a Complex Layout

In this exercise, you create a simple Windows 8 style application with a little more complex layout. You add a menu and divide the space to support a list with details.

1. Create a new Windows 8 style application using Visual Studio 2012. Choose the Blank App (XAML) template.

2. In the Solution Explorer window, double-click the `MainPage.xaml` file.

3. On the designer surface, divide the `Grid` into the Main Columns, as shown in Figure 7-7.

FIGURE 7-7: Adding columns to the Grid panel using the Visual Studio 2012 designer

4. On the designer surface, divide the Grid into two rows, as shown in Figure 7-8.

FIGURE 7-8: Adding rows to the Grid panel using the Visual Studio 2012 designer

5. From the ToolBox, drag a StackPanel to the first row.

6. Open the Properties window and ensure that the StackPanel is selected.

7. On the Properties window, open the Layout section. Set the following properties:

➤ HorizontalAlignment: Left

➤ VerticalAlignment: Bottom

➤ RowSpan: 1

➤ ColumnSpan: 2

➤ Row and Columns: 0.

➤ Width and Height: Auto

➤ Margin: 30 (Left),0,0,0

8. Open the Documents Outline window and pin it.

9. Ensure that the StackPanel is selected, as shown in Figure 7-9.

10. On the Properties window, set the Orientation property of the StackPanel to Horizontal.

11. On the Toolbox, find the TextBlock element and double-click it to add it to the StackPanel. Repeat this three times to end up with four TextBlocks.

12. Select all the TextBlocks in the StackPanel and, in the Properties window, set the following properties:

➤ Margin: 15 (Left), 0,0,0

➤ FontSize: 36

➤ Text: MenuItem

13. Select the Grid panel that contains the StackPanel.

14. Find the Rectangle in the Toolbox and double-click it.

15. Set the following properties on the Rectangle:

➤ HorizontalAlignment: Stretch

➤ VerticalAlignment: Stretch

➤ RowSpan and ColumnSpan: 1

➤ Column: 0

➤ Row: 1

➤ Width and Height: Auto

➤ Margin: 20

FIGURE 7-9: The Document Outline window

16. On the Properties window, select the Brush section and set the Fill property to any shade of red.

17. Select the Grid panel that contains the StackPanel.

18. Find the StackPanel in the Toolbox and double-click it.

19. Set the following properties on the new StackPanel:

➤ HorizontalAlignment: Stretch

➤ VerticalAlignment: Stretch

➤ RowSpan and ColumnSpan: 1

➤ Column: 1

➤ Row: 1

➤   `Width` and `Height`: `Auto`

➤   `Margin`: `20`

➤   `Background`: `#FFD4D4D4`

20. Press F5 to run the application. Figure 7-10 shows the result you should see.

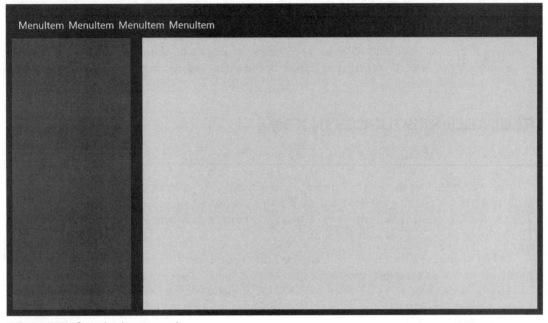

FIGURE 7-10: Complex layout result

How It Works

By clicking slightly above and slightly to the left side of the `Grid` panel, you instruct Visual Studio to add two rows and two columns to the `Grid`.

The first `StackPanel` is used as a menu container. It has a `ColumnSpan` property set to 2, because you want the menu to span over the columns. The `Orientation` is set to `Horizontal` to ensure that the menu items are arranged horizontally. By setting the alignment properties, you can ensure that the panel menu will be positioned in the bottom-left corner of the first row and column.

The menu is represented by four `TextBlock`s. Setting the left `Margin` ensures that there is some whitespace between the menu items.

The `Rectangle` serves as a placeholder. Later in this chapter, you replace it with a `ListBox`. Setting the `Rows` property to 1 moves the rectangle to the second row. Setting the `Margin` to 20 provides some whitespace on all four sides.

The second `StackPanel` will be populated in later exercises. Fow now, it is a placeholder for the item details.

> **NOTE** *In this excercise, you used the Visual Studio 2012 visual designer to build the UI. You could have achieved the same result using a XAML editor as well. Sometimes it is faster and more convenient to set properties using a XAML editor. If you prefer visual designers, Expression Blend is a much more effective tool to use to create user interfaces. In Chapter 8, you'll use Expression Blend to customize the user interface.*

Now that you know how to create layouts, you'll want to add controls and customize the UI. When trying to create a consistent UI, soon you'll feel the need to have shared objects across the applications, such as a common visual appearance, or some data objects. In the next section, you learn how to create such resources.

REUSABLE RESOURCES IN XAML

When building the UI using XAML, you'll need different objects like colors, styles, templates, data objects, or anything you can imagine to be used as reusable components. You can think of *resources* as a big dictionary container into which you can put whatever you want, and then later reference anything from it from XAML or code using a single key. Resources are of type `ResourceDictionary` defined on the `FrameworkElement` class, which means that every panel or control has a `Resources` section you can use.

Adding items into a `Resources` collection is fairly simple. The following code demonstrates two `SolidColorBrush` resource items added to the `Grid` panel's `Resources` section. Note that both resource items have the `x:Key` attribute set. This property is used to reference the resources.

```
<Grid.Resources>
    <SolidColorBrush x:Key="foregroundBrush" Color="White"/>
    <SolidColorBrush x:Key="backgroundBrush" Color="Black"/>
</Grid.Resources>
```

Referencing Resources

To use a resource, you must reference it using the `StaticResource` markup extension. As its name suggests, this reference is static, which means that it is not possible to change the reference to a different resource during run time. However, changing properties on the referenced resource is certainly possible. The following code shows how to reference resources:

```
<Button Content="Click Me"
    Background="{StaticResource backgroundBrush}"
    Foreground="{StaticResource foregroundBrush}"/>
```

> **NOTE** *Referencing a resource that does not exist will not cause a compiler error by itself, although you'll get warnings from the designer. If a referenced resource is not found with the provided key, you'll get an exception during run time while the view is trying to initialize inside the `InitializeComponent` method. This can lead to nasty errors, so you should always ensure that all referenced resources are accessible.*

The Hierarchy of Resources

You should think of resources as objects that are just a part of the UI hierarchy like any other controls, because they are defined on controls that are part of the visual tree. When setting a reference to a resource on a control's property, you must ensure that the resource is accessible and visible to the given control.

You can define resources at three different levels:

> ➤ **Application resources** — In `App.xaml`, there is a `Resource` section on the application object. A resource added to this section is visible anywhere in your application.

> ➤ **Page resources** — In every page you create on the top-level control, you can define resources. A resource added to this section is visible for every control on the page, but invisible to any other control placed on a different page.

> ➤ **Local resources** — Because the `Resources` property is defined on the `FrameworkElement` class, you can add resources to controls or panels. These resources are local resources, and are accessible only by elements inside the given control or panel.

Resource Dictionaries

If you are doing a good job, most of your XAML code will be part of a `Resource` section, and only the layout and controls will be placed inside the `Children` and `Content` sections. You'll soon discover that the resources sections are huge and very difficult to maintain. To solve this issue, you can use separate `ResourceDictionary` files.

`ResourceDictionary` files are sperate XAML files containing only resource objects. The visibility and hierarchy of `ResourceDictionary` files are determined by the merging location. By default, resources in these separate files are not visible. You must merge them into a `Resource` section on any level you think appropriate. After merging the files into a `Resource` section, you can think of the assets located in the separate file as though they were defined directly in the given `Resource` section. The following code sample demonstrates the contents of a resource dictionary:

```
<ResourceDictionary
    xmlns="http://schemas.microsoft.com/winfx/2006/xaml/presentation"
    xmlns:x="http://schemas.microsoft.com/winfx/2006/xaml">
    <SolidColorBrush x:Key="brBrush" Color="Red" />
</ResourceDictionary>
```

`ResourceDictionary` files are a great tool to use to partition your resources. The following code shows how to merge a `ResourceDictionary` file into the `Application.Resources` section:

```
<Application.Resources>
    <ResourceDictionary>
        <ResourceDictionary.MergedDictionaries>
            <ResourceDictionary Source="MyResource.xaml"/>
        </ResourceDictionary.MergedDictionaries>
    </ResourceDictionary>
</Application.Resources>
```

System Resources

Resources are a common way to reuse brushes, styles, and other objects on many pages. Earlier, you learned how you can define your own resources. However, when building a Windows 8 style application, you may want to ensure that the design of your application conforms to the design of the native operating system. To accomplish that, it would make sense to use the same colors, fonts, and font styles as Windows 8 does. You can do this by referencing built-in system resources. You can use tons of resources — brushes, colors, font styles and sizes, and many other shared objects.

The best and probably the easiest way to explore these system resources is to use the Visual Studio 2012 Properties window, as shown in Figure 7-11. For example, if you want to ensure that a rectangle has the same color as the background of the app bar you can start Visual Studio 2012, click the `Rectangle`, find the `Fill` property, and click System Resources. You are presented with a list of applicable system-wide brush resources. All you have to do is to choose one like the `AppBarBackgroundThemeBrush`.

In the next exercise, you learn how to create and reuse existing resources throughout your application.

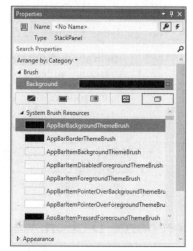

FIGURE 7-11: System Resources in the Properties window

TRY IT OUT Using Resources

In this exercise, you create a brush resource and place it in the page's `Resources` section. Then you reference it from a rectangle.

1. Open the previous project.

2. Select the gray `StackPanel`. On the Properties window, set the `Name` property to **detailsPanel**.

3. On the Properties window, select the `Brush` section.

4. Select the `Background` property.

5. On the right side of the color bar of this property, there is a small light gray square called Advanced Properties. Click it.

6. Select "Convert to New Resource."

7. On the pop-up dialog box, provide the name **lightBrush** for your new resource.

8. Ensure that this document is selected and the `Page` option is also selected in the `ComboBox`.

9. Click OK.

10. Select the red rectangle and select its `Fill` property.

11. In the `Brushes` section, locate a series of icons under the `Stroke` property. Click the last one, `Brush Resources`.

12. On the Brush Resources tab, you can see the local and the system-wide resources.

13. Click `lightBrush`.

14. Press F5 to run the application. You should see the result shown in Figure 7-12.

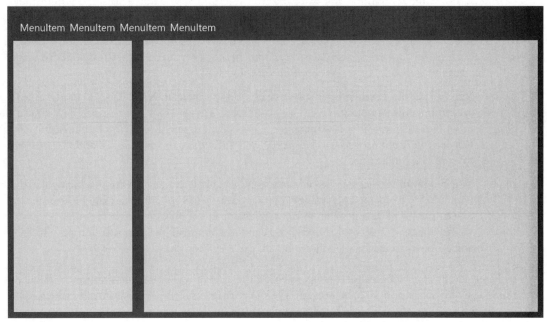

MenuItem MenuItem MenuItem MenuItem

FIGURE 7-12: Using Resources result

How It Works

The "Convert to New Resource Window" creates a new resource and saves the resource to a location you specify. In this case, you saved it to the current document, which is the current `Page.Resources` section.

This is how the `Page.Resources` section should look:

```
<Page.Resources>
    <SolidColorBrush x:Key="lightBrush" Color="#FFD4D4D4"/>
</Page.Resources>
```

Later, you can reuse resources by referencing them from code, creating the reference using the Advanced Properties option, or, if you are working with brushes, you can use the `Brush Resources` panel as well.

BASIC CONTROLS IN WINDOWS 8 STYLE APPLICATIONS

For Windows 8 style application development, there are simple controls that you can use to build your UI. These controls can be divided into two main categories.

The first category contains the `ContentControls`. These types of controls can contain only one single child element. You can add this child using the `Content` property of the `ContentControl`. The `ContentControl` itself is a base class, but you can also use it in your UI to group or separate a part of the UI. You can put anything you want into the `Content`. If you add a string, it will display text; if you add a `UIElement`, it will render it. A `UIElement` is a component that can be displayed visually.

The second category contains the `ItemsControls`. These types of contols can contain a list of elements. Just like the `ContentControl`, you can use the `ItemsControl` directly as well. You have two different ways to populate an `ItemsControl` with items:

➤ **You can set the `Items` property** — Usually, this happens in XAML. An `ItemsControl` can accept any type of object in its `Items` collection. This enables you to create any kind of list or UI. For example, if you want to have a social wall where you can place text, images, and videos, you could use an `ItemsControl` and add `TextBlocks`, `Images`, and `MediaElements` to the `Items` collection.

➤ **You can set the `ItemsSource` property** — Whereas the `Items` collection is manipulated directly within XAML or from code using the `Items.Add()` method, the `ItemsSource` property is set to a collection of data items in most cases. You can use only one of these properties at once. If you set the `ItemsSource` property, you cannot manipulate the `Items` collection directly. If you add elements to the `Items` collection, you can't set the `ItemsSource` property.

Basically, every single control derives from either the `ContentControl` class or the `ItemsControl` class. The only exceptions are the `Border`, the `TextBlock`, and the `Image` controls, which are technically not even controls! This is something you don't really have to worry about. It's just a simple technical detail. The normal use of these elements is very similar to the control-derived elements.

Controls with Simple Values

In Windows 8 style applications, it is not just `ContentControls` versus `ItemsControls`. There are other types of controls that do not belong to these categories.

The Border Element

Using the `Border` element, you can draw a border and/or a background around your other controls. The `Border` element is just a `FrameworkElement`, which also is a base class for every control. The `Border` element can have only a single child element, so if you need to group more controls into a border, consider grouping them into a panel first, and then add the panel to the `Border` as a child.

Table 7-1 shows the most important properties for the `Border` class.

TABLE 7-1: Important Properties of the Border Class

PROPERTY	DESCRIPTION
CornerRadius	The `CornerRadius` property specifies the radius for the corners of the border. If you specify a single number, all of the corners are equally rounded. If you specify four numbers, the order is `TopLeft`, `TopRight`, `BottomRight`, and `BottomLeft`.

PROPERTY	DESCRIPTION
BorderThickness	Using the BorderThickness property, you can specify the thickness of the border lines on the four sides of the border. If you specify four numbers, the order is Left, Top, Right, and Bottom. Specifying only one number means the same value applies for all sides.

The following code sample demonstrates the use of the Border element:

```
<Border Width="400" Height="300" Background="LightBlue" CornerRadius="20"
    BorderThickness="1" BorderBrush="LightGray">
    <Grid>
        <!--....-->
    </Grid>
</Border>
```

> **NOTE** *In XML, you can use* `<!--` *to indicate that the following text is just a comment. You can end a comment section with* `-->`*.*

The Image Element

The Image element is used to display images. Using the Source property, you can point the element to the location of a picture. Supported image types include PNG, JPEG, GIF, TIFF, BMP, JPEG, and XR. If the Image can't open a picture, the ImageFailed event is fired. If loading the image is successful, the ImageOpened event is fired. The Image element can resize the picture to fill the space appropriately. You control this behavior using the Stretch property.

Table 7-2 shows the meanings of different Stretch values.

TABLE 7-2: Stretch Enumeration Values

VALUE	DESCRIPTION
None	The picture is displayed with the original size.
Fill	The picture fills the entire area occupied by the Image element. The original aspect ratio of the picture is not preserved.
Uniform	The picture is resized to fit in the area occupied by the Image element. The original aspect ratio of the picture is preserved.
UniformToFill	The picture fills the entire area occupied by the Image element. The original aspect ratio of the picture is preserved. The picture may be clipped if the aspect ratio of the control and the picture is different.

The TextBlock Element

`TextBlock` is a super-simple element that is designed to display simple text. If you want to display labels, titles, or just simple unformatted text, `TextBlock` can be a good choice. To display more complex formatted text, you should use the `RichTextBlock` control.

Table 7-3 shows the most important properties for the `TextBlock` class.

TABLE 7-3: Important Properties of the TextBlock Class

PROPERTY	DESCRIPTION
Text	The `Text` property represents the text content of the `TextBlock`. The `Text` property accepts simple text or something called `Inlines`. Using `Inlines`, you can add simple formatting to the text content.
TextWrapping	Using the `TextWrapping` enumeration, you can specify whether the text should be wrapped or truncated if there isn't enough horizontal space to display the entire content.
TextTrimming	Using the `TextTrimming` enumeration, you can specify whether the text should be trimmed if there isn't enough space to display the entire content.
IsTextSelectionEnabled	Using the `IsTextSelectionEnabled` property, you can specify whether or not text content can be selected and copied.

The TextBox Control

The `TextBox` control is the primary UI element for simple text input. The `TextBox` control and its functionality are designed in a way to support touchscreen, tablet, and standard PC (mouse and keyboard) scenarios just as well.

Table 7-4 shows the most important properties for the `TextBox` class.

TABLE 7-4: Important Properties of the TextBox Class

PROPERTY	DESCRIPTION
Text	The `Text` property represents the text content of the `TextBox`. The `Text` property accepts simple text.
InputScope	The `InputScope` property determines what kind of keyboard should be presented for touchscreen or tablet scenarios. Consider setting this property often, because it can improve the user experience.
IsSpellCheckEnabled	Using the `IsSpellCheckEnabled` property, you can set whether or not the content of the `TextBox` should be spellchecked.

PROPERTY	DESCRIPTION
IsTextPredictionEnabled	Using the IsTextPredictionEnabled property, you can set whether or not text prediction should be enabled while typing.
SelectedText	Using the SelectedText property, you can get the currently selected text in the TextBox.

In the following code sample, you can see the use of TextBox with InputScope:

```
<TextBox x:Name="InputTextBox" IsTextPredictionEnabled="True">
    <TextBox.InputScope>
        <InputScope>
            <InputScope.Names>
                <InputScopeName NameValue="Url"/>
            </InputScope.Names>
        </InputScope>
    </TextBox.InputScope>
</TextBox>
```

The PasswordBox Control

The PasswordBox control is another text input control, but it is specialized for accepting passwords. The behavior of this control is pretty much the same as what you encounter on the login screen of Windows 8.

Table 7-5 shows the most important properties of the PasswordBox class.

TABLE 7-5: Important Properties of the PasswordBox Class

PROPERTY	DESCRIPTION
Password	The Password property represents content of the control. Using this property, you can get the entered password.
PasswordChar	The PasswordChar property represents the character to display instead of the real characters of the password.
IsPasswordRevealButtonEnabled	Using the IsPasswordRevealButtonEnabled property, you can set whether or not the user can reveal the real characters of the password. This is controlled using a special button on the PasswordBox control.

Displaying Progress with the ProgressBar and ProgressRing Controls

The ProgressBar and ProgressRing controls are both designed to represent a running background process, but they are quite different controls in terms of use.

The ProgressRing control is designed to represent that the screen has something to load. In Windows 8 style applications, you'll see this control pop up whenever the logic behind has to load some data to display on the screen. So, there is an unknown time increment to wait, but the user should be aware that there is something going on in the background. The `ProgressRing` control has one important property: the `IsActive` property. When this property is set to `true`, the `ProgressBar` is displayed; when `false`, it is not visible.

On the other hand, the `ProgressBar` control represents the progress of an operation. Typically, there is a bar that animates a filled area as the progress continues.

Table 7-6 shows the most important properties of the `ProgressBar` class.

TABLE 7-6: Important Properties of the ProgressBar Class

PROPERTY	DESCRIPTION
Minimum	The `Minimum` property represents the minimum possible value for the control.
Maximum	The `Maximum` property represents the maximum possible value for the control.
Value	The `Value` property represents the current value of the control.
IsIndeterminate	Using the `IsIndeterminate` property, you can set the control to display progress when the `Minimum`, `Maximum`, and `Value` property values are not available.

Content Controls

The previous items were controls that did not belong to the family of ContentControls or ItemsControls. In this section we'll discuss the familiy of ContentControls.

The Button Control

The `Button` control is probably the most simple control you can use. It is a `ContentControl`, so the content of the `Button` can be anything (and not just simple text).

One member you should be aware of regarding the `Button` control is the `Click` event. Events are designed in Windows 8 style applications in such way that they respond well for both touchscreen and mouse input. So, handling just the `Click` event will work great for touch-enabled devices and in a standard PC environment as well.

The following code sample demostrates the use of the `Button` control in XAML:

```
<Button Content="Click Me" Click="Button_Click"/>
```

The following code sample demostrates the event handler for the `Click` event in the code-behind file:

```
private void Button_Click(object sender, RoutedEventArgs e)
{
    //TODO insert code here
}
```

The CheckBox and the RadioButton Controls

The CheckBox and the RadioButton controls are two very similar controls, because both represent options to select. The main difference between the controls is that the CheckBox is usually designed to let the user select more than one option, whereas the RadioButton is designed to let the user select only one of many. You can achieve this behavior by setting the GroupName property of the RadioButton, because RadioButtons with the same GroupName value are mutually exclusively selected. Both controls have an IsChecked Boolean property to represent whether or not they are selected.

The following code sample demostrates the use of the RadioButton control:

```
<StackPanel>
    <RadioButton GroupName="Settings" IsChecked="True"/>
    <RadioButton GroupName="Settings"/>
    <RadioButton GroupName="Settings"/>
</StackPanel>
```

The ScrollViewer Control

By defining dynamic layouts, you can prepare yourself for different screen dimensions and resolutions. However, some parts of a screen always need to display more data than the screen can actually display. You can solve this issue by grouping that area into a ScrollViewer control. Types derived from ItemsControl like the ListBox use ScrollViewer internally as well.

Table 7-7 shows the most important properties of the ScrollViewer class.

TABLE 7-7: Important Properties of the ScrollViewer Class

PROPERTY	DESCRIPTION
HorizontalScrollBarVisibility	Using the HorizontalScrollBarVisibility property, you can set whether the horizontal ScrollBar is always visible, never, or only when needed.
VerticalScrollBarVisibility	Using the VerticalScrollBarVisibility property, you can set whether the vertical ScrollBar is always visible, never, or only when needed.

The ToggleSwitch Control

As its name suggests, the ToggleSwitch control is a simple switch. It has two states: On and Off. You can find a lot of ToggleSwitch controls on the Control Panel of Windows 8.

Table 7-8 shows the most important properties of the ToggleSwitch class.

TABLE 7-8: Important Properties of the ToggleSwitch Class

PROPERTY	DESCRIPTION
IsOn	The IsOn property determines whether the switch state is On or Off.
OnContent	The OnContent property determines what to display when the control is in the On state.
OffContent	The OffContent property determines what to display when the control is in the Off state.

The following code sample demostrates the use of the ToggleSwitch class:

```
<ToggleSwitch OnContent="It's on" OffContent="It's Off" IsOn="True"/>
```

In the next exercise, you create a simple UI to display the details for a football player.

TRY IT OUT Using Basic Controls to Build the User Interface

In this exercise, you create the Details view for a player, and also create a ListBox for the list of players:

1. Open the previous project or you can open the SimpleControlsDemo - Start solution.

2. Select the StackPanel on the right. On the Properties window, name the panel **detailsPanel**.

3. From the Toolbox, add a TextBlock, an Image, and another TextBlock to the StackPanel, in this order, either by dragging and dropping, or by double-clicking each item.

4. Switch to the XAML editor by clicking the XAML tab on the bottom of the designer area.

5. Find the detailsPanel.

6. Replace its current content with the following code:

```
<TextBlock x:Name="txtTitle" HorizontalAlignment="Left" TextWrapping="Wrap"
    Text="This is a placeholder for Title" FontSize="32"/>
<Image x:Name="playerPhoto" HorizontalAlignment="Center" Height="150" Width="200"
    Margin="0,20,0,20"/>
<TextBlock x:Name="txtContent" HorizontalAlignment="Stretch" TextWrapping="Wrap"
    Text="This is a placeholder for the biography"/>
```

7. Switch back to the Designer view.

8. From the Toolbox, select the ListBox control.

9. Draw a ListBox exactly over the Rectangle.

10. Name the new ListBox **lboxPlayers**.

11. Press F5 to run the application. You should see the result shown in Figure 7-13.

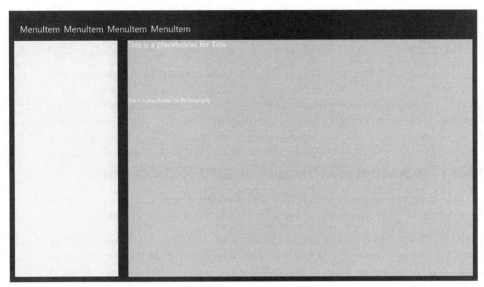

FIGURE 7-13: Completed user interface

How It Works

You have many ways to add controls to the UI. You can select a target and double-click the New Item option, or you can use drag and drop. Selecting the item to be added and then drawing it on the designer surface works just as well.

Adding three controls to the `StackPanel` arranges them automatically according to the `Orientation` property, which, by default, is set to `Vertical`.

Adding a `Margin` to the image creates some whitespace between the controls.

You can switch back and forth between the Designer and the XAML Editor view. If you want to see both areas, you can choose the split option. In this exercise, you used a mixed approach to set the properties. You can choose whether you prefer the designer-friendly approach, or if you prefer typing code directly in XAML.

WORKING WITH DATA

Most of time, you want to display data on your UI and accept user input, then write it back into your data model. Without *data binding*, you would be required to manage a lot of plumbing code.

For example, say you have a `TextBox` that represents the `FirstName` of a `Person` object. Say that you want to update the value of the `FirstName` property whenever the `Text` property of the `TextBox` changes. You must subscribe to the `TextChanged` event of the `TextBox` and update the `FirstName` property on the `Person` instance manually.

The opposite approach is just as cumbersome. Whenever the FirstName property changes, you must update the Text property of TextBox manually. If you have more controls on the UI displaying the same FirstName property, you must update all of them manually.

With data binding, you can forget about all of this. The data-binding mechanism can serve as a glue between the properties of the controls and the data objects. In the previous example, you could bind the Text property of TextBox to the FirstName property of the Person instance. Whenever one side's value changes, the other side gets notified and updated automatically, saving you from writing a lot of additional code to keep the two sides synchronized.

Data Binding Dependency Properties and Notifications

There is one important rule of data binding. The target property of the data binding must be a dependency property, and the target object must be derived from the DependencyObject class.

Figure 7-14 shows the concept of binding. Most of the time, you don't have to worry about this constraint, because most of the properties defined on controls are all dependency properties, and all controls are derived from the DependencyObject class.

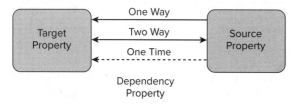

FIGURE 7-14: Data binding between objects

You can define data binding either declaratively in XAML, or imperatively in code using the Binding class. The Binding class has a number of useful properties that provide more control over the binding mechanism. Table 7-9 shows the most important properties.

TABLE 7-9: Important Properties of the Binding Class

PROPERTY	DESCRIPTION
Path	The Path property specifies the source property you want to bind to. This could be any public property.
Mode	Using the Mode property, you can specify a BindingMode that determines the direction of the binding. You can learn more about this in the, "Binding Modes and Directions," section later in this chapter.
Source	The Source property specifies the class instance you want to bind to.
ElementName	You can also define bindings between different controls on the UI. The ElementName property references the source control by its Name property.
Converter	This property accepts an IValueConverter instance that can serve as a proxy between incompatible properties.

The following code demonstrates the use of data binding in XAML. A `Person` instance is added to the `Resources` section of a `Grid`. The `Text` property of `TextBox` is bound to the `FirstName` property of the `Person`. The source object is specified using the `Source` property on the `Binding` object, and the source property is specified using the `Path` property.

```
<Grid x:Name="LayoutRoot">
    <Grid.Resources>
        <local:Person x:Key="personData"/>
    </Grid.Resources>

    <TextBox Text="{Binding Path=FirstName, Source={StaticResource personData}}"/>
</Grid>
```

> **NOTE** You can omit the `Path` keyword if the first parameter on the `Binding` is the source property you want to bind to.

The main feature of data binding is that whenever the source property notifies the `Binding` object about changes, it updates the target property. However, sending notifications about the changes of the source property is not the responsibility of the `Binding` object. This must be performed by the object containing the source property.

The notification mechanism is built on an interface called `INotifyPropertyChanged`. This interface defines a single event called `PropertyChanged`. The source object must implement this interface and fire the `PropertyChanged` event whenever the source property changes. The following code demonstrates the implementation of this interface:

```
public class Person : INotifyPropertyChanged
{
    private string firstName;

    public string FirstName
    {
        get { return firstName; }
        set
        {
            firstName = value;
            RaisePropertyChanged("FirstName");
        }
    }

    private string lastName;

    public string LastName
    {
        get { return lastName; }
        set
        {
            lastName = value;
            RaisePropertyChanged("LastName");
        }
    }
}
```

```
        // Helper method the raise the event
        protected void RaisePropertyChanged(string propertyName)
        {
            if (PropertyChanged != null)
                PropertyChanged(this, new PropertyChangedEventArgs(propertyName));
        }

        public event PropertyChangedEventHandler PropertyChanged;
    }
```

Binding Modes and Directions

When you create a binding, you can specify the binding direction. Using the `Mode` property, you can choose between the following three binding modes:

➤ **OneWay** — This option ensures that the binding updates the target object whenever it gets a change notification from the source property. Changing the value of the target property has no effect on the source property.

➤ **TwoWay** — This option ensures that the binding synchornizies both the target and source properties whenever it gets a change notification from any of them.

➤ **OneTime** — This option is very similar to the `OneWay` mode, except that it only updates the target property immediately after the binding happens. However, after that, it stops monitoring the changes. Most of the time, you don't need to use this option. However, in some exceptional cases, this could help to improve performance.

The following code demonstrates the use of `TwoWay` bindings:

```
<TextBox Text="{Binding Path=FirstName, Source={StaticResource personData},
    Mode=TwoWay}"/>
```

The DataContext Property

Another imporant property that is substantial in the data-binding mechanism is called `DataContext`. The `DataContext` property is defined with an option called *property value inheritance*. This means that if you build a UI structure and you set the `DataContext` property on a `FrameworkElement`, all its children and descendants in the visual tree automatically inherit the value of the `DataContext`.

For example, if you have a `Grid` panel containing a list of controls setting the `DataContext` on the panel, `DataContext` for all of the controls would be set to the value of the parent panel's `DataContext` property.

The following code demonstrates this scenario:

```
<Grid x:Name="LayoutRoot">
    <Grid.Resources>
        <local:Person x:Key="personData"/>
    </Grid.Resources>

    <StackPanel DataContext="{StaticResource personData}">
```

```
            <TextBox Text="{Binding Path=FirstName, Mode=TwoWay}"/>
            <TextBox Text="{Binding Path=LastName, Mode=TwoWay}"/>
        </StackPanel>
    </Grid>
```

The binding on the TextBox control doesn't need to reference the source anymore, because DataContext of the parent StackPanel is referencing it instead. The TextBox is a child of the StackPanel, so it inherits the DataContext, which means that the binding will get the source object from the inherited DataContext value.

Changing the Data in the Binding Pipeline Using Value Converters

Describing the binding as a glue between the target and the source properties indicates how tight this connection is. As a matter of fact, thinking about binding as a pipeline mechanism would be more appropriate.

Sometimes you need to have better control over this pipeline. As an example, think about building a UI that displays currency rates with changes in percentage. If the percantage is positive, you could use green as the foregound color of the font displaying the value. If it is negative, you could display the value in red.

The data object you want to bind to has a Change property of type Double that represents the change in percentage. In this case, you must bind the Foreground color property to the Change property directly. A Color to Double binding doesn't seem to make much sense. Luckily, there is a transformation step in the data-binding pipeline. It's called *value conversion*. Using *converters*, you can inject some custom code to transform one value to a different value or type.

Converters are classes implementing the IValueConverter interface. The interface defines two methods:

➤ Convert is called when reading the source property's value.

➤ ConvertBack is called when writing back the value of the target property into the source property.

The following code demonstrates the implementation of an IValueConverter. If the price is more than 9.99, the Foreground of the TextBlock property should be red; otherwise, it should be green. Converting a color back to a price value doesn't really make sense, so the ConvertBack method is not implemented. The converter can be added as a resource and be referenced later by the binding with the Converter parameter of the Binding class.

```
// Value converter class
public class PriceToColorConverter : IValueConverter
{
    public object Convert(object value, string typeName, object parameter,
        string language)
    {
        var price = (double)value;
```

```
            if (price > 9.99) return Colors.Red;
            else return Colors.Green;
        }

        public object ConvertBack(object value, string typeName, object parameter,
            string language)
        {
            throw new NotImplementedException();
        }
    }
}
```

You can use this converter from XAML, as shown here:

```
<Grid x:Name="LayoutRoot">
    <Grid.Resources>
        <!-- ... -->
        <local:PriceToColorConverter x:Key="priceConverter"/>
    </Grid.Resources>

    <StackPanel DataContext="{StaticResource salesData}">
        <TextBlock Foreground="{Binding Path=Price,
            Converter={StaticResource priceConverter}}"
                Text="{Binding Path=Price}"/>
    </StackPanel>
</Grid>
```

The previous code sample uses a `PriceToColorConverter` to ensure that the `TextBlock`'s foreground is painted with the appropriate color according to the value of price. The converter is placed into the resources section of the grid, and is referenced by an XML namespace named `local`. The "local" prefix is mapped to the CLR namespace of the `PriceToColorConverter` class.

The `Convert` and `ConvertBack` methods support other parameters in addition to the value:

➤ **typeName** — Type of the target property for which you want to convert the data.

➤ **Parameter** — You can add a converter parameter in the binding mechanism when using converters. You can use this property for any converter logic you want.

➤ **Language** — This is the language of the conversion. Some conversion logic might be specific to a language and region. You can use this parameter to decide what kind of logic to apply.

Binding to Collections

Most of the time, you will have to deal with lists of data. `ItemsControls` are designed to display and visualize any collection of data. So, if you have a data source with a collection, you can easily data bind to it. As easy as it may seem, there is a little catch.

Your data can change at any time, and the UI (in this case, the `ItemsControl`) should be aware of any changes made to its source collection. You notify a `Binding` about a property change by using the `PropertyChanged` event of the `INotifyPropertyChanged` interface. The same logic applies to changing collections, except that this time, the collection must implement the `INotifyCollectionChanged` interface and fire the `CollectionChanged` event on every single change.

You should know that simple collections like the generic `List` do not implement this functionality. However, there is a new collection called `ObservableCollection` that was designed with this behavior in mind. So, every time you bind a collection to the `ItemsSource` property of an `ItemsControl`, you should ensure that the collection is an `ObservableCollection`.

In the next exercise, you create a very simple master-details scenario where you can explore binding to collections and displaying details.

TRY IT OUT   **Simple Master-Details Scenario**

In this exercise, you populate a `ListBox` with a list of players, and bind the details view and its controls that represent the selected player's data.

1. Open the previous project, or you can open the `DataBindingDemo - Start` project from this book's downloadable code at www.wrox.com.

2. On the Solutions Explorer window, right-click Project and select the Add Class option.

3. Name the file **Player.cs**.

4. Add the following code to the `Player` class:

```
public class Player : INotifyPropertyChanged
{
    private string playerName;

    public string PlayerName
    {
        get { return playerName; }
        set
        {
            playerName = value;
            RaisePropertyChanged("PlayerName");
        }
    }

    private string photoUrl;

    public string PhotoUrl
    {
        get { return photoUrl; }
        set
        {
            photoUrl = value;
            RaisePropertyChanged("PhotoUrl");
        }
    }

    private string biography;

    public string Biography
    {
        get { return biography; }
        set
        {
```

```
            biography = value;
            RaisePropertyChanged("Biography");
        }
    }

    protected void RaisePropertyChanged(string propertyName)
    {
        if (PropertyChanged != null)
            PropertyChanged(this, new PropertyChangedEventArgs(propertyName));
    }
    public event PropertyChangedEventHandler PropertyChanged;
}
```

5. Add another class named **PlayerDataSource.cs** to the project.

6. Add the following code to the PlayerDataSource class:

```
public class PlayerDataSource
{
    public PlayerDataSource()
    {
        LoadPlayers();
    }

    private ObservableCollection<Player> players;

    public ObservableCollection<Player> Players
    {
        get { return players; }
        set { players = value; }
    }


    private void LoadPlayers()
    {
        players = new ObservableCollection<Player>
        {
            new Player
            {
                PlayerName = "Sample Player 1",
                PhotoUrl = "/Assets/Player1Photo.jpg",
                Biography = "Sample Biography"
            },
            new Player
            {
                PlayerName = "Sample Player 2",
                PhotoUrl = "/Assets/Player2Photo.jpg",
                Biography = "Sample Biography"
            }
        };
    }
}
```

7. On the Document Outline window, click the root Grid panel.

8. Open the Properties window and find the DataContext property.

9. Click the New button. On the Select Object dialog box, select the `PlayerDataSource` class. Click the OK button.

10. Click the `ListBox` and on the Properties window. Find the `ItemsSource` property, and click Advanced Properties. Select Create Data Binding. From the Path window, select `Players` and click the OK button.

11. Click the `Details` panel and find the `DataContext` property.

12. Click Advance Properties and select Create Data Binding.

13. Change the `Binding Type` to Element Name.

14. From the Element Name TreeView select the `ListBox`.

15. From the Path TreeView, select the `SelectedItem` property.

16. Click the OK Button.

17. Click `txtTile`, find the `Text` property in the Properties window,. and select Advanced Properties. Choose Create Data Binding and select the `PlayerName` property from the Path TreeView. Click the OK button.

18. Click `playerPhoto`, find the `Source` property in the Properties window, and select Advanced Properties. Choose Create Data Binding and select the `PhotoIUrl` property from the Path TreeView. Click the OK button.

19. Click `txtContent`, find the `Text` property in the Properties window, and select Advanced Properties. Choose Create Data Binding and select the `Biography` property from the Path TreeView. Click the OK button.

20. Press F5 to run the application.

How It Works

The `Player` class implements the `INotifyPropertyChanged` interface every time a property of the `PropertyChanged` event is fired. This way, if any data changes inside this class, the binding is notified, and it can update the UI.

The `PlayerDataSource` class defines a `Players` collection of type `ObservableCollection<Player>`. This collection is ready to notify the binding if there is a change inside the collection.

By assigning the `PlayerDataSource` as the `DataContext` of the main `Grid` panel, the entire page and all the controls inside it inherit the `PlayerDataSource` as `DataContext`.

The `ListBox` is bound to the `Players` collection, which is located in the `DataContext`. (Remember the `DataContext` right now is the `PlayerDataSource`.)

With *UI-to-UI binding*, the `DataContext` of `detailsPanel` is bound to the `SelectedItem` of the `ListBox`. So, whenever the selected item changes in the `ListBox` the `DataContext` of the `detailsPane` is updated. This means that the `DataContext` of the `detailsPanel` is always a `Player` instance.

The controls inside the `detailsPanel` are bound to the properties of a player. Because the `DataContext` of the `detailsPanel` is a `Player`, the controls inside share the same `Player` instance as their `DataContext`.

Whenever the `ListBox`'s `SelectedItem` changes, the contents of the `detailsPanel` are updated automatically through the binding engine.

SUMMARY

You can develop Windows 8 style applications using XAML-based solutions. XAML provides a declarative way to describe the UI.

A new and very flexible control model has been introduced to fit the needs of new-generation UIs. The new control model enables you to customize the UI and the controls any way you want.

Among the new concepts, a new layout management system was introduced that is based on panels. Many panels are implemented to fit the developer's needs, such as `Grid`, `StackPanel`, `Canvas`, and `VariableSizedWrapGrid`.

You can use a powerful data-binding engine to tie your data objects and your UI together. Simple objects and collections are also supported. The bindings are updated automatically if the models notify the binding about changes using the `INotifyPropertyChanged` and the `INotifyCollectionChanged` interfaces.

In Chapter 8, you learn about more complex controls that can handle a large amount of data and represent them in various ways. You also learn about other important UI concepts, such as animations and the templating engine that enables you to customize the controls and the visual representation of the data.

EXERCISES

1. How can you share a predefined brush within the application?

2. How can you notify a binding about changes of the source property?

3. Which panel enables you to position its elements freely using relative coordinates?

4. How can you ensure that there will be some whitespace between elements inside a `StackPanel`?

5. How does a binding update a `ListBox` when the underlying collection changes?

6. How can you ensure that a binding updates both the source and the target properties as well?

> **NOTE** *You can find answers to the exercises in Appendix A.*

▶ **WHAT YOU LEARNED IN THIS CHAPTER**

TOPIC	KEY CONCEPTS
eXtensible Application Markup Language (XAML)	XAML is an XML-based language that you can use to describe the user interface (UI) declaratively. It provides great support for designer tools, and allows developers to separate the UI from code.
`StaticResource`	You can share resources in an application on many levels to reuse them at any point. Most of the time, you share styles, colors, brushes, and converters. You can reference these objects in XAML using the `StaticResource` property.
Panels	The layout system is built on top of panels. Panels are responsible for arranging their own children according to certain logic. Panels are a powerful tool used to build complex UIs.
Data binding	Using data binding, you can represent a "live connection" between two objects. Whenever an object is changed, the other object is synchronized as well. Most of the time, you bind UI control properties to data object properties.
`INotifyPropertyChanged`	To update a binding, it must be notified about changes. You can do this by firing the `PropertyChanged` event defined in the `INotifyPropertyChanged` interface. So, you must ensure that the source object containing the source property implements this interface.
`ObservableCollection`	Just like simple objects, collections must notify the binding about collection changes. In the case of collections, this happens using the `CollectionChanged` event defined in the `INotifyCollectionChanged` interface. `ObservableCollection` implements this interface.
`DataContext`	`FrameworkElement`s define a property called `DataContext`. This is a special property, because its value is inherited by the child elements inside the `FrameworkElement`. As its name suggests, if you set this property to a data object, every element in the visual tree under this object will also inherit that value, which means they'll share the same context of data.
Converters	The binding mechanism enables you to bind two properties together that have completely different types. To ensure that these bindings make sense and work, you can add a converter to the binding pipeline.
`BindingMode`	Using `BindingMode`, you can specify the direction of updates. `OneWay` bindings only update the target, whereas `TwoWay` bindings can update the source as well.

continues

TOPIC	KEY CONCEPTS
ContentControl	This is the simplest type of control. `ContentControl`s have a `Content` property that represents the inner visual content of the controls. The property is of type `object`, so you can add anything to it.
ItemsControl	`ItemsControl`s represent visual lists. You can add any type of items within the collection and the `ItemsControl` will display it. This is the base class for every list-based control in the framework.

Working with XAML Controls

WHAT YOU WILL LEARN IN THIS CHAPTER:

➤ Understanding and creating animations and transitions in Windows 8 style applications

➤ Understanding and applying transformations

➤ Understanding how to change the visual look of controls

➤ Getting acquainted with Microsoft Expression Blend

➤ Getting acquainted with the powerful Windows 8 style-specific complex controls

WROX.COM CODE DOWNLOADS FOR THIS CHAPTER

You can find the wrox.com code downloads for this chapter on the Download Code tab at www.wrox.com/remtitle.cgi?isbn=012680. The code is in the Chapter8.zip download and individually named, as described in the corresponding exercises.

In this chapter, you learn some more exciting features of Windows 8 style applications that enable you to create more stunning user experiences. This chapter begins with a look at how to create animations using the Animation Library, and how to create custom animations. You also learn about important concepts such as transformations, visual customization, and a tool called Microsoft Expression Blend. By the end of this chapter, you'll have learned how to create a custom visual experience for your user interface (UI), and will be familiar with how to present complex controls in Windows 8 style applications.

USING ANIMATIONS IN YOUR APPLICATION

Animations can make your UI come alive. With carefully designed animations, you can make your application look fast, fluid, and responsive. Additionally, animations can help the user learn how to use your application much faster. For example, when you add a new item to a list, the new item animates into its place (instead of just simply popping up in the list control), while other items animate to a new position. Your UI ensures that the new item has enough room to display. These small (but meaningful) animations can help the user understand the performed action much more easily.

Although animations can add great value to your application, they also should be carefully designed. Animations and transitions should be consistent throughout the application and the operating system. They also should be smooth, fast, and fluid. Stuttering animations can be really disappointing.

When building Windows 8 style applications, you can choose from two different types of animations:

➤ **Dependent animations** — If you create custom animations, there's a good chance that they'll run as dependent animations. Dependent animations run on the UI thread. The UI thread is often busy with handling user input or with some drawing logic, so it might not be able to produce a consistent frame rate for your animations, thus making them stutter a little.

➤ **Independent animations** — Independent animations run independently from the UI thread. The work is offloaded from the CPU to the graphics processing unit (GPU). GPUs are optimized hardware units to deliver beautiful, rich graphics at a consistent frame rate. This means that if you want to have smooth and glitch-free animations, you should use independent animations, because they will perform much better.

> **NOTE** *Diving deeper into the inner workings of independent animations is out of the scope of this book. However, to learn more about creating custom independent animations, see the article at* `http://msdn.microsoft.com/en-us/library/windows/apps/hh994638.aspx`.

One way to make sure you are using an independent animation that is consistent with other Windows 8 style applications is to use the Animation Library.

Animation Library

The Animation Library contains a set of predefined animations that are high-performing, smooth, and consistent with the look and feel of Windows animations. You don't have to worry about making them fast and fluid, or even consistent. They are already taking advantage of the platform's independent animation capability, and are used throughout the Windows operating system UI. Think of the Animation Library as a palette of animations that you can use whenever you want, and are already adjusted to the requirements of a great Windows 8 style UI.

The Application Library supports two types of animations:

➤ **Theme transitions** — These transitions are triggered automatically by the layout system. They are triggered in response to the changes of the active layout of the page. These are typically animations used to provide visuals for loading, unloading, or changing the location of objects.

➤ **Theme animations** — These animations are triggered manually from code, and you can specify a target for the animations.

Theme Transitions

Theme transitions are a great way to create simple animations that won't annoy the user of your application, while still making it attractive and likeable. Typically, you'll apply theme transitions to animate the adding, removing, or reordering of items, or the changing of the content of controls. The following code snippet demonstrates the use of a transition called `EntranceThemeTransition`:

```
<Button Content="Animated Button" HorizontalAlignment="Center">
    <Button.Transitions>
        <TransitionCollection>
            <EntranceThemeTransition/>
        </TransitionCollection>
    </Button.Transitions>
</Button>
```

By using this code snippet, you can animate a button to slide into its place, instead of just appearing when it is rendered for the first time. As you can see from the code snippet, you can apply more than one transition to a `UIElement`. Actually, you can have as many as you want (provided that doing so makes sense to the user).

Some transitions provide a certain degree of customization by enabling you to set a couple of properties on the transition. Customization should be performed with great care, because these transitions are designed to be simple, easy to use, and, most importantly, consistent.

The previous sample code snippet is not that interesting, because it applies only to a single `Button` control. The real fun starts when you start to apply these transitions to containers of other elements. In the following code sample, the transition is defined on the panel:

```
<WrapGrid>
    <WrapGrid.ChildrenTransitions>
        <TransitionCollection>
            <EntranceThemeTransition/>
            <RepositionThemeTransition/>
        </TransitionCollection>
    </WrapGrid.ChildrenTransitions>
    <Rectangle Fill="Red" Width="100" Height="100" Margin="10"/>
    <Rectangle Fill="Red" Width="100" Height="100" Margin="10"/>
    <Rectangle Fill="Red" Width="100" Height="100" Margin="10"/>
    <Rectangle Fill="Red" Width="100" Height="100" Margin="10"/>
    <Rectangle Fill="Red" Width="100" Height="100" Margin="10"/>
```

```
        <Rectangle Fill="Red" Width="100" Height="100" Margin="10"/>
        <Rectangle Fill="Red" Width="100" Height="100" Margin="10"/>
        <Rectangle Fill="Red" Width="100" Height="100" Margin="10"/>
        <Rectangle Fill="Red" Width="100" Height="100" Margin="10"/>
    </WrapGrid>
```

Every child contained in the `WrapGrid` panel slides into its place when first rendered. This is achieved by using `EntranceThemeTransition`. `RepositionThemeTransition` ensures that whenever you add or remove a child element, the rest are repositioned and slide into their new places with a smooth and nice animation.

When using a complex control like a `GridView` or a `ListView` (which you learn more about later in this chapter), you don't have to worry about configuring transitions. These controls are designed to support them by default.

Table 8-1 describes the supported transitions.

TABLE 8-1: Supported Theme Transitions

THEME TRANSITION	DESCRIPTION
AddDeleteThemeTransition	Animates the transition for item additions or removals. Typically applied to item containers.
ContentThemeTransition	Animates the transitions when the content of a control is changing.
EntranceThemeTransition	Provides the transition when an item is first displayed.
ReorderThemeTransition	Provides the transition when the order of the items changes in a list control. Typically used with drag and drop.
RepositionThemeTransition	Provides the transition when controls are repositioned to a new location.

Theme Animations and Storyboards

Theme transitions are a great way to create simple animations, but you may need more control over the animation process while still being consistent with Windows operating system animations.

Storyboards are objects that can control multiple animations. You can think of storyboards like having a video player. You can start, stop, pause, resume, and seek animations using a storyboard. You will need to write code using event handlers to control a `Storyboard` object. Storyboards also support targets. This means that when you add an animation to a storyboard, you can set a target for the animation. The target represents the object that should be animated.

The following code snippet demonstrates the use of theme animations with storyboards:

```
<Grid>
    <Grid.Resources>
        <Storyboard x:Name="hideStoryboard">
```

```
                    <FadeOutThemeAnimation Storyboard.TargetName="targetRectangle"  />
            </Storyboard>
        </Grid.Resources>
        <Rectangle x:Name="targetRectangle" PointerPressed="Rectangle_Tapped"
            Fill="Blue" Width="200" Height="300" />
    </Grid>
```

Let's take a closer look at this code sample. The `Grid` panel contains a single blue rectangle. The `PointerPressed` event is handled on the rectangle. The event handler looks like the following:

```
private void Rectangle_Tapped(object sender, PointerRoutedEventArgs e)
{
    hideStoryboard.Begin();
}
```

This code ensures that whenever a user clicks or taps on the rectangle, the `Storyboard` called `hideStoryboard` is started.

This storyboard contains a single animation called `FadeOutThemeAnimation`, which, as the name suggests, is a theme animation, and is responsible for a smooth fade-out animation to hide the target element. On the animation object, the target object is defined by setting the `Storyboard` `.TargetName` attached property. The value of this property is set to the value of the `Name` property of the targeted `UIElement`.

NOTE *Attached properties are described in more detail in Chapter 7.*

This means that whenever a user taps or clicks the rectangle, a fade-out animation is applied to the rectangle.

Table 8-2 describes some of the supported theme animations.

TABLE 8-2: Most Important Supported Theme Animations

THEME ANIMATION	DESCRIPTION
FadeInThemeAnimation	Opacity animation for controls on first appearance.
FadeOutThemeAnimation	Opacity animation for controls that are removed or hidden from the UI.
PopInThemeAnimation	Translation and opacity animation for UI components as they appear. This is a pop-up-like animation.
PopOutThemeAnimation	Translation and opacity animation for UI components as they are closed with a pop-up-like animation.
TapUpThemeAnimation	Animation that runs just after an element is tapped.
TapDownThemeAnimation	Animation that runs when an element is tapped.

As you can see, you'll most likely need quite a few supported animations to build stunning and exciting UIs. You should remember that using animations and transitions from the Animation Library guarantees that the animation will be an independent animation.

Getting to Know Visual States

An additional (and really useful) feature of animations is called *visual states*. Visual states are meant to describe the visual state of the view, and the transitions between different states of the view. Visual states use simple storyboard objects to describe the states and transitions. A good example is the states defined in the Button control. The Button control has pressed states and mouse-over states, among many others.

The following code snippet demonstrates the use of visual states:

```
<Grid x:Name="mainGrid">
    <VisualStateManager.VisualStateGroups>
        <VisualStateGroup x:Name="VisibilityGroup">
            <VisualState x:Name="Visible">
                <Storyboard>
                    <FadeInThemeAnimation Storyboard.TargetName=
                        "targetRectangle"  />
                </Storyboard>
            </VisualState>
            <VisualState x:Name="Hidden">
                <Storyboard>
                    <FadeOutThemeAnimation Storyboard.TargetName=
                        "targetRectangle"  />
                </Storyboard>
            </VisualState>
        </VisualStateGroup>
    </VisualStateManager.VisualStateGroups>

    <Rectangle x:Name="targetRectangle" Fill="Blue" Width="200" Height="300" />
</Grid>
```

As you can see, a visual state contains storyboards to represent the state of the control. You can define visual states any time. Visual states must be placed into VisualStateGroups. Your control can be only in one state at a same time inside a VisualStateGroup, but it can be in two or more states if all states are located in a different VisualStateGroup.

The previous code sample defines two different states in the same group. The group is called VisibilityGroup, and it contains the Visible and the Hidden states. You can change states from code using the GoToState() method of the VisualStateManager class. The following code sample demonstrates how to change that current visual state:

```
VisualStateManager.GoToState(this, "Hidden", true);
```

The first parameter of the GoToState method is the control that contains the visual state. In this case, you can specify this as the control, which is a reference to the current Page control. The second parameter of the GoToState method is the name of the visual state to which you want to switch. The third and final parameter is a boolean value to decide whether or not you want to use *visual transitions*. Visual transitions are a more advanced concept of visual state management. They are meant to differentiate animations between state changes based on the original and the new target visual states. `true` means to use transitions when available.

> **NOTE** *You can read more about visual transitions at* `http://msdn.microsoft` `.com/en-us/library/windows/apps/windows.ui.xaml.visualtransition` `.aspx`.

By setting a visual state, the contained storyboard is started automatically. There is no need to start it manually. In this case, if you switch to the `Visible` state, a `FadeInThemeAnimation` is used to display the `targetRectangle`. If you switch to `Hidden` state, a `FadeOutThemeAnimation` is used to hide the `targetRectangle`.

Visual states are a great way to define multiple states for your views. For example, you could define two different visual states for a page based on the logged-in state of the user.

In the following exercise, you apply animations from the Animation Library to create a nice visual and smooth experience.

> **NOTE** *You can find the complete code to download for this exercise on this book's companion website at* `www.wrox.com` *in the* `AnimationLibraryDemo` *folder.*

TRY IT OUT   Using the Animation Library

In this exercise, you use `EntranceThemeTransition`, `AddDeleteThemeTransition`, and `RepositionThemeTransition` to animate item additions and removals in a panel.

1. Create a new project using the Blank App (XAML) template.

2. Open `MainPage.xaml`.

3. Locate the `Grid` inside the `Page` control and add a `VariableSizedWrapGrid` named **itemsContainer** inside the `Grid`, as shown here:

```
<VariableSizedWrapGrid x:Name="itemsContainer"/>
```

4. Add two buttons above the `itemsContainer`:

```
<StackPanel Orientation="Horizontal" HorizontalAlignment="Center"
        VerticalAlignment="Top">
  <Button Content="Add"/>
  <Button Content="Remove" Margin="0,0,0,0"/>
</StackPanel>
<VariableSizedWrapGrid x:Name="itemsContainer" Margin="0,50,0,0"/>
```

5. Subscribe to the `Click` events of the buttons:

```
<Button x:Name="btnAdd" Content="Add" Click="btnAdd_Click_1"/>
<Button x:Name="btnRemove" Content="Remove" Click="btnRemove_Click_1"
    Margin="8,0,0,0"/>
```

6. Open `MainPage.xaml.cs` and locate the `OnNavigatedTo` method. Place code inside it to add 20 red rectangles to the `itemContainer`. Each rectangle should be 100 pixels wide and 100 pixels tall, and should have a margin of 8 pixels on each side, as shown here:

```
protected override void OnNavigatedTo(NavigationEventArgs e)
{
    for (int i = 0; i < 20; i++)
    {
        var rectangle = new Rectangle();
        rectangle.Width = 100;
        rectangle.Height = 100;
        rectangle.Fill = new SolidColorBrush(Colors.Red);
        rectangle.Margin = new Thickness(8);
        itemsContainer.Children.Add(rectangle);
    }
}
```

7. Add code to the `btnAdd`'s event handler to add new rectangles:

```
private void btnAdd_Click_1(object sender, RoutedEventArgs e)
{
    itemsContainer.Children.Add(new Rectangle
    {
        Width = 100,
        Height = 100,
        Fill = new SolidColorBrush(Colors.Red),
        Margin = new Thickness(8)
    });
}
```

8. Add code to the `btnRemove`'s event handler to remove the second rectangle:

```
private void btnRemove_Click_1(object sender, RoutedEventArgs e)
{
    itemsContainer.Children.RemoveAt(1);
}
```

9. Press F5 to run the application.

10. Click the Add and Remove buttons. Observe the behavior of the items.

11. Switch back to Visual Studio 2012 and stop debugging by pressing Shift+F5.

12. Add animation for the first appearance, as shown here:

```
<VariableSizedWrapGrid x:Name="itemsContainer">
    <VariableSizedWrapGrid.ChildrenTransitions>
        <TransitionCollection>
            <EntranceThemeTransition/>
        </TransitionCollection>
    </VariableSizedWrapGrid.ChildrenTransitions>
</VariableSizedWrapGrid>
```

13. Press F5 to run the application. Observe the behavior of items at start.

14. Click the Add and Remove buttons. Observe the behavior of the items.

15. Switch back to Visual Studio 2012 and stop debugging by pressing Shift+F5.

16. Add animation for item removal, addition, and reposition by adding the following code:

```
<VariableSizedWrapGrid x:Name="itemsContainer">
    <VariableSizedWrapGrid.ChildrenTransitions>
        <TransitionCollection>
            <EntranceThemeTransition/>
            <AddDeleteThemeTransition/>
            <RepositionThemeTransition/>
        </TransitionCollection>
    </VariableSizedWrapGrid.ChildrenTransitions>
</VariableSizedWrapGrid>
```

17. Click the Add and Remove buttons. Observe the behavior of the items.

18. Press F5 to run the application.

How It Works

In the first couple of steps, you build the layout (as you should be used to doing by now). The interesting part of this exercise starts at Step 6. The OnNavigatedTo method runs when you navigate to the page. At start, the MainPage is the first page to be opened, so as navigation takes place, the OnNavigatedTo method is invoked.

In Step 6, from code, you add 20 rectangles with 100 × 100 dimensions. The rectangles are filled with a SolidColorBrush, which is created with a red color. Then you create some whitespace between the elements using the Margin property. As soon as the rectangle is ready, you add it to the itemsContainer, which is the VariableSizedWrapGrid panel.

In Steps 7 and 8, the btnAdd_Click_1 event handler adds a new rectangle with the same parameters. The btnRemove_Click_1 event handler removes the second rectangle from the Children collection of the itemsContainer.

When you run the application for the first time, there is no animation, and no visual hint as to what is really happening.

In Step 12, you add the EntranceThemeTransition. When you run the application, you'll see that the rectangles animate to their places with a smooth slide animation. However, item removals, additions, and repositions are still not animated.

Finally, in Step 16, you add the AddDeleteThemeTransition (which animates the new item when it is added, and animates the old item when it is removed), and the RepositionThemeTransition (which rearranges the items located after the removed item).

When you run the application, you see that the item removals and additions are now animated. Figure 8-1 shows the result.

FIGURE 8-1: Animation during repositioning after item removal

It is that easy to light up your UI with simple, consistent, and smooth animations from the Animation Library.

Custom Animations

The Animation Library is really useful and quite powerful, but it can't cover every possible animation scenario. If you want to create an animation that cannot be done with a theme animation or theme transition, you should create your own custom animation.

In most cases, custom animations are dependent animations. This means that you should use them with care. With custom animations, you have the freedom to create any kind of animation you want. You can animate any property that is a dependency property.

> **NOTE** *Dependency properties are described in detail in Chapter 7.*

Following are some common animation types for which you can use animation classes to animate different types of properties:

➤ **DoubleAnimation** — DoubleAnimation is great to animate properties of type double. For example, you could animate an Opacity property, or a double property of a transformation object (such as rotation).

➤ **ColorAnimation** — ColorAnimation is a simple way to change the color of objects when something happens. For example, you could animate to a much lighter color to represent a highlighted item.

➤ `ObjectAnimation` — Sometimes objects have a somewhat more complex property that should be changed using animations. The most common usage of this type of animation is to hide and show controls using the `Visibility` enumeration.

> **NOTE** *Other types of animations exist, such as animations using key frames and animations using easing functions. Covering all types of animations is out of the scope of this book. If you are interested in creating more complex animations, you should read the article at* http://msdn.microsoft.com/en-us/library/windows/apps/br243232.aspx.

Most of the time, you'll probably use `DoubleAnimation`s and animate properties like `Opacity`, or you'll animate a property of a transformation. Using this set of animation techniques, you can create most of the animations you'll want to perform. The following code snippet demonstrates the use of a `DoubleAnimation`:

```
<Grid>
    <Grid.Resources>
        <Storyboard x:Name="hideStoryboard">
            <DoubleAnimation Storyboard.TargetName="targetRectangle"
                Storyboard.TargetProperty="Opacity" Duration="00:00:00.5"
                To="0"/>
        </Storyboard>
    </Grid.Resources>
    <Rectangle x:Name="targetRectangle" PointerPressed="Rectangle_Tapped"
        Fill="Blue" Width="200" Height="300" />
</Grid>
```

This code snippet hides a rectangle by animating the `Opacity` property of the `targetRectangle` to 0 in 0.5 seconds. As you can see, you can use a custom animation just like you would use an animation from the Animation Library. You create a `Storyboard` and add an animation to it, and then you set the `Storyboard.TargetName`. However, this time you also set the name of the property you want to animate.

Animations in the Animation Library are predefined animations. Everything is specified on those types of animations (such as durations, properties to animate, and so on). With custom animations, you must specify all of this information.

The previous code sample sets the `Storyboard.TargetProperty` to the `Opacity` property and the `Duration` to 0.5 seconds. So, when the storyboard is playing, it will animate the opacity to 0 in 0.5 seconds. The desired value after the storyboard completes is defined using the `To` property. If you need to define the start value of the animation, you can use the `From` property as well.

Transformations

Now you know how to animate objects' properties with custom animations. However, most of the time, you'll animate transformation properties to slide, scale, or rotate controls. In Windows 8 style applications, these animations are called *render transformations*. These types of transformations are applied without affecting the layout, so you don't have to worry about performance issues, or funny, continuously changing layouts.

The following transformation types are supported:

➤ `TranslateTransform`

➤ `ScaleTransform`

➤ `RotateTransform`

➤ `SkewTransform`

> **NOTE** *You could create much more complicated transformations using matrices. If you want to dive deeper into the world of transformations, you can find more information on the subject at* `http://msdn.microsoft.com/en-us/library/windows/apps/windows.ui.xaml.media.matrixtransform.aspx.`

Origin of Transformations

Transformations must have a *center point*. This point determines the origin of transformations. For example, if you want to specify that you want to rotate a rectangle around its center, you should set the `RenderTransformOrigin` property to `(0.5,0.5)`.

These coordinates are relative coordinates to the top-left corner of the `UIElement`:

➤ `(0,0)` is the top-left corner.

➤ `(1,1)` is the bottom-right corner.

➤ `(0.5, 0.5)` is the exact center of `UIElement`.

You might be wondering about an ellipse, which has no visual top-left corner. However, from a layout point of view, every `UIElement` is placed on the UI in a bounding rectangle that represents the minimal width and height the `UIElement` requires. You should set the `RenderTransformOrigin` properties with this bounding rectangle in mind.

Every `UIElement` you place into your XAML page has a property called `RenderTransform`. Assign any of the previously described transformations to this property and you'll get a transformed `UIElement`. The following code sample shows an example:

```
<Rectangle Width="200" Height="200" Fill="Red" RenderTransformOrigin="0.5,0.5">
    <Rectangle.RenderTransform>
        <RotateTransform Angle="45"/>
    </Rectangle.RenderTransform>
</Rectangle>
```

This code sample rotates the rectangle 45 degrees around its center point. Figure 8-2 shows the rotated rectangle.

FIGURE 8-2: Rectangle rotated 45 degrees

Applying Multiple Transformations

If you want to apply more than one transformation to a UIElement, you can use a TansformGroup like this:

```
<Rectangle Width="200" Height="200" Fill="Red" RenderTransformOrigin="0.5,0.5">
    <Rectangle.RenderTransform>
        <TransformGroup>
            <RotateTransform Angle="45"/>
            <TranslateTransform X="100"/>
        </TransformGroup>
    </Rectangle.RenderTransform>
</Rectangle>
```

These transformations are quite effective, but are also limiting at the same time. They are limited to the two-dimensional (2-D) space. Unfortunately, to create a real three-dimensional (3-D) space would require the use of DirectX and a lot of complicated code. But if you can cope with just a little cheating, PlaneProjections can come to the rescue.

Transformations in the 3-D Space

If you want to create 3-D-like transformations, you can simulate them in the 2-D space using PlaneProjections. PlaneProjections behave exactly like render transformations — they won't affect the layout.

In the next exercise, you create a custom animation using PlaneProjections to rotate a panel in 3-D.

> **NOTE** You can find the complete code to download for this exercise on this book's companion website at www.wrox.com in the RotatingPanelIn3D folder.

Creating a 3-D Rotating Panel

In this exercise, you create a panel that rotates in 3-D. As soon as you click the Start Rotation button, the panel starts rotating 360 degrees. You use custom animations and `PlaneProjections` to achieve this.

1. Create a new project named **RotatingPanelIn3D**. Use the Blank App (XAML) template.

2. Open `MainPage.xaml` and locate the `Grid` panel inside.

3. Add a `Border` with an orange background color to the grid and place simple text content inside the `Border` control. Use a `TextBlock` to display text. Add the following code:

```xml
<Border Width="500" Height="350" Background="Orange"
        HorizontalAlignment="Center" VerticalAlignment="Center">
    <Grid>
        <TextBlock Foreground="White" FontSize="40" HorizontalAlignment=
            "Center" VerticalAlignment="Center" Text="Rotating in 3D"/>
    </Grid>
</Border>
```

4. Add a Next `Button` inside the main `Grid` panel and subscribe to the `Click` events:

```xml
<Grid Background="{StaticResource ApplicationPageBackgroundThemeBrush}">
    <Button x:Name="startButton" Content="Start Rotation" HorizontalAlignment=
        "Center" VerticalAlignment="Top"
            Click="startButton_Click_1"
            />

    <Border Width="500" Height="350" Background="Orange"
            HorizontalAlignment="Center" VerticalAlignment="Center">
        <Grid>
            <TextBlock Foreground="White" FontSize="40" HorizontalAlignment=
                "Center" VerticalAlignment="Center" Text="Rotating in 3D"/>
        </Grid>
    </Border>
</Grid>
```

5. Define a `PlaneProjection` on the `Border`. Name it **rotateTransform**.

```xml
<Grid Background="{StaticResource ApplicationPageBackgroundThemeBrush}">
    <Button x:Name="startButton" Content="Start Rotation" HorizontalAlignment=
        "Center" VerticalAlignment="Top"
            Click="startButton_Click_1"
            />

    <Border Width="500" Height="350" Background="Orange"
            HorizontalAlignment="Center" VerticalAlignment="Center">
        <Border.Projection>
            <PlaneProjection x:Name="rotateTransform"/>
        </Border.Projection>
        <Grid>
            <TextBlock Foreground="White" FontSize="40" HorizontalAlignment=
                "Center" VerticalAlignment="Center" Text="Rotating in 3D"/>
        </Grid>
    </Border>
</Grid>
```

6. Create a `Storyboard` to rotate the panel. Name it **rotateStoryboard**.

```
<Page.Resources>
    <Storyboard x:Name="rotateStoryboard">
        <DoubleAnimation Storyboard.TargetName="rotateTransform"
                         Storyboard.TargetProperty="RotationY"
                         To="360"
                         Duration="00:00:00.5"/>
    </Storyboard>
</Page.Resources>
```

7. Open `MainPage.xaml.cs`. In the `startButton_Click_1` event handler, start the storyboard with the following code:

```
private void startButton_Click_1(object sender, RoutedEventArgs e)
{
    rotateStoryboard.Begin();
}
```

8. Press F5 to run the application and click the Start Rotation button.

How It Works

In Step 3, you added a `Border` control with explicit height and width values, and aligned it to the center of the screen. You set the border's background to a shade of orange, and placed a `TextBlock` inside. The `TextBlock` is not directly added to the `Border`. It is wrapped into a `Grid` panel. This way, you can ensure that you are able to add more items inside the border, instead of just a single `TextBlock`.

In Step 5 you defined the `Projection` property on the `Border` control. The `PlaneProjection` object is named `rotateTransform`. At this point, you didn't specify any other properties, because at the beginning, there is nothing else to do. Adding a name to a transformation is very useful when you want to animate it using a `Storyboard`.

In Step 6 you added a storyboard to the page's `Resources` section. The storyboard uses a single `DoubleAnimation` to animate the `rotateTransform` object's `RotationY` property. The `To` value determines the desired value of the object after the animation completes. Using the `Duration` property, you specified how long it should take to complete the animation. In this case, it will take 500 milliseconds (ms).

In Step 7, you referenced the storyboard by its name, `rotateStoryboard`. You can do so because, in the `Page.Resource` section, you specified the `x:Name` property on the storyboard. There is nothing else to do besides starting the storyboard using the `Begin()` method and the application is ready to run.

DESIGNING THE VISUAL LOOK OF A CONTROL

Creating visually appealing, beautiful UIs plays a very important role in the success of your application. Designing your application with the Windows 8 style principles in mind, using the built-in Windows 8 specific controls can help your cause quite a lot. But in many cases, you will want to change the visual appearance of a control.

In Windows 8 style applications, the control model is so flexible that, in fact, the controls only have a default look. This is what you see when you just use a built-in control. But their visual look can be overridden at any time.

Every control has a property called `Template`. This property represents the look and inner visual structure of a control. If you could take a look at the inside structure of a control (which, as a matter of fact, you can, as you see later in the next "Try it Out" exercise), you'd see borders, rectangles, panels, and other primitive controls that, as a whole, represent the control itself. To change the inside of a control, you must set the `Template` property of the control to something else you think is more appropriate.

The following code snippet demonstrates the use of control templates when designing a button:

```
<Button Content="This is the Content" Width="200" Height="200" FontSize="20">
    <Button.Template>
        <ControlTemplate TargetType="Button">
            <Grid>
                <Ellipse Fill="Orange"/>
                <ContentPresenter/>
            </Grid>
        </ControlTemplate>
    </Button.Template>
</Button>
```

The `Template` property is of type `ControlTemplate`. That's why you add a `ControlTemplate` to the `Template` property. On the `ControlTemplate`, you should specify the `TargetType` property, which determines what controls can use this structure as a template.

In this case, the `ControlTemplate` contains a `Grid` panel and an orange `Ellipse` that serves as the background for the `Button`. The `ContentPresenter` is a new element.

Let's say you have a `ContentControl` and you want to redesign its template. You plan to add a lot of visuals to make it fancy. How can the run time decide which element will display the content of the `ContentControl`? The answer is simple — you explicitly create a placeholder to display the content. For `ContentControls`, the placeholder is called `ContentPresenter`; for `ItemsControls`, it's called `ItemsPresenter`. All you have to do is to place this component inside the template to mark where to put the valuable content of the control.

> **NOTE** `ContentControls` and `ItemControls` are described in more detail in Chapter 7.

In this case, the "This is the Content" text will be displayed where the `ContentPresenter` is located. However, this template is super simple. Figure 8-3 shows the redesigned `Button` control.

This means that although the default look of this button has been changed, if you start using the button, you'll notice that it's missing all the visual feedback for interactions.

Connecting the Control with the Inside

The template created in the previous section is not flexible at all. The `Button` control has a couple of important properties, such as the `Background` property (which determines the background color of the control), and the `HorizontalContentAlignment` and `VerticalContentAlignment` properties (which determine the alignment of the button's content). Although these properties worked before redefining the template, now they are useless.

FIGURE 8-3: The redesigned Button control

How could a button know which visual element serves as a background for the control? Is it the background of a border or a panel? Or is it a fill of a shape? You will have to be explicit about this information.

The challenge is to tell the Button control that the Background property is tied to the ellipse's Fill property. You can use a familiar concept called *template binding*. It's pretty much like data binding (which was discussed in detail in Chapter 7), but this one is designed for use in a control template. The following code sample demonstrates the use of TemplateBinding:

```
<Button Content="This is the Content" Width="200" Height="200" FontSize="20"
        Background="#FFFB6C09">
    <Button.Template>
        <ControlTemplate TargetType="Button">
            <Grid>
                <Ellipse Fill="{TemplateBinding Background}"/>
                <ContentPresenter HorizontalAlignment="{TemplateBinding
                    HorizontalContentAlignment}"
                    VerticalAlignment="{TemplateBinding
                    VerticalContentAlignment}"/>
            </Grid>
        </ControlTemplate>
    </Button.Template>
</Button>
```

This code sample ensures that the fill of the ellipse is tied to the background of the button, and the content's alignment can be adjusted using the button's HorizontalContentAligment and VerticalContentAlignment properties. Figure 8-4 shows the button with the refined template.

Responding to Interactions

So far, the redesigned button doesn't react visually to any changes or interactions. There is no visual change to indicate that the mouse is over the control, or that it is being pressed. The Button control itself supports a couple of visual states you could hook up to. Implementing these states would mean that every time a button reacts to any interaction, it changes its visual state, and your storyboards would start.

FIGURE 8-4: The button with the refined template

By default, the Button control supports the following visual states:

➤ **Normal** — This is the default state.

➤ **Pressed** — The Pressed state is applied when the user clicks the button or touches the control.

➤ **Disabled** — The Disabled state is applied when the control's IsEnabled property is false.

➤ **PointerOver** — The PointerOver state is applied when the mouse cursor is over the control.

These visual states belong to the CommonStates visual state group. Button also supports visual states for focus changes.

If you decide you want to implement any of the visual states, Button will use your implementations. You don't have to support all the states, only the ones you are interested in.

The following code snippet demonstrates the use of visual states in the control template:

```
<Button Content="This is the Content" Height="200" Width="200"
        Background="#FFFB6C09" FontSize="20">
    <Button.Template>
        <ControlTemplate TargetType="Button">
            <Grid x:Name="grid" RenderTransformOrigin="0.5,0.5">
                <Grid.RenderTransform>
                    <CompositeTransform/>
                </Grid.RenderTransform>
                <VisualStateManager.VisualStateGroups>
                    <VisualStateGroup x:Name="CommonStates">
                        <VisualState x:Name="Normal"/>
                        <VisualState x:Name="Pressed">
                            <Storyboard>
                                <DoubleAnimation Duration="0" To="0.9"
                                  Storyboard.TargetProperty=
                                  "(UIElement.RenderTransform).
                                  (CompositeTransform.ScaleX)"
                                  Storyboard.TargetName="grid"
                                  d:IsOptimized="True"/>
                                <DoubleAnimation Duration="0" To="0.9"
                                  Storyboard.TargetProperty=
                                  "(UIElement.RenderTransform).
                                  (CompositeTransform.ScaleY)"
                                  Storyboard.TargetName="grid"
                                  d:IsOptimized="True"/>
                            </Storyboard>
                        </VisualState>
                        <VisualState x:Name="Disabled"/>
                        <VisualState x:Name="PointerOver">
                            <Storyboard>
                                <ObjectAnimationUsingKeyFrames
                                  Storyboard.TargetProperty="
                                  (UIElement.Visibility)"
                                  Storyboard.TargetName="mouseOverEllipse">
                                    <DiscreteObjectKeyFrame KeyTime="0">
                                        <DiscreteObjectKeyFrame.Value>
                                            <Visibility>Visible</Visibility>
                                        </DiscreteObjectKeyFrame.Value>
                                    </DiscreteObjectKeyFrame>
                                </ObjectAnimationUsingKeyFrames>
                            </Storyboard>
                        </VisualState>
                    </VisualStateGroup>
                    <VisualStateGroup x:Name="FocusStates"/>
                </VisualStateManager.VisualStateGroups>
                <Ellipse Fill="{TemplateBinding Background}"/>
                <ContentPresenter HorizontalAlignment="{TemplateBinding
                    HorizontalContentAlignment}"
                    VerticalAlignment="{TemplateBinding
                    VerticalContentAlignment}"/>
                <Ellipse x:Name="mouseOverEllipse" Visibility="Collapsed">
                    <Ellipse.Fill>
                        <LinearGradientBrush EndPoint="0.5,1" StartPoint="0.5,0">
                            <GradientStop Color="#FFFFE800" Offset="1"/>
```

```
                        <GradientStop Color="Transparent" Offset="0"/>
                    </LinearGradientBrush>
                </Ellipse.Fill>
            </Ellipse>
        </Grid>
    </ControlTemplate>
  </Button.Template>
</Button>
```

This code has some exciting ideas that need some explanation.

First, take a look at the real visual content, and forget about the visual states. You'll see that the new control template is very similar to the previous one. It has an ellipse that serves as the visual representation of the control, and has a ContentPresenter as well to support the content.

But this new version also has a new ellipse called mouseOverEllipse with a gradient fill. The gradient at the bottom of the ellipse displays the color #FFFFE800, which is a shade of yellow. At the top of the ellipse, the gradient changes to Transparent. Basically, this new ellipse is used to create a highlighted visual element for the button. By default, the mouseOverEllipse is collapsed, so it is not visible.

Now, let's investigate the visual states of this template. You can find the visual states discussed earlier in the CommonStates VisualStateGroup. The PointerOver state defines a storyboard with an object animation to change the mouseOverEllipse's Visibility property to Visible. Whenever the mouse cursor is over the button control, the PointerOver state is activated, and the Visibility property of the mouseOverEllipse is set to Visible. When the mouse cursor leaves the area of the Button control, the control switches back to the Normal visual state while reverting back all the property changes. You get this behavior for free when using visual states.

If you investigate further, you'll see that the Pressed state is implemented as well. The Pressed state uses a storyboard to control two DoubleAnimations. These animations animate the ScaleX and the ScaleY properties of a CompositeTransform object defined on the template's root grid. This means that when you press the button, it shrinks a bit to provide some nice visual feedback for the Click event. Figure 8-5 shows the button in two different states.

FIGURE 8-5: The Button in Normal and PointerOver states.

> **NOTE** Most of the time, you'll want to reuse the control templates, or use them as defaults for a certain type of control. You should place these templates in resources so that you can reuse them. A quite common practice is to place the control template in a style, and make the style the default for a control type.

You must be thinking that this is quite a lot of complicated code to achieve simple things and modifications. You might also be wondering how to know what kind of visual states a control supports, and how to modify the default templates without redefining the whole control's template.

In most cases, you'll just want to adjust the template of the control to your own custom design, and you don't want to start from scratch. Unfortunately, Visual Studio 2012 doesn't do much to support this scenario. If you need a visual designer to create a new control template, or to edit an existing one, you should use Microsoft Expression Blend.

Visual Studio and Expression Blend share the same project structure, which means that you can load your project into Blend. Blend was primarily designed for interaction designers, but developers can also take advantage of this tool.

Working with Expression Blend

Microsoft Expression Blend does a great job in revealing the original template of the control, or showing you what kind of visual states the control supports. On the designer surface, you can easily adjust the visual structure, or create animations to customize the control. Figure 8-6 shows how Microsoft Expression Blend looks.

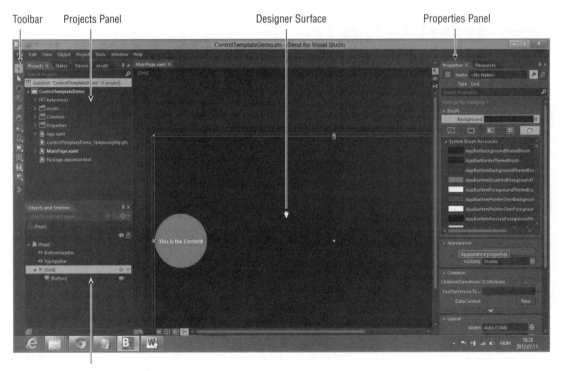

FIGURE 8-6: Microsoft Expression Blend

The Toolbar

Figure 8-7 shows the Expression Blend toolbar.

FIGURE 8-7:
The Expression
Blend toolbar

On the toolbar, you'll find some really useful tools that will help you build UIs more easily. The most important tool is the selection tool, which is the first icon with a mouse cursor. If this tool is active, you can select and move items on the designer surface.

If you add a control to the UI, you'll switch into "drawing mode." This means that when you click the designer surface (or any item on the designer surface), you'll start drawing the same control you added before. If you want to switch back to selection mode, you should click the selection tool on the toolbar (or press V).

> **NOTE** *You learn more about the designer surface and its modes shortly.*

On the bottom half of the toolbar, you can find controls as well. If you press and hold the Button, the TextBlock, the Grid, or the Rectangle controls, you are presented with other options (that is, other controls from the same category). If you just click these toolbar items, you switch into drawing mode. You can draw these controls on the designer surface just like you'd do in Microsoft Paint.

The Projects Panel

The Projects panel shown in Figure 8-8 is basically the Blend version of Visual Studio's Solution Explorer. You can see the files associated with your solutions.

The Assets Panel

The Assets panel shown in Figure 8-9 contains everything you can add to your UIs, grouped into multiple categories. You can find controls, panels, shapes, media elements, styles, and so on in this panel. It also supports searching for controls. If you need a `Button` control, just locate it, and drag and drop it on the designer surface.

FIGURE 8-8: The Expression Blend Projects panel

FIGURE 8-9: The Expression Blend Assets panel

The States Panel

The States panel shown in Figure 8-10 displays the visual states supported by your controls. If you select a visual state, the designer surface switches to that state. Any property you change is added as an animation inside a storyboard to the active visual state. A red border around the designer surface and a message warns you that you are in visual state editing mode.

The Device Panel

The Device panel shown in Figure 8-11 helps you simulate different properties of Windows 8 devices. You can simulate orientations, snap states, resolutions, themes, and options where to deploy the application: remote device, local, or simulator.

FIGURE 8-10: The Expression Blend States panel

FIGURE 8-11: The Expression Blend Device panel

The Objects and Timeline Panel

The Objects and Timeline panel shown in Figure 8-12 displays the visual tree of controls on your page. You can see the entire hierarchy you've built. Selecting any node of the tree also selects the control on the designer surface. You can drag and drop items on the tree as well. This panel also offers an option to switch into Timeline mode, and to create and manage sophisticated storyboards.

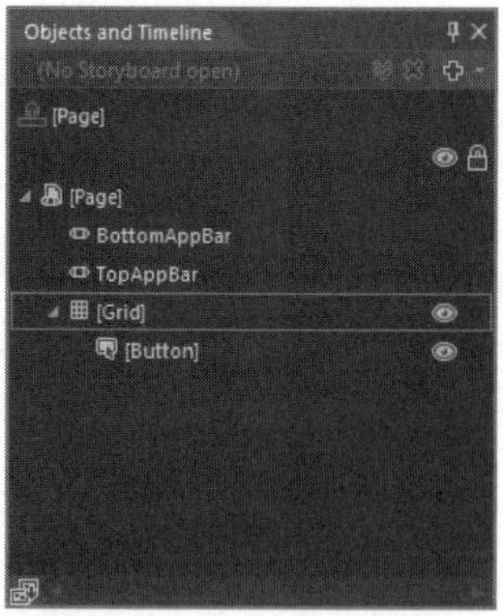

The Designer Surface

The designer surface shown in Figure 8-13 supports three different modes:

➤ **Design mode** — In this mode, you are in full visual designer mode, and you see no XAML.

➤ **Code mode** — In this mode, you can see and edit the XAML code, but you can't see the visual representation.

FIGURE 8-12: The Expression Blend Objects and Timeline panel

➤ **Split mode** — In this mode, you can see both the XAML code editor and the visual designer, and you can edit both sides, while Expression Blend keeps the two views in sync.

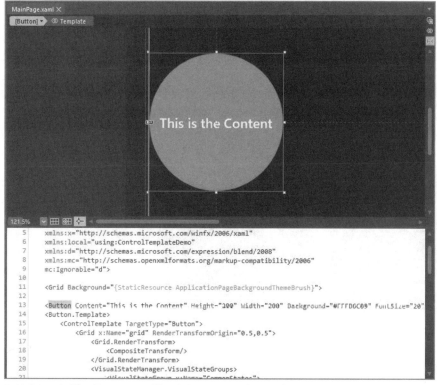

FIGURE 8-13: The Expression Blend designer surface in Split mode

The Properties Panel

The Properties panel shown in Figure 8-14 is very similar to the one you'll find in Visual Studio 2012. Actually, Visual Studio adopted the Expression Blend Properties panel. When an element is selected, all the properties are listed in this section. The Properties panel is also the place where you can subscribe to events when you switch it to events mode. However, this option is rarely used, because most coding is done in Visual Studio 2012.

The Resources Panel

The Resources panel shown in Figure 8-15 enables you to get an overview of all of your resources in your entire application. On this panel, you can move resources between sections, and some resources can be edited in place as well. Using drag and drop, you can apply resources to elements located on the designer surface.

FIGURE 8-14: The Expression Blend Properties panel

FIGURE 8-15: The Expression Blend Resources panel

> **NOTE** *The fact that you can work with Expression Blend and Visual Studio at the same time provides great value for a software developer. All you have to do is to open your project in both applications. But be very careful! Keep in mind that if you change anything using Expression Blend, you'll have to save your file before you switch back to Visual Studio. Otherwise, Visual Studio will override all the changes you made. Of course, this is true for switching from Visual Studio to Expression Blend as well. If you save your file in your active IDE, when you switch to the other IDE, it will warn you that you should reload the file, because it was changed by another application. In this case, you should accept the reload action.*

In the next exercise, you use Expression Blend to create the button you designed earlier.

> **NOTE** *You can find the complete code to download for this exercise on this book's companion website at* `www.wrox.com` *in the* `ControlTemplateDemo` *folder.*

TRY IT OUT   Customizing Templates with Expression Blend

1. Open Expression Blend and select New Project.

2. In the New Project dialog box, ensure that the XAML option is selected. Select the Blank App (XAML) template.

3. Name the application **ControlTemplateDemo**. Click (or tap) the OK button.

4. On the toolbar, select the `Button` control. Figure 8-16 shows the `Button` control on the toolbar.

5. Using the mouse, draw a `Button` onto the designer surface.

6. Click the Properties panel to view the properties of the new button.

7. Click the Background property and select an orange shade of color from the color palette.

8. On the Properties panel, find the Layout section and set both the `Width` and `Height` properties to **200**.

9. On the Properties panel, find the Text section and set the FontSize to **20**.

10. Right-click the `Button` and select Edit Template from the context menu.

11. Edit Template offers a number of choices. Select "Edit a Copy."

12. Enter **MyButtonTemplate** as the name of the resource and click OK.

Button Control

FIGURE 8-16: The Button control on the toolbar

13. Take a look at the Objects and Timeline panel. You can see the original inner structure of the `Button` control.

14. On the Objects and Timeline panel right-click the top item below the Template root item. Select Delete from the context menu.

15. On the toolbar, double-click the Grid panel. Figure 8-16 shows the Grid panel on the toolbar.

16. On the toolbar, press and hold the rectangle, then select the ellipse from the list.

17. Double-click the ellipse.

18. Click the Assets panel to activate it.

19. In the Search TextBox, start typing the word **contentpresenter**. As soon as the result list finds the `ContentPresenter` control, double-click it.

20. On the toolbar, click and hold on the rectangle tool, then select the ellipse from the pop-up menu. Double-click the ellipse. Figure 8-18 shows the Rectangle tool on the toolbar.

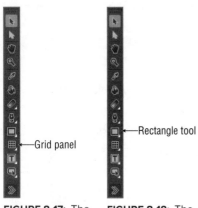

FIGURE 8-17: The Grid Panel on the toolbar

FIGURE 8-18: The Rectangle tool on the toolbar

21. On the Properties panel, enter **mouseOverEllipse** in the Name TextBox.

22. On the Objects and Timeline panel, select the first ellipse. On the Properties panel, locate the `Fill` property. Next to the `Fill` property, there is a little gray rectangle that displays the text "Default" in the tooltip when the mouse is over it. Click the rectangle and select the Template Binding option. In the list offered in the Template Binding option, select Background.

23. On the Objects and Timeline panel, select the `ContentPresenter`. On the Properties panel, in the Search `TextBox`, start typing the word **horizontalcontentalignment**. Next to the `HorizontalContentAlignment` property, there is a little gray rectangle that displays the text "Default" in the tooltip when the mouse is over it. Click the rectangle and select the Template Binding option. In the list offered in the Template Binding option, select `HorizontalAlignment`.

24. On the Properties panel, in the Search TextBox, start typing the word **verticalcontentalignment**. Next to the VerticalContentAlignment property, there is a little gray rectangle that displays the text "Default" in the tooltip when the mouse is over it. Click the rectangle and select the Template Binding option. In the list offered in the Template Binding option, select VerticalAlignment.

25. On the Objects and Timeline panel, select the mouseOverEllipse. On the Properties panel, ensure that the Search TextBox is empty.

26. Click the Fill property. Select the "Gradient brush" option.

27. Below the color palette editor, there is an indicator line. The little shapes (arrows) represent the gradient stops. Click the left one and enter 0 into the TextBox next to the A (Alpha) value.

28. Click the right one, and then select a light yellow color on the color palette.

29. On the Properties panel, find the Appearance section, and set the Visibility property to Collapsed.

30. Click the States panel to activate it.

31. Select the PointerOver visual state, and then set the Visibility property to Visible.

32. On the top of the designer surface, on the breadcrumbs menu, click [Button] to exit the template editing mode.

32. Press F5 to run the application. Move the mouse over the button to test the state changes.

How It Works

In this exercise, you did exactly the same as you did in pure XAML. The only difference is that, in this case, you are using Expression Blend to do the same without writing a single line of code.

From Step 1 to Step 9, you just add some properties to the Button control (such as width and height, background color, and font size).

From Step 10 to Step 21, you create the control template for the Button control (at least the visual structure for it).

From Step 22 to Step 24, you apply Template Bindings to ensure that some properties (such as the background color of the Button control) are tied to the properties of the appropriate controls in the template.

From Step 25 to Step 31, you configure the mouseOverEllipse to behave as a highlighting visual over the Button control, and use visual states to do the transitions.

These are the main steps you performed during the exercise. However, some steps are important to understand, because you can learn a lot about Expression Blend from them. Let's walk through the most important steps.

In Step 2, you chose the XAML option. However, you could have chosen the HTML option, too. Expression Blend supports both XAML- and HTML-based development, which makes it quite powerful and unique.

In Step 4, you selected the Button control. This action sends Expression Blend into drawing mode. Your cursor changes to a cross-hair when over the designer surface. When you draw a new item, it is added automatically to the selected item in the Objects and Timeline panel. Also, it makes the new item the selected item. The Properties panel now displays the properties of the new `Button` control.

In Step 8, you located the Layout section. The properties on the Properties panel are grouped into distinct sections, which can be collapsed and expanded.

In Step 10, you can click the `Button` on the designer surface, or on the Objects and Timeline panel. Both react the same way when performing right-clicks. The Edit Template option enables you to enter into the template of the control and customize it. By selecting the "Edit a copy" option, the original content and structure of the `Button` will be visible. It is a great option if you want to make fine adjustments. The new dialog box is the Resource dialog box. You must specify the name of the resource, because the new control template will be saved as a resource.

In Step 15, after you emptied the original content, you can add a new panel to the template by double-clicking the Grid panel on the toolbar.

In Step 22, you used the property options to access advanced features such as template binding, data binding, or referencing resources. The Template Binding option presents you only with the suitable properties of the parent control you can bind to.

In Step 31, you activated the `PointerOver` visual state. As soon as you click it, the designer surface displays a red border and a message that state recording is on. Everything you set now on the Properties panel will be part of an animation that will run when the state is activated.

This might have seemed like quite a few steps. But, rest assured, once you get to know Expression Blend and get some practice using it, this process can take less than a minute, which makes it very effective when customizing the UI.

WORKING WITH COMPLEX CONTROLS

One of the great benefits of the Windows 8 style application design principles and the basic set of controls with default styles is the capability to create a consistent user experience across applications and the Windows operating system. As you use more and more Windows 8 style applications, you'll notice major similarities and familiar concepts in the UIs. These applications might use similar list controls, with similar layout. The interaction modes and gestures with these controls are the same. This is really good from the user experience point of view, especially when thinking about the learning curve of using applications confidently.

This similarity is coming from some well-established UI patterns formed by built-in complex controls like the `GridView`, `ListView`, `FlipView`, `SemanticZoom`, or `AppBar` controls. Using these controls, you can make your application easier to understand and more familiar for the user.

Getting to Know the ListViewBase Controls

Complex list controls are derived from the `ListViewBase` class (except `ListBox`). This class contains all the logic that a complex Windows 8 style list control needs. Classes derived from

`ListViewBase` support features such as touch- and mouse-optimized interaction modes, on-demand asynchronous loading, grouping, multi-selection, and semantic zoom (among many others).

`ListView` and `GridView` controls are derived from `ListViewBase`, which means that, with these controls, you'll get the features previously mentioned for free. One other (rather interesting) aspect of the `ListView` and `GridView` controls is that they are pretty much the same. These controls don't invent additional properties in `ListViewBase`, but they are quite different when presenting data.

Using the GridView Control

The `GridView` control shown in Figure 8-19 represents a horizontally scrolling grid of items. You can see this layout in many applications where photos must be arranged. Typically, news and photo applications prefer this layout format.

FIGURE 8-19: The GridView control in the USA Today app

Binding to Data

The `GridView` control is an `ItemsControl`, and, as such, it exposes properties like `Items` and `ItemsSource` that you can use to specify a list of items as a data source. Binding a `GridView` to a collection is as simple as binding any `ItemsControl` to a collection.

> **NOTE** *Chapter 7 provides more detail on* `ItemsControl, Items,` *and* `ItemsSource.`

The following code demonstrates binding to a `GridView`:

```
<Page.Resources>
    <local:PlayersCollection x:Key="players"/>
<Page.Resources>

<GridView ItemsSource="{Binding Source={StaticResource players}}"
  Margin="0,120,0,0" MaxHeight="500">
    <GridView.ItemTemplate>
        <DataTemplate>
            <StackPanel Margin="20">
                <TextBlock Text="{Binding Name}" FontWeight="Bold" />
                <TextBlock Text="{Binding BirthDate}"/>
                <CheckBox Content="Complete" IsChecked="{Binding
                        IsTeamCaptain}" IsEnabled="False"/>
            </StackPanel>
        </DataTemplate>
    </GridView.ItemTemplate>
</GridView>
```

This code snippet binds to a collection of players. The collection is located in the `Page.Resources` section. When setting the `ItemsSource` property using a binding, the `Source` can be referenced as a `StaticResource`. This `GridView` is also configured to display items using a custom `ItemTemplate`. All this functionality works exactly the same as it does with simple `ItemsControls`.

If you have a lot of data to display, you may want to group it visually so the user can process the presented information more easily. Grouping is not a feature specific to `GridView`. It is also supported by the `ListViewBase` class.

Grouping Data

Grouping to visually and logically partition data is quite common. However, changing the original structure and content of the data collection would be very expensive in terms of performance. It would also take quite a lot of code to write. To work around this issue, you can use a class called `CollectionViewSource`.

`CollectionViewSource` wraps your original collection and leaves it intact, no matter what you are doing — sorting, grouping, or filtering. Sorting, grouping, and filtering rules can be changed, added, or removed, and your original collection is not changed at all.

To enable grouping on `CollectionViewSource`, perform the following steps:

1. Set the `Source` property of the `CollectionViewSource` object to the grouped data.

2. Set the `IsSourceGrouped` property to `true`. This enables grouping for your data.

3. Set the `ItemsPath` property to the name of the property that represents the items in the group.

The following code demonstrates the use of the `CollectionViewSource` class:

```
<Page.Resources>
    <CollectionViewSource x:Name="teamsList" IsSourceGrouped="True"
        ItemsPath="Players"/>
```

```
<Page.Resources>

<GridView ItemsSource="{Binding Source={StaticResource teamsList}}"
  Margin="0,120,0,0" MaxHeight="500">
    ...
</GridView>
```

In this case, you have a collection of Team objects. Every Team object has a collection of Player objects. What you want to do here is to use the teams as groups, and use the players as group items. This code snippet configures the CollectionViewSource to support this scenario.

Note that, in the previous code snippet, the Source property is not set. This is because, in most cases, you'll do this using code in the code-behind file. You can set the Source property to any collection.

Defining Visual Groups

Although your CollectionViewSource is ready to be displayed in a grouped view, the GridView still requires some refinement. The GridView needs to know which property should be used to display the grouping headers. You can specify this using the GroupStyle property.

The GroupStyle property enables you to completely customize the visual representation of grouping. The GroupStyle property defines a HeaderTemplate to customize the look of the header.

The following code demonstrates the definition of a GroupStyle:

```
<Page.Resources>
    <CollectionViewSource x:Name="teamsList" IsSourceGrouped="True"
        ItemsPath="Players"/>
<Page.Resources>

<GridView ItemsSource="{Binding Source={StaticResource teamsList}}"
  Margin="0,120,0,0" MaxHeight="500">
    <GridView.ItemTemplate>
        <DataTemplate>
            <StackPanel Margin="20">
                <TextBlock Text="{Binding Name}" FontWeight="Bold" />
                <TextBlock Text="{Binding BirthDate}"/>
                <CheckBox Content="Complete" IsChecked="{Binding
                    IsTeamCaptain}" IsEnabled="False"/>
            </StackPanel>
        </DataTemplate>
    </GridView.ItemTemplate>

    <GridView.GroupStyle>
        <GroupStyle HidesIfEmpty="True">
            <GroupStyle.HeaderTemplate>
                <DataTemplate>
                    <Grid Background="LightGray">
                        <TextBlock Text='{Binding TeamName}'
                                Foreground="Black" Margin="30"
                                Style="{StaticResource HeaderTextStyle}"/>
                    </Grid>
                </DataTemplate>
```

```
            </GroupStyle.HeaderTemplate>

            <GroupStyle.Panel>
                <ItemsPanelTemplate>
                    <VariableSizedWrapGrid/>
                </ItemsPanelTemplate>
            </GroupStyle.Panel>
        </GroupStyle>
    </GridView.GroupStyle>

</GridView>
```

This code sample displays the `Players` grouped by `Teams`. On the `GroupStyle`, several properties are defined:

➤ The `HidesIfEmpty` property defines whether or not to display the group when no items are in the group.

➤ The `HeaderTemplate` property defines what data should be displayed in the header of the groups. It is bound to the `TeamName` property.

➤ The `TextBlock`'s style representing the header text is referencing the `HeaderTextStyle` system resource.

➤ The default panel for the group is overridden. Using the `GroupStyle.Panel` property, it is set to use a `VariableSizedWrapGrid`.

As you can see, you can use many properties and options to customize the grouping functionality of the `GridView` control.

Using the ListView Control

The `ListView` control is a vertically arranged scrollable list of items. It is designed to represent items one after the other, while supporting features that make it easy to use and learn for the user. By default, `ListView` does not have a visual representation; only the items are rendered. Figure 8-20 shows the `ListView` control in use in the PC Settings application. The settings groups are represented as a vertical list of items.

Comparing ListView to ListBox

`ListBox` and `ListView` are both `ItemsControls`, and they share a very similar behavior. Both controls are meant to visually arrange a list of items. By default, these controls display these items vertically stacked.

However, subtle (but very important) differences exist between these two. Technically, they have different base classes. `ListBox` is inherited directly from the `Selector` class, whereas the `ListView` is inherited from the `ListViewBase` class. But still, their important differences come from their default visual look.

The `ListView` was designed with the Windows 8 style principles and touch applications in mind, whereas the `ListBox` control is more of a heritage. By default, the `ListView` control provides more room for its items in order to make it more comfortable for touch, and it does not have a visual look like the `ListBox` does.

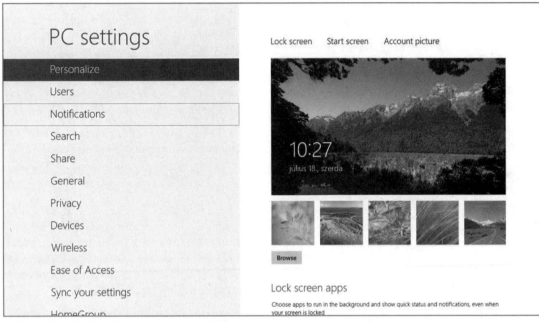

FIGURE 8-20: The ListView control in the PC Settings

When it comes to touch and selection, their behavior is quite different as well. When you try to scroll the contents of a `ListBox`, you'll notice that it highlights the element you tapped first. Because the scrolling and selection actions start with the same touch gesture, the `ListBox` control simply cannot tell the difference at the beginning.

The `ListView` has a completely different gesture and mouse action for selection, so this problem just does not occur in that case. `ListView` also supports transitions and animations from the Animation Library to help the user understand more easily what happens when you add or remove an item from the list.

These are subtle, yet very important, differences between the two controls. It is recommended to prefer the `ListView` control in Windows 8 style applications.

The following code shows how to use the `ListView` control:

```
<ListView ItemsSource="{Binding Source={StaticResource players}}">
    <ListView.ItemTemplate>
        <DataTemplate>
            <Grid Height="100" Margin="8">
                <Grid.ColumnDefinitions>
                    <ColumnDefinition Width="Auto"/>
                    <ColumnDefinition Width="*"/>
                </Grid.ColumnDefinitions>
                <Border Width="100" Height="100">
                    <Image Source="{Binding PlayerPhoto}" Stretch="UniformToFill"/>
                </Border>
                <StackPanel Grid.Column="1" VerticalAlignment="Top"
                        Margin="8,0,0,0">
```

```
                <TextBlock Text="{Binding Name}"/>
                <TextBlock Text="{Binding BirthDate}"/>
                <TextBlock Text="{Binding TeamName}"/>
            </StackPanel>
        </Grid>
    </DataTemplate>
  </ListView.ItemTemplate>
</ListView>
```

This code displays a list of players vertically. Every item has an `Image` displaying the photo of the `Player`. Next to the photo, the name, birth date, and team name information is displayed.

Using the FlipView Control

The `FlipView` control is an `ItemsControl` that is designed to display only one item at a time. As odd as it may sound, the concept of `FlipView` is really useful — concentrate only on one item of a list. You can think of this control as one that represents a details view with many pages.. When using a touch device, the `FlipView` control provides a smooth transition when the user changes the current item with a swipe gesture. When the user is using the mouse as an input device, the control provides pager controls on both sides. Figure 8-21 shows the `FlipView` control in use.

FIGURE 8-21: The FlipView control in the Photos application

The following code snippet demonstrates the use of the `FlipView` control:

```
<FlipView Width="480" Height="250 ItemsSource="{Binding Photos}"/>
    <FlipView.ItemTemplate>
        <DataTemplate>
```

```
<Grid>
    <Image Width="480" Height="250" Source="{Binding Image}"
        Stretch="UniformToFill"/>
    <Border Height="80" VerticalAlignment="Bottom">
        <TextBlock Text="{Binding ImageTitle}"/>
     </Border>
</Grid>
        </DataTemplate>
    </FlipView.ItemTemplate>
</FlipView>
```

Notice how the `FlipView` control uses the `ItemTemplate` property to define how a single item should be displayed. Still, it displays only one item at a time.

Using SemanticZoom

`SemanticZoom` control is definitely the coolest feature in Windows 8 style applications. `SemanticZoom` enables you to define two different zoom levels to represent the same set of data. This means that if you have a lot of data, you can create a detailed zoom level where you can see every piece of data, and you can define an overview presentation of the data. `SemanticZoom` offers nice transitions between the levels, and gesture support as well. You can use the pinch and the zoom gestures to switch between the zoom levels.

`SemanticZoom` has two properties corresponding to two zoom levels:

➤ `ZoomedOutView`

➤ `ZoomedInView`

You can add any control to these properties that implement the `ISemanticZoomInformation` interface. The XAML framework provides two controls that implement this interface: `GridView` and `ListView`. Figure 8-22 shows the Windows 8 Start menu using `SemanticZoom`.

> **NOTE** *Don't confuse* `SemanticZoom` *with optical zoom.* `SemanticZoom` *provides different representations for the same set of data, whereas optical zoom does not change views. It simply magnifies the viewable area.*

The following code sample shows how to use `SemanticZoom`:

```
<SemanticZoom>
    <SemanticZoom.ZoomedOutView>
        <!-- GridView or ListView for the zoomed out view here. -->
    </SemanticZoom.ZoomedOutView>
    <SemanticZoom.ZoomedInView>
        <!-- GridView or ListView for the zoomed in view here. -->
    </SemanticZoom.ZoomedInView>
</SemanticZoom>
```

In the next exercise, you learn to use the new controls in Windows 8, and learn more about the prepared application templates.

> **NOTE** *You can find the complete code to download for this exercise on this book's companion website at* www.wrox.com *in the* ComplexControlsDemo *folder.*

FIGURE 8-22: The Windows 8 Start menu using SemanticZoom

TRY IT OUT Using Complex Controls in Windows 8

1. Open Visual Studio 2012 and select File ➪ New ➪ Project.

2. The New Project dialog box offers numerous XAML application templates for Windows 8 style applications. Select the GridApp (XAML) template.

3. Name the project **ComplexControlsDemo**. Click (or tap) the OK button.

4. Press (or tap) F5 to run the application.

5. Try scrolling the application. Then select a GridViewItem and click it.

6. The details page is a FlipView. Try to change the currently active item using the arrows on the left and right edge of the screen, or using swipe gestures.

How It Works

As you can see, this template creates a sample application and a baseline structure for you to get started. Now, it is very important to understand every bit of this code so that you can improve it or reuse it.

First, let's investigate the data model. The solution has a `DataModel` folder that contains the `SampleDataSource.cs` file. If you open the file, you'll see a `SampleDataSource` class. This class exposes only a single property called `AllGroups`. The `AllGroups` property is of type `ObservableColle ction<SampleDataGroup>`, which means that every item in the group is a `SampleDataGroup` instance.

The `SampleDataGroup` class exposes two collections: `Items` and `TopItems`. Both of these collections contain `SampleDataItems`. Every `SampleDataItem` has `Content` and a reference to its `Group`. Both `SampleDataGroup` and `SampleDataItem` inherit from `SampleDataCommon`.

This base class contains the common properties (`Title`, `Subtitle`, `Description`, `Image`, `UniqueId`) for these classes. So, both groups and items have `Title` and `Subtitle`. The `SampleDataSource` class creates a lot of sample data for this model hierarchy.

Now, open the `GroupedItemsPage.xaml`. This is where the `GridView` is located. Locate the `Page .Resources` section. In the section, you'll find a configured `CollectionViewSource`. Because you want to present grouped data, `CollectionViewSource` is a very handy object to help you achieve your goal.

You can see that the `Source` property is bound to the `Groups` property, the `IsSourceGrouped` property is set to `true`, and the `ItemsPath` property is bound to `TopItems`:

```
<CollectionViewSource
        x:Name="groupedItemsViewSource"
        Source="{Binding Groups}"
        IsSourceGrouped="true"
        ItemsPath="TopItems"
        d:Source="{Binding AllGroups, Source={d:DesignInstance
            Type=data:SampleDataSource, IsDesignTimeCreatable=True}}"/>
```

If you bind a `GridView` to this `CollectionViewSource`, it will be bound to a grouped collection of data that was examined earlier.

Now, locate the `GridView` named `itemGridView`. Its `ItemsSource` is bound to the `CollectionViewSource`. The `IsItemClickEnabled` property is set to `true`, so the `ItemClick` event will fire when clicking or touching an item in the `GridView`. You are subscribed to this event with the `ItemView_ItemClick` event. If you take a closer look on the `GridView`, you'll find that a couple of other things are set as well, such as a custom `GroupStyle` or a custom panel for the `GridView`.

```
<GridView
    x:Name="itemGridView"
    AutomationProperties.AutomationId="ItemGridView"
    AutomationProperties.Name="Grouped Items"
    Grid.Row="1"
    Margin="0,-3,0,0"
    Padding="116,0,40,46"
    ItemsSource="{Binding Source={StaticResource groupedItemsViewSource}}"
    ItemTemplate="{StaticResource Standard250x250ItemTemplate}"
    SelectionMode="None"
    IsItemClickEnabled="True"
    ItemClick="ItemView_ItemClick">

    <GridView.ItemsPanel>
        <ItemsPanelTemplate>
```

```xml
                    <VirtualizingStackPanel Orientation="Horizontal"/>
            </ItemsPanelTemplate>
        </GridView.ItemsPanel>
        <GridView.GroupStyle>
            <GroupStyle>
                <GroupStyle.HeaderTemplate>
                    <DataTemplate>
                        <Grid Margin="1,0,0,6">
                            <Button
                                AutomationProperties.Name="Group Title"
                                Content="{Binding Title}"
                                Click="Header_Click"
                                Style="{StaticResource TextButtonStyle}"/>
                        </Grid>
                    </DataTemplate>
                </GroupStyle.HeaderTemplate>
                <GroupStyle.Panel>
                    <ItemsPanelTemplate>
                        <VariableSizedWrapGrid Orientation="Vertical"
                            Margin="0,0,80,0"/>
                    </ItemsPanelTemplate>
                </GroupStyle.Panel>
            </GroupStyle>
        </GridView.GroupStyle>
    </GridView>
```

In the code-behind file, the event handler looks like the following:

```csharp
void ItemView_ItemClick(object sender, ItemClickEventArgs e)
{
    // Navigate to the appropriate destination page, configuring the new page
    // by passing required information as a navigation parameter
    var itemId = ((SampleDataItem)e.ClickedItem).UniqueId;
    this.Frame.Navigate(typeof(ItemDetailPage), itemId);
}
```

This means that if you click an item of the GridView, the ItemClickEventArgs will tell you which item was clicked through the ClickedItem property. It is still an object, so you must cast to the appropriate type, which is the SampleDataItem type. Then you can start the navigation to the ItemDetailPage while passing the UniqueId as a parameter for the new page.

The ItemDetailPage works in a very similar fashion. It uses a CollectionViewSource, but this time it is bound to a FlipView control. The FlipView control in its ItemTemplate defines a whole UserControl to display all the contents of the currently selected (displayed) item.

> **NOTE** It's worth investigating this template further. It demonstrates additional capabilities of a Windows 8 style application that are not covered in this chapter. It also introduces some really nice and useful patterns that you can later use in your applications.

Using the AppBar Control

In many cases, you'll face a situation where you'll want to add extra functionalities, commands, or operations to your UI, but you don't want to dedicate space and extra visuals on your content area. Windows 8 style applications offer a great solution for this issue. Using a Windows 8 style pattern, the AppBar control, you can build a uniform solution to this problem.

Every Page has two AppBar regions: a TopAppBar and a BottomAppBar. If you adhere to the Windows 8 style application design principles, you'll use the TopAppBar to add navigation controls (such as a back button) and use the BottomAppBar to show commands and tools related to your application and the current page. Figure 8-23 shows the AppBar control in action.

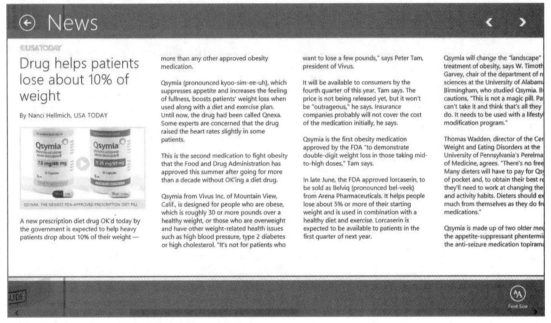

FIGURE 8-23: The AppBar control

The following code sample shows how to use the AppBar control:

```
<Page.TopAppBar>
    <AppBar>
        <StackPanel Orientation="Horizontal" HorizontalAlignment="Right">
            <Button Style="{StaticResource RemoveAppBarButtonStyle}"
                Click="RemoveButton_Click"/>
            <Button Style="{StaticResource AddAppBarButtonStyle}"
                Click="AddButton_Click"/>
        </StackPanel>
    </AppBar>
</Page.TopAppBar>
```

SUMMARY

Animations make your applications come alive. Using the Animation Library, you can create smooth and consistent user experiences, but you still have the power to create a custom animation.

Using transformations and projections, you can apply any kind of animation you can think of while still keeping your application performance. You can even create a sense of using 3-D-like tranformations.

Using a control template, you have the power to completely change the visual look of a control, while still preserving all the functionality a control offers.

In Windows 8 style applications, you have lot of exciting ways to display data using specific complex controls such as GridView, ListView, FlipView, or SemanticZoom.

In Chapter 9, you learn about more integration with the operating system using controls and services offered by it. You also learn about other important features like data persistence, localization, notification, and Live Tiles.

EXERCISES

1. What is the difference between independent and dependent animations?

2. What is the Animation Library?

3. What is a render transformation?

4. How can you bind a control's property to another property inside its template?

5. Why should you use a CollectionViewSource when binding a collection to a GridView?

6. What is the purpose of SemanticZoom?

> **NOTE** *You can find answers to the exercises in Appendix A.*

► **WHAT YOU LEARNED IN THIS CHAPTER**

TOPIC	KEY CONCEPTS
Independent animations	Independent animations are fast and smooth animations calculated on the GPU.
Dependent animations	Dependent animations might not be smooth, because they are calculated on the CPU. Most custom animations are dependent animations, so you should use them with great care.
Animation Library	The API offers a set of predefined animations and transitions that are independent animations, and are consistent with the behavior of Windows 8.
Storyboard	Animations are controlled using a storyboard. A single storyboard can control multiple animations at the same time.
Visual states	You can assign different visual states to a control. For every visual state, you can define how the UI looks. Visual states are described using storyboards. When changing states, animations are responsible for transitioning into the new state.
Render transformation	Most of the time, you will animate transformations. Render transformation is applied after the layout logic was executed, so it will not affect the layout. You can apply one or more transformations to a single `UIElement`.
Control template	To change the visual look of a control, you can assign a new control template to the control's `Template` property. It will enable you to redefine the inner visual structure of the control without affecting the behavior and logic of the control.
`ContentPresenter`	In case of `ContentControls` inside a `ControlTemplate` you should explicitly define a placeholder for the control where it can display its content. You can use `ContentPresenter` to mark where the content should be placed inside the control.
`CollectionViewsource`	`CollectionViewSource` serves as a view over a collection of data. It supports grouping, sorting, and filtering without affecting the underlying original collection. It is a great way to present data for complex controls like `GridView` or `ListView`.
Grouping	`ItemsControls` represent visual lists. The items in the list can be grouped visually by any property using `GroupStyles` and `HeaderTemplates`.

Building Windows 8 Style Applications

WROX.COM CODE DOWNLOADS FOR THIS CHAPTER

You can find the wrox.com code downloads for this chapter on the Download Code tab at www.wrox.com/remtitle.cgi?isbn=012680. The code is in the Chapter09.zip download and individually named, as described in the corresponding exercises.

In Chapters 7 and 8, you learned about creating a user interface (UI) for your Windows 8 style apps using eXtensible Application Markup Language (XAML), and about the fundamental UI controls. Windows 8 style applications use a set of patterns to provide a uniform user experience. In this chapter, you learn about patterns that determine how your application can implement the same user interaction experience as the Windows 8 apps that are shipped as a part of Windows 8. You also learn important details about integrating your apps with the operating system's Start screen.

THE LIFECYCLE OF A WINDOWS 8 APPLICATION

In any previous version of Windows, or even in the Desktop mode of Windows 8, users can run multiple applications simultaneously that all display information in their corresponding windows. In this mode, each running application consumes resources, although the user probably focuses on only one of the apps most of the time.

With Windows 8 style apps, there is always a foreground application owning the screen and managing user interactions, and the other applications are hidden. The Windows 8 operating system manages resources with a very simple policy. The application in the foreground gets the resources to provide the best user experience, whereas applications somewhere in the background (which are momentarily invisible to the user) are frozen in memory, and they do not get other resources except the memory they stay in. When the user switches among applications, and brings another app back to the foreground, the newcomer gets the resources, and the one pushed into the back is frozen (that is, it does not get resources).

> **NOTE** *When an application goes to the background, Windows 8 does not suspend it immediately. The operating system will wait about 5 seconds before suspending an app to prevent unnecessary suspensions, and resumes when apps are changed quickly.*

As you can see, Windows 8 apps have a different lifecycle model than desktop applications. This model helps the user feel as though your application is always alive.

Application Lifecycle States

As shown in Figure 9-1, Windows 8 applications can be in one of four states: *not running*, *running*, *suspended*, and *terminated*. From the lifecycle point of view, the "not running" and terminated states actually have the same meaning — the application either has not been started, or was closed for any reason.

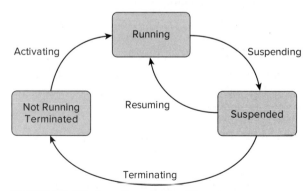

FIGURE 9-1: Windows 8 application lifecycle

When an application is started (either by the user or by another app), it is activated and goes into the running state. In this state, the running application that is in the foreground gets available resources to make it responsive, fluent, and, thus, attractive. Generally, there is only one application in the running state — or, in the snapped mode (when two apps are side-by-side on the screen), two apps are in the running state.

When you switch to another app, as the one in the foreground is sent to the back, its state goes to suspended. A suspended application does not receive CPU or other system resources, which prevents system resources from being drained from the foreground app. The suspended state means that the application keeps the memory it occupies, but that's the only resource it possesses.

If the user launches many applications, suspended apps can reserve too much memory, and jeopardize the overall operation and responsiveness of the foreground app. In this case, the operating system terminates one or more suspended applications to ensure that the foreground app has the required resources. The stopped apps go into the terminated state — Windows 8 closes them and reclaims the memory they hold.

The result of this lifecycle is that foreground applications always have the maximum resources the system can provide, and the battery power is still conserved. While the foreground application waits for user input, it consumes very few CPU cycles. Even the suspended apps are frugal with system resources, because they only consume memory.

Managing Application State Changes

From an application development point of view, the Windows 8 app lifecycle model has a few issues. Assume that an application displays stock exchange rates and refreshes them every 30 seconds. While this app is in the foreground, the user can peruse the changes. However, if the app goes into the background, its code cannot run, and it does not refresh the rates. So, when the user switches back to this app after 10 minutes, the app displays the information that is 10 minutes old, and it may take 30 more seconds for the current rate to be displayed.

Assume that, while another app is in the foreground, this application is terminated by Windows 8 because of a low level of system resources. Say that, when the user activates the application, he or she would like to see the ticker information displayed from the last time he or she viewed the app. From an application point of view, this activation is just like starting it after it was explicitly closed by the user. The app should know that it has been activated after a termination so that it can display the last ticker information instead of a welcome screen.

These situations can be handled with the help of events the operating system sends to the application when changing its state. As described in Table 9-1, these events can be caught and handled in your application class (generally called App in a new Visual Studio project).

TABLE 9-1: Application Lifecycle Events

APPLICATION EVENT	STATE TRANSITION IN FIGURE 9-1	DESCRIPTION
OnLaunched	Activating	The application has been launched either by the user or by some other application. The event-handler method receives an argument of type `LaunchActivatedEventArgs`. You can examine the `Kind` property of the argument to find out the way the app has been launched. The `PreviousExecutionState` property tells you the state of the app before this activation. Its value (one of the `ApplicationExecutionState` enumeration) is `Terminated` or `ClosedByUser`, suggesting that previously the app was closed by the system, or by the user, respectively.
Suspending	Suspending	The system suspends your application because the user switched to another app. The event-handler method receives a `SuspendingEventArgs` argument. In this event handler, you generally save the state of the application so that you can restore it in case the application gets terminated by the system. You can also release unnecessary resources to the system.
Resuming	Resuming	When the user switches back to your suspended application, this event handler is invoked. This is where you can reclaim resources released in the `Suspending` event handler.
No event	Terminating	When the system needs resources and decides to terminate your application, it does not allow you to intercept the termination process, so it does not provide you any event handler to respond to the termination event.

Suspending, Resuming, and Closing the Application

Windows 8 requires you to keep the policies of suspending and resuming your application. When you switch to another application, it does not suspend your application immediately. It allows you a few seconds to reconsider and switch back to the app. After a few seconds, if your application is still in the background, the operating system suspends it, and the application object receives the `Suspending` event.

You should carry out several activities in this event-handler method:

➤ You can save the application state. For example, you can save the information about the last ticker data used in your finance app.

➤ If you hold any exclusive lock on resources (for example, you lock a file used within the application), you can release the lock and provide access to the file for other apps while the finance app is suspended.

➤ If it is possible, you can reduce memory usage. For example, if you keep a large matrix in memory to accelerate certain operations, you can save it on disk, and release the memory it occupies.

The operating system is very stringent with your app. It has up to 5 seconds to carry out all activities. If the Suspending event does not return within 5 seconds, the app will be terminated. The app should not start operations that may block execution (such as popping up a message and waiting for user input, or uploading data to the Internet).

When you switch back to your suspended application, the operating system brings it to the foreground, and the application immediately receives the Resuming event. This is the time when you can restore everything that you need to continue the normal operation of your application:

➤ You can restore the application state.

➤ You can reload the data into the memory, which was saved in the Suspending event to reduce memory usage.

When resuming your application from its suspended state, the operating system does not constrain the time you have for restoring the application's data and the UI.

Windows 8 enables you to save the state of your application when closing it. If the user closes the application explicitly (by pressing Alt+F4, or using the close gesture), the app immediately goes into the background. However, it does not get closed immediately. The operating system waits a few seconds, and then suspends the application. The application receives a Suspending event, and has 5 seconds to save its state. When returning from the event handler (or the 5 seconds elapses), the operating system closes the application process.

Now that you are familiar with the fundamentals of Windows 8 app lifecycle management, it is time to use it in practice.

Using Application Lifecycle Events

Let's create a non-functional application that demonstrates how you can handle the lifecycle events. The application provides the following features:

➤ It traces application lifecycle events, and saves them.

➤ When activating the application, it restores the saved state.

➤ It can emulate a faulty suspension event handler that exceeds the 5-second response time allowed by the operating system.

To examine the lifecycle events, you start from a prepared application, the AppLifeCycleDemo Start solution, that you can find in the Chapter09.zip download.

> **NOTE** *You can find the complete code to download for this exercise on this book's companion website at* www.wrox.com *in the* AppLifeCycleDemo Complete *folder.*

TRY IT OUT   Using Application Lifecycle Events

To complete the prepared application and examine lifecycle events, follow these steps:

1. With the File ⇨ Open Project (Ctrl+Shift+O) command, open the AppLifeCycleDemo.sln file from the AppLifeCycleDemo   Start folder of this chapter's download. The solution contains an EventTracer.cs file with a static class responsible for logging trace messages. The MainPage .xaml.cs and the App.xaml.cs files are prepared with empty methods. You complete them in this exercise.

2. In Solution Explorer, double-click the App.xaml.cs file to open it. Insert the following boldfaced code into the body of the default constructor:

```
public App()
{
    this.InitializeComponent();
    this.Suspending += OnSuspending;
    this.Resuming += OnResuming;
    DelayOnSuspending = TimeSpan.FromMilliseconds(100);
}
```

3. In the code editor, scroll down to the OnSuspending method. This is invoked just before the operating system suspends this application. Copy the following boldfaced code into the method body, and add the async modifier to the method header:

```
private async void OnSuspending(object sender, SuspendingEventArgs e)
{
    var deferral = e.SuspendingOperation.GetDeferral();
    EventTracer.WriteLine("Application is being suspended.");
    await Task.Delay(DelayOnSuspending);
    EventTracer.WriteLine("The app has {0} ms left after saving its state.",
        (e.SuspendingOperation.Deadline - DateTime.Now).TotalMilliseconds);
    deferral.Complete();
}
```

4. To trace when the app is resumed, scroll down to the OnResuming method, and copy the following boldfaced code into the method body:

```
void OnResuming(object sender, object e)
{
    EventTracer.WriteLine("Application is being resumed.");
}
```

5. When your application is launched, it can restore its saved state. To achieve this, navigate to the `OnLaunched` method. Copy the following boldfaced code into the method body:

```
protected override void OnLaunched(LaunchActivatedEventArgs args)
{
    EventTracer.WriteLine(
        "Application launched. (Kind='{0}', PreviousExecutionState='{1}')",
        args.Kind, args.PreviousExecutionState);

    if (args.PreviousExecutionState == ApplicationExecutionState.Running)
    {
        Window.Current.Activate();
        return;
    }

    var rootFrame = new Frame();
    if (!rootFrame.Navigate(typeof(MainPage)))
    {
        throw new Exception("Failed to create initial page");
    }

    Window.Current.Content = rootFrame;
    Window.Current.Activate();
}
```

6. At this point the code in the `App.xaml.cs` file should look like this (comments are removed for the sake of brevity):

```
using System;
using System.Threading.Tasks;
using Windows.ApplicationModel;
using Windows.ApplicationModel.Activation;
using Windows.UI.Xaml;
using Windows.UI.Xaml.Controls;

namespace AppLifeCycleDemo
{
    sealed partial class App : Application
    {
        private const string APP_DATA_FILE = "MyAppData.txt";

        public App()
        {
            this.InitializeComponent();
            this.Suspending += OnSuspending;
            this.Resuming += OnResuming;
            DelayOnSuspending = TimeSpan.FromMilliseconds(100);
        }

        protected override void OnLaunched(LaunchActivatedEventArgs args)
        {
            EventTracer.WriteLine(
                "Application launched. (Kind='{0}', PreviousExecutionState='{1}')",
```

```
            args.Kind, args.PreviousExecutionState);

        if (args.PreviousExecutionState == ApplicationExecutionState.Running)
        {
            Window.Current.Activate();
            return;
        }

        var rootFrame = new Frame();
        if (!rootFrame.Navigate(typeof(MainPage)))
        {
            throw new Exception("Failed to create initial page");
        }

        Window.Current.Content = rootFrame;
        Window.Current.Activate();
    }

    public static TimeSpan DelayOnSuspending { get; set; }

    private async void OnSuspending(object sender, SuspendingEventArgs e)
    {
        var deferral = e.SuspendingOperation.GetDeferral();
        EventTracer.WriteLine("Application is being suspended.");
        await Task.Delay(DelayOnSuspending);
        EventTracer.WriteLine("The app has {0} ms left after saving its state.",
            (e.SuspendingOperation.Deadline - DateTime.Now).TotalMilliseconds);
        deferral.Complete();
    }

    void OnResuming(object sender, object e)
    {
        EventTracer.WriteLine("Application is being resumed.");
    }
  }
}
```

7. With these modifications, the application is ready to run. Before starting it, launch Task Manager by pressing Ctrl+Alt+Delete and then clicking or tapping Task Manager. When it has started, click the Details tab.

8. Switch back to the Visual Studio IDE, and launch the application by pressing Ctrl+F5. As shown in Figure 9-2, the application starts and displays an event trace message as the result of executing the OnLaunched event handler.

FIGURE 9-2: The app displays the launch trace message.

9. Press Alt, and without releasing it, press Tab several times while you switch to the Task Manager, and then release Alt. The Task Manager shows that AppLifeCycleDemo is still running, as shown in Figure 9-3.

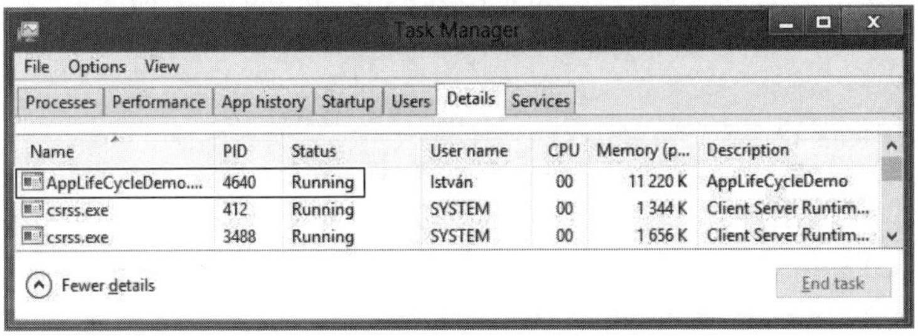

FIGURE 9-3: The app is still in running state.

10. Wait for a few seconds. Now, the AppLifeCycleDemo Windows 8 app is not in the foreground, so the operating system suspends it. The status of the app changes in Task Manager, as shown in Figure 9-4.

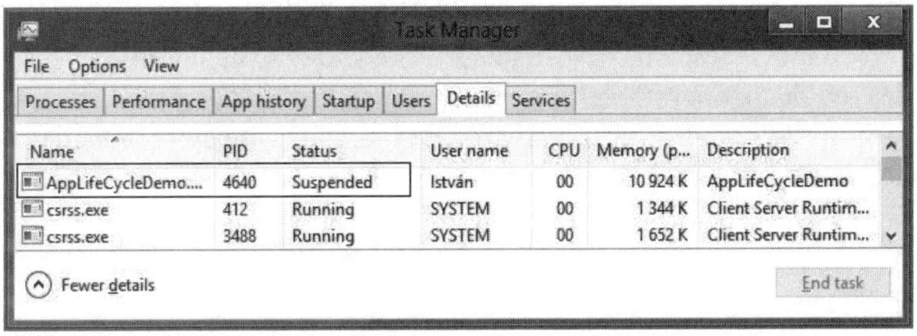

FIGURE 9-4: The app gets suspended.

11. Switch back to the app. The app is immediately resumed, and the trace messages belonging to the Suspending and Resuming events are displayed, as shown in Figure 9-5.

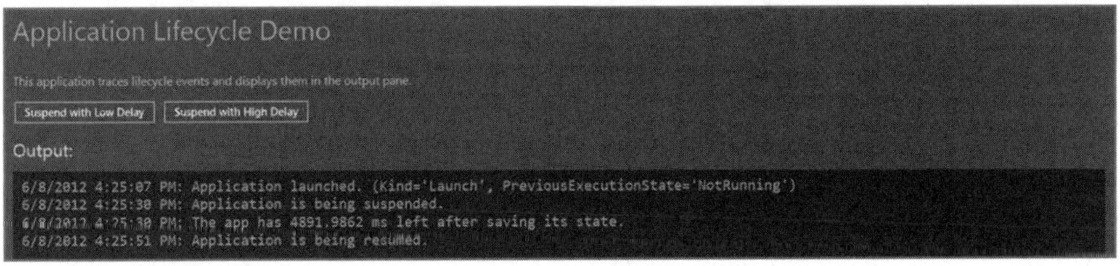

FIGURE 9-5: The app displays the Suspending and Resuming trace messages

12. Close the application by pressing Alt+F4.

How It Works

When you started the application from Visual Studio, the `OnLaunched` method was called, and it displayed the trace message you saw in Figure 9-2. In Step 8, when you switched to Task Manager, the operating system kept the application active for a few seconds before suspending it. When the application received the Suspending event, the following code lines were executed (within the body of the `OnSuspending` method):

```
var deferral = e.SuspendingOperation.GetDeferral();
EventTracer.WriteLine("Application is being suspended.");
await Task.Delay(DelayOnSuspending);
EventTracer.WriteLine("The app has {0} ms left after saving
    its state.",
    (e.SuspendingOperation.Deadline -
    DateTime.Now).TotalMilliseconds);
deferral.Complete();
```

The code obtained a deferral object, because it was about to execute asynchronous method calls. As you learned in Chapter 5, the `await Task.Delay()` call would return from the `OnSuspending` method immediately, because the operating system would not know that there is an asynchronous call in the current context. Getting a deferral object signals this fact, and the caller of the `OnSuspending` method knows that it should wait for the `deferral.Complete()` operation as the signal of completion.

This code snippet displayed two trace messages. The first displayed the start of the method; the second displayed the time remaining after the delay operation. The remaining time was calculated from the `DeadLine` property of the event argument's `SuspendingOperation` object. The delay task made the application wait for 100 milliseconds.

In Step 10, when the application was resumed, the `OnResuming` event was fired, and it displayed a new trace message, as was shown in Figure 9-5.

> **NOTE** You can try running the application and clicking the "Suspend with High Delay" button. As a result, the Suspending event is 7 seconds longer. You can check with the Task Manager that the operating system will terminate your application, because it does not respond to the Suspending event in a timely manner.

You already learned that Visual Studio builds and deploys your application, so you can start it by pressing F5 (when you intend to debug it) or Ctrl+F5 (without debugging). It is now time to learn an important step in this process — deploying the application.

DEPLOYING WINDOWS 8 APPS

In previous Windows versions, when you built applications, you could immediately run them by starting their executable files. In Windows 8, applications run in an application sandbox, so you cannot run their executables without deploying the application. The deployment process prepares the application by registering it with the operating system. This process also registers capabilities that determine how the application runs in the sandbox — for example, whether it can use a webcam, whether it can access the document library, and so on. Applications can add extensions to the operating system (for example, they can extend the search charm). Registering these extensions is also part of the deployment process.

> **NOTE** *A sandbox is a security mechanism that separates running applications, and prevents them from accessing system resources they are not allowed to use. A sandbox prevents programs from communicating with each other directly with an arbitrary mechanism. Thus, only predefined (and, so, from a security point of view, controlled) ways of communication and access are allowed. As a result, a sandbox can protect the system from accidental programming mistakes that would breach the intended security level of an application, and also from malicious or untrusted programs (such as spyware and computer viruses).*

Application Packages

Instead of writing installation utilities for Windows 8 style apps, you must package your application and let the operating system install it. Normally, only applications submitted to the Windows Store can be installed on a Windows 8 computer, but by installing Visual Studio 2012 on your computer, you obtain a special developer certificate that allows deploying your apps on your machine.

> **NOTE** *You learn about the Windows Store and the related submission process in Chapter 16.*

This application package is a container based on the Open Packaging Convention (OPC) standard. It is a structure that stores your application, its resources, and related information using a standard .zip file. When you run your application in Visual Studio, the IDE creates and deploys the application package behind the scenes. You can create a standalone package that later can be submitted to the Windows Store.

In the next exercise, you learn how to create an application package, just for the sake of discovering its structure.

TRY IT OUT Creating an Application Package

To create and examine an application package, follow these steps:

1. Open the AppLifeCycleDemo solution you created in the previous exercise. You can also find this solution in the AppLifeCycleDemo Complete folder of this chapter's download.

2. Use the Store ⇨ Create App Package command. The Create App Package dialog box appears and asks you whether you want to build a package to upload to the Windows Store, as shown in Figure 9-6. Select No, and click Next.

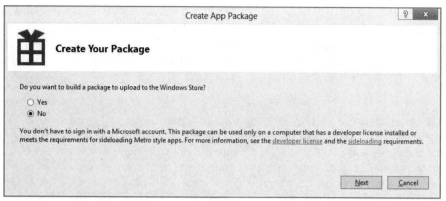

FIGURE 9-6: The Create App Package dialog box

3. On the next page of the dialog box, you can specify package settings, as shown in Figure 9-7. Leave all settings as provided by default, and click Create.

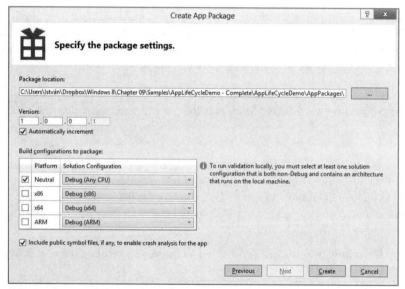

FIGURE 9-7: Specifying package settings

4. The IDE builds the `AppLifeCycleDemo` project, and creates the package in a few seconds. The Create App Package dialog box pops up again with a hyperlink to the folder that contains the application package, as shown in Figure 9-8. Click the hyperlink to open the folder in Windows Explorer.

5. In the package folder, you can see a folder ending with `Debug_Test`. Open this folder, and locate the package file with the `.appx` filename extension, as shown in Figure 9-9. Rename this file's extension to `.zip`. When the shell asks whether you are sure you want to change the file extension, select Yes.

FIGURE 9-8: The hyperlink to the newly created package

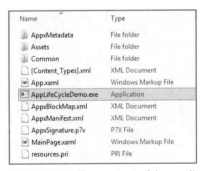

FIGURE 9-9: The application package file

6. Double click the `.zip` file to open its content. You can immediately recognize the application's executable file, as shown in Figure 9-10, and other resources and assets, such as the `Common` folder, and the `App.xaml` and `MainPage.xaml` files. You can also find an `AppxManifest.xml` file here, which plays an important role in application deployment, as you will soon learn.

Name	Type
AppxMetadata	File folder
Assets	File folder
Common	File folder
[Content_Types].xml	XML Document
App.xaml	Windows Markup File
AppLifeCycleDemo.exe	Application
AppxBlockMap.xml	XML Document
AppxManifest.xml	XML Document
AppxSignature.p7x	P7X File
MainPage.xaml	Windows Markup File
resources.pri	PRI File

FIGURE 9-10: The content of the application package file

How It Works

The package you created in Step 4 used the OPC standard, and it's actually a `.zip` file. So, when you renamed the `.appx` extension to `.zip`, you were able to examine its structure.

The Application Package Manifest

The deployment process of the application does a lot of things besides simply unzipping the package and copying the related files. It checks the application's integrity, prepares the sandbox the application will run in, registers the extension the app proffers, and carries on other important steps.

There is a very important file that holds all information that is used during the deployment process. This file is the application package manifest file. You can find it in Solution Explorer with the name `Package.appxmanifest`, as shown in Figure 9-11.

This file is an XML file, but Visual Studio provides a designer to edit this file. When you double-click `Package.appxmanifest`, the designer opens, as shown in Figure 9-12.

FIGURE 9-11: The application package manifest file

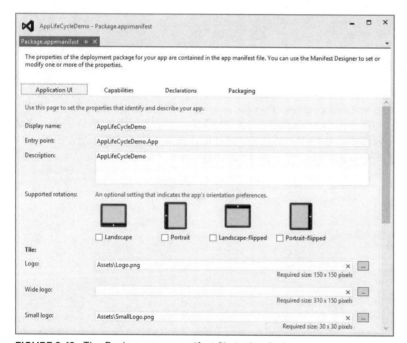

FIGURE 9-12: The Package.appxmanifest file in the designer

> **NOTE** You can examine the content of the `Package.appxmanifest` file. In Solution Explorer, right-click it, and select the View Code command from the context menu. The `Package.appxmanifest` file opens in the code editor, and you can examine its XML structure.

The application package manifest designer contains four tabs: Application UI, Capabilities, Declarations, and Packaging. JavaScript applications have an additional tab, titled Content URIs. Each tab is a container for a specific kind of information, as summarized in Table 9-2.

TABLE 9-2: Application Package Manifest Editor Tabs

TAB	DESCRIPTION
Application UI	In this tab, you can specify information that identifies your application package, and describes properties influencing the app's appearance. Among the other things, you can declare the logos and text used in the application's Live Tile, define the splash screen artwork, and specify a badge logo used in the lock screen. (You learn more about a badge logo later in this chapter.)
Capabilities	As you already learned, Windows 8 apps run in a sandbox. In this tab, an app can declare the capabilities it intends to use. The sandbox prevents the app from using any capability it does not declare explicitly. This feature prevents malicious code (that somehow managed to infect your app) from using unwanted capabilities. For example, if you did not declare the Microphone capability in this tab, your app cannot turn on the microphone. If it were to try, an exception would be raised.
Declarations	Your application may provide extensions to be used by other applications. In this tab, you can declare the types of extensions your application proffers. For example, if you add a Search declaration, the system registers the app as a search provider, and users will be able to search the app from anywhere in the system. Another declaration, the File Open Picker, registers your app as a file open picker, making the content in the app available to other Windows 8 apps.
Packaging	To deploy a package, you must provide information that identifies it in the Windows Store. In this tab, you can specify these attributes of your app.
Content URIs	In this tab, you can configure network boundaries for your JavaScript app. You can add, modify, and remove Uniform Resource Identifiers (URIs) that have access to web standards for geolocation and clipboard access.

Installation, Update, and Removal

Windows requires that applications be signed with a trusted signature. This signature enables Windows to confirm the identity of the signer, and verify that the contents of the package haven't been tampered with. If someone changed the content of your application (for example, changed the executable in the .zip file representing your package), the signature would become invalid. Because of security reasons, Windows won't deploy an unsigned package.

> **NOTE** *Windows 8 keeps a list of trusted certification authorities — third parties who create certificates used to sign code and documents digitally. When your application is signed with a certificate coming directly or indirectly from a trusted certification authority, this signature is taken into account as trusted.*

Generally, users browse the Windows Store on the Internet, or directly from their computers using the Store application. After they purchase an app (or download it for free), they receive a license that enables them to install the app. When you are using Visual Studio, you have a special developer license that allows you to install your app without packaging.

> **NOTE** *You can check the unpackaged files used by the installation process with a developer license. After building your app in Visual Studio, in Solution Explorer, right-click the project node and select the Open Folder in Windows Explorer command. In Windows Explorer, navigate to the* `bin\Debug\AppX` *folder. The files in this folder are used during installation.*

In contrast to previous Windows versions, Windows 8 does not need elevated rights to install an app — you do not need to be logged in your computer as an administrator. No custom actions are required during the install, because everything Windows needs to install the app is contained in the package. It makes the whole installation user experience quick and simple; the user won't be prompted for any additional information. The user does not even have to be aware of things such as the registry or program files. Getting an application is just like buying a beer at the supermarket — you take it from the shelf, pay for it, and drink it.

If a user does not like an application, or simply does not want to use it anymore, he or she can uninstall it easily. Just like installation, application removal is a simple thing that does not require any user interaction. Because an application can be installed for multiple users on the same computer, when a user uninstalls it, the application will be removed only from that user's context. When the last user uninstalls the app, the installation files will be removed from the computer.

Applications may be updated by their authors. Windows Update observes that an application has an updated version, and notifies users about the availability of newer versions. Although updates are observed by the system, they are not installed automatically. Users must choose to install any updated versions of an app.

You have now learned about the basics of the Windows 8 application lifecycle. It's time to get acquainted with adding commanding surfaces to your app.

COMMANDING SURFACES

Desktop applications have standard elements such as menus and toolbars that can be used to execute commands. These adornments consume UI estate and often confuse the user, because they provide too many options to execute in a particular context.

Windows 8 applications are about the full-screen experience that is free from unnecessary embellishments that do not add functional value to the application. While you interact with an application, you have several ways to express your intentions by touching or clicking the visual elements of the UI. A great user experience design builds on intuition and conventions (usage patterns) that are used commonly by all applications.

Each application may use commands that cannot be easily attached to any elements on the UI, because there is no appropriate visual component. Such commands may include opening a document, moving a contact card to a new folder, or printing an e-mail. Of course, you can always put button controls on the UI that trigger the command, but they always consume screen real estate, and may be disturbing, because they are there even when they are not needed.

Windows 8 has several usage patterns to cope with this issue. These patterns fit in perfectly with the Windows 8 design principles, and, as you learn in this section, you can use them easily.

Using the Context Menu

A *context menu* is a lightweight menu that you can attach to UI elements. The user can immediately access the menu by right-clicking the particular element, or using the "tap and hold" gesture. A few controls (such as text boxes and hyperlinks) provide a predefined context menu, but you can replace the default ones and display your own custom commands.

You should use context menus to show commands that are directly relevant to users, and that cannot be easily accessed otherwise. Typical usage is to display clipboard comments, and to show commands that operate on UI components that cannot be selected. The key type of displaying and using the context menu is the `PopupMenu` class that is defined in the `Windows.UI.Popups` namespace, as you learn in the next exercise.

FIGURE 9-13: The shuffled puzzle

To examine the commanding surfaces (including the context menu), you use a prepared solution (`SimplePuzzle`) that you can find in the `Chapter09.zip` download. This is a very simple puzzle game that shuffles a few puzzle pieces marked with numbers, and your task is to restore their order by moving them, as shown in Figure 9-13.

The prepared project contains all the code that controls the game, and in the next exercise, you add a context menu that starts a new game or restarts the current one.

> **NOTE** *You can find the complete code to download for this exercise on this book's companion website at* www.wrox.com *in the folder* SimplePuzzle ContextMenu *within the* Chapter09.zip *download.*

TRY IT OUT Adding Context Menu to an Application

To add a context menu to the prepared sample application, follow these steps:

1. With the File ⇨ Open Project (Ctrl+Shift+O) command, open the `SimplePuzzle.sln` file from the `SimplePuzzle Start` folder of this chapter's download.

2. Build and start the application by pressing Ctrl+F5. When it starts, it immediately creates a new puzzle, and shuffles the pieces randomly. You can move the pieces adjacent with the empty puzzle cell by clicking or tapping the piece. Try to solve the puzzle (the solution is shown in Figure 9-13). When you manage to solve it, a new game is started.

3. Close the application by pressing Alt+F4.

> **NOTE** *If the puzzle is too difficult to solve, you can make it easier. Open the* `GameController.cs` *file, and locate the* `StartNew` *method. In the middle of the method body, find the* `await Shuffle(10)` *statement, and change it to* `await Shuffle(4)`. *Start this exercise again from Step 2. In this case, the puzzle will be really easy to solve.*

4. In Solution Explorer, double-click `Mainpage.xaml` to open it. In the designer, go to the XAML pane, and select the `<Grid x:Name="LayoutRoot"...>` node, and add the following boldfaced attribute to it:

```
<Grid x:Name="LayoutRoot" Background="#124372" RightTapped=
    "MainPageRightTapped">
```

5. While in the XAML editor, right-click the `RightTapped` word in the modified code line, and select the "Navigate to Event Handler" command. The IDE creates an empty method. Add the `async` modifier to the method, and copy the following boldfaced code into the method body:

```
private async void MainPageRightTapped(object sender,
    RightTappedRoutedEventArgs e)
{
    var menu = new PopupMenu();
    menu.Commands.Add(new UICommand("New Game", command =>
        {
            _game.StartNew(_height, _width);
        }));
    menu.Commands.Add(new UICommandSeparator());
    menu.Commands.Add(new UICommand("Restart Game", command =>
        {
            _game.RestoreStartPositions();
        }));
    var point = e.GetPosition(null);
    await menu.ShowForSelectionAsync(new Rect(point,
        new Size(0, 0)));
}
```

6. Run the application by pressing Ctrl+F5. Right-click anywhere on the screen (or use the "tap and hold gesture") to display the context menu, as shown in Figure 9-14.

7. Click or tap the New Game command, and you'll be given a new puzzle.

8. Move a few puzzle pieces. Then display the context menu again, and use the Restart Game command. The puzzle pieces will be reset to the same state as at the beginning of the new game.

9. Close the `SimplePuzzle` application.

FIGURE 9-14: The context menu is displayed on the screen.

How It Works

The prepared project contains a `GameController.cs` file that defines the `GameController` type responsible for implementing the logic of the puzzle game. In Step 4, you added an event handler to the

LayoutRoot grid, and in Step 5, you defined the body of the event-handler method. Any time you right-clicked on the application screen (or used the "tap and hold" gesture), the context menu was displayed.

In the body of the MainPageRightTapped method, you prepared the context menu by creating a PopupMenu instance and adding two UICommand objects and a UICommandSeparator object to the PopupMenu's Commands container:

```
var menu = new PopupMenu();
menu.Commands.Add(new UICommand("New Game", command =>
    {
        _game.StartNew(_height, _width);
    }));
menu.Commands.Add(new UICommandSeparator());
menu.Commands.Add(new UICommand("Restart Game", command =>
    {
        _game.RestoreStartPositions();
    }));
```

Each UICommand constructor accepted two arguments. The first was the name of the command to display; the second was the method to execute as the response when the user triggers the command. In this case, both commands were defined with lambda expressions, where the command argument referred to the UI command triggered by the user. These commands used the _game member that is a GameController instance to start and restart the game, respectively. The UICommandSeparator declared a simple separator line between the two commands.

You displayed the prepared PopupMenu with the following statements:

```
await menu.ShowForSelectionAsync(new Rect(point, new Size(0, 0)));
```

Displaying the context menu and waiting for user input is an asynchronous operation, as await suggests. The ShowForSelectionAsync method accepted a Rectangle argument that specified the placement of the context menu. The positions were calculated with the following code line where the GetPosition method obtained the mouse (or touch) coordinates relative to the screen:

```
var point = e.GetPosition(null);
```

As you have just seen, using the context menu is quite easy, but (to be honest) it is misused in this exercise. The main issue with the context menu is that it is not really intuitive. The user does not know that this menu exists at all, unless he or she tries a right-click (or a "tap and hold" gesture).

It would be much better to use some more intuitive commanding solutions. Windows 8 provides a better way for incorporating these commands — by placing them in the app bar.

Using the App Bar

The app bar is a more intuitive way of presenting commands to the user on-demand. The app bar is not visible by default. It appears only when a user swipes a finger from the top or bottom edge of the screen. The app bar can also appear programmatically on object selection or on right-click. When you start a new Windows 8 app project in Visual Studio, your application is programmed to show the app bar not only for swiping your finger from the screen edges, but also for right-clicking the screen, or pressing the Windows+Z key combination.

Adding an app bar takes a few more steps than creating a context menu, but from a programming point of view, it's a bit easier, as you learn in the next exercise.

TRY IT OUT   Adding an App Bar to Your Screen

In this exercise you add a few commands to the app bar of the `SimplePuzzle` application.

To add the app bar with the commands to the application, follow these steps:

1. With the File ⇨ Open Project (Ctrl+Shift+O) command, open the `SimplePuzzle.sln` file from the `SimplePuzzle   Start` folder of this chapter's download. If you modified this project in the previous exercise, use the `Chapter09.zip` download to extract this project so that you can start working with its original state.

2. In Solution Explorer, double-click the `MainPage.xaml` file to open it in the designer.

3. In the XAML pane, type the following code just before the `<Grid x:Name="LayoutRoot"...>` node:

```
<Page.BottomAppBar>
    <AppBar x:Name="CommandBar">
        <Grid>
            <Grid.ColumnDefinitions>
                <ColumnDefinition/>
                <ColumnDefinition/>
            </Grid.ColumnDefinitions>
            <StackPanel Orientation="Horizontal">
                <Button x:Name="NewGameButton" Height="84" VerticalAlignment="Top"
                    &#xE0B4;
                    <AutomationProperties.AutomationId>
                        NewGameButton
                    </AutomationProperties.AutomationId>
                    <AutomationProperties.Name>
                        New Game
                    </AutomationProperties.Name>
                </Button>
            </StackPanel>
            <StackPanel Grid.Column="1" HorizontalAlignment="Right"
                Orientation="Horizontal">
                <Button x:Name="ResetGameButton" Height="84"
                    VerticalAlignment="Top"
                    Style="{StaticResource AppBarButtonStyle}">
                    &#xE102;
                    <AutomationProperties.AutomationId>
                        RestartGameButton
                    </AutomationProperties.AutomationId>
                    <AutomationProperties.Name>
                        Restart
                    </AutomationProperties.Name>
                </Button>
            </StackPanel>
        </Grid>
    </AppBar>
</Page.BottomAppBar>
```

4. Run the application by pressing Ctrl+F5. When it starts, right-click it (or swipe your fingers from the bottom edge of the screen). The app bar appears with two buttons, one aligned to the left and one aligned to the right, as shown in Figure 9-15. As you see, the first button looks weird.

FIGURE 9-15: The app bar displayed on the screen

5. Close the application.

6. In the `MainPage.xaml` file, add a `Style` attribute to the first `<Button>` node (with the name `NewGameButton`), as the following boldfaced code shows:

```
<Button x:Name="NewGameButton" Height="84" VerticalAlignment="Top"
    Style="{StaticResource AppBarButtonStyle}">
    &#xE0B4;
    <AutomationProperties.AutomationId>
        NewGameButton
    </AutomationProperties.AutomationId>
    <AutomationProperties.Name>
        New Game
    </AutomationProperties.Name>
</Button>
```

7. Run the application again. This time the first button appears properly, as shown in Figure 9-16.

8. Close the application.

How It Works

The layout of the command bar is defined by the long XAML fragment you inserted in Step 3. The skeleton of the layout is simple:

FIGURE 9-16: Now the first button appears as expected

```
<Page.BottomAppBar>
    <AppBar x:Name="CommandBar">
        <Grid>
            <Grid.ColumnDefinitions>
                <ColumnDefinition/>
                <ColumnDefinition/>
            </Grid.ColumnDefinitions>
            <StackPanel Orientation="Horizontal">
                <!-- Left aligned buttons -->
            </StackPanel>
            <StackPanel Grid.Column="1" HorizontalAlignment="Right"
                Orientation="Horizontal">
                <!-- Right aligned buttons -->
            </StackPanel>
        </Grid>
    </AppBar>
</Page.BottomAppBar>
```

The `Page` has a `BottomAppBar` property, and the `AppBar` control is assigned to this property. The control uses a two-column grid with one `StackPanel` in each column, the second aligned to right. The buttons are put into the appropriate `StackPanel`, depending on their alignment.

The definition of a button in the app bar looks like this:

```
<Button x:Name="NewGameButton" Height="84" VerticalAlignment="Top"
    Style="{StaticResource AppBarButtonStyle}">
    &#xE0B4;
    <AutomationProperties.AutomationId>
        NewGameButton
    </AutomationProperties.AutomationId>
    <AutomationProperties.Name>
        New Game
    </AutomationProperties.Name>
</Button>
```

This definition is not very obvious, so let's see how it displays an app bar button. The key of the appearance is the `Style` attribute that uses the `AppBarButtonStyle` resource. This resource is defined in the `StandardStyle.xaml` file, and it is responsible for displaying an app bar button as you saw in Figure 9-16. When you typed the XAML fragment in Step 3, the `NewGameButton` did not have the `Style` attribute, so that was why you saw a weird button in Figure 9-15.

The `<AutomationProperties.AutomationId>` element defines an identifier that can be used by Windows 8 automation to access the app bar button. The `<AutomationProperties.Name>` element sets the name to be displayed for the button. The interesting thing is that the content of the `<Button>` element is a simple character denoted by a hexadecimal code, such as `&#xE0B4`. This strange code is a character in the Segoe UI Symbol font type (the `AppBarButtonStyle` assigns this font to an app bar button), as shown in Figure 9-17.

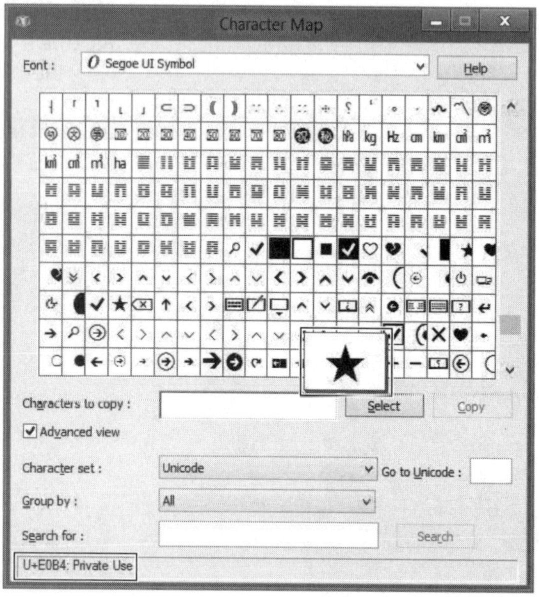

FIGURE 9-17: The Segoe UI Symbol font in Character Map

> **NOTE** *You can use the Segoe UI Symbol font in Windows 8 that provides hundreds of predefined Windows 8 style icons. Open the Character Map application to browse this font. The code for a particular character is shown at the bottom-left side of the app window, as highlighted in Figure 9-17.*

As you saw in this exercise, app bar buttons are standard button controls with a predefined style. It is not surprising that you can respond to app bar button events just as you can with normal buttons. In the next exercise, you add event handlers to the New Game and Restart Game buttons.

TRY IT OUT Responding to App Bar Button Events

To add event handlers to the app bar buttons, follow these steps:

1. Open the solution you worked with in the previous exercise, unless it is still open in Visual Studio.

2. Open the `MainPage.xaml` file, and in the XAML pane of the editor, navigate to the `<Button>` element representing the `NewGameButton`. Add the `Tapped` attribute to this element, as shown in the following boldfaced code:

```
<Button x:Name="NewGameButton" Height="84" VerticalAlignment="Top"
    Style="{StaticResource AppBarButtonStyle}"
    Tapped="NewGameButtonTapped">
```

3. In the XAML pane, right-click the `Tapped` attribute and select the "Navigate to Event Handler" command. The IDE creates the skeleton of the event-handler method. Type its body, as indicated in the following boldfaced code snippet:

```
private void NewGameButtonTapped(object sender,
    Windows.UI.Xaml.Input.TappedRoutedEventArgs e)
{
    _game.StartNew(_height, _width);
}
```

4. Turn back to the `MainPage.xaml` file, and now navigate to the `<Button>` element representing the `ResetGameButton`. Add the `Tapped` attribute to this element, as shown in the following boldfaced code:

```
<Button x:Name="ResetGameButton" Height="84" VerticalAlignment="Top"
    Style="{StaticResource AppBarButtonStyle}"
    Tapped="ResetGameButtonTapped">
```

5. In the XAML pane, with the "Navigate to Event Handler" command, set the body of the event-handler method, as shown in the following boldfaced code snippet:

```
private void ResetGameButtonTapped(object sender,
    Windows.UI.Xaml.Input.TappedRoutedEventArgs e)
{
    _game.RestoreStartPositions();
}
```

6. Run the application by pressing Ctrl+F5. Move a few puzzle pieces, and then right-click or use the Windows+Z key combination to display the app bar. Click the Restart and the New Game buttons to check that these functions work.

7. Close the application.

How It Works

In this exercise, you assigned event-handler code to the app bar buttons in the same way as you learned in Chapter 8. This time, however, you used the Tapped event.

Because of the asynchronous manner in which SimplePuzzle works, when you run the application, you can use the Restart command while the app is shuffling the puzzle pieces. It may lead to errors, so it would be better to disable the Restart app bar button during this initialization phase. Another thing you can observe is that after clicking the New Game or Restart buttons, the app bar remains displayed on the screen. In the following exercise, you learn how to manage these issues.

> **NOTE** You can find the complete code to download for this exercise on this book's companion website at www.wrox.com in the folder SimplePuzzle AppBar within the Chapter09.zip download.

TRY IT OUT   Polishing the App Bar Behavior

To solve the Restart button issue, and hide the app bar, follow these steps:

1. Open the solution you worked with in the previous exercise, unless it is still open in Visual Studio.

2. Open the GameController.cs file, navigate to the StartNew method, and change the await Shuffle(10) statement to this one:

```
await Shuffle(height * width * 10);
```

This change extensively shuffles the puzzle pieces, and takes more time than the previous solution, so it provides you with time to check that Restart is disabled while the puzzle is initialized.

3. Open the MainPage.xaml.cs file, and extend the body of the Page_Loaded method with the bold-faced code as shown here:

```
private void Page_Loaded(object sender, RoutedEventArgs e)
{
    _game = new GameController(PuzzleCanvas);
    _game.GameStarted += (s, arg) => VisualStateManager
        .GoToState(this, "InProgress", true);
    _game.ShuffleStarted += (s, arg) => ResetGameButton.IsEnabled = false;
    _game.ShuffleCompleted += (s, arg) => ResetGameButton.IsEnabled = true;
    _game.GameCompleted += GameCompleted;
    _height = 3;
    _width = 3;
    StartNewGame();
}
```

4. Run the application by pressing Ctrl+F5. Right-click the screen, or use the Windows+Z key combination to display the app bar, and then click the New Game button. Observe that the Restart button is disabled while the puzzle is being shuffled, then it is enabled again. Close the app.

5. In the `MainPage.xamle.cs` file, append the following code snippet to the body of the `NewGameButtonTapped` method, and then the same snippet to the body of the `ResetGameButtonTapped` method:

```
CommandBar.IsOpen = false;
```

6. Run the application by pressing Ctrl+F5. Right-click the screen, or use the Windows+Z key combination to display the app bar, and then click the New Game button. Observe that the app bar hides immediately after you clicked the button. Close the app.

How It Works

In Step 3 you added statements that disabled the Restart button when the puzzle game entered into the initialization phase (the `ShuffleStarted` event was raised). Similarly, when the puzzle was ready to be solved (the `ShuffleCompleted` event was raised), the button was enabled again.

Setting the `IsOpen` property of the app bar to `false` in Step 5 hid the app bar as soon as you clicked either of the two buttons.

Now, you cannot use the Restart button anytime, because it gets disabled while shuffling puzzle pieces. However, you can use the New Game button. If you incidentally click it, your almost-solved puzzle may be dropped. It would be much better if the app could ask for user confirmation. In the next section, you learn how to create simple dialog boxes that can be used for this purpose (among other things).

Using Message Dialog Boxes

Your application may often use messages to notify the user of something (such as successfully saving a file, telling the user that a long process has been completed, and so on). Also, there may be situations when the application waits for a confirmation (such as deleting a picture, moving a folder, and so on).

The `Windows.UI.Popups` namespace defines a `MessageDialog` class that can display a simple message with a title. You can add buttons with related actions to the `Commands` container of a `MessageDialog` class. Using the `DefaultCommandIndex` property, you can mark the command that should be executed when the user presses the Enter key. Similarly, the `CancelCommandIndex` property marks the command to execute when the user presses the Esc key.

Using a `MessageDialog` is fairly easy, as you learn in the next exercise.

> **NOTE** *You can find the complete code to download for this exercise on this book's companion website at* `www.wrox.com` *in the folder* `SimplePuzzle Messages` *within the* `Chapter09.zip` *download.*

TRY IT OUT Adding Message Dialog Boxes to an App

In this exercise, you add three messages to your application. The first two are used to confirm the New Game and Restart actions, respectively; the third one is displayed when you solve the puzzle. To add these messages to the app, follow these steps:

1. Open the solution you worked with in the previous exercise, unless it is still open in Visual Studio.

2. Open the `MainPage.xaml` file, and append the following line to the end of the `using` directives in the top of the file:

```
using Windows.UI.Popups;
```

3. Add the `async` modifier to the header of the `NewGameButtonTapped` method and insert the following boldfaced code into the method body:

```
private void NewGameButtonTapped(object sender,
    Windows.UI.Xaml.Input.TappedRoutedEventArgs e)
{
    if (_game.State == GameState.InProgress || _game.State == GameState.Shuffle)
    {
        bool abort = true;
        var messageDialog = new MessageDialog(
            "Are you sure you want abort this game and start a new one?",
            "Game is in progress");
        messageDialog.Commands.Add(
            new UICommand("Yes", (command) => { abort = true; }));
        messageDialog.Commands.Add(
            new UICommand("No", (command) => { abort = false; }));
        messageDialog.DefaultCommandIndex = 1;
        await messageDialog.ShowAsync();
        if (!abort) return;
    }
    _game.StartNew(_height, _width);
    CommandBar.IsOpen = false;
}
```

4. Navigate to the `ResetGameButtonTapped` method. Add the `async` modifier to its header, and insert the following boldfaced code into the method body:

```
private async void ResetGameButtonTapped(object sender,
    Windows.UI.Xaml.Input.TappedRoutedEventArgs e)
{
    if (_game.State == GameState.InProgress)
    {
        bool restart = true;
        var messageDialog = new MessageDialog(
            "Are you sure you want to restart this game?",
            "Game is in progress");
        messageDialog.Commands.Add(
            new UICommand("Yes", (command) => { restart = true; }));
        messageDialog.Commands.Add(
            new UICommand("No", (command) => { restart = false; }));
        messageDialog.DefaultCommandIndex = 0;
```

```
        messageDialog.CancelCommandIndex = 1;
        await messageDialog.ShowAsync();
        if (!restart) return;
    }
    _game.RestoreStartPositions();
    CommandBar.IsOpen = false;
}
```

5. Add the `async` modifier to the `GameCompleted` method, and change its body as shown in the following boldfaced code:

```
private async void GameCompleted(object sender, EventArgs e)
{
    VisualStateManager.GoToState(this, "Completed", true);
    var messageDialog = new MessageDialog(
        "You have successfully solved the puzzle!",
        "Game Completed");
    messageDialog.Commands.Add(
        new UICommand("OK"));
    await messageDialog.ShowAsync();
    _game.StartNew(_height, _width);
}
```

6. Run the app by pressing Ctrl+F5. In the app bar, click the New Game button. The confirmation message specified in Step 3 appears, as shown in Figure 9-18.

FIGURE 9-18: The message dialog box appearing when you click New Game

7. Click Yes, and solve the puzzle. When it's completed, a message dialog box appears telling you that you solved the puzzle. While this message is displayed, the puzzle is rotated in the background, indicating that the message dialog box does not block the UI, as shown in Figure 9-19.

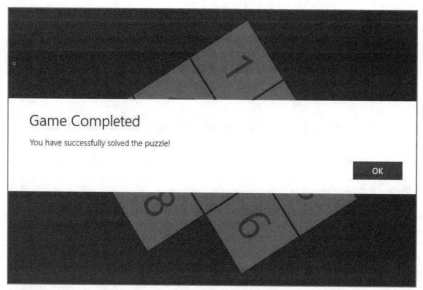

FIGURE 9-19: Message dialog box appearing when you solve the puzzle

How It Works

In Step 3, you instantiated a `MessageDialog` by passing two strings to the constructor. The two string arguments declared the message and the title, respectively. Then you added two `UICommand` instances to the `Commands` container of the dialog box. Each instance represented a command, with the "Yes" and "No" text, respectively. The second parameter of the `UICommand` constructor accepted a lambda expression that set the `abort` flag. The `DefaultCommandIndex` property was set to 1, which was the second ("No") button, because index values are zero-based. The dialog box was displayed asynchronously with the `ShowAsync` method.

In Step 7, you could observe the asynchronous operation, because the puzzle was rotated in the background while the message dialog box still waited for the OK button to be clicked.

In Step 4, you used the same approach to display the dialog box as you did in Step 3.

The `SimplePuzzle` application can handle different table dimensions, not just 3 × 3 puzzles. In the next section, you learn about changing the table dimensions using the settings charm.

Using the Settings Charm in Your App

By convention, Windows 8 style apps should integrate management of the UI with application-wide settings incorporated in the settings charm. The `Windows.UI.ApplicationSettings` namespace offers the `SettingsPane` class for this purpose. Using this class, your application can add custom commands to the settings charm, and respond to them when the user clicks or taps any of them.

> **NOTE** *For apps that you intend to submit to the Windows Store, using the settings charm for application-wide settings is a requirement, and it is checked by the approval process.*

You can harness the SimplePuzzle game with predefined table size settings using the SettingsPane class, as you learn in the next exercise. Although this exercise uses simple commands, when you have many settings, you generally add commands that display application settings panels.

TRY IT OUT   Integrating with the Settings Charm

In this exercise, you start from a prepared sample. To integrate SimplePuzzle with the settings charm, follow these steps:

1. With the File ➪ Open Project (Ctrl+Shift+O) command, open the SimplePuzzle.sln file from the SimplePuzzle Settings folder of this chapter's download.

2. Open the MainPage.xaml.cs file, and scroll down to the end of the file. You can find two new methods there, SettingsCommandsRequested and OnSettingsCommand, as shown in the following code snippet:

```
void SettingsCommandsRequested(SettingsPane sender,
    SettingsPaneCommandsRequestedEventArgs args)
{
    var size3By3 = new SettingsCommand(SIZE3BY3, "3x3", OnSettingsCommand);
    args.Request.ApplicationCommands.Add(size3By3);
    var size3By4 = new SettingsCommand(SIZE3BY4, "3x4", OnSettingsCommand);
    args.Request.ApplicationCommands.Add(size3By4);
    var size4By4 = new SettingsCommand(SIZE4BY4, "4x4", OnSettingsCommand);
    args.Request.ApplicationCommands.Add(size4By4);
}

void OnSettingsCommand(IUICommand command)
{
    var id = command.Id.ToString();
    _height = id == SIZE4BY4 ? 4 : 3;
    _width = id == SIZE3BY3 ? 3 : 4;
}
```

These methods use constant values that can be found at the beginning of the class definition, such as SIZE3BY3 and others.

3. Add the following boldfaced code to the beginning of the Page_Loaded method:

```
private void Page_Loaded(object sender, RoutedEventArgs e)
{
    SettingsPane.GetForCurrentView().CommandsRequested +=
        SettingsCommandsRequested;
    // --- Other lines omitted from this code snippet
}
```

4. Start the application by pressing Ctrl+F5. You see a puzzle displayed with three rows and three columns.

5. Press the Windows+C key combination to display the charms bar, and click the Settings button. You can see the available table sizes there, as shown in Figure 9-20.

6. Click 4x4. Press the Windows+Z key combination and click New Game. Select Yes, and as you can see, the new game uses a table with four rows and four columns.

7. Close the application.

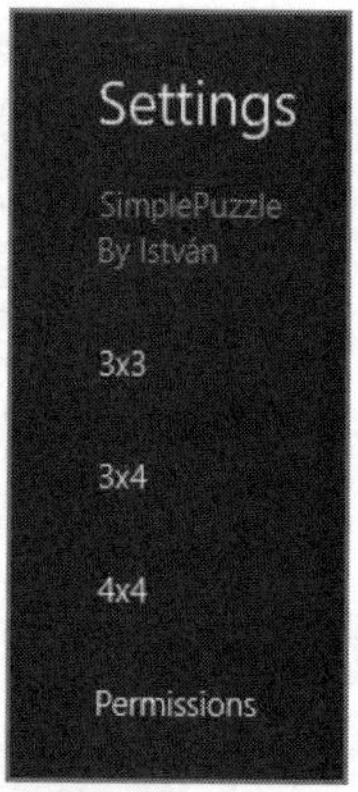

How It Works

In Step 3 you declared that the `SettingsCommandsRequested` event-handler method should be called when the settings charm is to be displayed from your application. This method used the `Request.ApplicationCommands` container of the event argument to add commands to the charm. For example, the 3x3 command was added with these two statements:

FIGURE 9-20: Table sizes are shown in the settings charm.

```
var size3By3 = new SettingsCommand(SIZE3BY3, "3x3", OnSettingsCommand);
args.Request.ApplicationCommands.Add(size3By3);
```

The command was represented by a newly created `SettingsCommand` instance that accepted three arguments: the command identifier (the `SIZE3BY3` constant), the command text (`"3x3"`), and the command event handler (`OnSettingsCommand`).

In Step 6, when you clicked 4x4, the `OnSettingsCommand` method was invoked. It extracted the identifier of the command from the method argument, and set table dimensions accordingly.

It may take a long time to solve the puzzle. Wouldn't it be great if you could save the state of the game and continue from that state later? In the next section, you learn how to modify the `SimplePuzzle` application to allow this feature.

PERSISTING APPLICATION DATA

Most applications store per-user data, such as preferences, game states, highest scores, widget layouts, and so on. When you install an app, the system gives it its own per-user data stores for application data. You don't need to know where or how this data is stored, because the system undertakes the responsibility for managing the physical storage. To read, write, or delete the data, you can use the application data API, which makes it fairly simple for you to work with this data.

It is important to know that the lifetime of the application data is tied to the lifetime of the app. If you remove the app, all of the application data will be removed, too. Application data is not suitable for storing your app's persistent data, such as user information, or other valuable and irreplaceable data that should be persisted in a database. If you remove an application and you lose the color scheme settings, it's okay. However, losing all your contacts stored in an application may be disastrous.

Application Data Stores

Windows 8 provides three application data stores, as summarized in Table 9-3. When designing data management for your app, you should decide which store is the appropriate one for a particular kind of application data.

TABLE 9-3: Application Data Stores

DATA STORE	DESCRIPTION
Local	This store keeps data that exists only on your current device. You should keep data here when it does not make sense to roam to other devices, or requires a large size that makes it unsuitable for roaming.
Roaming	The data stored here exists on all devices on which you installed the app. It is stored in the cloud, and a replication mechanism takes care of synchronizing the data among your devices. Because Windows limits the size of the application data that each app may roam, it is a best practice to use roaming data only for user preferences, links, and small data files.
Temporary	The data in this store does not roam and could be removed at any time (for example, when the user starts the Disk Cleanup utility). So, you should store temporary information during an application session here, using this store like a cache. There is no guarantee that this data will persist beyond the end of the application session, because the system might reclaim the used space if needed.

You can use settings and files in the application stores. Settings have small size (up to a few kilobytes), and are physically stored in the system registry. You can organize your settings into logical containers up to 32 hierarchy levels, and you can store compound settings (for example, a string and integer pair). You can add files to the stores, and they are physically stored in the filesystem, under your user profile. You can organize these files into folders (up to 32 levels).

> **NOTE** *You can optionally version the application data for your app. This would enable you to create a future version of your app that changes the format of its application data without causing compatibility problems with the previous version of your app. For more details, see* `http://msdn.microsoft.com/en-us/library/windows/apps/windows.storage.applicationdata.setversion-async.aspx.`

The ApplicationData Class

Windows Runtime provides the `ApplicationData` class, found in the `Windows.Storage` namespace. This class is a hub to all application data stores, settings, and files. Table 9-4 summarizes the most important members of this class.

TABLE 9-4: Important ApplicationData Members

MEMBER	DESCRIPTION
ClearAsync	This method removes all application data from the local, roaming, and temporary app data stores.
Current	This property provides access to the app data store associated with the current app.
DataChanged	This event is raised when roaming application data is synchronized.
LocalFolder	This gets the root folder in the local app data store.
LocalSettings	This gets the application settings container in the local app data store.
RoamingFolder	This gets the root folder in the roaming app data store.
RoamingSettings	This gets the application settings container in the roaming app data store.
RoamingStorageQuota	This gets the maximum size of the data that can be synchronized to the cloud from the roaming app data store.
TemporaryFolder	This gets the root folder in the temporary app data store.
Version	This gets the version number of the application data in the app data store.

When you use the `ApplicationData` class, it takes only a few steps to save and restore the puzzle table in the `SimplePuzzle` application. There is a prepared sample in the `SimplePuzzle ManageState` folder of this chapter's download that demonstrates how you can use `ApplicationData`. This sample saves the state of the application any time it is suspended or closed. When you start `SimplePuzzle`, it recognizes if there is a game that can be resumed, and offers the user the option to resume the saved game, or start a new one. When a puzzle is solved, it removes the previously saved state.

The lion's share of the work can be found in the `App.xaml.cs` file, as shown in Listing 9-1 (code file: `App.xaml.cs`). For the sake of brevity, a part of the unchanged code and related comments are omitted.

LISTING 9-1: The App.xaml.cs file (extract)

```
sealed partial class App : Application
{
    // --- Application state constants
    private const string PUZZLE_STATE = "PuzzleState";
    private const string TABLE_ROWS = "TableRows";
    private const string TABLE_COLS = "TableCols";
    private const string EMPTY_CELL = "EmptyCell";
    private const string TABLE_CELLS = "TableCells";

    public App()
```

```
    {
        this.InitializeComponent();
        this.Suspending += OnSuspending;
        this.Resuming += OnResuming;
    }

// --- A few methods omitted

    private void OnSuspending(object sender, SuspendingEventArgs e)
    {
        if (Game.State != GameState.Completed)
        {
            SavePuzzleState();
        }
    }

    private void OnResuming(object sender, object e)
    {
        RestorePuzzleState();
    }

    internal static GameController Game { get; set; }

    internal static void SavePuzzleState()
    {
        var puzzleState = new ApplicationDataCompositeValue();
        puzzleState[TABLE_ROWS] = Game.Height;
        puzzleState[TABLE_COLS] = Game.Width;
        puzzleState[EMPTY_CELL] = Game.EmptyPosition;
        var cellValues = "";
        for (int i = 0; i < Game.Height * Game.Width; i++)
        {
            if (Game[i] != null)
            {
                cellValues += String.Format("{0}:{1};", i,
                    Game[i].PuzzleId);
            }
        }
        puzzleState[TABLE_CELLS] = cellValues;
        ApplicationData.Current.LocalSettings.Values[PUZZLE_STATE] = puzzleState;
    }

    internal static bool IsStateSaved()
    {
        var data = ApplicationData.Current.LocalSettings.Values[PUZZLE_STATE]
            as ApplicationDataCompositeValue;
        return data != null;
    }

    internal static void RestorePuzzleState()
    {
        var puzzleState = ApplicationData.Current
            .LocalSettings.Values[PUZZLE_STATE]
            as ApplicationDataCompositeValue;
```

continues

LISTING 9-1 *(continued)*

```
            if (puzzleState == null) return;
            Game.Height = (int)puzzleState[TABLE_ROWS];
            Game.Width = (int)puzzleState[TABLE_COLS];
            Game.InitEmptyTable();
            Game.EmptyPosition = (int)puzzleState[EMPTY_CELL];
            var cellValues = ((string)puzzleState[TABLE_CELLS])
                .Split(new char[] { ':', ';' }, StringSplitOptions.RemoveEmptyEntries);
            for (int i = 0; i < cellValues.Length-1; i += 2)
            {
                Game.AddPuzzle(int.Parse(cellValues[i]),
                    int.Parse(cellValues[i + 1]));
            }
        }

        internal static void RemovePuzzleState()
        {
            ApplicationData.Current.LocalSettings.Values.Remove(PUZZLE_STATE);
        }
    }
}
```

The key methods in this code are `SavePuzzleState`, `IsStateSaved`, `RestorePuzzleState`, and `RemovePuzzleState`.

`SavePuzzleState` uses an `ApplicationDataCompositeValue` instance (`puzzleState`) to store the table height, table width, the empty cell position, and the puzzle pieces in each cell. When `puzzleState` is assembled, it is saved to the `ApplicationData.Current.LocalSettings` data store using the `Values` container.

`IsStateSaved` examines if the `LocalSettings` store contains a value with the `PUZZLE_STATE` key, which is used to save the game state.

`RestorePuzzleState` works in a similar way as `SavePuzzleState`, but it reads data values from the `LocalSettings` store, and initializes the puzzle accordingly. Because the `Values` container stores `object` values, data elements read from this container should be cast to the appropriate type.

With the `Remove` method of the `Values` container, you can remove application data settings, as `RemovePuzzleState` demonstrates.

> **NOTE** When you load the solution in the `SimplePuzzle ManageState` folder, it is worth having a look at the `MainPage.xaml.cs` file to discover how these methods are utilized there.

Any time you started the `SimplePuzzle` application during the previous exercises, it displayed a default logo. In real applications, you might like to have a more attractive logo. In the next section, you learn how to integrate your app with the Start screen, and how to change the logo of `SimplePuzzle`.

APPLICATIONS AND THE START SCREEN

It may sound a bit weird, but the Start screen is the vital part of Windows 8 apps. When using Windows 8, you can see the application Live Tiles in the main screen. Even if an application is not started, Live Tiles share information that can be important for you. When you design your application, you should design it with Start screen in mind. In this section, you learn the fundamental design principles and tools that make your app integrate with the Start screen perfectly.

Application Logo and the Splash Screen

When you create a new Windows 8 app with Visual Studio, it automatically creates a splash screen and several logos that are placed into the `Assets` folder of the application project. When your application is deployed, the logo information is extracted from the application manifest zipped into the application package.

By editing the `Package.appxmanifest` file, you can declare these logos. The Application UI tab of the package manifest editor contains the logo information (as shown in Figure 9-21), as well as the splash screen information. You can set the logo that is displayed in Windows Store on the Packaging tab.

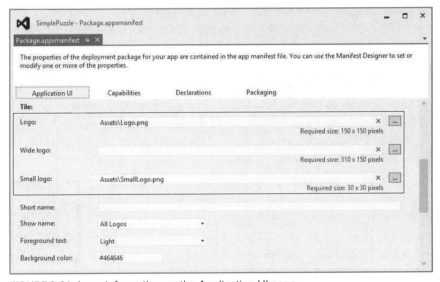

FIGURE 9-21: Logo information on the Application UI page

The Windows 8 UI design guidelines define the expected dimensions of logos (width and height, in pixels), as summarized in Table 9-5. Although you can use logos with other sizes, because Windows 8 resizes them to the correct size, they may look unprofessional, so always use the appropriate sizes.

TABLE 9-5: Windows 8 App Logos

LOGO	SIZE	DESCRIPTION
Small logo	30 × 30	The logo displayed in the Start screen in All Apps and Search views
Normal logo	150 × 150	The logo displayed in the Start screen, when the app Live Tile is set to small (default)
Wide logo	310 × 150	The logo displayed in the Start screen, when the app Live Tile is set to wide
Windows Store logo	50 × 50	The app logo displayed in the Windows Store

> **NOTE** You learn about the Windows Store in Chapter 16.

Applications can be set to display small or wider Live Tiles. If the application does not have a wide logo, the Live Tile cannot be set wide. In the next exercise, you set up the `SimplePuzzle` application so that it has a wide logo.

TRY IT OUT Adding a Wide Logo to the SimplePuzzle App

In this exercise, you start from a prepared sample. To add a wide logo to the `SimplePuzzle` app, follow these steps:

1. With the File ➪ Open Project (Ctrl+Shift+O) command, open the `SimplePuzzle.sln` file from the `SimplePuzzle  Logo` folder of this chapter's download.

2. In Solution Explorer, double-click the `Package.appxmanifest` file to open it in the designer. On the Application UI page, scroll down to the "Wide logo" field, and type **Assets\WideLogo.png** in the text box.

3. Run the application by pressing Ctrl+F5. The application uses a new splash screen with SimplePuzzle text, instead of the default text.

4. Press the Windows key to switch to the Start screen. The application has a new logo on its Live Tile, as shown in Figure 9-22.

FIGURE 9-22: The new logo of SimplePuzzle

5. Right-click the `SimplePuzzle` tile or select it with the swipe gesture, and from the Start screen app bar, select Larger. Now, the app Live Tile is displayed in a wider size and with a different logo (with a W in the middle), as shown in Figure 9-23.

6. Start typing `SimplePuzzle`. After a few keystrokes, the app is shown in the Search screen, as shown in Figure 9-24. Here the small logo of the app is displayed.

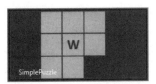

FIGURE 9-23: The wide logo of SimplePuzzle

FIGURE 9-24: The small logo of SimplePuzzle

7. Switch back to the `SimplePuzzle` application, and close it.

How It Works

The prepared app contained four logos in its `Assets` folder. In Step 2, you declared that the `Assets\WideLogo.png` file should be used as the app logo for `SimplePuzzle` in wide tile mode. Because you assigned a wide logo to the application manifest, in Step 5, you could use the Larger command to display a wide logo.

Changing the logo is only one way you can customize the app Live Tile. You have much more control over the Live Tile. For example, you can make it live, as you will soon learn.

> **NOTE** Try the `SimplePuzzle` application after changing several properties on the Application UI page of the `Package.appxmanifest` file, such as names, background color, foreground text, and so on.

Vivifying App Tiles with Notifications

One of the most characteristic distinguishing factors of Windows 8 compared to other iconographic operating systems (such as the iOS running on Apple iPad and iPhone) is the capability to display Live Tiles that may show up-to-date information about the app right on the Start screen. For example, the Video and Music application Live Tiles can show information about the video or music being played, respectively. You can also make your app's Live Tile more vivid with notifications. You can add text blocks, images, and badges to the Live Tile, as you learn in this section.

FIGURE 9-25: The TileSquareText02 template

A number of predefined templates describe the layout of your app's Live Tile. For example, as shown in Figure 9-25, the `TileSquareText02` template enables you to specify two text blocks to display in the Live Tile. As shown in Figure 9-26, another template, `TileWideImageAndText01`, lets you specify an image (at the top of the Live Tile) and a text block. You can set the placeholders in the template with concrete text and image elements, and update your app's Live Tile accordingly.

FIGURE 9-26: The TileWideImageAndText01 template

You can also enable notification queuing. When it is enabled, a maximum of five tile notifications can automatically cycle on the Live Tile. The queue is FIFO (first in, first out), so that when it is full and a new notification arrives, the oldest notification is removed.

You can also enable scheduled (periodic) updates. In this case, the operating system periodically (the shortest interval is half an hour, and the longest is one day) polls a uniform resource identifier (URI) to obtain the description of the Live Tile to display.

Tile Notification Format

The tile notification is an XML document that defines the concrete layout of the tile to display. This XML format is very simple, and you can easily peek into the file using the `TileUpdateManager` `.GetTemplateContent()` method, as shown in this code snippet:

```
var tileXml = TileUpdateManager.GetTemplateContent(
    TileTemplateType.TileWideImageAndText01);
var xmlText = XDocument.Parse(tileXml.GetXml()).ToString();
```

The argument of this method is a `TileTemplateType` enumeration value, and it returns an `XmlDocument` instance that represents the template with empty placeholders. If you run this code snippet, it results in this XML document:

```
<tile>
  <visual>
    <binding template="TileWideImageAndText01">
      <image id="1" src="" />
      <text id="1"></text>
    </binding>
  </visual>
</tile>
```

> **NOTE** The `XDocument.Parse` method is used to format the XML document nicely with line breaks and indents.

The structure of the tile notification XML is easy to understand. In the previous XML snippet, `<image>` is the placeholder of the image in the tile and `<text>` is the placeholder of the text block.

Updating Tile Notifications

The `Windows.UI.Notifications` namespace provides the `TileUpdateManager` type that is responsible for handling tile updates. The usage pattern of `TileUpdateManager` is fairly simple, as shown in the following code snippet:

```
// --- Obtain tile notification template XML
var tileXml = TileUpdateManager.GetTemplateContent(
    TileTemplateType.TileSquareText04);
// --- Update tile notification template with the text specified by the user
tileXml.GetElementsByTagName("text")[0].InnerText = Message.Text;
// --- Create a TileNotification instance
```

```
var notification = new TileNotification(tileXml);
// --- Update the app's tile
TileUpdateManager.CreateTileUpdaterForApplication().Update(notification);
```

This scenario uses two key methods:

➤ `CreateTileUpdaterForApplication()` provides an object that is responsible for managing tile notification updates belonging to your app.

➤ `Update(notification)` performs the notification update according to the `TileNotification` instance passed as the argument.

Using this pattern, your only task is to modify the XML document describing the tile layout.

> **NOTE** *To get acquainted with all tile templates, see* `http://msdn.microsoft` `.com/en-us/library/windows/apps/windows.ui.notifications` `.tiletemplatetype.aspx.`

Removing Tile Notifications

If you do not have any notifications to display, you can easily restore the original state of the tile with the `Clear()` method, as shown in this code snippet:

```
TileUpdateManager.CreateTileUpdaterForApplication().Clear();
```

Managing Normal and Wide Tile Notifications

The application Live Tile can be either small (square) or large (wide). Notification templates are applied either to square or wide Live Tiles, as indicated by the template name. When you try to use a wide template for a square tile (or vice versa), the Live Tile won't be updated. But you should know in advance whether an app tile is currently square or wide, and so you can't guess whether you need to apply a square or a wide template!

You can create a tile notification that contains two templates, one for the square and another for the wide template, just like this one:

```
<tile>
  <visual>
    <binding template="TileSquareText04">
      <text id="1">Hello from SimplePuzzle</text>
    </binding>
    <binding template="TileWideText04">
      <text id="1">Hello from SimplePuzzle</text>
    </binding>
  </visual>
</tile>
```

This example uses two `<binding>` elements with two templates. When the app tile has the normal size, the `TileSquareText04` template is used; otherwise, `TileWideText04` is applied.

Using Tile Images

You can display images in application Live Tiles with any of the predefined templates that allow an image tag, such as the `TileWideImageAndText01` template mentioned earlier:

```
<tile>
  <visual>
    <binding template="TileWideImageAndText01">
      <image id="1" src="" />
      <text id="1"></text>
    </binding>
  </visual>
</tile>
```

The `src` attribute defines the source of the tile image. You can use three different types of sources, as summarized in Table 9-6.

TABLE 9-6: Tile Image Sources

SOURCE	DESCRIPTION
App image	This type of image is the part of the application (it is deployed with the app). These images are accessed with the "`ms-appx:///`" prefix, followed by the relative path of the image within the application package. For example, the `Logo.png` image in the `Assets` folder can be accessed as "`ms-appx:///Assets/Logo.png`."
Local image	This kind of image can be found in the current user's local folder. These images are accessed with the `ms-appdata:///local/` prefix, followed by the relative path of the image within the application package. For example, the `SmallLogo.png` image can be accessed as `ms-appdata:///local/SmallLogo.png`.
Web image	This type of image can be accessed through web URIs, such as `http://mysite.com/myLogo.png`.

Other Live Tile Features

A few other features of tiles can be useful in your apps:

➤ Just as you can display tile notifications, you can add badges to your app's Live Tile. A badge can be a number between 0 and 99 (numbers greater than 99 are displayed as 99), or a glyph that can be selected from a predefined set.

➤ Tile notifications can have an expiration setting. When a notification expires, it is automatically cleared, just as if you did it programmatically.

➤ Applications can pin secondary Live Tiles to the screen — with the confirmation of the active user. Secondary Live Tiles are shortcuts to your app. When you start or activate your application with a secondary Live Tile, the Live Tile can pass an argument to the app, and the app's logic can process that argument. For example, the secondary Live Tiles of the Weather app represent locations. When you start Weather through a location, the app launches while showing the weather information for the particular location.

Tile Notification Samples

You can find a sample of tile notifications in this chapter's code download, in the `LiveTiles` folder. This sample demonstrates a number of scenarios to display tile notifications. Open the `LiveTiles` `.sln` solution in Visual Studio and examine the `MainPage.xaml` and `MainPage.xaml.cs` files to get acquainted with these scenarios' details.

SUMMARY

Windows 8 provides a very simple resource-management policy for Windows 8 apps. While the application is in the foreground, it can consume resources (such as the CPU, memory, network, and so on) to provide the best user experience. When an app goes to the background, it gets suspended, and has no more access to resources. Your app can catch the events when it gets suspended and later resumed, and use these events to save and restore the application's state.

In Windows 8 apps, you place only the frequently used commanding controls to the app's screen permanently. For commands that are used only in a specific context, you can use the app bar and the context menus. You can integrate your app's settings with the settings charm.

The Start screen is probably the most important part of the user experience in Windows 8. Your application Live Tiles do not have to be simple icons; you can make them more vivid with tile notifications.

In Chapter 10, you learn about another set of application patterns, using multiple pages and navigating among them, respectively.

EXERCISES

1. When does Windows 8 terminate a Windows 8 app?

2. What key can be used to display the app bar?

3. Which application data store allows keeping information on all devices of a user?

4. Which object is responsible for updating tile notifications?

> **NOTE** *You can find answers to the exercises in Appendix A.*

▶ WHAT YOU LEARNED IN THIS CHAPTER

TOPIC	KEY CONCEPTS
Running state	The Windows 8 app that is in the foreground is in running state. In this state, the application gets available resources to allow it to be continuously responsive.
Suspended state	When a Windows 8 app goes into the background (that is, another Windows 8 app is brought into the foreground), its state goes to suspended. A suspended application does not receive CPU cycles or other system resources. Otherwise, system resources could be drained from the foreground app.
App termination	The operating system can terminate a suspended application to free memory so that the foreground application can have enough memory and resources to provide overall operation and responsiveness.
Application package	Before deployment, Windows 8 apps are packaged into an application package that contains the app's executable files and resources. This package is deployed to user machines. Installation is a simple copy operation of the files within the package.
Sandbox	A sandbox is a security mechanism that separates running applications, and prevents them from accessing system resources they are not allowed to use.
Application package manifest	The application package manifest file describes the information about the package to be deployed. This file contains information about the sandbox in which the app runs (that is, the kinds of resources the application can use), the extensions the app proffers to other Windows 8 applications, and the visual attributes of the particular app (such as logos, splash screen, and so on).
Context menu	Context menus are UI control-specific menus with operations that can be executed on the particular user control in the current context (such as clipboard operations). Context menus are shown when the use right-clicks them (or applies the "tap and hold" gesture).
App bar	App bars are context menus that provide application-specific functions for the user (such as creating a new item, saving information, opening an image, and so on). The app bar can be located at the bottom and at the top of the screen, and it opens when the user swipes a finger from the top or bottom edge of the screen, or presses the Windows+Z key combination.

TOPIC	KEY CONCEPTS
Message dialog	Message dialog boxes can be popped up to display information to the user, or to ask for confirmation of a specific operation. Although message dialog boxes wait for user input, they do not block the UI.
Application data stores	An application data store persists application-wide information for each user the app is installed for. The local store keeps data that exists only on the user's current device. The roaming store keeps data that is synchronized among all devices of the user. The temporary store works like a cache in that the data kept there can be removed by the system if space is needed.
Tile notifications	An application can send notifications to its Live Tile on the Start screen. These notifications can use text blocks and images. Generally, these notifications reflect the changes within an application, and let the user know the state of the app merely by having a look at its Live Tile on the Start screen.

10

Creating Multi-Page Applications

WHAT YOU WILL LEARN IN THIS CHAPTER:

➤ Understanding the fundamental navigation patterns used in Windows 8 apps

➤ Getting to know the Page class and understanding the navigation mechanism among pages

➤ Starting other applications through file associations from your app

➤ Using the Split Application and Grid Application templates to create apps with your custom content

WROX.COM CODE DOWNLOADS FOR THIS CHAPTER

You can find the wrox.com code downloads for this chapter on the Download Code tab at www.wrox.com/remtitle.cgi?isbn=012680. The code is in the Chapter10.zip download and individually named, as described in the corresponding exercises.

In Chapter 9, you learned about a number of important Windows 8 app user interface (UI) patterns, such as using the context menus and the app bar, integrating your app with the settings charm, saving the application state, using dialog box messages, and so on. The samples in those exercises were simple applications with one screen — or, following the Windows 8 style app terminology, with one page.

Real applications often use more than one page. In this chapter, you learn how to create applications with multiple pages. First, you will study the navigation concepts used in Windows 8 apps, and you will get acquainted with the UI controls that support paging.

With Visual Studio, Microsoft provides two project templates — the Grid Application template and the Split Application template — that are great for starting your multi-page apps. In this chapter, you will discover the details surrounding these templates and learn how to create your own content with them.

NAVIGATION BASICS

Content is a key factor in the design of Windows 8 style applications. If your app presents its content in a way that users perceive as a great experience, your app will be successful and popular; otherwise, it will be just another app hidden in a crowd. You can use many elements to provide an excellent user experience, such as clean layout and typography, great animations, intuitive UI controls, and so on. These are all very important elements, but a more essential one rules them all — navigation.

Navigation Patterns

When users browse app content, they use navigation to roam from one content element to another. The designers of the Windows 8 language created a number of navigation patterns that are fairly intuitive, and users can use these to find the content they are looking for.

Hub Navigation

Probably the most frequently used pattern is the *hub navigation*. In this case, the content is placed into a *hub page* that can be scrolled horizontally with the keyboard (using the PgUp and PgDown keys), with the mouse wheel, or even with touch using slide gestures. The hub page is a virtually wide page that is several times wider than the screen. As you slide or scroll the hub page, the content flies in. The content is built up so that the user always knows there is more content to discover.

For example, when you start the Finance app, you see a screen similar to the one shown in Figure 10-1. You can see that the content on the right side overflows the screen. Intuitively, you can guess that scrolling or sliding the screen to the left provides more content. When you're using touch and you reach the edges of the hub page, you'll see a bouncing effect, indicating that there is no more content to scroll to.

FIGURE 10-1: The hub page of the Finance app

Direct Navigation

The hub page is often combined with *direct page navigation*. In this case, you can select the type of content you would like to see using a navigation control, such as the app bar. For example, the Finance app provides a top app bar that enables you to select a page directly, as shown in Figure 10-2. The app bar shows a list of available pages, displaying the Today page with a white background indicating that this page is the current one. For example, when you select the Currencies page, you navigate directly to it without the need to slide or scroll the hub page.

FIGURE 10-2: The app bar of the Finance app provides direct navigation

Hierarchical Navigation

In many apps, you are presented with so much information that using the hub pattern simply does not work. You might have hundreds or thousands of information elements that simply cannot be scrolled fast enough to find your topic of interest in a few seconds.

The solution for this situation is *hierarchical navigation*. You present the content in a hierarchy, where separate pages display separate hierarchy levels. During the navigation, you can move up and down among the nodes in this hierarchy and look at the content on the current node. For example, when you start the Store app, its first screen displays app categories in a hub page, as shown in Figure 10-3. This is the root level of the hierarchy. When you select an item, you get to a lower hierarchy level that displays apps in the selected category, as shown in Figure 10-4.

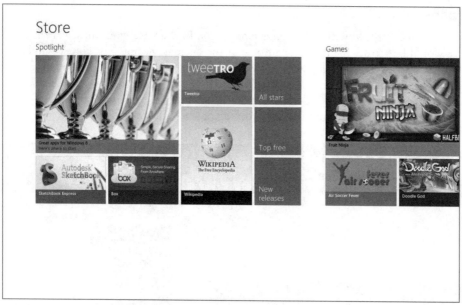

FIGURE 10-3: The top hierarchy level of the Store app's content

FIGURE 10-4: Applications in a selected app category

Semantic Zoom

Windows 8 provides a feature called *semantic zoom*. You can use this feature to accelerate navigation when you have many items that would be difficult to view with scrolling and sliding. Semantic zoom uses the pinch gesture to zoom in or out in a list with lots of items. You can also use the Ctrl key together with the + and – keys on the numeric keyboard to zoom in and out, respectively, or click the zoom icon in the bottom-right corner of the Start screen.

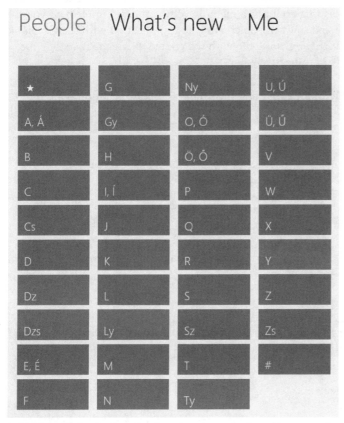

FIGURE 10-5: Contacts in the People app as displayed by semantic zoom

For example, the People app displays contacts. Most users who regularly use any kind of social app generally have hundreds or thousands of contacts. With semantic zoom, it's easier to navigate among them. The People application uses the semantic zoom to display an alphabet when you zoom out the list of your contacts, as shown in Figure 10-5. When you click or tap an item, you immediately zoom in the contact list displaying your contacts filed under the corresponding letter.

In this chapter, you will learn about using these patterns (except semantic zoom) for creating multipage applications.

> **NOTE** You learned about semantic zoom in Chapter 8, during the discussion of the `GridView` control.

WORKING WITH PAGES

Every Windows 8 app you created earlier in the exercises of this book used pages. In these examples, you had filenames ending with Page, such as BlankPage.xaml or MainPage.xaml. The Page control is one of the fundamental controls that contains a plethora of functions to implement your apps quickly with only a few lines of code. When you create a new application with the C# Blank Application template, it provides a MainPage.xaml file with the related MainPage.xaml.cs file, as shown in Listing 10-1 and Listing 10-2, respectively.

LISTING 10-1: The MainPage.xaml file of an app created with the Blank Application template

```
<Page
    x:Class="MyApp.MainPage"
    IsTabStop="false"
    xmlns="http://schemas.microsoft.com/winfx/2006/xaml/presentation"
    xmlns:x="http://schemas.microsoft.com/winfx/2006/xaml"
    xmlns:local="using:MyApp"
    xmlns:d="http://schemas.microsoft.com/expression/blend/2008"
    xmlns:mc="http://schemas.openxmlformats.org/markup-compatibility/2006"
    mc:Ignorable="d">

    <Grid Background="{StaticResource ApplicationPageBackgroundThemeBrush}">

    </Grid>
</Page>
```

LISTING 10-2: The MainPage.xaml.cs file of an app created with the Blank Application template (comments omitted for the sake of brevity)

```
using System;
using System.Collections.Generic;
using System.IO;
using System.Linq;
using Windows.Foundation;
using Windows.Foundation.Collections;
using Windows.UI.Xaml;
using Windows.UI.Xaml.Controls;
using Windows.UI.Xaml.Controls.Primitives;
using Windows.UI.Xaml.Data;
using Windows.UI.Xaml.Input;
using Windows.UI.Xaml.Media;
using Windows.UI.Xaml.Navigation;

namespace MyApp
{
    public sealed partial class MainPage : Page
    {
        public MainPage()
        {
            this.InitializeComponent();
        }

        protected override void OnNavigatedTo(NavigationEventArgs e)
```

```
            {
            }
        }
    }
```

The `MainPage.xaml` file contains a `Page` control that embeds a `Grid` control. The grid is a placeholder for the UI elements of the page. When you take a look at the Document Outline tool window, you can see that the page also has a placeholder for a top and a bottom app bar, as shown in Figure 10-6.

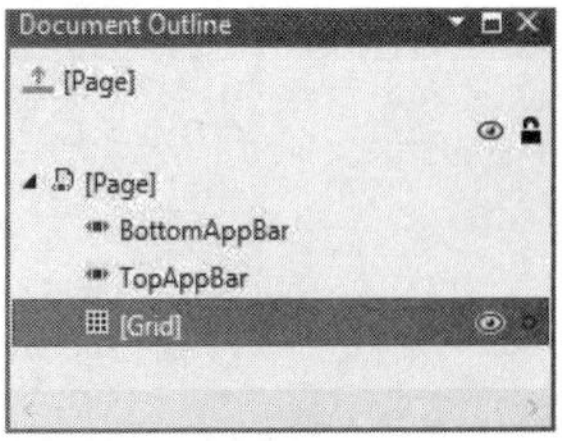

The `MainPage.xaml.cs` file contains two methods by default:

FIGURE 10-6: The Document Outline of an empty page

➤ The `MainPage` constructor initializes all controls according to the XAML description.

➤ The `OnNavigatedTo` method is invoked whenever the user navigates to this page. One such occasion is when your application launches.

The `Page` class has the entire infrastructure required to implement navigation among pages, as you learn in the next section.

Navigating Backward and Forward

The simplest form of page navigation is sequential navigation, when you start your task with a page and navigate sequentially to other pages (unless the task is entirely finished). In the next exercise, you will learn about the implementation details of such an easy navigation pattern. You start with a prepared app that simulates the steps of recoding a scuba dive log entry in a diver's digital logbook. The application does not let you enter data because it is just for demonstrating the navigation. This log entry task uses four pages.

> **NOTE** You can find the complete code to download for this exercise on this book's companion website at www.wrox.com in the DiveLog - PageByPage folder.

TRY IT OUT Navigating Among Pages

To complete the simple application that simulates the entry of a scuba dive log, follow these steps:

1. With the File ⇨ Open Project (Ctrl+Shift+O) command, open the `DiveLog.sln` file from the `DiveLog Start` folder of this chapter's download. In a few seconds, the solution loads into the IDE.

2. In Solution Explorer, select the `DiveLog` project node, and add a new item with Ctrl+Shift+A. In the Add New Item dialog box, select the Blank Page template, enter the name **Step2.xaml**, and click Add.

3. The `Step2.xaml` file opens in the designer. In the XAML pane, remove the `<Grid>` element (including the `</Grid>` closing tag), and replace it with the following code snippet:

```
<Grid Background="{StaticResource PageBackgroundBrush}">
    <Grid.RowDefinitions>
        <RowDefinition Height="140"/>
```

```
            <RowDefinition Height="*"/>
        </Grid.RowDefinitions>
        <!-- Back button and page title -->
        <Grid>
            <Grid.ColumnDefinitions>
                <ColumnDefinition Width="Auto"/>
                <ColumnDefinition Width="*"/>
            </Grid.ColumnDefinitions>
            <Button x:Name="backButton" Click="GoBack"
                    IsEnabled="{Binding Frame.CanGoBack, ElementName=PageRoot}"
                    Style="{StaticResource BackButtonStyle}" />
            <TextBlock x:Name="pageTitle" Grid.Column="1"
                    Text="Step 2: Depth and Bottom Time"
                    Style="{StaticResource PageHeaderTextStyle}"
                    Foreground="{StaticResource TitleForegroundBrush}"/>
        </Grid>
        <StackPanel HorizontalAlignment="Left" Height="557.927" Margin="116,0"
                Grid.Row="1" VerticalAlignment="Top" Width="1240.652">
            <TextBlock HorizontalAlignment="Left" TextWrapping="Wrap"
                Style="{StaticResource H2Style}"
                Text="Specify the maximum depth and the bottom time." />
            <Button x:Name="NextButton" Margin="0,24,0,0"
                    Style="{StaticResource ButtonStyle}"
                    Click="NextButtonClicked">Next</Button>
        </StackPanel>
    </Grid>
```

4. In the XAML pane, right-click the `Click` attribute of the `<Button>` element (named `NextButton`) at the bottom of the code, and select the "Navigate to Event Handler" command.

5. Type the following boldfaced code into the method body:

```
private void NextButtonClicked(object sender, RoutedEventArgs e)
{
    Frame.Navigate(typeof(Step3));
}
```

6. Add the following new method to the `Step2.xaml.cs` file:

```
private void GoBack(object sender, RoutedEventArgs e)
{
    if (this.Frame != null && this.Frame.CanGoBack) this.Frame.GoBack();
}
```

7. Open the `Step1.xaml.cs` file in the editor. Scroll down to the `NextButtonClicked` method, and add the following boldfaced code to its body:

```
private void NextButtonClicked(object sender, RoutedEventArgs e)
{
    Frame.Navigate(typeof(Step2));
}
```

8. Run the app by pressing Ctrl+F5. When it launches, the first page is displayed, as shown in Figure 10-7. Click the Start Dive Log Entry button, and the app moves to the next page, as shown in Figure 10-8.

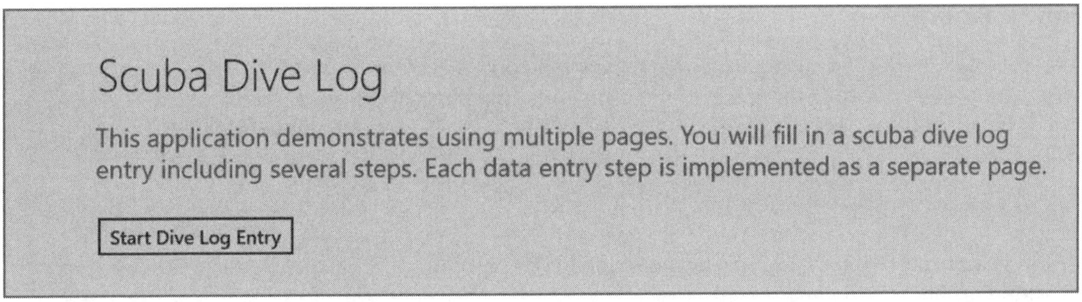

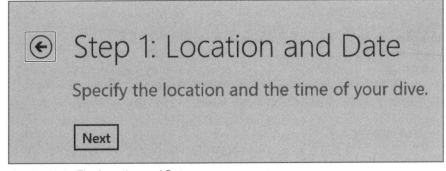

FIGURE 10-7: The first page of the DiveLog app

Step 1: Location and Date

Specify the location and the time of your dive.

Next

FIGURE 10-8: The Location and Date page

Because this is the second page, you can see the back button (as highlighted in Figure 10-8) that takes you back to the first page. Try it!

9. Now, you're in the first page again. Click the Start Log Entry again, and then as you proceed with the pages, click Next, Next, and Start Next Entry again. You arrive back to the first page. In this case, you can see the back button there, as shown in Figure 10-9.

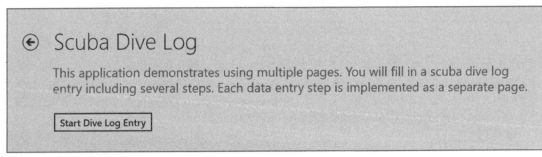

FIGURE 10-9: The back button is shown on the first page

10. Close the app.

How It Works

The `DiveLog.sln` solution from which you started contained three pages (`MainPage.xaml`, `Step1.xaml`, and `Step3.xaml`) with preset navigation code. In Step 2 and Step 3, you added a new page file, `Step2.xaml`, and set up its content. In Step 5, you added the code to navigate from the `Step2` page to the `Step3` page:

```
Frame.Navigate(typeof(Step3));
```

`Frame` is a property on a `Page` object that controls the content of the page. You use the `Navigate` method with an argument value of `typeof(Step3)` to set the content of the page to an instance of the specified type — in this case, `Step3`.

In Step 7, you used to same approach to navigate from the `Step1` page to the `Step2` page.

In the `Step2.xaml` file, you defined the back button with the following markup:

```
<Button x:Name="backButton" Click="GoBack"
        IsEnabled="{Binding Frame.CanGoBack, ElementName=PageRoot}"
        Style="{StaticResource BackButtonStyle}" />
```

The `IsEnabled` property is bound to the `Frame.CanGoBack` property of the `PageRoot` element. (This element represents the `Page` instance itself.) The result of this data binding is that you can use the back button on the `Step2` page only if there is a page to go back to. The same approach is used to enable the back button on all other pages. That is why the back button was hidden in Figure 10-7 (that was the first page, so there were no pages to go back to) and shown in Figure 10-9 (you navigated to the first page from the `Step3` page, so there was a page to go back to).

All pages used the same `GoBack` method — to navigate back to the previous page — as you added in Step 6:

```
private void GoBack(object sender, RoutedEventArgs e)
{
    if (this.Frame != null && this.Frame.CanGoBack) this.Frame.GoBack();
}
```

The body of this method checked to see if there was a previous page to go back to (`Frame.CanGoBack`) and invoked the `Frame.GoBack` method to return to that page.

Parameters and Navigation Events

The pages displayed in a Windows 8 app can accept parameters. These parameters can be used when rendering the content of the page. In the previous exercise, the `Navigate` method was called with a single argument that accepted the type of the page. However, `Navigate` can be called with two arguments, where the second one is an optional `System.Object` instance that is the parameter of the page.

Navigation Event Arguments

Every time you navigate to a page, the target page's `OnNavigatedTo` method is called with a `NavigationEventArgs` argument that has a number of properties, as summarized in Table 10-1.

TABLE 10-1: NavigationEventArgs Properties

PROPERTY	DESCRIPTION
Content	Gets the root node of the target page's content.
NavigationMode	Gets a value that indicates the direction of movement during navigation. This property takes its value from the NavigationMode enumeration: ➤ New — Navigation is to a new instance of a page (not going forward or backward in the stack of visited pages). ➤ Back — Navigation is going backward in the stack. ➤ Forward — Navigation is going forward in the stack. ➤ Refresh — Navigation is to the current page (perhaps with different data).
Parameter	Gets any parameter object passed to the target page for the navigation (the second argument of the Frame's Navigate method).
SourcePageType	This property's name is a bit confusing. It's called SourcePageType, but it gets the data type of the target page.
Uri	Gets the uniform resource identifier (URI) of the target. This property contains a non-null value when you are using JavaScript.

Using Navigation Parameters

It is very easy to use the Navigate and OnNavigatedTo methods to pass and process page parameters, as demonstrated in a prepared sample that you can find in the DiveLog - Parameters folder of this chapter's download. This sample contains a modified version of the DiveLog app that adds a few text blocks to the pages, as shown in Figure 10-10.

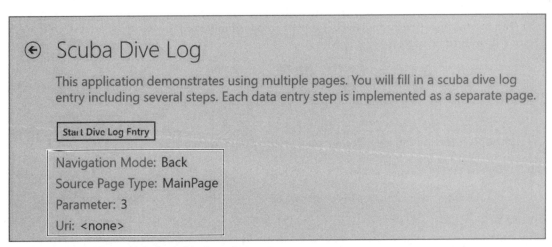

FIGURE 10-10: Additional labels on DiveLog pages

The button click event-handler code of each page uses the `Frame.Navigate` method with two arguments:

```
Frame.Navigate(typeof(PageType), Frame.BackStackDepth);
```

The `PageType` is the type representing the target page. The navigation logic behind `Frame` keeps a stack of visited pages as you go forward and back. The `Frame.BackStepDepth` property indicates the depth of this stack, and the code uses this value as the page parameter. In Figure 10-10, this value is shown in the Parameter label. The value "3" indicates that the depth of this stack was 3 when navigating to the `MainPage` page.

The labels in Figure 10-10 are refreshed in the `OnNavigatedTo` methods that happen to be the same in each page:

```
protected override void OnNavigatedTo(NavigationEventArgs e)
{
    NavigationModeLabel.Text = e.NavigationMode.ToString();
    SourcePageLabel.Text = e.SourcePageType.Name;
    ParameterLabel.Text = (e.Parameter ?? "<none>").ToString();
    UriLabel.Text = e.Uri == null ? "<none>" : e.Uri.ToString();
}
```

Navigating Away from Pages

When you run this sample, you can see how the depth of the navigation stack increases or decreases as you move forward and back among the pages. The value of the Navigation Mode label tells you the direction, too, as shown in Figure 10-10.

In many situations, it is important to know when you are about to leave a page. If the user enters information on the page, you may not allow navigating away unless the data is valid. You can override the `OnNavigatingFrom` method that accepts a `NavigationCancelEventArgs` argument. Set the `Cancel` property of the argument to `true` to prevent leaving the page.

It can be also useful to catch the moment before you leave the page. Your page may allocate memory for its data that is not required when leaving the page. Because the page is not disposed as you leave it (you may navigate back to it later), it is your responsibility (and in your best interest) to free temporarily unused resources.

You can override the `OnNavigatedFrom` method that accepts a `NavigationEventArgs` argument just like the `OnNavigatedTo` method. The `Step3.xaml.cs` file in the sample solution demonstrates using these methods, as shown in Listing 10-3.

LISTING 10-3: Navigating away from a page in the Step3.xaml.cs file

```
public sealed partial class Step3 : Page
{
    private static bool _lastCancelled;

    public Step3()
    {
        this.InitializeComponent();
```

```
        _lastCancelled = false;
    }

    protected async override void OnNavigatedFrom(NavigationEventArgs e)
    {
        var dialog = new MessageDialog(
            "You are leaving Step 3 page.",
            "Navigation Message");
        dialog.Commands.Add(new UICommand("OK"));
        await dialog.ShowAsync();
        base.OnNavigatedFrom(e);
    }

    protected override void OnNavigatingFrom(NavigatingCancelEventArgs e)
    {
        _lastCancelled = !_lastCancelled;
        e.Cancel = _lastCancelled;
        if (_lastCancelled) NavigationModeLabel.Text = "Navigation Cancelled";
        base.OnNavigatingFrom(e);
    }

    // --- Other methods omitter for the sake of brevity
}
```

The OnNavigatingFrom method is implemented so that, every second time, it prevents leaving the page by setting the e.Cancel flag (through the _lastCancelled flag) to true, and signals the canceled state on the screen. The OnNavigatedFrom method pops up a dialog box on the screen every time you successfully navigated away from the Step3 page.

> **NOTE** The OnNavigatedFrom *event shows a dialog message that is displayed asynchronously, so it does not block the UI. Although it works well in this sample, generally you should avoid the coding practice where you display dialogs and messages in navigation events.*

> **NOTE** *In the code, you can catch navigation events of other page objects. Of course, in this case, you cannot use any of the protected* OnNavigatedTo, OnNavigatingFrom, *or* OnNavigatedFrom *methods. Instead, you should subscribe to the* NavigatedTo, NavigatingFrom, *and* NavigatedFrom *events of the corresponding page objects, respectively.*

Using App Bars for Navigation

As you learned earlier in this chapter, you can use the direct navigation pattern with the app bar to explicitly select a page to navigate to, instead of sequentially traversing through pages. As you saw in Figure 10-2, the Finance app uses this model. You can use the same approach to create an app bar, as you learned in Chapter 9. However, using app bars with page navigation is a bit trickier than you would think, as you learn from the next exercises.

The Intuitive Solution

In the next exercise, you start from a prepared sample (going on with the DiveLog application) that adds an app bar to the MainPage object. The app bar contains four buttons, one for each page.

TRY IT OUT Using an App Bar with Page Navigation

To complete the prepared application, follow these steps:

1. With the File ⇨ Open Project (Ctrl+Shift+O) command, open the DiveLog.sln file from the DiveLog - AppBar folder of this chapter's download.

2. Open the MainPage.xaml file in the designer. The file contains an app bar displayed at the top of the page, defined with the following XAML snippet:

```
<Page.TopAppBar>
    <AppBar x:Name="CommandBar" Style="{StaticResource AppBarStyle}">
        <StackPanel Orientation="Horizontal">
            <Button x:Name="NewEntryButton"
                Style="{StaticResource TopAppBarButtonStyle}"
                Tapped="NewEntryButtonTapped" Content="New Entry">
            </Button>
            <Button x:Name="LocationButton"
                Style="{StaticResource TopAppBarButtonStyle}"
                Tapped="LocationButtonTapped" Content="Location &amp; Time">
            </Button>
            <Button x:Name="DepthButton"
                Style="{StaticResource TopAppBarButtonStyle}"
                Tapped="DepthButtonTapped"
                Content="Maximum Depth &amp; Bottom Time">
            </Button>
            <Button x:Name="CompletedButton"
                Style="{StaticResource TopAppBarButtonStyle}"
                Tapped="CompletedButtonTapped" Content="Completed">
            </Button>
        </StackPanel>
    </AppBar>
</Page.TopAppBar>
```

3. Open the MainPage.xaml.cs file, and add the following boldfaced code to the event-handler methods of the app bar buttons:

```
private void NewEntryButtonTapped(object sender, TappedRoutedEventArgs e)
{
    Frame.Navigate(typeof(MainPage), Frame.BackStackDepth);
}

private void LocationButtonTapped(object sender, TappedRoutedEventArgs e)
{
    Frame.Navigate(typeof(Step1), Frame.BackStackDepth);
}

private void DepthButtonTapped(object sender, TappedRoutedEventArgs e)
```

```
{
    Frame.Navigate(typeof(Step2), Frame.BackStackDepth);
}

private void CompletedButtonTapped(object sender, TappedRoutedEventArgs e)
{
    Frame.Navigate(typeof(Step3), Frame.BackStackDepth);
}
```

4. Run the application by pressing Ctrl+F5. When the main page appears, right-click the screen, or use the Windows+Z key combination to display the app bar (or swipe your fingers from the top edge of the screen). The app bar displays the four buttons, as shown in Figure 10-11.

FIGURE 10-11: The app bar with buttons representing pages

5. Click or tap the "Maximum Depth & Bottom Time" app bar button. You are sent directly to the Step2 page. The Parameter label displays 0, indicating that this is the first page on the navigation stack, so you get here directly from the Start Page, as shown in Figure 10-12. If you navigated to the Step2 page sequentially (first from MainPage to Step1, and then to Step2), the Parameter label would display 1.

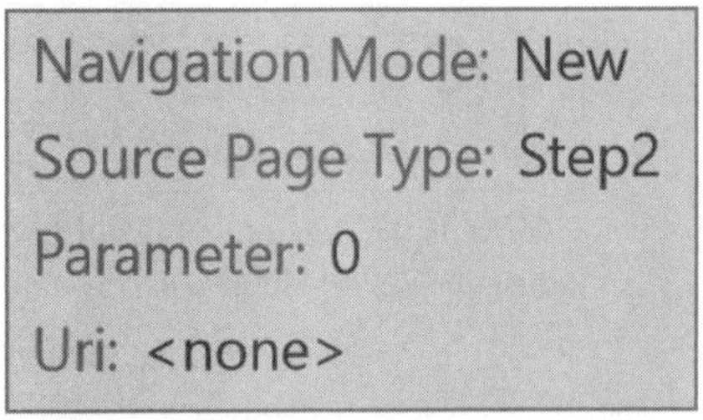

Navigation Mode: New

Source Page Type: Step2

Parameter: 0

Uri: <none>

FIGURE 10-12: The Parameter value of the Step2 page is 0

6. Now, right-click the screen (or press the Windows+Z key combination) to display the app bar again. No app bar will be shown on page Step2!

7. Press the back button to get back to the first page, and try displaying the app bar there again. It appears exactly as shown in Step 4.

8. Close the DiveLog app.

How It Works

When the application started, the main page was displayed by the following code snippet, which is in the App xaml.cs file:

```
var rootFrame = new Frame();
if (!rootFrame.Navigate(typeof(MainPage)))
{
    throw new Exception("Failed to create initial page");
}
Window.Current.Content = rootFrame;
Window.Current.Activate();
```

As the result of this code, the hierarchy of layout containers was as shown in Figure 10-13.

When you tried to display an app bar, Windows Runtime searched for an app bar starting from `Window.Current` traversing down to `Frame`, and then to the page within `Frame`. `Frame` held a `MainPage` instance that had an app bar, and so this app bar was displayed. If the app bar had not been found, the search would have continued traversing the hierarchy with the `Frame` within `MainPage`, unless an app bar had been found or the hierarchy had been ended.

After you navigated from `MainPage` to `Step2` — as a result of the `Frame.Navigate(typeof(Step1)` call — the layout hierarchy was changed, as shown in Figure 10-14.

In this hierarchy, the search algorithm did not find any app bar, so that is why it was not displayed in Step 6.

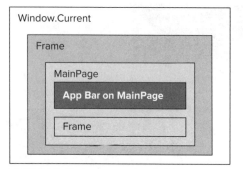

FIGURE 10-13: Layout container hierarchy when displaying MainPage

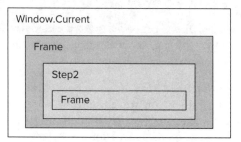

FIGURE 10-14: Layout container hierarchy when displaying the Step2 page

Of course, you can fix this issue, as you learn in the next exercise.

Fixing the App Bar Issue

The key to fixing this issue of a missing app bar is to utilize the traversal mechanism you just learned about. Instead of using the layout hierarchy shown in Figure 10-13 and Figure 10-14, you should create another one, as depicted in Figure 10-15.

This hierarchy contains a new `Page` object called `LogEntryPage`. This page holds the app bar, and it nests a new `Frame` object, named `LocalFrame`. When navigating among pages, `LocalFrame` will be used instead of the `Frame` of `Windows.Current`. So, when you navigate to the `Step2` page, the layout hierarchy would be the one shown in Figure 10-16. As you can see, the search algorithm would find and display the app bar of `LogEntryPage`.

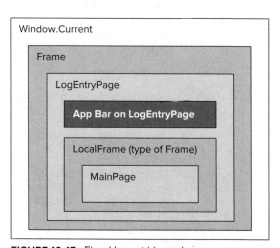

FIGURE 10-15: Fixed layout hierarchy

TRY IT OUT **Fixing the App Bar Issue**

To apply the layout hierarchy changes and fix the app bar issue, follow these steps:

1. If you closed Visual Studio after the previous exercise, open it and load the `DiveLog.sln` file you used the last time.

2. In Solution Explorer, select the `DiveLog` project node and add a new page with the Project ⇨ Add New Item dialog box using the Blank Page template. Name it **LogEntryPage**.

3. When the new page opens in the designer, replace the `<Grid>` element (including the `</Grid>` closing tag) with the following `Frame` definition:

```
<Frame x:Name="LocalFrame" />
```

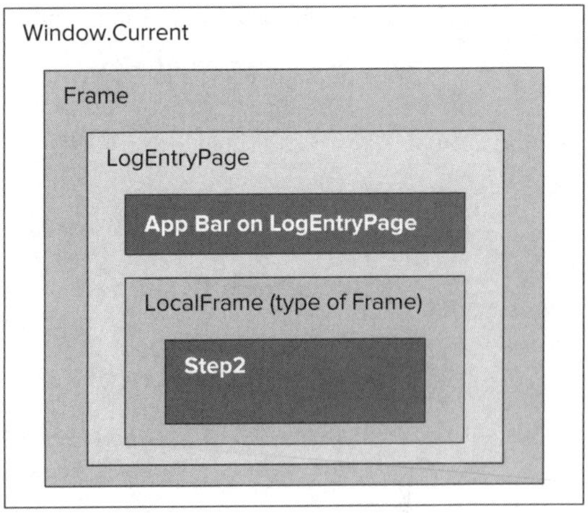

4. Open the `MainPage.xaml` file in the designer. In the XAML pane, select the whole `<Page.TopAppBar>` fragment (from the beginning to the last character of the `</Page.TopAppBar>` closing tag) and cut it by pressing Shift+Del. Switch back to `LogEntryPage.xaml`, and position the cursor at the beginning of the `<Frame>` definition you added in the previous step. Press Ctrl+V to paste the `<Page.TopAppBar>` definition.

FIGURE 10-16: Fixed layout hierarchy after navigating to the Step2 page

5. Open the `MainPage.xaml.cs` file, and select the code belonging to the last four methods (`NewEntryButtonTapped`, `LocationButtonTapped`, `DepthButtonTapped`, and `CompletedButtonTapped`). Cut this code by pressing Shift+Del.

6. Open the `LogEntryPage.xaml.cs` file, and place the cursor before the closing brace of the class definition. Paste the code you cut in the previous step by pressing Ctrl+V.

7. Change all occurrences of `Frame` in the pasted code to `LocalFrame`. You have two occurrences in each of the four methods, so altogether you must change eight occurrences.

8. Append the following code line to each of the four methods pasted in Step 6:

```
CommandBar.IsOpen = false;
```

9. Type the following boldfaced code into the body of the `OnNavigatedTo` method:

```
protected override void OnNavigatedTo(NavigationEventArgs e)
{
    LocalFrame.Navigate(typeof(MainPage));
}
```

Now, the completed code of `LogEntryPage.xaml.cs` should be as follows (comments and unused `using` directives are removed for the sake of brevity):

```
using Windows.UI.Xaml.Controls;
using Windows.UI.Xaml.Input;
```

```
using Windows.UI.Xaml.Navigation;

namespace DiveLog
{
    public sealed partial class LogEntryPage : Page
    {
        public LogEntryPage()
        {
            this.InitializeComponent();
        }

        protected override void OnNavigatedTo(NavigationEventArgs e)
        {
            LocalFrame.Navigate(typeof(MainPage));
        }

        private void NewEntryButtonTapped(object sender, TappedRoutedEventArgs e)
        {
            LocalFrame.Navigate(typeof(MainPage), LocalFrame.BackStackDepth);
            CommandBar.IsOpen = false;
        }

        private void LocationButtonTapped(object sender, TappedRoutedEventArgs e)
        {
            LocalFrame.Navigate(typeof(Step1), LocalFrame.BackStackDepth);
            CommandBar.IsOpen = false;
        }

        private void DepthButtonTapped(object sender, TappedRoutedEventArgs e)
        {
            LocalFrame.Navigate(typeof(Step2), LocalFrame.BackStackDepth);
            CommandBar.IsOpen = false;
        }

        private void CompletedButtonTapped(object sender, TappedRoutedEventArgs e)
        {
            LocalFrame.Navigate(typeof(Step3), LocalFrame.BackStackDepth);
            CommandBar.IsOpen = false;
        }
    }
}
```

10. Open the `App.xaml.cs` file, and locate the following line within the body of the `OnLaunched` method:

```
if (!rootFrame.Navigate(typeof(MainPage)))
```

11. Replace `MainPage` with `LogEntryPage`, as shown here:

```
if (!rootFrame.Navigate(typeof(LogEntryPage)))
```

12. Run the application by pressing Ctrl+F5. You can navigate to every page using the app bar, because now it is displayed on every page — unlike in the previous exercise. Try navigating among the pages using the app bar.

13. Close the application.

How It Works

In Step 2, you added the `LogEntryPage` file to your project to implement the layout concept depicted in Figure 10-15. In Step 3, you created the `LocalFrame` element. In the subsequent steps (from Step 4 to Step 8), you moved the app bar and the related event-handler methods to `LogEntryPage`. In Step 9 and Step 10, you set `LogEntryPage` as the root page of the application. You modified the `App.xaml.cs` file so that the application would use `LogEntryPage` instead of `MainPage`. The code you added in Step 9 forwarded your app to `MainPage` right after it had been launched.

As you can see, you did not modify the code of the existing pages, except for moving the app bar code. As a result of the changes, the application now works as expected.

By now, you've used only page navigation in this chapter. However, you can navigate to web pages, and open files through associated apps, as you learn in the next section.

Launching Files and Web Pages

You can launch other files from your currently running app with any of the apps associated with the file extension. The `Windows.System` namespace contains a `Launcher` object responsible for this. Using the `Launcher` object is very easy, as the `LaunchFiles.sln` sample solution in the `LaunchFiles` folder of this chapter's download demonstrates.

`Launcher` is a static class with two methods:

➤ `LauchFileAsynch` accepts a file (an `IStorageFileObject`) argument and opens the application associated with the specified file type.

➤ `LaunchUriAsync` accepts an `Uri` argument and starts the default (or specified) browser with the given `Uri`.

Both methods have an overload that accepts a second argument with a type of `LauncherOptions`. Using this option, you can specify several options to launch a file association or a URI.

Let's take a look at a few examples of using `Launcher`. To start the default application associated with the `.png` file extension, use this simple code snippet:

```
const string FILE = @"Assets\Surface.png";
// ...
var file = await Package.Current.InstalledLocation.GetFileAsync(FILE);
if (file != null)
{
    bool success = await Launcher.LaunchFileAsync(file);
    if (success)
    {
        // --- Application launched successfully
    }
    else
    {
        // --- Application has not been launched
    }
else
```

```
    {
        // --- There are issues accessing the file
    }
```

Starting a URI follows the same pattern:

```
const string URI = "http://msdn.com";
// ...
bool success = await Launcher.LaunchUriAsync(file);
if (success)
{
    // --- URI launched successfully
}
else
{
    // --- URI has not been launched
}
```

Using the `LauncherOptions` argument, you can ask for a confirmation from the user before starting the app, as the boldfaced code in the following snippet indicates:

```
const string FILE = @"Assets\Surface.png";
// ...
var file = await Package.Current.InstalledLocation.GetFileAsync(FILE);
if (file != null)
{
    var options = new LauncherOptions();
    options.TreatAsUntrusted = true;
    bool success = await Launcher.LaunchFileAsync(file);
    if (success)
    {
        // --- Application launched successfully
    }
    else
    {
        // --- User did not allow to start the app
    }
}
else
{
    // --- There are issues accessing the file
}
```

Using `LauncherOptions`, you can even let the user launch the associated app using the Open With dialog box:

```
const string FILE = @"Assets\Surface.png";
// ...
var file = await Package.Current.InstalledLocation.GetFileAsync(FILE);
if (file != null)
{
    var transform = StartOpenWithButton.TransformToVisual(null);
    var popupLocation = transform.TransformPoint(new Point());
    popupLocation.Y += StartOpenWithButton.ActualHeight;
    var options = new LauncherOptions();
    options.DisplayApplicationPicker = true;
```

```
        options.UI.PreferredPlacement = Placement.Below;
        options.UI.InvocationPoint = popupLocation;
        bool success = await Launcher.LaunchFileAsync(file, options);
        // --- Handle launch status
    }
    // --- Handle file issues
```

This code sets the `DisplayApplicationPicker` property to `true`, and this setting causes the Open With picker dialog box to pop up. In this dialog box, you can select the application with which to open the specified file. The `PreferredPlacement` property is set to `Placement.Below`, and so the `InvocationPoint` property is taken into account as the upper-left position of the picker dialog box. This position is calculated according to the position of the button (`StartOpenWithButton`) used to run this code snippet.

> **NOTE** *You can find all the samples of the previous code in the* `MainPage.xaml.cs` *file under the* `LaunchFiles` *folder in this chapter's download.*

Now, you've learned the fundamental concepts and details of navigation. It's time to get to know the behavior of two great Visual Studio application templates — the Split Application and the Grid Application templates.

USING THE SPLIT APPLICATION AND GRID APPLICATION TEMPLATES

The Windows 8 team at Microsoft places a lot of emphasis on making it easy for developers to follow the Windows 8 design patterns — including content representation and navigation. To support these patterns, Visual Studio provides two Windows 8 application templates that boost your application development by providing a fast start:

➤ The *Split Application* template supports hierarchical navigation. It is a two-page project for an app that navigates among grouped items, as shown in Figure 10-17. The first page allows group selection, and the second displays an item list alongside details for the selected item.

➤ The *Grid Application* template supports hierarchical navigation, as shown in Figure 10-18. It is a three-page project for an app that navigates among groups of items. The first page allows group selection, and the two other pages are dedicated to displaying group and item details, respectively.

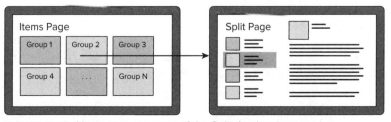

FIGURE 10-17: Navigation structure of the Split Application template

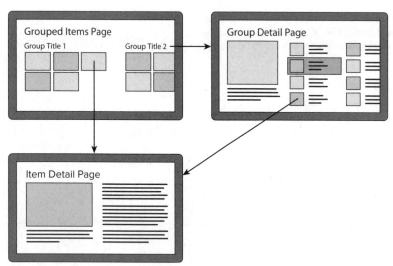

FIGURE 10-18: Navigation structure of the Grid Application template

These templates are harnessed with useful tools that manage the behavior of your application:

➤ **Sample data source** — Templates provide sample data at design time. This helps you to preview the UI without running your application.

➤ **Application layout** — The pages in these templates manage the different visual states of the application. When you rotate your device (for example, from landscape to portrait view), or you snap two apps on the screen, the page layout accommodates the new visual state.

➤ **State management** — You do not have to worry about saving and restoring your application's state (remember the discussion about the Windows 8 app lifecycle in Chapter 9). These templates handle the `Suspending` and `Resuming` application events.

➤ **Navigation support** — Your app handles the keyboard and mouse navigation events automatically. For example, when the user presses the Alt+Left or Alt+Right key combinations, your application navigates backward or forward, respectively. Also, when your mouse supports the back and forward buttons, those are correctly used for page navigation.

Before you create apps with the Split Application or Grid Application templates, it is worth getting acquainted with the structures and the toolsets they provide.

The Structure of the Templates

When you create a new app with either the Split Application or Grid Application template, your project is equipped with a number of useful code files, as shown in Figure 10-19. Although you see an app built on the Split Application template in this figure, these files have the same content for both templates. Table 10-2 summarizes the role of these code files.

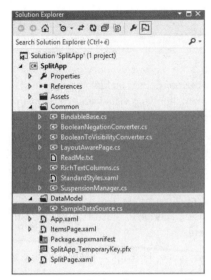

FIGURE 10-19: Code infrastructure files created by the Split and Grid Application templates

TABLE 10-2: Common Infrastructure Files in the Split and Grid Application Templates

FILE	DESCRIPTION
BindableBase.cs	This file contains the `BindableBase` abstract class that is a helper class to implement the `INotifyPropertyChanged` interface — it has a key role in XAML data binding, as you learned in Chapter 8. You can use this class to derive your model classes (that is, classes that represent data to be displayed in the app). The model classes in the `SampleDataSource.cs` file derive from this class.
BooleanNegationConverter.cs	This is a data-binding converter class that negates the value of a boolean flag. It is not used in the templates directly.
BooleanToVisibilityConverter.cs	This is a data-binding converter class that translates the boolean `true` and `false` values to the `Visible` and `Collapsed` values of the `Visibility` enumeration. Although this converter is not used directly in the templates, it is very convenient when you want to bind the visibility of a UI element to a boolean value.

continues

TABLE 10-2 *(continued)*

FILE	DESCRIPTION
LayoutAwarePage.cs	This file implements the LayoutAwarePage class that adds functionality to your pages, including application lifecycle management, handling visual state, and navigation. You learn more about this class later.
Readme.txt	This file contains a very short generic description of the files in the Common folder.
RichTextColumns.cs	This file contains the RichTextColumns class that helps you manage multiple columns of rich text and related scrolling tasks. This class is used only in the Grid Application template.
StandardStyles.xaml	This file contains predefined resources (styles, data templates, and so on).
SuspensionManager.cs	This file contains an implementation of the SuspensionManager class that captures global session states to simplify app lifetime management.
SampleDataSource.cs	This class defines a sample data source for your app that can be used at design time.

In addition to the common files, the Split Application and Grid Application templates contain their own page files, as summarized in Table 10-3 and Table 10-4, respectively.

TABLE 10-3: Split Application Template Pages

PAGE FILE	DESCRIPTION
ItemsPage.xaml	This is the Start Page of the app. It displays item groups in a GridView (or in a ListView in snapped mode).
SplitPage.xaml	Selecting a group in the ItemsPage view navigates to this page. It contains the list of items on the left, and the details of the selected item on the right. In snapped mode, this view works as if the list and the item details were two separate pages.

TABLE 10-4: Grid Application Template Pages

PAGE FILE	DESCRIPTION
GroupedItemsPage.xaml	This is the Start Page of the app. It displays all groups and their items in a GridView (or in a ListView in snapped mode).

PAGE FILE	DESCRIPTION
GroupDetailPage.xaml	Selecting a group header in the GroupedItemsPage view navigates to this page. It contains the detailed information about the group and its items.
ItemDetailPage.xaml	Selecting an item in the GroupedItemsPage view or in the GroupDetailPage view navigates to this page. It contains the details of the selected item.

Just like most Windows 8 apps, these templates use the *Model-View-ViewModel* (*MVVM*) design pattern to separate the responsibilities of objects composing the application. If you want to understand these templates better, you cannot avoid having a basic overview about MVVM.

To handle the cooperating components of your application as loosely coupled as possible, MVVM suggests that you divide the build of your application components around the three roles of Model, View, and ViewModel. The *Model* represents an object that retrieves your content (application data) and writes back the modifications to a store (database). The *View* is the UI that displays the application content. In the case of Windows 8 apps using XAML, the View is the XAML code representing your UI.

To separate the Model and the View from each other, the data is transferred through a *ViewModel* between them. When the Model is queried for a kind of content, it retrieves a ViewModel representing that content. The View uses the ViewModel to display data coming from the Model. When the user modifies some information on the UI, the View uses a ViewModel object and sends it to the Model to persist it.

> **NOTE** *The Microsoft Pattern and Practices team published a great article about MVVM (*http://msdn.microsoft.com/en-us/library/gg430869(v=PandP.40).aspx*) that provides an in-depth approach through an application sample. Although this sample uses Silverlight, it can be applied easily to Windows 8 applications written in C#.*

When you start working with a new Split Application or Grid Application, these templates contain a Model, and a number of ViewModel and several View (one view for each page type) components. If you want to customize the application, you must carry out the following steps:

1. Modify the Model to retrieve the type of content you want to display. You can also modify the Model to save modified content.

2. As your Model evolves, specify the ViewModel classes that represent the data retrieved from the Model or to be persisted by the Model.

3. Change the predefined UI (template pages) according to your app's content, and use XAML data binding to tie the ViewModel with your UI.

4. Optionally change the styles, content, and data templates to provide your own visual design.

5. Optionally add new pages to your app and implement their navigation logic.

You can find two prepared sample applications in the `FamilyTripsSplit` and `FamilyTripsGrid` folder of this chapter's download that were created with the Split Application template and the Grid Application template, respectively. These apps display photos with their descriptions, as shown in an example in Figure 10-20.

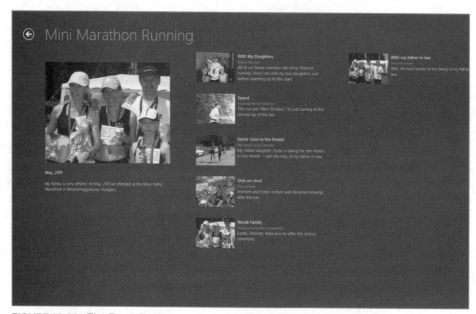

FIGURE 10-20: The FamilyTrips app — based on the Grid Application template

As you learn in the next section, it is worth opening these sample apps and regularly comparing them with the freshly created (and non-customized) versions of Split and Grid apps.

Managing Sample Data and Runtime Data

The `DataModel` folder contains a `SampleDataSource.cs` file that represents the content of the template app in memory, just as if it were read from a database (or queried from an Internet data source). Table 10-5 summarizes the types in this file and their roles.

TABLE 10-5: Types in the SampleDataSource.cs File

TYPE	DESCRIPTION
SampleDataCommon	A type representing an abstract ViewModel class for items with a unique ID, a title, a subtitle, a description, and an image.
SampleDataItem	A data item (ViewModel) inheriting the attributes from `SampleDataCommon` and adding a `Content` property.

TYPE	DESCRIPTION
SampleDataGroup	A data item (ViewModel) inheriting the attributes from SampleDataCommon, and adding an Items property that represents SampleDataItem instances that belong to that group.
SampleDataSource	The Model class that has several (read-only) operations, such as GetGroups GetGroup, and GetItem.

The SampleDataSource class is used as sample data during the design of pages. This behavior is defined in a CollectionViewSource resource in the XAML files of application pages:

```
<!-- d:Source is broken into three separate lines for better readability, -->
<!-- however, is should be types as one line! -->
<CollectionViewSource
    x:Name="itemsViewSource"
    Source="{Binding Items}"
    d:Source="{Binding AllGroups,
        Source={d:DesignInstance Type=data:SampleDataSource,
        IsDesignTimeCreatable=True}}"/>
```

The d:source attribute of the <CollectionViewSource> element indicates that the AllGroups property of SampleDataSource should be used during design time. The Source attribute defines the runtime data source.

The data is bound to UI elements through the ItemsSource property of UI controls. For example, ItemsPage.xaml contains a GridView and a ListView element that refer to the CollectionViewSource by its name (itemsViewSource):

```
<GridView
    <!-- ... -->
    ItemsSource="{Binding Source={StaticResource itemsViewSource}}"
    <!-- ... -->
/>

<ListView
    <!-- ... -->
    ItemsSource="{Binding Source={StaticResource itemsViewSource}}"
    <!-- ... -->
/>
```

The Split Application and Grid Application templates use the SampleDataSource class not only at design time, but also as a runtime data source. The runtime assignment is done in the LoadState method of the apps' starting pages:

```
protected override void LoadState(Object navigationParameter,
        Dictionary<String, Object> pageState)
{
    var sampleDataGroups = SampleDataSource.GetGroups((String)navigationParameter);
    this.DefaultViewModel["Items"] = sampleDataGroups;
}
```

Putting `sampleDataGroups` in the `"Items"` element of the `DefaultViewModel` container binds the data to the `CollectionViewSource`, because of the `Source={Binding Items}` declaration.

> **NOTE** The `FamilyTrips` *sample apps (both the Split- and Grid-based ones)*
> *contain a* `TripDataSource` *class representing the design-time and runtime*
> *data source of the app.* `TripDataSource` *is built with a very similar structure as*
> `SampleDataSource`.

Layout Management

Both templates derive all page classes from the `LayoutAwarePage` class that is located in the `Common` folder. This class undertakes the responsibility of managing the layout of the application. As you rotate the screen of a mobile device, or snap apps beside your app, the screen layout is managed for you automatically.

As soon as the page inheriting from `LayoutAwarePage` is loaded, it subscribes to the current window's `SizeChanged` event. When this event is triggered, `LayoutAwarePage` automatically moves the page to the appropriate visual state. When the window size changes, not only does the size of existing controls change but sometimes the whole layout of the page. For example, when an app based on the Split Application template is snapped on the screen, the layout of the `ItemsPage` view changes from the `GridView` to a `ListView`, because of the boldfaced markup in the following declaration:

```xml
<VisualStateManager.VisualStateGroups>
    <VisualStateGroup x:Name="ApplicationViewStates">
        <VisualState x:Name="FullScreenLandscape"/>
        <VisualState x:Name="Filled"/>
        <VisualState x:Name="FullScreenPortrait">
            <!-- Details omitted for the sake of brevity -->
        </VisualState>
        <VisualState x:Name="Snapped">
            <Storyboard>
                <!-- The animation of the Back button and the Title is omitted -->
                <ObjectAnimationUsingKeyFrames
                        Storyboard.TargetName="itemListView"
                    Storyboard.TargetProperty="Visibility">
                    <DiscreteObjectKeyFrame KeyTime="0" Value="Visible"/>
                </ObjectAnimationUsingKeyFrames>
                <ObjectAnimationUsingKeyFrames
                        Storyboard.TargetName="itemGridView"
                    Storyboard.TargetProperty="Visibility">
                    <DiscreteObjectKeyFrame KeyTime="0" Value="Collapsed"/>
                </ObjectAnimationUsingKeyFrames>
            </Storyboard>
        </VisualState>
    </VisualStateGroup>
</VisualStateManager.VisualStateGroups>
```

This markup sets the `Visibility` property of the `ListView` to `Visible` (and so displays it) and the `Visibility` property of the `GridView` to `Collapsed` (and so hides it). You can use a similar solution to alter the layout of your apps adaptively as the window size changes.

Using Logical Pages

The Split Application template's `SplitPage` view has a trick. Originally, it divides the screen into two panes — a list view on the left, and a detail view on the right. However, when the window's layout changes to portrait or to snapped, the width of the remaining window is not enough to display both panes.

In this case, this page allows internal navigation between the list view and the detail view, as if the one physical page were actually two. The `SplitPage` view is handled as two logical pages. When the user navigates from the list to an item, the list view is hidden, and only the detail view is shown. When the back button is used on the detail pane, it navigates back only to the list view.

Using Rich Text Columns

The Grid Application template's `ItemDetailPage` view uses a `FlipView` control to represent its content. The `FlipView`'s template contains a `ScrollView` (to enable you to scroll long content horizontally) that uses the `RichTextColumns` control to display the content in multiple columns on the screen:

```
<common:RichTextColumns x:Name="richTextColumns" Margin="117,0,117,47">
    <RichTextBlock x:Name="richTextBlock" Width="560"
        Style="{StaticResource ItemRichTextStyle}">
        <Paragraph>
            <Run FontSize="26.667" FontWeight="Light" Text="{Binding Title}"/>
            <LineBreak/>
            <LineBreak/>
            <Run FontWeight="SemiBold" Text="{Binding Subtitle}"/>
        </Paragraph>
        <Paragraph LineStackingStrategy="MaxHeight">
            <InlineUIContainer>
                <Image x:Name="image" MaxHeight="480" Margin="0,20,0,10"
                    Stretch="Uniform" Source="{Binding Image}"/>
            </InlineUIContainer>
        </Paragraph>
        <Paragraph>
            <Run FontWeight="SemiLight" Text="{Binding Content}"/>
        </Paragraph>
    </RichTextBlock>

    <common:RichTextColumns.ColumnTemplate>
        <DataTemplate>
            <RichTextBlockOverflow Width="560" Margin="80,0,0,0">
                <RichTextBlockOverflow.RenderTransform>
                    <TranslateTransform X="-1" Y="4"/>
                </RichTextBlockOverflow.RenderTransform>
            </RichTextBlockOverflow>
        </DataTemplate>
    </common:RichTextColumns.ColumnTemplate>
</common:RichTextColumns>
```

The `Width` attribute of the `<RichTextBox>` element defines that the first column's width is 560 pixels. The first `<Paragraph>` element nests the title, subtitle, and description of the item. The second `<Paragraph>` contains the image, and the third one nests the content that can be very long, even consuming multiple columns.

When the content of the `<RichTextColumns>` element does not fit into one column on the page, additional columns are automatically added where the content can overflow to. The `<common:RichTextColumns.ColumnTemplate>` element defines a template for the additional rich text columns. It uses a `<RichTextBlockOverFlow>` element of 560 pixels wide — the same width as the first column. If you change it to 280, you will recognize the overflow columns, as shown in Figure 10-21, because they were narrower than the first column.

FIGURE 10-21: Overflow columns are narrower than the first column

> **NOTE** The `FamilyTrips` sample apps do not modify the original layout mechanism. However, they change a few styles in the `StandardStyles.xaml` resource file to customize the page design.

Other Features to Study

You can get some great ideas from studying the Split Application and Grid Application templates. Here are a few things that are worth examining:

➤ Look at the constructor of `LayoutAwarePage`, and study the methods in the `Visual state switching` section to determine how window size changes are managed within this class.

➤ You can use the `SuspensionManager` class in your other apps as well. Look at it to understand how it saves and loads application changes.

➤ The `RichTextColumns` class implements a panel control that creates additional columns on demand for overflown rich text. It does quite a complex job with a relatively small amount of code.

➤ The `StandardStyles.xaml` file contains a great variety of resource styles and templates you can use in other applications as well.

SUMMARY

Most applications have multiple screens — or, using the Windows 8 terminology, pages. Several navigation patterns help users intuitively browse app content — expanding multiple pages. These patterns include hub navigation, direct navigation, hierarchical navigation, and semantic zoom.

The key object in multi-page scenarios is the `Page` object, the basic UI element that represents an application page. Each `Page` instance has an associated `Frame` object (which can be accessed through the `Frame` property) that controls the content of the page. You can use the `Frame` property to navigate to other pages, passing the type representing the target page.

You can handle events related to navigation, such as `NavigatingFrom`, `NavigatedFrom`, and `NavigatedTo`. If you want to handle these events within a `Page`-derived class, you can override the `OnNavigatingFrom`, `OnNavigatedFrom`, and `OnNavigatedTo` methods, respectively.

You do not need to start building your apps from empty pages. The Split Application and Grid Application templates provide a quick start that suits a number of scenarios. These templates are equipped with great predefined helper tools. They manage (among other things) a sample data source, a visual state that changes with the application window's size (for example, rotating the device or snapping apps on the screen), and an application lifecycle state.

In Chapter 11, you will learn about some great new features of Windows 8 that enable you to build connected apps — applications that work together with each other or with services on the Internet.

EXERCISES

1. What do you call the navigation pattern where you can select an item from a list of groups, and when you navigate to the group, you can select an item from a list to navigate to?

2. Which property of the `Page` object provides a key role in navigation?

3. How can you navigate from the current page to another one?

4. How can you prevent navigating away from a page?

5. Which predefined class provides functionality to manage window size changes in the Split Application and Grid Application projects?

> **NOTE** *You can find the answers to the exercises in Appendix A.*

▶ **WHAT YOU LEARNED IN THIS CHAPTER**

TOPIC	KEY CONCEPTS
Navigation patterns	The designers of the Windows 8 language created a number of navigation patterns that are fairly intuitive and help users easily find the content they are looking for. The most important patterns are hub navigation, direct navigation, hierarchical navigation, and semantic zoom.
Page control	The `Page` UI control is the key building block used in creating Windows 8 applications with navigation. Derive your app screens from `Page`, and you obtain implicit navigation support in your app, including forward and backward navigation with history and navigation events.
Frame control	The `Frame` property of a `Page` is an instance of the `Frame` class. `Frame` is a container that can hold and display pages. Navigating from one page to another means changing the content of a `Frame` to another `Page` instance.
Frame.Navigate method	The `Navigate` method of a `Frame` instance is the key operation in page navigation. This method accepts two arguments. The first argument is the type of the page to navigate to, and the second (optional) argument is an object used as the parameter or the page. This parameter can be used to pass data used in page initialization.
OnNavigatingFrom method, NavigatingFrom event	When you are about to navigate from one page to another, the `NavigatingFrom` event is raised on the source `Page` instance. This event can be handled within the source page by overriding the `OnNavigatingFrom` method. Set the `Cancel` property of the event argument to `true` if you want to prevent navigation.
OnNavigatedFrom method, NavigatedFrom event	When you have navigated from one page to another, the `NavigatedFrom` event is raised on the source `Page` instance. This event can be handled within the source page by overriding the `OnNavigatedFrom` method.
OnNavigatingTo method, NavigatedTo event	When you have navigated from one page to another, the `NavigatingTo` event is ralsed on the target `Page` instance. This event can be handled within the target page by overriding the `OnNavigatingTo` method.

TOPIC	KEY CONCEPTS
Launcher class	The `Launcher` class can be used to launch an app though a file associated with that application, or through a URI. This class provides the `LaunchFileAsync` and `LaunchUriAsynch` methods for this purpose, respectively.
Split Application template	The Split Application template supports hierarchical navigation. It is a two-page project for an app that navigates among grouped items. The first page allows group selection, and the second displays an item list alongside details for the selected item.
Grid Application template	The Grid Application template supports hierarchical navigation. It is a three-page project for an app that navigates among groups of items. The first page allows group selection. The two other pages are dedicated to displaying group and item details, respectively.

11

Building Connected Applications

WHAT YOU WILL LEARN IN THIS CHAPTER:

➤ Integrating your applications with well-known features of the operating system

➤ Communicating with other Windows 8 style apps

➤ Learning how your app can process feed data from the Internet easily

➤ Learning how your app can use the user's data stored in Microsoft's cloud

WROX.COM CODE DOWNLOADS FOR THIS CHAPTER

You can find the wrox.com code downloads for this chapter on the Download Code tab at www.wrox.com/remtitle.cgi?isbn=012680. The code is in the Chapter11.zip download and individually named, as described in the corresponding exercises.

Applications aren't islands. They live in an ecosystem that connects them to other applications and services — sometimes through the operating system, and sometimes through the Internet. It is important to know how to make your Windows 8 style apps use the features provided by the operating system to access certain resources, or to access data and services provided by other Windows 8 style apps. You will learn about these relevant integrating options in this chapter.

Also, you learn about various networking options in Windows 8 style applications. After reading this chapter, you'll be able to incorporate network information processing into your apps and to work with syndication feeds. The closing part of the chapter is about using a higher abstraction software development kit, the Live SDK, to integrate your apps into Microsoft's online services.

INTEGRATING WITH THE OPERATING SYSTEM AND OTHER APPS

Windows is just a shell that provides core features that enable you to use your PC or tablet. That is the purpose of an operating system. You can customize it to a certain extent, but what makes your computer truly yours, and what makes you productive when working with your computer, is the applications you use. Applications supply the features you need — you can read news feeds with an RSS reader, you can read and create documents with a word processor, and so on. But two disadvantages exist when certain features come in different apps.

> **NOTE** *RSS is an acronym for Really Simple Syndication. It is a standard that lets people create feeds from certain resources, like entries of a web log (blog), so other people can subscribe to it to receive updates. You learn about RSS and its usage later in this chapter.*

First, at least some of these apps are probably built by different companies and are designed by different user interface (UI) architects (if any). Therefore, their UIs are inherently diverse, which, in turn, could cause some confusion for a user when two applications attempt to present the same core functionality (such as opening or saving a file) in different ways.

Secondly, applications tend to behave like islands — they live on the same machine, but they are separated, and they don't (or can't) contact each other. Most of the time, they don't even know anything about each other. Imagine the possibilities if some mechanism would allow applications to work in concert. Your computer would provide more than just the sum of its parts, and those parts could work apart from each other.

However, there is a serious architectural difficulty when an app tries to contact other apps. How could it know all the publicly callable interfaces of an arbitrary number of other apps? The only way to solve this problem is to create one interface that every application can opt-in to support — and when one does, it becomes accessible to all the other apps.

The architects of Windows 8 identified these problems very early, so they've created pickers and contracts to solve them.

Pickers: Unified Design to Access Data

A lot of applications need to access files, either to store their own data, or to access and use the user's files. Resolving the first situation can be quite straightforward. Your app can create, modify, and delete files in its isolated storage. No other Windows 8 style app can reach another app's isolated storage, so interference is out of the question. But this is only good until your app needs to access the user's personal files.

For obvious security reasons, no Windows 8 style app can use these files without the user's permission. Users must authorize an application to open a file from their Documents library or other locations that may contain sensitive data.

The same is true for other resources, such as contact information. No one wants an app be able to delete or even read contacts without asking the user first. Applications must be regulated, and the user must always know what's happening with his or her data.

To this end, Microsoft requires that all apps either ask for permission to access sensitive information via contracts (which are discussed later in this chapter) or through pickers.

Pickers can be viewed as the descendants of dialog box windows from the older Windows or .NET APIs. Instead of the older OpenFileDialog from .NET, you can open files by using a class called FileOpenPicker. If you are acquainted with OpenFileDialog, you'll quickly understand the corresponding pickers. However, pickers are somewhat different from older dialog boxes. They aren't windowed; they take the full screen to present data. Harnessing this opportunity of having a lot of space, the current UI pickers are touch-optimized.

Another great addition to common dialog box windows is that applications can indicate by a contract that they provide some functionality that a picker can use to extend itself. You can read more about this feature later in this chapter.

Last but not least, pickers make access to restricted resources consistent. When an application defers file opening or contact picking to a picker, it's always the same — all apps present the same, well-known UI.

For the purposes of this chapter, there are four pickers you need to know: FileOpenPicker, FileSavePicker, FolderPicker, and ContactPicker. You can find the first three in the Windows .Storage.Pickers namespace, and the last is in the Windows.ApplicationModel.Contacts namespace. All can be simply instantiated using the new keyword, and they provide asynchronous methods to enable them to accomplish their work.

The following code sample shows how easy it is to open a file and load its contents to a StorageFile object using a FileOpenPicker:

```
async void OpenFile(object sender, RoutedEventArgs e)
{
    FileOpenPicker foPicker = new FileOpenPicker();

    StorageFile file = await foPicker.PickSingleFileAsync();
    if (file != null)
    {
        //do something with the file
    }
}
```

FileOpenPicker is used to open one or multiple files — even from locations that are out of reach for the application because of security regulations. Table 11-1 describes the FileOpenPicker's key properties. Some of them are shared with the FileSavePicker class.

TABLE 11-1: Important Properties of the FileOpenPicker Class

PROPERTY	DESCRIPTION
ViewMode	Defines how the picker shows files. You can set it to `Thumbnail` or `List`.
FileTypeFilter	Sets the file types that are available to the user when he or she wants to filter the files.
SuggestedStartLocation	This is the location the picker will open when shown. You can use only well-known locations (such as the desktop, the `Documents` library, the `Pictures` library, or `Videos` library).

After setting its properties to the desired values, you should call one of the two methods that make the picker appear. As its name indicates, `PickSingleFileAsync` is used to open a single file. The method's return type is an `IAsyncOperation<StorageFile>`, but by using the `await` keyword, it'll seemingly return a `StorageFile` object, so you don't have to wait in your code for the background processing (the `IAsyncOperation`) to complete, and after that, extract the result of the operation (the `StorageFile`) manually. This instance of the `StorageFile` class can be used to read and manipulate properties and content of the file chosen by the user. But, keep in mind that if an app opened a file using a `FileOpenPicker` from an otherwise restricted location, it won't be able to save changes to that file without using a `FileSavePicker`.

The other way to show the `FileOpenPicker` is by calling the `PickMultipleFileAsync` method. When you use the `await` keyword, it returns a read-only list of `StorageFile` objects. This list contains all the files the user chose as `StorageFile` objects.

Figure 11-1 shows the `FileOpenPicker` in action.

`FileSavePicker` can be used to save a file to a location and with a name chosen by the user. Among others, it shares the `SuggestedStartLocation` property with the `FileOpenPicker` class. Table 11-2 shows the other key properties of `FileSavePicker`.

TABLE 11-2: Important Properties of the FileSavePicker Class

PROPERTY	DESCRIPTION
DefaultFileExtension	The default extension string that the `FileSavePicker` appends to the filename upon saving the file.
FileTypeChoices	A list containing the possible choices of file type and extension.
SuggestedFileName	A default filename that the user can overwrite after opening the picker.
SuggestedSaveFile	With this property, you can have the picker suggest not just a name and an extension, but an existing file to the user.

Using this picker is relatively simple. After creating a `FileSavePicker` and setting its properties, you just have to call the `PickSaveFileAsync` method. When you use the `await` keyword, it returns with a `StorageFile` object. Modify the contents of the file freely — all the modifications will be saved. To add the content to a `StorageFile`, you can use the `FileIO` class, which you can find in the `Windows.Storage` namespace.

Files outside of an isolated storage can be seen by virtually any app — either by using contracts or a picker. This means that there is a chance that more than one app tries to update a file at the same time. To avoid conflicts, you should indicate to the operating system that it should not update the file until your app has finished working on it. When working with files outside of a Windows 8 style app's isolated storage, you should use the `CachedFileManager` class (in the `Windows.Storage` namespace) to signal to the operating system when not to update a file.

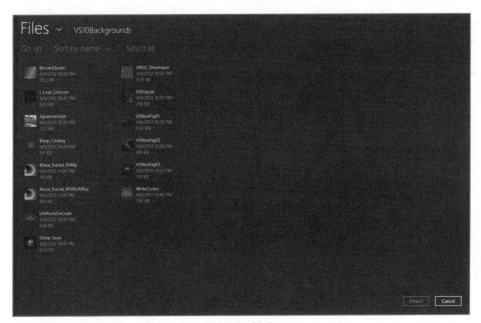

FIGURE 11-1: The FileOpenPicker opened by the Mail app

The third picker class worth mentioning is `FolderPicker`. With this class, you can let the user select not files but whole folders. You can find all of its important properties in the previous two picker classes. To use it, after creating a `FolderPicker` object and setting its properties, call the `PickSingleFolderAsync` method. When you use the `await` keyword, it returns with a `StorageFolder` object. This can be used to access all the data about and in a directory: name, creation date, attributes, and, of course, the files in it.

The last picker is the `ContactPicker`, which is a bit different from the previous three. It lets your app access the contacts of the current user. When an application uses a `ContactPicker`, it can either present its own UI to the user to pick the contacts, or direct the user to another application — one that can read contacts and, so, act as a contact picker. The Contacts Windows 8 style app that is preinstalled on every Windows 8 machine is the default contact picker application. If you don't want to create a customized UI to pick contacts, you can rely on the Contacts app.

Using the `ContactPicker` is even simpler than using a file or folder picker. After creating a `ContactPicker` object and setting its properties, you must call either the `PickSingleContactAsync` or the `PickMultipleContactsAsync` method. When you use the `await` keyword, the former returns a `ContactInformation` object that represents the contact the user picked. The latter returns a read-only list of `ContactInformation` objects.

The two important properties of the `ContactPicker` are `SelectionMode` and `DesiredFields`. `SelectionMode` controls whether the picker shows contacts as standalone objects, or as a collection of the fields they contain. `DesiredFields` indicates in which parts of the contact information your app is interested.

In the following exercise, you write an app that can open one or more contacts, and then save the names of these contacts in a text file, outside the app's isolated storage.

> **NOTE** You can find the complete code to download for this exercise on this book's companion website at www.wrox.com in the folder `PickerSample\End` within the `Chapter11.zip` download.

TRY IT OUT Using Pickers

To see how to use the pickers to open contacts and save files, follow these steps:

1. Open the solution located in the `PickerSample\Begin` directory of this book's `Chapter11.zip` file (which you can download from www.wrox.com). Familiarize yourself with the UI.

2. Open `MainPage.xaml.cs` by double-clicking it in the Solution Explorer. Insert the following `using` directives under the ones already there at the top of the file:

```
using Windows.ApplicationModel.Contacts;
using Windows.Storage;
using Windows.Storage.Pickers;
using Windows.Storage.Provider;
using Windows.UI.Popups;
```

3. Add a List of `ContactInformation` objects to the `MainPage` class, as shown in bold here:

```
public sealed partial class MainPage : Page {
    List<ContactInformation> contacts = null;

    public MainPage() {
...
```

4. In `MainPage.xaml`, locate the declaration of the two buttons, and add an event-handler subscription to both of their `Click` events. The markup you need to add is boldfaced in the following code:

```
<Button Click="OpenContacts">Open Contacts</Button>
<Button Click="SaveContactsToFile">Save to file</Button>
```

5. In `MainPage.xaml.cs`, create the `OpenContacts` method, as shown here:

```
async void OpenContacts(object sender, RoutedEventArgs e)
{
```

```
ContactPicker cp = new ContactPicker();
var res = await cp.PickMultipleContactsAsync();
if (res.Count > 0)
{
    contacts = new List<ContactInformation>(res);
    lbxFiles.Items.Clear();
    foreach (var item in contacts) lbxFiles.Items.Add(item);
    tbkStatus.Text = string.Format("{0} contacts selected", res.Count);
}
}
```

6. Create the `SaveContactsToFile` method. For the time being, it'll stay empty.

```
async void SaveContactsToFile(object sender, RoutedEventArgs e)
{
}
```

7. Build the application by pressing the F6 button or clicking "BUILD - Build Solution" on the main menu of Visual Studio. If the Errors window appears and shows that there are errors in the code, try to resolve them by following the suggestions in the aforementioned window. If you can't resolve an error, open the `PickerSample\End` solution in the companion code, and compare your code to the one in the working solution. Start the application, and test that the first button works as it should. Click or tap it, choose a few contacts, and then click or tap the OK button. Figure 11-2 shows the look of the application after choosing two contacts.

FIGURE 11-2: Two contacts picked

8. Add code to the previously created `SaveContactsToFile` method to use a `FileSavePicker`. The difference is boldfaced in the following code:

```
async void SaveContactsToFile(object sender, RoutedEventArgs e)
{
    if (contacts != null)
    {
        FileSavePicker fsp = new FileSavePicker { SuggestedFileName = "contacts",
            DefaultFileExtension = ".txt" };
        fsp.SuggestedStartLocation = PickerLocationId.Desktop;
        fsp.FileTypeChoices.Add("Plain text", new List<string>() { ".txt" });
        StorageFile sf = await fsp.PickSaveFileAsync();


    }
    else await new MessageDialog("No contacts selected.", "Error").ShowAsync();
}
```

9. Modify the code of the `SaveContactsToFile` method to do the actual writing to the file. The code you need to add is boldfaced:

```
async void SaveContactsToFile(object sender, RoutedEventArgs e)
{
    if (contacts != null)
    {
        FileSavePicker fsp = new FileSavePicker { SuggestedFileName = "contacts",
            DefaultFileExtension = ".txt" };
        fsp.SuggestedStartLocation = PickerLocationId.Desktop;
        fsp.FileTypeChoices.Add("Plain text", new List<string>() { ".txt" });
        StorageFile sf = await fsp.PickSaveFileAsync();

        if (sf != null)
        {
            CachedFileManager.DeferUpdates(sf);
            await FileIO.WriteLinesAsync(sf, contacts.Select(c => c.Name));
            if (await CachedFileManager.CompleteUpdatesAsync(sf) ==
                    FileUpdateStatus.Complete)
                tbkStatus.Text = sf.Name + " was saved";
            else await new MessageDialog("Error while saving file",
                    "Error").ShowAsync();
        }
        else await new MessageDialog("No file selected.", "Error").ShowAsync();
    }
    else await new MessageDialog("No contacts selected.", "Error").ShowAsync();
}
```

10. Build the application by pressing the F6 button or clicking "BUILD - Build Solution" on the main menu of Visual Studio. If the Errors window appears and shows that there are errors in the code, try to resolve them by following the suggestions in the aforementioned window. If you can't resolve an error, open the `PickerSample\End` solution in the companion code, and compare your code to the one in the working solution.

11. Run the app by pressing F5, choose a few contacts as you did before in Step 7, and click or tap the "Save to file" button. The exact view depends on the contents of your desktop, but Figure 11-3 shows approximately what you should see. Pay attention to the lower part of the `FileSavePicker`.

There you can set the name and type of the file you'd like to save. Save the file, and check that it has been created on the location you chose.

FIGURE 11-3: The `FileSavePicker`, showing the contents of the desktop

How It Works

The `Windows.ApplicationModel.Contacts` namespace that you added to `MainPage.xaml.cs` in Step 2 contains the `ContactPicker` class that you used in the `OpenContacts` method in Step 5. After calling the `PickMultipleContactsAsync` method in Step 5, the result (`res`) is saved into the `contacts` field and added to the `ListBox`.

Saving the contact names into a file is a bit more complex. In Step 8, you created a `FileSavePicker`, set it up to show the user's desktop when opened, and made the default filename "contacts." Still in Step 8, you also set the default file extension that will be appended to the filename to ".txt" and filtered the view to plain text files only. After these, you called the `PickSaveFileAsync` method in Step 8 to show the `FileSavePicker` to the user.

The code you added in Step 9 is responsible for actually writing to the file that the user selected with the `FileSavePicker`. `WriteLinesAsync` receives a `StorageFile` object to write to, and an enumerable object (a list or array) of strings. The two calls in Step 9 to the `CachedFileManager` class that surround `WriteLinesAsync` (`DeferUpdates` and `CompleteUpdatesAsync`) are needed to ensure that there won't be any conflicts caused by multiple updates to the file at the same time.

Understanding the Concept of Contracts

Windows 8 builds heavily on Windows 8 style apps, which run in some kind of a sandboxed environment — not as restricting as Microsoft's mobile phone apps' environment, but there is some resemblance. To unleash the power of inter-application communication, Windows 8 breaks away from the totally island-like application management scheme and lets apps contact each other in a clean, easy-to-understand fashion.

Along with this, apps can execute a few select actions only after getting permission from the operating system and the user to do so. These actions include running background tasks, accessing restricted resources such as the printer(s), and registering to be associated with certain file types and protocols.

The notion of *contracts* is that the apps must remain separated while contacting each other or when contacting the operating system to use select operating system features. When an app tries to send or receive some data to or from another app, it must not need to have intricate knowledge about the other app's internal workings. In lieu of knowing the other one, an app must know a global connection point that the operating system provides. This way, all the apps can work in concert, not just ones that were programmed to know each other.

When an app tries to integrate with the operating system, it should do it in a managed way — that is, without relying on techniques like P/Invoke — through a unified, global connection point, and it should indicate the intent in advance to the operating system and the user. (The user will be automatically notified of the intent before installing the app.)

Many of these global connection points exist, and each of them has a corresponding contract that your app must adhere to in order to exchange data, files, and so on.

For example, if an app such as a SkyDrive app can be used to access files, it can declare this capability, and when another app uses a `FileOpenPicker` to access a file, the picker will list the SkyDrive app as a possible source to open a file. The other app doesn't have to know anything about SkyDrive or the SkyDrive app, because the two apps are contacting each other solely through the API provided by Windows Runtime.

Another example is sharing. When an app can use certain kinds of data (plain texts, URLs, and so on), and wants to indicate that this data can come from other apps, using a contract lets the operating system step in and connect this app with all the others that can provide the data.

Many contracts are available — some of them are easier to use, and some can get really complex. In the following sections, you learn how to use contracts in general and how to use some more common ones specifically.

Using Contracts

You can make any application use a contract by completing a few steps.

First, you must indicate to the operating system that your app would like to participate in communicating with other apps or the operating system itself. You can do this by editing the `Package.appxmanifest` file that every Windows 8 style app has by default. Under the Declarations tab, you can declare which contracts the app wants to use.

After declaring that the app can participate in the data or feature exchange described by a certain contract, you must respond to specific lifecycle events, or expand the app with new components corresponding to the contract. For example, if you stated that your app can work as a contacts picker, you can add a contact picker page to the app that will be shown to any app that tries to pick a contact using your app.

Figure 11-4 shows the Declarations tab of a Windows 8 style app. You can choose to add declarations under Available Declarations. You can use some declarations in an app only once; some of them you can add multiple times with different settings. You can view, edit, and delete the added declarations under the Supported Declarations list. The app shown in Figure 11-4 declares that it adheres to the File Save Picker contract. This means that the app adheres to the requirements the contract specifies, and it appears in other Windows 8 style apps when they try to save a file through a `FileSavePicker`.

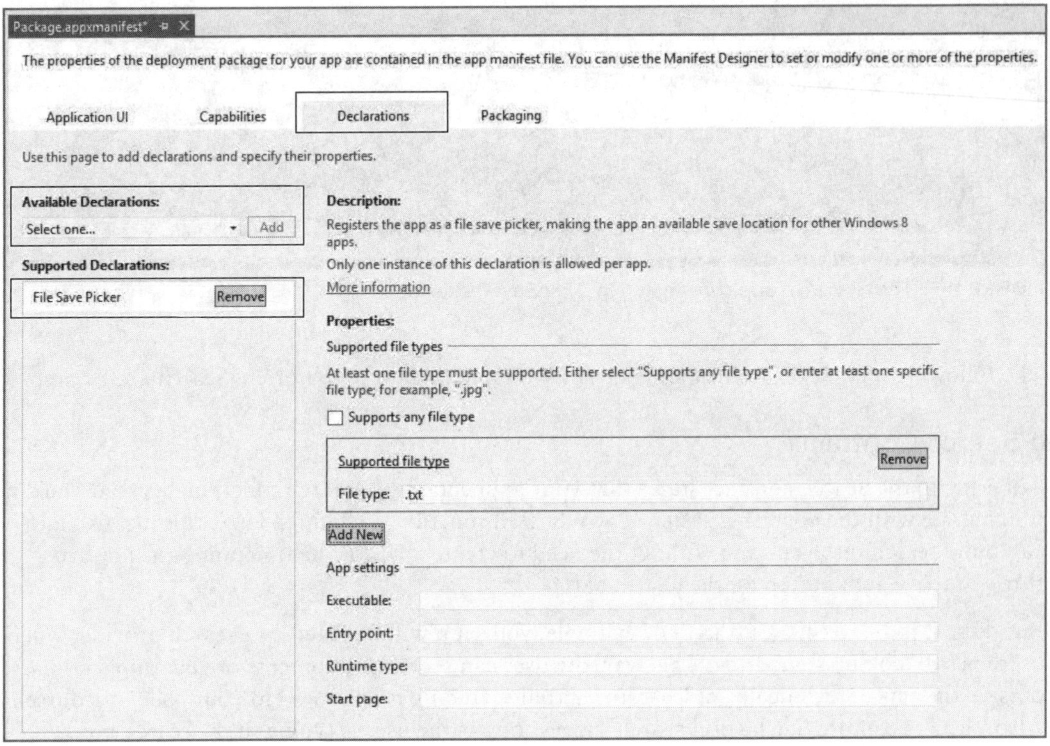

FIGURE 11-4: Declaring adherence to contracts

After an app that was declared to be able to operate as a file saver has been installed on a Windows 8 system, it will appear in every app's `FileSavePicker` UI. You can switch between apps to save the file by clicking the name of the file saver app. Figure 11-5 shows that the SkyDrive app is listed as a possible "save location," because it declared to the system that files can be saved with it.

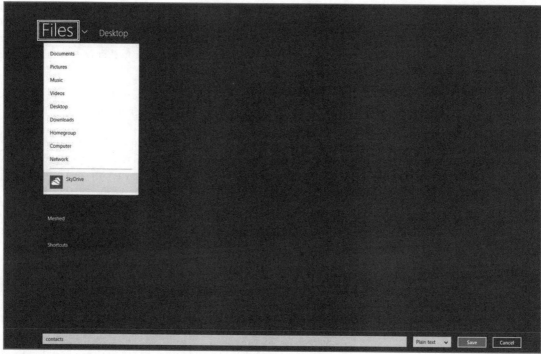

FIGURE 11-5: The SkyDrive app showing up in a FileSavePicker UI

The following sections examine two contracts you might want to use often: Search and Share.

The Search Contract

Adhering to the Search contract states that your application has search functionality that you'd like to integrate with the operating system's own Search function. On a high level, this means that you can build search into your app without the need to create a UI for the function — it'll be accessible through the Search button on the charm bar.

But there is more to this contract. For example, your app will be listed as a search provider when the user tries to look up something. This way, the user can search the contents of your application from outside the app — technically, at least (the actual searching is delegated to your code, of course). Also, the app can provide helpful search suggestions as the user is typing in the search box.

The basics of integrating with search functionality are relatively simple. After declaring that your app uses the Search contract, it must respond to the lifecycle event that corresponds to the event of the user searching for something in Windows. You can do this by overriding the `OnSearchActivated` method of the `Application` class. To access higher-level capabilities of the Search contract, you can use the `SearchPane` class.

In the next exercise, you learn how to add search functionality to an app by implementing the Search contract.

> **NOTE** *You can find the complete code to download for this exercise on this book's companion website at* www.wrox.com *in the folder* ContractsSample\ SearchEnd *within the* Chapter11.zip *download.*

TRY IT OUT Using the Search Contract

1. Open the ContractsSample\Begin app from the companion code in Chapter11.zip. (You can download it from www.wrox.com.) Familiarize yourself with the UI, and note that some features (such as adding or deleting notes) are not implemented. Don't try to build or run the project just yet, because it won't work until you have executed the steps in this exercise.

2. Double-click Package.appxmanifest in Solution Explorer. In the editor window, click the Declarations tab, and add the Search contract to the Supported Declarations list. Save the project, and close the editor window.

3. Open MainPage.xaml.cs, and add the following using directive under the others:

```
using Windows.ApplicationModel.Search;
```

4. Create two fields in the MainPage class — a SearchPane and a list of NoteItems. Add the following boldfaced code to achieve this:

```
public sealed partial class MainPage : Page
{
    SearchPane sp = null;
    List<NoteItem> notes = null;

    public MainPage()
    {
    ...
```

5. In the constructor, create an instance of the SearchPane. Add the following boldfaced code only:

```
public MainPage()
{
    this.InitializeComponent();
    ...

    sp = SearchPane.GetForCurrentView();
}
```

6. Open App.xaml.cs, and add the following method to the class:

```
protected override void OnSearchActivated(SearchActivatedEventArgs args)
{
    ActivateMainPage(args);
    Page.ShowSearchResults(args.QueryText);
}
```

7. Close this file after saving it, and switch back to `MainPage.xaml.cs`. Implement the method you called in the previous step by adding the following code to the `MainPage` class:

```
internal void ShowSearchResults(string searchText)
{
    tbkFilter.Text = "Filtered to notes containing " + searchText;
    lbxNotes.Items.Clear();
    foreach (var n in notes)
    {
        if (n.Title.ContainsSubstring(searchText))
            lbxNotes.Items.Add(n);
    }
    btnRemoveFilter.IsEnabled = true;
}
```

8. In `MainPage.xaml`, locate the `Button` called `btnRemoveFilter` and add a subscription to its `Click` event by adding the following boldfaced markup:

```
<Button Name="btnRemoveFilter" HorizontalAlignment="Stretch" IsEnabled="False"
    Click="RemoveFilter">Remove filter</Button>
```

9. Back in `MainPage.xaml.cs`, create the `RemoveFilter` method by adding the following code to the class:

```
void RemoveFilter(object sender, RoutedEventArgs e)
{
    btnRemoveFilter.IsEnabled = false;
    tbkFilter.Text = string.Empty;
    lbxNotes.Items.Clear();
    foreach (var n in notes) lbxNotes.Items.Add(n);
}
```

10. Override the `OnNavigatedTo` and `OnNavigatedFrom` methods of the `MainPage` class. Add the following code:

```
protected override void OnNavigatedTo(NavigationEventArgs e)
{
    base.OnNavigatedTo(e);
    sp.SuggestionsRequested += sp_SuggestionsRequested;
}

protected override void OnNavigatedFrom(NavigationEventArgs e)
{
    base.OnNavigatedFrom(e);
    sp.SuggestionsRequested -= sp_SuggestionsRequested;
}
```

11. Add the `sp_SuggestionsRequested` method to complete the class, as shown here:

```
void sp_SuggestionsRequested(SearchPane sender,
    SearchPaneSuggestionsRequestedEventArgs args)
{
```

```
foreach (var s in lbxNotes.Items.OfType<NoteItem>().Select(n => n.Title))
{
    if (s.ContainsSubstring(args.QueryText) &&
        args.Request.SearchSuggestionCollection.Size < 5)
        args.Request.SearchSuggestionCollection.AppendQuerySuggestion(s);
}
}
```

12. Build the application by pressing the F6 button or clicking "BUILD - Build Solution" on the main menu of Visual Studio. If the Errors window appears and shows that there are errors in the code, try to resolve them by following the suggestions in the aforementioned window. If you can't resolve an error, open the `ContractsSample\SearchEnd` solution in the companion code, and compare your code to the one in the working solution.

13. Run the application by pressing F5. Open the charm bar and click or tap the Search button on it, as shown in Figure 11-6.

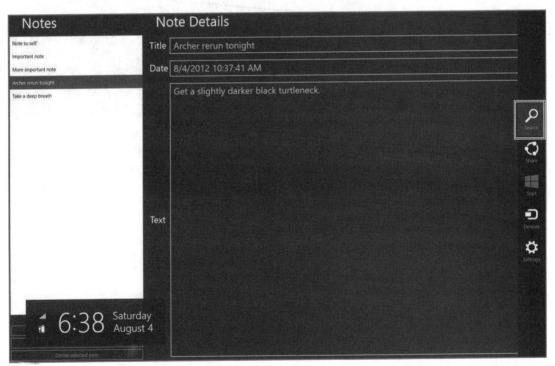

FIGURE 11-6: Opening the Search pane while the app is running

14. Start to type **note** into the search box. Notice that titles of `NoteItems` from the application appear as suggestions under the search box, as shown in Figure 11-7.

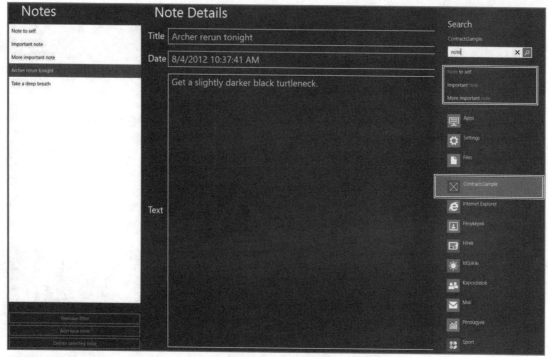

FIGURE 11-7: Search suggestions from the app show up on the Search pane

15. After pressing Enter (or clicking/tapping the magnifier icon), the contents of the `ListBox` are filtered down to the `NoteItems` that have the query text in their title, as shown in Figure 11-8. Clicking or tapping the "Remove filter" button nullifies the effect of the search.

16. Save the project; you'll need it in the next "Try It Out" exercise.

How It Works

With your actions in Step 2, you made your app indicate to the operating system that it would like to integrate searching with it. When the app is deployed, Windows 8 recognizes this intent and shows the app's icon when the user searches using the Search charm.

In Step 6, you subscribed the app to the lifecycle event of the application being opened by the Search feature of Windows. This method (`OnSearchActivated`) is called when the user clicks or taps your app's icon while looking for something using the Search charm. The current contents of the method make the app filter the contents of the `ListBox`. This is the purpose of the `ShowSearchResults` method you added in Step 7.

In Steps 4 and 5 you created the `SearchPane` object that lets you access the system's Search feature from your application. This object was used later to hook up a handler method to the event when your app can provide search suggestions (Step 10). When the user uses the Search feature of Windows and selects your app, it will send five suggestions at most to the operating system. (These include `NoteItems` with a `Title` containing the text the user typed into the search box.) You added this in Step 11.

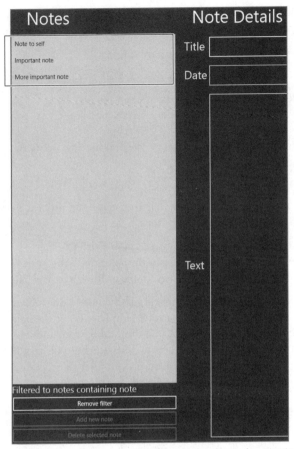

FIGURE 11-8: ListBox in the app showing filtered contents

The Share Target Contract

Applications often work with data that can be useful to other apps as well. For example, if you open a website in Internet Explorer, another app could use the address of that website to download all the images from it or simply send the address to your friends with your comments on the site.

Windows 8 style apps can share data using a global connection point in Windows Runtime. When an app tries to share some data with others, Windows looks for all the other Windows 8 style apps that declared adherence to the Share Target contract.

Making an application a share target is relatively simple, because Visual Studio provides a template that you can use to add all the needed components to an app. A key point is to override the OnShareTargetActivated method of the Application class. This method is invoked by Windows Runtime when an app tries to share information with your application. You can get the shared data from the second argument of the method, which is an instance of ShareTargetActivatedEventArgs. You can then do anything with this data.

It is important that the sharing occurs without the user leaving the share source app — it's not like copy and paste when the user copies something in an app, switches to another, and pastes the data.

In the following exercise, you learn how to make an application a share target.

> **NOTE** *You can find the complete code to download for this exercise on this book's companion website at* www.wrox.com *in the folder* ContractsSample\ ShareEnd *within the* Chapter11.zip *download.*

TRY IT OUT   Using the Share Target Contract

To see how to use the Share Target contract to make your application able to receive and process data from other applications using Windows 8's Share charm, follow these steps:

1. Open the ContractsSample app that you developed in the previous "Try It Out" ("Using the Search Contract"). If you haven't finished it, you could just open the solution that's in the ContractsSample\SearchEnd directory of the companion code available at the Wrox website.

2. Right-click the project node (ContractsSample) in Solution Explorer, and choose Add ➪ New Item. In the Add New Item window, choose the Share Target Contract template. Enter the name **ShareTargetPage.xaml** in the Name text box, as in Figure 11-9. Click the Add button, and let Visual Studio add all the additional files and references that the app will need. After you've added the file, you can open the Package.appxmanifest file of the project. As you'll see, Visual Studio already added the Share Target contract to the declarations.

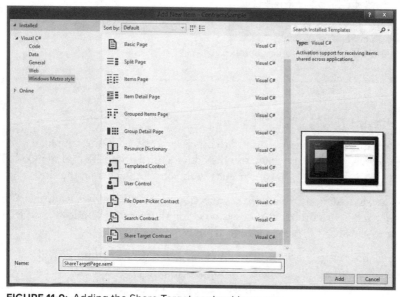

FIGURE 11-9: Adding the Share Target contract to an app

3. Open `MainPage.xaml.cs`, and add a method named `AddNote` that can create a new `NoteItem`, and add it to the existing notes collection. Insert the following code into the class:

```
public async void AddNote(string title, DateTime createdAt, string text)
{
    if (Dispatcher.HasThreadAccess)
    {
        notes.Add(new NoteItem { Title = title, TakenAt = createdAt, Text = text });
        lbxNotes.Items.Clear();
        foreach (var n in notes) lbxNotes.Items.Add(n);
    }
    else
    {
        await Dispatcher.RunAsync(Windows.UI.Core.CoreDispatcherPriority.High,
            new Windows.UI.Core.DispatchedHandler(() => {
                notes.Add(new NoteItem { Title = title, TakenAt = createdAt, Text =
                    text });
                lbxNotes.Items.Clear();
                foreach (var n in notes) lbxNotes.Items.Add(n);
            }));
    }
}
```

4. Open the newly added `ShareTargetPage.xaml`, and locate the only text box that the template contains. Set its `Text` property's `Binding` to `TwoWay` mode by modifying the code as shown here in bold:

```
<TextBox
    Grid.Row="1"
    Grid.ColumnSpan="2"
    Margin="0,0,0,27"
    Text="{Binding Comment, Mode=TwoWay}"
    Visibility="{Binding SupportsComment, Converter={StaticResource
        BooleanToVisibilityConverter}}"
    IsEnabled="{Binding Sharing, Converter={StaticResource
        BooleanNegationConverter}}"/>
```

5. Switch to the code-behind file (`ShareTargetPage.xaml.cs`), and insert the following boldfaced code to the `ShareButton_Click` method:

```
async void ShareButton_Click(object sender, RoutedEventArgs e)
{
    this.DefaultViewModel["Sharing"] = true;
    this._shareOperation.ReportStarted();

    var url = await _shareOperation.Data.GetUriAsync();

    ((App)Application.Current).Page.AddNote((string)DefaultViewModel["Comment"],
        DateTime.Now, url.AbsoluteUri);

    this._shareOperation.ReportCompleted();
}
```

6. That's it! Build the application by pressing the F6 button or clicking "BUILD - Build Solution" on the main menu of Visual Studio. If the Errors window appears and shows that there are errors in the code, try to resolve them by following the suggestions in the aforementioned window. If you can't resolve an error, open the `ContractsSample\ShareEnd` solution in the companion code, and compare your code to the one in the working solution. Begin testing the application by starting it, switching to the Start screen, and starting Internet Explorer. Navigate to a web page in Internet Explorer, and open the charm bar. Click or tap the Share button. Your application should be listed as possible share targets, as shown in Figure 11-10.

7. Choose the `ContactsSample` app as a target. In the page that appears (see Figure 11-11), enter a title for the new note, and click Share.

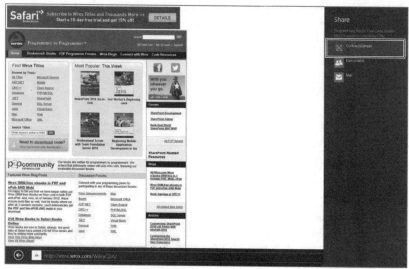

FIGURE 11-10: Share targets on the Share pane

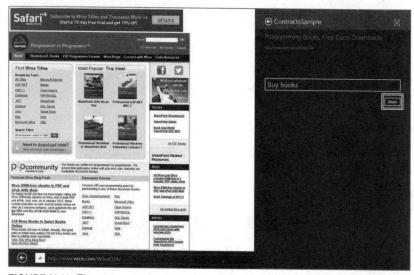

FIGURE 11-11: The `ShareTargetPage` in action

8. Switch back to the `ContactsSample` app from Internet Explorer, and make sure the new note was added, as shown in Figure 11-12.

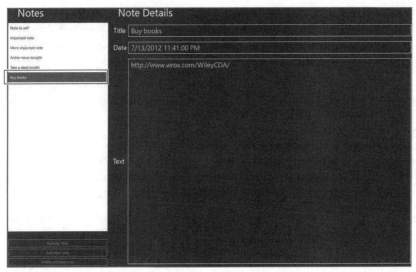

FIGURE 11-12: The new note in the `ContactsSample` app

How It Works

In Step 2, you added a page to your app. This, in turn, added to the app a few extra files with resources, and, more importantly, indicated to the operating system that your app can receive certain kinds of data through the Share feature. This results in the application appearing as a possible share target when the user tries to share something from another app. You can view (and modify) the accepted data formats by opening the manifest editor and clicking the Declarations tab.

Modifying the `TextBox`'s binding to be `TwoWay` in Step 4 was important, because you'd like to save the text that the user will enter on the `TextBox` when sharing something. The two-way binding makes the `TextBox` update the underlying business object that controls and, in this case, stores the data (this is called the ViewModel).

The few lines of code you added to the `ShareButton_Click` method in Step 5 are responsible for getting the data from Windows (which, in turn, goes to the data from the share source app), and sending it to another part of the application for processing, by calling the `AddNote` method. Here, it is assumed that the data is a URI (uniform resource identifier). This is the reason behind the call to `GetUriAsync`. Applications can share many other kinds of data, so it is a good custom to not just get it in one format, but check that it is in the correct one.

The `AddNote` method (which you added in Step 3) can accept the three parts that make up a `NoteItem`. Then it adds the new `NoteItem` to the backing collection and to the `ListBox`. Because this method can (and will) be invoked from outside the UI thread of the `Page`, and it makes modifications to the UI, it is imperative to ensure that it'll succeed in doing so. You can do this by checking its access to the UI (`HasThreadAccess`), and when it does not, run the code through the `Dispatcher`.

ACCESSING THE INTERNET

Windows 8 style applications are capable of connecting to the underlying operating system and to other applications. But some applications require "stepping out" of the device and reaching out to websites, online services, and databases on the Internet. Windows Runtime provides classes to do this. You can build apps that can communicate with any website or service and access online databases.

In the following sections, you'll learn about handling the changes of a device's connectivity, creating an app that can process syndication feeds, and connect to Microsoft's online services using the Live SDK.

Detecting the Changes of Internet Connectivity

When building an application that needs to use the Internet, the first and most important task is to make the application capable of detecting whether or not the device is online, and making the app capable of recognizing changes in the status of the Internet connection.

Windows Runtime makes all the basic information on the status of the current connection (or lack of it) accessible through a static class called `NetworkInformation`. This type is in the `Windows .Networking.Connectivity` namespace.

By subscribing to the only event of this class, `NetworkStatusChanged`, you can get automatic updates when network connectivity changes. The event itself, however, doesn't send you any information on the network status or properties. You can get the current network information by querying the current network's profile by calling the `GetInternetConnectionProfile` method on the same class. This will return with a `ConnectionProfile` object. The return value will be `null` if there is no active connection.

`ConnectionProfile` objects enable you to acquire the details of the current network connection. For example, you can identify the networks, or get the level of connectivity available, and query the security settings of the network(s).

In the following exercise, you learn how to read connection information in your Windows 8 style apps.

> **NOTE** You can find the complete code to download for this exercise on this book's companion website at www.wrox.com in the folder `NetworkSample\ NetInfoEnd` within the `Chapter11.zip` download.

TRY IT OUT   Acquiring Network Information

To see how to use the Network Information API to read current connectivity information, and to ensure that your app will be updated when the network status changes, follow these steps:

1. Open the solution that you find in the `NetworkSample\NetInfoBegin` directory of the companion code for Chapter 11. Quickly familiarize yourself with the UI. You will use this application in the next "Try It Out" exercise, too. Actually, the only element of the UI that you'll use in this exercise is the `TextBlock` in the lower-left corner of the application, called `tbkNetStatus`.

2. Open `MainPage.xaml.cs`, and add the following `using` statements to the code, under the ones already present:

```
using Windows.Networking.Connectivity;
using System.Text;
```

3. Override the `OnNavigatedTo` and `OnNavigatedFrom` methods by adding the following code to the `MainPage` class:

```
protected override void OnNavigatedTo(NavigationEventArgs e)
{
    NetworkInformation.NetworkStatusChanged +=
        NetworkInformation_NetworkStatusChanged;
    RefreshNetworkInfo();
}

protected override void OnNavigatedFrom(NavigationEventArgs e)
{
    NetworkInformation.NetworkStatusChanged -=
        NetworkInformation_NetworkStatusChanged;
}
```

4. Create the `NetworkInformation_NetworkStatusChanged` method you used in the previous step:

```
void NetworkInformation_NetworkStatusChanged(object sender)
{
    RefreshNetworkInfo();
}
```

5. Create the `RefreshNetworkInfo` method by adding the following code to the class:

```
async void RefreshNetworkInfo()
{
    ConnectionProfile profile = NetworkInformation.GetInternetConnectionProfile();
    StringBuilder sb = new StringBuilder();

    if (profile != null)
    {
        sb.Append("Connected to ");
        sb.Append(profile.GetNetworkNames()[0]);
        sb.Append(". Connectivity level is ");
        sb.Append(profile.GetNetworkConnectivityLevel().ToString());
        sb.Append(".");
    }
    else sb.Append("Disconnected.");

    await Dispatcher.RunAsync(Windows.UI.Core.CoreDispatcherPriority.Normal,
        () => tbkNetStatus.Text = sb.ToString());
}
```

6. Build the application by pressing the F6 button or clicking "BUILD - Build Solution" on the main menu of Visual Studio. If the Errors window appears and shows that there are errors in the code, try to resolve them by following the suggestions in the aforementioned window. If you can't resolve an error, open the `NetworkSample\NetInfoEnd` solution in the companion code, and compare your code to the one in the working solution.

7. Run the application. Notice that, in the lower-left corner, the network status appears right after opening the page. Figure 11-13 shows a state when the device is connected to a network called `SubCommSatFour`, and the Internet is accessible. (Of course, you will see "Disconnected" if the device has no network connectivity.)

FIGURE 11-13: Connection information

8. Try turning the Wi-Fi connection off and on again to see how the UI updates accordingly.

9. Save the `NetworkSample` project; you are going to need it for the next "Try It Out" exercise.

How It Works

The method that does the heavy lifting is the one you added in Step 6: `RefreshNetworkInfo`. When called, it gets the current network's profile information by calling the `GetInternetConnectionProfile` method. If it's `null`, it means that there is no active connection. If there is a connection, the method queries its name and the level of connectivity (whether it has access to the Internet or not).

Registering to the `NetworkStatusChanged` event in Step 3 was necessary to get automatic status updates when there is a change in connectivity. The subscribed method (`NetworkInformation_NetworkStatusChanged`) merely calls the `RefreshNetworkInfo` method. But, because this would refresh the UI (show the information) only if there is a change, you must call the `RefreshNetworkInfo` method once when the `Page` is ready — this is the reason behind the extra call to the method in `OnNavigatedTo`.

Using Feeds

If you ever wanted to remain updated about a blog, a news channel, or some topic in an Internet forum, you probably subscribed to a feed.

Feeds can be described basically as lists of items containing information on one subject. The subject itself, as well as the exact content of the feed items, can be broad. Some feeds contain plain text, some of them are formatted using HTML tags, and some may even include images or embedded videos. However, every feed item — a blog post or a new answer to a forum thread — has loads of additional metadata (such as information on the authors, a date when it was published, keywords, links, or other identifiers).

Very early, standards were created to regulate the format of feeds and feed items. Today, the most prevalent of these are the Really Simple Syndication (RSS) and Atom. These two are based on Extensible Markup Language (XML), so, essentially, feeds created to adhere to one of these formats are text strings.

SYNDICATION FORMATS

It is good to know how RSS or Atom documents look when you work with them. Because of their relatively simple nature, the easiest way to get to know them is to do some "reverse engineering."

Open a feed in your web browser of choice, and look at the markup — the structure will be clear to you in no time. (If the browser implicitly processes and presents the feed and won't show the raw XML markup behind it, right-clicking the document and choosing "Source" or "View source" should do the trick.)

If you want to learn about these by reading detailed documents and samples, here are a few links you might consider visiting:

➤ RSS — `http://www.rssboard.org/rss-specification/`

➤ Atom — `http://www.atomenabled.org/developers/syndication/`

In the past, when you were creating an application that had to work with feeds, you needed to have knowledge about these standard formats, and you either had to write a parsing engine that transforms the raw XML into your own business objects, or you may have built your software on one of the available (free or paid) parsing engines. Because feeds are becoming more and more common, the need to handle them becomes more and more common as well. To alleviate the pain of creating a robust, fast parsing engine and corresponding software infrastructure, Windows Runtime comes with one built in.

The `Windows.Web.Syndication` namespace contains the relevant types when you're trying to embed feed support into your application. The namespace contains a lot of types if you want to exploit every little feature of feeds, but the most crucial class is `SyndicationClient`.

This type is responsible for contacting the server, retrieving the requested feed, and processing it. Here, processing means *parsing* — transforming the retrieved XML into manageable business objects. You can use `SyndicationClient`'s `RetrieveFeedAsync` method to do so. When you use the `await` keyword (in other words, using the `await` keyword in front of the method call), this method returns with a `SyndicationFeed` object. `SyndicationFeed` contains all the data of the RSS or Atom feed, including the title, the list of authors, and, of course, the items.

You can access feed items with the `Items` property. The list contains `FeedItem` instances. Each `FeedItem` object corresponds to a blog post or a forum post, depending on the subject of the feed. To access the contents of the item, you can use `FeedItem`'s properties such as `Authors`, `Title`, `PublishedDate`, or `Content`. Be aware that some of these aren't core objects (like `string`, `int`, `DateTime`, and so on), so you have to do some additional processing.

Contacting servers and downloading data is considered an action that the user must know about, so when building an app that will work with syndication feeds, always ensure that the "Internet (Client)" capability is enabled in the `Package.appxmanifest`.

In the next exercise, you expand the app that you've been working on in the previous "Try It Out" exercise with feed-reading capabilities.

> **NOTE** *You can find the complete code to download for this exercise on this book's companion website at* www.wrox.com *in the folder* NetworkSample\ FeedEnd *within the* Chapter11.zip *download.*

TRY IT OUT   Using Feeds

To see how to use the Syndication API to enrich your application with support for RSS and Atom feeds, follow these steps:

1. Open the `NetworkSample` solution from the previous "Try It Out" exercise ("Acquiring Network Information"). If you haven't done it yet, you can open the solution from the `NetworkSample\ NetInfoEnd` folder of the chapter's companion code available at www.wrox.com.

2. Double-click the `Package.appxmanifest` file in Solution Explorer to open the manifest editor. Click the Capabilities tab, and ensure that the "Internet (Client)" capability is checked, as shown in Figure 11-14. Save, and close the editor.

3. Open `MainPage.xaml.cs`, and add the following using directives after the others:

   ```
   using Windows.Web.Syndication;
   using Windows.UI.Popups;
   ```

4. Switch to `MainPage.xaml`. Locate the `Button` with the content `"Get feed"`, and add an event handler to its `Click` event by inserting the following boldfaced markup:

   ```
   <Button Click="GetFeed" HorizontalAlignment="Stretch" Content="Get feed" />
   ```

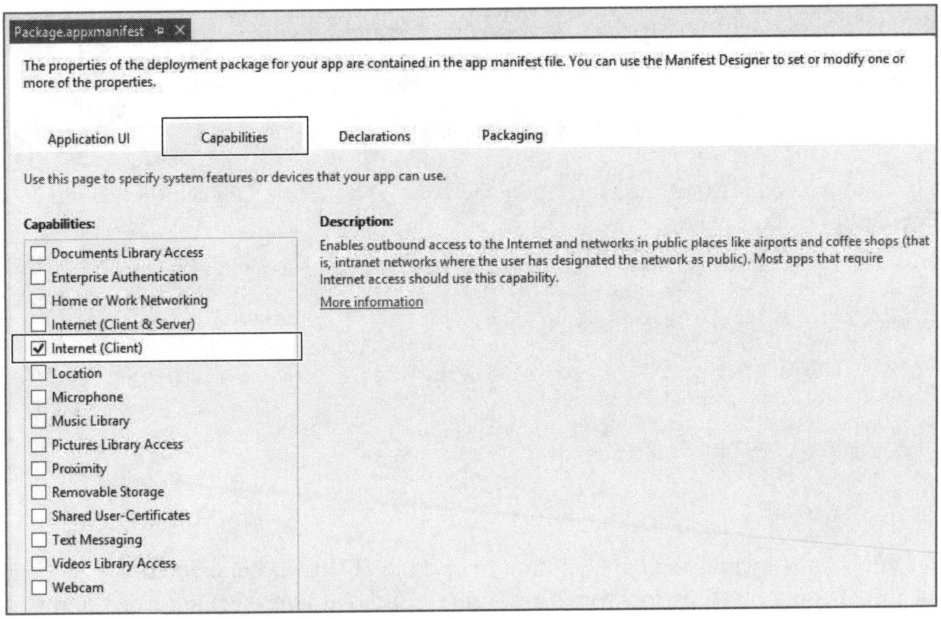

FIGURE 11-14: The Capabilities panel of the manifest editor

5. Switch back to `MainPage.xaml.cs`, and create the `GetFeed` method. Add the following code to the class:

```
async void GetFeed(object sender, RoutedEventArgs e)
{
    if (!string.IsNullOrWhiteSpace(tbFeedUrl.Text) &&
        Uri.IsWellFormedUriString(tbFeedUrl.Text.Trim(), UriKind.Absolute))
    {
        SyndicationClient client = new SyndicationClient();
        try
        {
            tbkFeedStatus.Text = "Downloading feed";
            var feed = await client.RetrieveFeedAsync(new Uri(
                tbFeedUrl.Text.Trim(), UriKind.Absolute));

            tbkFeedStatus.Text = "Feed downloaded";
            lbxPosts.Items.Clear();
            foreach (var item in feed.Items) lbxPosts.Items.Add(item);
        }
        catch (Exception ex)
        {
            tbkFeedStatus.Text = "Error: " + ex.Message;
        }
    }
}
```

6. Switch to `MainPage.xaml`. Locate the `ListBox` in the file and subscribe a handler method to its `SelectionChanged` event. Insert the following boldfaced part into the markup:

```
<ListBox Grid.Row="1" Name="lbxPosts" DisplayMemberPath="Title.Text" MaxWidth="350"
    SelectionChanged="lbxPosts_SelectionChanged" />
```

7. Switch back to `MainPage.xaml.cs`, and create the `lbxPosts_SelectionChanged` method. Add the following code to the class:

```
void lbxPosts_SelectionChanged(object sender, SelectionChangedEventArgs e)
{
    if (lbxPosts.SelectedIndex > -1)
    {
        SyndicationItem post = lbxPosts.SelectedItem as SyndicationItem;
        tbkTitle.Text = post.Title.Text;
        tbkPublishedDate.Text = post.PublishedDate.ToString();
        wvSummary.NavigateToString(post.Summary.Text);
    }
}
```

8. Build the application by pressing the F6 button or clicking "BUILD - Build Solution" on the main menu of Visual Studio. If the Errors window appears and shows that there are errors in the code, try to resolve them by following the suggestions in the aforementioned window. If you can't resolve an error, open the `NetworkSample\FeedEnd` solution in the companion code, and compare your code to the one in the working solution.

9. Run the application for testing. Enter a feed address into the `TextBox` (or use the default one that's already there), and click or tap the Get Feed button. Notice that the application reports in one of the `TextBlocks` on the bottom of the UI that it has initiated, and later, completed downloading the feed. Also, when the download is complete, the feed items (their titles to be precise) appear in the `ListBox`. If you click or tap one, its contents show up on the right side of the app, as shown in Figure 11-15.

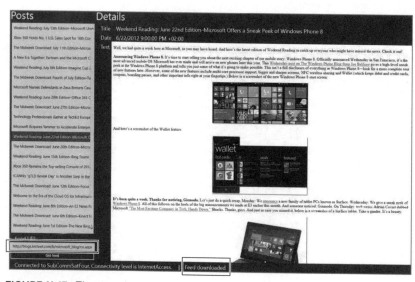

FIGURE 11-15: The app showing a feed

How It Works

Checking the "Internet (Client)" capability (Step 2) is usually not needed; Windows 8 style applications have this capability by default.

The GetFeed method you created in Step 5 (which is called when the user clicks or taps the corresponding Button) is responsible for contacting the server, processing the feed, and showing it on the UI. The SyndicationClient's RetrieveFeedAsync method contacts the server (specified by the Uri it needs as an argument) and turns the retrieved raw XML data into a SyndicationFeed, called feed. This is an asynchronous method, so using the await keyword is a good practice if you want to keep the UI responsive during the XML processing in the background. When all data has been parsed, the GetFeed method simply iterates through all the elements of the Items collection of feed and pushes every item into the ListBox.

Registering to the ListBox's SelectionChanged event in Step 7 is needed to refresh the details pane (the right side of the application) with the selected feed item's contents. The subscribed method simply takes the selected item from the ListBox and sets the three controls' contents. The WebView control (wvSummary) is particularly handy here because the Summary of the FeedItem tends to contain not plain text but formatted text. The WebView can display this rich content without any trouble.

A couple of other things are worth noting when working with SyndicationClient.

First, SyndicationClient can use the local cache. Therefore, when a user tries to get a feed, there is a chance that the SyndicationClient object won't return the actual feed — if it finds it in the local cache, it'll return that. Usually, this isn't a problem, but if you want to control this behavior, set the BypassCacheOnRetrieve property of the client to false.

The second thing is that some servers provide different feeds to different clients. Browsers tend to interpret and display a few parts of the data differently, so if a server can identify the exact engine behind the client, it can send a feed tailored to that exact client. Usually, this isn't a problem either, so you don't have to worry about it. However, if a server refuses to send the feed to your app because it doesn't specify its type, use the SetRequestHeader method to do so. The first parameter to be passed to this method is the string "User-Agent", and the second is an identifier of a browser engine.

> **NOTE** The types in the Windows.Web.Syndication *namespace were created for reading feeds. However, if the website that manages the feed supports the Atom Publishing Protocol, you can create applications that can not only retrieve and display feeds but send new items and modify or delete existing ones. Types for this purpose are in the* Windows.Web.AtomPub *namespace.*

ACCESSING WINDOWS LIVE

Windows Live is a Microsoft brand that identifies the public online services and web-based applications the company freely provides to everyone. Among others, services include features like e-mail (Hotmail); Instant Messaging (Messenger); file storage, synchronization, and sharing (SkyDrive); and scheduling (Calendar).

Needless to say, these are all connected to each other. For example, when attaching pictures or other files to an e-mail, you can choose to send it via SkyDrive instead, so the recipient won't have to download a potentially large file. He or she will receive a link to your online storage and can retrieve the file from there with any web browser.

Apart from these services, a handful of native, client-side applications are collectively downloadable in the Windows Live Essentials package. With Windows 8, some of these applications become redundant (for example, you don't need Live Messenger because you can connect to the instant messaging service with the built-in Messaging app instead), and some of them remain just as useful as they have been in the past (like Movie Maker).

> **NOTE** *These services and applications are available to anyone with a Microsoft Account (formerly called Live ID). You can freely create one (or more) on* `http://live.com`*.*

The importance of the Windows Live services becomes clear when you start using Windows 8 with a Microsoft Account. The operating system connects you to these services immediately when you sign in. The Mail app downloads your e-mails, the Messaging app connects to your IM account, and so on.

These apps were built by Microsoft, so the tight integration with Microsoft's online services is evident, just as is the benefit to the user from this integration. But, fortunately, Microsoft lets you integrate your apps with Windows Live just as tightly as its own apps. The company provides the means to integrate apps with Windows Live in a downloadable package called the Live SDK (Software Development Kit).

Enhancing your app with Windows Live integration starts with downloading the Live SDK from the Live Connect Developer Center and installing the package. Then you can add a reference of the Live SDK dynamic link library (DLL) to your app. After this, you can use all the types that make it easy to access almost anything the user has on Windows Live.

Of course, these resources can be private or restricted — something that the user might not want to share with an app. Authorization to use these resources consists of two steps.

First, you must register your app on Windows Live. You get an identifier that Windows Live will use to recognize which application tries to contact it. You can register your app by navigating to `https://manage.dev.live.com/`, clicking the "My apps" link, logging in with your Microsoft

Account, and creating an app. After this, you can request an identifier for your app to be able to contact the Live Connect service. The identifier is a package name that you must swap with the original one in your app's `Package.appxmanifest`.

The second step of authorization is done by the user. When you build an app that must connect to Windows Live, you must specify which parts of the user's data the app wants to use — contacts, files, calendar, and so on. When the user starts the app for the first time, and it connects to Windows Live, he or she will be asked by Windows Live to confirm that the app can access the resources it wants to use. If the user agrees, there will be no further sign-ins or confirmations needed. The next time, Windows Live will know that this particular user enabled this particular app to access a particular set of resources. The user can revoke the access rights at any time, of course.

The Live SDK for Windows 8 style apps comes with a single control called `SignInButton`. This button can be placed on the UI of the app to let the user sign in or out of Microsoft's online services. Scopes (the parts of the Live profile that the app would like to access) can be managed with this button. Also, its `SessionChanged` event can signal to the app that the user has chosen to sign in or out.

When the user is connected, the app can create a `LiveConnectClient`, which can be used to manage the session and to retrieve or modify data and files in the Live Service. These manipulations occur with the user's consent. Windows Live only asks the user once (at the first attempt to connect to Microsoft's online services) to let the application work.

In the next exercise, you learn how to create a Windows 8 style application that can connect to Windows Live and retrieve the user's name and Live profile picture. Also, you see how to access SkyDrive and upload files to it. This exercise may seem a bit longer than usual, but don't be afraid. It's not that difficult to execute.

> **NOTE** You can find the complete code to download for this exercise on this book's companion website at www.wrox.com in the folder LiveSample\End within the Chapter11.zip download. However, the package name is missing — you have to create one if you try to use the application.

TRY IT OUT   Integrating Your App with Windows Live Services

Note that, for this exercise, you'll need a Microsoft Account to use these services, and you might be asked to confirm your identity more than once. To see how to use the Live SDK to integrate Live Services with your app, follow these steps:

1. Download and install the Live SDK for Windows 8 style apps. Navigate to `http://msdn.micro-soft.com/en-us/live/`, and click the Downloads link. On the following page, choose the SDK version that was built for Windows 8, and initiate downloading. When the browser asks for further instructions, click Run. Figure 11-16 may help you with this, but be aware that Microsoft may change the layout of this page at any time. After the download is complete, the installer will start. Follow the onscreen instructions to install the SDK.

FIGURE 11-16: Downloading the Live SDK for Windows 8

2. Create a C# Windows 8 style application with the Blank App template in Visual Studio 2012. Name it **LiveSample**.

3. Open `Package.appxmanifest` by double-clicking it in Solution Explorer. Click the Packaging tab to see the package information. You'll need two of these shortly: the package display name and the publisher.

4. Switch back to your browser, and register your Windows 8 style app on Live Connect. Click the "My apps" link in the Developer Center, and then click the link that reads "application management site for Windows 8 style apps." Carefully read what the site says, and follow the steps depicted there. You'll find two `TextBoxes` on the bottom of the page — you must copy and paste the parts of the package information here. Click the "I accept" button to advance to the next two steps.

5. Your app is registered now. Under Step 3 on the page, you can see your package name. Copy this package name, and switch back to Visual Studio's manifest editor. Overwrite the package name of your application with the one you got from the Developer Center website. Save the project, and close the manifest editor.

6. Add the Live SDK DLL to your project. To do so, right-click the References node in Solution Explorer, and choose Add Reference. In the following window, choose the Windows tab on the left menu, and Extensions under that. Live SDK should show up in the list in the middle of the window, as shown in Figure 11-17. Check it, and click OK.

7. Add a new class called `LiveItemInfo` to the project's `Common` folder by right-clicking the Common node in Solution Explorer, and choose Add ⇨ Class. Overwrite the file's contents with the following code.

```
namespace LiveSample.Common
{
    class LiveItemInfo
    {
        public string Id { get; set; }
        public string Name { get; set; }
        public string Source { get; set; }

        public override string ToString()
        {
            return this.Name;
        }
    }
}
```

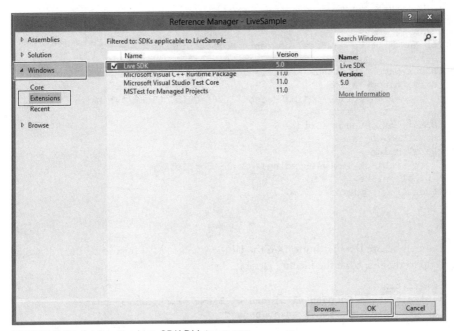

FIGURE 11-17: Adding the Live SDK DLL to an app

8. Open `MainPage.xaml`, and modify the `<Page>` tag by adding the following boldfaced line:

```
<Page
    x:Class="LiveSample.MainPage"
    IsTabStop="false"
    xmlns="http://schemas.microsoft.com/winfx/2006/xaml/presentation"
    xmlns:x="http://schemas.microsoft.com/winfx/2006/xaml"
    xmlns:d="http://schemas.microsoft.com/expression/blend/2008"
    xmlns:mc="http://schemas.openxmlformats.org/markup-compatibility/2006"
    xmlns:LiveControls="using:Microsoft.Live.Controls"
    mc:Ignorable="d">
```

9. Delete everything between the opening and closing `Page` tags (`<Page...>` and `</Page>`), and add the following markup under the `Page` tag:

```
<Grid Background="{StaticResource ApplicationPageBackgroundThemeBrush}">
    <Grid.RowDefinitions>
        <RowDefinition Height="Auto"/>
        <RowDefinition/>
    </Grid.RowDefinitions>
    <Grid Grid.Row="0" Height="128">
        <Grid.ColumnDefinitions>
            <ColumnDefinition Width="Auto" />
            <ColumnDefinition Width="Auto" />
            <ColumnDefinition/>
            <ColumnDefinition Width="Auto" />
            <ColumnDefinition Width="138" />
        </Grid.ColumnDefinitions>
        <Button Name="btnGetFolder" Content="Read root folder" Click="btnGet_Click"
            Grid.Column="1" />
        <Button Name="btnUploadFile" Content="Upload picture"
            Click="btnUploadFile_Click" Grid.Column="2" />
        <TextBlock Name="tbkStatus" FontSize="24" VerticalAlignment="Center"
            Grid.Column="3" />
        <Image Name="imgProfilePic" MaxHeight="128" Grid.Column="4" Margin="5,0" />
    </Grid>
    <ListBox Name="lbxContents" Grid.Row="1">
        <ListBox.ItemTemplate>
            <DataTemplate>
                <TextBlock Text="{Binding}" FontSize="20" />
            </DataTemplate>
        </ListBox.ItemTemplate>
    </ListBox>
</Grid>
```

10. Add a `SignInButton` before the first button on the UI (`btnGetFolder`) by adding the following boldfaced markup to the file. Save the file and close it.

```
</Grid.ColumnDefinitions>
<LiveControls:SignInButton Scopes="wl.signin wl.basic wl.skydrive_update"
    SessionChanged="SignInButton_SessionChanged" />
<Button x:Name="btnGetFolder" Content="Read root folder" Click="btnGet_Click"
    Grid.Column="1" />
```

11. In `MainPage.xaml.cs`, add the following `using` directives to the file:

```
using LiveSample.Common;
using Microsoft.Live;
using Microsoft.Live.Controls;
using Windows.UI.Xaml.Media.Imaging;
using Windows.Storage.Pickers;
using Windows.Storage;
```

12. Add a `LiveConnectClient` called `client` to the `MainPage` class by copying the following bold-faced code into the file:

```
public sealed partial class MainPage : Page
{
```

```
LiveConnectClient client = null;

public MainPage() …
```

13. Add the following method to the class:

```
void SignInButton_SessionChanged(object sender,
    LiveConnectSessionChangedEventArgs e)
{
    if (e.Status == LiveConnectSessionStatus.Connected)
    {
        client = new LiveConnectClient(e.Session);
        LoadProfile();
    }
    else if (e.Error != null) tbkStatus.Text = e.Error.Message;
}
```

14. The previous method called the `LoadProfile` method, which doesn't exist yet. Add it to the class, as shown here:

```
async void LoadProfile()
{
    LiveOperationResult lor = await client.GetAsync("me");
    tbkStatus.Text = "Welcome, " + lor.Result["name"].ToString();
    lor = await client.GetAsync("me/picture");
    imgProfilePic.Source = new BitmapImage(new
        Uri(lor.Result["location"].ToString()));
}
```

15. Create the `btnGet_Click` method by adding the following code to the class:

```
async void btnGet_Click(object sender, RoutedEventArgs e)
{
    if (client.Session != null)
    {
        LiveOperationResult lor = await client.GetAsync(@"/me/skydrive/files");
        lbxContents.Items.Clear();
        foreach (var item in (dynamic)lor.Result["data"])
        {
            lbxContents.Items.Add(new LiveItemInfo
            { Name = item.name, Id = item.id, Source = item.source });
        }
    }
}
```

16. Add the last method, `btnUploadFile_Click`, to the class.

```
async void btnUploadFile_Click(object sender, RoutedEventArgs e)
{
    var picker = new FileOpenPicker {  ViewMode = PickerViewMode.List,
        SuggestedStartLocation = PickerLocationId.Desktop };
    picker.FileTypeFilter.Add(".jpg");
    picker.FileTypeFilter.Add(".jpeg");
    picker.FileTypeFilter.Add(".png");
    StorageFile file = await picker.PickSingleFileAsync();
```

```
if (file != null)
{
    tbkStatus.Text = "Uploading image...";
    try
    {
        await client.BackgroundUploadAsync("me/skydrive", file.Name, file);
        tbkStatus.Text = "Image uploaded.";
    }
    catch (LiveConnectException ex)
    {
        tbkStatus.Text = ex.Message;
    }
}
}
```

17. Build the application by pressing the F6 button or clicking "BUILD - Build Solution" on the main menu of Visual Studio. If the Errors window appears and shows that there are errors in the code, try to resolve them by following the suggestions in the aforementioned window. If you can't resolve an error, open the `LiveSample\End` solution in the companion code, and compare your code to the one in the working solution. Please be aware that even though the sample application contains no errors, it won't compile unless you've installed the Live SDK for Windows 8 style apps, added the reference to the DLL, and swapped the package name to the one you got from the Live Development Center, as instructed in Steps 1 and 3 through 6.

18. Start the app, and wait until the `SignInButton` becomes enabled. Click or tap it to log in to Windows Live. Figure 11-18 shows the window that should appear.

FIGURE 11-18: Windows Live asks the user to let the app access the required resources

19. After clicking or tapping the Yes button, the app should download your profile picture, show it in the upper-right corner, and greet you with text containing your name. Click or tap the "Read root folder" button. After a while (a few seconds, depending on the speed of your Internet connection and the state of the Live servers), the contents of your SkyDrive's root directory should show up. Figure 11-19 shows approximately how the UI should now look. (Of course, your name, the contents of your SkyDrive, and the profile picture will be different.)

FIGURE 11-19: The UI, after the app accessed the Live profile and the user's SkyDrive

20. Click or tap the "Upload picture" button. Choose an image in the `FileOpenPicker` that appears, and then click or tap the Open button on the bottom of the picker. After the application indicates that the image has been uploaded, click or tap the "Read root folder" button again. The newly uploaded picture's name should appear among the other files and folders. You can navigate to `http://skydrive.live.com` using Internet Explorer or some other web browser to confirm that the image is really there and is intact.

How It Works

The first five steps were required to set up the environment and make Windows Live acquainted with your app. When your app contacts Microsoft's online services, it will be able to identify the application by the package name.

In Step 6, you referenced the Live SDK to the application. This is needed to be able to use the types working with the Windows Live services.

Adding the extra `xmlns` attribute to the `Page` tag is required to enable using the `SignInButton` class — which you did in Step 10. The `SignInButton` contains the scopes. With these, you can declare which parts of the user's data you want to access. Here, your app states that it needs to access the basic profile information and needs full access (reading and writing) to SkyDrive. When the user starts the app for the first time (actually, when the app tries to connect to Microsoft's online services for the first time), Windows Live enumerates these access requests. This is what you saw in Figure 11-18.

You can read more about what kinds of scopes are available at `http://msdn.microsoft.com/en-us/library/live/hh243646.aspx`.

When there is a change in the session with Windows Live services (for example, the application connects to Windows Live), the `SignInButton` raises the `SessionChanged` event. The code you added in Step 13 responds to the session change by creating a `LiveConnectClient` and loading the profile information if the app is connected.

The `LoadProfile` method that you added in Step 14 uses this `client`'s `GetAsync` method to download the profile information (`"me"`), and then the profile picture (`"me/picture"`). The picture's `location` property contains the `Uri`, which makes the image accessible to the application.

Likewise, the `btnGet_Click` method that you added in Step 15 uses the `GetAsync` method to get the contents of the root directory of the user's SkyDrive (`"/me/skydrive/files"`). Then it iterates through the data and adds each item to the `ListBox` as a new `LiveItemInfo` object. Casting the `lor.Result` object to `dynamic` is needed to use the indexer (the `[]` operator) on the object.

The `btnUploadFile_Click` method that you added in Step 16 first sets up a `FileOpenPicker`, and then uses the `client`'s `BackgroundUploadAsync` method to upload the file to the root of the user's SkyDrive (`"me/skydrive"`) with the same filename as it has on the local computer.

SUMMARY

In this chapter, you learned about how to connect and integrate your application to the ecosystem that surrounds it.

First, you were introduced to the concept of pickers. With these classes, all apps can maintain a unified design and UI when the user tries to access resources (for example, opening a file or a contact, saving an image, using the camera, and so on).

Contracts are needed so that Windows 8 can know a few important things about an application, such as the need to access select folders of the user (`Documents`, `Music`, and so on) programmatically, run background tasks, or be associated with file types. Apart from these, contracts declare integration with the operating system and other apps — for example, an app can display itself on the Search pane of Windows 8, it can be a share source or target, and it can provide other apps with its file opening or saving capabilities through the aforementioned pickers and corresponding contract declarations.

After integrating with Windows, you learned about handling input from the Internet. First you saw how to acquire network information and changes to it. Then you learned about feeds and how to process them with the Syndication API.

The last part of the chapter introduced the Live SDK. With this downloadable extension, you can integrate your apps into Microsoft's online ecosystem. Your app can use the user's data stored in the cloud, and it can even manipulate the data.

In Chapter 12, you will learn how to build applications that can acquire the user's position, and how to enhance your apps to handle input from the various sensors a tablet device has to offer.

EXERCISES

1. What is the purpose of the pickers?

2. How can you build easily accessible search functionality into an app?

3. What's the simplest way to prepare your app to be a share target?

4. How can you transform Internet feeds into business objects?

5. How can your app ask Windows Live for permissions to access the app's user's data in Windows Live services?

> **NOTE** *You can find answers to the Exercises in Appendix A.*

▶ **WHAT YOU LEARNED IN THIS CHAPTER**

TOPIC	KEY CONCEPTS
Picker	This is a kind of a class that can let apps access a certain set of resources (such as files or contacts) with the user's knowledge and permission.
Contract	A contract is a declaration that the app wants to use certain features of the operating system and adheres to the requirements the contract specifies. When a user installs an app, he or she is warned about these.
Feed	A feed is an XML-based representation of coherent data objects. The most well-known kinds of feeds are RSS and Atom.
Windows Live	This is the brand name of Microsoft's free online services. These include mail, IM, calendar, and cloud-based file storage.
Live SDK	This is a freely downloadable extension to your app that enables it to contact Windows Live, retrieve and process the user's data, or upload (or modify) the data.

12

Leveraging Tablet Features

WHAT YOU WILL LEARN IN THIS CHAPTER:

➤ Understanding how tablets are different from traditional desktop or laptop PCs

➤ Incorporating location, movement, and device attitude data into your apps

➤ Using Windows Runtime APIs to enhance the user experience with sensory input

WROX.COM CODE DOWNLOADS FOR THIS CHAPTER

You can find the wrox.com code downloads for this chapter on the Download Code tab at www.wrox.com/remtitle.cgi?isbn=012680. The code is in the Chapter12.zip download and individually named, as described in the corresponding exercises.

Computers running a Windows operating system are traditionally desktop or laptop devices equipped with a mouse and a keyboard. Because of this, every application written to run on Windows was optimized for these kinds of input devices.

Now, Windows opens up for the tablet form factor, too, bringing many new users — your potential customers — to the scene. But they'll expect more from a tablet application in terms of input than mere support for the touchscreen. Tablet users usually hold their devices in their hands while using them. By means described in this chapter, you can use the device's attitude and movement information to create more engaging apps that respond to changes in these properties, and even let the users control the apps by moving the tablet.

Also in this chapter, you learn how to access and use the location information provided by a tablet device. Tablets are often equipped with a Global Positioning System (GPS) that can pinpoint their location on Earth. But as you'll see, the location API in Windows 8 can do much more than just channel the GPS data. By incorporating location data into your app, you can create a better user experience that is customized to the current location of the user.

ACCOMMODATING TABLET DEVICES

Despite the fact that they now share the same operating system, tablet devices are very different from desktop PCs, and even from laptops. Today's tablet devices were created for a purpose that is different from that of traditional computers. Tablets are considered to be primarily content-consuming devices — meaning that their purpose is to let you browse the web, read documents, watch videos, and consume content in an easy, natural, and fun way.

Consuming content with a tablet usually entails a casual activity by the user. People want to consume content (and, thus, use tablet devices) in many situations that are unsuitable for the work environment (for example, when lying in bed or using public transportation).

At the hardware level, tablets were designed to be used casually in these situations. They are lightweight, so they can be held even with one hand. Their screens are relatively small, but because they lack a hardware keyboard (at least most of them), this 7-inch to 10-inch touchscreen provides the main means of interaction between the user and the tablet.

The inherent restrictions of peripherals for external user interaction would lead to an uneasy handling of such devices if the operating system and the applications didn't support this new means of interaction. But the operating system can achieve this only in concert with additional hardware. This is the reason why the touchscreen and touch input are so important, and why you should incorporate multi-touch gesture support into your apps when it's appropriate.

Although the handling of touch events is mandatory for all Windows 8 style apps, tablet devices come with a slew of additional built-in input hardware that a developer can use to enable rich, novel ways of user interaction. These are called *sensors*.

Most of the time, you can build apps without having to worry about sensors, but in some situations — everyday situations — processing sensor data can make your application easier to use, or even more fun to use. Remember that not all Windows 8 style apps are going to be work-related apps, and people who aren't paid to use your app won't use if it's not easy to use, or they'll find a better one on the Windows Store. Regardless of its purpose, the more comfortable an app is to use, the more likely users will pay for it.

In terms of sensors, when writing apps for tablet devices designed for Windows 8 (or Windows RT, the ARM-version of Windows 8), you'll have data from an accelerometer, a gyroscope, a magnetometer, and an ambient light sensor at your disposal.

Apart from using the sensors, you can access a device's geolocation readings, too. This lets you build apps that (if the user permits) can build and customize their services according to the user's current location. Every tablet device designed for Windows 8 has an Assisted GPS receiver.

Laptop and desktop computers usually don't have these sensors, but some may contain them. Therefore, when building an application, always provide a way to access each and every function without sensors.

BUILDING LOCATION-AWARE APPLICATIONS

As mentioned, Windows 8 computers and devices may provide a means to access location information. The Windows Runtime API enables you to test whether or not the appropriate hardware is present and to use its data.

The concept of determining the location of a device is referred to as *location* (or *geolocation*) in Windows. This is because the location can be determined by different and distinct means.

In situations where accuracy isn't really relevant, the device or PC can determine its location by using IP address pinpointing, or by the nearby known Wi-Fi hotspots. This consumes far less energy and time than powering up a Global Positioning System (GPS) chip, waiting to acquire satellite signals, and then calculating the position. Furthermore, GPS signals cannot traverse concrete walls and ceilings, but a Wi-Fi's signal can, so information can't be acquired by GPS inside of a building.

If no well-known, registered Wi-Fi hotspots are in the area, but the device has a cell network connection, the Location API can use the nearby cell relay towers to triangulate the location of the device. Although the Wi-Fi location may not be very accurate, it may provide a suitable solution for many situations.

Windows 8 powers up the GPS chip in two situations (provided it's present, of course):

➤   When no well-known Wi-Fi hotspots exist and not enough cell towers are nearby

➤   When an application asks for more accurate location information than the aforementioned location techniques can provide

If your app states that accuracy is important, the Location API will use the GPS to pinpoint the device's location.

The Location API of Windows Runtime was built to provide location information based on either one of these technologies without you, the developer, having to worry about handling the different hardware and raw location data. You get one neat and clean programming interface to set up the environment for your needs (such as specifying the desired accuracy) and to get the location information.

Remember that your app must indicate in its manifest file that it requires access to the geolocation information, and when it does, the user must enable this feature, too. The first time the app wants to access the location data, the operating system will ask the user for this permission automatically. Figure 12-1 shows the default permission dialog box the user sees when an app tries to read the device's location information for the first time.

Using Geolocation

Building apps using the Location API in Windows Runtime is quite straightforward. All types belonging to this API are in the `Windows.Devices.Geolocation` namespace.

In your app, you should create an instance of the `Geolocator` class, and subscribe to its `PositionChanged` event. This event is raised when the device has new data for your app. In the event-handler method, you can examine the event arguments (that is, an instance of `PositionChangedEventArgs`), and process the data that is accumulated in the `Position` property (that is, an instance of the `Geoposition` class).

Alternatively, if you don't want to track the user's location continuously, you can call the `GetGeopositionAsync` method on the geolocator. This method returns an instance of the `Geoposition` class.

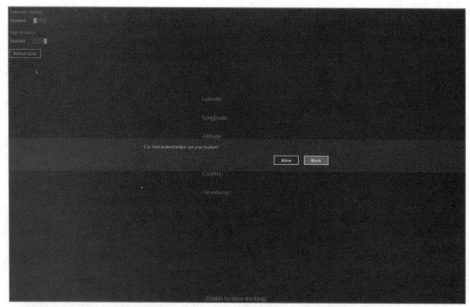

FIGURE 12-1: An app asking for permission to read location information

The said class contains two important properties: `Coordinate` and `CivicAddress`. The `Coordinate` property is an instance of the `Geocoordinate` class, and it contains the properties described in Table 12-1.

TABLE 12-1: Instance Properties of the Geocoordinate Class

NAME	TYPE	DESCRIPTION
Latitude	double	Gets the latitude of the coordinates in degrees
Longitude	double	Gets the longitude of the coordinates in degrees
Accuracy	double	Gets the maximum error of the latitude and longitude in meters
Altitude	double?	If present, gets the altitude of the position in meters
AltitudeAccuracy	double?	Gets the maximum error of the altitude reading in meters
Heading	double?	Represents the heading to the geographical North Pole in degrees
Speed	double?	If present, gets the speed of the device in meters per second
Timestamp	DateTimeOffset	Gets the time when the location was calculated

> **NOTE** *In Table 12-1, you see a type named "double" and another named "double?". These are not the same types. Double is a double-precision float-ing-point value, which means it can contain any number (integer or fraction) in a wide range. When you see a value type that has a question mark after its name, it is a nullable value type. Instances of a nullable type can contain any value that the original type can, but additionally, they can be assigned to be* null, *indicating that they don't have any defined value. Instances of plain value types like double cannot be* null; *they must always have a value. You can read more about nullable types at* http://msdn.microsoft.com/en-us/library/1t3y8s4s(v=vs.110).aspx.

The CivicAddress class, which is the type of the CivicAddress property, holds a Timestamp (a DateTimeOffset instance with the same purpose as the Timestamp of the Geocoordinate class) and four strings. These have mostly self-explanatory names: City, Country, PostalCode, and State.

> **NOTE** *Microsoft currently does not provide civic addresses through the Location API, so these should always be empty strings. Later, civic addresses may be included, but until then, if you want to use civic addresses in your app, you should rely on a third-party service to calculate the address from the coordinates.*

In the following exercise, you learn how to use the Location API and the Windows Simulator in concert to build and test location-aware applications. However, the current Windows Simulator has somewhat limited capabilities regarding simulating the change of location, so if possible, always test location-aware apps on a real tablet device before sending them to the Windows Store.

> **NOTE** *You can find the complete code to download for this exercise on this book's companion website at* www.wrox.com *in the folder* GeoLocSample\End *within the* Chapter12.zip *download.*

TRY IT OUT Using the Location API

To see how to use the Location API to incorporate location awareness into a Windows 8 style app, fol-low these steps:

1. Download and open the Ch12-GeoLoc-Begin project from this chapter's downloadable copy on the Wrox website (www.wrox.com). Quickly familiarize yourself with the user interface (UI) of the app. This is the skeleton to which you'll add working features.

2. Double-click the Package.appxmanifest file in the Solution Explorer to bring up the manifest's editor window. If you can't see the Solution Explorer, you can open it from the View menu. Figure 12-2 shows the Solution Explorer.

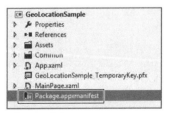

FIGURE 12-2: The Package.appx-manifest file in Solution Explorer

3. In the manifest editor window, switch to the Capabilities tab, and ensure that Location is checked in the Capabilities list box, as shown in Figure 12-3.

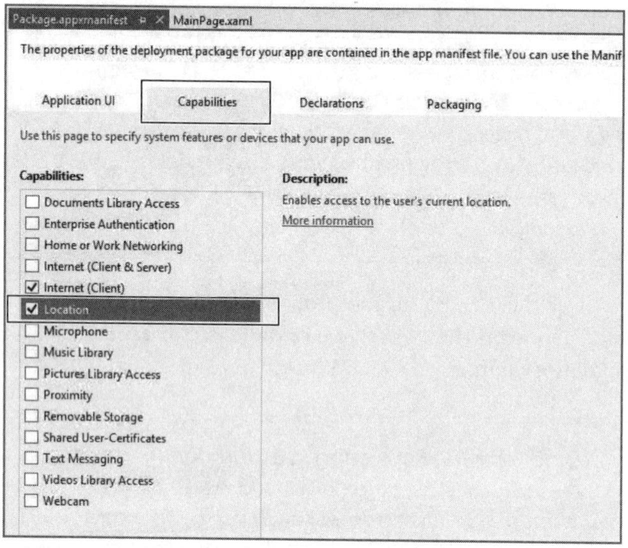

FIGURE 12-3: Editing capabilities

4. Open the `MainPage.xaml.cs` file to see the C# code-behind. Add the following lines under the `using` statements already there at the top of the file:

```
using Windows.Devices.Geolocation;
using Windows.UI.Core;
using System.Threading.Tasks;
```

5. Add the following line directly under the beginning curly brace of the `MainPage` class's declaration:

```
Geolocator locator = null;
```

6. Add the following lines to the constructor, after the call to `InitializeComponent()`:

```
locator = new Geolocator();
locator.StatusChanged += locator_StatusChanged;
```

7. Add the following method to the class:

```
async void locator_StatusChanged(Geolocator sender, StatusChangedEventArgs args)
{
    await Dispatcher.RunAsync(CoreDispatcherPriority.Normal,
        new DispatchedHandler(() =>
            tbkStatus.Text = "Geolocation service is " + args.Status.ToString()
    ));
}
```

8. Find the two ToggleSwitches named tsLocationTracking and tsAccuracy in the MainPage .xaml file, and add an event handler to their Toggled events. Also, locate the only Button in the XAML. Subscribe a method to its Click event. The markup you need to add is boldfaced.

```
<ToggleSwitch x:Name="tsLocationTracking" Header="Automatic tracking"
              HorizontalAlignment="Left"
              VerticalAlignment="Top" OffContent="Disabled" OnContent="Enabled"
              Toggled="tsLocationTracking_Toggled" />

<ToggleSwitch x:Name="tsAccuracy" Header="High Accuracy" HorizontalAlignment="Left"
              VerticalAlignment="Top" OffContent="Disabled" OnContent="Enabled"
              IsOn="True" Toggled="tsAccuracy_Toggled" />

<Button Content="Refresh now!" Click="RefreshData" />
```

9. In the code-behind file (MainPage.xaml.cs), locate the method you just added (tsLocation-Tracking_Toggled), and add the following boldfaced code to it. If you can't find the method, add the method declaration (the first line of the code that defines the method) with the curly braces, too. Also, create the tsAccuracy_Toggled and locator_PositionChanged methods, and the refreshUIAsync method that the latter calls.

```
void tsLocationTracking_Toggled(object sender, RoutedEventArgs e)
{
    if (tsLocationTracking.IsOn)
        locator.PositionChanged += locator_PositionChanged;
    else locator.PositionChanged -= locator_PositionChanged;
}

void tsAccuracy_Toggled(object sender, RoutedEventArgs e)
{
    if (locator != null)
    {
        locator.DesiredAccuracy = tsAccuracy.IsOn ?
            PositionAccuracy.High : PositionAccuracy.Default;
    }
}

async void locator_PositionChanged(Geolocator sender, PositionChangedEventArgs args)
{
    await refreshUIAsync(args.Position);
}

async Task refreshUIAsync(Geoposition pos)
{
    if (!Dispatcher.HasThreadAccess)
    {
        await Dispatcher.RunAsync(CoreDispatcherPriority.Normal,
            async () => await refreshUIAsync(pos));
    }
    else
    {
```

```
            tbkLat.Text = pos.Coordinate.Latitude.ToString();
            tbkLong.Text = pos.Coordinate.Longitude.ToString();
            tbkAlt.Text = pos.Coordinate.Altitude + " m";
            tbkAccuracy.Text = pos.Coordinate.Accuracy + "m";
            tbkCountry.Text = pos.CivicAddress.Country;
            tbkTimestamp.Text = pos.Coordinate.Timestamp.ToString("T");
        }
    }
```

10. Add the `RefreshData` method at the end of the `MainPage` class, as shown here:

```
async void RefreshData(object sender, RoutedEventArgs e)
{
    if (tsLocationTracking.IsOn)
        await refreshUIAsync(await locator.GetGeopositionAsync());
}
```

The code-behind file (`MainPage.xaml.cs`) should look like this (note that the exact order of the methods doesn't matter):

```
using System;
using Windows.UI.Xaml;
using Windows.UI.Xaml.Controls;
using Windows.Devices.Geolocation;
using Windows.UI.Core;
using System.Threading.Tasks;

namespace GeoLocationSample
{
    public sealed partial class MainPage : Page
    {
        Geolocator locator = null;

        public MainPage()
        {
            this.InitializeComponent();
            locator = new Geolocator();
            locator.StatusChanged += locator_StatusChanged;
        }

        async void locator_StatusChanged(Geolocator sender,
            StatusChangedEventArgs args)
        {
            await Dispatcher.RunAsync(CoreDispatcherPriority.Normal,
                new DispatchedHandler(() =>
                    tbkStatus.Text = "Geolocation service is " +
                        args.Status.ToString()
            ));
        }

        void tsAccuracy_Toggled(object sender, RoutedEventArgs e)
        {
            if (locator != null)
            {
                locator.DesiredAccuracy = tsAccuracy.IsOn ?
```

```
                        PositionAccuracy.High : PositionAccuracy.Default;
        }
    }

    void tsLocationTracking_Toggled(object sender, RoutedEventArgs e)
    {
        if (tsLocationTracking.IsOn)
            locator.PositionChanged += locator_PositionChanged;
        else locator.PositionChanged -= locator_PositionChanged;
    }

    async Task refreshUIAsync(Geoposition pos)
    {
        if (!Dispatcher.HasThreadAccess)
        {
            await Dispatcher.RunAsync(CoreDispatcherPriority.Normal,
                async () => await refreshUIAsync(pos));
        }
        else
        {
            tbkLat.Text = pos.Coordinate.Latitude.ToString();
            tbkLong.Text = pos.Coordinate.Longitude.ToString();
            tbkAlt.Text = pos.Coordinate.Altitude + " m";
            tbkAccuracy.Text = pos.Coordinate.Accuracy + "m";
            tbkCountry.Text = pos.CivicAddress.Country;
            tbkTimestamp.Text = pos.Coordinate.Timestamp.ToString("T");
        }
    }

    async void locator_PositionChanged(Geolocator sender,
        PositionChangedEventArgs args)
    {
        await refreshUIAsync(args.Position);
    }

    async void RefreshData(object sender, RoutedEventArgs e)
    {
        if (tsLocationTracking.IsOn)
            await refreshUIAsync(await locator.GetGeopositionAsync());
    }
    }
}
```

11. Build the application by pressing the F6 button or clicking "BUILD - Build Solution" on the main menu of Visual Studio. If the Errors window appears and shows that there are errors in the code, try to resolve them by following the suggestions in the aforementioned window. If you can't resolve an error, open the GeoLocSample\End solution in the companion code, and compare your code to the one in the working solution.

12. Run the application. When you enable the Automatic tracking feature, the app updates its screen automatically (or, if you don't move, it's updated every 60 seconds). If you disabled High Accuracy, you might need to move your position more. Also, remember that if you run the app on the Windows Simulator, you can feed simulated location data to it without having to move around. The app should look like what you see in Figure 12-4. Note that, without GPS, the accuracy is somewhat limited.

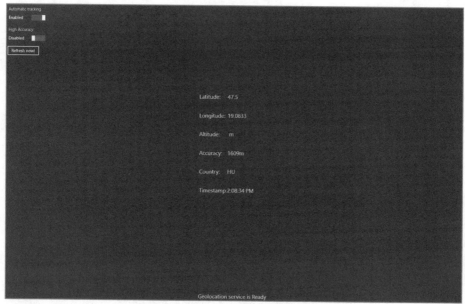

FIGURE 12-4: The working location-aware app

How It Works

In Step 3, you first indicated that your app would like to receive data on the device's location from the operating system. This is important, because, without this, the app won't run properly.

After adding the necessary namespaces and creating a `Geolocator`-type field to the class in Steps 4 and 5, you instantiated a `Geolocator` in Step 6 and subscribed to its `StatusChanged` event. The event-handler method, which you added in Step 7, writes the current status of the location service at the bottom of the page.

In Step 8, you subscribed with two event-handler methods on the two `ToggleSwitch` control's `Toggled` events.

The code you've added to the first `ToggleSwitch`'s event handler (`tsLocationTracking_Toggled`) in Step 9 make the `TextBlocks` in the middle of the page refresh their content every time the location service reports the current geolocation. This is done by the method you subscribe to the `Geolocator`'s `PositionChanged` event when the `ToggleSwitch` is turned on.

The code you added to the second `ToggleSwitch` in Step 9 is merely responsible for requesting lower or higher accuracy from the location service.

The last few lines of code that you added in Step 10 make the "Refresh now!" button refresh the contents of the screen when clicked or tapped by calling the `GetGeopositionAsync` method of the `Geolocator`. This won't make the location service "re-read" the location — it just receives the last reading.

> **NOTE** *While the location API is fairly simple and easy to use, you should consider a bit of advice Microsoft has for developers. You can read about this at* `http:// msdn.microsoft.com/en-us/library/windows/apps/xaml/hh465127.aspx.`

USING SENSORS

Users more often than not hold tablet devices (and even some laptops) in their hands. This gives app developers a great opportunity to introduce new, natural, and intuitive controlling mechanisms by leveraging a tablet's attitude and movement.

Just think of current mobile apps for phones that have a "shake to refresh" feature. When you shake your phone, the app starts downloading new information and automatically refreshes its UI.

Or, consider apps that are built with two color schemes — a light one that is best suited for bright environments, and a dark one that rests your eyes when using the app in a dim environment. If a device senses the strength of the ambient light in its surroundings, apps can automatically adapt to the lighting conditions by changing UI themes to provide a better view.

In the past, only a handful of mainstream PCs had sensors in them, so previous Windows versions had no (or limited) capabilities to provide sensor data to their apps in a unified, managed way — in other words, there was no broad need to do so. After the arrival of tablet devices, the PC world needed both hardware and software support to enable the same handy features. Windows 7 was the first Windows version that included a sensor and location platform baked into the system. This enabled developers to read and use the raw sensor data.

Windows 8 builds heavily on tablet devices. Channeling sensor input to applications is now more important than ever. Therefore, Windows 8 has a really sleek, simple, but powerful managed Sensor API in Windows Runtime — one that you'll understand in a few minutes if you've used the Sensor API in Windows Phone 7 and in only an hour if you haven't.

You can handle the sensory input in two ways:

➤ You can access the raw data coming from the device's actual sensor hardware.

➤ You can rely on the "logical sensors" that the Sensor API provides. These logical sensors calculate their data from the real readings, blending those readings into one simple aggregate, thus giving you an easier way to process complex orientations.

You will learn about both technologies in the following sections.

> **NOTE** *Be advised that you might not be able to see sensor apps in action. The current Windows Simulator cannot provide sensory input to your applications. Therefore, the apps described in the following discussions can only be tested properly using a real device that is equipped with sensors.*

Using Raw Sensor Data

As mentioned, Windows Runtime enables you to access the real sensors directly through the managed Sensors API. There are three sensors that you can access through this API:

➤ The accelerometer

➤ The gyroscope

➤ The ambient light sensor

There is one other hardware sensor that you cannot access directly: the magnetometer. This sensor is accessible only through the Sensor Fusion API, which you will learn about later in this chapter.

Using the Accelerometer

The *accelerometer* provides information about the moving device's change of speed in the three-dimensional (3-D) space.

As shown in Figure 12-5, the reading is divided into three values to represent the force on three axes: X, Y, and Z (relative to the device). The X and the Y axes are the same as the X and Y axes of the screen. The accelerometer's X axis overlaps with the horizontal side of a standing tablet. The Y axis overlaps with the vertical side of the screen. The third axis (Z) points to the user if he or she holds the

FIGURE 12-5: Axes of the accelerometer

tablet vertically and points upward when the tablet rests on a horizontal surface.

These values are normalized to Earth's gravity, so if you place the device on a flat, horizontal surface, the three values will tell you in which direction the ground is (that is, approximately –1 on the Z axis, and about 0 on the other two axes).

You can use the accelerometer through the `Accelerometer` class that resides in the `Windows.Devices` `.Sensors` namespace. You can't instantiate it, but it has a static method named `GetDefault`. This method returns an `Accelerometer` instance. If there is no such hardware present, this method returns `null`.

The `Accelerometer` object has two properties:

➤ `ReportInterval` enables you to set (or get) the interval of reading updates in milliseconds. The accelerometer will report changes of acceleration at this frequency (if there was any change at all). If you want to monitor broad movements (where precision isn't important), set this property to a larger value. When you want to analyze changes of acceleration more accurately, set `ReportInterval` to a smaller number.

➤ `MinimumReportInterval` indicates the minimum time (in milliseconds) the hardware can bear between two status updates, so do not set `ReportInterval` to a number smaller than this.

You can get the acceleration readings in two ways:

➤ If you want to be informed of any change in acceleration of the device, subscribe to the `ReadingChanged` event.

➤ If you want to know the device's timely acceleration in certain moments, you can call the `GetCurrentReading` method at any time. (Of course, if the time between two calls is smaller than the `MinimumReportInterval`, you're not going to see any change in the data.)

Both the event and the method provide you with an `AccelerometerReading` object. This object holds the three double values specifying the current acceleration of the device: `AccelerationX`, `AccelerationY`, and `AccelerationZ`. Also, this object contains a property called `Timestamp` (an instance of the `DateTimeOffset` class) that indicates the exact time the reading was taken.

`Accelerometer` provides another event called `Shaken`. Subscribing to this enables you to handle the event of the user moving the device rapidly while changing directions. In the event-handler method, all the parameters you get apart from the sender object (the `Accelerometer`) is an `AccelerometerShakenEventArgs` instance, which can tell you the exact time when the device was shaken (the usual `Timestamp` property). Handling this event is rather simple, because there is no additional information in the event arguments about how the device was shaken. So, you don't have to (and, in fact, you can't) process any more precise data.

In the following exercise, you learn how to use the accelerometer of a PC or tablet device.

> **NOTE** *You can find the complete code to download for this exercise on this book's companion website at* www.wrox.com *in the folder* AccelGyroSample\ EndAccelerometer *within the* Chapter12.zip *download.*

TRY IT OUT Using the Accelerometer

To see how to use the accelerometer to make a Windows 8 style app listen to and respond to changes in the device's acceleration, follow these steps:

1. Download the `Chapter12.zip` file from `www.wrox.com`, and open the solution under `AccelGyroSample\BeginAccelerometer`. This is the app you'll develop to test both accelerometer and gyro features.

2. Open the markup file (`MainPage.xaml`), and locate the first two buttons. Modify the markup by adding the following boldfaced event subscriptions to both buttons:

```
<Button Name="btnEnableDisableAccelerometer"
    Click="btnEnableDisableAccelerometer_Click"
    >Enable accelerometer</Button>
<Button Name="btnReadAccelerometer" Click="btnReadAccelerometer_Click"
    IsEnabled="{Binding ElementName=w, Path=AcmEnabled}"
    >Current accelerometer readings</Button>
```

3. Open `MainPage.xaml.cs` by double-clicking its name in the Solution Explorer window. Add the following `using` directives under the ones already there on the top of the file:

```
using Windows.Devices.Sensors;
using System;
using System.Threading.Tasks;
using Windows.UI.Popups;
```

4. Create an `Accelerometer` field in the `MainPage` class by adding the following boldfaced code to the class definition:

```
public sealed partial class MainPage : Page
{
        Accelerometer acm = null;
...
```

5. Add the following boldfaced code to the constructor, under the call to `InitializeComponent`:

```
public MainPage()
{
    this.InitializeComponent();
    acm = Accelerometer.GetDefault();
    if (acm != null) tbkAccelerometer.Text = "Accelerometer ready.";
    else tbkAccelerometer.Text = "Accelerometer not found.";
}
```

6. Add the following two methods to satisfy the event subscriptions from Step 2:

```
async void btnEnableDisableAccelerometer_Click(object sender, RoutedEventArgs e)
{
    if (acm != null)
    {
        if (!AcmEnabled)
        {
            acm.ReadingChanged += acm_ReadingChanged;
            AcmEnabled = true;
            btnEnableDisableAccelerometer.Content = "Disable Accelerometer";
        }
        else
        {
            acm.ReadingChanged -= acm_ReadingChanged;
            AcmEnabled = false;
            btnEnableDisableAccelerometer.Content = "Enable Accelerometer";
        }
    }
    else
    {
        await new MessageDialog("No accelerometer present.", "Error").ShowAsync();
    }
}


async void btnReadAccelerometer_Click(object sender, RoutedEventArgs e)
{
    await Task.Delay(1000).ContinueWith(async t =>
    {
```

```
        var reading = acm.GetCurrentReading();
        await Dispatcher.RunAsync(Windows.UI.Core.CoreDispatcherPriority.High, () =>
        {
            tbkAccelerometer.Text = string.Format("X: {0}, Y: {1}, Z: {2} @ {3}",
                reading.AccelerationX, reading.AccelerationY, reading.AccelerationZ,
                reading.Timestamp.Minute + ":" + reading.Timestamp.Second);
        });
    });
}
```

7. Add a third method after the previous two:

```
async void acm_ReadingChanged(Accelerometer sender,
    AccelerometerReadingChangedEventArgs args)
{
    await Dispatcher.RunAsync(Windows.UI.Core.CoreDispatcherPriority.Normal, () =>
    {
        var r = args.Reading;
        rectAcm.Width = 100 + Math.Abs(50 * r.AccelerationX);
        rectAcm.Height = 100 + Math.Abs(50 * r.AccelerationY);
        byte rgb = (byte)Math.Max(0, Math.Min(255, 128 + 10 * r.AccelerationZ));
        rectAcm.Fill = new SolidColorBrush(Color.FromArgb(255, rgb, rgb, rgb));
    });
}
```

The content of `MainPage.xaml.cs` should look like this now:

```
using Windows.UI;
using Windows.UI.Xaml;
using Windows.UI.Xaml.Controls;
using Windows.UI.Xaml.Media;
using Windows.Devices.Sensors;
using System;
using System.Threading.Tasks;
using Windows.UI.Popups;

namespace AccelGyroSample
{
    public sealed partial class MainPage : Page
    {
        #region DependencyProperties
        public bool AcmEnabled
        {
            get { return (bool)GetValue(AcmEnabledProperty); }
            set { SetValue(AcmEnabledProperty, value); }
        }
        public static readonly DependencyProperty AcmEnabledProperty =
            DependencyProperty.Register("AcmEnabled", typeof(bool),
            typeof(MainPage), new PropertyMetadata(false));

        public bool GyroEnabled
        {
            get { return (bool)GetValue(GyroEnabledProperty); }
            set { SetValue(GyroEnabledProperty, value); }
        }
        public static readonly DependencyProperty GyroEnabledProperty =
```

```
        DependencyProperty.Register("GyroEnabled", typeof(bool),
        typeof(MainPage), new PropertyMetadata(false));

#endregion

Accelerometer acm = null;


public MainPage()
{
    this.InitializeComponent();

    acm = Accelerometer.GetDefault();
    if (acm != null) tbkAccelerometer.Text = "Accelerometer ready.";
    else tbkAccelerometer.Text = "Accelerometer not found.";
}

async void btnEnableDisableAccelerometer_Click(object sender,
    RoutedEventArgs e)
{
    if (acm != null)
    {
        if (!AcmEnabled)
        {
            acm.ReadingChanged += acm_ReadingChanged;
            AcmEnabled = true;
            btnEnableDisableAccelerometer.Content = "Disable Accelerometer";
        }
        else
        {
            acm.ReadingChanged -= acm_ReadingChanged;
            AcmEnabled = false;
            btnEnableDisableAccelerometer.Content = "Enable Accelerometer";
        }
    }
    else
    {
        await new MessageDialog("No accelerometer present.",
            "Error").ShowAsync();
    }
}

async void btnReadAccelerometer_Click(object sender, RoutedEventArgs e)
{
    await Task.Delay(1000).ContinueWith(async t =>
{
    var reading = acm.GetCurrentReading();
    await Dispatcher.RunAsync(Windows.UI.Core.CoreDispatcherPriority.High,
        () =>
    {
        tbkAccelerometer.Text = string.Format("X: {0}, Y: {1}, Z: {2} @
            {3}",
            reading.AccelerationX, reading.AccelerationY,
                reading.AccelerationZ,
            reading.Timestamp.Minute + ":" + reading.Timestamp.Second);
    });
});
```

```
        });
    }

    async void acm_ReadingChanged(Accelerometer sender,
        AccelerometerReadingChangedEventArgs args)
    {
        await Dispatcher.RunAsync(Windows.UI.Core.CoreDispatcherPriority.Normal,
            () =>
        {
            var r = args.Reading;
            rectAcm.Width = 100 + Math.Abs(50 * r.AccelerationX);
            rectAcm.Height = 100 + Math.Abs(50 * r.AccelerationY);
            byte rgb = (byte)Math.Max(0, Math.Min(255, 128 + 10 *
                r.AccelerationZ));
            rectAcm.Fill = new SolidColorBrush(Color.FromArgb(255, rgb, rgb,
                rgb));
        });
    }
}
}
```

8. Build the application by pressing the F6 button or clicking "BUILD - Build Solution" on the main menu of Visual Studio. If the Errors window appears and shows that there are errors in the code, try to resolve them by following the suggestions in the aforementioned window. If you can't resolve an error, open the `AccelGyroSample\EndAccelerometer` solution in the companion code, and compare your code to the one in the working solution.

9. Run the app on a tablet device, click or tap the button that enables acceleration tracking, and move the device around to see the square on the left change its size based on the current movement on the three axes. Figure 12-6 shows what you should see.

10. Save the finished solution; you'll need it in the next exercise.

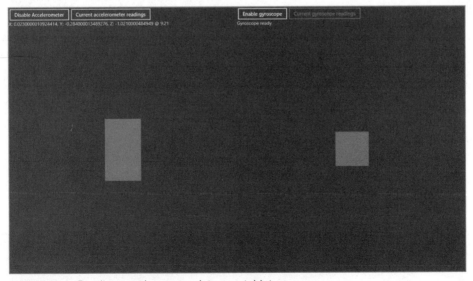

FIGURE 12-6: Reading accelerometer data on a tablet

How It Works

In Steps 3 through 5, you created the essential infrastructure to use the accelerometer.

The first method you added in Step 6 (`btnEnableDisableAccelerometer_Click`) tests whether there is an accelerometer in the PC, and if there is one, it subscribes the method you added in Step 7 to its `ReadingChanged` event. This event will fire (and, thus, the screen will be updated) every time the device changes its acceleration in some direction.

Acceleration on axis X makes the square grow horizontally. Acceleration on axis Y makes the square grow vertically, and acceleration on axis Z makes the square change its color.

Note that in `acm_ReadingChanged`, you should run the actual code through the `Dispatcher`. This is needed because this method will be called on a background thread, and changing the UI from that thread is forbidden. `Dispatcher` is responsible for running the code back on the UI thread to avoid such errors.

The second method you added in Step 6 (`btnReadAccelerometer_Click`) is called upon clicking or tapping the second button. It waits for a second, and then it catches the current readings from the accelerometer (so you don't have to click or tap the button while shaking the device).

Using the Gyroscope

Although the accelerometer can tell you the device's change of movement in space by sensing the movement forces that are having effects on the tablet, it can't tell you how the device is rotated. Some movement reported by the accelerometer on the X axis can mean that the device is being pushed away on a table, or it could mean that it's falling downward, depending on the device's rotation. Rotation speed might be approximated from continuously reading and processing data of the accelerometer, but that is a rather cumbersome calculation, and you can't really rely on its accuracy. Tablet devices come with other sensory hardware called the *gyroscope* (often abbreviated as gyro), which tells you the exact rotation speed of the device in the 3-D space.

Using a gyroscope is akin to using an accelerometer; their APIs are quite similar. You can access the gyroscope through the `Gyrometer` class of the `Windows.Devices.Sensors` namespace. Instantiation is prohibited, but you can get a `Gyrometer` object by calling the static `GetDefault` method on the class. Test the result for `null` to see if any gyroscope is included in the device.

When you have the `Gyrometer` object, you can use the `ReportInterval` property to set the minimum interval (in milliseconds) between two readings. The `MinimumReportInterval` property tells you the absolute minimum interval between two readings that the gyro can support.

To read the rotation speed, either subscribe to the `ReadingChanged` event (which is updated continuously when the gyro has new readings), or call the `GetCurrentReading` method (which gives you the current rotation speed).

The event has a parameter typed `GyrometerReadingChangedEventArgs`, which contains a `GyrometerReading` object called `Reading`. This is the same type of object that you get when calling the `GetCurrentReading` method.

GyrometerReading contains four properties. Timestamp is an instance of DateTimeOffset, and it gets you the time when the gyroscope reported the current reading. The other three properties are AngularVelocityX, AngularVelocityY, and AngularVelocityZ. These three double values tell you the rotation speed on the three axes in radians per second. If the device is resting (not being moved), all of them should read zero.

In the next exercise, you learn how to use the gyroscope by continuing the application from the previous exercise. Again, keep in mind that the current Windows Simulator can't feed synthetic sensor readings to your apps, so to see this example work, you should test it on an actual device with sensors.

> **NOTE** You can find the complete code to download for this exercise on this book's companion website at www.wrox.com in the folder AccelGyroSample\EndGyroscope within the Chapter12.zip download.

TRY IT OUT   Using the Gyroscope

To see how to use the gyroscope to make a Windows 8 style app listen and respond to changes in the device's rotation speed, follow these steps:

1. Open the AccelGyroSample from the previous "Try It Out" exercise called "Using the Accelerometer." If you haven't finished it yet, you can open the AccelGyroSample\EndAccelerometer solution from the companion code available at www.wrox.com.

2. Open MainPage.xaml, and locate the two buttons associated with the gyro (btnEnableDisableGyroscope and btnReadGyro). Add event handlers to the Click events of both buttons, as shown in the following boldfaced code:

```
<Button Name="btnEnableDisableGyroscope"
    Click="btnEnableDisableGyroscope_Click">Enable gyroscope</Button>
<Button Name="btnReadGyro" Click="btnReadGyro_Click" IsEnabled="{Binding
    ElementName=w, Path=GyroEnabled}">Current gyroscope readings</Button>
```

3. Open the MainPage.xaml.cs file, and add a Gyrometer field (boldfaced here) to the class definition of MainPage, under the Accelerometer field:

```
public sealed partial class MainPage : Page {
    ...
    Accelerometer acm = null;

    Gyrometer gyro = null;

    public MainPage() {
        this.InitializeComponent();
    ...
```

4. Add the following boldfaced code to the constructor:

```
public sealed partial class MainPage : Page
{
    ...
```

```
    Gyrometer gyro = null;

    public MainPage()
    {
        this.InitializeComponent();

        acm = Accelerometer.GetDefault();
        if (acm != null) tbkAccelerometer.Text = "Accelerometer ready.";
        else tbkAccelerometer.Text = "Accelerometer not found.";

        gyro = Gyrometer.GetDefault();
        if (gyro != null) tbkGyro.Text = "Gyroscope ready";
        else tbkGyro.Text = "Gyroscope not found";
    }
```

5. Add the two event-handler methods you created subscriptions for in Step 2, as shown here:

```
async void btnEnableDisableGyroscope_Click(object sender, RoutedEventArgs e)
{
    if (gyro != null)
    {
        if (!GyroEnabled)
        {
            gyro.ReadingChanged += gyro_ReadingChanged;
            GyroEnabled = true;
            btnEnableDisableGyroscope.Content = "Gyro enabled";
        }
        else
        {
            gyro.ReadingChanged -= gyro_ReadingChanged;
            GyroEnabled = false;
            btnEnableDisableGyroscope.Content = "Gyro disabled";
        }
    }
    else
    {
        await new MessageDialog("No gyroscope present.", "Error").ShowAsync();
    }
}


async void btnReadGyro_Click(object sender, RoutedEventArgs e)
{
    await Task.Delay(1000).ContinueWith(async t =>
{
    var r = gyro.GetCurrentReading();
    await Dispatcher.RunAsync(Windows.UI.Core.CoreDispatcherPriority.High, () =>
    {
        tbkGyro.Text = string.Format("X: {0}, Y: {1}, Z: {2} @ {3}",
            r.AngularVelocityX, r.AngularVelocityY, r.AngularVelocityZ,
            r.Timestamp.Minute + ":" + r.Timestamp.Second);
    });
});
}
```

6. Add a third method after the previous two, as shown here:

```
async void gyro_ReadingChanged(Gyrometer sender, GyrometerReadingChangedEventArgs
    args)
{
    await Dispatcher.RunAsync(Windows.UI.Core.CoreDispatcherPriority.High, () =>
    {
        var r = args.Reading;
        rectGyro.Width = 100 + Math.Abs(r.AngularVelocityX);
        rectGyro.Height = 100 + Math.Abs(r.AngularVelocityY);
        byte rgb = (byte)Math.Max(0, Math.Min(255, 128 + 15 * r.AngularVelocityZ));
        rectGyro.Fill = new SolidColorBrush(Color.FromArgb(255, rgb, rgb, rgb));
    });
}
```

The contents of `MainPage.xaml.cs` should look like this:

```
using Windows.UI;
using Windows.UI.Xaml;
using Windows.UI.Xaml.Controls;
using Windows.UI.Xaml.Media;
using Windows.Devices.Sensors;
using System;
using System.Threading.Tasks;
using Windows.UI.Popups;

namespace AccelGyroSample
{
    public sealed partial class MainPage : Page
    {
        #region DependencyProperties
        public bool AcmEnabled
        {
            get { return (bool)GetValue(AcmEnabledProperty); }
            set { SetValue(AcmEnabledProperty, value); }
        }
        public static readonly DependencyProperty AcmEnabledProperty =
            DependencyProperty.Register("AcmEnabled", typeof(bool),
            typeof(MainPage), new PropertyMetadata(false));

        public bool GyroEnabled
        {
            get { return (bool)GetValue(GyroEnabledProperty); }
            set { SetValue(GyroEnabledProperty, value); }
        }
        public static readonly DependencyProperty GyroEnabledProperty =
            DependencyProperty.Register("GyroEnabled", typeof(bool),
            typeof(MainPage), new PropertyMetadata(false));

        #endregion

        Accelerometer acm = null;

        Gyrometer gyro = null;

        public MainPage()
```

```
{
    this.InitializeComponent();

    acm = Accelerometer.GetDefault();
    if (acm != null) tbkAccelerometer.Text = "Accelerometer ready.";
    else tbkAccelerometer.Text = "Accelerometer not found.";

    gyro = Gyrometer.GetDefault();
    if (gyro != null) tbkGyro.Text = "Gyroscope ready";
    else tbkGyro.Text = "Gyroscope not found";
}

private async void btnEnableDisableAccelerometer_Click(object sender,
    RoutedEventArgs e)
{
    if (acm != null)
    {
        if (!AcmEnabled)
        {
            acm.ReadingChanged += acm_ReadingChanged;
            AcmEnabled = true;
            btnEnableDisableAccelerometer.Content = "Disable Accelerometer";
        }
        else
        {
            acm.ReadingChanged -= acm_ReadingChanged;
            AcmEnabled = false;
            btnEnableDisableAccelerometer.Content = "Enable Accelerometer";
        }
    }
    else
    {
        await new MessageDialog("No accelerometer present.",
            "Error").ShowAsync();
    }
}

async void btnReadAccelerometer_Click(object sender, RoutedEventArgs e)
{
    await Task.Delay(1000).ContinueWith(async t =>
{
    var reading = acm.GetCurrentReading();
    await Dispatcher.RunAsync(Windows.UI.Core.CoreDispatcherPriority.High,
        () =>
    {
        tbkAccelerometer.Text = string.Format("X: {0}, Y: {1}, Z: {2} @
            {3}",
            reading.AccelerationX, reading.AccelerationY,
                reading.AccelerationZ,
            reading.Timestamp.Minute + ":" + reading.Timestamp.Second);
    });
});
}

async void acm_ReadingChanged(Accelerometer sender,
    AccelerometerReadingChangedEventArgs args)
```

```
{
    await Dispatcher.RunAsync(Windows.UI.Core.CoreDispatcherPriority.Normal,
        () =>
    {
        var r = args.Reading;
        rectAcm.Width = 100 + Math.Abs(50 * r.AccelerationX);
        rectAcm.Height = 100 + Math.Abs(50 * r.AccelerationY);
        byte rgb = (byte)Math.Max(0, Math.Min(255, 128 + 10 *
            r.AccelerationZ));
        rectAcm.Fill = new SolidColorBrush(Color.FromArgb(255, rgb, rgb,
            rgb));
    });
}


async void btnEnableDisableGyroscope_Click(object sender, RoutedEventArgs e)
{
    if (gyro != null)
    {
        if (!GyroEnabled)
        {
            gyro.ReadingChanged += gyro_ReadingChanged;
            GyroEnabled = true;
            btnEnableDisableGyroscope.Content = "Gyro enabled";
        }
        else
        {
            gyro.ReadingChanged -= gyro_ReadingChanged;
            GyroEnabled = false;
            btnEnableDisableGyroscope.Content = "Gyro disabled";
        }
    }
    else
    {
        await new MessageDialog("No gyroscope present.",
            "Error").ShowAsync();
    }
}

async void btnReadGyro_Click(object sender, RoutedEventArgs e)
{
    await Task.Delay(1000).ContinueWith(async t =>
{
    var r = gyro.GetCurrentReading();
    await Dispatcher.RunAsync(Windows.UI.Core.CoreDispatcherPriority.High,
        () =>
    {
        tbkGyro.Text = string.Format("X: {0}, Y: {1}, Z: {2} @ {3}",
            r.AngularVelocityX, r.AngularVelocityY, r.AngularVelocityZ,
            r.Timestamp.Minute + ":" + r.Timestamp.Second);
    });
});
}

async void gyro_ReadingChanged(Gyrometer sender,
```

```
                GyrometerReadingChangedEventArgs args)
        {
            await Dispatcher.RunAsync(Windows.UI.Core.CoreDispatcherPriority.High,
                () =>
            {
                var r = args.Reading;
                rectGyro.Width = 100 + Math.Abs(r.AngularVelocityX);
                rectGyro.Height = 100 + Math.Abs(r.AngularVelocityY);
                byte rgb = (byte)Math.Max(0, Math.Min(255, 128 + 15 *
                    r.AngularVelocityZ));
                rectGyro.Fill = new SolidColorBrush(Color.FromArgb(255, rgb, rgb,
                    rgb));
            });
        }
    }
}
```

7. Build the application by pressing the F6 button or clicking "BUILD - Build Solution" on the main menu of Visual Studio. If the Errors window appears and shows that there are errors in the code, try to resolve them by following the suggestions in the aforementioned window. If you can't resolve an error, open the AccelGyroSample\EndGyroscope solution in the companion code, and compare your code to the one in the working solution.

8. Run the app on a tablet device, and rotate the device to see the square on the right change its size (and color) based on the current rotation around its three axes. Click (or tap) the "Current gyroscope readings" button to see the current rotation data. Figures 12-7 and 12-8 show the change on the user interface you should see. Notice the difference in the size of the rectangle on the right.

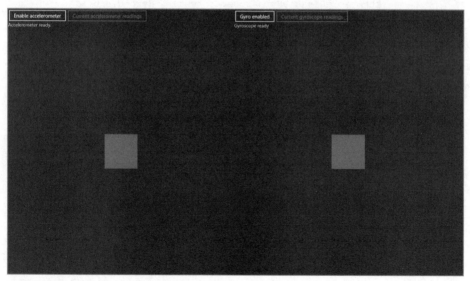

FIGURE 12-7: The application's UI when there is no movement

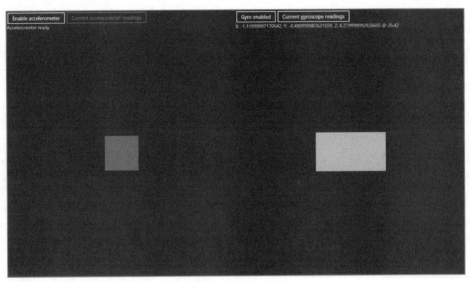

FIGURE 12-8: Reading gyroscope data on a tablet

How It Works

In the previous exercise ("Using the Accelerometer"), you inserted the necessary using directives. In Step 3 and Step 4 of this exercise, you added and instantiated the Gyrometer that lets you use the data coming from the gyroscope hardware. In Step 5, you added functionality to two buttons.

The first method (btnEnableDisableGyroscope_Click) checks whether or not there is a gyroscope in the device, and, if so, subscribes to its ReadingChanged event (and unsubscribes when you click or tap the button again).

The method that runs when the gyro has new data is the one you added in Step 6. If there is rotation around axis X of the device, that will appear in the horizontal size of the square. Rotation on axis Y grows the height of the rectangle, and rotation around axis Z changes the rectangle's color.

The second method you added in Step 5 (btnReadGyro_Click) waits for a second (so you don't have to click or tap the button while rotating the device), and then writes the gyro's current readings to a TextBlock under the buttons.

Using the Ambient Light Sensor

Tablet devices are capable of determining the average luminosity of their surrounding environments with the ambient light sensor hardware. Windows Runtime has a corresponding class for this sensor, which you can use to make your apps aware of and respond according to the lighting conditions. For example, if your app processes the reading of the ambient light sensor, you can automatically switch to a dark theme when the environment's lighting changes.

Because Microsoft likes to keep its APIs simple and consistent, the light sensor can be programmed just as easily as the previous two sensors were.

To access the light sensor, call the GetDefault method on the LightSensor class in the Windows .Devices.Sensors namespace. It returns null if no light sensor hardware is present.

On the `LightSensor` object, you find a double property called `ReportInterval`, which you can use to tell the sensor the minimum interval in milliseconds in which you'd like to see the status updates on the lighting conditions. `MinimumReportInterval` is a read-only property that gives you the physical minimum of the reporting interval supported by the hardware.

You can access the readings through the usual two ways: subscribing to the `ReadingChanged` event, and calling the `GetCurrentReading` method. If you subscribe to the event, the second event argument will be an instance of `LightSensorReadingChangedEventArgs`, which contains a `Reading` property, an instance of `LightSensorReading`. `GetCurrentReading` returns an instance of this class, too.

`LightSensorReading` contains the usual `Timestamp` (a `DateTimeOffset` that tells you when the reading was taken), and a float-type property called `LuminanceInLux`. (Float type is like the double type you encountered in the first exercise of this chapter; the only difference is that it's less precise.) This number tells you the strength of ambient light that the sensors detect. You can easily find what kind of environment-specific luminance values correspond to, but here are some rough estimates to get you started:

➤ This value is above about 25,000 if the device is in direct sunlight.

➤ Between 1,000 and 25,000, it's daylight (cloudy on the lower end), but not direct.

➤ When outside, a reading less than 100 means it's nighttime.

➤ In a building, lighting could vary from about 50 to 500 with the lights turned on.

> **NOTE** The `LightSensor` class returns values in lux. This is the SI unit of illuminance. You don't have to know anything about the measurement of illuminance to be able to use this sensor, but if you're interested in it, see http://en.wikipedia.org/wiki/Lux.

Using Sensor Fusion Data

The hardware movement sensors (the accelerometer and the gyro) are useful if you find yourself in a situation where being aware of acceleration or rotation information is desired. But, most of the time, you don't want to give the user feedback based on this information — you just want to know how the user holds the device. Calculating this seemingly simple data from the readings of multiple movement sensors can be a mess. Because of this, Microsoft created a higher-level abstraction layer on the Sensor APIs, which can answer common questions about the device's orientation and attitude. This is the Sensor Fusion API.

The Sensor Fusion API defines new "logical sensors"—they aren't tied to one hardware sensor like the ones described previously. Fusion sensors calculate their readings using multiple hardware sensors.

The API defines four of these logical sensors:

➤ The compass

➤ The inclinometer

➤ Two device-orientation sensors

Using the Magnetometer through the Compass

Some apps need to have information about the direction of the North Pole. For example, if you build an app that contains a map, you may want to present the map to the user in such a way that it always points to north, so the user can always be aware of his or her heading while following the directions on the map. To this end, tablet devices contain a *magnetometer* sensor, which can tell the strength of the magnetic fields around the device.

The magnetometer has no low-level API like the accelerometer or the gyroscope, so you can't use the magnetometer to actually measure the power of the said magnetic fields. However, the Sensor Fusion API lets you use the Compass class. With this class, you can read the heading to the magnetic and the geographic North Pole, calculated from the readings of all the necessary hardware sensors.

Using the Compass is fairly straightforward after you have become familiar with the accelerometer or the gyro APIs. You can access the Compass by calling the GetDefault method on the Compass class. If it's null, there is no compass in the device.

After you have the Compass, you can set the ReportInterval to indicate how often you want to be informed about changes in the direction of the North Pole. MinimumReportInterval tells you the minimum value in milliseconds.

If you subscribe to the ReadingChanged event, you get a notification every time the compass has new headings. If you call the GetCurrentReadings method, you get the current headings at the moment of the method call.

ReadingChanged has a CompassReadingChangedEventArgs class event argument, which contains a CompassReading object in the Reading property. GetCurrentReadings also gives you a CompassReading as a return value.

CompassReading specifies three useful properties. One is the usual Timestamp, which gives you the exact time when the reading was taken. The other two contain the actual compass data. HeadingMagneticNorth is a double value that gives the angle of the device relative to the magnetic North Pole. HeadingTrueNorth is a nullable double value that gives you the angle of the device relative to the true geographic North Pole. If the Sensor Fusion API cannot determine the location of the geographic North Pole, this property reads null.

Using the Inclinometer

The *inclinometer* can tell you the way the user holds the device by calculating the angular offset on each and every axis. The values are referred to as *pitch*, *roll*, and *yaw*. The easiest way to visualize and remember what these three properties mean is to imagine an airplane:

➤ Pitch tells you how hard the plane's nose points up or down to climb up or lose altitude.

➤ Roll is how much the plane rolls to one of its sides (that is, the difference in altitude between the ends of its wings).

➤ Yaw tells you how much the plane turns to the right or left, based on its original direction.

On a tablet device, if these values are 0, 0, and 0, that means that the tablet is resting on a flat surface with its screen up. As shown in Figure 12-9, pitch represents the inclination on axis X of the screen; roll represents the angular offset on axis Y; and yaw is the angular offset on axis Z. Of course, these values are represented in degrees (0 to 360) as single-precision floating-point numbers.

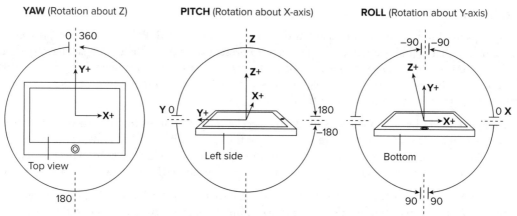

FIGURE 12-9: Pitch, roll, and yaw on a tablet device

Using the inclinometer is quite the same as processing raw sensor data — only the data can turn out to be more useful. You can get the Inclinometer object by calling GetDefault on the Inclinometer class. To specify the minimum interval in which you'd like to get status updates, set the ReportInterval property to the desired quantity of milliseconds. The other double-typed property, MinimumReportInterval, gives you the absolute minimum to which you can set the ReportInterval. Setting the ReportInterval on other sensors like the accelerometer has no effect on the inclinometer.

Subscribing to the ReadingChanged event gives you the option to receive automatic updates when there is a change in the device's attitude. Event-handler methods to this event have a method parameter of type InclinometerReadingChangedEventArgs. Instances of this type contain an InclinometerReading object in the Reading property, which holds the valuable data.

The other way to get an InclinometerReading object is to call the GetCurrentReading of the Inclinometer instance at any time. This returns with an InclinometerReading.

InclinometerReading holds four properties. PitchDegrees, RollDegrees, and YawDegrees indicate the angular offset of the device on the three axes (X, Y, and Z, respectively). Timestamp is a DateTimeOffset that holds the time the reading was taken.

Detecting Device Orientation in a Simple Way

An inclinometer can radically simplify your job when it comes to calculating attitude of the device. But many applications need even less precise and verbose information. When you just want to know whether the device faces up or down (meaning that it rests on its back or on its screen), processing all the inclinometer data is overkill. To accommodate apps in this situation, Microsoft created another logical sensor, called the *simple orientation sensor.*

The SimpleOrientationSensor class is in the Windows.Devices.Sensors namespace. You can get an instance of the class by calling the GetDefault method on it. After you have the SimpleOrientationSensor, you can either subscribe to the OrientationChanged event or call the GetCurrentOrientation method. The event handler's second argument will be an instance of

SimpleOrientationSensorOrientationChangedEventArgs. (No, this is not the longest class name in Windows Runtime.) This object contains a Timestamp — the usual DateTimeOffset specifying the exact time the orientation changed — and a property called Orientation. Its type is an enumeration, named SimpleOrientation.

Table 12-2 describes the possible values of SimpleOrientation.

TABLE 12-2: Values of the SimpleOrientation Enumeration

NAME	DESCRIPTION
NotRotated	The user holds the device in his or her hands normally, like a portrait (the shorter edge of the screen is parallel to the ground).
Faceup	The device rests on a flat, horizontal surface with its screen upward.
Facedown	The device rests on a flat, horizontal surface with its screen downward (the user cannot see it).
Rotated90DegreesCounterclockwise	The user holds the device with its longer edge parallel to the ground. The original bottom of the device (defined by NotRotated mode) is on the left.
Rotated180DegreesCounterclockwise	The user holds the device like a portrait, with its shorter edge parallel to the ground but upside down.
Rotated270DegreesCounterclockwise	The user holds the device with its longer edge parallel to the ground. The original bottom of the device (defined by NotRotated mode) is on the right.

Other Options for Detecting Device Orientation

Readings from the simple orientation sensor and the inclinometer are more than enough most of the time. However, some applications require a more exact, complete representation of the attitude, orientation, and position of the device.

You may have come across this with some augmented reality (AR) apps when using a smartphone, even if you didn't know about this category of apps. AR apps use your surroundings (environment) as a base of representation, and they add additional information to this representation. In most cases, this means that the app channels the (altered or original) image feed from the device's camera to the screen, and, in the process, it recognizes objects on the image and decorates them with the additional info.

Real image recognition on small, handheld devices can be really slow (not fast enough for a real-time app), so these apps rely on sensor data from multiple sensors to calculate what the user actually sees. The GPS can tell you on which street you are located, the compass (or magnetometer) can tell you the direction you're looking, and the inclinometer can tell you at what building you are pointing the camera. From this small chunk of data, a backend server can tell what building you should see on the screen, and draw additional information about that building (such as when it was built, who built it, and so on).

Another example would be the numerous "skymap" apps. You point your phone (or in this case, tablet) at the night sky, and the app draws the known star formations on the screen, so you know what are you looking at. And, of course, many more kinds of these augmented reality apps exist.

Building real-time AR apps can be difficult enough, so Windows Runtime tries to alleviate part of the pain by giving you a logical sensor that accumulates data from nearly all the hardware sensors and presents it in one, universal format. This is called the *orientation sensor*. It collects information from the accelerometer, the gyro, and the magnetometer, and with this information, it can place the device in the 3-D space. You only need to add the location information to this mix, and you can tell what the user is looking at when he or she points the device's camera at something. (Of course, you need a database to tell what there is.)

You can access the orientation sensor through the `OrientationSensor` class in the `Windows.Devices.Sensors` namespace. Its API strongly resembles the other sensor APIs you've learned about in this chapter.

Again, this sensor is most useful when you build heavy-duty AR apps — something that is way beyond the boundaries of a beginning book. Because of this, this sensor is not examined in further detail. But it's good to know that when you find yourself in need of a quaternion and a rotation matrix, there is a sensor to give you all this data without you having to calculate it by yourself, using the lower-level sensor APIs.

SUMMARY

In this chapter, you learned about the advantages of developing apps for tablet devices. Tablets are used quite differently from other traditional PCs — users hold them in their hands. With the presence of sensor hardware in these devices, this provides an opportunity to enable additional, natural control methods in your apps. Of course, not all tablet devices may be equipped with sensors, but they most likely will be.

The Location API can determine a device's location by IP address, triangulating from the distance of cell towers, or known Wi-Fi hotspots. It turns on the GPS receiver only when you need more precision, or when other methods have failed.

Tablets incorporate new hardware parts collectively called sensors. The accelerometer, the gyro, and the light sensor are accessible directly, so you can easily determine the current strength of forces having effects on the device and the strength of ambient light. Windows Runtime also provides an API for logical sensors, including the compass, the inclinometer, and the device-orientation sensors. These accumulate data from multiple physical sensors and refine that data to be more usable in common scenarios.

In Chapter 13, you will learn about creating Windows 8 applications with C++. Using this slightly more complex language, you can access more features of the underlying framework as opposed to simply using C#, Visual Basic, or JavaScript.

EXERCISES

1. Why is it important to incorporate sensory input in your apps when targeting tablet devices?

2. What are the possible settings of precision of the geolocator, and what is the result of using either of them?

3. What is the difference between the accelerometer and the gyroscope?

4. Why do you need logical sensors (apart from physical ones)?

5. When should you use the `SimpleOrientationSensor` instead of other ones?

> **NOTE** *You can find the answers to the exercises in Appendix A.*

▶ **WHAT YOU LEARNED IN THIS CHAPTER**

TOPIC	KEY CONCEPTS
Location or geolocation	This is the concept of determining the position of a device by using multiple techniques, including IP pinpointing, triangulation from the distances of cell towers, Wi-Fi hotspots, or by GPS.
Location-aware app	This is an application that uses the Location API to obtain data on the device's current location and customize its services according to it.
Sensors	These are hardware parts in a PC (or tablet) that feed data on the environment of the device (such as lighting conditions, magnetic field strength, movement, and attitude or orientation).
Raw sensor data	This is data coming from the physical sensors. In Windows Runtime, these are the accelerometer, the gyro, and the ambient light sensor.
Sensor Fusion API	This application programming interface defines logical sensors and lets you access the data coming from them. These logical sensors calculate their readings from the data coming from physical sensors and present this data differently to save you from writing algorithms to do the heavy lifting.

PART III
Advancing to Professional Windows 8 Development

13

Creating Windows 8 Style Applications with C++

WHAT YOU WILL LEARN IN THIS CHAPTER:

➤ Understanding the scenarios where the C++ programming language is the right choice

➤ Getting to know the most important recent enhancements to the C++ language

➤ Getting acquainted with the new features that make it possible to write Windows 8 style applications in C++

WROX.COM CODE DOWNLOADS FOR THIS CHAPTER

You can find the wrox.com code downloads for this chapter on the Download Code tab at www.wrox.com/remtitle.cgi?isbn=012680. The code is in the Chapter13.zip download and individually named, as described in the corresponding exercises.

Although the title of this chapter may suggest that it is only for C++ developers, this is not true. In this chapter, if you are a C#, Visual Basic, or JavaScript developer, you learn in which scenarios C++ is the best choice of available Windows 8 languages. If you have had experience with C++ in the past (even if it was frustrating), this chapter demonstrates that C++ has become a modern, fast, clean, and safe language, as well as a first-class citizen in Windows 8 style application development.

First, you learn about the renaissance of C++, and then you are presented with an overview of recent improvements to the programming language. In most of this chapter, you learn about new features that Microsoft has added to its C++ implementation in Visual Studio 2012, additions that support Windows 8 style application development and integration with Windows Runtime. After learning about all these new things and extensions, you work with a small sample application to see how the theory works in practice.

> **NOTE** *Teaching you the C++ programming language is far beyond the scope of this book. If you are interested in learning this language, a good starting point is Ivor Horton's* Beginning Visual C++ 2012 *(Indianapolis: Wiley, 2012). If you want to obtain more reference information about the elements or standard libraries of the language, see* `http://cppreference.com`*.*

MICROSOFT AND THE C++ LANGUAGE

Although circumstances may show that .NET languages (C# and Visual Basic) are the standard programming languages for Microsoft (and, thus, are used in most products), this is not the situation. Most product development within Microsoft still happens with C++, and it seems as though this development will go on with this language for a long time.

Why is this so? Does Microsoft not believe in its own managed runtime environment (.NET Framework), and is that why it does not utilize it? Does Microsoft not want to (or can't) leverage the productivity benefits of .NET? No! C++ provides two things that challenge managed programming languages: performance and fine-grained control over system resources.

When you work with the managed languages of the .NET Framework, the compiler creates executable programs that contain Microsoft Intermediate Language (MSIL) code, or instructions from an intermediate language. When this program runs, MSIL instructions are compiled to CPU-specific instructions on the fly with a just-in-time (JIT) compiler, and then this CPU-specific code is executed. Although the managed languages and MSIL contain constructs that make software development really productive, it is circuitous to describe low-level instructions (such as bit-level operations), which are very easy to declare with CPU-specific instructions. So, although an algorithm's performance benefits significantly from low-level constructs, managed languages have challenges.

Of course, using native languages (including C++) has its drawbacks. By controlling all the details in order to achieve performance, you often must deal with many subtle things. For example, if you want to have total control over memory consumption, you must allocate and dispose of resources explicitly. This activity requires a lot of attention to avoid memory leaks, or to reuse disposed resources.

Earlier, you learned that the beginning of the Windows era was about C and C++ programming. At that time, productivity of developers was very low in contrast to productivity achieved by using the managed languages emerging with .NET in 2002. Managed languages always had a performance penalty in exchange for productivity. For a long time, with great hardware (especially at the server side), it was an acceptable trade-off, because buying hardware with about 20 percent more performance was cheaper than paying developers to tune the app for a few more months.

Smartphones, new-generation tablets, and ultra-mobile devices totally changed the rules of the game. The CPUs in these devices are generally less powerful than in desktop computers, so the same algorithms may run longer on them. To keep the device weight low, these devices work with batteries that have limited capacity. The more performance you use, the shorter the time the battery holds on. Moreover, consumers want to have a great user experience with these devices, so they prefer responsive user interfaces (UIs), and do not like bitty animations.

The key to writing well-behaving applications for these mobile devices is efficiency. The applications should carry out many activities in a short time, with as little CPU usage as possible. They must be frugal with memory and other hardware resources. This is the point at which native coding can be drawn into the scene, because these requirements are exactly the ones where native programming languages (including C++) perform their best.

So, it is not surprising that Microsoft wanted to support the C++ language as a first-class citizen in Windows 8 style application development. Microsoft not only solved Windows 8 style development in C++, but also modernized the language by making it clean and safe.

Clean and Safe

Most programmers either love or hate C++. No one would say, "I like it a bit," or "It's OK, but I don't like that feature." Lovers of C++ like it because of the full control this language provides over the application's execution. It's a kind of excitement to almost know in advance what instructions will be executed on the CPU as a result of a certain C++ programming construct. Those who hate C++ hate the low-level constructs and the common pitfalls coming from them.

With the newest C++ implementation (the one you can find in Visual Studio 2012), Microsoft invested a lot to make C++ a modern language by means of productivity, while still keeping the opportunity to maintain full control over the application's execution. Microsoft implemented a number of new features in C++11. Moreover, Microsoft extended the language to support Windows 8 style applications and Windows Runtime integration.

> **NOTE** The C++ programming language was developed by Bjarne Stroustrup in 1979 at Bell Labs. At that time, it was named "C with classes." The language went through its first standardization process in 1998 (C++98), then later in 2003 (C++03). The latest major revision of the standard is C++11, approved by the International Organization for Standardization Organization/International Electrotechnical Commission (ISO/IEC) on August 12, 2011.

To understand what kind of features make C++ more productive than it ever was before, let's take a look at a code sample written with C++03 (the previous revision of the C++ standard), as shown in Listing 13-1 (code file: `LegacyCpp\LegacyCpp.cpp`).

LISTING 13-1: A simple C++ program — using the old style

```
// --- Create a vector of 10 rectangles
vector<rectangle *> shapes;
for (int i = 1; i <= 10; i++)
{
    shapes.push_back(new rectangle(i * 100, i * 200));
}

// --- This is the rectangle we are looking for
```

continues

LISTING 13-1 *(continued)*

```
rectangle* searchFor = new rectangle(300, 600);

// --- Iterate through all rectanges
for (vector<rectangle*>::iterator i = shapes.begin(); i != shapes.end(); i++)
{
    (*i)->draw();
    if (*i && **i == *searchFor)
    {
        cout << "*** Rectangle found." << endl;
    }
}

// --- Dispose resources held by this program
for (vector<rectangle*>::iterator i = shapes.begin(); i != shapes.end(); i++)
{
    delete *i;
}
delete searchFor;
```

This program creates a `vector` of ten `rectangle` objects (stored in `shapes`), and then draws them in a `for` loop and checks if any of these rectangles matches with the one stored in the `searchFor` variable. A few points add disturbing complexity to this simple task:

➤ The `shapes` variable is a vector of pointers to `rectangle` objects. The first `for` loop that goes from 1 to 10 creates `rectangle` objects and attaches them to `shapes`. The programmer must keep in mind that these objects must be disposed of at a certain point of the program. The last `for` loop with the `delete i` body performs this cleanup.

➤ The `searchFor` variable holds a pointer to a `rectangle` object. This object is disposed of with the `delete searchFor` statement in the last line.

➤ Two `for` loops use an iterator object that goes through the elements of the vector. Although the intention of this cycle is really clear, the code expressing it seems a bit lengthy.

➤ The `*i && **i == *searchFor` conditional expression is simple, but still difficult to decode. In this expression, `i` is an iterator and `*i` represents the pointer to a `rectangle` object the iterator is currently referring to. The `**i` expression is the rectangle the iterator points to, and `*searchFor` is the `rectangle` object the cycle is looking for. This condition says that, if the iterator is pointing to a `rectangle` object, and that rectangle has the same value as the one you search for, it is a match. Although the meaning is trivial for seasoned C++ developers, it's still difficult to read.

A potential pitfall with such a program is that the programmer ought to take the full control of the heap where `rectangle` objects are stored. It is not always entirely clear who is responsible for managing the `rectangle` objects stored in `shapes`. In Listing 13-1, it is clear, because the code disposes of them. But if you see only the `for` loop allocating these objects, this intention is not trivial at all.

With the new C++ language that now is available in Visual Studio 2012, this program can be written in a more elegant way, as shown in Listing 13-2 (code file: `ModernCpp\ModernCpp.cpp`).

LISTING 13-2: A simple C++ program — using the new style

```cpp
// --- Create a vector of 10 rectangles
vector<shared_ptr<rectangle>> shapes;
for (int i = 1; i <= 10; i++)
{
    shapes.push_back(shared_ptr<rectangle>(
        new rectangle(i * 100, i * 200)));
}

// --- This is the rectangle we are looking for
auto searchFor = make_shared<rectangle>(300, 600);

// --- Iterate through all rectangles
for_each(begin(shapes), end(shapes), [&](shared_ptr<rectangle>& rect)
{
    rect->draw();
    if (rect && *rect == *searchFor)
    {
        cout << "*** Rectangle found." << endl;
    }
});
```

This program contains a few elements that resolve the issues noted in Listing 13-1:

➤ The `shapes` vector holds reference-counted `rectangle` objects (as is indicated by `shared_ptr`). One or more objects can hold such a pointer to a rectangle. When the last object is destroyed (which owns the pointer), the rectangle is freed.

➤ The `auto` keyword before the `searchFor` variable declaration automatically infers the type of this variable from the initialization expression. If you did not use `auto`, you should know that `make_shared<rectangle>` creates a `shared_ptr<rectangle>` and use this type instead of the `auto` keyword.

➤ The `for_each` method clearly tells that it's a loop that traverses through the items of the `shapes` vector. The first two arguments of the method are `begin(shapes)` and `end(shapes)`, respectively, making it clear that the loop goes from the first to the last element. The third argument is a lambda expression (a new feature in C++11) that draws the rectangle and checks for matching. Comparing the body of the lambda expression with Listing 13-1, you can see that here `rect` is a reference to a rectangle, and so the `*rect == *searchFor` is easier to understand than `**i == *searchFor`.

Listing 13-2 does not contain any statement to explicitly dispose of the memory held by the rectangles in `shapes`. The behavior of `shared_ptr` type reclaims the memory automatically; developers do not have to explicitly do it.

This little code snippet was just one example of the changes in C++ that make the language modern and productive. Microsoft also implemented numerous new features in its C++ compiler, according to the C++11 standard.

> **NOTE** *It's been a long time since the C++03 standard (released in 2003) was revised and the new C++11 standard was approved in August 2011. The world of software development has changed a lot, and C++ had to accommodate to these changes. Although Microsoft has not implemented all C++11 features, in Visual Studio, you can use the ones that deliver the best improvements in productivity. You can find detailed information about these features in the Visual C++ Team Blog on MSDN (*`http://blogs.msdn.com/b/vcblog/archive/2011/09/12/10209291.aspx/`*).*

C++ AND WINDOWS 8 APPS

In Chapter 3, you learned that by creating an independent stack of layered components for Windows 8 style applications, Microsoft has introduced a new concept that re-images the idea of Windows API and language run times. As shown in Figure 13-1, these components allow C++, C#, Visual Basic, and the HTML5/CSS3/JavaScript technology stack to be first-class citizens in programming Windows 8 apps.

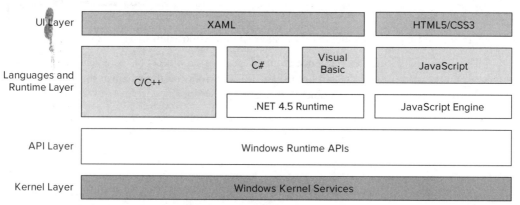

FIGURE 13-1: Windows 8 style application technology layers

Let's dive deeper into this figure and see what types of Windows 8 apps can be implemented with the direct or indirect utilization of C++.

Privileges of C++ in Windows 8 Apps

Figure 13-1 shows the four programming languages (C/C++, C#, Visual Basic, and JavaScript/HTML/CSS3) as if they were co-equal. But, in reality, C++ is "more equal" than the others. The C++ language has a few privileges in terms of accessing Windows 8 system resources that are unavailable in the other programming languages:

> ➤ You can still use a narrow set of Win32 API services (Windows Kernel Services) from C++. These do not go through Windows Runtime. They are available through system dynamic link libraries (DLLs).

➤ You can easily use DirectX technologies (Direct2D, Direct3D, DirectWrite, XAudio2, and so on) from C++. These use the graphics processing unit (GPU) and sound devices directly with amazing performance.

➤ A brand-new technology, C++ Accelerated Massive Parallelism (C++ AMP) enables you to use today's massively parallel hardware — that is, GPUs and audio processing units (APUs). C++ AMP enables you to run parts of your C++ program on the GPU in your computer.

As Figure 13-1 points out, you can use C++ entirely to write Windows 8 apps with the XAML UI. However, you have other scenarios where C++ is also a great choice:

➤ You can write Windows 8 style games that use DirectX and C++. Because most games need to squeeze out the last drops of performance that the CPU and the GPU can provide, C++ seems the perfect tool for game development.

➤ You can write hybrid Windows 8 apps that use C++ components, but are implemented either in C#, Visual Basic (of course, using .NET Framework in the back, and XAML for the UI), or in JavaScript with HTML5/CSS3 UI. In this case, C++ components can undertake those tasks that require direct system resource access and/or solid performance.

Let's take a look at how Windows Runtime and C++ work together.

Windows Runtime and C++

Almost every chapter in this book mentions Windows Runtime, and it would be difficult to avoid using its objects and operations. As you have already learned, Windows Runtime objects have been implemented in native (C++ and assembly) code. However, it has scarcely been mentioned that these objects utilize a new version of the old component object model (COM).

COM is an almost 20-year-old binary interface standard developed by Microsoft in 1993. Its original aim was to enable a wide range of programming languages to create their own dynamic objects and proffer them to other processes — even written in a different programming language. COM itself became an umbrella term that embraces other related technologies, such as distributed component object model (DCOM), Object Linking and Embedding (OLE), OLE automation, COM+, and ActiveX.

Although this binary standard is technically great, using it is often a pain, especially from C++:

➤ Objects and their interfaces must be registered in the Windows system registry, which is a main source of deployment issues.

➤ The lifetime management of COM objects is based on reference counting. When the address of an object is assigned to a new variable, a reference counter must be increased manually. When the object is detached from this variable, or the variable is disposed of, this counter must be decreased. When the counter reaches zero, the COM object is automatically disposed of. You can imagine what confusion could be caused when this manual reference counting is misused!

➤ Exceptions are handled through the HRESULT values (32-bit integers) retrieved from method calls. Callers of COM operations always must check these values to check whether operations are successful.

Now, Windows Runtime uses a new version of COM that does not require interface and object registration, and provides a transparent way to manage reference counting — as you learn in the next section.

Managing Windows Runtime Objects in C++

In Visual Studio 2012, Microsoft added new features to C++ to manage Windows Runtime objects with the ease that developers have used to handle .NET Framework objects in C# and Visual Basic. This set of new language extensions is called C++ *for Windows Runtime.*

The objects of Windows Runtime are strongly typed, and implement automatic reference counting. Instead of HRESULT values, you can use structured exception handling to catch and manage operation failures. Windows Runtime objects are deeply integrated with the STL, so all functions, collections, and algorithms implemented in the STL still work together with Windows Runtime types. There is a boundary between Windows Runtime and the external world; the new version of COM is a well-defined binary contract between these two domains. This brings up some obvious questions.

When and how should C++ programmers use these language extensions? Should they use these new types for every Windows 8 app? How can old-fashioned C++ types and the STL be used?

The answer to these questions is really simple! You should use the Windows Runtime types when you need to cross this boundary — either when you want to call Windows Runtime operations, or when you want to provide services for other languages. Figure 13-2 shows the programming style you need to follow.

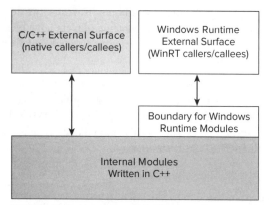

FIGURE 13-2: Using C++ with Windows Runtime objects

So, you can write a C++ module (assuming you are already a C++ programmer) just as you've been doing it, and these modules can be consumed directly by native C or C++ callers and callees. The same module can consume Windows Runtime objects or proffer operations to other Windows Runtime objects or other languages through a thin boundary layer that passes all data to and fro through Windows Runtime compatible objects.

To allow this kind of boundary crossing, C++ comes with *component extensions* (C++/CX) that provide bindings to foreign type systems such as the ones used by .NET or the JavaScript engine. Table 13-1 summarizes the new data types in C++/CX.

TABLE 13-1: New C++ Component Extensions Data Types

TYPE	DESCRIPTION
Value types	Value type instances are always stored in the call stack or in the static data of an application. Value structures (declared using the `value struct` keyword) contain only public data fields. Value classes (declared with the `value class` keyword), which are less frequently used, contain only public data fields and methods.
Reference types	Reference type instances are always allocated dynamically (and disposed of) in the memory space of the application. A reference class can be declared with the `ref class` keyword, and it can contain public, protected, and private function members; data members; and even nested classes. A reference structure is signified with the `ref struct` keyword. It is the same as a reference class, except that a `ref class` declares a runtime class that, by default, has public accessibility.
Interface classes	Interface classes (declared with the `interface class` keyword) are very similar to the native C++ interfaces. However, they have a number of specialties: ➤ All members are implicitly public. ➤ Fields and static members are not permitted. ➤ Their members can include properties, methods, and events. ➤ Types that are used as parameters can only be Windows Runtime types.
Generic types	Now you can use generic interface classes in C++ following the same semantics as generic types in the .NET Framework. They are declared with the `generic<typename T1, …, typename Tn> interface class` construct. Generic interfaces can be implemented with C++ template definitions, too. However, these templates can use only `typename` parameters. Non-type parameters are not supported.
Properties	The standard C++ does not support properties. With the `property` keyword of the C++/CX, now you can define a property with the same GET/SET semantics as used by the .NET languages.
Delegates	Delegates declare type-safe function pointers, and so they resemble a function declaration, except that a delegate is a type. They are declared with the `delegate` keyword.
Events	Events are special types (you may call them "delegate properties") that have add/remove semantics just as .NET events have. They are declared with the `event` keyword. In addition to the add/remove semantics, they contain a *raise accessor* that defines the way an event is signed.

As you learned earlier, Windows Runtime types are COM types, and so they are inherently reference counted. To avoid the manual work of managing reference counters, there is a special notation for pointers referencing Windows Runtime types. They use the ^ ("hat" or "handle") character to signify they are reference counted, and they must be allocated with the `ref new` keyword, as this sample code snippet shows:

```
Map<String^, int>^ MainPage::CreateMap()
{
    map<String^, int> myMap;
    myMap.insert(pair<String^, int>("One", 1));
    myMap.insert(pair<String^, int>("Two", 2));
    myMap.insert(pair<String^, int>("Three", 3));
    return ref new Map<String^, int>(move(myMap));
}
```

Here, the `CreateMap()` method creates an associative dictionary of integer values with string keys. Both `Map` and `String` are Windows Runtime types. The method returns a reference-counted pointer to a `Map`, so the `ref new` operator is used, and the return value has the `^` notation. Also, the keys of the map use reference-counted pointers to a `String`, so these are declared as `String^`.

> **NOTE** The `^` notation and the `ref new` keyword are simple compiler tricks. Without these notations, the programmer would have to increment and decrement the reference counter of COM (Windows Runtime) objects. Now, with these extensions, the compiler undertakes all these challenges and generates the appropriate code. Note that you cannot use the `*` (pointer) notation with a Windows Runtime object. If you try, the compiler will raise an error message.

Defining Runtime Classes

When writing Windows 8 apps in C++, in addition to consuming Windows Runtime objects, you create Windows Runtime types. For example, the application and its pages are also represented with these runtime classes. From the implementation point of view, these should be reference classes with a few restrictions, as this code snippet shows:

```
public ref class Customer sealed
{
public:
    Customer(String^ firstName, String^ LastName);
    Customer(String^ lastName);
    property String^ FullName
    {
        String^ get();
    }
    void MarkAsKeyAccount();
    ~Customer();
private:
    std::wstring m_firstName;
    std::wstring m_LastName;
};
```

The runtime classes must be marked with the `public` modifier so that they can be consumed by external applications and other languages. Although the parameters and return values of function members can be any arbitrary C++ types, public members can use only Windows Runtime types. You also must apply the `sealed` keyword to prevent derivation from these classes.

> **NOTE** The `public` keyword in the class definition also forces the compiler to put the metadata (about public functions and data members) into the `.winmd` file exposed to the external world. If you do not remember what a `.winmd` file is, refer to Chapter 3 (in the, "Metadata Format," section) to refresh your knowledge. In Chapter 14, you learn how to create and consume `.winmd` files. You can omit the `sealed` modifier, but, in this case, the compiler will issue a warning telling you that the runtime type won't be consumable from JavaScript, because it is not marked `sealed`.

You can instantiate your own runtime class with the `ref new` operator, just like any other Windows Runtime class:

```
Customer^ myCustomer = ref new Customer("John", "Doe");
```

Using a runtime class as a simple local variable also provides automatic life-cycle management:

```
{
    Customer myOtherCustomer("Jane", "Doe");
    myOtherCustomer.MarkAsKeyAccount();
    // ...
    // Process customer data, i.e. query it, modify it, etc.
    // ...
}   // ~Customer() is automatically invoked
```

In this code snippet, `myOtherCustomer` is a local variable. The compiler manages its life cycle, and automatically destroys it, as soon as the variable exits its scope. In this case, the `~Customer()` destructor is invoked when the control flow of the application leaves the statement block.

Exceptions

Managing COM exceptions was a laborious task, because COM operations returned HRESULT error codes. For example, when you passed a wrong argument to an operation, an HRESULT value with E_INVALIDARG code was retrieved. If you did not check the return value for this code and allowed the program to flow ahead, sooner or later you might have caused an application crash.

Windows Runtime still uses COM, but now it also allows structured exception handling. Instead of dealing with HRESULT codes directly, you can now catch and handle exceptions that represent the HRESULT codes. Table 13-2 shows these COM-specific exception types with the HRESULT codes they represent.

TABLE 13-2: Windows Runtime Exceptions with Related HRESULT Codes

EXCEPTION TYPE	HRESULT CODE
InvalidArgumentException	E_INVALIDARG
NotImplementedException	E_NOTIMPL
AccessDeniedException	E_ACCESSDENIED
NullReferenceException	E_POINTER
InvalidCastException	E_NOINTERFACE
FailureException	E_FAIL
OutOfBoundsException	E_BOUNDS
ChangedStateException	E_CHANGED_STATE
ClassNotRegisteredException	REGBD_E_CLASSNOTREG
DisconnectedException	E_DISCONNECTED
OperationCanceledException	E_ABORT
OutOfMemoryException	E_OUTOFMEMORY

> **NOTE** You can find all these exceptions in the `Platform` namespace.

You do not need to care about how HRESULT codes are wrapped into exceptions; the runtime environment does it for you. If you want to handle potential issues with using Windows Runtime objects, you can follow this pattern:

```
void MyWIndowsRTOperation(String^ parameter1, int parameter2)
{
    OtherRuntimeObject^ otherObj = ref new OtherObj();
    try
    {
        otherObj->SimpleOperation(parameter1);
        // ...
        otherObj->AnotherOperation(parameter2);
        // ...
        otherObj->CompountOperation(parameter1, parameter2)
        // ...
    }
    catch (NotImpelentedException^ ex)
    {
        // Respond to the issues when an operation is not implemented
    }
    catch (InvalidArgumentException^ ex)
```

```
    {
        // Log that the operation was invalid
        throw ex;
    }
    catch (COMException^ ex)
    {
        // Examine ex->HResult values and decide what to do
    }
    catch (...)
    {
        // Decide what to do with any other exceptions
    }
}
```

The first two catch blocks handle a specific COM exception. The third catch block accepts a pointer to a COMException instance. Because all exception types in Table 13-2 derive from COMException, this block catches all of them except NotImplementedException and InvalidArgumentException, because these two are handled with the previous catch blocks. In this block, you can examine the HResult property of the exception instance to decide how to go on. The fourth catch block traps any other exceptions. In this pattern, you can see that the most-specific exceptions are always caught first, and the least-specific ones at the end.

Because these exceptions derive from COMException, you might be tempted to create your own COM-specific exception with your own failure code by inheriting a new class from COMException. Well, because of internal implementation details, it will not work. In this case, you need to raise a COMException and pass the HRESULT code to the constructor, as shown in this code snippet:

```
    void MyOperation(int param)
    {
        if (param == 0)
        {
            throw ref new COMException(MY_ERROR_CODE);
        }
        // ...
    }
    // ...

    try
    {
        // ...
        MyOperation(0);
        // ...
    }
    catch (COMException^ ex)
    {
        if (ex->HResult == MY_ERROR_CODE)
        {
            // Handle your own error code
        }
        // ...
    }
```

The `COMException` instance can be caught only in the `catch (COMException^ ex)` branch. Even if you raise a `COMException` instance with a known failure code that has a corresponding exception class in Table 13-2, you cannot catch it with that exception, only with `COMException`:

```
try
{
    // ...
    throw ref new COMException(E_FAIL)
    // ...
}
catch (FailureException^ ex)
{
    // The COMException above cannot be caught here
}
catch (COMException^ ex)
{
    if (ex->HResult == E_FAIL)
    {
        // This is where to handle the COMException above
    }
}
```

You've now learned enough about C++ and Windows 8 apps. It's time to try out these features with Visual Studio.

DISCOVERING C++ FEATURES WITH VISUAL STUDIO

Visual Studio provides great support for C++ applications. You can find all important productivity enhancement tools in the IDE, just like for the other programming languages. In this section, you learn a few things about creating and editing C++ applications. You also get to know some new C++ features.

In the previous chapters, you learned some important things about creating a Windows 8 application UI, so, in this section, you start with a prepared sample, and add new code snippets to that application in each exercise. Before you start to play with the sample, let's have a look at creating C++ projects.

Creating C++ Projects

You can create C++ programs in Visual Studio with the File ⇨ New Project command (Ctrl+Shift+N), just as you already learned. Of course, you need to select the Visual C++ node under Templates, as shown in Figure 13-3. In the middle of this figure you can see the types of Windows 8 style templates supported by C++ in Visual Studio 2012 Express for Windows 8.

> **NOTE** *The other (non-free) editions of Visual Studio 2012 contain additional C++ project templates to create desktop applications and components.*

C++ supports the same standard Windows 8 application templates as the other languages (Blank Application, Grid Application, and Split Application), and a few additional ones, as described here:

➤ **Blank Dynamic-Link Library** — Use this project type to create a library that is compiled into a .dll file. Although this library has the same extension as .NET component library assemblies, it's in native code, so you cannot reference it from C# or Visual Basic projects.

➤ **Blank Static Library** — With this project type, you can compile libraries with a .lib extension. You can link these libraries statically with executable files of your other projects.

➤ **Unit Test Library** — As the name of this template suggests, you can create unit test projects for your C++ applications and libraries.

➤ **WinRT Component DLL** — This project type enables you to create native Windows Runtime components that can be referenced from any other languages. In addition to the component library, this project creates a .winmd file that contains metadata information about your public classes.

➤ **Direct2D Application and Direct3D Application** — These templates help you to start creating applications using the Direct2D and Direct3D technologies, respectively.

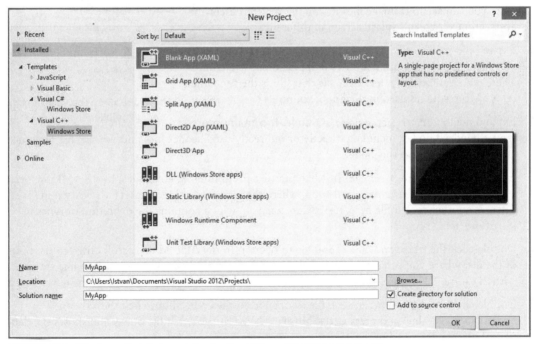

FIGURE 13-3: Windows 8 style templates for the C++ programming language

To specify the attributes of your projects, the New Project dialog box provides you with the same options (for example, solution and application name, location, and solution creation mode) as the other programming languages.

Elements of a C++ Project

To examine the elements of a project, you use the CppDemo Start solution, which you can find in the Chapter13.zip download. The structure of a C++ project is very similar to the one created with other programming languages. However, slight differences exist, as you learn from the next exercise.

TRY IT OUT Examining the Elements of a C++ Project

To examine the structure of a simple C++ project, follow these steps:

1. With the File ⇨ Open Project (Ctrl+Shift+O) command, open the CppDemo.sln file from the CppDemo Start folder of this chapter's download. In a few seconds, the solution loads into the IDE, and its structure is displayed in the Solution Explorer window, as shown in Figure 13-4.

2. Under the Solution 'CppDemo' node, you will find the CppDemo project node (this solution contains only one project). Click the small triangle to the left of the Assets folder to expand its content. You can see four image files in Assets that represent the application's logo and splash screen in different sizes.

3. Expand the Common folder. It contains various C++ and header files that are part of your Windows 8 application's skeleton. There is a StandardStyles.xaml file that holds the fundamental XAML resources used in the application.

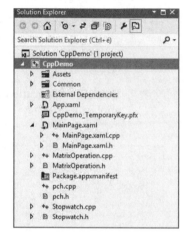

FIGURE 13-4: The CppDemo project in Solution Explorer

4. Expand the External Dependencies node. It contains more than a hundred nodes, including directly or indirectly used header files and .winmd file references in your project. Collapse this node.

5. Expand the MainPage.xaml file. Just like in other programming languages, this XAML file nests a code-behind file, MainPage.xaml.cpp, where the .cpp extension suggests it's written in C++. There is another nested file here, MainPage.xaml.h, which contains the definition of types in MainPage.xaml.cpp.

6. Double-click the MainPage.xaml.cpp file to open it. In the code editor, scroll down to the bottom of the file, where you can see several methods with an empty body and a comment line starting with "Feature." These are the placeholders of the code you are going to write in the next exercises.

7. Double-click the MainPage.xaml.h file to open it. In the code editor, click the #include "MainPage.g.h" line and press Ctrl+Shift+G. The MainPage.g.h file opens and shows the definition of objects described in the MainPage.xaml file.

8. Use the Debug ⇨ Start Without Debugging command (Ctrl+F5) to build and immediately start the application. It takes a few seconds to compile and link the project files, and then the application starts with the screen shown in Figure 13-5.

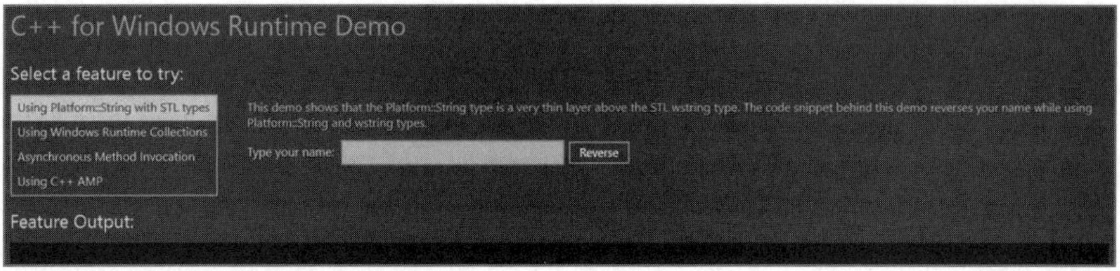

FIGURE 13-5: The CppDemo application in action

9. Now you can select an item from the feature list to display the specified scenario's input panel to the right of the list. In this initial version of the project, all buttons are non-functional.

10. Close the application by pressing Alt+F4.

How It Works

While examining the structure of the CppDemo project, you may recognize that is very similar to projects created with other programming languages, although folders have different names.

C++ has a very tight integration with XAML. As you discovered in Step 5, MainPage.xaml has code-behind files. The MainPage.xaml.cpp file is there for you to create your code, and the MainPage.g.h file is automatically generated every time you modify and save the MainPage.xaml file. Behind the scenes, the IDE generates a MainPage.xaml.hpp file that initializes your components when constructing the MainPage object.

When you started the CppDemo application in Step 9 after building it, the IDE also created the deployment package of the app (using the Pakage.appmanifest file) and installed it, just as you already experienced with other applications in the exercises shown in previous chapters.

You are now ready to modify this simple C++ application.

Using the Platform::String type

To provide a way to pass character strings to Windows Runtime components, and retrieve strings from Windows Runtime operations, Microsoft created a new String type that is located in the Platform namespace. This new type is a very thin wrapper type that enables the construction of immutable string objects with a few operations. The great thing about this type is that it totally cooperates with the STL's wstring type, as you learn in the next exercise.

> **NOTE** *If you are not a C++ programmer, you should know that C++ uses the* :: *scope-resolution operator to separate the namespace and type elements. So, the qualified type name of Windows Runtime's* String *class is* Platform::String, *because it is declared in the* Platform *namespace.*

Using the Platform::String Type

To get acquainted with the `Platform::String` type, follow these steps:

1. Open the `CppDemo` solution from the `CppDemo   Start` folder, unless it is still open in the Visual Studio IDE.

2. In Solution Explorer, double-click the `MainPage.xaml.cpp` file (expand the `MainPage.xaml` node if it is collapsed), and locate the `ReverseStringButton_Tapped` method with an empty body.

3. Insert the following boldfaced code into the method body:

`C++`

```cpp
void MainPage::ReverseStringButton_Tapped(Object^ sender, TappedRoutedEventArgs^ e)
{
    String^ yourName = YourName->Text;
    Feature1OutputText->Text += "Your name: " + yourName + "\n";
    wstring inputString(yourName->Data());
    wstring reverseString(inputString.rbegin(), inputString.rend());
    String^ yourReversedName = ref new String(reverseString.c_str());
    Feature1OutputText->Text += "Reversed: " + yourReversedName + "\n";
}
```

In this code, `yourName` is a reference-counted pointer (as the ^ indicates) that is set to the content of the `YourName` text box. You can use this variable to concatenate it with string literals because of the + operators declared by the `String` class, and set the `Text` property of the `Feature1OutputText` block.

4. Run the application by pressing Ctrl+F5. In the feature list, the first item is selected. Type your name (or any other text) into the text box and click the Reverse button. The Feature output writes out the text in reverse order. For example:

```
Your name: My nickame is DeepDiver
Reversed: reviDpeeD si emankcin yM
```

5. Close the application.

How It Works

You can use the `String` type directly with other Windows Runtime types, including XAML controls. This is how the code snippet set the content of the `Feature1OutputText` variable. However, `String` implements only a few operations. Whenever you want to carry out more complex operations, you can use the STL's `wstring` type in connection with `String`. To set up its initial content, `inputString` in the previous code snippet (it is a `wstring`) uses the `String::Data()` method to obtain a pointer to a C++ null-terminated string.

In the next line, `reverseString` uses the `wstring` constructor that iterates through a range of characters to create its content. Thanks to the `rbegin()` and `rend()` methods, this iterator traverses from the last character of the string to the first one, so it constructs the reverse of the original string. To write back the reversed string to the output, you need a `String^` instance. The `yourReversedName` variable instantiates a new `String` (with the `ref new` operator), and uses the `c_str()` method to obtain the content of the `reverseString` variable.

This type of cooperation between Windows Runtime types and STL types is a common pattern. You can use Windows Runtime collections together with STL collections in a similar way, as you learn in the next exercise.

Using Runtime Collections

The C++ STL defines a number of collections with a plethora of related operations. Moreover, as you learned earlier from Table 13-1, C++11 adds new collection types to the STL. You can use the STL collections everywhere, but you cannot pass them to Windows Runtime objects directly.

The solution is to use the Windows Runtime collections that are found in the `Platform::Collections` namespace. In the next exercise, you learn to utilize the `Vector` and the `VectorView` collections.

TRY IT OUT **Using the Vector and VectorView Collections**

To learn how to use these collection classes, follow these steps:

1. Open the `CppDemo` solution from the `CppDemo   Start` folder, unless it is still open in the Visual Studio IDE.

2. In Solution Explorer, double-click the `MainPage.xaml.cpp` file, and locate the `CreateRandomVector()` method that returns `nullptr`.

3. Insert the following boldfaced code into the method body:

```
col::Vector<int>^ MainPage::CreateRandomVector()
{
    vector<int> myNumbers;
    srand((unsigned)time(0));
    for (int i = 0; i < 10; i++)
    {
        myNumbers.push_back(rand()%100 + 1);
    }
    return ref new col::Vector<int>(move(myNumbers));
}
```

This method uses a `for` loop to set up a `vector<int>` collection — it is declared in the STL — with random numbers. The `return` statement in the last code line creates a new `Vector<int>` collection that uses the `move` method to take the ownership of the random vector.

4. Locate the `SumAVectorButton_Tapped` method and copy the following boldfaced code into its body:

```
void MainPage::SumAVectorButton_Tapped(Object^ sender, TappedRoutedEventArgs^ e)
{
    wstringstream streamVal;
    WFC::IVectorView<int>^ vv = CreateRandomVector()->GetView();
    int sum = 0;
    int index = 0;
    for_each(begin(vv), end(vv), [&](int value)
    {
```

```
            streamVal << "Number " << ++index << " is " << value << endl;
            sum += value;
        });
        streamVal << "Sum of these values is " << sum;
        Feature2OutputText->Text = ref new String(streamVal.str().c_str());
    }
```

This method invokes `CreateRandomVector()` and uses its `GetView()` method that creates a snapshot of the random vector. The `for` loop summarizes the elements of this view, and writes them to the `streamVal` stream. When the sum is calculated, the stream's content is sent to the `FeatureOutput2Text` block that displays the output of this exercise.

5. Run the application by pressing Ctrl+F5. In the feature list, select the Using Windows Runtime Collections item and click or tap the "Sum Up a Vector" button.

6. In the output pane, the program displays a random vector and the sum of its elements. Close the application.

How It Works

The `CreateRandomVector()` operation uses the STL's `vector` class to generate its values, and wraps it into a `Vector` object only when returning the values. The `SumAVectorButton_Tapped` method wants to read the values of this vector without changing them, so it uses a `VectorView` object (that implements the `IVectorView` interface). The `WFC` identifier is an alias for the `Windows::Foundation::Collections` namespace defined at the beginning of the `MainPage.xaml.cpp` file.

In the last code line, you can also see a good example of using the `String` class. All the output in this exercise was written into the `streamVal` string stream. In the last line, it was converted to a `String` so that it could be assigned to the output text block.

> **NOTE** *Windows Runtime defines a relatively small set of collection classes, each living and acting together with the STL collection classes. You can find a list of them on the MSDN web page at* `http://msdn.microsoft.com/en-us/library/windows/apps/hh710418(v=vs.110).aspx`*.*

Using Asynchronous Operations

In previous chapters, you saw many examples using asynchronous method calls. In C#, the new `async` and `await` keywords performed magic with the compiler, and enabled you to consume asynchronous methods as if they were synchronous — while keeping the UI responsive. In JavaScript, you can use the Common JavaScript Promises pattern, as you learned in in Chapter 5.

Well, C++ does not have such a compiler trick like C#, but it has a great component, the Parallel Pattern Library (PPL), which helps you to invoke asynchronous operations with a relatively simple pattern, as you learn in the next exercise.

TRY IT OUT **Writing to a File Asynchronously**

To create a simple text file with a short text message asynchronously, follow these steps:

1. Open the CppDemo solution from the CppDemo Start folder, unless it is still open in the Visual Studio IDE.

2. In Solution Explorer, double-click the MainPage.xaml.cpp file, and locate the WriteFileButton_Tapped method.

3. Insert the following boldfaced code into the method body:

```cpp
void MainPage::WriteFileButton_Tapped(Object^ sender, TappedRoutedEventArgs^ e)
{
    Feature3OutputText->Text += "File creation has been started.\n";
    StorageFolder^ documentsFolder = KnownFolders::DocumentsLibrary;

    // --- Start file creation
    task<StorageFile^> createTask(documentsFolder->CreateFileAsync(
        "MySample.txt", CreationCollisionOption::ReplaceExisting));
    createTask.then([this](StorageFile^ file)
    {
        Feature3OutputText->Text += "File " + file->Name + " has been created.\n";
        // --- Start writing into the file
        task<void> writeTask(FileIO::WriteTextAsync(file, YourMessage->Text));
        writeTask.then([this](void)
        {
            Feature3OutputText->Text += "Text '" + YourMessage->Text +
                "' has been written to the file.\n";
        });
    });
}
```

This code snippet chains two asynchronous operations: createTask that creates the MySample.txt file, and writeTask that outputs the message specified by the user. Each task uses its then method with a lambda expression to define the continuation of the particular task.

4. Run the application by pressing Ctrl+F5. In the feature list, select the Asynchronous Method Invocation item. Type a message into the text box, and click (or tap) the "Write Message to File" button.

6. In the output pane, the program displays a few lines of output telling you that the file has been created and the message has been written.

7. Start Windows Explorer and select the Documents node under Libraries. Locate the MySample.txt file, and double-click to open it. You can check that the message is really written there.

8. Return to the running CppDemo application and close it.

How It Works

The code in this exercise uses the task<TResult> template to create and start an asynchronous task, where TResult is the type of the result the task is expected to retrieve. The argument of the task is an object implementing the IAsyncOperation<TResult> interface.

`createTask` uses the `CreateFileAsync` operation that retrieves a `StorageFile^` object. `writeTask` invokes the `WriteTextAsync` operation that does not retrieve any object. These tasks are chained — the continuation (the `then` method) of `createTask` instantiates the `writeTask` with the `file` result of `createTask`.

You can see that the lambda expressions in continuation methods capture the `this` pointer, and so they access all UI elements. This is how these methods write messages to the output pane.

> **NOTE** *You can use several asynchronous patterns with C++. For more information, see* `http://msdn.microsoft.com/en-us/library/windows/apps/` `hh780559.aspx`.

Using Accelerated Massive Parallelism

Most computers contain not only a CPU, but also a very high-performance GPU and other processing units (such as APUs). Many operations can be executed much faster on these units, because they have special architecture that allows a high level of concurrency of special operations. Microsoft's C++ Accelerated Massive Parallelism (AMP) is an open specification implementing data parallelism directly in C++.

The Direct2D and Direct3D technologies use the GPU for rendering complex graphics. GPUs have an architecture that can process pixels and vectors in a very fast way. They can carry out many operations simultaneously. You can use this power not only to draw graphics, but also for processing data. C++ AMP is a technology that extends C++ with its own library and a compiler that is able to generate code that executes on GPUs and other accelerator units.

> **NOTE** *It is far beyond the scope of this book to discuss C++ AMP in detail. If you are interested, you can find more details on MSDN. Start your discovery at* `http://msdn.microsoft.com/en-us/library/hh265137(v=vs.110)`.

You can use C++ AMP in Windows 8 apps, as you learn in the next exercise. In this exercise you multiply float-number matrices with 1,000 rows and 1,000 lines. This is a complex operation because of the size of matrices. For calculating the 1 million cells altogether, this operation requires 1,000 multiplications of float-number pairs, and then summing up the result of these multiplications. In total, this results in 2 billion operations.

In the next exercise you implement this operation both with the traditional sequential algorithm and with C++ AMP.

> **NOTE** *You can refresh your knowledge about matrix multiplication by reading the article at* `http://en.wikipedia.org/wiki/Matrix_multiplication`.

TRY IT OUT Using C++ AMP in Windows 8 Apps

To compare the sequential and C++ AMP matrix multiplication algorithms, follow these steps:

1. Open the CppDemo solution from the CppDemo Start folder, unless it is still open in the Visual Studio IDE.

2. In Solution Explorer, double-click the MainPage.xaml.cpp file and fill up the body of the CalculateSerialButton_Tapped method with the following boldfaced code:

```C++
void MainPage::CalculateSerialButton_Tapped(Object^ sender,
    TappedRoutedEventArgs^ e)
{
    Feature4OutputText->Text += "Sequential matrix multiplication started...\n";
    CalculateSerialButton->IsEnabled = false;
    MatrixOperation matrixOp;
    task<unsigned long long> matrixTask (matrixOp.MultiplyMatrixSeriallyAsync());
    matrixTask.then([this](unsigned long long elapsed)
    {
        CalculateSerialButton->IsEnabled = true;
        wstringstream streamVal;
        streamVal << "Sequential operation executed in " << elapsed << "ms.\n";
        Feature4OutputText->Text += ref new String(streamVal.str().c_str());
    });
}
```

3. Copy the following boldfaced code into the body of the CalculateWithAMPButton_Tapped method:

```C++
void MainPage::CalculateWithAMPButton_Tapped(Object^ sender,
    TappedRoutedEventArgs^ e)
{
    Feature4OutputText->Text += "AMP matrix multiplication started...\n";
    CalculateWithAmpButton->IsEnabled = false;
    MatrixOperation matrixOp;
    task<unsigned long long> matrixTask (matrixOp.MultiplyMatrixWithAMPAsync());
    matrixTask.then([this](unsigned long long elapsed)
    {
        CalculateWithAmpButton->IsEnabled = true;
        wstringstream streamVal;
        streamVal << "AMP operation executed in " << elapsed << "ms.\n";
        Feature4OutputText->Text += ref new String(streamVal.str().c_str());
    });
}
```

4. In Solution Explorer, double-click the MatrixOperation.cpp file, and fill up the body of the MultiplySequential method with the following boldfaced code that uses the sequential approach:

```C++
void MatrixOperation::MultiplySequential(vector<float>& vC,
    const vector<float>& vA, const vector<float>& vB,
```

```
        int M, int N, int W)
{
    for (int row = 0; row < M; row++)
    {
      for (int col = 0; col < N; col++)
      {
        float sum = 0.0f;
        for(int i = 0; i < W; i++)
          sum += vA[row * W + i] * vB[i * N + col];
        vC[row * N + col] = sum;
      }
    }
}
```

5. Copy the following boldfaced code into the body of the `MultiplyAMP` method:

```
void MatrixOperation::MultiplyAMP(vector<float>& vC,
    const vector<float>& vA, const vector<float>& vB,
    int M, int N, int W)
{
    concurrency::array_view<const float,2> a(M, W, vA);
    concurrency::array_view<const float,2> b(W, N, vB);
    concurrency::array_view<float,2> c(M, N, vC);
    c.discard_data();
    concurrency::parallel_for_each(c.extent,
    [=](concurrency::index<2> idx) restrict(amp) {
      int row = idx[0]; int col = idx[1];
      float sum = 0.0f;
      for(int i = 0; i < W; i++)
        sum += a(row, i) * b(i, col);
      c[idx] = sum;
    });
}
```

6. Build and start the application by pressing Ctrl+F5. In the feature list, select the Using C++ AMP item, and click or tap the Multiply Matrices Sequentially button. Depending on your computer's performance, it will take about 5 to 20 seconds before you get a message about the successful operation that indicates the execution time.

7. Now, click or tap the "Multiply Matrices with C++ AMP" button. This operation will take less time, as you can see from the message. Depending on your computer and GPU, it should be about 10 to 25 times faster than the sequential execution.

8. Close the application.

> **NOTE** You can find the complete code to download for this exercise on this book's companion website at www.wrox.com in the CppDemo Complete folder.

How It Works

The code you created in Step 2 and Step 3 is quite simple — in relation to the techniques you learned in the previous exercises. These code snippets call the serial and AMP-based matrix multiplication in an asynchronous way. The lion's share of the work is done by the `MultiplySequential` and `MultiplyAMP` methods of the `MatrixOperation` class, which you created in Step 4 and Step 5.

Both methods represent matrices with flat vectors. The `MultiplySequential` method works totally according to the simplest matrix multiplication algorithm; it does not require further explanation.

However, `MultiplyAMP` is different. It is not really straightforward at first sight. The first three lines define that the `vA`, `vB`, and `vC` vectors should be managed on the GPU as two-dimensional float arrays (matrices), through the `a`, `b`, and `c` variables, respectively:

```
concurrency::array_view<const float,2> a(M, W, vA);
concurrency::array_view<const float,2> b(W, N, vB);
concurrency::array_view<float,2> c(M, N, vC);
```

The `array_view` type is responsible for managing the data movement between the CPU and the GPU. The `c.discard_data()` method declares that the `c` matrix on the GPU should not be copied back to the `vC` vector. The next two lines declare the `parallel_for_each` construct to be executed on the GPU with a lambda expression:

```
concurrency::parallel_for_each(c.extent,
[=](concurrency::index<2> idx) restrict(amp) {
```

It declares that this parallel loop should go through all the cells of the `c` matrix (`c.extent`), and within the loop's body the current cell is identified with the `idx` index that has two dimensions (the row and the column index of a matrix cell). The `restrict(amp)` clause tells the compiler two things. First, the body of the loop should be compiled to code that can run on AMP-compatible hardware (for example, a GPU with DirectX11 driver). Second, only those statements and constructs are allowed in the body that can be managed by AMP. For example, you cannot open files in the loop body, because this operation is not viable on the GPU. The body of the loop simply calculates the cell value referenced with `idx`.

The great thing is that this parallel construct lets the DirectX11 driver and the GPU decide about the level of the concurrency. For example, if the GPU supports 128 independent processing channels, 128 cell values can be calculated simultaneously.

SUMMARY

C++ is a co-equal programming language with the others (C#, Visual Basic, and JavaScript) when creating Windows 8 apps. Because of new devices such as tablets, smartphones, and ultra-mobile computers, C++ has experienced a renaissance — sort of. These devices have less powerful CPUs and GPUs than desktop computers, and they also must be frugal with their batteries, while user expectations (most importantly, the responsiveness of the UI) are very high. Application performance is a key in these devices. The lower-level constructs of C++ and its capability leverage underlying hardware capabilities directly, which makes C++ the best programming language for these new devices.

In the past, C++ never had greater productivity than other (especially managed) languages. However, the C++11 standard added new features to the language that made it cleaner, faster, and more robust. To make it a first-class citizen for Windows 8 app development, Microsoft extended the language with new features. These provide seamless integration with Windows Runtime, and new constructs (such as generics, value, reference types, and so on) make C++ as strong as managed languages.

C++ has some unique features in Windows 8 app development. It can use DirectX technologies, and create Windows 8 apps that leverage Direct2D, Direct3D, DirectWrite, and XAudio2, among others. Microsoft created a new technology for leveraging hardware-accelerated devices such as GPUs and APUs, called C++ AMP, which can be accessed only from C++.

In Chapter 14, you learn advanced techniques that help you create hybrid applications (apps with mixed programming languages) and perform often-used chores, such as running background tasks or managing network status changes.

EXERCISES

1. Why does the C++ programming language have such an important role in mobile Windows 8 style application development?

2. Which new C++ feature allows converting functors into anonymous functions with state management?

3. What is the role of the ^ (hat) operator?

4. Which operator can you use to create reference-counted Windows Runtime types?

5. How can you mix the types declared in the C++ Standard Template Library (STL) with the Windows Runtime types?

6. What technology would you use to create a very fast C++ function to invert the colors of a large bitmap?

> **NOTE** You can find answers to the exercises in Appendix A.

▶ WHAT YOU LEARNED IN THIS CHAPTER

TOPIC	KEY CONCEPTS
C++11	The latest major revision of the C++ standard is C++11, approved by ISO/IEC on August 12, 2011.
auto keyword	This new feature of C++11 implements an automatic type deduction, provided that an explicit initializer is given. The compiler infers the type of the variable from the initialization value.
Smart pointers in C++11	C++11 deprecates the `auto_ptr`, and introduces three new smart pointers: `unique_ptr` (sole ownership of an object), `shared_ptr` (shared ownership of an object), and `weak_ptr` (non-owning reference to an object).
Rvalue references	C++11 uses the `&&` notation to bind rvalue (right-hand side value) references to identifiers.
Move semantics	C++11 introduces move semantics to improve the performance in such situations where a large amount of data should be copied between caller and callee methods. Move semantics allow moving the ownership of the data instead of the data itself.
Lambda functions	Lambda functions are anonymous functions that allow capturing variables from the enclosing scope of the expression.
C++ for Windows Runtime	In Visual Studio 2012, Microsoft added new features to C++ in order to manage Windows Runtime objects with the ease that developers are used to in the .NET Framework. This set of new language extensions is called C++ for Windows Runtime.
C++Component Extensions	Microsoft provides C++ Component Extensions (C++/CX) to provide bindings to foreign type systems, such as the ones used by .NET or the JavaScript engine.
Reference counter management	Windows Runtime types are COM types and so inherently they are reference counted. There is a special notation for pointers referencing Windows Runtime types. The `^` ("hat" or "handle") character signifies that they are reference counted, and they must be allocated with the `ref new` keyword. Using `^` and `ref new`, the compiler takes over the responsibility of managing reference counting and object disposal automatically.
COM exceptions	Windows Runtime still uses COM, but now it also allows structured exception handling. Instead of dealing with `HRESULT` codes directly, you can now catch and handle exceptions representing those `HRESULT` codes.

TOPIC	KEY CONCEPTS
Creating C++ projects in Visual Studio	Use the File ⇨ New Project command (Ctrl+Shift+N) and select Visual C++ node under Templates to list the available C++ templates. Set the solution properties, and click OK to create the selected project.
`Platform::String`	This Windows Runtime type is a very thin wrapper around the STL's `wstring` type, and it is used to pass reference-counted immutable string values crossing the Windows Runtime boundary.
Windows Runtime Collections	You can use these types to pass reference-counted collections crossing the Windows Runtime boundary. They can be used in cooperation with the STL's standard collection types.
Parallel Pattern Library (PPL)	This library provides useful types to implement asynchronous operations in C++, using the task pattern with continuations.
C++ AMP	Accelerated Massive Parallelism (AMP) is a unique feature of C++. It is able to use hardware-accelerated devices (such as GPUs and APUs) to execute programs written in C++. It may provide a great performance boost for methods running on these devices.

14

Advanced Programming Concepts

WHAT YOU WILL LEARN IN THIS CHAPTER:

➤ Understanding the scenarios in which solutions using more than one programming language (hybrid solutions) are advantageous

➤ Getting acquainted with the role and implementation of background tasks in Windows 8

➤ Learning how to query for the capabilities of internal and external input devices connected to your computer

WROX.COM CODE DOWNLOADS FOR THIS CHAPTER

You can find the wrox.com code downloads for this chapter on the Download Code tab at www.wrox.com/remtitle.cgi?isbn=012680. The code is in the Chapter14.zip download and individually named, as described in the corresponding exercises.

As the title suggests, in this chapter you learn several concepts that enable you to develop more advanced Windows 8 apps. By now, you should be familiar with all four Windows 8 languages (C++, C#, Visual Basic, and JavaScript). In previous chapters, you used them as exclusive choices to implement apps. Here you learn how you can mix these languages to provide an optimal solution in terms of productivity, user experience, and performance.

In Windows 8, for the sake of providing the best available user experience, only the application in the foreground receives resources from the system. Applications in the background (that is, suspended apps) cannot run code. However, in some situations even the suspended apps should have a connection with the external world, such as checking new e-mails, downloading information from the Internet, and so on. Windows 8 provides the concept of background tasks, as described in this chapter.

Windows 8 supports many input devices. A great app is prepared to use different input devices, depending on availability, device features, and on the user's choice. In this chapter, you learn how to query about input device capabilities so that you'll be able to provide the best user experience in your apps.

BUILDING SOLUTIONS WITH MULTIPLE LANGUAGES

In previous chapters, you learned about peculiarities for each Windows 8 programming language. You already know that HTML and JavaScript are great for utilizing your existing web programming knowledge. C# and Visual Basic are great with XAML, especially if you already have Silverlight and/or Windows Presentation Foundation (WPF) experience. C++ is about performance and direct access to system resources.

When you're about to design an application and prepare the development project, one of your most important decisions is the choice of a programming language. It is often difficult to choose the best trade-off when selecting the right language for a certain application, because you have multiple choices. For example, say that you would like to create a web-page like application and use your HTML/JavaScript knowledge, but you still have a large amount of the existing codebase written in C#. Or, say that you must create a very fast algorithm with a great user interface (UI), and you know C# and XAML, but you guess C++ Accelerated Massive Parallelism (AMP) would provide the best solution.

Well, you are not tied to a single programming language when creating Windows 8 apps! You can create solutions that allow the mixing of programming languages. If you have an existing codebase, you can reuse it with minimal effort. You can decompose your application into components, and you can use different programming languages for each of them. Visual Studio 2012 supports the mixed-language model.

Hybrid Solutions

Solutions using multiple programming languages are often referred as *hybrid solutions*. A Visual Studio hybrid solution contains at least two projects with two different programming languages. Of course, a single Visual Studio project may use only one programming language, because the project is the smallest physical compilation unit. However, each project can use already built binary components that can be created with another language.

An application generally can be decomposed into software layers. Following is one possible separation:

> ➤ **The UI layer of the application** — This layer is responsible for rendering and displaying the UI, and allowing user interactions (including navigation).

> ➤ **The application logic layer** — This layer implements the logic (workflows, algorithms, and rules) of your application, generally using a more detailed component model.

> ➤ **Data and service access layer** — This layer provides access to the data and services used by your app. Either data or services can belong to your application, or can be provided by third parties.

> ➤ **Device access layer** — In certain cases, you must access special devices (such as bar-code readers, security devices, special hardware, and so on) from your application.

You can choose a separate programming language for each software layer. Moreover, if you have more than one physical component in one layer, you can implement each component in its own programming language.

If you actively use .NET Framework, you already know that assemblies written in separate .NET languages can easily refer to each other. In a Visual Studio solution, you can add a project (written in Visual Basic) as a referenced project to another one (written in C#), and so types and operations in the referenced project can be accessed in the host project. For example, a C# project can invoke an operation implemented in a Visual Basic project.

The Windows 8 programming languages are more diverse. C++ is compiled to CPU-specific code. .NET languages use an intermediate language that is compiled to machine instructions only when running the application. JavaScript provides a third approach, because it has its own run-time engine. How is it possible that such dissimilar languages can cooperate and access each other's objects and operations?

The answer is Windows Runtime. Each programming language is capable of consuming Windows Runtime objects. If you want to utilize a component in any other language, expose the functionality through Windows Runtime objects! With Visual Studio, it is fairly easy.

Creating a Hybrid Solution with C# and C++ Projects

To learn how to work with hybrid solutions, let's create a very simple Windows 8 app that displays prime numbers between 1 and 5,000. Assume that you are expected to create an app with great performance that still uses low memory. You decide to use the Sieve of Eratosthenes to collect prime numbers between 2 and an upper-bound value that can be specified by the user. If the upper-bound value is n, this algorithm uses an array of n Boolean values. You choose C++, because it provides the best performance, and you can also be frugal with the memory representing eight flags in a single byte. However, you are a seasoned C# developer, so you decide to create the UI of this Windows 8 app in C#.

> **NOTE** To refresh your knowledge about Sieve of Eratosthenes, see `http://www.en.wikipedia.org/wiki/Sieve_of_Eratosthenes`.

In the following exercise you start with a prepared sample, which you can find in the `CSharpHybrid Start` folder within the `Chapter14.zip` download. This project contains the skeleton of the UI, and you extend it with a C++ project that implements the Sieve of Eratosthenes.

TRY IT OUT Creating a Hybrid Solution with C# and C++ Projects

To extend the prepared C# solution with a new C++ project, follow these steps:

1. In Visual Studio, open the `CSharpHybrid Start` solution. In Solution Explorer, you can see that it contains a single C# project, named `CSharpHybrid`. This solution was created with the C# Blank Application template and expanded with a few custom styles.

2. In Solution Explorer, select the Solution (root) node. Use the File ➪ Add New Project command. When the Add New Project dialog box opens, select the Visual C++ node under the Installed node, and choose the Windows Runtime Component template, as shown in Figure 14-1.

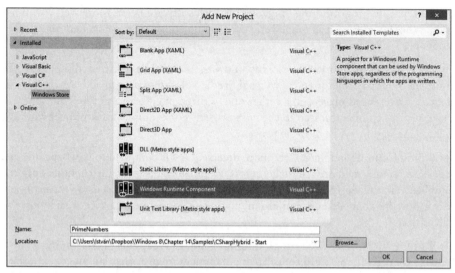

FIGURE 14-1: Creating a new project with the C++ Windows Runtime Component DLL template

3. Name the project **PrimeNumbers,** and click OK. The IDE adds this new project to the solution, which now contains two projects, one in C# and another one in C++. These projects are independent from each other.

4. In Solution Explorer, expand the `CSharpHybrid` (C#) project node, and right-click the References node. From the context menu, select the Add Reference command. The Reference Manager dialog box opens.

5. In this dialog box, select the Solution node and check the `PrimeNumbers` project, as shown in Figure 14-2. Click OK to add this project reference to `CSharpHybrid`. The `PrimeNumbers` project immediately appears in the References node of the `CSharpHybrid` project, as shown in Figure 14-3.

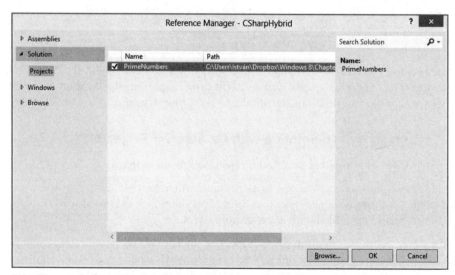

FIGURE 14-2: Referencing the PrimeNumbers project from CSharpHybrid

6. Build the solution by pressing F7.

7. In Solution Explorer, right-click the Solution node, and select the "Open Folder in Windows Explorer" command. In Windows Explorer, navigate to the Debug\PrimeNumbers folder. In this folder, you will find the PrimeNumbers.winmd file with the Windows Runtime metadata of the C++ project, in addition to PrimeNumbers.dll, as shown in Figure 14-4.

8. In Solution Explorer, expand the MainPage.xaml node, and double-click MainPage.xaml.cs to open it. In the code editor, navigate to the first empty line following the last using directive. Start typing **using P**, and IntelliSense displays a list of possible continuations, including the PrimeNumbers namespace, as shown in Figure 14-5.

FIGURE 14-3: PrimeNumbers among the references of CSharpHybrid

FIGURE 14-5: IntelliSense offers the PrimeNumbers continuation

Name	Date modified	Type	Size
PrimeNumbers.dll	5/22/2012 5:01 PM	Application extens...	126 KB
PrimeNumbers.exp	5/22/2012 5:01 PM	Exports Library File	1 KB
PrimeNumbers.ilk	5/22/2012 5:01 PM	Incremental Linke...	728 KB
PrimeNumbers.lib	5/22/2012 5:01 PM	Object File Library	2 KB
PrimeNumbers.pdb	5/22/2012 5:01 PM	Program Debug D...	923 KB
PrimeNumbers.pri	5/22/2012 5:01 PM	PRI File	2 KB
PrimeNumbers.winmd	5/22/2012 5:01 PM	WINMD File	11 KB

FIGURE 14-4: PrimeNumbers.dll with the related .winmd file

9. Press Tab, and close the line with a semicolon, as shown here:

```
using PrimeNumbers;
```

10. Now, the CSharpHybrid project (C#) has a valid reference to a C++ project. Press F7 to check that the solution still builds.

How It Works

The solution you opened in Step 1 contained the UI layer. To implement the Sieve of Eratosthenes, in Step 2 you added a C++ project to the solution with the WinRT Component DLL template. This template compiles to a Windows Runtime component with a metadata file, as you saw in Figure 14-4.

To utilize the PrimeNumbers component, you referenced it from the CSharpHybrid project. After you built the solution in Step 7, the metadata became available in the IDE. IntelliSense used it in Step 8, and offered the continuation of the using directive.

Your hybrid project's skeleton is ready, but you must implement the prime number collection algorithm, and integrate it with the UI.

Creating and Consuming Windows Runtime Components

Windows Runtime components can be consumed from any Windows 8 language. So, if you want to create reusable artifacts that can be utilized from any Windows 8 app independently of the programming language implementing a particular application, implement them as Windows Runtime components. You can use C++, C#, and Visual Basic for this purpose, but, because of its nature, you can't create these components in JavaScript.

Windows Runtime components are compiled into a .dll file, and the build process always generates a .winmd (Windows Metadata) file that exposes information about the public types of the component library. Although you can use this internally at any time in your Windows Runtime component projects, restrictions exist about types and members you intend to publish.

These restrictions are specific to the programming language used to implement the component. However, the most important rule is that public types and their members (including fields, properties, operations, parameters, and return values) must be Windows Runtime types — and it's independent from the language used.

> **NOTE** *The rules and restrictions about creating Windows Runtime components in C++ are detailed on the MSDN library page at* `http://msdn.microsoft.com/en-us/library/windows/apps/hh441569(v=vs.110).aspx.` *You can also use C# and Visual Basic. These languages have other restrictions, because the .NET and Windows Runtime type systems are different. See* `http://msdn.microsoft.com/en-us/library/windows/apps/br230301(v=vs.110).aspx` *for more information.*

Fortunately, the build process always raises an error when you're trying to expose an invalid type or member on the public interface of a Windows Runtime component. If you experience unusual errors and warnings for code that otherwise (compiled as a non-Windows Runtime component) are not raised, there is a high likelihood that you have violated a restriction.

In the next exercise, you implement the PrimeNumbers component you prepared in the previous exercise.

TRY IT OUT Implementing a Windows Runtime Component in C++

To implement the PrimeNumbers component in C++, follow these steps:

1. In Visual Studio, open the CSharpHybrid Start solution, unless it is still open.

2. In Solution Explorer, expand the PrimeNumbers node, and double-click the WinRTComponent.h file to open it. In the code editor, type the following boldfaced code to create the definition of the prime number collection algorithm.

```
C++
```

```cpp
#pragma once

#include <collection.h>

namespace PrimeNumbers
{
    public ref class Prime sealed
    {
    public:
        Prime();
        Windows::Foundation::Collections::IVectorView<unsigned long long>^
            GetPrimes(int upperBound);
    };
}
```

3. Open the `WinRTComponent.cpp` file. Delete its content and type the following code to implement the algorithm:

```
C++
```

```cpp
#include "pch.h"
#include "WinRTComponent.h"
#include <cmath>

using namespace PrimeNumbers;

Prime::Prime() {}

Windows::Foundation::Collections::IVectorView<unsigned long long>^
    Prime::GetPrimes(int upperBound)
{
    // ~DH- Create an array of bits and initialize all of them to 1
    int length = upperBound/8 + 1;
    char* numberFlags = new char[length];
    for (int i = 0; i < length; i++) numberFlags[i] = (char)0xff;

    // ~DH- Use Sieve of Eratosthenes
    int seekLimit = (int)sqrt(upperBound);
    for (int i = 2; i <= seekLimit; i++)
    {
        if (numberFlags[i>>3] & (0x80 >> i % 8))
        {
            for (int j = i + i; j < upperBound; j += i)
            {
                numberFlags[j>>3] &= ~(0x80 >> j % 8);
            }
        }
    }

    // ~DH- Collect prime numbers
    std::vector<unsigned long long> primeNumbers;
```

```
        for (int i = 2; i < upperBound; i++)
        {
            if (numberFlags[i>>3] & (0x80 >> i % 8)) primeNumbers.push_back(i);
        }
        return (ref new Platform::Collections::
            Vector<unsigned long long>(move(primeNumbers)))->GetView();
    }
```

4. Build the solution by pressing F7. Now, the `PrimeNumbers` Windows Runtime component is ready to be consumed.

5. In Solution Explorer, expand the `CSharpHybrid` project, and open the `MainPage.xaml.cs` file. In the code editor, type the following boldfaced code into this file:

C#

```
using Windows.UI.Xaml.Controls;
using Windows.UI.Xaml.Input;
using System.Text;
using PrimeNumbers;

namespace CSharpHybrid
{
    public sealed partial class MainPage : Page
    {
        public MainPage()
        {
            this.InitializeComponent();
        }

        private void DisplayPrimesButton_Tapped(object sender,
            TappedRoutedEventArgs e)
        {
            var builder = new StringBuilder("Prime numbers between 1 and 5000:\n");
            var primes = new Prime().GetPrimes(5000);
            bool appendComma = false;
            foreach (var prime in primes)
            {
                if (appendComma) builder.Append(", ");
                builder.Append(prime);
                appendComma = true;
            }
            OutputText.Text = builder.ToString();
        }
    }
}
```

6. Build and run the project by pressing Ctrl+F5. Click or tap the Display Prime Numbers button, and you will immediately see the results, as shown in Figure 14-6.

7. Close the application.

> **NOTE** You can find the complete code to download for this exercise on this book's companion website at www.wrox.com in the CSharpHybrid ⇨ Complete folder.

How It Works

In Step 2 you declared the class implementing the prime number collection algorithm as `public ref class Prime sealed`. In this declaration, `public ref class` tells the compiler that this reference class should be exposed on the component interface. The `sealed` modifier is required so that you can use this component from JavaScript code, too.

The `GetPrimes` method accepts an `int` argument, which is not a Windows Runtime type, but the C++ compiler automatically wraps it into the Windows Runtime representation of a 32-bit integer. The method returns with an `IVectorView<usingned long long>` that is an appropriate type to cross the Windows Runtime boundary.

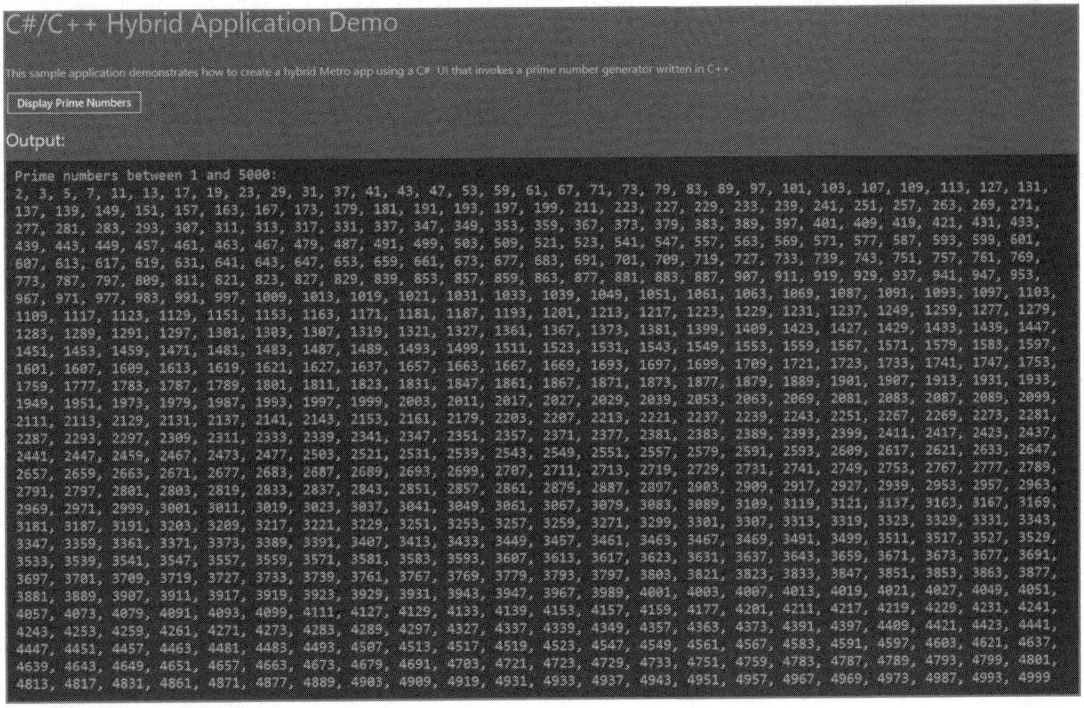

FIGURE 14-6: The CSharpHybrid project in action

The algorithm you specified in Step 3 uses a `char` array, where each bit represents a number. The Sieve of Eratosthenes uses this array, and at the end, it transforms the numbers stuck in the sieve into a vector, and retrieves the related `IVectorView` object with the `GetView` method.

The `DisplayPrimesButton_Tapped` method uses a `StringBuilder` object and iterates through the results to display each number collected by the algorithm.

Hybrid solutions are very useful, because they provide a way to combine the best features of Windows 8 programming languages into a great application. In the next section, you learn how to harness your application with background tasks that may run automatically, even if your app is not in the foreground.

BACKGROUND TASKS

As you already learned in Chapter 9, Windows 8 introduces a new model of application behavior. Windows 8 apps are in the foreground while the user interacts with them, and they get the system resources to provide great user experience with continuous responsiveness. However, when an application is not in the foreground, it is suspended, and cannot run any code. When the user again brings the application into the foreground, the app can continue its work. In some situations, a suspended app is terminated because of limited system resources. This model ensures that the user experience is not impacted by delays or lags, because applications running somewhere in the background cannot gobble up resources.

However, sometimes suspended apps still must be able to communicate with the outside world. For example, a mailing app must be able to check your inbox, even if it is not in the foreground. Moreover, this mail app should be able to display the number of new messages when you see the Windows 8 lock screen, without explicitly starting the app.

> **NOTE** *The lock screen is the screen that you see right after Windows is started (before you log in), or when you lock your device either using the Windows key+L key sequence, or pressing Ctrl+Alt+Del and then selecting Lock.*

Several mechanisms in Windows 8 make an app update its content even when the app is not in the foreground (that is, when it is suspended):

➤ You can play audio in the background with Playback Manager. (For more information on developing audio-aware apps and using Playback Manager, see `http://msdn.microsoft.com/en-us/library/windows/apps/hh452724.aspx`.)

➤ With the Background Transfer API, you can download and upload files in the background. (The article on the MSDN page at `http://msdn.microsoft.com/en-us/library/windows/apps/hh452979.aspx` will help you use this feature.)

➤ You can keep the app tiles updated with push notifications, as you learned in Chapter 9.

These mechanisms are optimized for system performance and battery life, but they are specialized for a particular kind of task. Windows 8 also offers the capability to create background tasks. With them, suspended applications can run their own code to execute tasks and keep the suspended application's content up-to-date.

Understanding Background Tasks

Most developers know that the Windows operating system has a concept called *Windows services* to run background tasks. Many components of the operating system run in Windows services, and a lot of programmers develop Windows services as a part of their systems. Well, Windows services are still available in Windows 8, and they are still a fundamental part of the operating system. So, the obvious question is why does Windows 8 have a separate concept for background tasks?

Windows services are kings in their own fiefdoms, and although the operating system has full control over them, they can devour system resources. They exist to implement heavy background processing tasks, such as parsing and executing SQL queries, compressing files, providing a web server, and so on.

In contrast to Windows services, background tasks are lightweight constructs that use a limited amount of system resources to carry out a certain chore. They are primarily designed for real-time class applications, such as chat, e-mail, voice over IP (VOIP), financial dashboards, weather displays, and so on.

Background Tasks and System Resources

Because of the limited amount of system resources, you should use background tasks for small task items that do not require user interaction, and provide only the necessary minimal effort to keep an application up to date (such as downloading new e-mails, sending a chat message typed in by the user, or downloading ticker information from a stock exchange portal). Compressing an image taken by a tablet's camera, or executing heavy and time-consuming mathematical operations, are definitely not for background tasks.

Background tasks can interact with the Windows 8 lock screen. This is very important from the point of view of a user's experience, because the lock screen is a perfect place to catch the user's attention. For example, displaying the number of unread e-mails, incoming chat messages, friend requests from a social portal, and so on, can shepherd the user immediately to the relevant application without having to browse applications one by one just to see what's new.

How Background Tasks Work

A background task can run while the application is suspended. But, if the application is suspended, it cannot run any code. So, how does a background task know when to run? Of course, the suspended application cannot start it! Background tasks are run by the operating system. They are tied to a trigger that signals the task to run, and they can be tied to an optional set of conditions, too.

For example, there is a trigger called `UserPresent`. This trigger represents the event when a user logs in to the computer, or returns from a break while there was no user activity on the computer for a while. Combined with this trigger, the `InternetAvailable` condition means that the background task will start as soon as a user is present and the Internet is available. If the user returns to the computer, but the Internet is not available, the background task will not launch.

Of course, the operating system must know that an application has one or more background tasks, and it also must know the trigger and conditions the specific task is bound to. It is the responsibility of an application to negotiate with the operating system the scenarios concerning its own background tasks. As shown in Figure 14-7, the whole process takes the following steps:

1. The application that contains the background task registers the details about the trigger that should launch the background task. In this particular case, the application registers with the `UserPresent` trigger, which is a system event trigger.

2. The application registers with the system infrastructure the class that implements the background task. During this phase, the app passes the details about the trigger specified in the previous step.

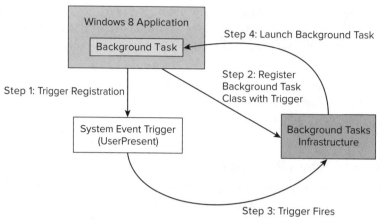

FIGURE 14-7: Registering and triggering a background task

3. When the event is raised (in this case, the UserPresent event), the system notifies the background tasks infrastructure.

4. The infrastructure knows all background classes that should be launched in the case of a specific event (because of the registration), and launches the appropriate task by instantiating the specified background task class.

Trigger Events and Task Conditions

The Windows 8 background task infrastructure defines more than a dozen trigger events. Most of them are system event triggers. Following are a few of them:

➤ **UserAway** — The user is away (for example, he or she leaves the computer while having a coffee break).

➤ **UserPresent** — The user is present (for example, he or she returns from the coffee break, unlocks the device, and resumes working).

➤ **TimeZoneChange** — The time zone changes on the device (for example, when the system adjusts the clock for daylight saving time, or the user changes the current time zone in the Control Panel).

➤ **NetworkStatusChange** — A network change occurs, such as a change in cost (for example, moving from the wireless company network to a paid cellular network) or connectivity (for example, the Internet becomes unavailable).

> **NOTE** *You can get the full list of system event triggers supported by Windows 8 from* http://msdn.microsoft.com/en-us/library/windows/apps/windows
> .applicationmodel.background.systemtriggertype.aspx.

Table 14-1 summarizes the roles of a few other trigger events.

TABLE 14-1: Special Trigger Events

TRIGGER NAME	DESCRIPTION
TimeTrigger	Represents a time event that triggers a background task to start.
PushNotificationTrigger	Represents an event that invokes a background task item of the app in response to the receipt of a raw notification (that is, a push notification that does not involve the UI).
ControlChannelTrigger	Enables real-time communication to be received in the background for several network transports, primarily the ones in the Windows .Networking.Sockets namespace.
MaintenanceTrigger	The operating system periodically executes maintenance tasks, provided that the system is on AC power. This event is raised when such background tasks should be launched.

When registering a trigger, you can optionally add conditions, as summarized in Table 14-2.

TABLE 14-2: Background Task Conditions

CONDITION NAME	SATISFIED WHEN
InternetAvailable	The Internet is available.
InternetNotAvailable	The Internet is unavailable.
SessionConnected	The session is connected.
SessionDisconnected	The session is disconnected.
UserNotPresent	The user is away.
UserPresent	The user is present.

The Lock Screen and Background Tasks

Users can add applications to the lock screen, and these applications can display important status information (such as the number of unread e-mails, the number of chat messages, the number of newly connected friends, and so on). By placing these applications on the lock screen, the user indicates that those applications are especially important for him or her.

Background tasks are the keys to communicating between the lock screen and the apps. The application for which particular status information is displayed may not run when the user sees the lock screen, so adding the background task to the lock screen is the way to display up-to-date information in real time.

Certain triggers are restricted to only applications on the lock screen. If an app that is not on the lock screen tries to use such a trigger, the background task will not be launched, even if the event is triggered. All triggers except `SystemTrigger` and `MaintenanceTrigger` require the app to be added to the lock screen. This means, for example, that you cannot use a `TimeTrigger` to periodically execute a background task, unless the app is assigned to the lock screen.

> **NOTE** *One of the* `SystemTrigger` *types,* `SessionStart`, *does need the app to be on the lock screen.*

The BackgroundTaskHost.exe Program

As mentioned previously, background tasks can be triggered even when their host application does not run. This means that these tasks should be hosted in such a way so that the operating system can manage them separately from their owner app (in other words, from the app that the tasks provide services for).

Background tasks are implemented in a class library, and this class library can run either within its main application, or in a system-provided executable, `BackgroundTaskHost.exe`. When you create your application, in the package manifest file, you must declare the host to let the system know your intention. However, several rules exist for background task trigger types and host processes:

➤ Tasks registered with `TimeTrigger`, `SystemTrigger`, or `MaintenanceTrigger` must be hosted in `BackgroundTaskHost.exe`.

➤ Tasks listening with `ControlChannelTrigger` can run only in the hosting application.

➤ Background tasks working with `PushNotificationTrigger` events can be hosted either in the main app, or within the `BackgroundTaskHost.exe`.

> **NOTE** *As a rule of thumb, host your tasks within the* `BackgroundTaskHost.exe`, *unless your application does not require hosting it directly.*

Communicating between Foreground Applications and Background Tasks

Background tasks can communicate with the main application in two ways:

➤ The progress of the background task can be reported back to the application.

➤ The application can be notified about the completion of tasks.

Both mechanisms assume that the main application is running in the foreground; otherwise, notifications coming from the background tasks cannot be caught by the main app. These notifications are implemented as events, so event handlers must be used in the foreground app to respond to them. These event handlers are generally used to update the UI.

Because background tasks may run even when the foreground application is terminated, there is a mechanism to rebuild the event handlers when the foreground application starts. The app in the foreground can query its own background tasks and re-associate the completion and progress event handlers.

Canceling Background Tasks

In some situations (such as a low battery level, disconnected network, and so on), the system can cancel a background task. To save battery power and CPU bandwidth, canceled tasks should finish their own work as soon as possible, and they also have the opportunity to save their state. To receive cancelation notifications, background tasks should register a cancelation event handler. A task must respond to this cancelation notification — and return from the handler — in 5 seconds; otherwise, the application gets terminated.

A well-behaving application uses the cancelation notification to save its state, so that later, when the background task is launched again, the task can continue from the saved state.

Application Updates

Background tasks are registered in the system so that they persist across application updates. This registration contains the entry points of these tasks by means of the full name of a Windows Runtime class responsible for servicing the task. However, when an application is updated, there is no guarantee that the background task that existed in the previous version still exists in the updated version, too.

Applications can register a background task for the ServicingComplete trigger (it's a type of SystemTrigger) to be notified when the application is updated. When the notification arrives, the application can unregister those background tasks that are no longer valid in the new application version.

Now that you have learned all basics required to create background tasks, the best way to proceed with this knowledge is to try it out in a few exercises.

Implementing Background Tasks

A background task is a Windows Runtime object that implements the IBackground interface located in the Windows.ApplicationModel.Background namespace. Background tasks are declared in the application manifest, where the full name of the Windows Runtime type is passed as the task entry point. A task is registered with its entry point, and from this registration, the system knows exactly where to find and launch that task.

Creating a Simple Background Task

In the following exercise, you learn the basic steps for creating and using a background task. You create a task that is triggered when the Internet connection becomes available, and reports it back to the foreground application. To implement this task, you use the InternetStatusTaskSample - Start solution, which you can find in the Chapter14.zip download.

TRY IT OUT Creating a Background Task

To create a background task that communicates with the main application, follow these steps:

1. With the File ⇨ Open Project (Ctrl+Shift+O) command, open the InternetStatusTaskSample .sln file from the InternetStatusTaskSample - Start folder of this chapter's download. In a few seconds, the solution loads into the IDE.

2. In Solution Explorer, select the Solution node, and use the File ⇨ Add New Project command to add a C# Windows Runtime Component project to the solution. Name this project **InternetStatusTask**.

3. Expand the `InternetStatusTask` node, and remove the `Class1.cs` file from the project.

4. In Solution Explorer, double-click the `Package.appxmanifest` file. In the manifest editor, click the Declarations tab, and select Background Tasks from the Available Declarations combo box. Click the Add button.

5. Under the Supported Types, click the "System event" check box. Type **InternetStatusTask .StatusWatcherTask** into the "Entry point" box, as shown in Figure 14-8.

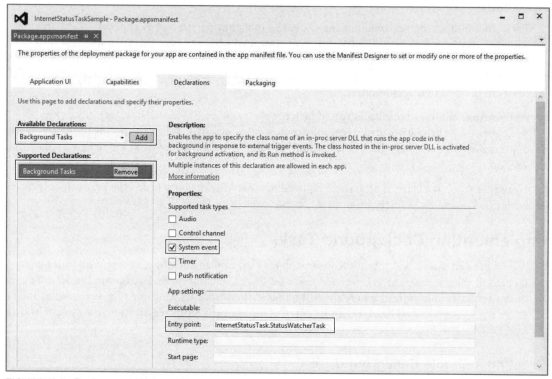

FIGURE 14-8: Background Task manifest properties

6. In Solution Explorer, select the `InternetStatusTaskSample` project and add a reference to the `InternetStatusTask` project.

7. Add a new code file to the `InternetStatusTask` project, and name it **StatusWatcherTask.cs**. Type the following code into this file:

```csharp
using System;
using System.Diagnostics;
using Windows.ApplicationModel.Background;
```

```
using Windows.Storage;

namespace InternetStatusTask
{
    public sealed class StatusWatcherTask : IBackgroundTask
    {
        public void Run(IBackgroundTaskInstance taskInstance)
        {
            var settings = ApplicationData.Current.LocalSettings;
            var key = taskInstance.Task.TaskId.ToString();
            settings.Values[key] = string.Format(
                "StatusWatcherTask invoked at {0}", DateTime.Now);
        }
    }
}
```

8. Open the `MainPage.xaml.cs` file, and type in the following boldfaced code:

`C#`

```
using System;
using Windows.UI.Core;
using Windows.UI.Xaml;
using Windows.UI.Xaml.Controls;
using Windows.UI.Xaml.Input;
using Windows.ApplicationModel.Background;
using Windows.Storage;

namespace InternetStatusTaskSample
{
    public sealed partial class MainPage : Page
    {
        private CoreDispatcher StatusDispatcher;

        public MainPage()
        {
            this.InitializeComponent();
            StatusDispatcher = Window.Current.CoreWindow.Dispatcher;
            UnregisterTaskButton.IsEnabled = false;
        }

        private void RegisterTask_Tapped(object sender, RoutedEventArgs e)
        {
            var builder = new BackgroundTaskBuilder();
            builder.Name = "StatusWatcherTask";
            builder.TaskEntryPoint = "InternetStatusTask.StatusWatcherTask";
            builder.SetTrigger(new SystemTrigger(
                SystemTriggerType.NetworkStateChange, false));
            IBackgroundTaskRegistration task = builder.Register();
            task.Completed += OnCompleted;
            RegisterTaskButton.IsEnabled = false;
            UnregisterTaskButton.IsEnabled = true;
            OutputText.Text += "StatusWatcherTask registered.\n";
        }
```

```
private void UnregisterTask_Tapped(object sender, TappedRoutedEventArgs e)
{
    foreach (var cur in BackgroundTaskRegistration.AllTasks)
    {
        if (cur.Value.Name == "StatusWatcherTask")
        {
            cur.Value.Unregister(true);
            OutputText.Text += "StatusWatcherTask unregistered.\n";
        }
    }
    RegisterTaskButton.IsEnabled = true;
    UnregisterTaskButton.IsEnabled = false;
}

private async void OnCompleted(IBackgroundTaskRegistration task,
    BackgroundTaskCompletedEventArgs args)
{
    await  StatusDispatcher.RunAsync(CoreDispatcherPriority.Normal,
        () =>
        {
            try
            {
                var key = task.TaskId.ToString();
                var settings = ApplicationData.Current.LocalSettings;
                OutputText.Text += settings.Values[key].ToString() + "\n";
            }
            catch (Exception ex)
            {
                OutputText.Text += ex.ToString() + "\n";
            }
        });
}
    }
}
```

9. Run the application by pressing Ctrl+F5. Click the Register Background Task button.

10. Disconnect from the Internet by removing the network cable from your computer, or using the Settings charm in Windows 8 to disconnect from your wireless network. The application displays a message about the lost Internet availability.

11. Connect back to the Internet by plugging the network cable back to your computer, or connecting to the appropriate wireless network using the Settings charm.

12. Click the Unregister Background Task button. Your application should display messages, as shown in Figure 14-9.

13. Close the application.

> **NOTE** You can find the complete code to download for this exercise on this book's companion website at www.wrox.com in the InternetStatusTaskSample ⇨ Simple folder.

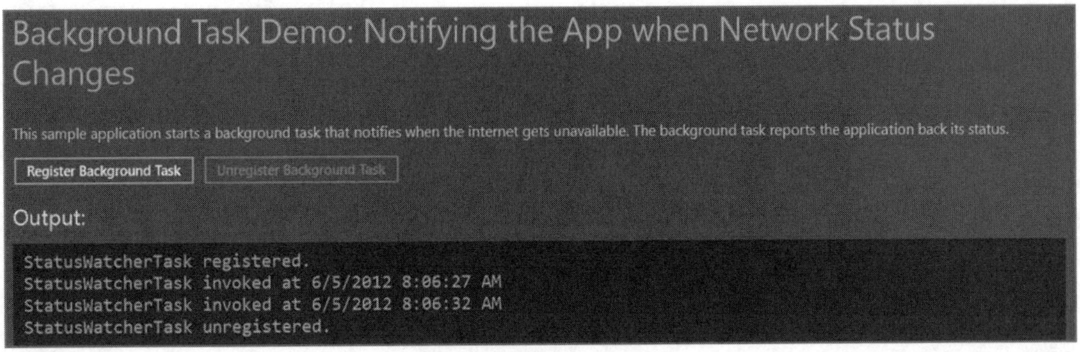

FIGURE 14-9: The InternetStatusTaskSample application in action

How It Works

As you have learned, background tasks are implemented as Windows Runtime classes. In Step 4, when you changed the project output type to WinMD File, you declared that you wanted to create a Windows Runtime DLL and a related `.winmd` file.

The code you typed in Step 6 implemented the `Run` method of the `IBackgroundTask` interface. It simply saved the fact that the Internet was unavailable into the application settings.

Registering the background task required a few steps:

```
var builder = new BackgroundTaskBuilder();
builder.Name = "StatusWatcherTask";
builder.TaskEntryPoint = "InternetStatusTask.StatusWatcherTask";
builder.SetTrigger(new SystemTrigger(
    SystemTriggerType.NetworkStateChange, false));
IBackgroundTaskRegistration task = builder.Register();
task.Completed += OnCompleted;
```

The key component was the `BackgroundTaskBuilder` class. You set up the name, entry point, and trigger information before calling the `Register()` method that retrieved the task registration instance. In this code snippet, you used the `SetTrigger()` method of the builder to associate the task with the event when Internet access becomes unavailable. You intended to handle the event when the task completes, so you set up the `Completed` event.

Unregistering the class required finding the background task by its name:

```
foreach (var cur in BackgroundTaskRegistration.AllTasks)
{
    if (cur.Value.Name == "StatusWatcherTask")
    {
        cur.Value.Unregister(true);
        OutputText.Text += "StatusWatcherTask unregistered.\n";
    }
}
```

The `AllTasks` collection of `BackgroundTaskRegistration` provided you with the list of tasks registered by your application. The code iterated through this collection and removed the `StatusWatcherTask` instance.

The `OnCompleted` method seemed a bit long. However, it was not very complex. The most important thing was that it used a `CoreDispatcher` instance named `StatusDispatcher` to invoke the `RunAsync` method to execute the event handler asynchronously. This was required, because the thread reporting back the completion was not the UI thread, and so it was not able to access the elements of the UI. `StatusDispatcher` executed the specified lambda method on the UI thread.

The body of the lambda method extracted the event parameters, checked them, and obtained the status information saved by the task to set the message on the UI:

```
var key = task.TaskId.ToString();
var settings = ApplicationData.Current.LocalSettings;
OutputText.Text += settings.Values[key].ToString() + "\n";
```

This program would not work without registering the background task in the application manifest file, as you did in Step 8 and Step 9.

As you saw, both disconnecting from and connecting to the network triggered the background task.

Managing Task Progress and Cancelation

The background task in the previous exercise was a very lightweight one. It simply saved a message. In real life, background tasks are often more complex, and sometimes they need several seconds (or even a minute) to complete, so it is a great feature to have background tasks report their progress back to the UI. If your task runs for a long time, it is always subject to cancelation (for example, the task may become unregistered). Your task can catch the cancelation notification and stop the task gracefully.

TRY IT OUT **Reporting Background Task Progress and Handling Cancelation**

To add progress reporting and cancelation management to the `StatusWatcherTask`, follow these steps:

1. Open the `InternetStatusTaskSample` solution from the `InternetStatusTaskSample   Start` folder, unless it is still open in the Visual Studio IDE.

2. Open the `StatusWatcherTask.cs` file, and replace the existing code with the following:

```
C#    using System;
      using System.Diagnostics;
      using Windows.ApplicationModel.Background;
      using Windows.Storage;
      using Windows.System.Threading;

      namespace InternetStatusTask
      {
          public sealed class StatusWatcherTask : IBackgroundTask
          {
              private volatile bool _cancelRequested = false;
              private BackgroundTaskDeferral _taskDeferral = null;
              uint _progress = 0;
```

```
        ThreadPoolTimer _timer = null;
        IBackgroundTaskInstance _instance;

        public void Run(IBackgroundTaskInstance taskInstance)
        {
            taskInstance.Canceled +=
                new BackgroundTaskCanceledEventHandler(OnCanceled);
            _taskDeferral = taskInstance.GetDeferral();
            _instance = taskInstance;
            _timer = ThreadPoolTimer.CreatePeriodicTimer(
                new TimerElapsedHandler(TimerCallback),
                TimeSpan.FromMilliseconds(2000));
        }

        private void OnCanceled(IBackgroundTaskInstance sender,
            BackgroundTaskCancellationReason reason)
        {
            _cancelRequested = true;
        }

        private void TimerCallback(ThreadPoolTimer timer)
        {
            if (_cancelRequested == false && _progress < 100)
            {
                _progress += 10;
                _instance.Progress = _progress;
            }
            else
            {
                _timer.Cancel();
                var settings = ApplicationData.Current.LocalSettings;
                var key = _instance.Task.TaskId.ToString();
                settings.Values[key] = _cancelRequested
                    ? "Task cancelled." : "Task completed.";
                _taskDeferral.Complete();
            }
        }
    }
}
```

3. Open the `MainPage.xaml.cs` file, and add the following boldfaced code to the `RegisterTask_Tapped` method:

`C#`
```
IBackgroundTaskRegistration task = builder.Register();
task.Completed += OnCompleted;
task.Progress += OnProgress;
```

4. Add the `OnProgress` method directly after the `OnCompleted` method:

`C#`
```
private async void OnProgress(IBackgroundTaskRegistration task,
    BackgroundTaskProgressEventArgs args)
{
    await StatusDispatcher.RunAsync(CoreDispatcherPriority.Normal,
```

```
        () =>
        {
            try
            {
                OutputText.Text += String.Format("Background task progress: {0}%\n",
                    args.Progress);
            }
            catch (Exception ex)
            {
                OutputText.Text += ex.ToString() + "\n";
            }
        });
}
```

5. Run the application by pressing Ctrl+F5. Click the Register Background Task button.

6. Disconnect from the Internet by removing the network cable from your computer, or using the Settings charm in Windows 8 to disconnect from your wireless network. The application starts displaying progress messages every 2 seconds. Wait while all status messages are displayed (that is, the progress reaches 100%).

7. Click the Unregister Background Task button. Your application should display messages, as shown in Figure 14-10.

8. Connect back to the Internet by plugging the network cable back in to your computer, or connecting to the appropriate wireless network using the Settings charm.

9. Click the Register Background Task button, and then disconnect from the Internet. When the progress messages start to be displayed, click the Unregister Background Task button. In a few seconds, the task is canceled, as shown in Figure 14-11.

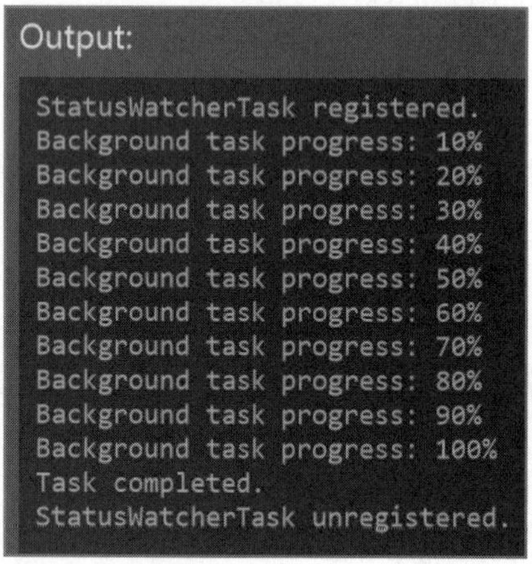

```
Output:

StatusWatcherTask registered.
Background task progress: 10%
Background task progress: 20%
Background task progress: 30%
Background task progress: 40%
Background task progress: 50%
Background task progress: 60%
Background task progress: 70%
Background task progress: 80%
Background task progress: 90%
Background task progress: 100%
Task completed.
StatusWatcherTask unregistered.
```

FIGURE 14-10: The
InternetStatusTaskSample application
reports progress

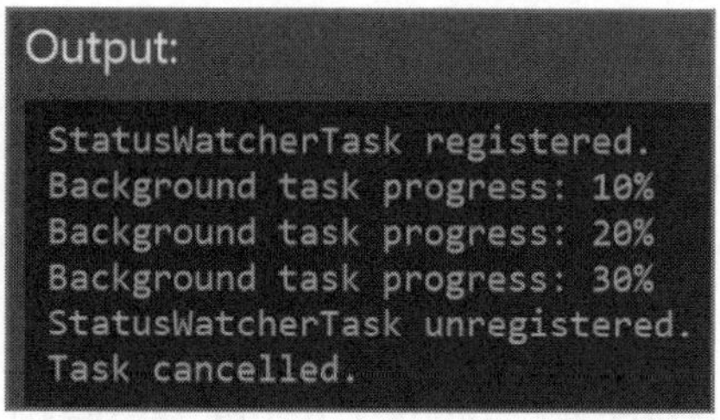

```
Output:

StatusWatcherTask registered.
Background task progress: 10%
Background task progress: 20%
Background task progress: 30%
StatusWatcherTask unregistered.
Task cancelled.
```

FIGURE 14-11: The background task is
canceled

10. Connect back to the Internet, and close the application.

> **NOTE** You can find the complete code to download for this exercise on this book's companion website at www.wrox.com in the InternetStatusTaskSample ⇨ Reporting folder.

How It Works

The StatusWathcerTask's Run() method used a timer object to emulate a long-running task that uses the CPU slightly. The timer was set up to invoke the TimerCallback method every 2 seconds (or 2,000 milliseconds):

```
taskInstance.Canceled += new BackgroundTaskCanceledEventHandler
    (OnCanceled);
_taskDeferral = taskInstance.GetDeferral();
_instance = taskInstance;
_timer = ThreadPoolTimer.CreatePeriodicTimer(
    new TimerElapsedHandler(TimerCallback),
    TimeSpan.FromMilliseconds(2000));
```

However, before activating the timer, it set the Cancelled event handler in order to get cancelation notifications. Normally, a task is completed when the Run() method returns. But, in this method, Run() would return immediately after setting up the timer, without completing the task. To signal this situation, the code snippet obtained an object with the GetDeferral() method. As a result of this call, the completion of the task was deferred while the _taskDeferral object's Complete() method was called. The OnCanceled event handler simply set the _cancelRequested flag.

The lion's share of the work was done in the TimeCallback method that first checked for cancelation or completion. In both cases, it meant the task was about to be finished. Unless the task was finished, it increased the progress counter. Then it canceled the timer, and set the response messages according to whether the task was canceled or completed. Most importantly, it called the _taksDeferral .Complete() method to signal that the task finished its job:

```
_timer.Cancel();
var settings = ApplicationData.Current.LocalSettings;
var key = _instance.Task.TaskId.ToString();
settings.Values[key] = _cancelRequested
    ? "Task cancelled." : "Task completed.";
_taskDeferral.Complete();
```

The current progress of the task was handled by the OnProgress method. Its structure was very similar to the OnCompleted method. The StatusDispatcher object was used to direct the activities to the UI thread. The progress was refreshed in the UI with a simple statement:

```
OutputText.Text += String.Format("Background task progress:
        {0}%\n",
    args.Progress);
```

In Step 6, when you disconnected from the Internet the first time, the task was completed. However, in Step 9, when you disconnected a second time, you unregistered the background task before it was completed, and unregistering it caused the system to cancel the task.

Now that you know the basics of background tasks, let's learn about input devices.

INPUT DEVICES

When you create an application, you must be prepared for several input devices. In contrast to desktop computers where the keyboard and mouse are the essential input devices, portable devices and tablets have pens and touch or similar digitizer devices. A great Windows 8 app should be prepared to provide the best user experience available on a particular device.

Without knowing what kinds of input devices are available for your application, it is not easy to select the best for your user. Windows Runtime provides you with easy-to-use objects to enumerate input devices and their capabilities.

Querying Input Device Capabilities

The `Windows.Devices.Input` namespace encapsulates a few object types that help you to query specific device capabilities. Table 14-3 describes these types.

TABLE 14-3: Helper Classes to Query Input Device Capabilities

TYPE	DESCRIPTION
KeyboardCapabilities	You can use this class to determine the capabilities of any connected hardware keyboard, including wired and wireless keyboard devices.
MouseCapabilities	You can use this class to query the capabilities of any connected mouse devices.
TouchCapabilities	You can use this class to determine the capabilities of any connected touch digitizers.

Each class has a set of properties to access device capability information. Using these properties, you can obtain all information about input devices.

Keyboard Capabilities

The `KeyboardCapabilities` class has a single integer property named `KeyboardPresent`. When this integer value is 0, there is no hardware keyboard connected to your computer; otherwise, there is. Technically, you can connect more than one keyboard to your computer, but from the point of view of input capabilities, it does not matter how many of them you have, as long as there is at least one connected.

This code snippet shows that it is easy to work with `KeyboardCapabilities`. (This code may be found in the `InputDevices\MainPage.xaml.cs` downloadable code file.)

```
var output = new StringBuilder();
// ...
output.Append("\n~DH- Querying keyboard capabilities\n");
```

```
var keyboardCaps = new KeyboardCapabilities();
output.Append(keyboardCaps.KeyboardPresent == 0
    ? "No keyboard device is present.\n"
    : "There is a keyboard device present.\n");
// ...
OutputText.Text = output.ToString();
```

Mouse Capabilities

The `MouseCapabilities` class has a few properties, as summarized in Table 14-4.

TABLE 14-4: Properties of MouseCapabilities

PROPERTY NAME	DESCRIPTION
MousePresent	This property gets an integer value indicating whether the mouse is present on the computer. A value of 0 indicates that no mouse is connected to the computer; 1 indicates there is at least one mouse connected. The value does not indicate the number of mice that are present.
NumberOfButtons	This property gets a value representing the number of buttons on the mouse. If multiple mice are present, it returns the number of buttons of the mouse that has the maximum number of buttons. Some mice have programmable buttons. This property gets only the number of buttons reported by the mouse driver, which may be different from the actual number of physical buttons.
SwapButtons	This property gets a value indicating whether any of the mice connected to the computer has swapped left and right buttons. Left-handed users often swap mouse buttons.
HorizontalWheelPresent	This property's value indicates whether any of the mice connected to the computer has a horizontal wheel.
VerticalWheelPresent	This property's value indicates whether any of the mice connected to the computer has a vertical wheel.

This code snippet shows a brief sample of using `MouseCapabilities`. (This code may be found in the `InputDevices\MainPage.xaml.cs` downloadable code file.)

```
var output = new StringBuilder();
// ...
output.Append("\n~DH- Querying mouse capabilities\n");
var mouseCaps = new MouseCapabilities();
output.Append(mouseCaps.MousePresent == 0
    ? "No mouse is present.\n"
    : "There is a mouse present.\n");
output.AppendFormat("The mouse has {0} buttons.\n", mouseCaps.NumberOfButtons);
output.AppendFormat("The user has {0}swapped the mouse buttons.\n",
```

```
        mouseCaps.SwapButtons == 0 ? "not " : "");
output.Append(mouseCaps.VerticalWheelPresent == 0
    ? "No vertical mouse wheel is present.\n"
    : "There is a vertical mouse wheel present.\n");
output.Append(mouseCaps.HorizontalWheelPresent == 0
    ? "No horizontal mouse wheel is present.\n"
    : "There is a horizontal mouse wheel present.\n");// ...
// ...
OutputText.Text = output.ToString();
```

Touch Device Capabilities

The `TouchCapabilities` class has only two properties, as summarized in Table 14-5.

TABLE 14-5: Properties of TouchCapabilities

PROPERTY NAME	DESCRIPTION
TouchPresent	This property indicates whether the computer has any touch digitizer device (pen or human touch). Any non-zero value means that there is at least one touch digitizer device connected.
Contacts	This property gets the minimum number of contacts supported by all touch devices. This property returns the value 1 in most cases, even if the device allows multi-finger touch, because often pen devices are also enabled, which support only one contact.

Here is a short code snippet demonstrating the use of `TouchCapabilities`. (This code may be found in the `InputDevices\MainPage.xaml.cs` downloadable code file.)

```
var output = new StringBuilder();
// ...
output.Append("~DH- Querying touch capabilities\n");
var touchCaps = new TouchCapabilities();
output.Append(touchCaps.TouchPresent == 0
    ? "No touch device is present.\n"
    : "There is a touch device present.\n");
output.AppendFormat("The touch device supports {0} contacts.\n",
    touchCaps.Contacts);
// ...
OutputText.Text = output.ToString();
```

Querying Pointer Device Information

Your computer may have one or more pointer devices. In many applications, it is important to know which devices are available. The `Windows.Devices.Input` namespace has a class named `PointerDevice` that you can use to query pointer device information. You can invoke the static `GetPointerDevices()` method to enumerate all pointer devices installed on your system. The use

of this class is best explained by this code snippet. (This code may be found in the `InputDevices\`
`MainPage.xaml.cs` downloadable code file.)

```
var output = new StringBuilder();
// ...
output.Append("\n~DH- Querying pointer device information\n");
var index = 0;
foreach (var device in PointerDevice.GetPointerDevices())
{
    string deviceType;
    switch (device.PointerDeviceType)
    {
        case PointerDeviceType.Mouse:
            deviceType = "mouse";
            break;
        case PointerDeviceType.Pen:
            deviceType = "pen";
            break;
        case PointerDeviceType.Touch:
            deviceType = "touch";
            break;
        default:
            deviceType = "unknown";
            break;
    }
    output.AppendFormat("Device #{0} is an {1} {2} device with {3} contacts.\n",
        index, device.IsIntegrated ? "internal" : "external",
        deviceType, device.MaxContacts);
    var rect = device.PhysicalDeviceRect;
    output.AppendFormat(
        "Device #{0} supports the [{1},{2}]-[{3},{4}] rectangle.\n",
        index,
        rect.Left, rect.Top, rect.Right, rect.Bottom);
    index++;
}
OutputText.Text = output.ToString();
```

> **NOTE** *You can find the previous code snippets in the* `InputDevices` *folder of this chapter's download.*

Each device is represented by a `PointerDevice` instance, and the `foreach` loop iterates through
them. The `PointerDeviceType` property indicates the type of a particular device that can be any
of the `Mouse`, `Pen`, or `Touch` values. Devices can be built into the computer hardware, or can be
connected to the machine (for example, through a Bluetooth controller). The `IsIntegrated` property indicates whether the device is integrated with the hardware, or it is an external one. Touch
devices can have a number of contacts, as indicated by the `MaxContacts` property. A touch device
can address virtual points in a two-dimensional coordinate system that can be queried with the
`PhysicalDeviceRect` property.

Querying all device capabilities on a Windows 8 tablet with an external keyboard and mouse will result in the information shown in Figure 14-12. The output of the program tells a few important facts:

Three pointer devices are attached to the tablet, as you can see at the bottom of Figure 14-13. One of them (Device #2) is an external mouse; the other two internal devices are pen and touch, respectively. At the top of the figure, the message says that "The touch device supports 1 contacts," although the touch device (Device #1) can handle up to 8 contacts. Remember, the message at the top was the value of the Contacts property coming from TouchCapabilities, and this property retrieves the minimum number of contacts of any touch devices. It is one, because the pen (Device #0) has only one contact.

```
--- Querying touch capabilities
There is a touch device present.
The touch device supports 1 contacts.

--- Querying keyboard capabilities
There is a keyboard device present.

--- Querying mouse capabilities
There is a mouse present.
The mouse has 4 buttons.
The user has not swapped the mouse buttons.
There is a vertical mouse wheel present.
No horizontal mouse wheel is present.

--- Querying pointer device information
Device #0 is an internal pen device with 1 contacts.
Device #0 supports the [0,0]-[971.716552734375,548.031494140625] rectangle.
Device #1 is an internal touch device with 8 contacts.
Device #1 supports the [0,0]-[1000.06298828125,551.055114746094] rectangle.
Device #2 is an external mouse device with 1 contacts.
Device #2 supports the [0,0]-[1366,768] rectangle.
```

FIGURE 14-12: Device capabilities of a Windows 8 tablet

Another interesting thing is that pointer devices use different coordinate maps. Whereas the mouse device retrieves [0,0][1366,768] (or the exact resolution of the screen), other devices use different values, depending on the resolution and sensitivity of the particular device.

SUMMARY

You are not constrained to using a single programming language when creating Windows 8 apps, because with Visual Studio, you can create hybrid solutions using a mix of Windows 8 programming languages. If you create Windows Runtime component DLL projects, you can use C++, C#, and Visual Basic for this purpose. These projects can be referenced from any other programming languages, including JavaScript. Each language has its own strength, so using a mix of them enables you to leverage the best features out of them, and make you more productive.

Although suspended Windows 8 apps do not receive resources from the operating system, with background tasks, you can carry out activities while apps are not in the foreground. Background tasks can use only a limited amount of CPU time, and their network throughput is constrained when the computer runs on battery. So, they are suitable for lightweight tasks, such as checking e-mail, downloading small pieces of data, managing instant messages, and so on. Heavy tasks (such as background processing of pictures, or making CPU-intensive computations) are not for Windows 8 background tasks. In these cases, you should use Windows services.

Background tasks are assigned to triggers, such as when the user becomes present, the Internet becomes available, the time zone is changed, and so on. When you register a background task, the task is always associated with a trigger and with optional conditions. Background tasks can be added to the lock screen (assuming they are associated with a certain set of triggers), and these tasks can have roughly twice as many resources as background tasks not on the lock screens. Foreground applications can subscribe to the `OnCompleted` and `OnProgress` events, so they have a way to communicate with the task.

Windows 8 computers can have many input devices (mice, hardware keyboards, pens, and touch devices), depending on their form factors. For the best user experience, your application should use the input device (or a combination of them) that is best suited for a certain application function. The `Windows.Devices.Input` namespace provides you with a number of classes to query input device capabilities, such as the `KeyboardCapabilities`, `MouseCapabilities`, `TouchCapabilities`, and `PointerDevice` classes.

In Chapter 15, you learn several useful testing and debugging techniques that are great tools for creating solid Windows 8 apps, and also help you in troubleshooting.

EXERCISES

1. How should you set up a C# class library so that it can be referenced from any projects written in other programming languages?

2. Which system resources are constrained when you use background tasks?

3. How can background tasks communicate with foreground applications?

4. Can a background task run longer than 1 minute?

5. Why is it important to query input device capabilities?

> **NOTE** *You can find answers to the exercises in Appendix A.*

▶ **WHAT YOU LEARNED IN THIS CHAPTER**

TOPIC	KEY CONCEPTS
Hybrid solution	A solution in Visual Studio that contains a set of projects using different programming languages. For example, a foreground application project in this solution can be implemented in C#, while an embedded runtime component can be implemented in C++.
Windows Runtime component library	A project that contains reusable Windows Runtime objects. The main goal of such a component library is to produce objects that can be utilized in Windows 8 applications independently of the consuming programming language.
Creating Windows Runtime component library in C# and Visual Basic	Use the File ⇨ New Project command, and in the New Project dialog box, select C# or Visual Basic, then choose the Windows Runtime Component template.
Creating Windows Runtime components library in C++	Use the File ⇨ New Project command, and in the New Project dialog box, select Visual C++, and then choose the WinRT Component DLL template.
Background tasks	Windows 8 provides the concept of background tasks to allow suspended (or even terminated) applications to carry out lightweight background activities (such as checking e-mail messages, downloading small packets of data, and so on). Background tasks can use limited CPU time, and when they run on battery, their network throughput is constrained.
Trigger events	Background tasks are activated in response to triggered events (such as the user becoming present/absent, the Internet becoming available/unavailable, a certain amount of time expired, a change in the time zone, and many more).
Task conditions	Background tasks may have optional launch conditions in addition to triggers. For example, a task can be assigned to the "time zone changed" trigger with the "Internet is available" condition. The task will be launched only after the Internet becomes available when the time zone has been changed.
Lock screen applications	Applications can be assigned to the lock screen. The background tasks of these apps can have about twice as much resource consumption as the background tasks of applications not on the lock screen.
Communicating with foreground applications	Foreground tasks can subscribe to the `OnCompleted` and `OnProgress` events of their registered background tasks to manage when tasks are completed, or when they report progress, respectively. With the help of a `CoreDispatcher` instance, the UI can be refreshed from these event handlers.

TOPIC	KEY CONCEPTS
Cancelling background tasks	Background tasks can be canceled by the operating system after they are launched (for example, when their application unregisters them). Tasks can respond to cancelation by subscribing to the `OnCanceled` event.
Querying input device capabilities	The `Windows.Devices.Input` namespace defines a number of classes to query the capabilities of input devices connected to the computer, such as `KeyboardCapabilities`, `MouseCapabilities`, and `TouchCapabilities`.
Querying pointer devices	With the `PointerDevice` class of the `Windows.Devices.Input` namespace, you can query all pointer devices connected to the system, including the internal and external ones.

15

Testing and Debugging Windows 8 Applications

WHAT YOU WILL LEARN IN THIS CHAPTER:

- ➤ Understanding software quality and its importance
- ➤ Understanding the basics of the debugging process
- ➤ Getting to know the Windows Simulator and test the applications using it
- ➤ Understanding what unit testing is and how you can use it to create high-quality applications

WROX.COM CODE DOWNLOADS FOR THIS CHAPTER

You can find the wrox.com code downloads for this chapter on the Download Code tab at www.wrox.com/remtitle.cgi?isbn=012680. The code is in the Chapter15.zip download and individually named, as described in the corresponding exercises.

In this chapter, you learn why it is important to create high-quality software, and how to do it. This chapter begins with a look at how to find the root causes of malfunctions in your code. You learn about the tools you can use to make this process easier and more straighforward. You also learn how to write additional code to test your application logic to make sure that your code behaves exactly the way it should. By the end of this chapter, you should have a solid understanding of the principles and techniques of maintaining a high-quality codebase for your Windows 8 style applications.

THE QUALITY OF YOUR SOFTWARE

When you are writing code, you will inevitably make mistakes. Everyone makes mistakes — even professional developers with many years of coding experience. The only difference is that with experience you can reduce the number of those mistakes. This means that you don't have to be afraid or feel bad that there is some error in your code somewhere. You should accept that fact that there is no software without errors. You should prepare yourself for the fact that you will eventually make coding mistakes (if you haven't already).

In the world of enterprise application development, it is a bit easier to get away with bugs. Enterprise users (who are often forced to use certain applications) have grown accustomed to application errors. They accept the fact that all they can do is report the error and hope that there will be a fix soon. But enterprise application users do not stop using the software just because of the errors.

The consumer world is very different. No one is forcing a user to use your applications. A bad review or a bad rating can scare new users away. Those who try your application and find it difficult or annoying to use because of different malfunctions will leave your software in a second without any hesitation — and never look back. All they will do for you is to leave a low rating and a bad review in the Windows Store, which might scare away any new potential users.

When developing applications for the consumer market, creating high-quality software is more important than ever.

BECOMING FAMILIAR WITH DEBUGGING

You might have heard the expression "bug in the code." A *bug* is an error in the code you've written. After you discover that there is something wrong with the code, you must find the problem and indentify the root cause of the bug.

Modern development environments like Visual Studio 2012 offer great tools for investigating your codebase. There is a tool inside Visual Studio called the Debugger. You can attach the Debugger to a running instance of your application and debug your code. *Debugging* is the process of stepping through the lines of code you wrote one by one, while observing the values of variables and objects, and monitoring the execution of your code.

However, your codebase can be huge. Even a couple hundred lines of code would be difficult to step through. As an alternative, the Debugger enables you to concentrate on the critical parts of your code. When you run your application with debugging enabled, the application runs exactly the same way as before. However, you can add markers to your code to tell the Debugger to stop the normal run, and to switch into the debugging mode when it encounters a line with a marker.

This marker is called a *breakpoint*. You can add as many breakpoints to your code as you want by clicking the left side of the code editor (or by pressing F9) on the selected line. Figure 15-1 shows an active Debugger hit on a breakpoint.

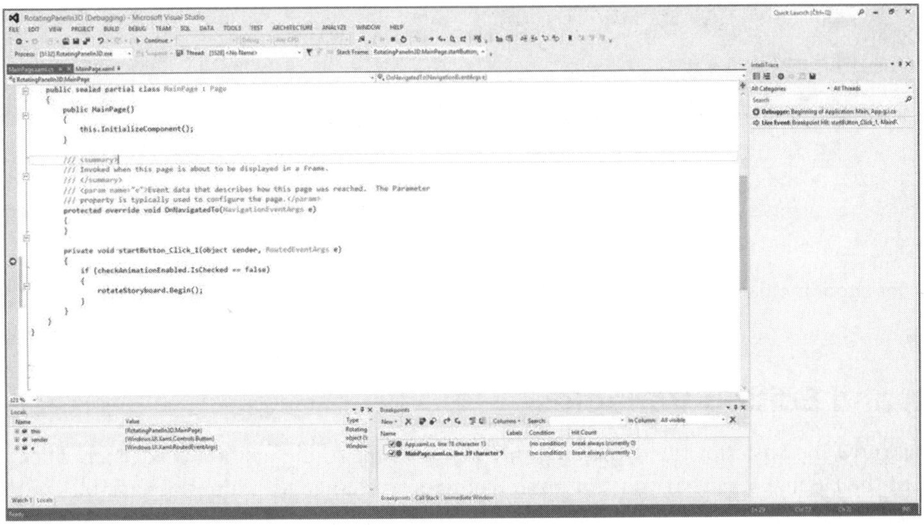

FIGURE 15-1: Debugger hit on a breakpoint

When you hit a breakpoint, the Debugger takes control of the program flow, and lets you read and write the current values of different variables. This is very useful when trying to identify the bug.

Controlling the Program Flow in Debug Mode

While you are in debug mode, you can enter various commands to step through the code.

- ➤ **Step Over** — This means that the Debugger should step to the next line of code. When the line on which the Debugger is positioned is a method, "step over" means not to step into the method's body, but just step over it. You can press F10 to step over the code.

- ➤ **Step Into** — This means that the Debugger should step to the next line of code. When the line on which the Debugger is positioned is a method, "step into" means to step into the method's body and investigate those lines of codes as well. You can press F11 to step into the method's body.

- ➤ **Step Out** — If you stepped into a method's body and you don't want to investigate it further, but you just want to return to the point of call, you can step out from the method's body by pressing Shift+F11.

- ➤ **Continue** — If you switched into debug mode and you want to continue normal running, just press F5.

- ➤ **Stop** — If you've finished debugging and running your app, just press Shift+F5 to stop the application and return to design mode in Visual Studio.

Rather than using shortcuts, you can alternatively use the command bar on the Visual Studio 2012 toolbar to control the Debugger. Figure 15-2 shows the Visual Studio 2012 Debugger toolbar.

FIGURE 15-2: Debugger toolbar in Visual Studio 2012

Monitoring and Editing Variables

Now that you know the basics of the debugging process, it's time to dig just a little deeper. The main benefit of the Debugger is that you can observe and even change the values of variables in the current context.

Several tool windows can help you to monitor the variables, the call stack, different threads, or to run code in the active context. In this section, you learn about the most important ones.

The Locals Window

The Locals window shown in Figure 15-3 is one of the most useful tool windows in terms of debugging. It displays the local variables in the current context. The context depends on which method body you are currently debugging.

Name	Value	Type
⊞ ● this	{RotatingPanelIn3D.MainPage}	Rotating
⊞ ● sender	{Windows.UI.Xaml.Controls.Button}	object {V
⊟ ● e	{Windows.UI.Xaml.RoutedEventArgs}	Window
⊟ ✦ OriginalSource	{Windows.UI.Xaml.Controls.Button}	dynamic
⊟ ● base	{Windows.UI.Xaml.Controls.Button}	Window
⊞ ● base	{Windows.UI.Xaml.Controls.Button}	Window
✦ ClickMode	Release	Window
✦ Command	null	System.\
✦ CommandParameter	null	dynamic
✦ IsPointerOver	true	bool
✦ IsPressed	true	bool
⊞ ● Static members		

Watch 1 | Locals

FIGURE 15-3: The Locals window in debugging mode

As you can see, you can observe any local variable in any desired depth. If a property on an object is editable, you can even overwrite its current value, thus changing the flow of program execution.

The Watch Window

The Watch window shown in Figure 15-4 is almost the same as the Locals window, but with a tiny difference. The Locals window displays all the local values (which can be a lot). Using the Watch window, you can specify which variable you are really interested in. You get the same functionality with the Watch window as you get with the Locals window.

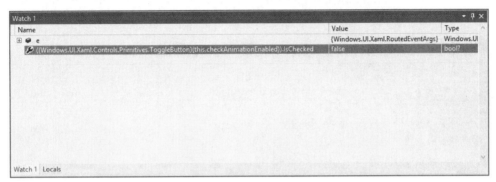

FIGURE 15-4: The Watch window in debugging mode

You can also add variables to the Watch window from the code editor by right-clicking the variable and choosing Add Watch. You can also use the Locals window to watch a variable by right-clicking the variable and choosing the Add Watch option.

The Immediate Window

The Immediate Window shown in Figure 15-5 is by far the most exciting tool window in Visual Studio 2012. When you are stepping through the code, you can decide to stop and investigate the code a little more by entering simple C# code into the Immediate window. The code will be executed and evaluated. For example, if you want to call a method with different values to see how it works, or to check the value of a global object, you can use the Immediate window to do so. Also you can change the values of the variables in the code. When you change the values, the app will use the new values while running.

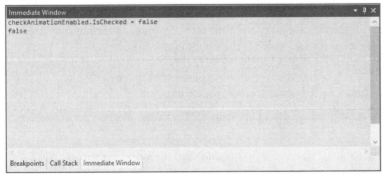

FIGURE 15-5: The Immediate Window in action

The Breakpoints Window

You'll probably set many breakpoints in your code, but you don't always want the Debugger to hit those breakpoints, nor do you want to remove them. You can activate the Breakpoints window in debug mode by selecting the Debug ➪ Windows ➪ Breakpoints menu item. You can then use the Breakpoints window shown in Figure 15-6 to list all your breakpoints. You can enable or disable them at any time, and you can jump to the relevant code as well. This serves as a really great overview on your breakpoints in use.

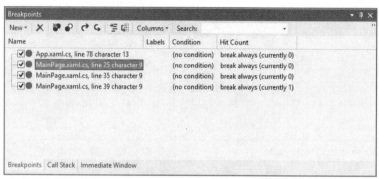

FIGURE 15-6: The Breakpoints window

In the next exercise, you investigate and fix a bug using the Visual Studio 2012 Debugger.

TRY IT OUT   Finding a Bug with the Debugger

To use the Debugger to find an error in code, follow these steps:

1. Run Visual Studio 2012 and open the `RotatingPanelIn3D` project. You can get the project by downloading `Chapter15.zip`. Extract the file and locate the `RotatingPanelIn3D` project.

2. Run the project by pressing F5. As you can see, if you click the Start Rotation button without the check box being enabled, the animation runs. If you check the check box, the animation is no longer running. This is the opposite behavior you want to achieve. So, you must fix this bug.

3. Open `MainPage.xaml.cs` and locate the `startButton_Click_1` event handler.

4. Click the `startButton_Click_1` method name, and then press F9 (or click the left gray area next to the code editor). This adds a red ellipse, which is the symbol for a breakpoint.

5. Press F5 to run the application.

6. Click the Start Rotation button. The Debugger stops at the breakpoint.

7. Press F10 until the cursor is positioned on the `if` statement. (The cursor is a yellow arrow on the left side of the code editor.)

8. Move your mouse cursor over the `IsChecked` property and read the value in the tooltip. You should see that the value is `False`.

9. Now, select the Locals window at the bottom of Visual Studio 2012.

10. Open `this` / `checkAnimationEnabled` / `base` / `IsChecked`. You can see the value is set to `False`.

11. Double-click the `False` value and change it to `True`.

12. Press F5 to let the application continue running. Now the animation is displayed.

13. Stop the application.

14. Change the `if` statement to compare with `true` instead of `false`.

15. Press F5 to run the application. The app should now work as expected.

How It Works

In Step 4, you add a breakpoint inside the button's event handler. This is enough for the debugger to know that it must stop and enter into debug mode when it hits the breakpoint.

In Step 8, you use the Locals window to investigate the problems with the code. As it turns out, the boolean value for the `IsChecked` property is wrong.

In Step 11, you overwrite the values of the `IsChecked` property, and you let the app continue to run. Now you know where the bug is.

In Step 14, you change the `if` statement to the opposite logic, which fixes the problem.

Changing the Code While Debugging

Undoubtedly, the best feature of modern debuggers is the capability to change the code while debugging. This is called the *Edit and Continue* feature.

Just to give you an example, imagine the following scenario. You encounter an exception while running your application. You can see the reason immediately, and all you have to do to fix the problem is to change a small part of the code. You could then go on running the application. You can choose to stop the application, fix the code, and restart it, but in some cases, that could cause a lot of work.

When you run the code with debugging enabled, as soon as you get an exception, Visual Studio offers you an option to intervene using the Debugger. A dialog box is displayed that provides the option to break and switch into debugging mode. Figure 15-7 shows the dialog box.

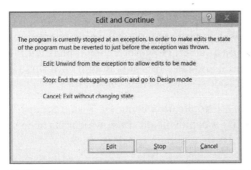

FIGURE 15-7: The "Edit and Continue" dialog box

After that, you can modify the code at will. Visual Studio will revert the state of the program to come out of the exception and run your modification. After you have fixed the code, you can press F5 to continue running.

> **NOTE** *You can't always perform "Edit and Continue." It's difficult to tell when you can do this exactly because it depends on the current state of the call stack, the language, and the capablility of the Debugger to change the current state without corrupting the process. Instead of analyzing whether or not it can be performed, you should just try it.*

Windows 8 Style Application-Specific Scenarios

Windows 8 style applications have a couple of interesting concepts that are exclusive to this technology, such as application lifecycle events, special sensors (like GPS or orientation-tracking with gyroscope), tablet hardware specifics (like different resolutions and aspect ratio), and so on. This section explores techniques that can help you test and debug these scenarios.

Debugging Application Lifecycle Events

Windows 8 style applications have a special lifecycle management. If you start the application for the first time, you'll activate the app using the Launched event. However, with task switching, you can't be sure that this event will fire again. Testing other lifecycle events like Suspend or Resume is not that easy because it's not quite deterministic when they'll run, which makes debugging really difficult.

Fortunatelly, in Visual Studio 2012, you have the option to trigger these events manually to ensure that your application behaves exactly the way it is supposed to.

To activate this feature, you must ensure that the Debugger Location toolbar is visible. Select View ➪ Toolbars ➪ Debug Location to add this toolbar to the visible toolbar area. If you run the application by pressing F5, you'll find the lifecycle event selector on the toolbar. By selecting a lifecycle event, you'll trigger it, and the event will fire. Then

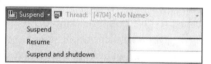

FIGURE 15-8: Debug Location toolbar options for suspending an application

you can start debugging the event handler. Figure 15-8 show the Debug Location toolbar options for suspending an application.

Specifying Deployment Targets

So far, you've run every application locally using your Windows 8 machine. However, that is most likely a PC, and you might rather test your application on a tablet. However, many tablets with many form factors exist, and you can't have them all. Still, you need to test your app with these different factors.

Visual Studio 2012 provides you with the option to run the application using the Visual Studio 2012 Simulator. When running the application, you can specify a deployment target, which has been the local machine so far. You can also change it to the Simulator, as shown in Figure 15-9.

FIGURE 15-9: The Simulator in Visual Studio 2012

The Simulator is a desktop application that simulates the environment while running a Windows 8 style app. Using the Simulator, you can specify many different factors:

➤ **Mouse mode** — This sets the interaction mode to mouse gestures (such as click, right-click, and mouse drag).

➤ **Basic touch mode** — This sets the interaction mode to a single finger touch mode. This includes tapping, swiping, and dragging. You can simulate touch input using your mouse.

➤ **Pinch/Zoom touch mode** — This sets the interaction mode to support pinch and zoom gestures. You can simulate touch input using your mouse. This is very useful if you don't have a touch-enabled device.

➤ **Rotation touch mode** — This sets the interaction mode to simulatate rotation using two fingers. You can simulate the touch input using your mouse.

➤ **Orientation** — This simulates clockwise and counter-clockwise rotations. This is great to simulate landscape and portrait layouts.

➤ **Change resolution** — This sets the screen resolutions and screen sizes. Using this option, you can test your user interface (UI) and layout on different display sizes and resolutions.

➤ **Set location** — This specifies simulated GPS coordinates for the Location API. If your device does not have a GPS built in, this is a great option to test the GPS usage.

Using the Simulator, you can easily test your Windows 8 style application to determine whether it works properly with tablets, all without having an actual device. However, the Simulator is not an isolated environment. Changes applied to the system through your application will affect your standard Windows environment as well. So, be careful about what you are doing.

> **NOTE** *So far, you have been introduced to two deployment targets: a local machine and the Simulator. There is a third option: a remote machine. Using the remote option, you can run and debug your application on a remote machine that is connected to your computer through a cable or a network. Setting up the remote debugging environment is out of the scope of this book, but you can learn more about it at* `http://msdn.microsoft.com/en-us/library/windows/apps/hh441469(v=vs.110).aspx`.

INTRODUCTION TO SOFTWARE TESTING

You've now learned how important it is to produce high-quality software, and so far in this chapter, you have learned how to fix a bug if you encounter one. But your main goal should always be to reduce the number of bugs as much as you can. This is where the applied tools and techniques of software testing come to your rescue.

Software testing has always been an integral part of professional software development. However, in professional teams, you have dedicated test professionals to ensure that your software stays high-quality by running manual and automated tests. You will probably need to wear that hat and perform some of those tests yourself. Although test professionals work in a very strict environment using test plans, scripts, and different tools, you might not need all that. A thorough "see if it works" approach and a couple of hours of manual testing and usage of your application might work as well, if it is not a big application.

Introduction to Unit Testing

There is an important part of software testing and development that will be useful for you as well. It's called *unit testing*. Writing unit tests is not a tester's task; it is the responsibility of the developer. A unit test is a method that runs a part of your code, and observes the ouput and behavior of your code based on different input. If done correctly, unit testing offers the following major benefits:

➤ **Better code quality** — Unit testing covers normal use and special cases as well. Thus, it helps you ensure that your code will not fail, and treats unexpected inputs properly.

➤ **Regression Tests** — If you apply changes to code written at an earlier time, you must be sure that you did not break it, and that it still works the same way when you introduce new code. This is called the *regression test*. Without existing unit tests, there is no way to ensure that your code is still right. But if you have unit tests covering those code parts, and after the modification, those tests still run successfully, there is a very good chance that your code is not broken, and it still works great.

➤ **Refactoring** — When you want to make your software testable, you should concentrate on making independent components that can be tested as an isolated unit. This will raise the quality of your code. Also, when creating unit tests, it can really point out the parts of your code that are not designed well. If they have a complicated API, they can't be tested easily, or too many things might depend on one another. This means that unit testing points out the need for restructuring your code. This process is called *refactoring*.

As you can see, unit testing offers many benefits while adding more work to your project, but this additional workload will pay off in later stages of the development process.

Unit Testing Windows 8 Style Applications

In Visual Studio 2012, there is a new project template for testing Windows 8 style applications. It's called Unit Test Library (Windows 8 style apps). A Unit Test Library can contain many test classes. Test classes are marked with the `TestClass` attribute. Test classes contain test methods, initialization code, and cleanup code.

➤ **Test method** — Test methods are marked with the `TestMethod` attribute. These methods run seperately one by one. Each method has a result that determines whether the test was successful, or if it failed.

➤ **Initialization** — Every test class can have a single method decorated with the `TestInitialize` attribute. This method runs before every test method to perform any intitialization needed. Unit tests should not use real data, network connections, or database access. If a component needs a data source, it is best to create a fake one. You can do this in the initialization stage so that every test method can use it.

➤ **Cleanup** — Every test class can have a single method decorated with the `TestCleanup` attribute. This method runs after every test method to clean up any changes after the test methods. You can ensure that every test method runs on the same environment and configuration.

In every test method, you should specify a condition that can be used to determine whether or not the unit test ran successfully. The Unit Testing Framework uses the `Assert` class to perform this check. The `Assert` class contains a number of methods to specify conditions like `Assert.IsTrue()`, `Assert.AreEqual()`, `Assert.InInstanceOfType()`, and so on. These methods accept a condition to evaluate, and a message to display, when the test fails. The following code snippet demonstrates the use of unit tests:

```
[TestClass]
public class CalculatorTest
{
    MyTestObject testInstance;

    [TestInitialize]
    public void Initialize()
    {
        testInstance = new MyTestObject();
        //You can perform any additional intialization here
    }

    [TestMethod]
    public void MyTestMethod()
    {
        double x = 0;
        double y = 1;
        double expected = 1;
        double result = testInstance.MethodZ(x, y);

        //Test the result
```

```
        Assert.AreEqual(expected, result, string.Format("Result should be
            {0}!", expected));
    }

    [TestCleanup]
    public void Cleanup()
    {
        //You can perform necessary cleanup here
    }

}
```

You can run the tests using the Test ➪ Run... ➪ All Tests menu item. There is a new window called the Test Explorer, which is shown in Figure 15-10. You can activate it using the Test ➪ Windows ➪ Test Explorer menu item. After you build your application, the Test Explorer discovers all the unit tests in your project. You can run tests using this window, too. The Test Explorer provides you with additional information as well, like grouping of passed and failed tests, run times, and, for each test method, a link to your unit test code.

If a test failed, the Test Explorer displays the error message shown in Figure 15-11 for your test.

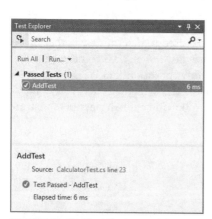

FIGURE 15-10: Test Explorer with a successful test run

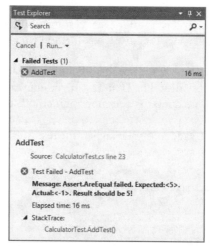

FIGURE 15-11: Test Explorer with a failed test run

In the next exercise, you create a unit test for a `Calculator` class.

TRY IT OUT **Unit Testing the Calculator Class**

To create a unit test for a `Calculator` class, follow these steps:

1. Run Visual Studio 2012 and open the `CalculatorDemo` project. You can get the project by downloading `Chapter15.zip`. Extract the archive and find the `CalculatorDemo` project.

2. Right-click the solution file in Solution Explorer and choose Add ➪ New Project.

3. Select the Unit Test Library project template. Name the project **CalculatorTests**.

4. Right-click the `UnitTest1.cs` file and select Rename. Set the new name to **CalculatorTest.cs**. Visual Studio 2012 shows a dialog box to determine whether you want to rename the class name as well in the file. Select Yes.

5. Right-click the References node of the `CalculatorTests` project. Select Add Reference. From the new dialog box, select Project under the Solution node, and choose the `CalculatorDemo` project. Click OK.

6. Open `CalculatorTest.cs` and find the `CalculatorTest` class. Replace it with the following code snippet:

```
[TestClass]
public class CalculatorTest
{
    CalculatorDemo.Calculator calculator;

    [TestInitialize]
    public void Initialize()
    {
        calculator = new CalculatorDemo.Calculator();
        //You can perform any additional intialization here
    }

    [TestMethod]
    public void AddTest()
    {
        double a = 2;
        double b = 3;
        double expected = 5;
        double result = calculator.Add(a, b);

        Assert.AreEqual(expected, result, string.Format("Result should be
            {0}!", expected));
    }
}
```

7. Select the Test ⇨ Windows ⇨ Test Explorer menu item.

8. Build the solution.

9. Click Run All in the Test Explorer window. You'll see that the test failed.

10. Open `Calculator.cs` and locate the `Add` method. Change the operation between a and b from substraction to addition.

11. Click Run All again in the Test Explorer window.

12. The test passes this time.

How It Works

In Step 4 you created a new unit test project. It enables you to create new unit tests. By default, the new project does not know anything about the `CalculatorDemo` project. This is why you must add a reference to it.

In Step 6, the code sample creates a new `Calculator` object, which you can use in later tests as well. You call the `Add` method with the values 2 and 3 and expect a result of 5. The `Assert.AreEqual()` method checks whether or not the expected values and the real result values are equal. If not, the string message is displayed.

After you fix the bug in Step 10, the new test run turns to green, because the test is passed.

SUMMARY

To create high-quality software, it is important to embrace the tools and methodologies of software testing and bug fixing.

The integrated Debugger tool in Visual Studio 2012 offers you many options to observe and sometimes change your code while running. Stepping through your code line by line makes it much easier to discover and fix bugs in your application.

Using deployment targets, you can specify where you want to run your application. The Simulator offers a great opportunity to test your applications on different screen sizes, and to simulate sensors that your development machine may not have.

Writing unit tests along with the development of your main codebase is the most reliable way to decide whether your code works, and that changes do not break it. This ensures that your work will result in high-quality, well-structured code. The additional work will pay off in later and critical stages of your development process.

In Chapter 16, you learn about the Windows Store. At this point, you know how to write your Windows 8 style app. In the Chapter 16, you learn how to sign up as a developer, how to publish your app, the main requirements that your app must meet, and how to use the services offered by the Windows Store (such as trials and app purchases).

EXERCISES

1. What is a breakpoint?

2. How can you step into a method while debugging?

3. How can you read and write the values of variables during debugging?

4. What is "Edit and Continue"?

5. How can you test your Windows 8 style app for multiple screen dimensions?

6. What are the main components of a unit test class?

> **NOTE** *You can find answers to the exercises in Appendix A.*

▶ WHAT YOU LEARNED IN THIS CHAPTER

TOPIC	KEY CONCEPTS
Debugging	Debugging is the process of stepping through the lines of code you wrote one by one while observing the values of variables and objects, and monitoring the execution of your code.
Debugger	The Debugger is a tool that can attach to your application and support the process of debugging.
Breakpoint	A breakpoint is a marker for the Debugger indicating that the normal run should be stopped, and Visual Studio should switch to debugging mode when this marker is hit.
"Edit and Continue"	"Edit and Continue" enables you to modify the codebase while the application is running and is in debug mode. It's a great way to recover from exceptions and to fix small bugs.
Deployment targets	Deployment targets determine where the applications should be deployed and run. You can choose the local machine, the Simulator, or a remote machine as a deployment target.
Simulator	The Simualtor is a desktop application that simulates the environment for a Windows 8 style app. Using the Simulator, you can specify many different factors for many different environments.
Debug locations	Using the Debugger Location toolbar, you can manually trigger application lifecycle events for debugging.
Unit tests	A unit test is a method that runs a part of your code, and observes the ouput and behavior of your code based on different inputs.

16

Introducing the Windows Store

WHAT YOU WILL LEARN IN THIS CHAPTER:

➤ Understanding what the Windows Store is and how to use it

➤ Understanding your options on how to make money with your application

➤ Learning how you can publish your application to the Windows Store from start to finish

WROX.COM CODE DOWNLOADS FOR THIS CHAPTER

You can find the wrox.com code downloads for this chapter on the Download Code tab at www.wrox.com/remtitle.cgi?isbn=012680. The code is in the Chapter16.zip download and individually named, as described in the corresponding exercises.

In this chapter, you learn about the new Windows Store, where you can publish and download Windows 8 style applications. This chapter begins with a look at the most important concepts of the Windows Store, and you learn how customers can meet your app for the first time. You also learn how to make money with your applications by using trials, in-app purchase techinques, and advertisements. By the end of this chapter, you should have a solid understanding of the process for publishing your Windows 8 style applications to the Windows Store.

GETTING TO KNOW THE WINDOWS STORE

Every application developer's dream is to make an application that is successful, widely known, recognized, loved, and, most importantly, makes a lot money. However, the process of selling an application has never been easy.

Selling an application requires a lot of work in addition to coding, and beginning developers are not qualified for this most of the time. You should understand how to reach the global market, how to advertise your application, how to build the required channels from the ground up to sell your application, how to interact with your customers to make your app better (or notify your users that there is a new, much better, and safer version of your application), and so on. As you can see, you have many things to handle that may be outside of your comfort zone, and many battles to fight in unknown territory.

Today, this process is somewhat different for the consumer market. Of course, this doesn't mean that the work described previously does not have to be done. It means that most of this work is done for you. With the introduction of "application stores," developers have been given the opportunity to publish their applications to a global application marketplace where consumers can find and get them easily.

Apple and Google have proven how viable this solution can be. You can find many great and unbelievable success stories out there. Just a couple of simple and great ideas with some solid craftsmanship have redefined success and raised many people (and companies) to unknown heights. Simple applications like Angry Birds, Instagram, or Cut the Rope have provided huge success, making their developers millionaires in the process.

Windows 8 can once again redefine success. Millions of computers and users out there are capable of running Windows 8, and many more will come. All of these people will have access to Microsoft's own application store, called the *Windows Store*. Many business analysts agree that this market is going to be huge, and many agree that it would be foolish not to jump on this train.

How Customers See an App in the Windows Store

The Windows Store is Microsoft's private application store where you can publish and download Windows 8 style applications. This is the main channel to distribute your apps and updates, to interact with your customers, to sell your apps, and make money with them. This is why it is extremely important to ensure that a potential customer's first encounter with your app is perfect.

The first encounter with an application does not involve using the application itself, but rather its *app details page*. Everything is decided on this page. If customers like the details and overview of your application, they may download or buy it. If the overview is not convincing for potential customers, they will leave and never come back. This is why it is very important to make a good first impression through the details page.

Application Details

When you submit an application, you are required to provide details and information about your app. Most of this information is displayed on the app details page of the application, and is visible for your customers. Figure 16-1 shows the app details page.

The app details page is divided into two sections. The left section contains the following information:

- ➤ **Ratings** — This is the average rating by a number of customers. This is very important information for a potential customer. If a rating is low, it is less likely that the customer will download the app.

- ➤ **Price** — This displays the price of the application or the text "Free."

- ➤ **Technical information** — This is additional information on what kind of sensors and features are used by this application.

FIGURE 16-1: The app details page

On the right side of the app details page is a multi-tab area that provides additional information about the app. The following information is displayed on the right side:

➤ **Overview** — The Overview tab is probably the most important tab on this page. It gives potential customers an overall impression about your application. On this tab, customers can find screenshots of your application (which you should carefully choose to make a good first impression), a short description, and features that your application provides.

➤ **Details** — Details contains technical information about your app, such as the processor types your app supports, supported languages, application capabilities, accessibility information, information about the terms of use, update information (if there is an update), and recommended hardware.

➤ **Reviews** — The Reviews tab contains customer reviews about your applications. This is very important feedback information. Bad reviews can adversely impact your application, whereas good reviews can potentially increase your sales.

Making Money with Your App

You can upload your application as a free application without any option to make money from it. Sometimes it may seem foolish to work for free, but, if successful, free applications can make your name stand out. It is more likely that customers will find and buy an application created by you if you have already earned a good reputation with a great free application.

At some point, you will want to realize a profit from your investments (in this case, from the hard work you put into developing your app). That's why it is important to understand the different models for application offerings.

Full-Featured Apps

Full-featured apps can be downloaded with the full set of functionality and without any restrictions. Full-featured apps can be free, or sold for a price. For free apps, this option makes the most sense. In the case of paid applications, you can simply create an application, set a price for it, and sell it for money.

Though this model definitely works, you'll get considerably fewer app downloads for a paid application than you would get with a free application. Right now, you're probably thinking that this is not an issue. Free applications don't make money, so losing those downloads is not relevant. This is not entirely true. With paid applications, you also lose the option for a customer to try and get to like your application. The potential customer must decide whether or not to buy the application based solely on ratings, the app listings page, and some reviews.

Free Trial Period

In the case of paid applications, *free trial periods* make the most sense. The customer can download your application and use it with a limit. You can apply a limit in various ways:

➤ **Time limit** — Customers can use your application with its full power and features until a period of time expires. When the time limit ends, customers are prompted with a message saying that they must purchase the application to use it again.

➤ **Feature limit** — During the trial period, customers can use only a limited set of functionality. If users buy the application, all features will be unlocked. For example, in the case of a game, you could enable, say, three maps for the customer to play during the trial period. When the customer buys the game, all the maps would be unlocked and available.

➤ **Feature-enabled limit** — During the trial period, customers can use all the features in your application. As soon as the trial period ends, you restrict the use of some important features. If the customer buys the app, all the restrictions will be removed again.

Creating a Trial Version

The state of the license is stored in the `LicenseInformation` property of the `Windows .ApplicationModel.Store.CurrentApp` object. The problem with this object during development time is that it requires the app to be uploaded in the Windows Store. This makes it difficult to test and debug trial modes.

You can use another class in the API for testing during development. It is the `Windows .ApplicationModel.Store.CurrentAppSimulator` object. It is basically the same class as the `CurrentApp`, except that it is designed for testing and debugging.

> **NOTE** *Remember that you must change the `CurrentAppSimulator` object to the `CurrentApp` object before publishing to the Windows Store; otherwise, your app will fail the application certification process (which you learn about later in this chapter).*

The `LicenseInformation` class provides a number of properties that will help you to create trial apps. Table 16-1 shows the most important properties.

TABLE 16-1: LicenseInformation Properties

PROPERTY NAME	DESCRIPTION
ExpirationDate	Gets the expiration date of the license
IsActive	Indicates whether or not the license is active
IsTrial	Indicates whether or not the license is a trial license
ProductLicenses	Provides a list of licenses for the feature that can be bought through in-app purchase
LicenseChanged	An event is raised when the licensing status of the app changes

The following code snippet demonstrates the use of the `LicenseInformation` property:

```
void EvaluateLicense()
{
    var licenseInformation =
        Windows.ApplicationModel.Store.CurrentAppSimulator.LicenseInformation;

    if (licenseInformation.IsTrial && licenseInformation.IsActive)
    {
        // Show the features that are available during trial only.
    }
    else if (licenseInformation.IsTrial && !licenseInformation.IsActive)
    {
        // The trial period is expired
    }
    else
    {
        // Show the features that are available only with a full license.
    }
}
```

Using In-App Purchases

One of the best ways to make money with your application is to use an *in-app purchase*. People like to download and use applications. Making them pay for an application can scare them away, even if the price of an app is less than a cup of coffee. Using trials and restrictions can create discomfort in users — it has a negative psychological effect, which people don't like. Instead of buying the app, they might leave it for good and look for alternatives.

However, with an in-app purchase, the psychology and the options are entirely different. It suggests that you have a fully functioning app without any restrictions that provides everything you need, but it can do even more if you are willing to pay for it.

In-app purchase solutions have been widely successful. For example, Instagram allows you to take photos and publish them on the Instagram wall. But, before you publish a photo, you can edit it by applying some neat visual effects (filters). You get a fully functioning app with some basic visual effects, but you can do even more if you buy more filters using the in-app purchase options.

Be very careful when combining in-app purchases with paid options. Although this combination is certainly possible, it might lead to general dissapointment with your product. Remember that your customer already has paid for your app. Locking essential functionalities with an in-app purchase can frustrate the customer. Using in-app purchases with free applications is definitely the best way to go.

Implementing an In-App Purchase

In-app purchases are basically feature and item purchases. To be able to identify an in-app purchase item, you must set a unique token for each in-app purchase option. Make it a meaningful name to easily identify the feature while you are coding it.

You can access the in-app purchase licenses through the `ProductLicenses` property of the `LicenseInformation` class. The following code snippet demontrates how to check the license for an in-app purchase:

```
void CheckInAppPurchaseLicense()
{
    var licenseInformation =
        Windows.ApplicationModel.Store.CurrentAppSimulator.LicenseInformation;

    if (licenseInformation.ProductLicenses["MyFeatureName"].IsActive)
    {
        // The feature is already bought the user can access it
    }
    else
    {
        // The customer did not buy the feature, it can't be accessed
    }
}
```

This code sample checks whether the user has already bought the `MyFeatureName` feature through in-app purchase. You can make this determination by using the `IsActive` property for the selected product license.

Now, let's change the previous code to display the in-app purchase dialog box for the user if he or she didn't buy the feature previously. This requires changing the `else` section, as shown here:

```
void CheckInAppPurchaseLicense()
{
    var licenseInformation =
        Windows.ApplicationModel.Store.CurrentAppSimulator.LicenseInformation;

    if (licenseInformation.ProductLicenses["MyFeatureName"].IsActive)
    {
        // The feature is already bought the user can access it
    }
```

```
    else
    {
        try
        {
            // The user didn't buy the feature previously,
            // show the purchase dialog.
            await Windows.ApplicationModel.Store.CurrentAppSimulator
                .RequestProductPurchaseAsync("MyFeatureName");

            // The in-app purchase was successful
        }
        catch (Exception)
        {
            // The in-app purchase was not completed because the user
            // cancelled it or an unknown error occurred.
        }
    }
}
```

On the app side, you're finished. When you submit an app to the Windows Store, you must configure each in-app offer on the "Advanced features" page in the Windows Store. On this page, you can set the tokens for the features, the price for each feature, and the lifetime of the offer. After you upload the package for your app, you must add descriptions for each feature. If your app supports more languages, you must provide the descriptions in each language. This information will be displayed on your app listing page.

Asking for money for the application you wrote is not the only model you can rely on. Ever since there have been consumers, web, and media, there have been alternative ways to make profit with your products.

Displaying Advertisements

One of the easiest ways to get money for a full-featured, free application is to use built-in *advertisements*. These models are quite simple. You get money after users "click" the advertisements.

However, you should know that advertisements really have a negative effect on the overall experience for your applications, and most users despise them. This can easily trigger a negative attitude toward your application.

It is best to combine advertisements with paid options. This means that if a user buys your application, no advertisement is displayed, whereas for free versions, you can display ads. This gives users the option to get rid of the annoying advertisements and use the app in its full power, while users not willing to pay for your app still can use the full functionality, but they need to accept some inconvenience.

> **NOTE** *You can use any ad platform provider, or you can use the Microsoft Advertising SDK. You are free to choose as long as you follow the certification requirements. For more information about advertising, see* `http://advertising .microsoft.com/windowsadvertising/developer`*.*

Let's Talk About the Money

Another thing you should know is that you get 70 percent of the purchase price of the app, and the rest goes to Microsoft. This means that if your application costs $2.00, you get $1.40 for every sold instance. If you get lucky and successful, and your application makes more than $25,000, you get 80 percent of the app earnings from then on.

You can't sell a paid app for less than $1.49, and the minimal amount of increments is $0.50.

To be a registered developer who is able to submit and sell applications in the Windows Store, you'll have to pay an annual account registration fee. In the United States, it is $49 for individuals and $99 for companies. You can read more about registration fees in different countries at `http://msdn` `.microsoft.com/en-us/library/windows/apps/hh694064.aspx`.

In the next excersise, you add a trial mode to your application, which adds time restrictions. Then you add support for buying the app.

TRY IT OUT   Adding a Trial Mode and Providing Support

To add a trial mode to your application and provide support for in-app purchases, follow these steps:

1. Open Visual Studio 2012 and open the project called `LicensingDemo`. You can get this project by downloading `Chapter16.zip`. Uncompress the archive and you'll find the `LicensingDemo` project.

2. Create a new folder called `Data`.

3. Inside the `Data` folder add an XML file called `trial.xml` with the following content:

```xml
<?xml version="1.0" encoding="utf-16" ?>
<CurrentApp>
  <ListingInformation>
    <App>
      <AppId>9fbf66bd-9670-4ba2-809d-843043b5b45c</AppId>
      <LinkUri>http://apps.microsoft.com/app/29fbf66bd-9670-809d-
          843043b5b45c</LinkUri>
      <CurrentMarket>en-US</CurrentMarket>
      <AgeRating>3</AgeRating>
      <MarketData xml:lang="en-us">
        <Name>LicenseDemo</Name>
        <Description>Demo app demonstrating license management</Description>
        <Price>1.99</Price>
        <CurrencySymbol>$</CurrencySymbol>
      </MarketData>
    </App>
  </ListingInformation>
  <LicenseInformation>
    <App>
      <IsActive>true</IsActive>
      <IsTrial>true</IsTrial>
      <ExpirationDate>2013-01-01T00:00:00.00Z</ExpirationDate>
    </App>
  </LicenseInformation>
</CurrentApp>
```

4. Open `MainPage.xaml.cs` and locate the `NavigatedTo` method.

5. Replace the `OnNavigatedTo` method with the following code:

```
protected async override void OnNavigatedTo(NavigationEventArgs e)
{
    //Configure the CurrentAppSimulator with fake data
    var proxyDataFolder = await
        Package.Current.InstalledLocation.GetFolderAsync("data");
    var proxyFile = await proxyDataFolder.GetFileAsync("trial.xml");
    await CurrentAppSimulator.ReloadSimulatorAsync(proxyFile);

    //Get the license info
    var licenseInfo = CurrentAppSimulator.LicenseInformation;

    //Refresh the UI
    RefreshLicenseDisplayInfo(licenseInfo);
}

private void RefreshLicenseDisplayInfo(LicenseInformation licenseInfo)
{

    if (licenseInfo.IsActive && licenseInfo.IsTrial) //It is a trial
    {
        txtLicenseStatus.Text = "Trial use expires on " +
            CurrentAppSimulator.LicenseInformation.ExpirationDate;
        btnBuyApp.Visibility = Visibility.Visible;
    }
    else if (licenseInfo.IsActive && !licenseInfo.IsTrial) //It is a full license
    {
        txtLicenseStatus.Text = "Full featured app";
        btnBuyApp.Visibility = Visibility.Collapsed;
    }
    else //Error occured or the trial is expired
    {
        txtLicenseStatus.Text = "Trial expired";
        btnBuyApp.Visibility = Visibility.Visible;
    }
}
```

6. Press F5 to run the application. As you can see, a text display indicates that the app is in trial mode, and it will expire on 01/01/2013.

7. Stop the application. Open `MainPage.xaml.cs` and locate the `buttonBuyApp_Click_1` event handler.

8. Replace the event handler with the following code:

```
private async void btnBuyApp_Click_1(object sender, RoutedEventArgs e)
{
    await CurrentAppSimulator.RequestAppPurchaseAsync(false);
}
```

9. Locate the `OnNavigatedTo` method, and add the following code at the end of the method:

```
//Subscribe to license changes
licenseInfo.LicenseChanged += () =>
{
    Dispatcher.RunAsync(Windows.UI.Core.CoreDispatcherPriority.Normal, () =>
    {
        RefreshLicenseDisplayInfo(licenseInfo);
    });
};
```

10. Press F5 to run the application. When you click the Buy button, you should select the S_OK option. Click OK. Your app now shows that this is a full-featured app.

How It Works

In Step 3, you created an XML file that represents information about the application. This information is the same as what comes from the Window Store. The `ListingInformation` section is basic information about the application. The exciting part is the `LicensingInformation` element. That's the part where the Windows Store provides the license status of the application. In this case, it is a trial application. This XML will be used to simulate information from the Windows Store.

In Step 5, the XML file is read into memory, and then it is loaded into the `CurrentAppSimualtor` using the `ReloadSimualtorAsync` method. This method reads the data from the XML with the license information. Next, you just print the license info on the screen.

In Step 6, when you run the application, the trial info is displayed and you also see a Buy button, which does nothing at this point.

In Step 8, using the `RequestPurchaseAsync` method, you send a request to the Windows Store to buy this app. Of course, in this case, you are just simulating the purchase, since you are using the `CurrentAppSimulator` class.

In Step 10, when you run the application and you click the Buy button, a dialog appears. This dialog helps you with debugging the communication with the Windows Store. In a dialog box, you can choose between different responses from the store. S_OK represents a scenario when the purchase was successful.

THE DEVELOPER REGISTRATION PROCESS

As a potential Windows 8 style application developer, you must register in the Windows Store to publish and sell applications through the Store.

The registration process is simple and straightforward. Open the Windows Dev Center portal (`http://msdn.microsoft.com/en-us/windows/apps`) and choose to sign in.

During the registration process, you must provide the following information:

➤ **Account name** — You can use your existing Windows Account (formerly known as Windows Live ID), or you can register a new one.

➤ **Publisher display name** — This is the name under which your application will be listed in the Windows Store. Customers will see this name when buying and browsing through your app. Make sure that the publisher name doesn't belong to someone else. Your account might be closed if it violates a trademark or copyright.

➤ **Developer account info** — This describes the details and contact information for the developer of the account. This contact will recieve information and notifications about this account.

➤ **Company account info** — If you are registering as a company, you must provice additional information, such as value-added tax (VAT) identification number, and an approver.

➤ **Agreement approval** — You must read and accept the aggreement to create a developer account.

➤ **Payment** — Here you provide information on payment details.

➤ **Confirmation** — You can review your order, and you must click the Purchase button to confirm registration.

As soon as the account is created, the annual account registration fee is deducted. Figure 16-2 shows the screen for the payment step in the registration process.

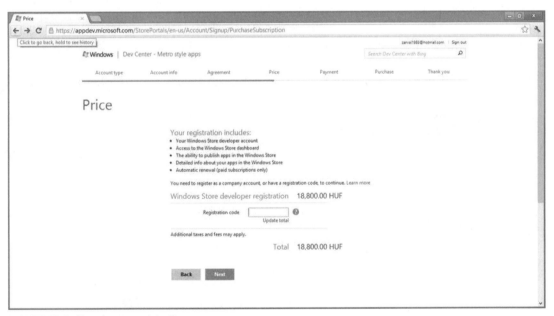

FIGURE 16-2: Developer registration process

Submitting the Application

Submitting an application to the Windows Store is a straightforward process. The first step you should perform way before submitting your app is to check whether or not the name you gave to your application is available. There is a chance that someone else has already reserved it. You can also reserve names by using the Project ⇨ Store ⇨ Reserve App Name menu item in Visual Studio 2012.

If you click the Reserve App Name menu item, you are directed to the Windows Store portal. You won't be directed to the application name reservation section, but rather to an overview page of the submission process. This will give you a good overview of what's to come:

➤ **Name** — This is where you can reserve the name for your app.

➤ **Selling details** — You can define the properties of your app, such as the price, category, and distribution details about where you want to sell your app.

➤ **Advanced Features** — You can configure `Push` notifications, Live Services, and in-app offers on this page.

➤ **Age rating and rating certificates** — You can declare the audience of your app on this page.

➤ **Cryptography** — You can set whether or not your application is using cryptography.

➤ **Packages** — You can upload your app on this page.

➤ **Description** — You can describe your application to your potential customers.

➤ **Notes to testers** — Your app will be tested by human testers as well. You can send a brief note to the tester.

Figure 16-3 shows the application submission page.

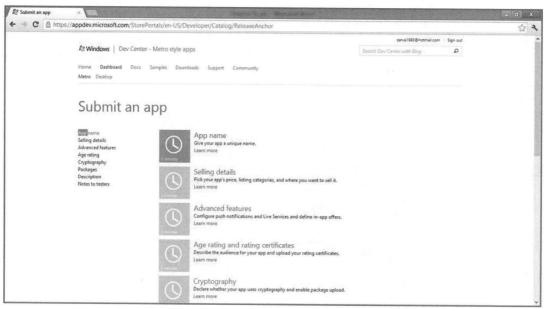

FIGURE 16-3: Application submission page

The Application Certification Process

After you submit your application, it goes through the application certification process. Following are the steps for the certification process:

1. **Pre-Processing** — At this step, all the details that the Windows Store will need to publish your application are checked. Your developer account is validated as well. This step usually takes about an hour.

2. **Security Test** — Your package is checked for malware and viruses. This step usually takes about three hours.

3. **Technical compliance** — Microsoft uses the Windows App Certification Kit to validate that your package complies with the technical policies. This is exactly the same step that you can run locally. This test usually takes about six hours.

4. **Content compliance** — A team of testers looks at your app to check that the contents of your app comply with Microsoft's content policies. This step can take five days.

5. **Release** — If you specified a specific publish day, the process will be stuck at this step until that day comes. If you didn't specify any specific day for release, this step is passed very quickly.

6. **Signing and publishing** — Your package is signed with a trusted certificate that matches the details of your developer account. Then your app is published to the Windows Store.

> **NOTE** *You can track the status of your app within the certification process by using the Windows Store portal.*

The Windows App Certification Kit

In this chapter, the certification process has already been mentioned a couple of times. However, an extensive part of those steps should be validated before application submission. That includes content validation and technical validation.

During the certfication process, your app is validated against the application certification requirements. These requirements are a set of rules that secure the comfort and interests of customers, and encourages you to create compelling, high-quality applications.

> **NOTE** *You can read the Windows 8 app certification requirements at* `http://msdn.microsoft.com/en-us/library/windows/apps/hh694083.aspx`. *You should spend some time reading through the certification requirements document before you start developing your app, because it might affect your application and your content considerably.*

The easiest way to ensure that your application complies with the certification requirements is to run the Windows App Certification Kit locally. This is the same tool that runs during the submission process. However, you should know that even if the test is passed locally, it might fail on the server. The test might run with different options in different circumstances during the submission process. Still, it is a very good idea to run the test locally to reduce the possibility of failure.

Figure 16-4 shows the Windows App Certification Kit in action.

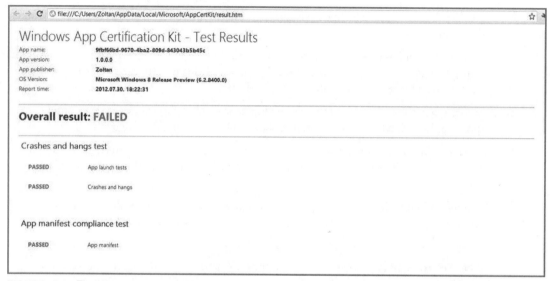

FIGURE 16-4: The Windows App Certification Kit

SUMMARY

When developing Windows 8 style applications, some of your main goals are to make your application available for as many potential customers as possible, and to sell it. The Windows Store helps you to distribute your apps to a wide audience, manages payments and reviews, and provides details and information for your customers.

To make money with your apps, you can choose from a wide variety of pricing models. You can use trials, in-app purchases, and ads to get the most out of your hard work, while balancing between creating a likeable product versus an annoying product.

To submit your application to the Windows Store, you must be a registered developer. After you submit your app, it goes through a certification process to ensure that your app does not violate the rules of the certification requirements, and to ensure that it works the way it should. You can use the Windows App Certification Kit to ensure that your application meets the requirements.

EXERCISES

1. What is the Windows Store?

2. What are your options for making money with your app?

3. How can you test that your application is probably passing the certification tests before submitting it?

4. What do you have to do to support in-app purchases?

5. How can you test licensing information during development?

> **NOTE** *You can find answers to the exercises in Appendix A.*

▶ **WHAT YOU LEARNED IN THIS CHAPTER**

TOPIC	KEY CONCEPTS
Windows Store	The Windows Store is Microsoft's private application store where you can publish, sell, and download Windows 8 style applications.
Full-featured application	Full-featured applications are fully functioning apps with no restrictions. They can be paid or free apps.
In-app purchase	Using in-app purchases, you can sell extra features for your application.
Trial application	In the case of paid applications, free trial periods make the most sense. The customer can download your application and use it with a limit. The limit can be time- or feature-based.
CurrentAppSimulator	Using the `CurrentApp` class, you can get information about the license status. However, `CurrentApp` works only when the app is deployed to the Windows Store. `CurrentAppSimulator` is designed to work during development.
LicenseInformation	Using this class, you can get detailed information about the license status, expiration dates, and trial modes.
Certification requirements	After you submit your app to the Windows Store, it goes through a certification process. During this process, your application is checked to see whether or not it violates any of the certification requirements. These requirements are a collection of rules protecting the interests of the customers.
Windows App Certification Kit	The certification process can take days, so it is important to ensure (or at least to try your best to ensure) that your app won't be rejected during the process. Using the Windows App Certification Kit, you can test your application in advance.

PART IV
Appendices

Answers to Exercises

This appendix provides the answers to Exercises found at the conclusion of each chapter.

CHAPTER 1 EXERCISE ANSWERS

Following are the answers to the exercises in Chapter 1.

Answer to Question 1

This operating system was Windows Phone 7, released in October 2010. Microsoft created it to utilize a first-class user (consumer) experience over any other operating system feature.

Answer to Question 2

Windows 8 style applications possess the full screen, thus allowing the user to focus on one application at a time. Because of this approach, there is no need for a window caption or a sizing border. A Windows 8 style application does not utilize any accessory (chrome) to manage the size or position of the application window.

Answer to Question 3

Following are the most frequently used programming languages for Windows:

- ➤ C, C++
- ➤ Visual Basic
- ➤ C#, Visual Basic .NET
- ➤ Delphi (Object Pascal)

Of course, many other programming languages are used for creating Windows applications, but they are not as frequently utilized as these. Other languages include F#, Python, Ruby, Perl, COBOL, FORTRAN, and several more.

Answer to Question 4

Web developers can use HTML5 and its powerful accessories, Cascading Style Sheets 3 (CSS3) and JavaScript, to create Windows 8 style applications. They can use exactly the same API as the other languages, so the HTML5 stack of languages can coexist with the others.

CHAPTER 2 EXERCISE ANSWERS

Following are the answers to the Exercises in Chapter 2.

Answer to Question 1

To return to the previous application, use the swipe gesture to go the left edge of the screen.

Answer to Question 2

Open the charm bar, click (or tap) the Search button, and start typing. Alternatively, just open the Start screen, and start typing on your keyboard.

Answer to Question 3

Mark the Live Tile (that is, right-click it or swipe it) and choose "Turn live tile off" on the context bar.

Answer to Question 4

Grab the top of the app, and then click and hold the left mouse button, or tap and hold with one finger. Then, move the cursor or finger all the way down to the bottom edge of the screen, and release it.

Answer to Question 5

Both the share source and the share target apps must be able to participate in the sharing process. While running the source app, open the charm bar, and click or tap the Share button. Select the target app from the list.

Answer to Question 6

To switch to the desktop, click or tap the Desktop app's Live Tile on the Start screen. (If it is missing from the Start screen, you can use the app search feature to find it.) Alternatively, if you start any desktop application, it will immediately start and switch to the Desktop app.

CHAPTER 3 EXERCISE ANSWERS

Following are the answers to the Exercises in Chapter 3.

Answer to Question 1

The programming languages are C/C++, C#, Visual Basic, and JavaScript.

Answer to Question 2

You can use HTML with CSS when you select JavaScript as your programming language. In C++, C#, and Visual Basic, you can use XAML to declare and implement the UI.

Answer to Question 3

It is Windows Runtime.

Answer to Question 4

While Win32 API is a flat API with thousands of operations, Windows Runtime groups operations into meaningful objects, and encapsulates data structures used by those operations. Win32 is not self-descriptive and does not use namespaces, whereas Windows Runtime provides metadata and groups objects into clear hierarchical namespaces.

Answer to Question 5

Windows Store is an online service. Application developers can upload their Windows 8 style applications in order to monetize them or deploy them free. Users can search the Windows Store for applications, buy applications, or try them. Users do not need to have any prior knowledge about the installation process, because Windows 8 installs and removes the application seamlessly.

CHAPTER 4 EXERCISE ANSWERS

Following are the answers to the Exercises in Chapter 4.

Answer to Question 1

This tool is Visual Studio 2012 Express for Windows 8, a free version of the Visual Studio 2012 family. It includes all features you may need to create Windows 8 applications.

Answer to Question 2

You can download the applications from the MSDN Samples Gallery (`http://code.msdn.microsoft.com/`). Here, you can browse samples by technologies, programming languages, Visual Studio versions, and by other categories.

If you are in the Visual Studio IDE, you do not need to visit this site, because the Sample Gallery is integrated with the New Project dialog box. Simply select the Online tab, and when the IDE lists the online galleries, select the Samples tab to browse the available samples.

Answer to Question 3

It is the Solution Explorer tool window. Its root node represents the solution that may contain zero, one, or more Visual Studio projects. You can use the hierarchy nodes to drill down in the structure of the source code.

Answer to Question 4

You can start applications from Visual Studio with two commands. The Debug ➪ Start With Debugging command (F5) launches your application in debug mode. In this mode, the application stops at every breakpoint, so you can analyze its execution. The Debug ➪ Start Without Debugging command (Ctrl+F5) launches the application outside of the IDE. In this case, you cannot debug it.

Answer to Question 5

This is the Quick Launch feature. You can find the Quick Launch search box in the top-right corner of the IDE's main window. As you are typing a search expression, the IDE automatically lists menu commands, options, or open documents matching the search key. Selecting an item in the result list automatically invokes the corresponding command, shows the related option page, or switches to the selected document.

You can access Quick Launch with the Ctrl+Q keyboard shortcut.

Answer to Question 6

This is the storyboard object. With a storyboard, you can define the states of objects in a certain point of the storyboard timeline. You need to describe these states only in discrete time points, and the engine behind the storyboard will compose a fluent animation interpolating property values for each frame to display.

CHAPTER 5 EXERCISE ANSWERS

Following are the answers to the exercises in Chapter 5.

Answer to Question 1

The new Windows 8 design language was designed by Microsoft to follow the infographic design principle. Although every application has its own appearance, the Windows 8 design language defines the common patterns and common themes that help users to understand and use them in a similar way.

Answer to Question 2

In the flat system, all pages reside at the same hierarchical level. This pattern is best for applications that contain only a small number of pages, and the user must be able to switch between tabs. Games, browsers, or document-creation applications often fall into this category.

The hierarchical pattern is best for applications that have a large number of pages that can be grouped into multiple sections.

Answer to Question 3

In the threaded model, each task is executed on a separate thread. The threads are fully managed by the underlying operating system that takes care of dedicating a CPU or a CPU core to every thread.

In the asynchronous programming model, multiple tasks are executed on the same thread. However, long tasks are divided into smaller units to ensure that they don't block the thread for a long time. Although, in this way, the tasks will not be completing faster, your application will be more pleasant to the user.

Answer to Question 4

C# 5.0 has two new keywords, `async` and `await`, that you can use to create asynchronous logic. With the `async` keyword, you can mark a method as asynchronous, and with the `await` keyword, you can create asynchronous code while keeping the linear flow of control.

Answer to Question 5

A promise is a JavaScript object that returns a value at some time in the future, just like tasks in C#. All asynchronous Windows Runtime APIs that are exposed to Windows 8 style applications are wrapped in promise objects, so you can work with them in a natural way in JavaScript.

CHAPTER 6 EXERCISE ANSWERS

Following are the answers to the exercises in Chapter 6.

Answer to Question 1

You can sort the new HTML5 elements into the following four categories:

➤ Semantic and structural elements

➤ Media elements

➤ Form elements and input types

➤ Drawing

Answer to Question 2

The Windows Library for JavaScript (WinJS) is a code library that enables developers to create Windows 8 style applications in a JavaScript-friendly way. The WinJS publishes several system-level features of Windows 8 through JavaScript objects and functions, and also provides helpers for common JavaScript coding patterns.

Answer to Question 3

With data binding, you can connect the data structures to the UI components, so when the underlying data changes, the UI elements are updated automatically. You can define and control data binding in the HTML markup, or by using JavaScript code.

Answer to Question 4

Media queries enable you to create media-dependent style sheets, and target your CSS settings more precisely to specific output devices without changing the content or using JavaScript code. A media query contains logical expressions that rely on device features (such as screen resolution or aspect ratio), and the browser applies the specified CSS settings only if the condition resolves to `true`.

Answer to Question 5

The Windows 8 Animation Library is an integrated part of the WinJS and contains the key animations for Windows 8 style applications. With these built-in animations, you can easily provide a natural Windows 8 style application experience to your users using device-optimized and standards-based CSS3 transitions and animations.

CHAPTER 7 EXERCISE ANSWERS

Following are the answers to the exercises in Chapter 7.

Answer to Question 1

Using the `Resources` collection, you can place a `Brush` object anywhere. To ensure that the resource is available in the entire application, you should add the `Brush` to the `Application.Resources` collection so that you can reference it as a `StaticResource` from anywhere.

Answer to Question 2

The source object containing the source property must implement the `INotifyPropertyChanged` interface. In the setter of the source property, you should always fire the `PropertyChanged` event so that when the property is set, the binding is always notified through this event.

Answer to Question 3

The `Canvas` panel doesn't have an automatic layout strategy. On the elements inside, you can set the `Canvas.Left` and `Canvas.Top` properties to ensure that you place the elements in the correct positions.

Answer to Question 4

The StackPanel arranges its elements horizontally or vertically. By default, there is no space between the elements. However, by setting the Margin property on the elements inside, you can ensure that there will be some whitespace between the elements. If the Orientation property is set to Horizontal, you should set the left or right margins; otherwise, setting the top or bottom margin should accomplish the task.

Answer to Question 5

Just like with simple objects, the collections must notify the bindings about the changes as well. You can do this using the INotifyCollectionChanged interface. Whenever the collection changes, the CollectionChanged event must be fired. So, you must use a collection that implements this interface. The ObservableCollection class might be a good choice.

Answer to Question 6

By setting the BindingMode property on the binding itself, you can control the direction of the binding. If set to TwoWay, any change on any side is reflected automatically on the other side of the binding.

CHAPTER 8 EXERCISE ANSWERS

Following are the answers to the exercises in Chapter 8.

Answer to Question 1

Independent animations are calculated using the GPU, which will ensure that the animation is smooth. Dependent animations are calculated on the UI thread running on the CPU, which might cause a less smooth experience.

Answer to Question 2

The Animation Library provides a set of predefined theme animations and theme transitions. These animations are independent animations, and also are consistent with the animations used in Windows 8.

Answer to Question 3

Every UIElement has a RenderTransform property that enables you to apply any kind of transformation you want. It is called RenderTransform because the transformation process is happening just before rendering, and right after the layout calculations have been performed. This means render transformations do not affect the layout.

Answer to Question 4

In the control template, you can apply TemplateBinding to bind a control's property to a property defined on the templated control itself.

Answer to Question 5

`CollectionViewSource` provides a view over a collection of items. The view supports grouping, sorting, and filtering without affecting the underlying collection. It is a fast and safe way to bind your collection to a complex control.

Answer to Question 6

`SemanticZoom` provides two different levels of view over the same set of data. Using zoom and pinch gestures, you can switch between the zoom levels.

CHAPTER 9 EXERCISE ANSWERS

Following are the answers to the exercises in Chapter 9.

Answer to Question 1

If the user starts many applications, suspended ones can reserve too much memory and jeopardize the overall operation and responsiveness of the foreground app. In this case, the operating system terminates one or more suspended applications and reclaims the resources (such as memory and exclusively locked resources) to ensure that the foreground app continues to be responsive.

Answer to Question 2

You can use the Windows+Z key combination to display the app bar. In many applications, you can right-click the app screen to display the app bar, too. On touchscreens, you can swipe your finger from the top or bottom edges of the screen to show the app bar.

Answer to Question 3

This is the roaming application data store. It is stored in the cloud, and a replication mechanism takes care of synchronizing the data among your devices.

Answer to Question 4

This object is the `TileUpdateManager` that is defined in the `Windows.UI.Notifications` namespace. Use the `TileUpdateManager.CreateTileUpdaterForApplication()` method to obtain an object that is responsible for managing tile notification updates belonging to your app. Use the `Update()` method of this object to change tile notifications on the Start screen.

CHAPTER 10 EXERCISE ANSWERS

Following are the answers to the exercises in Chapter 10.

Answer to Question 1

This kind of navigation is called hierarchical navigation. You present the content in a hierarchy, where separate pages display separate hierarchy levels. During the navigation, you can move up and down among the nodes of this hierarchy, and take a look at the content at the current node.

Answer to Question 2

This is the `Frame` property, which holds an instance of the `Frame` object. The `Frame` object controls the content of the page, and it provides operations and events in regard to navigation.

Answer to Question 3

You can call the `Navigate` method of the page's `Frame` property, and pass the type of the page you intend to navigate to, as shown here:

```
Frame.Navigate(typeof(NextPageType))
```

You can also pass a second optional argument that can be used on the target page, as shown here:

```
Frame.Navigate(typeof(NextPageType), "Page Title")
```

Answer to Question 4

You must override the `OnNavigatingFrom` method of the page (or subscribe to the `NavigatingFrom` event). The (event handler) method has an argument of type `NavigationCancelEventArgs`. Set the `Cancel` property of the argument to `true` to prevent navigating away from the current page.

Answer to Question 5

This is the `LayoutAwarePage` class (found in the `Common` folder), the common base class of pages in the Split Application and Grid Application templates. As soon as the page (which is derived from `LayoutAwarePage`) is loaded, it subscribes to the current window's `SizeChanged` event. When this event is triggered, `LayoutAwarePage` automatically moves the page to the appropriate visual state.

CHAPTER 11 EXERCISE ANSWERS

Following are the answers to the exercises in Chapter 11.

Answer to Question 1

Pickers provide a unified UI for every app to access otherwise restricted resources. Also, some of them support app integration. An application can include itself in the picker, and other applications can use its features.

Answer to Question 2

Implementing the search functionality is more or less a matter of programming. But you can make your app's search functionality more accessible if you integrate your app with Windows 8's Search feature by declaring adherence to the Search contract, and implementing the needed code.

Answer to Question 3

Use the Share Target Contract template to add the contract and the custom share page to your app.

Answer to Question 4

Although you have many ways to do so (including parsing the XML manually), the most straightforward and efficient way to transform an XML feed into objects is by using the Syndication API's SyndicationClient class.

Answer to Question 5

Your app can use the Live SDK. Then, when it connects to Microsoft's online services, it should declare which "scopes" of the user's data it wants to use.

CHAPTER 12 EXERCISE ANSWERS

Following are the answers to the exercises in Chapter 12.

Answer to Question 1

Most of the time, users hold their tablets in their hands. Sensors enable extra and natural controlling mechanisms that enhance an app. It is far easier to drive a racing car in a game by rotating your tablet than by pressing buttons on the screen.

Answer to Question 2

You have two options: Default and High. Using Default makes the device try to determine its location less accurately, but faster, and by consuming less power. If low-energy methods have failed, or you've set the precision to High, the device powers up its GPS receiver, and determines the location more accurately.

Answer to Question 3

The accelerometer gives you the device's current acceleration (change of velocity) on its three coordinate axes. The gyroscope can tell you how much the device rotated around these axes since the previous reading.

Answer to Question 4

You don't exactly need them, but they are very handy. In most situations, to make use of raw data from physical sensors, you must process it by writing somewhat complex calculations. Logical sensors gather data from multiple physical sensors and do the processing themselves, so you can focus on building your application logic, rather than typing in long algorithms.

Answer to Question 5

You should use the `SimpleOrientationSensor` when you want to know how the user holds the device. Use this class when you aren't interested in the exact degrees of attitude, and you'd just rather know whether the device is lying on a table, or it is in landscape mode or portrait mode, and it is rotated by about 90, 180, or 270 degrees.

CHAPTER 13 EXERCISE ANSWERS

Following are the answers to the Exercises in Chapter 13.

Answer to Question 1

Because of the less-powerful CPUs and GPUs in mobile devices, and the still high user expectations (such as the responsiveness of the UI), application performance is a key factor. The C++ programming language provides you with the best possible performance among the available Windows 8 app languages.

Answer to Question 2

Lambda expressions in C++ (a new feature in C++11) provide you with anonymous functions that can capture variables from the enclosing scope to manage state. You can use lambda expressions instead of functors.

Answer to Question 3

The ^ (hat) operator marks a reference-counted pointer used for keeping references to Windows Runtime types. When you use ^, the compiler generates code that automatically tracks references to the pointed object, and disposes of the object when the reference counter reaches zero.

Answer to Question 4

This is the `ref new` operator. You can use it to instantiate Windows Runtime objects that are reference-counted. You can use this operator in tandem with the ^ operator, as shown in the following example:

```
Vector<int>^ numbers = ref new Vector<int>(myNumbers);
```

Answer to Question 5

You can mix STL and Windows Runtime types interchangeably in your C++ applications, but you must use Windows Runtime types to cross Windows Runtime boundaries. In practice, this means that you can use STL types everywhere, but you must wrap them into Windows Runtime types when crossing the boundary.

Answer to Question 6

The best technology choice would be C++ AMP. This would enable you to run the pixel-color-inverting algorithm directly on the GPU with a high scale of parallelism, and so it would be much faster than running it on the CPU.

CHAPTER 14 EXERCISE ANSWERS

Following are the answers to the Exercises in Chapter 14.

Answer to Question 1

When creating your project, you should select the C# Windows Runtime Component template. This setting ensures that the project is built as a Windows Runtime component library. Windows Runtime component libraries can be used from any Windows 8 language.

Answer to Question 2

Background tasks have CPU and network throughput limits. The CPU limit is 1 second per 15 minutes or 2 seconds per 2 hours for standard and lock-screen applications, respectively. Network throughput is limited only when the computer runs on battery, but it is not limited when AC power is used.

Answer to Question 3

Foreground tasks can subscribe to background task notifications. The OnCompleted event handler of a registered background task is triggered when a task is completed. The OnProgress event handler is triggered when the background task changes its progress value. These event handlers can update the UI of the foreground application.

Answer to Question 4

Yes, it can, unless it does not consume more than 1 second of CPU time while it's running. For example, assume it downloads 500 pieces of data packets, and it takes about 1 millisecond of CPU time to start downloading a packet, but the task has to wait 2 seconds for each download. Altogether the task lasts a bit more than 1,000 seconds, but it consumes only 500 milliseconds of CPU time.

Answer to Question 5

A Windows 8 computer may have several input devices, including the mouse, keyboard, pen, or touch. Knowing the available input devices lets you select the best way of input in terms of the user experience. Your application will be able to accommodate the capabilities of the available devices, and use the interaction model best suited for the app.

CHAPTER 15 EXERCISE ANSWERS

Following are the answers to the exercises in Chapter 15.

Answer to Question 1

A breakpoint is a marker for the Debugger indicating that the normal run should be stopped, and Visual Studio should switch to debugging mode when this marker is hit.

Answer to Question 2

You can press the F11 button or the "Step into" option on the Debugger toolbar.

Answer to Question 3

You can use the Locals window to observe and change values for local variables. You can also use the Watch window to perform these operations on local variables under watch.

Answer to Question 4

"Edit and Continue" enables you to modify the codebase while the application is running and is in debug mode. It's a great way to recover from exceptions and to fix small bugs.

Answer to Question 5

You can use the Simualtor to simulate the environment for a Windows 8 style app. Using the Simulator, you can specify many different factors, among which are different screen sizes and resolutions.

Answer to Question 6

Test classes contain test methods, initialization code to run before every test method, and cleanup code to run after every test method.

CHAPTER 16 EXERCISE ANSWERS

Following are the answers to the exercises in Chapter 16.

Answer to Question 1

The Windows Store is Microsoft's private application store where you can publish, sell, and download Windows 8 style applications. Users can get an overview of your application, detailed descriptions, and reviews by other users.

Answer to Question 2

You can publish full-featured applications with a set price. The best way is to use trial modes for your applications. In-app purchases also provide a good way to make money with your app. Another alternative is to add advertisements to your application, whereas you'll get paid after the user opens the ads.

Answer to Question 3

Before submitting the app to the Windows Store, you should test your application with the Windows App Certification Kit to ensure that your app does not violate the rules of the certification requirements. However, you still can't be sure that your app will pass the process.

Answer to Question 4

You can use the `LicenseInformation.ProductLicenses` collection to check for the status of the in-app purchase licenses. You must also ensure that you register every in-app purchase token with detailed descriptions on the Windows Store portal during submission.

Answer to Question 5

Using the `CurrentApp` class, you can get information about the license status. However, `CurrentApp` works only when the app is deployed to the Windows Store. `CurrentAppSimulator` is designed to work during development.

B

Useful Links

So far in this book, you have learned the basics of Windows 8 style application development. The topics treated in this book and the related exercises have provided an overview and a taste of the new style of apps, and you should now understand the essence of creating them. You can find many ways to enhance and improve your knowledge, and this appendix provides useful links to web pages and articles that contain more detail about Windows 8 app development.

CODE SAMPLES

The best way to understand Windows Runtime APIs and the fundamental techniques is to take a look at prepared samples. Table B-1 provides links within the MSDN Developer Code Samples Gallery to download sample source code.

TABLE B-1: Code Samples Links

LINK	DESCRIPTION
http://code.msdn.microsoft.com/	This is the homepage of the MSDN Developer Code Samples. Here you can browse for samples by platforms, Visual Studio versions, programming language, tags, and other attributes.
http://code.msdn.microsoft.com/ Windows-8-Modern-Style-App-Samples	This link contains a download for packages of all Windows 8 style app samples. You can download these samples separately for your preferred programming language, or all in one package.
http://code.msdn.microsoft. com/windowsapps/XAML-controls-sample-pack-7ae99c95	This code sample demonstrates how to use predefined Windows 8 controls. You can download these samples separately for your preferred programming language, or all in one package.

GUIDELINES

When you are ready to create your own Windows 8 style apps, the guidelines summarized in Table B-2 provide indispensable resources to get you started.

TABLE B-2: Application Design Guidelines Links

LINK	DESCRIPTION
http://msdn.microsoft.com/en-us/ library/windows/apps/hh464920.aspx	This article provides an overview about what makes your Windows 8 style app great. The principles treated here help you understand the essence of Windows 8 design.
http://msdn.microsoft.com/en-us/ library/windows/apps/hh465427.aspx	This article provides a guideline that helps you plan your Windows 8 style apps — from deciding what your app is great at, to validating your design.
http://msdn.microsoft.com/en-us/ library/windows/apps/hh465424.aspx	Use this link as a starting hub for understanding user experience patterns and principles. It collects links to all user experience guidelines that are indispensable when designing the user interface (UI) and user interactions for your apps.
http://msdn.microsoft.com/en-us/ library/windows/apps/hh465415.aspx	Windows 8 focuses a great deal on touchscreen devices. This article explains the basics of touch interaction design.
http://msdn.microsoft.com/ en-us/library/windows/apps/ Hh452681(v=win.10).aspx; http://msdn.microsoft.com/en-us/ library/windows/apps/xaml/ Hh452680(v=win.10).aspx	These two links provide guidelines to help you design and implement accessibility in your apps, using HTML/JavaScript and C#/Visual Basic, respectively.
http://msdn.microsoft.com/en-us/ library/windows/apps/hh465413.aspx	This link points to an index of white papers for Windows 8 style apps. Visit them to obtain practical guidelines and hints to developing your apps.

WINDOWS RUNTIME

Windows Runtime is the cornerstone of Windows 8 style application development. The links summarized in Table B-3 provide the most important information you need to take advantage of the great features of this fundamental component.

TABLE B-3: Windows Runtime Reference Links

LINK	DESCRIPTION
http://msdn.microsoft.com/en-us/library/windows/apps/br211377.aspx	This link is the index of Windows Runtime API references for Windows 8 style apps.
http://msdn.microsoft.com/en-us/library/windows/apps/br230301(v=vs.110).aspx; http://msdn.microsoft.com/en-us/library/windows/apps/hh441569(v=vs.110).aspx	With Visual Studio, you can develop your own Windows Runtime components. These links helps you with component development, using C#/Visual Basic and C++, respectively.
http://msdn.microsoft.com/en-us/library/windows/apps/hh464945.aspx	From this article, you can learn which features of the Windows API you can use in a Windows 8 style app, and which APIs to use as alternatives for those that you cannot.

LANGUAGE REFERENCES

You can develop Windows 8 style apps with four languages — C++, C#, Visual Basic, and JavaScript. In many apps, you can mix these languages to provide a great user experience by leveraging the strength of each individual language. Table B-4 summarizes the links of references to these programming languages, and additionally, to XAML.

TABLE B-4: Language Reference Links

LINK	DESCRIPTION
http://msdn.microsoft.com/en-us/library/windows/apps/hh699871.aspx	Visual C++ Language Reference (Component Extensions, C++/CX)
http://msdn.microsoft.com/library/618ayhy6(VS.110).aspx	C# Language Reference
http://msdn.microsoft.com/library/25kad608(VS.110).aspx	Visual Basic Language Reference
http://msdn.microsoft.com/en-us/library/windows/apps/d1et7k7c(v-vs.94).aspx	JavaScript Language Reference
http://msdn.microsoft.com/en-us/library/windows/apps/hh700351.aspx	Basic XAML Syntax Guide

CONTROLS

Windows 8 style controls are the basic building blocks of each app's UI. The links summarized in Table B-5 point to information that helps you to choose the right control for specific tasks, as well as to understand their implementation details.

TABLE B-4: Useful Links for Windows 8 Style Controls

LINK	DESCRIPTION
http://msdn.microsoft.com/en-us/ library/windows/apps/xaml/ Hh465351(v=win.10).aspx; http://msdn.microsoft.com/ en-us/library/windows/apps/ Hh465453(v=win.10).aspx	These two links list all controls available for Windows 8 style application development. The first link uses the XAML notation for controls (to be used from C#, Visual Basic, or from C++). The second one provides HTML notation (to be used from JavaScript).
http://msdn.microsoft.com/en-us/ library/windows/apps/xaml/ Hh465381(v=win.10).aspx; http://msdn.microsoft.com/ en-us/library/windows/apps/ Hh465498(v=win.10).aspx	You can totally change the visual style of built-in Windows 8 controls. These two links point to articles describing a quick start for C++/C#/Visual Basic apps, and HTML/JavaScript apps, respectively.

INDEX

I

J

X

X–Y–Z